Cumberland County Pennsylvania

CEMETERY RECORDS

Collected by Jeremiah Zeamer

Wilbur J. McElwain

HERITAGE BOOKS
2012

HERITAGE BOOKS
AN IMPRINT OF HERITAGE BOOKS, INC.

Books, CDs, and more—Worldwide

For our listing of thousands of titles see our website
at
www.HeritageBooks.com

Published 2012 by
HERITAGE BOOKS, INC.
Publishing Division
100 Railroad Ave. #104
Westminster, Maryland 21157

Copyright © 1994 Wilbur J. McElwain

Other Heritage Books by the author:

*A Documentary and Genealogical History of the Family of Andrew McElwain
and Mary Mickey of Cumberland County, Pennsylvania*

Cumberland County, Pennsylvania Cemetery Records Collected by Jeremiah Zeamer

Genealogical Data Abstracted from History of Middle Spring Presbyterian Church, Middle Spring, Pennsylvania, 1738–1900

Genealogical Data Abstracts from the History of the Big Spring Presbyterian Church, Newville, Pennsylvania, 1737–1898

United States Direct Tax of 1798: Tax Lists for Cumberland County, Pennsylvania

United States Direct Tax of 1798: Tax Lists for the City of Philadelphia, Pennsylvania: New Market Ward

*United States Direct Tax of 1798: Tax Lists for the City of Philadelphia, Pennsylvania:
Upper Delaware, Lower Delaware, High Street, Chestnut Street, Walnut and Dock Wards*

United States Direct Tax of 1798: Tax Lists for Washington County, Pennsylvania

All rights reserved. No part of this book may be reproduced or transmitted in any form or by any means,
electronic or mechanical, including photocopying, recording or by any information storage and retrieval system
without written permission from the author, except for the inclusion of brief quotations in a review.

International Standard Book Numbers
Paperbound: 978-0-7884-0075-9
Clothbound: 978-0-7884-3413-6

TABLE OF CONTENTS

Introduction	vii
Abbreviations	x
Jeremiah Zeamer	xi
Vita	xi

Tables of Inscriptions

    Carlisle

Ashland Cemetery	1
Meeting House Springs Grave Yard	24

    Dickinson

Barnitz M. E. Church Graveyard	26
Line Graveyard	26
Martin Farm Graveyard	26
Mount Zion Lutheran Church Graveyard	27
Old Associate Reformed Church Yard	31
Old LIne Graveyard	31

    Frankford

Bloserville Reformed Church Graveyard	33
Entlerville Graveyard	34
Gayman Farm Graveyard	35
Lutheran and Reformed Stone Church Graveyard	36
Lutheran Brick Church Graveyard	46
Possum Hill Church Graveyard	58

    Hopewell

Hanna Graveyard	60
Hoover Graveyard	62
Mount Tabor Church Graveyard	62
Newburg Church of God Graveyard	63
Stouffer Farm Graveyard	67
Zion Reformed Church Graveyard	68

Table of Contents

Lower Allen
Eberly's Mills Graveyard	74
Lisburn Cemetery	77
Monroe Woods Farm Graveyard	80

Middlesex
Carlisle Springs Church Graveyard	81
Dunker Church Graveyard	88
Letort Spring Church Graveyard	90
Mennonite Graveyard at Balfour	97
Old Hoffer Farm Graveyard	97
Peter Albright Farm Graveyard	97

Mifflin
Bethany Church Graveyard	98
Bethel Church Graveyard	100
Center Church Graveyard	101
Mount Hope Cemetery	105
Snoke Graveyard	106
Zeigler's Church Graveyard	107

Newton
Irishtown Church Graveyard	108
Oakville U. B. Cemetery	111
Old Roads Graveyard	112
Stoughstown Lutheran Church Graveyard	113

Newville
Big Spring Presbyterian Graveyard	114
Newville Cemetery	137
Prospect Hill Cemetery	149
United Presbyterian Church Graveyard	160
Zion Lutheran Church Graveyard	163

North Middleton
Bethel Church Graveyard	165
Wagner's Church Graveyard	166

South Middleton
Flint Ridge Chapel Graveyard	169
Garber Graveyard	169
Mount Victory Graveyard	170
Strickler Graveyard	170

Table of Contents

Penn
Centerville Lutheran Church Graveyard	171
Cummingstown Campbellite Church Graveyard	177
Dickinson Presbyterian Church Graveyard	178
Hisner Graveyard	183
Huntsdale Dunker Cemetery	184

Upper Allen
Lantz's School House Cemetery	193

West Pennsboro
Bear Graveyard	194
Bitner Farm Graveyard	195
Diller Mennonite Church Graveyard	195
Francis Bear Farm Graveyard	200
Graveyard on hill	200
Heikes Farm Graveyard	201
Jonathan Bear Farm Graveyard	202
Ker Farm Graveyard	202
Mt. Rock Graveyard	203
Old Shellenberger Farm Graveyard	204
Plainfield Bethel Church Graveyard	205
Plainfield Lutheran Church Graveyard	209
Riggleman Farm Graveyard	212
Seitz Farm Graveyard	213
Springfield Graveyard	214
William A. Lindsey Farm Graveyard	216

unknown location
Oyster's Point Graveyard	216

Narrative of Jeremy Zeamer's Visits to Cemeteries in Cumberland County, Pennsylvania	217
Index to Surnames of Interred Persons	233
Index to Names of Relatives of Interred Persons	262
Index to Cemeteries in Narrative	265
Index to Narrative	266

INTRODUCTION

In the years 1901 through 1909 Jeremiah Zeamer of Carlisle visited cemeteries located in Cumberland County, Pennsylvania and recorded the inscriptions on the gravestones. His compilation eventually came into the possession of the State Library of Pennsylvania in Harrisburg. In 1960 Helen I. Harmon, Pennsylvania State Chairman of the Genealogical Research Committee of the Daughters of the American Revolution transcribed the material collected by Mr. Zeamer, prefacing her work with these remarks:

> Mr. Jere Zeamer's Books of Cemetery Records
> reproduced here from brittle and crumbling pages
> have been carefully copied, completely checked and
> corrected, and fully indexed with great care. Mr.
> Zeamer's records all written in same handwriting.

Mrs. Harmon made five copies which were placed in historical societies and libraries. Subsequently one of these transcripts was microfilmed for the Family History Library of the Mormon church, and it is presently available in that form at branch libraries of the church. This work was compiled from this microfilm. Its purpose is to make this vast repository of information more widely available and to provide it in a form more convenient than microfilm.

GEOGRAPHICAL COVERAGE OF ZEAMER'S COLLECTION

Jeremiah Zeamer's collection of inscriptions are from seventy-three cemeteries located in twelve townships and two boroughs.

Of the then existing townships no listings were made for Cooke, East Pennsboro, Hampden, Monroe, Silver Spring, or Southampton. Frankford, Mifflin, and Newton were split into two townships each in 1920, but the cemeteries have been listed under the name in use between 1902 and 1909.

Obviously, despite the great amount of work done by Zeamer, the more than 9,000 names in his collection represent a comparatively small portion of the inscriptions within the limits of Cumberland County. How he selected cemeteries for visitation cannot now be ascertained, but, as is evident, he did not visit any Catholic or Jewish cemeteries.

ORGANIZATION OF THE INSCRIPTIONS

The original work and the Harmon transcript were organized with a section devoted to each cemetery. Within each section the inscriptions were organized in a partially alphabetized sequence, according to the initial letter of the surname. Beyond that surnames were sometimes further alphabetized and sometimes not. There was no alphabetization by given names. Nor is there any indication of location through notation of plot numbers.

To compile this work each inscription was entered into a computer data base. Once this was accomplished it was possible to produce the tables in any of a number of forms. A strictly alphabetical listing, whether by cemetery or for the entire collection was quickly ruled out, since this would result in the loss of information conveyed by proximity. Husbands, wives, and children are often grouped together, though these relationships may not be noted in the inscriptions; a researcher somewhat familiar with a family might recognize relationships not obvious to everyone.

It seemed most useful to keep surname groupings together with names within the group kept in the original sequence. Surname groups have been alphabetized, using the spelling of the initial entry for each group to determine placement in the sequence, even though that results in placement based upon a variant spelling.

Introduction

ARRANGEMENT OF THE CEMETERIES

It is difficult to determine the organizational method in the arrangement of the original material. The cemeteries are grouped according to townships or boroughs, but there are several sections for some divisions, sometimes rather widely separated. Within the sections the cemeteries are not in alphabetical order, nor are they strictly in the order in which Zeamer made his visits.

To facilitate reference to this work all cemeteries within a given township or borough have been brought together. Within each section the cemeteries appear in alphabetical order, using the cemetery name given in the table of contents in the Harmon transcript. The townships and boroughs have been alphabetized, except for South Middleton, which immediately follows North Middleton.

The cemeteries which are listed under the boroughs of Carlisle and Newville are not all within the borough limits. Apparently, nearby cemeteries were listed under the boroughs because they were used by residents of that borough.

The names of the cemeteries seem not always to be strictly the official names. It seems unlikely, for example, that "Lutheran and Reformed Stone Church " or "Lutheran Brick Church" are official names. Graveyards located on private property were probably unnamed; Zeamer evidently solved this problem by adopting such designations as "Ker Farm Graveyard" and similar names.

NARRATIVE

Accompanying each list of inscriptions is narrative and descriptive material which provides a variety of information on the cemetery, and the people and the institution connected with it. This material has been gathered into a chronological narrative which enables the reader to follow Mr. Zeamer in his peregrinations about Cumberland County.

Each description passage has been headed with the date of the visit, the name of the cemetery, and its location. The material is reproduced as it appears in the Harmon transcript, edited with only the lightest hand.

INDEXES

The main index is an index to surnames of interred persons. An index of complete names--surnames and given names--would greatly increase the size of this volume and would serve little purpose. To make the index more useful each surname is listed separately for every cemetery in which it appears, and the township in which the cemetery is located is also given as part of the entry.

A second index is provided for relatives named in the inscriptions when their surname differs from that of the person interred.

There are also two separate indexes for the narrative of the visits made by Mr. Zeamer to the cemeteries. One of these indexes the cemeteries, the second various references in the narrative.

FORMAT OF NAMES OF INDIVIDUALS

Names of individuals in the all of the tables are in reverse form, with surname given first.

Given names which are abbreviated in the original have been expanded to their full form when the abbreviation is a standard one. A few doubtful abbreviations have been retained in their abbreviated form.

Introduction

CONTENTS OF THE TABLES

Surname — Arranged in alphabetical order by surname groups, with a very few exceptions. These exceptions can be found through the index.

Names are given with surname first and given names last, separated by a comma.

Given Name — These appear in the original order, which is not alphabetized.

Death — Death dates are given as Month.Day | Year. In the original transcript month names were used; here they were converted to numerals to facilitate computations in the data base.

Birth — The format is the same as for death dates

Attained Age — Many inscriptions provide the age at death, either with or without the birth and death dates. These ages may be given in either of two ways. Most commonly age is expressed as attained age, that is, the age at the last birthday: "he died at age eighty" for example. Less commonly, but not rarely, age is expressed as the year of one's age: "he died in the eightieth year of his age," or he "died in his eightieth year." This number is that of the next birthday. When age at death is so expressed in the inscriptions it has been converted to attained age in this column.

Computed Age — So that the reader will have the age at death for each person readily available without having to do a mental calculation, the data base was programed to provide this information. The age given here is the year in which the person is living, not the attained age. The chief reason for this is that it avoids giving the age for a child who died before its first birthday as zero. The age given here is, of course, one year greater than that given in the Attained Age column.

If Attained Age is given, that age is used to derive the Computed Age. If Attained Age is not given, Computed Age is determined by a comparison of the year of birth and the year of death. If month and day of both birth and death are given, the result will be exact. If month and day of either birth or death is not given, the result will be approximate. If the data available is insufficient for a calculation the field will contain be blank.

Page & Number — The page number is that in the Harmon transcript; number is the position of the entry on that page. This will be of use to anyone wishing to refer to the transcript.

Other Information — Information in this column is of several kinds:

1. Most of the entries give information on relatives mentioned in the inscriptions. All names are given with last name first, followed by the given name, title, and relationship. Commas separate each category. This arrangement makes for easy sorting in the data base, but does result in some unpleasantly convoluted sequences, for example: "Murray, J. P., Maj. Gen. & E., of Benpoort, Hampshire, England, son of."

2. Places of birth or death when mentioned

3. Cause of death, given in a few inscriptions

4. Military rank and related service information

5. Titles of various sorts

Introduction

6. Language of the inscription, if foreign (only German is mentioned)

7. Description of the tombstone (it is difficult to say why some stones are described; most are not).

8. Occupation

9. Place of residence

10. Birth year, given in parenthesis

    A small number of birth years are so given. The significance of this, if any, is not clear, but the fact is indicated by the inclusion of the year in parenthesis in this column.. The year is also included in the birth year column.

11. Dates and ages which are not useable in the calculation of age from the data columns. For example, "21 years, --months, 15 days" would be entered in the data columns as 21 years, and would also be entered in the Other Information column; -- years, 4 months, 3 days would be entered only in the Other Information column.

12. Comments by the compiler of this volume appear in brackets.

    a. When a reading is doubtful the date or word appears with the doubtful portion indicated.

    b. Spellings are reproduced as given in the Harmon transcript, except for a few obvious errors. Unusual spellings, which might appear to be transcription errors in this work are bracketed with the notation " (sic)" to indicate that the Harmon transcript spelling has been reproduced exactly.

    c. Question marks indicate that the reading of the previous word is doubtful.

    d. When surname spelling varies for the same person this is noted.

    e. Other useful notes--self-explanatory, it is hoped

ABBREVIATIONS

Abbreviations have not been used except where a definite saving of space would result, or where the use of the abbreviation is customary. The meaning of most of those used is probably obvious, but they are here given so that no reader may be mystified.

b.	born	Gen.	General	Brig.	Brigade
d.	died	Col.	Colonel	Regt.	Regiment
dau.	daughter	Maj.	Major	Co.	Company
Ch.	Church	Capt.	Captain	Res.	Reserves
Pa.	Pennsylvania	Lt.	Lieutenant	V.	Volunteers
Presb.	Presbyterian	Lieut.	Lieutenant	Vol.	Volunteers
Prof.	Professor	Sgt.	Sergeant	Vols.	Volunteers
Ref.	Reformed			C.	Cavalry
Rev.	Reverend			Inf.	Infantry

Introduction

Township and borough abbreviations

CARL	Carlisle	MDSX	Middlesex	SMID	South Middleton
DICK	Dickinson	MIFF	Mifflin	PENN	Penn
FRAN	Frankford	NEWT	Newton	UALN	Upper Allen
HOPE	Hopewell	NEWV	Newville	WPEN	West Pennsboro
LALN	Lower Allen	MMID	North Middleton		

JEREMIAH ZEAMER

The Harmon transcript provides no information on Mr. Zeamer, but something of his life may be gleaned from the 1900 and 1910 censuses, between which years Zeamer made his compilation of cemetery records.

Jeremiah Zeamer was born in Pennsylvania in April 1842. Isabella, his wife, was born in May 1846, also in Pennsylvania. They were married about 1872 and had two children both of whom were living with them at the time of the 1900 census. Maud was born in September 1874, and Jay S. in August 1880, both in Pennsylvania.

In the 1900 census the Zeamers were living at 658 North Hanover Street in Carlisle. The family then included Mr. and Mrs. Zeamer, their son, their daughter and her son, and a sister-in-law, whose name was Levina Benner. Whether Benner was a married name is not known.

In 1910, Mr. and Mrs. Zeamer were living with their daughter and grandson. The son was not listed as a resident of the household, nor was the sister-in-law.

The 1900 census gives the occupation of Jeremiah Zeamer as "editor".

Jeremiah Zeamer died August 26, 1911, at age 69.

VITA

Wilbur J. McElwain was born at Chicago, Illinois, on February 8, 1923. He completed his elementary and secondary education Chicago, Illinois.

He received the degree of Bachelor of Science, with a major in English Literature, from Northwestern University, Evanston, Illinois in 1950. In 1958 he received the degree of Master of Arts (English) from the University of Miami, Coral Gables, Florida. His thesis was entitled The Development of the Social and Political Thought of James Fenimore Cooper. He received the degree of Doctor of Education from Florida Atlantic University, Boca Raton, Florida in 1976. His dissertation was entitled Academic Achievement of Students Earning Credit through the College Level Examination Program General Examinations.

Mr. McElwain taught in the Dade County Public School Adult Education Division from 1952 to 1960. He joined the faculty of Miami-Dade Community College in 1960 and held the position of Associate Dean for Adult, Military, and Off-Campus Education at the South Campus from 1967 to 1986.

He retired in 1986 and moved to his present address, 10122 Northeast 126 Street, Kirkland, Washington, 98034.

Carlisle - Ashland Cemetery

CARLISLE BOROUGH

ASHLAND CEMETERY

Surname	Given Name	Death Mo/Dy	Year	Birth Mo/Dy	Year	Att. Yr	Age Mo/Dy	Cm Ag	Pg	No	Other Information
Aberly	Frederick	4.25	1885			63		64	001	04	
Aberly	William F.	10.28	1882			36		37	001	05	
Abrams	Hannah	2.11	1863			36		37	001	01	
Abrahims	Samuel	11.02	1882			80		81	001	02	
Abrahims	Elizabeth	2.11	1886	2.27	1807			79	001	03	Abrahims, Samuel, wife of
Achenbaugh	Frederick	4.02	1871			59	9.15	60	001	06	
Addams	William	6.19	1875	5.15	1802			74	001	10	
Adams	Howard Elmer	4.08	1881	12.23	1867			14	001	11	Adams, N. J. & H. E., son of
Ahl	Carey W.	11.02	1885	2.22	1811			75	001	07	
Ahl	Catharine Williams	8.27	1897	7.06	1817			81	001	08	Ahl, Carey W., wife of
Ahl	Myra Jane	6.01	1858	2.07	1851			8	001	09	
Albert	Jacob J.	8.07	1879						001	12	
Albert	Melinda	2.12	1872						001	13	
Albert	Julia Adams	10.29	1866						001	14	Albert, Jacob H., wife of
Albert	Annie M. Searight	10.26	1885						001	15	Albert, Jacob H., wife of
Alexander	William	6.10	1865	5.07	1790			76	001	24	
Alexander	Samuel A.	10.11	1856	8.13	1837			20	001	25	
Alexander	Mary	11.30	1850	12.05	1803			47	001	26	
Alexander	John B.	9.20	1866	11.25	1832			34	001	27	
Alexander	William G.	1.25	1880	10.07	1834			46	001	28	
Alexander	Jane M.	6.23	1877	11.13	1828			49	001	29	
Allen	Jane	8.28	1865	4.22	1790			76	001	16	
Allen	James M.	9.17	1892	1.09	1816			77	001	17	
Allen	Elizabeth B.	9.06	1876	10.07	1818			58	001	18	
Allen	Edward Biddle	11.29	1867	4.08	1855			13	001	19	Allen, James M. & E. B., son of
Allen	William Spottswood	12.06	1849				7.00	1	001	20	Allen, James M. & Elizabeth B., son of
Allen	Charles Penrose	2.07	1858	6.20	1857			1	001	21	Allen, James M. & Elizabeth B., son of
Allen	Edward Biddle	11.26	1849			13	1.25	14	001	22	
Allen	John A.	9.21	1821			14	5.09	15	001	23	Allen, J. M. & Jane, son of
Armstrong	Henry Saxton	7.21	1878				9.11	1	001	30	Armstrong, B. F. & Sallie C., son of
Baird	Samuel	7.27	1833			45		46	001	33	d. in Reading, Pa. (b. 1787)
Baird	Lydia M.	6.03	1871	7.04	1797			74	001	34	Baird, Samuel, wife of; Biddle, Wm. M. & Lydia, dau. of; b. Phila. d. Carlisle
Baird	Samuel	10.12	1884	4.20	1821			64	001	35	Baird, Samuel & Lydia M. B., second son of; b. Reading, PA; d. Carlisle
Baird	William M.	10.19	1872	8.04	1817			56	001	36	
Baird	Robert	9.07	1897	5.10	1857			41	001	37	Baird, William M. & Harriet H., son of
Baker	John, Sr.	3.11	1887	2.28	1814			74	001	31	
Baker	Philip	3.30	1875			46	5.22	47	001	32	
Barnitz	Jane R.	10.08	1842			17		18	001	38	
Barnitz	Henry	12.14	1860	9.05	1800			61	001	39	[d. 1860 ?]
Barnitz	J. Elder	9.18	1890	12.10	1809			81	001	40	
Barnitz	Susan	11.02	1884	10.29	1807			78	001	41	
Beatty	Erourius	3.08	1880	5.06	1817			63	003	05	
Beetem	Abram	8.12	1833			43	11.15	44	002	06	Captain
Beetem	Elizabeth	2.04	1872			77	6.07	78	002	07	Beetem, Abram, Captain, wife of

Carlisle - Ashland Cemetery

Surname	Given Name	Death Mo/Dy	Year	Birth Mo/Dy	Year	Att. Age Yr	Mo/Dy	Cm Ag	Pg	No	Other Information
Beetem	George	1.03	1852	11.23	1792			60	002	08	
Beetem	Hannah	11.18	1878	1.14	1801			78	002	09	Beetem, George, wife of
Beetem	Hannah	3.13	1830	3.17	1801			29	002	10	Beetem, George, wife of; Zinn, George & Mary, daughter of
Beetem	Samuel T.	9.07	1844			20	7.07	21	002	11	Beetem, George & Hannah, son of
Beetem	Mary Ann	8.13	1854				11.13	1	002	12	Beetem, John & E. A., daughter of
Beetem	William M.	7.26	1865	4.14	1820			46	002	13	
Beetem	Joseph	2.18	1894	12.16	1830			64	002	14	
Beetem	Hetty			6.28	1836				002	15	Beetem, Joseph, wife of: (not dead)
Beetem	George S.	5.30	1892	1.08	1824			69	002	16	
Beetem	Mary E.	10.20	1855	12.27	1854			1	002	17	
Beetem	Samuel			8.17	1816				002	43	[death date not given]
Beetem	Almira	8.20	1894	1.06	1818			77	002	44	
Beetem	William H.	10.20	1889	9.06	1844			46	002	45	Beetem, Samuel & A., son of
Beetem	Laura								002	46	Beetem, Samuel & Elmira, daughter of
Beetem	Elizabeth A.	10.04	1867			40	5.02	41	003	01	Beetem, John, wife of
Beetem	Mary A.	5.12	1889	7.13	1835			54	003	02	Beetem, Abram, wife of
Beetem	Alice Louise	11.05	1897	12.04	1885			12	003	03	Beetem, Jacob Redsecker & Alice Gardner, daughter of
Beetem	Mary J.	5.02	1901						003	04	Beetem, Abraham & Elizabeth, daughter of
Beidler	Sophia Zeigler								003	06	Beidler, John K., wife of [no dates]
Beisel	Anna					1	7.00	2	004	11	Beisel, A. B. & S. R., only daughter of
Beltzhoover	Catharine E. T.	10.08	1856	12.25	1833			23	003	07	
Beltzhoover	Charles	12.04	1862	5.15	1825			38	003	08	
Beltzhoover	M. G.	1.01	1873	1.14	1792			81	003	09	
Beltzhoover	A. M. Herman	5.30	1871	11.12	1799			72	003	10	Beltzhoover, M. G., wife of
Beltzhoover	C. H.	2.27	1875	8.27	1826			49	003	11	
Bender	Mary Alberta	7.06	1870	1.15	1870			1	002	31	Bender, John Godfrey & A. M., child of
Bender	Anna Margaretta	2.19	1876	6.05	1868			8	002	32	Bender, John Godfrey & A. M., child of
Bender	John Godfrey	12.05	1882	5.31	1823			60	003	12	
Bender	Anna Margaretta	9.08	1882	2.06	1824			59	003	13	Bender, John Godfrey, wife of
Bender	John	6.08	1870	6.02	1844			27	003	14	
Bender	Anna Mary	8.23	1877	10.03	1792			85	003	15	
Bentz	John	2.01	1885			69		70	002	33	
Bentz	Mary R.	11.29	1884			72		73	002	34	Bentz, John, wife of
Bentz	George Z.	5.14	1887	11.20	1822			65	002	35	
Bentz	Jane E.	3.16	1883	9.03	1825			58	002	36	Bentz, George Z., wife of
Bentz	George W. H.	8.12	1874	7.03	1854			21	002	37	
Bentz	William	4.13	1881			70	3.14	71	002	38	
Bentz	Anna	12.03	1881			70	1.02	71	002	39	
Bentz	Martin G.	8.31	1873	9.25	1843			30	002	40	
Bentz	Sadie A.	7.22	1880	6.03	1841			40	002	41	Bentz, Martin, wife of
Bentz	Robert M.	12.18	1884	8.17	1881			4	002	42	Bentz, I. C. & A. [?] M., son of
Bergman	Herman H.	3.15	1867			23		24	002	19	1st Sgt. Permanent Troop, Carlisle Barracks; fell at Carlisle [?]
Bergner	Mary Ann M.					23	2.19	24	002	28	Bergner, G., consort of
Bergner	Thadeus					2	9.07	3	002	29	Bergner, Mary & G., child of
Bergner	Henrietta						6.26	1	002	30	Bergner, Mary & G., child of
Berie	Dionysius	9.23	1867			41	6.05	42	002	18	
Biddle	Edward	11.26	1849			13	1.25	14	003	16	

Carlisle - Ashland Cemetery

Surname	Given Name	Death Mo/Dy	Death Year	Birth Mo/Dy	Birth Year	Att. Yr	Age Mo/Dy	Age Ag	Cm	Pg	No	Other Information
Biddle	Lydia, Mrs.	3.28	1858	1.16	1766			93	003	17		Biddle, William M., of Philadelphia, widow of; Spencer, Elihu, Rev. D. D., of Trenton, N. J., daughter of
Biddle	Edward M.	5.13	1888	7.27	1808			80	003	18		
Biddle	Charles P.	3.25	1890	7.21	1847			43	003	19		
Bird	Frederick Stanley					1.00		1	003	20		Bird, Samuel R. & Mary E., son of
Bitner	Henry		1884		1804			81	003	21		
Bitner	Sarah		1862		1806			57	003	22		
Bixler	Mary E.	9.09	1872	2.29	1848			25	003	26		Bixler, S. & Lydia, daughter of
Blair	William	5.20	1852			38		39	002	01		
Blair	Jane		1890						002	02		Blair, William, wife of
Blair	Mary	8.30	1864			74		75	002	03		Blair, William, wife of
Blaney	Mary E. D. Biddle	9.04	1879						001	42		Blaney, Geo., Maj., Corps of Engineers, USA., wife of; b. Phila.; d. Carlisle
Blaney	William Biddle	2.18	1862	9.26	1832			30	001	43		Blaney, Geo. & Mary E. D., only son of; b. Smithville, NC; d. St. Louis, MO
Bohme	Emanuel	4.16	1871			37		38	003	42		a native of the Kingdom of Hanover
Booth	John P.	7.30	1884	2.12	1859			26	003	37		
Bosh	Lewis	8.22	1872	11.25	1835			37	003	36		
Bosler	Abraham	12.21	1883			77	4.03	78	003	27		(b. 8.18 1806)
Bosler	Eliza Herman	12.07	1885			75	2.07	76	003	28		Bosler, Abraham. wife of
Bosler	James Williamson	12.17	1883			50	7.13	51	003	29		
Bosler	Helen Beltzhoover	10.05	1890	5.15	1833			58	003	30		Bosler, James W., wife of
Bosler	Charlie	12.23	1870	8.27	1864			7	003	31		Bosler, James W. & Helen, son of
Bosler	J. Herman	11.18	1897	12.14	1830			67	003	32		
Bosler	Nellie					1	3.00	2	003	33		Bosler, J. H. & M. J., child of
Bosler	Jessie						11.00	1	003	34		Bosler, J. H. & M. J., child of
Bosler	Eddie						5.00	1	003	35		Bosler, J. H. & M. J., child of
Bowers	James Patton								003	38		Bowers, S. A. & R. M., child of
Bowers	William Edward								003	39		Bowers, S. A. & R. M., child of
Bowman	George W.	9.12	1887	5.20	1809			79	003	40		General
Bowman	Ann	2.22	1885	2.05	1813			73	003	41		
Bratton	John Beatty	4.27	1892						002	04		
Bratton	Mary Ellen Boyd	3.13	1893						002	05		Bratton, John B., wife of
Brenneman	Melchoir	12.04	1862			71	11.11	72	002	20		[Melchoir (sic)]
Brenneman	Mary	3.25	1881			95	2.29	96	002	21		Brenneman, Melchoir, wife of
Brenneman	Isaac		1895		1824			72	002	22		
Brenneman	Margaret		1896		1820			77	002	23		Brenneman, Isaac, wife of
Brenneman	W. Heagy		1900		1879			22	002	24		
Bretz	Edward B.	6.07	1878	5.06	1851			28	002	25		
Bretz	Jacob		1896		1806			91	002	26		
Bretz	Mary		1883		1809			75	002	27		Bretz, Jacob, wife of
Brightbill	Carrie L. Mumma	5.04	1886	12.14	1864			22	003	25		Brightbill, George B., wife of
Brill	Joseph	5.28	1893			55	5.03	56	004	12		(seaman)
Brindle	Abner C.	9.23	1898	9.17	1837			62	003	23		
Brindle	Miriam E.	7.12	1880	1.30	1880			1	003	24		
Brougher	Mary E.	4.05	1867			27	5.00	28	003	43		Brougher, G. W., wife of
Brubaker	Maria	6.29	1886	5.22	1824			63	004	08		
Brubaker	Annie M.	9.04	1887			35	8.08	36	004	09		Brubaker, Levi, wife of
Brubaker	Nina	5.09	1872						004	10		

Carlisle - Ashland Cemetery

Surname	Given Name	Death Mo/Dy	Year	Birth Mo/Dy	Year	Att. Age Yr	Cm Mo/Dy	Pg Ag	No	Other Information
Brubaker	Percy M.	4.02	1878				6.17	1	004 13	Brubaker, Levi & Annie, child of
Brubaker	Ellis M.	9.11	1880				5.11	1	004 14	Brubaker, Levi & Annie, child of
Burkholder	Ella		1883		1864			20	004 06	[the following entry reads "Burkholder, J. Earley & Ella B."; possibly an error; these may be parents of Ella]
Bushman	Henry	9.22	1886			85	4.08	86	003 44	
Bushman	Mary	9.12	1861			61	11.16	62	004 01	Bushman, Henry, wife of
Bushman	William Henry	9.09	1854	11.13	1836			18	004 02	Bushman, Henry & Mary, son of
Bushman	Ida	5.06	1889	8.08	1863			26	004 03	
Bushman	Eli		1898		1826			73	004 04	
Bushman	Alfadore	7.18	1858	7.13	1858			1	004 05	Bushman, Eli & Jane, son of
Butler	Edward Biddle	11.29	1867	4.08	1855			13	004 07	Butler, James M. & E., son of
Cameron	Elmer L.	12.22	1892			23	11.12	24	004 18	
Cameron	Ralph M.	1.05	1881			7	1.05	8	004 19	Cameron, L. & E, child of
Cameron	Bessie W.	10.07	1887			2	1.00	3	004 20	Cameron, L. & E, child of
Campbell	Mary	6.14	1859	9.08	1833			26	004 15	Campbell, John, wife of
Campbell	W. K.	9.24	1885						004 16	Dr.
Campbell	Belle Hitner	11.12	1880	1.03	1838			43	004 17	
Carr	Henry G.	12.18	1890	11.28	1822			69	004 21	
Cart	George	1.12	1878	7.04	1802			76	004 22	
Cathcart	Alexander	10.03	1882			83		84	004 23	
Cathcart	Elmira J. King	8.03	1843			31	3.25	32	004 24	Cathcart, Alexander, wife of
Cathcart	Susan L.	5.10	1889	9.29	1840			49	004 25	
Cathcart	Robert	6.07	1883			49	11.00	50	004 26	
Cheston	H. C.	11.27	1882			48	1.28	49	004 34	Rev.
Coble	John E.	9.12	1867			41	6.00	42	004 35	
Collins	Caroline M.	11.18	1893	4.10	1845			49	004 36	
Condon	Charles E.	10.03	1863				10.22	1	004 39	Condon, J. & D., infant son of
Corbett	Jacob L.	2.16	1891			40		41	004 37	
Corbett	John W.	4.30	1895			42		43	004 38	
Cornman	John P.	2.17	1887			43	8.16	44	004 40	
Cornman	David	1.30	1875	1.17	1794			82	004 41	
Cornman	Elizabeth	3.03	1893	8.31	1800			93	004 42	Cornman, David, wife of
Cornman	Jacob W.					7		8	004 43	
Cornman	David M.					1	9.18	2	004 44	
Cornman	William M.						7.05	1	004 45	
Coyle	Samuel M.	8.23	1879						005 01	
Craighead	William L.	12.02	1874	3.04	1828			47	004 29	
Craighead	George S.	4.23	1869			3		4	004 30	Craighead, W. L. & M. B., son of
Craighead	Reynolds						8.00	1	004 31	Craighead, R. R. & M., child of
Craighead	Maggie R.						3.00	1	004 32	Craighead, R. R. & M., child of
Craighead	Sallie B.						2.00	1	004 33	Craighead, R. R. & M., child of
Crane	Benjamin	11.12	1831			62		63	004 27	
Crane	Catharine	12.14	1863			103		104	004 28	Crane, Benjamin, wife of
Crouse	Mary	9.01	1857			27		28	005 02	Crouse, Adam, consort of
Crozier	John T.	12.15	1880	3.17	1845			36	005 03	
Culver	Hannah M.	1.19	1871			28		29	005 04	
Culver	Martha	3.18	1898	2.07	1809			90	005 05	
Dale	William W.	2.24	1891	11.15	1817			74	005 06	M. D.
Dale	Sarah Martin	6.07	1895	6.20	1821			74	005 07	Dale, William W., wife of

Carlisle - Ashland Cemetery

Surname	Given Name	Death Mo/Dy	Year	Birth Mo/Dy	Year	Att. Age Yr	Mo/Dy	Ag	Cm	Pg	No	Other Information
Dale	W. James	10.28	1888			38			39	005	08	
Danner	Mary Ann	9.11	1861			52	7.07	53		005	10	Danner, Joseph, wife of
Danner	Uriah	2.23	1866			26	6.21	27		005	11	
Dare	A. Dale Filbert	8.03	1892	7.19	1864			29		005	09	Dare, William K., wife of
Darr	John David	2.16	1869			18	7.05	19		005	25	
Darr	Rachel E.	10.18	1867			23	6.03	24		005	26	Darr, John H. & Elizabeth, daughter of
Darr	John H.	1.18	1871			58	11.13	59		005	27	
Darr	Elizabeth	9.28	1896			77	0.16	78		005	28	Darr, John H., wife of
Davidson	Eliza	2.25	1875			74	1.24	75		005	12	
Delancey	John	4.27	1833			80			81	005	21	Esquire
Delancey	Catharine	3.03	1821			48			49	005	22	Delancey, John, Esq., wife of and 10 ch.
Delancey	Oliver	2.16	1835			36			37	005	23	Delancey, John & Catharine, son of
Delancey	John	1.05	1835			1	5.20	2		005	24	Delancey, Oliver & Sarah, son of
Derland	Asbury		1898		1837			62		005	14	
Derland	Mary	3.27	1867			36	3.00	37		005	15	Derland, Asbury, wife of
Derland	Carroll Maxwell	8.11	1867				5.00	1		005	16	Derland, Asbury & Mary, son of
Derr	Wilhelmina	6.04	1884	5.04	1857			28		005	13	Derr, Thomas, wife of; nee Smith
Dewalt	Solomon	10.08	1888	5.12	1818			71		005	17	
Dewalt	Susan	12.31	1892	11.23	1823			70		005	18	
Dewalt	Harry E.	4.22	1878	1.08	1863			16		005	19	
Diehl	Charles E.	12.21	1892	2.24	1849			44		005	34	
Dinkle	Emma L.	10.13	1897	10.07	1852			46		005	29	
Dinkle	Essie									005	30	[no dates given]
Dinkle	Daniel									005	31	[no dates given]
Dinkle	George									005	32	[no dates given]
Dinkle	Frank									005	33	[no dates given]
Diven	Thomas P.					33			34	005	20	Captain, 1st Regt., Pa. Reserves
Dixon	William B.	10.27	1884	11.10	1840			44		005	35	Co. A, 7th Pa. Reserves
Dobson	Sarah M.		1859							005	36	[1859 is not designated as death date]
Dobson	John R.		1849							005	37	[1849 is not designated as death date]
Dobson	Samuel	7.19	1856							005	38	[death year could be 1836]
Dobson	Jane		1887		1822			66		005	39	
Dunkle	Susan M.	2.04	1889			69	8.19	70		005	40	Dunkle, Jacob, wife of
Dunkle	Ellie	3.30	1869			12		13		005	41	
Earley	S. W.	1.10	1874			37			38	005	42	
Earley	Eliza	7.18	1884							005	43	Earley, S. W., wife of
Earley	Susan	2.18	1870			56		57		005	44	Earley, John, wife of
Eckles	John C.	5.22	1896	4.13	1824			73		005	45	
Eckels	Frank Kenyon	3.25	1887	9.07	1856			31		006	01	has a child buried in Mechanicsburg cem.
Eckels	Lucinda	7.31	1865			23	5.07	24		006	02	Eckels, T. H. B., wife of
Eckels	Mamie									006	03	Eckels, J. C. & M. L., daughter of
Edmonds	Danford R.		1895		1839			57		006	08	
Edmonds	Lucy G.		1900		1833			68		006	09	
Egbert	Issacher R.	5.23	1894	10.28	1810			84		006	04	[month given as "10th" and "5th"]
Egbert	Sarah C.	4.06	1890	1.25	1809			82		006	05	[month given as "4th" and "1st"]
Egbert	Naomi	6.12	1890	1.22	1837			54		006	06	[month given as "6th" and "1st"]
Egbert	W. Oscar	1.15	1854	3.28	1853			1		006	07	[month given as "1st" and "3rd"]
Eisenhower	Ellen W.	3.16	1870	11.04	1822			48		006	35	Mrs.
Elliott	Margaretta A.	5.09	1875			64			65	006	10	Elliott, Abram, wife of
Elliott	Charles H.						2.29	1		006	11	Elliott, Abram & M. A., son of

Carlisle - Ashland Cemetery

Surname	Given Name	Death Mo/Dy	Year	Birth Mo/Dy	Year	Att. Age Yr	Mo/Dy	Ag	Cm	Pg	No	Other Information
Elliott	Abram L.									006	12	Elliott, A. & A. R., son of [no dates]
Elliott	Frances Caln Vaughn	12.22	1877	5.25	1791				87	006	13	Elliott, Jesse D., Commodore, wife of
Elliott	Catharine Howell	10.16	1839	4.18	1823				17	006	14	Elliott, J. D., Commodore & Frances, d. of; b. Norfolk, VA, d. Carlisle, PA
Elliott	-----									006	15	Elliott, W. L. & V. B., son of
Elliott	Sarah Ann									006	16	Elliott, J. D., Commodore & Frances, eldest daughter of; died of cholera on the Ohio River near Wheeling, separated from her relations
Eppley	John	8.05	1878			51	2.21	52		006	17	
Eppley	George	6.21	1852	2.21	1786				67	006	18	
Eppley	Susannah	12.14	1850	2.22	1800				51	006	19	Eppley, George, wife of
Eppley	Mary Ann	3.08	1860			23	10.28	24		006	20	Eppley, George & S., daughter of
Eppley	Jacob B.	12.22	1849	4.06	1823				27	006	21	Eppley, George & S., son of
Eppley	Abram	5.19	1846	6.15	1834				12	006	22	Eppley, George & S., son of
Eppley	Sarah A.	7.17	1885	12.21	1825				60	006	23	Eppley, George, wife of
Eppley	Joseph E.	1.02	1860			2	9.28	3		006	24	Eppley, George & S. A., son of
Eppley	Sarah E.	1.06	1860			6	7.06	7		006	25	Eppley, George & S. A., daughter of
Eppley	John L.	1.05	1850			1	9.19	2		006	26	Eppley, George & S. E., son of
Eppley	Annie M.	6.26	1892	6.04	1851				42	006	27	
Eppley	George Sheaffer					4	4.13	5		006	28	Eppley, J. & M., child of
Eppley	Susannah E.	7.23	1861			2	9.13	3		006	29	Eppley, J. & M., child of
Eppley	Clara	10.09	1862			1	8.19	2		006	30	Eppley, J. & M., child of
Eppley	George H.	3.17	1850	10.15	1848			2		006	31	Eppley, Samuel & Amanda, child of
Eppley	John Hoon	3.15	1861			6	5.21	7		006	32	Eppley, Samuel & Amanda, child of
Eppley	Susan Elizabeth	6.15	1884	6.16	1865				19	006	33	Eppley, Samuel & Amanda, child of
Ernest	John	5.26	1864							006	34	a native of Germany; a soldier of the U. S. Army; d. near Carlisle
Evans	Julia A.	9.23	1863			16	9.27	17		006	36	Evans, Samuel & Rebecca, daughter of
Evarts	George	10.26	1881							006	37	aged about 72 years
Ewing	Mary	1.15	1891	12.22	1820				71	006	38	
Faber	Lewis	4.10	1886	6.07	1827				59	007	01	
Faber	Lewis, Sr.	4.17	1868			67			68	007	02	
Faber	Maria	7.07	1858			55			56	007	03	Faber, Lewis, Sr., wife of
Faber	John L.	4.07	1857			1	2.00	2		007	04	Faber, L. & S. A., son of
Failor	Adam	2.16	1880	9.23	1804				76	007	05	
Failor	Sarah	4.03	1869			62	3.04	63		007	06	Failor, Adam, wife of
Fellman	Frederick	12.03	1874			47			48	007	28	
Fennicle	Sallie	11.25	1869			2	2.15	3		007	21	Fennicle, W. & M. A., child of
Fennicle	Anna M.	12.01	1869				1.12	1		007	22	Fennicle, W. & M. A., child of
Fickes	Samuel M.	9.30	1886			49			50	007	30	
Fickes	Laura A.	1.15	1885			17			18	007	31	
Fishburn	Anthony	8.02	1889	7.01	1815				75	007	33	
Fishburn	Philip Henry	2.11	1845	1.23	1843				3	007	34	
Fishburn	Annie Maria	3.03	1855	1.19	1851				5	007	35	
Fishburn	John	6.14	1895	7.13	1813				82	007	36	
Fishburn	Rachel	7.31	1839							007	37	Fishburn, John, wife of; b. 10.03, 18-7
Fishburn	Susan	4.21	1890	11.20	1821				69	007	38	Fishburn, John, wife of
Fishburn	Rachel C.	9.26	1839	6.17	1839				1	007	39	
Fishburn	Caroline Amelia	6.13	1853	8.28	1836				17	007	40	Fishburn, John & Rachel, daughter of

Carlisle - Ashland Cemetery

Surname	Given Name	Death Mo/Dy	Year	Birth Mo/Dy	Year	Att. Age Yr	Mo/Dy	Cm Ag	Pg	No	Other Information
Fishburn	Mary E.	12.20		4.09					007	41	Fishburn, Harvey M., wife of [error: b. 1870; d. 1880]
Fishburn	infant daughter	12.05	1888						007	42	Fishburn, H. & M. E., daughter of
Fishburn	Reuben	10.26	1890	7.05	1828			63	007	43	
Fishburn	Rebecca	8.05	1855	5.12	1827			29	007	44	Fishburn, Reuben, wife of
Fishburn	Adam			3.06	1826				007	45	
Fishburn	Catharine E. H.	11.17	1891	12.15	1832			59	007	46	Fishburn, Adam, wife of [H.=Hefflebower]
Fishburn	Jane Ellen	12.28	1854			24	9.14	25	008	01	Fishburn, Adam, wife of
Fishburn	Horace E.	6.02	1870	9.25	1869			1	008	02	
Fishburn	John	4.18	1861			76	4.06	77	008	03	
Fishburn	Catharine	3.15	1874			82	11.06	83	008	04	Fishburn, John, wife of
Fishburn	Philip	7.15	1842	1.16	1810			33	008	05	Fishburn, John & Catharine, son of
Fishburn	infant son	10.14	1860						008	06	Fishburn, Adam & C., child of
Fishburn	Elmer H.	4.04	1862	11.21	1861			1	008	07	Fishburn, Adam & C., child of
Fissel	Sallie A. Wetzel	4.09	1882	1.19	1856			27	007	32	Fissel, Niles N., wife of
Fleager	Charles	3.15	1875			75		76	007	07	
Fleager	Mary	3.16	1866	11.11	1807			59	007	08	Fleager, Charles, wife of
Fleager	Henry	11.12	1845			7	10.18	8	007	09	
Fleager	Benjamin F.	1.23	1846			1	2.19	2	007	10	
Fleager	Emm L.	9.27	1850			3	9.23	4	007	11	[Emm (sic)]
Fleager	Annetta	6.07	1853			3	0.01	4	007	12	
Fleager	Charles	6.14	1844			1	6.14	2	007	13	
Fleager	Annie	6.22	1831				9.02	1	007	14	Fleager, Charles & Mary, child of
Fleager	Sarah E.	8.30	1833			1	1.13	2	007	15	Fleager, Charles & Mary, child of
Fleager	John D.	9.07	1835			1	2.14	2	007	16	Fleager, Charles & Mary, child of
Fleager	Emanuel	3.29	1838			1	11.24	2	007	17	Fleager, Charles & Mary, child of
Fleager	Isabella	5.31	1844			4	6.13	5	007	18	Fleager, Charles & Mary, child of
Fleager	Mary A.	6.12	1844			3	1.01	4	007	19	Fleager, Charles & Mary, child of
Fleager	Charles	4.21	1838			7	8.22	8	007	20	Fleager, Daniel & Susan, son of
Foreman	James K.	12.28	1888	6.29	1837			52	008	08	
Frederick	Adam	4.17	1882	2.15	1815			68	007	23	
Frederick	George W.	6.15	1888			44		45	007	24	
Frederick	Adam J.	9.24	1877			5	9.02	6	007	25	Frederick, G. W. & C., son of
Frederick	David	6.29	1894	11.17	1820			74	007	26	
Frederick	Sarah E.	5.04	1896	3.17	1866			31	007	27	
Freeland	Margaret A.	5.01	1894	1.16	1837			58	007	29	
Galbraith	Thompson M.	12.29	1863	11.09	1813			51	008	24	
Galbraith	Elizabeth Woods	2.22	1893	7.25	1827			66	008	25	
Galbraith	Emma W.	3.25	1871	10.22	1853			18	008	26	
Garber	Jacob	8.08	1887	1.05	1845			43	008	09	
Garber	George A.	4.15	1890			19	8.00	20	008	10	
Garber	George	1.02	1894	7.20	1814			80	008	11	
Garber	Anna M.	4.11	1892	2.16	1839			54	008	12	Garber, George, wife of
Garber	Daisy M.	8.07	1896	4.30	1876			21	008	13	
Gardner	Franklin	11.00	1898	12.00	1820			78	008	14	
Gardner	Mary M.	10.19	1861			70		71	008	15	
Gardner	M. F.	4.25	1873			26		27	008	16	
Gardner	Israel		1879		1822			58	008	17	
Gardner	Elizabeth	2.18	1872						008	18	Gardner, Israel, wife of
Gardner	Hannah Abrahims	2.11	1863			36		37	008	19	

Carlisle - Ashland Cemetery

Surname	Given Name	Death Mo/Dy	Death Year	Birth Mo/Dy	Birth Year	Att. Age Yr	Att. Age Mo/Dy	Cm Ag	Pg	No	Other Information
Gardner	Frank	9.08	1871			1		2	008	20	Gardner, M. F., son of
Gardner	W. H.	10.11	1845			2		3	008	21	
Gardner	C. A.	1.11	1859			5		6	008	22	
Gardner	Lillie	3.29	1873			20	1.13	21	008	23	
Gebhart	Jacob	6.11	1867	10.02	1829			38	009	06	b. Gittersbach, Hesse Darmstadt
Gebhart	Jacob B.	10.24	1862	11.30	1861			1	009	07	
Gensler	Thudia J.	10.02	1877			2	8.05	3	008	32	Gensler, G. D. & M. B., son of
Geremyer	George L., Jr.	3.27	1891			36		37	009	02	
Gibson	David	2.11	1864	7.06	1842			22	009	08	
Gill	Sarah B.	5.06	1878			38	10.28	39	009	09	Gill, Samuel, wife of
Gill	Martha A.	5.27	1872			1	1.07	2	009	10	Gill, S. & S., daughter of
Ginter	Magdalena	12.01	1888	1.20	1835			54	009	11	
Given	Robert	2.09	1879	6.11	1810			69	009	12	
Given	Sarah H. Gibson	2.10	1887	12.26	1822			65	009	13	Given, Robert, wife of
Given	James S., Sr.	2.08	1841			75		76	009	14	
Given	Amelia Steele	5.23	1859			82		83	009	15	Given, James S., Sr., wife of
Given	Joseph					36		37	009	16	Given, James S. & Amelia Steele, ch. of
Given	John								009	17	Given, James S. & Amelia Steele, ch. of
Given	James								009	18	Given, James S. & Amelia Steele, ch. of
Given	Elizabeth								009	19	Given, James S. & Amelia Steele, ch. of
Given	Samuel	5.04	1892			87		88	009	20	Given, James S. & Amelia Steele, ch. of
Given	James	9.07	1862	9.27	1843			19	009	21	Given, Robert & Sarah, child of
Given	Samuel	5.11	1872	5.02	1848			25	009	22	Given, Robert & Sarah, child of
Given	Robert Hopkins	12.31	1872	7.15	1855			18	009	23	Given, Robert & Sarah, child of
Givler	Margie Teressa	5.00	1896	3.03	1869			28	009	24	Givler, Andrew Curtin, wife of
Glenn	William	3.01	1867	9.17	1813	53	5.00	54	008	33	[two entries for this person]
Glenn	Annie E.	2.23	1860			10	2.12	11	008	34	Glenn, William & Jane A., daughter of
Glenn	Jane A. McKeehan	9.16	1895	5.29	1819			77	008	35	Glenn, William, wife of
Good	John J.	12.13	1887	2.15	1849			39	009	30	
Goodrich	Mary	7.08	1896	12.21	1868			28	009	37	Goodrich, Joseph King, wife of; Kremer, James Brainard & Martha Nevin, dau. of
Goodyear	John	5.01	1891	9.22	1809			82	009	31	
Goodyear	Caroline	2.20	1895	4.18	1821			74	009	32	
Goodyear	Elmira Catharine	1.20	1858			19	5.07	20	009	33	Goodyear, J. C. & C., daughter of
Goodyear	Anna Regina	2.20	1850			9	10.23	10	009	34	Goodyear, J. C. & C., daughter of
Goodyear	Rowena Elmira	9.17	1858				4.19	1	009	35	Goodyear, J. C. & C., daughter of
Goodyear	Ida Sophia C.	12.24	1862			2	0.07	3	009	36	Goodyear, J. C. & C., daughter of
Gould	Samuel H.	12.27	1889	10.02	1826			64	009	38	
Graham	John	6.09	1866			85	5.21	86	008	27	
Graham	Polly	9.03	1861			73	7.19	74	008	28	Graham, John, wife of
Graham	Stuart Alexander	6.22	1843			25	6.01	26	008	29	Graham, J. & P., son of
Graham	Hettie E.	9.20	1862			1	8.15	2	008	30	Graham, J. E. B. & K., daughter of
Graham	Graham, I. H.					49		50	008	31	Captain, Co. I, 1st Regt., Pa. Reserves, 30th P. Vols.; [initials doubtful]
Greason	James A.	12.27	1880	3.14	1844			37	008	36	
Greason	Bennie					10		11	008	37	
Greason	Samuel	3.14	1897	3.27	1814			83	008	38	
Greason	Elmira J.		1889		1831			59	008	39	
Greason	Henry B.								008	40	dates given as: "May Sep 1868"
Bitner	Henry		1884		1804			81	008	41	(Indented under Greason)

Carlisle - Ashland Cemetery

Surname	Given Name	Death Mo/Dy	Death Year	Birth Mo/Dy	Birth Year	Att. Age Yr	Att. Age Mo/Dy	Cm Ag	Pg	No	Other Information
Bitner	Sarah		1862		1806			57	008	42	(Indented under Greason)
Greason	Margaret	10.28	1883						008	43	Greason, John & M., daughter of
Greason	Mary M.	7.12	1888	1.29	1846			43	009	01	Greason, Robert & M. A., daughter of
Greenfield	David M.	7.25	1870			5.00	1		009	03	Greenfield, L. T. & M. J., child of
Greenfield	Cora T.	7.19	1867			6.19	1		009	04	Greenfield, L. T. & M. J., child of
Greenfield	Lynda	6.11	1864			7.00	1		009	05	Greenfield, L. T. & M. J., child of
Grier	David	4.07	1865						009	28	
Grier	Mary Jane	10.07	1891						009	29	Grier, David, wife of
Grissinger	Samuel N.	10.25	1879	10.13	1799			81	009	25	
Grissinger	Anna M.	1.26	1871	3.13	1795			76	009	26	
Grissinger	Solomon W.	7.30	1875	8.07	1825			50	009	27	
Grove	Henry Beltzhoover	10.29	1865	2.09	1842			24	009	39	
Grove	Eliza Ann Beltzhoover	3.21	1876	12.22	1821			55	009	40	
Grove	Henry Hack	9.17	1870	4.21	1817			54	009	41	
Grube	Beuhla R.	2.06	1897			8.03	1		009	42	
Gutshall	John	9.12	1890	10.19	1818			72	009	43	
Gutshall	Catharine Wunderlich	12.25	1851	1.28	1825			27	009	44	Gutshall, John, wife of [1851 ?]
Gutshall	Hettie Graham	11.10	1876	5.28	1833			44	010	01	Gutshall, John, wife of
Gutshall	J. Charles	1.21	1860	1.28	1849			11	010	02	Gutshall, J. & C., son of
Gutshall	Peter	5.03	1865			73		74	010	03	
Gutshall	Willie C.	2.17	1860	9.22	1855			5	010	04	Gutshall, John & Hettie G., child of
Gutshall	Harry P.	9.01	1858	3.21	1858			1	010	05	Gutshall, John & Hettie G., child of
Gutshall	John	9.12	1863	4.28	1861			3	010	06	Gutshall, John & Hettie G., child of
Gutshall	Georgia E.	10.20	1885	3.12	1868			18	010	07	Gutshall, John & Hattie G., child of
Hackenberry	Henry	7.09	1894	7.19	1818			76	010	17	Rev.
Hackenberry	Hannah C.	1.30	1901	5.15	1825			76	010	18	Hackenberry, Henry, wife of
Haddock	Orison Lull	12.17	1879			35		36	010	08	
Hamman	John Jacob	8.25	1869	9.08	1798			71	010	20	
Hamman	Mary	5.04	1873	6.11	1805			68	010	21	Hamman, John J., wife of
Hamman	Margaret	12.24	1872	5.12	1841			32	010	22	Hamman, Philip, wife of
Hargis	J. H.	8.07	1895	5.07	1847			49	010	09	(D. D.)
Hargis	Sarah	9.15	1889	6.05	1875			15	010	10	
Harrison	Margaret	4.13	1852			5		6	010	19	Harrison, James & Mary Noble, dau. of
Hart	John E.	12.22	1879	9.06	1848			32	010	23	
Hartzler	Harry Herbert	1.22	1873	10.16	1871			2	010	11	Hartzler, H. B. & S. A., son of
Hastings	William M.	10.02	1874			35	6.16	36	010	12	
Hastings	Harry Snyder	7.24	1867	6.02	1866			2	010	13	Hastings, William M. & Caroline, son of
Hays	William R.	7.03	1883			76	8.00	77	010	14	
Hays	Mary			3.04	1815	83	9.27	83	010	15	Hays, William R., wife of
Hays	John Hoffman	7.04	1871	8.28	1847			24	010	16	Hays, William R. & Mary, son of
Heagy	William	12.01	1896	7.27	1820			77	010	26	
Heagy	Sarah A.	9.12	1877	1.25	1821			57	010	27	
Hemminger	Samuel	10.28	1881	1.28	1827			55	010	28	
Hemminger	Eliza	6.14	1883			81	10.11	82	010	29	
Hemminger	John	5.16	1878			89	7.04	90	010	30	
Hench	George	3.09	1892	1.31	1810			83	010	24	
Hench	George Allison	8.16	1899	10.04	1866			33	010	25	
Henderson	J. Wilson	3.25	1880	10.22	1824			56	010	34	
Henderson	Jane B.	3.23	1891	5.18	1825			66	010	35	
Henderson	Samuel Alexander	6.25	1886	1.15	1858			29	010	36	Henderson, J. Wilson & Jane B., son of

Carlisle - Ashland Cemetery

Surname	Given Name	Death Mo/Dy	Year	Birth Mo/Dy	Year	Att. Age Yr	Mo/Dy	Ag	Cm	Pg	No	Other Information
Henry	John L.	12.12	1898	5.20	1844			55	010	31		
Henwood	Annie C.	9.17	1888	5.22	1829			60	010	32		
Herbst	Hannah	3.28	1870			3	6.21	4	011	05		Herbst, A. & C., daughter of
Herebwont	Clara J.		1877		1856			22	010	33		
Herman	Martin Christian	1.19	1896	2.14	1841			55	010	37		
Herman	Martin C., Jr.		1878		1874			5	010	38		
Herman	Martin						4.00	1	010	39		
Hettrick	Abraham	10.15	1866			78	5.12	79	010	40		
Hettrick	Susanna	4.03	1848	12.13	1826			22	010	41		Hettrick, Abraham, child of
Hettrick	Martha	3.13	1848	2.01	1829			20	010	42		Hettrick, Abraham, child of
Hettrick	Henry	6.04	1836	12.03	1835			1	010	43		Hettrick, A. & M., son of
Hettrick	Eleanor Eliza	7.24	1835	3.22	1817			19	010	44		Hettrick, Abraham & Mary, daughter of
Hettrick	Jesse	6.15	1896	12.02	1833			63	011	01		
Hettrick	A. Matilda	2.10	1895	4.22	1837			58	011	02		
Hettrick	Ella E.	3.17	1900	4.02	1863			37	011	03		
Hettrick	Rebecca	12.28	1820	3.29	1820			1	011	04		
Hilton	George W.	3.20	1891	6.14	1816			75	011	09		
Hilton	Emeline Gibbs	7.21	1900	3.28	1830			71	011	10		
Hitner	George W.	4.03	1859	12.25	1802			57	011	06		
Hitner	Eliza Kennedy	1.29	1885	4.20	1802			83	011	07		
Hitner	Mary Kennedy	1.07	1894	7.04	1836			58	011	08		
Hocker	Adam	1.17	1881	6.09	1802			79	011	16		
Hocker	Mary	4.16	1875			66	2.07	67	011	17		Hocker, Adam, wife of
Hoerner	Melchoir	5.16	1828	10.18	1812			16	011	11		German
Hoerner	Ann Martha	11.21	1844	1.17	1783			62	011	12		Hoerner, Melchoir, wife of; German
Hoerner	Johann Peter	10.16	1836	3.31	1823			14	011	13		Hoerner, Melchoir, son of; German
Hoerner	Johannes	12.12	1824			17	1.01	18	011	14		German
Hoerner	Johann Melchoir	12.01	1850	2.16	1774			77	011	15		German
Hoffer	Joseph C.		1889		1829			61	011	31		
Hoffer	Anna R.		1895		1829			67	011	32		Hoffer, Joseph C., wife of
Hoffman	Ann Margaret	7.00	1850	1.03	1803			48	011	18		Hoffman, John W., Rev., consort of
Hoffman	Jacob	11.03	1880	6.07	1808			73	011	19		
Hoffman	Susan Powers	12.14	1891	12.10	1815			77	011	20		Hoffman, Jacob, wife of
Hoffman	George P.	2.09	1891			46		47	011	21		
Hoffman	John J.	3.18	1895			42		43	011	22		
Hoffman	Jacob					2	9.00	3	011	23		Hoffman, John J., son of
Hoffman	Lewis B.	11.30	1891	3.26	1850			42	011	24		
Hoffman	Lewis E.	12.02	1881	11.14	1880			2	011	25		
Hoffman	Emma M.	5.05	1892	2.02	1857			36	011	26		
Hoffman	George H.	4.08	1896	1.17	1880			17	011	27		
Hoffman	Anna M.	6.07	1881	2.05	1829			53	011	28		Hoffman, George B., wife of
Hoffman	Annie E.	11.22	1864			9	1.12	10	011	29		Hoffman, George B. & M. A.
Hoffman	Kate L.	11.12	1871			13	9.25	14	011	30		Hoffman, George B. & M.
Holmes	Margaretta W.	2.11	1881			64	4.27	65	011	35		
Hosler	John T.	4.13	1899			52	2.27	53	011	33		
Hosler	Elizabeth Mordorf	8.21	1876	11.07	1818			58	011	34		[Hosler appears as middle and last name]
Hull	Hannah	7.10	1857			34	5.11	35	011	36		Hull, Israel, wife of
Hull	Margaret M.	1.28	1885	5.29	1853			32	011	37		Hull, I. & H., daughter of
Humer	Stevy	10.06	1863			5	10.00	6	011	38		Humer, J. & E., son of
Humer	Sarah Jane	7.19	1848	4.24	1843			6	011	39		Humer, John & Emeline, daughter of

Carlisle - Ashland Cemetery

Surname	Given Name	Death Mo/Dy	Death Year	Birth Mo/Dy	Birth Year	Att. Age Yr	Att. Age Mo/Dy	Cm Ag	Pg	No	Other Information
Humer	Rosanna M.		1886		1810			77	011	40	
Humer	Peter		1877		1813			65	011	41	
Hunter	John	7.16	1886			68		69	011	42	Rev.
Hunter	Annie M.	4.24	1870			16	7.19	17	011	43	Hunter, John, Rev. & C., daughter of
Huston	John W.	5.30	1900	2.20	1828			73	011	44	
Huston	Albert L.		1858		1857			2	012	01	Huston, John W. & S. J., child of
Huston	John		1859		1859			1	012	02	Huston, John W. & S. J., child of
Huston	Sarah E.		1864		1860			5	012	03	Huston, John W. & S. J., child of
Huston	Samuel		1862		1861			2	012	04	Huston, John W. & S. J., child of
Huston	David W.		1865		1864			2	012	05	Huston, John W. & S. J., child of
Huston	Alfred J.		1882		1868			15	012	06	Huston, John W. & S. J., child of
Huyett	Daniel K.		1892		1844			49	012	07	
Hyer	Lewis	7.24	1848			79		80	012	08	
Hyer	Lewis, Jr.	5.09	1861						012	09	
Hyer	Eliza	2.27	1854						012	10	
Hyer	Julia Ann	2.15	1855			79		80	012	11	
Hyer	Sarah	1.25	1846						012	12	
Hyer	Annie T.	4.02	1869						012	13	
Hyer	Eli	8.14	1878			83		84	012	14	
Hyer	Harriet L.	1.13	1884						012	15	
Hyer	John		1889		1805			85	012	16	
Inhoff	Christian	4.26	1888	1.24	1810			79	012	17	
Inhoff	Christianna	12.21	1893	3.15	1817			77	012	18	
Inhoff	Edward P.	2.06	1870	9.20	1842			28	012	19	
Inhoff	Lizzie Dale	11.07	1878						012	20	Inhoff, E. P., wife of
Inhoff	Charles W.	5.06	1863			4	7.25	5	012	21	Inhoff, C. & C. A., son of
Inhoff	Henry S.								012	22	[no dates given]
Inhoff	Anna M.								012	23	[no dates given]
Irvine	James Ross	7.01	1879	9.18	1812			67	012	24	
Irvin	Robert	2.21	1881	9.16	1819			62	012	25	
Jacobs	Roger B.	11.01	1872			2	10.18	3	012	26	
Jamison	B. R.	7.11	1872	4.02	1833			40	012	27	
Jones	Harry M.	9.20	1882	1.27	1882			1	012	28	Jones, N. S. & E. L., child of
Jones	Annie C.	8.04	1870				10.24	1	012	29	Jones, N. S. & E. L., child of
Kauffman	Harrison F.								012	36	Kauffman, Henry & Rebecca, son of
Keepers	Stephen	3.16	1834			47	11.00	48	012	41	
Keepers	Mary Ann	9.05	1851			62		63	013	01	Keepers, Stephen, wife of
Keepers	Dewalt	11.30	1811						013	02	Keepers, Stephen & Mary Ann, child of
Keepers	John	6.06	1819						013	03	Keepers, Stephen & Mary Ann, child of
Keepers	George Willis	8.06	1833						013	04	Keepers, Stephen & Mary Ann, child of
Keigley	Anna R.	3.21	1886						013	10	
Keigley	Harriet	12.04	1887						013	11	
Keller	Anna								012	37	[no information other than name]
Keller	William								012	38	[no information other than name]
Keller	Mother								012	39	[no information other than name]
Keller	James								012	40	[no information other than name]
Keller	George	6.09	1859						013	17	
Kemper	Reuben	3.16	1899			72	0.06	73	013	05	
Kemper	Maria Ann	9.24	1864			6	4.19	7	013	06	
Kemper	Susanna	3.16	1865			2	1.05	3	013	07	

Carlisle - Ashland Cemetery

Surname	Given Name	Death Mo/Dy	Death Year	Birth Mo/Dy	Birth Year	Att. Age Yr	Age Mo/Dy	Cm Ag	Pg	No	Other Information
Kemper	John	4.05	1888	6.26	1799			89	013	08	
Kemper	Fannie	5.02	1872	11.09	1797			75	013	09	
Kernan	Elizabeth	5.05	1875			73	4.02	74	013	18	
Kernan	Furgus R.	2.04	1846			57		58	013	19	
Kernan	Thirza	3.15	1884	10.27	1827			57	013	20	
Kernan	John F. F.	6.27	1872	3.07	1842			31	013	21	["F. F." (sic)]
Kieffer	E.	5.11	1871	1.11	1812			60	013	14	Rev.
Kieffer	Sarah Elizabeth	5.07	1875			18	7.07	19	013	15	Kieffer, E. & M. M., daughter of
Kieffer	Benneville J.	1.03	1861			31		32	013	16	
Kiehl	John W.	3.23	1883			23	7.02	24	013	12	
Kiehl	Mary A. E.	11.27	1869	7.06	1863			7	013	13	Kiehl, John C. & Hannah, daughter of
King	Andrew	12.30	1849			47		48	013	22	Ordnance Sergeant, U. S. A.
Kissinger	George W.	10.12	1892	2.22	1866			27	013	23	
Kissinger	George	3.25	1892	11.14	1820			72	013	24	
Kissinger	Flora B.	6.14	1887	4.25	1858			30	013	25	Kissinger, Charles E., wife of: McLaughlin, William & Eliza A., dau. of
Kling	Zachariah T.	4.14	1891	8.11	1849			42	013	26	
Kling	Gracie V.	9.18	1887			2	9.09	3	013	27	Kling, Zachariah & L., daughter of
Kober	William	9.03	1862	8.19	1861			2	013	28	Kober, Charles & Mary, son of
Koch	Daniel A.	9.10	1867			32	1.19	33	013	29	
Kramer	Charles A.	4.21	1861	12.31	1860			1	012	30	Kramer, F. C. & Margaretta, child of
Kramer	Mary Matilda	5.21	1862	11.24	1858			4	012	31	Kramer, F. C. & Margaretta, child of
Kramer	Joseph Egbert	1.03	1870	4.10	1869			1	012	32	Kramer, F. C. & Margaretta, child of
Kramer	Carrie Estella	11.20	1877	4.02	1873			5	012	33	Kramer, F. C. & Margaretta, child of
Kremer	Amos H.	5.08	1894	11.03	1814			80	012	34	Rev.; D.D.; minister of the Gospel in Reformed Ch. in the U. S. for 55 years; Shippensbg, 1839-45; Carlisle, 1845-61 Lancaster, 1861-1877; Carlisle, 1877-94
Kremer	Martha Ellen	3.31	1898						012	35	Kremer, James Brainerd, wife of; Nevin, Wm. M., Prof. & Hannah McClay, dau. of
Kronenberg	Samuel	9.04	1893	8.24	1837			57	013	30	
Kronenberg	Henrietta	8.24	1886	9.09	1837			49	013	31	Kronenberg, Samuel, wife of
Kuhns	John F.	3.11	1864			45	8.07	46	013	32	
Kuhns	Mary	10.24	1889	12.07	1875			14	013	33	
Kuhns	George S.	10.03	1869			88	5.29	89	013	34	
Kuhns	Anna Mary	1.26	1835			46	8.24	47	013	35	Kuhns, George S., wife of
Kuhns	Elizabeth	8.06	1860	12.08	1789			71	013	36	Kuhns, George, wife of
Kuhns	Margaret	9.23	1880	9.23	1810			71	013	37	
Kutz	Mary C.	2.22	1862			28	3.22	29	013	38	Kutz, Daniel, wife of
Lamberton	Abram	1.29	1869	4.06	1801			68	013	42	
Lamberton	Elizabeth Clark	3.03	1886	6.08	1810			76	013	43	Lamberton, Abram, wife of
Lamberton	Ursula Wood		1859		1835			25	013	44	
Lamberton	Mary Ann		1876		1835			42	014	01	
Lamberton	James Ross		1841		1840			2	014	02	
Lamberton	Catharine W.		1848		1847			2	014	03	
Landis	Jacob		1886		1807			80	014	06	
Landis	Nancy		1883		1810			74	014	07	Landis, Jacob, wife of
Landis	Hattie A.		1900		1850			51	014	08	
Landis	Victor Merkle	12.30	1871	12.25	1871			1	014	09	Landis, J. B. & B. H., son of
Lane	William Blaney	6.24	1871	2.02	1865			7	014	04	Lane, Lydia S., & Wm. B., U.S.A., ch. of

Carlisle - Ashland Cemetery

Surname	Given Name	Death Mo/Dy	Death Year	Birth Mo/Dy	Birth Year	Att. Age Yr	Att. Age Mo/Dy	Cm Ag	Pg	No	Other Information
Lane	Valeria Blaney	4.09	1877	8.17	1871			6	014	05	Lane, Lydia B. & Wm. B, U. S. A., ch. of
Law	George Henry	4.29	1853			6	9.00	7	013	39	
Law	Robert Adair	2.17	1853			1		2	013	40	nearly 2 years
Lawton	Joseph	6.13	1897	2.02	1825			73	013	41	
Lee	Alfred F.	12.27	1864	11.17	1832			33	014	15	Lieutenant, 17th Pennsylvania Cavalry; killed near Gordonsville, VA
Lee	Charles	10.29	1867			37		38	014	16	
Lehman	Adam	5.25	1845			62	2.05	63	014	10	
Lehman	Magdalene	3.27	1871			79	3.10	80	014	11	Lehman, Adam, wife of
Lehman	Adam	7.20	1882	3.22	1814			69	014	12	
Lehman	Mary C.	7.01	1893			59		60	014	13	Lehman, Samuel, wife of
Lehman	Elizabeth	3.13	1830			14	2.26	15	014	14	
Leidich	Regenia E.	4.07	1873			46	10.17	47	014	17	Leidich, A. M., wife of
Lesher	Annie Mary	12.23	1877			7	6.11	8	014	18	Lesher, B. & K., only daughter of
Lesher	infant daughter								014	19	Lesher, David & Eliza C., daughter of
Lindsey	Eliza R.		1883		1871			13	015	01	Lindsey, M. H. & Elmira, daughter of
Lindsey	William A.	3.07	1873	3.27	1847			26	015	02	
Lindsey	Alexander	4.27	1875	4.11	1804			72	015	03	
Lindsey	Elizabeth	10.08	1878	8.01	1810			69	015	04	
Line	Emanuel	10.24	1871	4.15	1818			54	014	20	
Line	Catharine A.	8.13	1869	4.15	1821			49	014	21	
Line	Mary J.	3.31	1846	10.26	1845			1	014	22	
Line	Mary J.	12.25	1887	11.09	1854			34	014	23	
Line	Elizabeth A. C.	2.09	1851	7.08	1848			3	014	24	
Line	Samuel J.	1.19	1878	12.19	1877			1	014	25	
Line	Laura E.	8.26	1895	12.21	1888			7	014	26	Line, William H. & E. P., daughter of
Line	Samuel C.	2.15	1893	10.02	1840			53	014	27	
Line	Mary Simpson	4.17	1882						014	28	(Maria)
Line	Mary E. Ralston	11.12	1876	7.14	1832			45	014	29	Line, David, wife of
Line	Elizabeth	5.31	1869	3.17	1822			48	014	30	Line, A. A., wife of
Line	Cornelia	5.26	1899	9.13	1839			60	014	31	
Line	Laura McKim	10.03	1866	8.24	1848			19	014	32	
Line	George B.	5.17	1880	2.25	1850			31	014	33	
Line	William	11.16	1868	10.15	1785			84	014	34	Hon.
Line	Rebecca Wise	2.18	1826	6.20	1790			36	014	35	Line, William, Esq., consort of; Wise, J. Jacob & Anna Catharine, daughter of
Line	Catharine	1.24	1854	5.15	1795			59	014	36	Line, William, Esq., consort of; (Mrs. Luther, Hbg.)
Line	Ann Beggs	7.04	1870	5.22	1797			74	014	37	Line, Frederick, wife of
Line	George M.	12.15	1881			33	11.15	34	014	38	
Line	C. Mary					2	10.23	3	014	39	Line, George M. & Emma B., child of
Line	G. Wallace					1	4.27	2	014	40	Line, George M. & Emma B., child of
Line	Sarah R.	3.25	1879						014	41	Line, George M. & Emma B., child of
Line	John T.	7.05	1880						014	42	Line, George M. & Emma B., child of
Line	Clarence W.					4	1.02	5	014	43	Line, George M. & Emma B., child of
Lockard	John	1.14	1877	1.10	1802			76	015	13	
Lockard	Martha A.	5.02	1851			2	11.13	3	015	14	
Lockard	Richard Woods	12.09	1872			29	1.19	30	015	15	
Long	Marion L.	1.10	1870	3.21	1813			57	015	05	
Long	Edgar St. John	1.08	1870	5.06	1855			15	015	06	

Carlisle - Ashland Cemetery

Surname	Given Name	Death Mo/Dy	Year	Birth Mo/Dy	Year	Att. Age Yr	Mo/Dy	Ag	Cm	Pg	No	Other Information
Longsdorf	Ernest	7.07	1881			20	11.22	21	015	07		
Lord	Mary Helen Strock	12.25	1894	2.11	1859			36	015	08		Lord, David, Rev., wife of
Low	Jacob	7.05	1856			48	4.14	49	015	09		
Low	Catharine Low, Mrs	4.02	1888			79		80	015	10		[text reads "Low, Mrs. Catharine Low"]
Low	John S.	4.07	1891	6.02	1836			55	015	11		
Low	Rebecca	12.20	1892	9.15	1836			57	015	12		Low, John S., wife of
Maglaughlin	Charles	8.28	1859	8.01	1808			52	015	17		
Maglaughlin	Caroline	10.14	1878	9.26	1811			68	015	18		Maglaughlin, Charles, wife of
Maglaughlin	Henry	12.26	1885			34	6.27	35	015	19		
Maglaughlin	Mary C.	1.15	1848	9.25	1840			8	015	20		Maglaughlin, Charles & Caroline, dau. of
Maglaughlin	C. E.	4.26	1874	1.04	1839			36	015	21		
Maglaughlin	Charles Wilbur	8.04	1867			1	10.00	2	015	22		aged 22 months
Mapes	Eugene L.	6.22	1892	1.17	1845			48	015	16		Rev.; (D. D.); Pastor 1st Presbyterian Church, Carlisle
Marchand	John B.	4.13	1875	8.27	1808			67	015	38		Commodore, U. S. Navy
Mark	Cyrus K.		1899		1824			76	015	39		
Martin	Catharine	4.27	1871						015	28		Martin, Richard, wife of
Martin	Willie C.	9.08	1867			3	3.22	4	015	29		Martin, Simon & Mary E., child of
Martin	Clara C.	2.06	1868			2	0.21	3	015	30		Martin, Simon & Mary E., child of
Martin	Irvin O.	7.26	1881	12.09	1880			1	015	31		Martin, Simon & Mary E., child of
Martin	Chester A.	7.24	1881	12.09	1880			1	015	32		Martin, Simon & Mary E., child of
Martin	Jacob M.	1.23	1873			45	3.14	46	015	33		Martin, Simon & Mary E., child of
Martin	George	7.13	1879	2.09	1800			80	015	34		
Martin	Elizabeth	4.10	1885	2.16	1806			80	015	35		
Martin	Mary E.	12.06	1878			7	9.26	8	015	36		Martin, George & Annie, child of
Martin	Bessie C.	8.09	1895			5	10.02	6	015	37		Martin, George & Annie, child of
Matthews	Ann	1.23	1881	11.30	1811			70	015	23		
Matthews	Diller R.	3.19	1839	1.10	1838			2	015	24		
Matthews	Isabella	2.17	1844	5.17	1840			4	015	25		
Matthews	Fanny E.	5.23	1868	1.11	1836			33	015	26		
Matthews	Rohrer							0	015	27		(all) [?] [no other information given]
McCommon	Eliza J.	10.08	1870			23	5.09	24	016	37		
McCommon	Ann C.	1.13	1892			59		60	016	38		
McCommon	William Mc.	7.25	1870			7	4.18	8	016	39		
McCoy	G. W.	10.23	1883			65		66	016	40		
McCoy	Mattie J.	12.27	1894	12.30	1889			5	016	41		McCoy, W. & M., daughter of
McCoy	Parker H.	2.01	1878				8.21	1	016	42		McCoy, J. T. & M. B., son of
McDowell	Mary	8.12	1880			55		56	017	01		
McDowell	Jane	2.19	1892			71		72	017	02		
McFeely	George	4.06	1864			54		55	017	03		
McFeely	John	12.26	1876			54		55	017	04		
McFeely	George	1.12	1854			74		75	017	05		Colonel
McFeely	Margaret	1.08	1890			80		81	017	06		McFeely, George, Col., wife of
McGonegal	Matilda E.	7.08	1869	8.05	1859			10	017	07		
McGonelgal	Laura L.	12.05	1868	9.13	1868			1	017	08		[McGonelgal (sic)]
McGowan	Stewart	3.08	1867			69	4.17	70	017	09		
McIlhenny	Eliza J.	12.03	1888	8.26	1814			75	017	10		
McKeehan	George	11.24	1889	10.21	1815			75	017	11		
McKeehan	Joseph H.	7.31	1876			28		29	017	12		
McKeehan	Mary		1896		1852			45	017	13		

Carlisle - Ashland Cemetery

Surname	Given Name	Death Mo/Dy	Year	Birth Mo/Dy	Year	Att. Yr	Age Mo/Dy	Ag	Cm	Pg	No	Other Information
McKeehan	Ann Elizabeth		1860		1848			13	017	14		
McLaughlin	William	11.29	1887	10.20	1820			68	017	15		
Means	Joseph M.	6.08	1880	2.10	1796			85	015	40		
Means	Jane W.	1.08	1878	4.03	1799			79	015	41		Means, Joseph M., wife of
Means	Joseph James	4.07	1876			2	5.15	3	015	42		Means, James R. & Susan S., son of
Melester	Charles E.	10.15	1899			46	8.09	47	015	43		
Merchant	Charles Spencer	12.06	1879						015	44		Brigadier General, U. S. Army; a faithful soldier from 1814 to 1879
Merchant	Sarah	2.03	1884					0	015	45		Merchant, Charles Spencer, wife of
Merchant	Charles S.	2.15	1873	7.02	1872			1	015	46		
Miles	William A.	1.23	1885			66		67	016	08		
Miller	E. W.	9.07	1896	5.26	1830			67	016	01		
Miller	Anna C.					2		3	016	02		Miller, E. W. & F. M., child of
Miller	Carrie L.					16		17	016	03		Miller, E. W. & F. M., child of
Miller	Mary A.	12.31	1891	4.06	1842			50	016	04		Miller, Peter, wife of
Miller	Frank W.	12.05	1890	1.10	1884			7	016	05		
Miller	Mary	8.01	1852			1	6.24	2	016	06		Miller, John & Lucetta M., daughter of
Miller	W. H.	6.18	1877	1.15	1820			58	016	07		
Mishler	Mary C.	1.14	1897	12.11	1892			5	016	09		
Moist	George M.	8.04	1882	11.12	1881			1	016	25		Moist, J. F. & A. A., son of
Monosmith	Charles Edward					3		4	016	10		Monosmith, Samuel & Jane, only son of
Montgomery	Margaret	1.29	1865			19	10.06	20	016	21		Montgomery, A. W. & D. A., daughter of
Monyer	Noah V.	4.17	1848			2	7.04	3	016	11		Monyer, Peter & Annie E., daughter of [sic]
Morrison	John	9.06	1892	7.01	1818			75	016	12		
Morrison	Jane	3.23	1901	9.22	1818			83	016	13		Morrison, John, wife of
Morrison	Emma R.	10.17	1862			4	4.00	5	016	14		Morrison, John & Jane, daughter of
Morrison	Hermes	1.15	1874	11.08	1871			3	016	15		Morrison, W. H. & K. E., son of
Morrison	Sarah	2.20	1872			79		80	016	16		Morrison, William, wife of
Morrison	Mills Esby	1.02	1873			2	6.07	3	016	17		Morrison, W. D., son of
Morrow	Reginald Arthur	6.01	1890	12.17	1877			13	016	18		
Morrow	George Herbert	6.10	1890	12.06	1868			22	016	19		
Morrow	William Howett	7.03	1890	1.01	1873			18	016	20		
Motts	John S.			12.19	1821				016	22		(not dead)
Motts	Mary A.			10.30	1824				016	23		(not dead)
Motts	Joseph D.	4.12	1892	3.19	1853			40	016	24		
Mumau	Jacob	3.10	1899			75		76	016	33		
Mumau	Mary A.	11.10	1867			43	0.19	44	016	34		
Mumau	Kate M.	6.22	1894			68	5.28	69	016	35		
Munro	Elizabeth B. I.	2.20	1869	9.19	1827			42	016	26		Munro, John, wife of
Murray	Joseph A.	11.27	1889	10.02	1815			75	016	27		Rev.; (D. D.)
Murray	Ann Hays	9.04	1875	5.06	1819			57	016	28		(born Blair)
Murray	D. A.	7.19	1866			42	6.19	43	016	29		Colonel; Murray, J. P., Maj. Gen. & E., of Benpoort, Hampshire, England, son of
Musselman	Jacob	7.06	1876			79	11.26	80	016	30		
Musselman	Mary Ann	3.27	1882	8.20	1829			53	016	31		
Musselman	Jacob	11.08	1869			70	7.28	71	016	32		
Myers	James								016	36		[no dates given]
Nash	Albert G.	1.18	1896			14	4.00	15	017	16		
Natcher	Stuart	5.18	1845			1	7.14	2	017	17		

Carlisle - Ashland Cemetery

Surname	Given Name	Death Mo/Dy	Year	Birth Mo/Dy	Year	Att. Age Yr	Mo/Dy	Cm Ag	Pg	No	Other Information
Natcher	William, Jr.								017	18	Co. C, 5th U. S. Cavalry
Neff	John C.	6.01	1884			78		79	017	19	Dr.
Neff	Margaret A.	1.28	1890						017	20	
Neff	Mary Josephine	3.12	1840			7	2.00	8	017	21	
Neidich	William	5.11	1876			43	6.07	44	017	22	
Neidich	George C.	10.12	1881			21	5.00	22	017	23	
Neidich	Catharine	1.08	1884			88	10.16	89	017	24	
Neidich	George W.		1899		1835			65	017	25	
Neidich	Mary E.		1899		1834			66	017	26	
Noaker	Elizabeth		1839						017	33	child
Noaker	Tabitha		1846						017	34	child
Noaker	Anna		1851						017	35	child
Noaker	Kesia		1871						017	36	child
Noaker	Francis M.		1864						017	37	child
Noaker	Sarah E.		1887						017	38	child
Noaker	Maggie		1875						017	39	child
Noaker	infant daughter								017	40	child
Noble	Mary	1.06	1884	11.08	1808			76	017	27	
Noble	Margaret Harrison	4.13	1852			5		6	017	28	Noble, James & Mary, daughter of
Noffsinger	Jacob	5.14	1878			74		75	017	30	
Noffsinger	Catharine	4.20	1888			87		88	017	31	
Noggle	George E.	7.09	1866				3.28	1	017	32	Noggle, B. & S., son of
Norcross	George	12.28	1878						017	29	Norcross, George & L. J., son of
Ocker	William	5.12	1879			63	11.04	64	017	42	
Ocker	Susanna B.	5.09	1892			69	11.22	70	017	43	
Ogilby	Joseph		1900		1861			40	017	44	
Osburn	Ruth C.	1.00	1890			54	6.06	55	017	41	
Otto	John	3.16	1846			58	7.15	59	017	45	
Otto	Susanna	9.17	1882			86	6.12	87	017	46	
Otto	Henrietta	10.15	1835			54	11.03	55	017	47	Otto, George, wife of; [54:11.0<u>3</u> ?]
Pague	Samuel Augustus		1894		1833			62	018	01	
Pague	Wilmer J.		1891		1865			27	018	02	
Parker	William H.	2.07	1886	6.05	1850			36	018	05	
Paxton	Thomas	5.00	1887	5.00	1807			81	018	03	
Paxton	Thomas M.	8.00	1863	7.00	1862			2	018	04	
Pearson	Clara M.	4.26	1868			21	10.03	22	018	22	
Pearson	Sarah	10.14	1870			55		56	018	23	
Peffer	John	1.01	1888	12.22	1805			83	018	13	
Peffer	Margaret	1.20	1882	9.02	1815			67	018	14	Peffer, John, wife of
Peffer	Benjamin, Sr.	6.13	1866			80	3.28	81	018	15	
Peffer	B. K.	1.25	1899	6.03	1817			82	018	16	
Peffer	Annie Fickes	5.08	1892	10.00	1818			74	018	17	Peffer, B. K., wife of
Peffer	Diana J.		1896		1844			53	018	18	Peffer, I. Newton, wife of
Peffer	Ann Catharine	4.30	1867			23	4.18	24	018	19	Peffer, John & M., daughter of
Peffer	Peter	3.28	1866			49	9.01	50	018	20	
Peffer	Benjamin B.	9.01	1874			34	0.28	35	018	21	Peffer, Peter & J. A., son of
Pennington	Samuel	12.09	1878						018	26	
Penrose	W. M.	9.02	1872	3.29	1825			48	018	24	
Penrose	Charles Bingham	9.18	1895	8.29	1838			58	018	25	Major & Brevet Lieut. Col., U. S. A.
Peters	Charles A.		1898		1862			37	018	27	

Carlisle - Ashland Cemetery

Surname	Given Name	Death Mo/Dy	Year	Birth Mo/Dy	Year	Att. Age Yr	Mo/Dy	Cm Ag	Pg	No	Other Information
Piper	Ann Espy Elder	6.03	1886	2.26	1794			93	018	28	Piper, Alexander M., wife of
Plank	John	7.19	1890	1.02	1821			70	018	06	
Plank	Anna	11.22	1863	6.19	1819			45	018	07	Plank, John, wife of
Plank	Samuel	8.04	1874			79	8.28	80	018	08	
Plank	Sarah	2.04	1871			74	9.27	75	018	09	
Plank	James Elmer								018	10	[no dates given]
Plank	Bertha Ann								018	11	[no dates given]
Platt	Levi	2.23	1891						018	12	Co. K, 201 P. V.
Plough	Laura Annie	2.12	1882	11.25	1879			3	018	31	Plough, J. E. & Lizzie, daughter of
Plough	John E.	8.24	1887			48	11.26	49	018	32	
Porter	Henry	4.13	1863	5.18	1862			1	018	29	Porter, Henry & Virginia, son of
Province	Mary, Mrs.		1850			60		61	018	30	Ramsey, Mary Sterrett, Mrs., daughter of
Ralson	Mary E.	11.12	1876			44	8.28	45	018	37	Line, David, wife of [name difference ?]
Ramsey	Major Sterrett	7.23	1872			78		79	018	33	for 41 years purser in the U. S. Navy
Ramsey	Mary, Mrs.		1834			84		85	018	34	Sterrett, Ralph, of Sterretts Gap, d. of
Ramsey	William		1831						018	35	Hon.; 36 yrs. (?); member 20th & 21st Congresses and member elect of the 22nd
Ramsey	John		1835			43		44	018	36	Colonel; served as a private in the old Infantry Co. of Carlisle in the War of 1812 on the frontier of Canada
Reep	Mary E.	8.14	1876			20	0.10	21	018	38	Reep, John & Margaret, daughter of
Reighter	Mahalie	8.25	1898			17	2.19	18	019	07	Reighter, P. S. & S. E., daughter of
Reigle	John Adam	7.16	1842	2.11	1842			1	018	39	
Reigle	Anna Maria	3.06	1842	10.16	1817			25	018	40	Reigle, Levi, wife of
Reside	Martha R.	8.08	1885	10.26	1824			61	019	06	Reside, David, wife of
Rheem	Albert K.	2.26	1871	10.22	1839			32	019	01	
Rheem	E. B.	11.14	1890						019	02	Captain; U. S. A.
Rheem	Jacob		1899		1810			90	019	03	
Rheem	Susan E.	8.08	1874			57		58	019	04	Rheem, Jacob, wife of
Rheem	Mary C.	10.08	1878						019	05	
Rhoads	John	1.23	1890	9.15	1819			71	019	22	
Rhoads	Susan A.	4.26	1885	3.17	1823			63	019	23	Rhoads, John, wife of
Rhoads	Caroline	10.15	1875	5.24	1839			37	019	24	Rhoads, Henry, wife of
Rhoads	Sallie E.								019	25	Rhoads, H. & C., daughter of [no dates]
Rhoads	Ellen E.								019	26	Rhoads, Henry & C., dau. of [no dates]
Ricker	John	8.23	1871	4.18	1789			83	019	08	
Ricker	Hannah	12.02	1858			61	7.16	62	019	09	Ricker, John, wife of
Ricker	Margaret	8.30	1853	9.28	1833			20	019	10	Ricker, John & Hannah, child of
Ricker	Levina	4.03	1869	1.30	1830			40	019	11	Ricker, John & Hannah, child of
Ricker	Catharine	9.19	1886	12.26	1818			68	019	12	Ricker, John & Hannah, child of
Ringwalt	mother		1878						019	13	
Ringwalt	father		1864						019	14	
Ritter	Henry Samuel		1869		1817			53	019	15	
Ritter	Mary Wonderlich		1890						019	16	Ritter, Henry, daughter of; b. 18--
Ritter	Jane Ellen		1850		1844			7	019	17	
Ritter	Laura		1851		1849			3	019	18	
Ritter	Samuel A.		1860		1854			7	019	19	
Ritter	Laura	3.30	1851			1	4.00	2	019	20	
Ritter	Jane Ellen	11.21	1850			6	6.00	7	019	21	Ritter, Henry S. & Mary, daughter of
Roney	Scott Stewart	5.12	1881	6.18	1871			10	019	31	Roney, John C. & Eliza B., son of

Carlisle - Ashland Cemetery

Surname	Given Name	Death Mo/Dy	Year	Birth Mo/Dy	Year	Att. Age Yr	Cm Mo/Dy	Pg Ag	No	Other Information
Roush	George	3.04	1900			97	2.17	98	019	27	
Roush	Leah	8.30	1889			78	2.00	79	019	28	Roush, George, wife of
Royer	Benjamin	4.06	1870			64	1.20	65	019	29	
Royer	Rebecca	8.22	1890			69	2.27	70	019	30	
Sadler	Joshua	12.12	1862			61	3.00	62	019	32	
Sadler	Harriet Stehley	1.19	1868			52	3.04	53	019	33	Sadler, Joshua, wife of
Sadler	Mary	6.07	1848						019	34	Sadler, J. & H., infant child of
Sadler	Richard O.	3.21	1853						019	35	Sadler, J. & H., infant child of
Sadler	Isaac	9.05	1886			83		84	019	36	
Sadler	Isabella	12.30	1888			82		83	019	37	
Sadler	Anna M.	11.25	1866						019	38	
Sadler	Tommie T.	12.16	1848						019	39	
Sadler	Sarah Ellen Sterrett	1.10	1895	9.03	1841			54	019	40	Sadler, Wilbur F., wife of
Sanno	Charles P.	12.21	1887			49	3.03	50	019	41	Sergt., Co. C, 9th Pa. Vols.
Sanno	George M.	3.20	1865			87		88	019	42	Major
Sanno	Catharine	7.12	1854			57		58	019	43	Sanno, G. M., Major, wife of
Sanno	Samuel McCrosky	7.13	1844			12		13	019	44	
Sanno	Edward B.	12.09	1892			58		59	019	45	
Saxton	Henry		1882		1817			66	020	01	
Saxton	Anna M. A.		1897		1822			76	020	02	
Saxton	George Bentz	5.03	1872	5.17	1870			2	020	03	Saxton, D. B. & Laura, son of
Searight	Andrew K.	12.28	1873			50	10.00	51	021	01	
Searight	William A.	1.05	1897	8.22	1853			44	021	02	
Searight	Gilbert	2.15	1873				11.20	1	021	03	Searight, F. W. & K., child of
Searight	Clara	4.14	1874				11.06	1	021	04	
Sellers	George		1891		1838			54	021	18	
Sener	Sarah A.	9.13	1893			66	5.16	67	021	19	Sener, Alfred S., Sr., wife of
Shalley	Jesse V.	8.14	1872			36	0.02	37	020	12	
Shalley	Valentine	7.29	1865			70	6.22	71	020	13	
Shalley	Fanny	11.21	1886			90	4.26	91	020	14	Shalley, Valentine, wife of
Shalley	Samuel	6.17	1891			66	2.11	67	020	15	
Shalley	Susan W.	2.17	1891			61	10.21	62	020	16	
Shalley	George W.	12.15	1859			20	4.11	21	020	17	Shalley, Valentine & Fanny, child of
Shalley	Elizabeth C.	8.28	1858			24	6.16	25	020	18	Shalley, Valentine & Fanny, child of
Shapley	Rufus E.	2.28	1876	8.03	1816			60	020	04	
Shapley	Susan	5.13	1880	4.12	1818			63	020	05	Shapley, Rufus E., wife of
Shapley	Charles	12.16	1893	11.26	1821			73	020	06	
Shapley	William Wallace	8.12	1870	7.03	1843			28	020	07	Dr.; A. A. Surgeon U.S.A.; d. in Montana
Shapley	Alice		1853		1852			2	020	08	
Shapley	Minnie		1870		1867			4	020	09	
Sharpe	William C.	1.07	1883	11.06	1833			50	020	10	
Sharpe	Alexander Brady	12.25	1891	8.12	1827			65	020	11	
Sheaffer	Michael	4.21	1861			61		62	021	05	
Sheaffer	Susan	4.13	1873			60		61	021	06	Sheaffer, Michael, wife of
Sheaffer	Isaac	12.13	1850			26	10.17	27	021	07	Sheaffer, George & Susan, son of
Sheaffer	Mary E.	9.20	1877						021	08	
Sheaffer	Michael	4.21	1861			61		62	021	09	
Sheaffer	Susan	4.13	1873			60		61	021	10	Sheaffer, Michael, wife of
Sheaffer	David J.	9.29	1880			32	5.18	33	021	11	
Sheaffer	Anna M.	11.07	1880			26	9.09	27	021	12	

Carlisle - Ashland Cemetery

Surname	Given Name	Death Mo/Dy	Death Year	Birth Mo/Dy	Birth Year	Att. Age Yr	Att. Age Mo/Dy	Cm Ag	Pg	No	Other Information
Sheaffer	George	10.18	1880			66	10.23	67	021	13	
Shower	Mary Stewart	7.16	1887	9.15	1820			67	022	19	
Shrom	Jacob	4.25	1869	1.17	1798			72	022	16	
Shrom	Joseph	9.14	1838	11.18	1762			76	022	17	b. in York Co.
Shrom	Barbarah	9.18	1838	5.31	1766			73	022	18	Shrom, Joseph, wife of; b. York Co.; d. in Carlisle
Sipe	David		1883		1818			66	021	32	
Sipe	Ann C.		1898		1815			84	021	33	Sipe, David, wife of
Sipe	Mary I.		1850		1846			5	021	34	
Sipe	William D.		1851		1848			4	021	35	
Sipe	Robert E.		1881		1877			5	021	36	
Smead	Raphael C.	8.20	1848						021	14	Captain, 4th Regt., U. S. Artillery
Smead	John R.	8.30	1862	11.04	1830			32	021	15	Captain, 5th Regt., U. S. Artillery; killed at the Second Battle of Bull Run
Smead	Raphael C., Jr.	5.25	1869						021	16	
Smead	Sarah M.	10.20	1891						021	17	Smead, Raphael C., wife of
Smiley	James W.	3.22	1893	4.12	1824			69	021	43	Rev.
Smiley	Maria Emma	6.26	1869	3.06	1827			43	021	44	Smiley, James W., Rev., wife of
Smiley	Annie M.	11.20	1888	12.07	1864			24	022	01	
Smiley	Franklin	3.15	1892	4.24	1867			25	022	02	
Smiley	Rose Brooks	6.20	1892	2.17	1870			23	022	03	Smiley, Franklin, wife of
Smiley	Stephen					1		2	022	04	
Smiley	Willie					5		6	022	05	
Smiley	Minnie L.								022	06	[no dates given]
Smith	Henry	2.06	1882			90	9.20	91	021	37	
Smith	Susannah	4.17	1879			80	1.24	81	021	38	Smith, Henry, wife of
Smith	Henry	3.30	1835			11	6.24	12	021	39	
Smith	Samuel	8.02	1862			20	8.00	21	021	40	Smith, Henry & Susannah, child of; Co. A, 7th Regt., Pennsylvania Reserves
Smith	Emanuel	10.21	1864			25	4.10	26	021	41	Smith, Henry & Susannah, child of; Co. F, 17th Pennsylvania Cavalry
Smith	Susan A.	9.29	1876			41	10.07	42	021	42	Smith, George O., wife of
Sower	Beckie	7.05	1889			61	10.14	62	022	13	
Sower	Sarah	3.21	1889	10.09	1802			87	022	14	
Sower	Edwin W.	7.31	1865			23	5.07	24	022	15	
Spahr	John, Sr.	12.11	1876	11.03	1807			70	020	19	
Spahr	Elizabeth Stum	4.08	1875	3.00	1811			65	020	20	Spahr, John, wife of
Spahr	Annie E.	3.28	1871			30	0.19	31	020	21	Spahr, Peter, wife of
Spangler	Samuel	6.29	1880	5.04	1811			70	020	31	
Spangler	Philip	2.10	1867	9.13	1784			83	020	32	
Spangler	Mary	12.01	1867	1.06	1780			88	020	33	Spangler, Philip, wife of
Spangler	William	4.09	1847	3.12	1808			40	020	34	Spangler, Philip & Mary, son of
Spangler	John T.	10.23	1857			16	2.10	17	020	35	Spangler, William & Nancy, son of
Spangler	Maria	1.09	1891			80	9.29	81	020	36	
Spangler	Margaret	8.19	1831			13	7.03	14	020	37	
Spangler	Frances Rebecca	10.11	1854	1.25	1842			13	020	38	Spangler, Samuel & July Ann, dau. of
Spangler	Julia Ann	7.28	1889	11.04	1811			78	020	39	
Spangler	George	6.21	1846	9.11	1813			33	020	40	Spangler, Philip & Mary, son of
Spangler	Milton W.	2.16	1888	10.11	1872			16	020	41	Spangler, John K. & Margaret A., ch. of
Spangler	Katie	8.22	1863	10.28	1862			1	020	42	Spangler, John K. & Margaret A., ch. of

Carlisle - Ashland Cemetery

Surname	Given Name	Death Mo/Dy	Death Year	Birth Mo/Dy	Birth Year	Att. Age Yr	Att. Age Mo/Dy	Ag	Cm	Pg	No	Other Information
Speck	Daniel	1.04	1898	5.08	1824			74	021	20		
Speck	Delia E.	7.30	1898	2.16	1859			40	021	21		
Speck	Maria	11.25	1891	12.28	1827			64	021	22		Speck, Daniel, wife of
Sponsler	Alfred L.	1.29	1882	8.02	1822			60	022	08		
Sponsler	William D.	12.02	1892	5.28	1827			66	022	09		
Sponsler	Agnes	6.11	1869	5.15	1832			38	022	10		Sponsler, William D., wife of; Sterrett, Robert C. & Jane, dau. of
Spotts	Daniel	2.07	1895	9.21	1813			82	022	11		
Spotts	Louisa Ann	1.01	1878	10.04	1828			50	022	12		Spotts, Daniel, wife of
Stahl	Eliza	3.09	1891	1.07	1812			80	020	28		
Stahl	Willie E.	6.15	1888			8	2.09	9	020	29		killed by the Cumberland Fire Co.
Staller	Mary	3.06	1877						020	30		
Stauffer	Cora May	9.03	1887	11.10	1866			21	020	26		Stauffer, Enos & G. E., child of
Stauffer	Grace	4.30	1870			2	1.20	3	020	27		Stauffer, Enos & G. E., child of
Stayman	Christian	9.14	1881	11.22	1800	80		81	020	22		
Stayman	Agnes E.	11.24	1881	5.31	1842			40	020	23		Stayman, C. S., wife of
Stayman	C. S.								020	24		d. --- agd [no other information given]
Stayman	Eliza Coffman	3.29	1899						020	25		Stayman, Christian, wife of; b. --
Sterrett	Robert C.	4.08	1856	3.29	1803			54	021	23		
Sterrett	Jane	2.16	1884	3.15	1800			84	021	24		Sterrett,, Robert C., wife of
Sterrett	John S.	2.10	1868	6.03	1803			65	021	25		
Sterrett	Mary J.		1880		1817			64	021	26		Sterrett, John S., wife of
Sterrett	Alice I.		1863		1858			6	021	27		
Sterrett	J. Thomas		1898		1847			52	021	28		
Sterrett	David	6.21	1871	5.12	1801			71	021	29		Rev.
Sterrett	David Woods	7.24	1851	7.24	1839			13	021	30		Sterrett, David & Mary A., son of
Stock	Peter	11.10	1871			71	8.06	72	022	22		
Stock	Sibilla	2.28	1872			73	0.21	74	022	23		
Stock	Susanna	6.09	1893			62	2.11	63	022	24		
Stock	Jacob M.	5.03	1864			2	10.06	3	022	25		Stock, John & F., son of
Stonebraker	Joseph R.	10.09	1878	2.25	1876			3	022	26		Stonebraker, J. R. & M. C., son of
Stouffer	John	5.31	1871			68	0.25	69	021	31		
Strohm	Mary E.	12.14	1871	4.18	1838			34	022	20		Strohm, David, wife of
Strohm	Bessie	4.26	1892	7.11	1870			22	022	21		
Swigert	Martin L.	6.05	1879	5.16	1858			22	022	07		
Tennent	John Horace		1892		1839			54	022	27		b. Caroline Co., VA; d. in New York City
Tennent	Virginia Balfour								022	28		on same tombstone with John H. Tennent
Tennent	John Hunter								022	29		on same tombstone with John H. Tennent
Tennent	Elizabeth Upsher								022	30		on same tombstone with John H. Tennent
Thompson	Letitia	4.20	1849			3		4	022	35		Thompson, Joseph C. & Jane, child of
Thompson	John Stuart	3.10	1860			4	3.13	5	022	36		Thompson, Joseph C. & Jane, child of
Thompson	Nellie	4.26	1868			3	9.02	4	022	37		Thompson, Joseph C. & Jane, child of
Throne	Clarence					1	9.25	2	022	34		Throne, Samuel & B. J., son of
Thudium	Christian	1.16	1880	5.13	1800			80	022	38		
Thudium	Jacob		1891		1827			65	022	39		
Todd	Lemuel		1891		1817			75	022	32		Hon.
Todd	Edward I.		1896		1850			47	022	33		
Trego	Margret W.	3.30	1880	9.20	1809			71	022	31		[Margret (sic)]
Uhler	Sarah, Mrs.	10.26	1869			82		83	022	40		
Von Heilen	Ann		1884		1827			58	022	41		

Carlisle - Ashland Cemetery

Surname	Given Name	Death Mo/Dy	Death Year	Birth Mo/Dy	Birth Year	Att. Age Yr	Att. Age Mo/Dy	Cm Ag	Pg	No	Other Information
Von Heilen	Adolphus		1887		1858			30	022	42	
Wagoner	Jacob	8.30	1884	7.28	1809			76	023	02	
Wagoner	Anna	11.02	1887	3.18	1809			79	023	03	Wagoner, Jacob, wife of; nee Lehn
Wagoner	John L.	5.08	1870	10.01	1835			35	023	04	
Waggoner	Nancy J.	2.05	1893	1.04	1836			58	023	05	Waggoner, John L., wife of [sp. varies]
Waggoner	Anne E.					1	1.06	2	023	06	Waggoner, J. L. & N. J., daughter of
Wagner	George	12.07	1877	2.11	1811			67	023	07	
Wagner	Sarah	10.09	1897	10.16	1823			74	023	08	Wagner, George, wife of
Waggoner	Ida Bella	7.08	1867	11.14	1860			7	023	09	Waggoner, [sic] George & Sarah, dau. of
Wagner	Emma S. Jacoby	1.22	1861	4.03	1857			4	023	10	Wagner, Wilson J., wife of
Wagoner	Robert	1.10	1875			6	2.05	7	023	11	Wagoner, Alfred & Amanda, son of
Waggoner	H. H.		1900		1865			36	023	12	
Waggoner	Bruce	8.24	1897			30	4.17	31	023	13	
Walker	Sarah	1.20	1868			38		39	023	17	Walker, B. H., wife of
Wallace	Mabel	8.29	1875			1		2	023	14	Wallace, John M. & Maria, daughter of
Wallace	Florence	8.07	1881			2	11.07	3	023	15	Wallace, Isaac H. & Mary, child of
Wallace	Priscilla	8.21	1881				6.03	1	023	16	Wallace, Isaac H. & Mary, child of
Ward	James	6.27	1874			54		55	023	01	
Wareham	Adam	6.11	1866	3.08	1815			52	023	18	
Wareham	Susan	1.16	1896			77	0.04	78	023	19	Wareham, Adam, wife of
Wareham	Johnson	11.18	1896	12.06	1825			71	023	20	
Wareham	Catharine A.	2.28	1855			21	5.01	22	023	21	Wareham, Johnson, wife of
Wareham	Mary L.	2.22	1856						023	22	daughter [of Johnson & Catharine (?)]
Wareham	Philip	11.04	1873	11.07	1843			30	023	23	
Wareham	Susie A.	3.03	1874	1.18	1873			2	023	24	Wareham, Philip, infant daughter of
Wareham	Margaret	5.11	1876	2.11	1848			29	023	25	Wareham, William F., wife of
Wareham	Harry	2.22	1873	1.31	1872			2	023	26	Wareham, W. F. & M., son of
Weakley	James B.	2.28	1886	11.16	1819			67	023	32	
Weakley	Martha Eliza	2.12	1881	10.08	1822			59	023	33	Weakley, James B., wife of
Weibley	Mary		1862		1783			80	023	34	
Weibley	Peter		1859		1780			80	023	35	
Weibley	Jacob		1841		1813			29	023	36	
Weise	Charles E.	5.19	1868			19		20	024	01	
Weise	J. Curtis	4.24	1875			28		29	024	02	
Weise	George	6.04	1870			53		54	024	03	
Wise	Anna C.	4.09	1876			53		54	024	04	
Wert	William	6.17	1885	7.19	1812			73	023	27	
Wert	Mary Ann	6.22	1887	10.25	1813			74	023	28	Wert, William, wife of
Wert	Joseph E.	9.10	1850			2	0.21	3	023	29	Wert, W. & M. A., son of
Wert	William	6.17	1885	7.19	1812			73	023	30	
Wert	Mary Ann	6.22	1887	10.25	1813			74	023	31	Wert, William, wife of
Wetzel	Joseph	2.22	1890			54	2.19	55	023	37	
Wetzel	Susan M.								023	38	Wetzel, Joseph, wife of [no dates given]
Wetzel	Annetta	8.13	1848			5	3.30	6	023	39	Wetzel, John & Mary, daughter of
Wetzel	Nellie A.	9.17	1874						023	40	Wetzel, E. M. & M. E., daughter of
Wetzel	Charles E.	6.18	1881				10.22	1	023	41	Wetzel, H. M. [sic] & M. E., son of
Wherry	William	2.10	1885	2.11	1810			75	024	05	
Wherry	Elizabeth Stuart	7.16	1882	4.04	1824			59	024	06	Wherry, William, wife of
Wherry	Margaretta M.		1870		1848			23	024	07	
Wherry	Martha Jane		1872		1858			15	024	08	

Carlisle - Ashland Cemetery

Surname	Given Name	Death Mo/Dy	Year	Birth Mo/Dy	Year	Att. Age Yr	Mo/Dy	Cm Ag	Pg	No	Other Information
Wherry	Bessie Stuart		1884		1865			20	024	09	
Wherry	Nellie	5.01	1876	12.19	1864			12	024	10	Wherry, John & S. E., daughter of; b. b. Shanghai, China; d. Carlisle
Wilder	Barrens S.	3.17	1885	12.18	1833			52	024	20	
Willey	Harry								024	19	Willey, C. & C. A., son of; [no dates]
Williams	Frederick	10.15	1867			70	1.17	71	024	11	
Williams	Susannah	3.22	1832			18	7.07	19	024	12	Williams, Frederick, wife of
Williams	James Potter	4.27	1883	6.16	1837			46	024	13	
Williamson	Madeline Julia	4.12	1895	9.10	1803			92	024	14	
Wilson	John	1.11	1877			85	1.14	86	024	15	
Wilson	Elizabeth	9.20	1870			68	11.14	69	024	16	Wilson, John, wife of
Wilson	James H.	1.20	1867	2.28	1833			34	024	17	Wilson, John & E., son of
Wilson	Daniel R.	2.19	1882			47	3.09	48	024	18	
Wing	Conway Phelps	5.07	1889	2.12	1809			81	024	27	(D. D.)
Wing	Prudence Marie	5.03	1888	8.10	1811			77	024	28	Wing, Conway Phelps, wife of
Witmer	Jacob		1874		1815			60	024	21	
Witmer	Hannah Senseman				1819				024	22	Witmer, Jacob, wife of
Witmer	Robert Samuel		1899		1850			50	024	23	
Witmer	John A.		1850		1845			6	024	24	
Witmer	Mary R.		1849		1847			3	024	25	
Witmer	Abraham	10.17	1885			62		63	024	26	
Wolf	David W.	3.16	1876	11.29	1829			47	024	32	Rev.
Wolf	Miriam	5.15	1882					0	025	05	[date is not specified as that of death]
Wonderlich	John	3.30	1863	10.30	1790			73	025	06	
Wonderlich	Susannah	10.14	1865			73		74	025	07	Wonderlich, John, wife of
Wonderlich	W. D.					63	0.17	64	025	08	
Wonderlich	Mary M. Baker	2.24	1857				8.16	1	025	09	Wonderlich, W. D. & S. A., child of
Wonderlich	Frederick Edgar						6.23	1	025	10	
Wonderlich	J. Edward					1	8.13	2	025	11	Wonderlich, J. P. & H. F., child of
Wonderlich	Mervin F.	8.29	1886				5.14	1	025	12	Wonderlich, J. P. & H. F., child of
Wonderlich	Tolbert	11.18	1832			3	8.00	4	025	13	
Wonderlich	Grace						2.27	1	025	14	Wonderlich, W. W. & L. J., child of
Wonderlich	Herman						0.16	1	025	15	Wonderlich, W. W. & L. J., child of
Wonderlich	Emaline	11.08	1832			8	11.10	9	025	16	
Wunderlich	S. G.	5.15	1855	3.18	1828			28	025	17	
Wunderlich	B. D.	3.26	1850	11.21	1819			31	025	18	
Wunderlich	Simon	12.28	1843			58	8.02	59	025	19	
Wunderlich	Catharine	7.02	1856	3.04	1791			66	025	20	
Wunderlich	Jacob U.	4.18	1867	12.28	1834			33	025	21	
Woods	Richard	3.01	1872	3.03	1804			68	024	34	
Woods	Mary J. Sterrett	8.27	1882	11.16	1807			75	024	35	Woods, Richard, wife of
Woods	Mary C.					19		20	024	36	Woods, Richard & Mary Jane, daughter of
Woods	W. S.	10.08	1884	2.17	1829			56	024	37	
Woods	John Sterrett								024	38	Woods, W. S. & A. M., son of
Woods	Margaret R.	3.19	1886	7.31	1839			47	024	39	
Woods	Frances Jane					3		4	024	40	Woods, R. & M. J., child of
Woods	Sarah Ellen						10.00	1	024	41	Woods, R. & M. J., child of
Woods	Sarah Ann					1	8.00	2	024	42	Woods, R. & M. J., child of; aged 20 mo.
Woods	Mary Jane	2.03	1868			1	3.10	2	024	43	Woods, S. M. & E. M., daughter of
Woodward	R. C.	8.10	1877	3.14	1808			70	024	44	

Carlisle - Ashland Cemetery

Surname	Given Name	Death Mo/Dy	Year	Birth Mo/Dy	Year	Att. Age Yr	Mo/Dy	Cm Ag	Pg	No	Other Information
Woodward	S. E.	11.25	1865	2.24	1821			45	025	01	wife of [name not given] [d. 1865 (?)]
Woodward	R. S.	2.05	1876	6.19	1849			27	025	02	
Woodward	C. R.	3.13	1891	12.08	1844			47	025	03	
Woodward	C. R., Jr.	8.18	1888	2.22	1888			1	025	04	
Wormley	Isabella	11.25	1876	9.08	1801			76	024	33	
Wright	Thomas J.	4.29	1852	1.20	1832			21	024	29	Lieutenant, U. S. A.
Wright	Eliza Jones	7.06	1854	5.02	1805			50	024	30	
Wright	Joseph J. B.	5.14	1878	4.27	1801			78	024	31	Surgeon & Brevet Brig. Gen., U. S. A.
Zearing	Kate Witmer	2.02	1881			37	7.08	38	025	22	Zearing, J. S., wife of
Zearing	Nellie	8.19	1898			1	0.19	2	025	23	Zearing, J. S. & Kate H., daughter of
Zeigler	Jesse, Sr.	2.23	1881			76	11.08	77	025	24	
Zeigler	Mary A.	2.21	1895			87	6.16	88	025	25	Zeigler, Jesse, Sr., wife of
Zeigler	Samuel	1.09	1883	4.22	1801			82	025	26	
Zeigler	Abraham	2.27	1866			72	1.12	73	025	27	
Zeigler	Elizabeth H.	12.29	1890			81	1.06	82	025	28	
Zeigler	Elizabeth F.	1.22	1889	6.06	1815			74	025	29	
Zeigler	Philip	7.10	1862			49	10.06	50	025	30	
Zeigler	Mary Ann	4.10	1848	12.26	1818			30	025	31	Zeigler, Philip, wife of
Zeigler	Caroline M.	11.15	1850	10.16	1840			11	025	32	Zeigler, Philip & M. A., daughter of
Zeigler	Samuel	7.19	1867			17	1.05	18	025	33	Zeigler, Samuel & Elizabeth, son of
Zeigler	Abraham C.	1.03	1874				8.00	1	025	34	Zeigler, J. C. & I. M., son of
Zeigler	Elizabeth M.	7.08	1861			30	3.25	31	025	35	Zeigler, James A., wife of; Henwood, William & C., daughter of
Zeigler	Jacob B.	10.09	1892	3.23	1830			63	025	36	
Zeigler	Willie B.	4.16	1872				7.20	1	025	37	Zeigler, D. & A. C., son of
Zeigler	Maud Rebecca	1.10	1886			7	9.28	8	025	38	
Zeigler	Elmer Ellsworth	10.29	1882			10	1.28	11	025	39	
Zeigler	John Robert	1.22	1872			3	5.03	4	025	40	
Zeigler	David	5.23	1857			50	3.17	51	025	41	
Zeigler	Ann M.	6.06	1890			79	3.10	80	025	42	
Zeigler	Barbara	3.14	1884			40	9.08	41	026	01	Zeigler, Fred, wife of
Zeigler	Magdalene	7.23	1886			49	10.26	50	026	02	Zeigler, Philip, wife of
Zeigler	John	8.28	1897			58	5.16	59	026	03	
Zimmerman	William	8.22	1862	2.14	1834			29	026	04	Sergeant, Co. A., 7th Pa. Res. V.C.; d. from wounds received at White Oak Swamp
Zimmerman	Abraham	6.30	1894	8.23	1809			85	026	05	
Zimmerman	Keziah	1.18	1882	7.15	1806			76	026	06	Zimmerman, Abraham, wife of
Zitzer	Kate Mary	5.01	1853				3.03	1	026	07	Zitzer, L. & K., daughter of
Zug	Jacob	3.25	1877	2.12	1793			85	026	08	
Zug	Elizabeth	12.20	1846	10.17	1797			50	026	09	Zug, Jacob, wife of
Zug	John	5.18	1824	12.09	1793			31	026	10	
Zug	Margaret	9.10	1850	3.03	1797			54	026	11	Zug, John, wife of; mistake in date [?]
Zug	Margaret	7.28	1828	8.06	1820			8	026	12	Zug, Jacob & Elizabeth, child of
Zug	Theodore	5.19	1834	4.02	1834			1	026	13	Zug, Jacob & Elizabeth, child of
Zug	John	9.05	1843	3.28	1818			26	026	14	Zug, Jacob & Elizabeth, child of
Zug	Augustus	2.22	1862	5.25	1835			27	026	15	Zug, Jacob & Elizabeth, child of
Zug	infant								026	16	Zug, Jacob & Elizabeth, four infant children of

Carlisle - Meeting House Springs Graveyard

MEETING HOUSE SPRINGS GRAVEYARD

Surname	Given Name	Death Mo/Dy	Death Year	Birth Mo/Dy	Birth Year	Att. Age Yr	Att. Age Mo/Dy	Cm Ag	Pg	No	Other Information
Bear	Eliza	3.28	1896	2.08	1814			83	027	09	
Black	Isabella	10.24	1841			56	3.11	57	027	01	
Black	John	1.18	1842			63	10.14	64	027	02	
Black	Martha J.	2.24	1851			1	11.05	2	027	03	
Black	Eliza A.	12.10	1872			56	3.13	57	027	04	
Black	William E.	5.21	1860			2	1.19	3	027	05	Black, William C. & Susan, son of
Black	Martha J.	2.24	1851			1	11.07	2	027	06	
Black	Isabella	3.30	1860			6	6.19	7	027	07	
Black	Ann	1.12	1816			69		70	027	08	Forbes, John, Sr., niece of
Carothers	Elizabeth	12.05	1874			82	4.20	83	027	11	Carothers, William, wife of
Chambers	Ronald	12.24	1746		1686	60		61	027	13	sand stone slab on elevated foundation; a family crest is at the head of inscr.
Connelly	Jane	7.14	1864			72	6.20	73	027	12	
Coulter	Mary		1772		1716			57	027	14	
Crocket	Jane	1.25	1814		1766	48		49	027	10	Crocket, George, wife of
Denny	Daniel	10.18	1834			72		73	027	15	
Denny	John	10.03	1834			68		69	027	16	
Drennan	William	6.09	1831			77		78	027	17	Captain; [see note in narrative section]
Fleming	John	3.24	1814			54		55	027	27	
Forbes	Jane	10.03	1830			77	7.19	78	027	18	
Forbes	John	9.08	1823			77		78	027	19	
Forbes	James	5.17	1800			27		28	027	20	
Forbes	Jane	2.14	1802			20		21	027	21	
Forbes	Andrew	8.16	1854			70		71	027	22	
Forbes	John P.	9.01	1829			40		41	027	23	
Forbes	Richard	8.30	1823			32		33	027	24	
Forbes	Margaret	3.20	1870			74		75	027	25	
Forbes	John	9.08	1823			78	5.23	79	027	26	
Graham	William	4.24	1761			64		65	027	30	
Greason	William	11.22	1877	12.17	1805			72	027	28	
Greason	Mary	11.02	1854			67		68	027	29	Greason, James, wife of; [nee] Carothers [see note in narrative section]
Henderson	William M.	10.16	1886	5.28	1795			92	028	01	
Henderson	Elizabeth Parker	2.02	1860	4.03	1799			61	028	02	
Henderson	William M.	3.12	1862	12.14	1836			26	028	03	
Henderson	Sarah E.	2.04	1886	10.28	1828			58	028	04	
Henderson	Harriet S.	2.08	1838	9.23	1834			4	028	05	
Henderson	Robert M.	8.15	1863	11.20	1861			2	028	06	
Henderson	Robert M.	8.14	1868	9.27	1866			2	028	07	
Henderson	Richard Parker	2.10	1901	10.05	1838			63	028	08	
Johnston	William Dennison	5.04	1773			1	7.00	2	028	09	
Kinkead	Mary	8.17	1758			13		14	028	10	Kinkead, John, daughter of
Kinkead	John	8.04	1772			51		52	028	11	
Laird	Samuel	9.27	1806			70		71	028	12	Esq.
Laird	Mary	2.04	1833	10.31	1741			92	028	27	Laird, Samuel, Esq., wife of; Young, James, daughter of [see note in narr.]
Lindsey	Jane	3.29	1833			32	3.00	33	028	13	Lindsey, James, wife of
McAllister	Archibald	6.01	1858			84		85	028	16	

Carlisle - Meeting House Spring Graveyard

Surname	Given Name	Death Mo/Dy	Death Year	Birth Mo/Dy	Birth Year	Att. Age Yr	Att. Age Mo/Dy	Cm Ag	Pg	No	Other Information
McAllister	Eleanor	1.02	1858			74		75	028	17	
McAllister	James	4.23	1855			76		77	028	18	
McAllister	Andrew	11.00	1804			73		74	028	19	
McAllister	Margaret	8.00	1804			61		62	028	20	McAllister, Andrew, wife of
McCulogh	Alexander	1.15	1746			50		51	028	25	
McFarlane	James	10.31	1770	12.24	1695			75	028	21	
McFarlane	Hannah	5.31	1769	4.14	1766			4	028	22	
McKehan	John								028	23	[on same line as Alexander McKehan]
McKehan	Alexander								028	24	[on same line as John McKehan]
Morthland	Susannah	11.02	1899	3.28	1808			92	028	14	[months are expressed in numbers]
Myers	Mary	11.21	1842			39	5.00	40	028	15	Myers, Benjamin, wife of
O'Donnel	Mary	10.15	1747			60		61	028	26	
Parker	Alexander		1792		1753			40	028	28	Major; and his two children, Margaret and John
Parker	Margaret								028	29	Parker, Alexander, Major, child of
Parker	John								028	30	Parker, Alexander, Major, child of
Parker	Andrew					43		44	028	31	d. April 10, 1803 (1805)
Parker	Richard	3.04	1864			67		68	028	32	Parker, Andrew, son of
Ramsey	Mary Denny, Mrs.	4.27	1842			65		66	028	33	
Sanderson	John	8.12	1831			80		81	028	34	of North Middleton Twp.
Sanderson	Lydia	7.04	1813			60		61	028	35	of North Middleton Twp.
Sanderson	Alexander	6.14	1823			28		29	028	36	of North Middleton Twp.
Thomson	Janet	9.29	1744			33		34	028	37	Thomson, Samuel, Rev., wife of
Weakley	James	9.04	1777			1	1.00	2	029	02	Weakley, Samuel & Hetty, infant son of
Weakly	James	6.16	1772			68		69	029	03	
Weakley	Jane	11.30	1768			53		54	029	04	Weakley, James, wife of
Witherspoon	Thomas	3.22	1759			57		58	029	01	
Young	James	2.22	1747			79		80	029	05	"Senior"

Dickinson - Barnitz M. E. Church Graveyard
          Line Graveyard
          Martin Farm Graveyard

DICKINSON TOWNSHIP

BARNITZ M. E. CHURCH GRAVEYARD

Surname	Given Name	Death Mo/Dy	Death Year	Birth Mo/Dy	Birth Year	Att. Age Yr	Att. Age Mo/Dy	Cm Ag	Pg	No	Other Information
March	Catharine H.	3.23	1860			21	5.26	22	072	01	March, George P., wife of
March	John C.	7.21	1860				1.22	1	072	02	March, George P. & Catharine H., son of [apparent discrepancy between dates of birth of son and death of mother]
March	George W.	11.09	1862				6 0.04	7	072	03	

LINE GRAVEYARD

Surname	Given Name	Death Mo/Dy	Death Year	Birth Mo/Dy	Birth Year	Att. Age Yr	Att. Age Mo/Dy	Cm Ag	Pg	No	Other Information
Line	George	9.09	1877	3.05	1801			77	071	01	
Line	Rebecca (Myers)	3.04	1894	3.27	1820			74	071	02	
Line	Abraham	9.01	1848	7.04	1845			4	071	03	Line, George & Rebecca, child of
Line	Susannah F.	3.29	1852	2.08	1852			1	071	04	Line, George & Rebecca, child of
Line	Henry	5.19	1879			75	4.19	76	071	05	
Line	Frances Doner	4.19	1875			61	2.18	62	071	06	Line, Henry, wife of
Line	Elija Jane	12.05	1845				0.25	1	071	07	Line, Henry & Frances, daughter of
Line	Mary Martha	12.10	1870			5	10.19	6	071	08	
Long	Rebecca Jane								071	09	d. July 5, ---
Myers	Susanna	2.09	1873			83	0.20	84	071	10	Myers, Jacob, wife of; (b. 1790)

MARTIN FARM GRAVEYARD

Surname	Given Name	Death Mo/Dy	Death Year	Birth Mo/Dy	Birth Year	Att. Age Yr	Att. Age Mo/Dy	Cm Ag	Pg	No	Other Information
Houks	family								073	01	[see information in narrative section]

Dickinson - Mt. Zion Lutheran Church Graveyard

MT. ZION LUTHERAN CHURCH GRAVEYARD

Surname	Given Name	Death Mo/Dy	Death Year	Birth Mo/Dy	Birth Year	Att. Age Yr	Mo/Dy	Age	Cm	Pg	No	Other Information
Beam	James O.	5.11	1892			32	11.24	33		119	01	
Beam	Oceana	8.05	1883			24	7.21	25		119	02	Beam, James O., wife of
Beam	Grover H.	4.24	1902				0.22	1		119	03	Beam, H. R. & E. A., son of
Berkley	Mary	7.24	1884			68		69		119	04	Berkley, Lewis F., wife of
Blemler	John	2.20	1892			70	6.25	71		119	05	
Bonner	Joseph P.	1.02	1883							119	06	aged about 52 years; soldier; Co. F, 101st Pennsylvania Infantry
Bonner	Mary E.						0.04	1		119	07	Bonner, J. H. & S., daughter of
Bowers	Abraham	5.27	1873			49	5.07	50		119	08	
Bowers	Eleanor	7.06	1896			71	5.05	72		119	09	
Camp	Rebecca	1.24	1899			90	1.09	91		119	10	
Camp	Elizabeth	2.11	1881			75	7.22	76		119	11	
Camp	Hannah C.	7.18	1885			1	1.21	2		119	12	Camp, Peter W. & M. W., child of
Camp	Claude R.	7.05	1898				0.17	1		119	13	Camp, Peter W. & M. W., child of
Conrad	Eliza J.	5.06	1888			45	4.26	49		119	14	Conrad, H. G., wife of
Corbett	Martha B.	8.23	1886			40	3.11	41		119	15	Corbett, Benjamin, wife of
Corbett	Raphael	4.04	1891			14	7.00	15		119	16	Corbett, Benjamin M., son of
Corbett	Burton W.	9.25	1886				1.08	1		119	17	
Corbett	John	9.27	1871			78	4.15	79		119	18	(b. 1793)
Corbett	-----	8.19	1879			66	5.00	67		119	19	Corbett, John, wife of
Davis	Moses	2.11	1873	2.09	1805			69		119	20	
Davis	Mary D.	2.29	1876	4.00	1808			68		119	21	
Day	James	1.30	1873			59	7.16	60		119	22	
Day	Susannah	7.07	1897			79	9.14	80		119	23	
Day	John William W.	1.30	1873			23	3.20	24		119	24	
Day	Timothy F.									119	25	[no dates given]
Day	Mary B.	2.21	1895			45	6.12	46		119	26	Day, T. F., wife of
Day	Esther A.	4.13	1868				0.01	1		119	27	Day, T. F. & M., child of
Day	Leander	4.01	1869				1.02	1		119	28	Day, T. F. & M., child of
Day	Sarah E.	12.09	1871				1.25	1		119	29	Day, T. F. & M., child of
Day	Evey	3.20	1872				1.17	1		119	30	Day, T. F. & M., child of
Delp	Henry	7.14	1893							119	31	aged about 83 years
Delp	Mary A.	10.25	1894			74	6.19	75		119	32	Delp, Henry, wife of
Delp	Margaret J.	4.07	1870			22	4.07	23		119	33	
Delp	Annie G.	12.06	1876			1	8.16	2		119	34	Delp, Henry & Mary C., daughter of
Fanus	Moses	2.16	1891			77	0.23	78		120	01	
Fanus	Maria	1.07	1900			82	11.13	83		120	02	
Fanus	Howard T.	8.21	1874			1	8.28	2		120	03	Fanus, Henry & Eliza, son of
Fanus	Laura F.	8.20	1878			30	7.14	31		120	04	Fanus, Hiram J., wife of
Fanus	E. J.	8.14	1878	8.14	1878			1		120	05	Fanus, H. J. & L. F., son of
Fenner	Jacob	2.17	1895							120	06	aged about 62 years
Fenner	Godfrey	7.04	1874							120	07	aged about 73 years
Fanner	Sarah	4.00	1870			73	2.04	74		120	08	Fenner, Godfrey, wife of [sp. varies]
Fissel	Perse H.	7.11	1880			1	9.11	2		120	09	Fissel, H. A. & C. E., son of
Fissel	Caroline	5.13	1881			38	2.14	39		120	10	Fissel, H., wife of
Fissel	Perse H.	7.11	1880			1	9.11	2		120	11	Fissel, H. A. & C. E., son of; [dupl.]
Floyd	Charles A.	2.04	1883			29		30		120	20	Floyd, J. A. & M. A., son of
Frost	John A.	11.15	1880	1.20	1811			70		120	12	

Dickinson - Mt. Zion Lutheran Church Graveyard

Surname	Given Name	Death Mo/Dy	Year	Birth Mo/Dy	Year	Att. Age Yr	Mo/Dy	Ag	Cm	Pg	No	Other Information
Frost	Hannah M.	4.23	1876	10.05	1829			47	120	13		Frost, John A., wife of
Frost	Mary E.	12.13	1879			14	7.12	15	120	14		Frost, John & Anna M., daughter of
Frost	Rosy A.	7.14	1871	1.13	1871			1	120	15		
Frost	Henry	6.26	1882			22	9.03	23	120	16		
Frost	Sarah J.	6.01	1881			25	11.18	26	120	17		
Frost	John A.	5.02	1881			24	1.28	25	120	18		
Frost	E.					39		40	120	19		
Greenabaum	George	4.07	1873	11.15	1872			1	120	21		
Griffee	Emma E.	9.03	1889			13	0.05	14	120	22		Griffee, Abram & Sarah E., daughter of
Hart	George E.	5.12	1882			1	10.10	2	120	23		
Haskell	E. F.	5.18	1896			85	11.21	86	120	24		
Haskell	Eliza W.	12.25	1874			63	10.14	64	120	25		Haskell, E. F., wife of
Haskell	Rachel A.	7.30	1893			51	0.16	52	120	26		Haskell, H. F., wife of [H. F. (sic)]
Helsel	Joseph	7.01	1877			89	7.23	90	120	27		(b. 1788)
How	Abraham	5.15	1868			76	10.17	77	120	28		
How	Elizabeth	8.30	1868			67	1.17	68	120	29		How, Abraham, wife of
Howe	Philip G.	4.08	1889			53	2.08	54	120	30		
Howe	Wilson E.	5.22	1892			13	8.02	14	120	31		
Howe	Biddy	4.30	1873			3	7.11	4	120	32		Howe, James & A., daughter of
Howe	John E.	1.21	1896			29	4.29	30	120	33		Howe, James & A., son of
Humes	Eleanor	5.12	1884				1.12	1	120	34		Humes, Samuel & S. A., daughter of
Kuntz	Addy A.	8.23	1884				10.00	1	121	01		Kuntz, Conrad & Sarah A., child of
Kuntz	Charles L.	1.06	1893				1.08	1	121	02		Kuntz, Conrad & Sarah A., child of
Kuntz	Maria	6.06	1875				0.04	1	121	03		Kuntz, John B. & S. C., child of
Kuntz	Thomas F.	2.06	1881				3.14	1	121	04		Kuntz, John B. & S. C., child of
Kuntz	Goldie C.	10.10	1890			14	0.01	15	121	05		Kuntz, John B. & S. C., child of
Marsh	John Calvin	5.29	1872			1	1.29	2	121	06		Marsh, W. A. & R. E., son of
McBride	Abbie J.	1.09	1888			1	0.11	2	122	05		
McBride	Joseph A. R.	7.26	1895			65	5.14	66	122	06		Private, Co. B, 95th Regt., Pennsylvania Volunteer Infantry
McNew	Arnold B.	8.24	1887				6.20	1	122	07		McNew, J. W. & C. E., son of
McNew	Sarah Jane	1.28	1892						122	08		McNew, Basil, wife of; d. aged -- yrs., 4 mos., 11 days
Meals	Jeremiah	11.21	1900			67	1.15	68	121	07		
Meals	Sarah A.								121	08		Meals, Jeremiah, wife of; [no dates]
Meals	Samuel H. S.	11.23	1885			23		24	121	09		Meals, Jeremiah & Sarah A., son of; d. aged 23 yrs., - mos., 15 days
Mortorff	Jacob	1.13	1895			72	2.29	73	121	10		
Mortorff	B. F.				1856				121	11		
Mortorff	Annie E.		1902		1858			45	121	12		Mortorff, B. F., wife of
Mortorff	Daniel H.		1891		1890			2	121	13		Mortorff, B. F. & A. E., child of
Mortorff	Blanch I.		1894		1892			3	121	14		Mortorff, B. F. & A. E., child of
Mortorff	Jacob E.		1896		1879			18	121	15		Mortorff, B. F. & A. E., child of
Mortorff	Benjamin R.		1897		1876			22	121	16		Mortorff, B. F. & A. E., child of
Mortorff	Naomi C.		1897		1896			2	121	17		Mortorff, B. F. & A. E., child of
Murrey	Sarah A.	2.17	1869				5.02	1	121	18		Murrey, H. & L. A., child of
Murrey	Charlie E.	3.05	1872			5	8.27	6	121	19		Murrey, H. & L. A., child of
Murrey	John A.	3.17	1872			2	1.02	3	121	20		Murrey, H. & L. A., child of
Murray	Clarence E.	11.04	1902	1.25	1898			5	121	21		
Myers	Samuel C.	12.08	1882			73	8.04	74	121	22		

Dickinson - Mt. Zion Lutheran Church Graveyard

Surname	Given Name	Death Mo/Dy	Year	Birth Mo/Dy	Year	Att. Age Yr	Mo/Dy	Ag	Cm	Pg	No	Other Information
Myers	Susan	10.12	1886			75	0.10	76	121	23	
Myers	John C.	11.07	1882			78	8.20	79	121	24	
Myers	Elizabeth	4.21	1887			81	2.06	82	121	25	
Myers	Joseph	5.18	1888			68	0.08	69	121	26	
Myers	Lydia	2.22	1891			67	0.04	68	121	27	Myers, Joseph, wife of
Myers	Moses M.	1.15	1898			71	4.09	72	121	28	A Soldier
Myers	Margaret S.	10.29	1875			48		49	121	29	
Myers	Henry A.	11.27	1872			32		33	121	30	
Myers	Murven Elmer	10.13	1869				6.21	1	121	31	Myers, Henry A. & C. E., child of
Myers	Alice May	11.10	1872			5	6.04	6	121	32	Myers, Henry A. & C. E., child of
Myers	William Lester	1.19	1873				3.08	1	121	33	Myers, Henry A. & C. E., child of
Myers	George T.	8.15	1884			50	10.04	51	121	34	
Myers	Maria	2.03	1889			54	9.03	55	121	35	
Myers	Martha T.	2.12	1889			31	11.01	32	121	36	
Myers	Elmer E.	8.28	1876	8.28	1876			1	121	37	Myers, G. T. & M., son of
Myers	Clara Elsie	3.10	1873			2	7.22	3	121	38	Myers, Henry A. & C. E., daughter of
Myers	Mary E.	11.21	1871			3	10.00	4	121	39	Myers, Joseph & Lydia A., daughter of
Myers	Ida V.	1.21	1879			1	4.01	2	121	40	Myers, J. A. & S. S., daughter of
Myers	Anna M.	8.12	1882			31	11.13	32	121	41	Myers, W. O., wife of
Myers	Alice M.	4.14	1879			4	6.19	5	122	01	Myers, W. O. & A. M., child of
Myers	Benjamin L.	8.19	1882				3.15	1	122	02	Myers, W. O. & A. M., child of
Myers	Annie M.	4.22	1879			3	3.08	4	122	03	Myers, W. O. & A. M., child of
Myers	Otho Harrington	7.02	1892	2.20	1890			3	122	04	Myers, W. K. & Ella, son of
Naugle	George D.	8.26	1895			57	11.19	58	122	09	Priv., Co. F, 17th Regt., Pa. Volunteers Mounted Cavalry; Infantry [?]
Naugle	Mary	6.27	1876			32	11.14	33	122	10	Naugle, George D., wife of
Naugle	Anne M.	12.16	1872			1	2.09	2	122	11	Naugle, G. D. & M. F., daughter of
Nickel	John H.	4.22	1871			81	1.03	82	122	12	(b. 1790)
Nickel	John H.	2.25	1873			11	6.04	12	122	13	Nickel, Anna B., son of
Paxton	Martin W.	5.17	1902			28	6.28	29	122	14	
Paxton	Irvil	9.13	1882				3.15	1	122	15	Paxton, G. W. & A. M., son of
Paxton	Ellis W.	8.21	1900			24	9.14	25	122	16	
Paxton	Samuel C.	7.13	1879				2.22	1	122	17	Paxton, S. A. & J. S., child of
Paxton	Charles W.	7.30	1879				3.09	1	122	18	Paxton, S. A. & J. S., child of
Peters	Maranda	1.06	1876			49	0.09	50	122	19	Peters, Jacob, wife of
Rhodes	Nathan	9.29	1900			53		54	122	31	
Rhodes	Clayton J.	12.28	1902			35	3.02	36	122	32	
Richwine	Jacob	3.06	1888			72	1.21	73	122	20	
Richwine	Frances	10.16	1886			75		76	122	21	Richwine, Jacob, wife of
Richwine	Andrew T.	1.11	1903			80	6.22	81	122	22	
Richwine	Sarah A.	10.25	1892			69	1.07	70	122	23	Richwine, Andrew T., wife of
Richwine	Mary J.	2.28	1903	6.07	1869			34	122	24	
Rockey	W. M.	1.13	1879	5.19	1814			65	122	25	
Rockey	Hannah	4.16	1875	4.10	1818			58	122	26	Rockey, William, wife of
Rockey	James H.	6.21	1902			85	0.15	86	122	27	
Rockey	Lydia A.	6.06	1902			81	7.11	82	122	28	Rockey, J. H., wife of
Rockey	James A.	11.12	1900	3.22	1850			51	122	29	
Rockey	Edna E.	10.13	1895			6	5.16	7	122	30	Rockey, J. A. & F. P., dau. of; [E. ?]
Sease	Jeremiah	5.14	1893	8.29	1827			66	123	22	
Shoap	Rosie L.	3.06	1876	1.24	1876			1	123	26	

Dickinson - Mt. Zion Lutheran Church Graveyard

Surname	Given Name	Death Mo/Dy	Year	Birth Mo/Dy	Year	Att. Age Yr	Cm Mo/Dy	Ag	Pg	No	Other Information
Shoap	Florence R.	1.14	1890	11.29	1889			1	123	27	
Shoap	Martha W.	10.26	1902	3.13	1895			8	123	28	
Slusser	Susan	4.09	1876	1.14	1810			67	123	29	Slusser, Daniel, wife of
Smyers	Philip	7.25	1884			79	4.14	80	123	30	
Smyers	Sarah	8.10	1880			68	3.21	67	123	31	Smyers, Philip, wife of
Sowers	William W.	8.22	1898	1.10	1830			69	123	23	
Sowers	Sidney	6.02	1900	3.20	1841			60	123	24	Sowers, William W., wife of; [text gives husbands name as Sterner, Sidney; probably a transcription error]
Sowers	Magdalena	10.14	1872	2.04	1865			8	123	25	Sowers, W. W. & S., daughter of
Starner	Solomon	8.02	1896			75	9.14	76	123	01	
Starner	Leah	3.14	1887			64	2.25	65	123	02	Starner, Solomon, wife of
Starner	Wilhelmina Ida	7.27	1887			23	3.22	24	123	03	Starner, Solomon & Leah, daughter of
Starner	Moses	3.11	1897			73	3.01	74	123	04	
Starner	Elizabeth	12.06	1887			59	9.17	60	123	05	Starner, Moses, wife of
Starner	Jesse	8.12	1889			74	8.26	75	123	06	
Starner	Nathan	12.09	1869			70	1.28	71	123	07	
Starner	Elizabeth	4.30	1875			79	0.30	80	123	08	Starner, Nathan, wife of
Starner	Clarissa	4.03	1871				0.13	1	123	09	Starner, Moses & Elizabeth, child of
Starner	Sarah E.	12.24	1880			19	2.28	20	123	10	Starner, Moses & Elizabeth, child of
Starner	Nellie A.	10.07	1885			12	5.18	13	123	11	Starner, Moses & Elizabeth, child of
Starner	Andrew I.	7.04	1902			34	7.29	35	123	12	
Starner	Walter	4.29	1898				3.19	1	123	13	Starner, A. I. & E. G., son of
Starner	Hiram A.	11.17	1896			44	11.16	45	123	14	
Starner	George	8.19	1881			52	3.03	53	123	15	
Starner	Josiah F.	1.10	1874			1	4.26	2	123	16	Starner, J. T. & M. A., son of
Starner	Elizabeth	12.26	1872			16	3.06	17	123	17	Starner, C. & S., child of
Starner	Mary	1.21	1873			1	3.06	2	123	18	Starner, C. & S., child of
Sterner	Mary Ann	5.25	1883			38	5.10	39	123	19	Sterner, William A., wife of
Sterner	Leah	11.28	1881			28	8.00	29	123	20	Sterner, Benjamin F., wife of
Sterner	Kate	5.01	1887			32	5.28	33	123	21	Sterner, B. F., wife of
Walter	James H.	12.16	1883			47	8.28	48	123	32	
Walter	J. H.								123	33	Captain, Co. G, 138th Pennsylvania Inft.
Walter	Charles P. K.					2	1.23	3	123	34	Walter, J. W. & S. C., son of
Weigle	Stella May	4.04	1897			4	0.02	5	124	01	Weigle, Harvey & Hannah B., daughter of
Williams	Nicholas J.	1.31	1892						124	02	aged about 59 years; Private, Co. D, 2d Regiment, U. S. Vet. Vol. Infantry
Wolf	Mary	5.08	1880			61	1.04	62	124	03	Wolf, Isaac, wife of
Wolf	Sylvester A.	2.02	1885			31	3.20	32	124	04	
Zeigler	Jacob Francis	8.31	1872			2	1.20	3	124	05	Zeigler, J. & Rachel A., son of

Dickinson - Old Associate Reformed Church Yard
Old Line Graveyard

OLD ASSOCIATE REFORMED CHURCH YARD

Surname	Given Name	Death Mo/Dy	Year	Birth Mo/Dy	Year	Att. Yr	Age Mo/Dy	Cm Ag	Pg	No	Other Information
Moore	William	7.17	1834	11.14	1768			66	043	01	
Moore	Jane	8.29	1854			54		55	043	02	
Moore	James W.	9.04	1861	2.22	1827			35	043	03	
Moore	Elinor T.	8.14	1880	7.18	1817			64	043	04	

OLD LINE GRAVEYARD

Surname	Given Name	Death Mo/Dy	Year	Birth Mo/Dy	Year	Att. Yr	Age Mo/Dy	Cm Ag	Pg	No	Other Information
Black	Peter	2.24	1863			65		66	069	01	
Black	Sarah A.	3.17	1869			65		66	069	02	
Carothers	Ann Line	6.15	1838	2.02	1794			45	069	03	Carothers, William, wife of
Carothers	Ann R.	10.14	1866			34	7.24	35	069	04	Carothers, J. M., wife of
Carothers	Margaret Jane	3.08	1904			73	2.08	74	069	05	
Ferree	Susanna Peffer	8.15	1859			93		94	069	06	(b. 1765); ("Grandmother")
Givler	Rebecca	9.08	1872			77	7.19	78	069	10	Givler, Henry, wife of
Greason	Mary A.	6.15	1861			39	8.04	40	069	07	Greason, Robert, wife of
Greason	Robert H.					2	9.07	3	069	08	Greason, Robert & Mary A., son of; d. --
Greason	William E.	9.25	1862	12.14	1840			22	069	09	died from wounds received at the Battle of Antietam
Hemminger	Maria	12.03	1864			1	0.20	2	069	11	Hemminger, Samuel & Elizabeth M., dau. of
Huston	Matilda Line	4.27	1849	12.27	1827			22	069	12	Huston, James, wife of; Line, David & Sarah, daughter of
Line	George								069	13	native Swiss. One of the first settlers and proprietors of Lancaster County
Line	Salome Zimmerman								069	14	Line, George, consort of; born in Lancaster County, Pennsylvania
Line	William	6.12	1822	12.12	1749			73	069	15	
Line	Maria Bear								069	16	Line, William, consort of; born in Lancaster County, Pennsylvania
Line	Abraham	7.16	1820	2.20	1758			63	069	17	
Line	Christiana Eby	8.19	1820	1.17	1765			56	069	18	Line, Abraham, consort of
Line	John	1.08	1827	1.29	1763			64	069	19	
Line	Ann Barbara	8.18	1850			69	10.30	70	069	20	Line, John, consort of
Line	Emanuel, Sr.	1.30	1851	12.05	1781			70	069	21	
Line	Elizabeth	9.29	1838	1.12	1786			53	069	22	Line, Emanuel, consort of
Line	David	1.21	1864	8.30	1792			72	069	23	
Line	Sarah	6.01	1882	3.10	1801			82	069	24	
Line	John	5.11	1833			1	2.29	2	069	25	Line, David & Sarah, child of
Line	Frances R.	6.21	1855	9.10	1836			19	069	26	Line, David & Sarah, child of
Line	Gabriel	1.29	1849	9.26	1795			54	069	27	
Line	Mary	11.25	1872			72	4.18	73	069	28	Line, Gabriel, wife of
Line	Henry P.	5.23	1845	11.17	1833			12	069	29	Line, Gabriel & Mary, only son of

Dickinson - Old Line Graveyard

Surname	Given Name	Death Mo/Dy	Year	Birth Mo/Dy	Year	Att. Age Yr	Mo/Dy	Ag	Cm	Pg	No	Other Information
Line	Abraham	12.11	1823	10.06	1799			25		069	30	
Line	Salome	1.22	1852	12.21	1800			52		069	31	
Line	George Lefever	11.05	1885			60	10.10	61		070	01	
Line	Maria	11.27	1869	12.30	1807			62		070	02	
Line	William	3.28	1872			78		79		070	03	
Line	Isabel Jane	6.20	1905			81		82		070	04	Line, William, wife of
Line	David M.		1863		1862			2		070	05	Line, William, Dr. & S. F. Irwin, son of
Line	Miriam E.	8.17	1870				9.10	1		070	06	Line, J. A. & M. B., daughter of; [E ?]
Line	Albert G.	9.01	1878	8.06	1853			26		070	07	
Musselman	Nancy	9.11	1824			52		53		070	08	
Peffer	Warren L.	3.10	1850	4.10	1849			1		070	09	Peffer, Samuel & Mary Ann, son of
Stayman	Arthur Melvenda Eugene	2.28	1851	4.27	1850			1		070	10	Stayman, J., Dr. & S. M. B., son of

Frankford - Bloserville Reformed Church Graveyard

FRANKFORD TOWNSHIP

BLOSERVILLE REFORMED CHURCH GRAVEYARD

Surname	Given Name	Death Mo/Dy	Death Year	Birth Mo/Dy	Birth Year	Att. Age Yr	Cm Mo/Dy	Ag	Pg	No	Other Information
Auker	Anna Mary	10.27	1903			0	3.05	1	154	01	Auker, William H. & Sue H., daughter of
Baughman	John W.	4.04	1878	10.21	1877			1	154	02	Baughman, Jacob & A., son of; [d. 1878?]
Baughman	Annie May	1.25	1889			3	9.15	4	154	03	Baughman, J. W. [?] & A. J., daughter of
Chronister	Ida Alice	1.31	1883			23	0.09	24	154	04	Chronister, Charley, wife of; Mundorff, Elizabeth, daughter of
Derr	Martha Rachel	4.22	1904			1	8.00	2	154	05	Derr, J. A. & E. C., child of
Derr	Mary E [?]	4.11	1900			1	7.21	2	154	06	Derr, J. A. & E. C., child of
Ensminger	Samuel	12.25	1899			73	4.25	74	154	07	
Ensminger	Magdalena	1.22	1895			71	2.29	72	154	08	
Ensminger	Mariah H.	5.31	1857			7	8.18	8	154	09	Ensminger, S. & M., child of
Ensminger	Daniel P.	10.29	1859			1	2.08	2	154	10	Ensminger, S. & M., child of
Ensminger	Anna Mary	6.24	1860			9	2.02	10	154	11	Ensminger, S. & M., child of
Freet	Benjamin F.			10.31	1856				154	12	
Freet	Lola M.			5.04	1850				154	13	Freet, B. F., wife of
Freet	Susia Ellen	10.14	1895			9	9.14	10	154	14	Freet, B. F. & L. M., daughter of
Gensler	Hazel Olive	3.17	1899			1	1.10	2	154	15	Gensler, H. [?] N. & C. A., daughter of
Gutshall	Jacob			9.24	1840				154	16	
Gutshall	Elizabeth	11.17	1899	4.23	1834			66	154	17	Gutshall, Jacob, wife of
Hepple	William O.		1890		1865			25	154	18	
Hipple	Joseph	8.26	1892			73	8.03	74	154	19	
Hipple	Elizabeth		1857		1857			1	154	20	Hipple, Joseph & Sarah J., child of
Hipple	Jennie M.		1882		1858			25	154	25	Hipple, Joseph & Sarah J., child of
Hipple	Joseph A.		1863		1862			2	154	22	Hipple, Joseph & Sarah J., child of
Hipple	Charles S.		1868		1867			2	154	23	Hipple, Joseph & Sarah J., child of
Jumper	Minnie F.	8.23	1884			1	0.18	2	154	24	Jumper, Silas D. & Ida C., daughter of
Keck	Aaron	1.29	1894			48	5.21	49	154	25	Co. D, 187th Regt., Pa. Volunteers
Lutz	Sarah J.	9.11	1890			37	9.09	38	154	26	
Myers	Joseph	10.16	1829		1770	59	10.03	60	155	01	(b. 1770)
Myers	Fredericka	2.27	1901	9.24	1833			68	155	02	
Myers	Isaac M.	11.29	1884			9	2.02	10	155	03	Myers, Joseph & Fredericka, son of
Myers	Daniel		1905		1869			37	155	04	
Myers	Jessie Annie	3.01	1893			0	6.24	1	155	05	Myers, W. A. & A. M., daughter of
Myers	Samuel		1903		1856			48	155	06	
Myers	Lewis	3.16	1893			70	2.22	71	155	07	
Myers	Maria	12.12	1900			70	6.11	71	155	08	
Souder	Catharine	12.05	1890			65	10.10	66	155	09	
Souder	Sarah	3.27	1891			30	6.22	31	155	10	Souder, David, wife of
Souders	Alto F.	4.26	1886			0	8.15	1	155	11	
Souders	Maria	10.04	1886			32	1.23	33	155	12	
Stover	Florence May	1.07	1887			1	4.17	2	155	13	Stover, Samuel & Hetty, child of
Stover	Raymond Harper	10.07	1894			0	5.29	1	155	14	Stover, Samuel & Hetty, child of
Wagner	William	10.05	1889			62	4.02	63	155	15	
Wagner	Phebe A.	10.02	1887			62	4.00	63	155	16	
Waggoner	Jacob	8.23	1869			76	3.16	77	155	17	(b. 1793)
Waggoner	Catharine	5.30	1840	6.03	1835			5	155	18	
Waggoner	Elizabeth	12.17	1883	11.02	1800			84	155	19	Waggoner, Jacob, wife of

Frankford - Bloserville Reformed Church Graveyard
         Entlerville Graveyard

BLOSERVILLE REFORMED CHURCH GRAVEYARD (continued)

Surname	Given Name	Death Mo/Dy	Year	Birth Mo/Dy	Year	Att. Yr	Age Mo/Dy	Cm Ag	Pg	No	Other Information
Waggoner	Joseph	1.05	1834			1	8.15	2	155	20	Waggoner, Jacob & Elizabeth, child of
Waggoner	Theodore F.	5.15	1854			8	11.15	9	155	21	Waggoner, Jacob & Elizabeth, child of
Yeager	Elizabeth	12.25	1901		1859	42	0.19	43	155	22	
Yeager	Thomas H.	4.14	1894			37	0.29	38	155	23	
Zimmerman	Henry		1902		1829			74	155	24	
Zimmerman	Diana				1834				155	25	Zimmerman, Henry, wife of

ENTLERVILLE GRAVEYARD

Surname	Given Name	Death Mo/Dy	Year	Birth Mo/Dy	Year	Att. Yr	Age Mo/Dy	Cm Ag	Pg	No	Other Information
Barrick	Elizabeth	4.07	1875			69	0.01	70	152	01	
Brehm	John N.	9.18	1895			60	8.16	61	152	02	
Dewalt	Tobias	10.23	1869	4.25	1798			72	152	03	
Dewalt	Isabel	3.31	1876		1791	85	2.10	86	152	04	(b. 1791)
Dunbar	Rachel C.	1.25	1897	5.05	1845			52	152	05	
Dunbar	Elizabeth E.	4.22	1876		1819	57	0.06	58	152	06	
Dunbar	William V.	4.14	1874			3	5.03	4	152	07	Dunbar, Thomas & Alice, child of
Dunbar	Harry F.								152	08	Dunbar, Thomas & Alice, child of
Ferris	James V.	1.20	1890			65	2.15	66	152	09	
Feris	James H.	6.29	1893			39		40	152	10	
Feris	Sophia E.	1.26	1879			21		22	152	11	Feris, James H., wife of
Gensler	Peter V.	4.22	1904		1836	68	1.22	69	152	12	
Gensler	Margie E.	12.13	1889	12.28	1879			10	152	13	Gensler, Peter & Emily E., child of
Gensler	Floy G.	10.26	1879			1	2.21	2	152	14	Gensler, Peter & Emily E., child of
Hefflefinger	Lottie M.	9.01	1896			24		25	152	15	
Keck	Effie B.	2.23	1887			15	6.29	16	152	16	Keck, Andrew & Mary M., daughter of
Kennedy	W. T.		1870		1795			76	152	17	
Kennedy	Susannah		1881		1805			77	152	18	Kennedy, W. T., wife of
Miller	Henry	1.20	1891	11.20	1814			77	152	19	
Miller	Julian	4.11	1894	1.20	1826			69	152	20	
Miller	Harvey F.	9.07	1890				4.07	1	152	21	Miller, David & Laura, son of
Oiler	William	3.30	1879	11.27	1799			80	152	22	
Oiler	Mary	4.10	1885	1.22	1823			63	152	23	
Peck	Henry H.	1.21	1873			29	5.03	30	152	24	
Shuler	David M.	8.02	1880			7	8.29	8	152	26	Shuler, Reuben & Mary, son of
Strine	Lydia	2.09	1873			72	6.16	73	152	25	Strine, Henry, wife of
Thumm	William H.	8.24	1901			51	6.13	52	152	27	
Warner	John								153	01	Co. D, 187th Pa. Infantry [no dates]
Wolf	Barnett	5.27	1871			40	1.02	41	153	02	
Wolf	Ida F.	10.06	1887			21	4.29	22	153	03	

GAYMAN FARM GRAVEYARD

Surname	Given Name	Death Mo/Dy	Death Year	Birth Mo/Dy	Birth Year	Att. Age Yr	Att. Age Mo/Dy	Cm Ag	Pg	No	Other Information
Beinhower	Susan	11.20	1887	11.25	1838			49	151	01	
Doner	infant daughter	9.28	1847						151	02	Doner, J. & A., daughter of
Earnest	Mary	3.27	1831			29	5.01	30	151	03	Earnest, A., wife of
Gayman	Abraham	5.17	1862			51	3.00	52	151	04	
Gayman	Elizabeth	11.24	1877			65	7.19	66	151	05	
Mentzer	Henry	1.15	1861			64		65	151	06	(b. 1796)
Mentzer	Catharine	5.28	1871			73		74	151	07	Mentzer, Henry, wife of
Mentzer	William	9.11	1864			21	2.04	22	151	08	
Mosser	Jacob	9.03	1831		1747	84	4.00	85	151	09	(b. 1747); red sand headstone
Mosser	Catharine	4.03	1831			51	6.00	52	151	10	red sand headstone
Mowery	Martin	9.23	1862			57	1.08	58	151	11	
Mowery	Elizabeth	1.22	1891			81	3.16	82	151	12	Mowery, Martin, wife of
Mowreay	infant daughter			1.24	1839				151	13	Mowreay, Martin & Elizabeth, dau. of; gray sand headstone [spelling varies]
Mowreay	John	1.25	1834			3	0.06	4	151	14	red sand headstone
Mowery	Samuel H.	4.22	1871			2	11.18	3	151	15	Mowery, Benjamin & Mary M., son of
Mowry	Susannah	3.14	1846				11.16	1	151	16	gray sand headstone
Mowry	John Henry	8.17	1868				4.10	1	151	17	Mowry, A. & N., son of
Musser	Abraham	5.25	1829			45	2.14	46	151	18	red sand headstone
Musser	Catharine	3.24	1865			62	2.10	63	151	19	[62 [?], possibly 82 [?]
Musser	Mariah	9.09	1841			87	9.07	88	151	20	gray sand in good condition
Musser	Elizabeth	8.06	1839			27		28	151	21	red sand headstone
Musser	John	3.26	1844			68	9.25	69	151	22	red sand headstone
Plough	Caroline	4.30	1865	11.19	1840			25	151	23	Plough, John S., wife of

Frankford - Lutheran and Reformed Stone Church Graveyard

LUTHERAN AND REFORMED STONE CHURCH GRAVEYARD

Surname	Given Name	Death Mo/Dy	Death Year	Birth Mo/Dy	Birth Year	Att. Age Yr	Cm Mo/Dy	Ag	Pg	No	Other Information
Adams	Mary Wolf	10.22	1857			58	8.01	59	136	01	Adams, Joseph, wife of
Arnold	Barbara	7.22	1840			54	6.02	55	136	02	pale sand headstone
Auckarman	Henry	1.24	1863	6.22	1845			18	136	03	Aukarman, Henry & Sarah, child of
Auckarman	Catharine	2.07	1859	9.02	1841			18	136	04	Auckarman, Henry & Sarah, child of
Aukerman	Henry	2.20	1871			70	5.11	71	136	05	
Auckerman	Sarah	1.25	1899	9.23	1817			82	136	06	
Baker	John	3.24	1862			4	3.10	5	136	07	Baker, Philip & Ann, son of
Barley	Anna C.	7.23	1882			37	1.18	38	136	09	
Basehore	Susannah Orris	5.09	1856			40	3.18	41	136	08	Basehore, William, wife of
Baughman	Philip	10.29	1861			56	4.28	57	136	10	
Baughman	Mary	3.13	1888			62	5.20	63	136	11	
Beecher	Peter	8.01	1873			51	5.15	52	136	14	
Beecher	Catharine	8.12	1891			73	8.00	74	136	15	Beecher, Peter, wife of; aged 73 years, 8 mos., -- days
Beecher	Jonathan C.	2.11	1895			77		78	136	16	
Beecher	Catharine S.	2.26	1886			65	3.11	66	136	17	
Beecher	Sarah E.	10.23	1882	8.15	1855			28	136	18	Beecher, Peter & Catharine, child of
Beecher	Zacharia	6.15	1863	11.10	1862			1	136	19	Beecher, Peter & Catharine, child of
Beecher	Mary Jane	8.08	1879	6.30	1879			1	136	20	Beecher, David & Anna, daughter of
Beidler	Jacob L.	8.13	1847	5.13	1846			2	136	21	Beidler, J. & Catharine, son of
Beistlein	Michael	9.19	1829			75		76	136	22	German; brown sand headstone
Beistline	Peter	6.04	1865			1	10.22	2	136	23	Beistline, Michael & Sarah, son of
Bender	Simon	4.20	1864			30	5.01	51	136	24	[30?/05.01; possibly 50 years]
Blessing	Elizabeth Hall	4.21	1904	1.31	1835			70	136	25	
Braught	David	6.26	1862			79		80	136	12	
Braught	Anna Maria	3.18	1875	5.06	1782			93	136	13	
Brehm	Henry	4.11	1888			63	5.25	64	136	26	
Brehm	Sarah	8.11	1872			47	9.12	48	136	27	
Brehm	C. Mervin	7.31	1892			9	8.14	10	136	28	Brehm, J. T. & Alice A., son of
Brown	William	8.27	1826			52		53	136	29	
Brown	Ann	6.02	1832			51	4.23	52	136	30	Brown, William, wife of
Brown	William	3.12	1884			77	8.18	78	136	31	
Brown	Elizabeth	9.23	1882			73	9.21	74	136	32	Brown, William, wife of
Brown	George W.	12.14	1848	11.05	1844			5	136	33	Brown, Levring & Sarah, son of
Brymesser	Benjamin	5.12	1877			43	8.17	44	136	34	
Brymesser	Mary B.	5.04	1904			1	7.17	2	136	35	Brymesser, H. S. & A. J., daughter of
Clay	John	8.02	1846			38	4.24	39	137	01	
Clay	Elizabeth	7.21	1846			65		66	137	02	
Clay	Mathias	9.10	1846			63	5.24	64	137	03	pale sand headstone
Clay	John	8.02	1846	3.28	1808			39	137	04	
Clay	Catharine	12.25	1866	10.03	1808			59	137	05	Clay, John, wife of
Clay	Jacob	9.13	1864	9.05	1816			49	137	06	
Clay	Rachel	7.19	1857			40	4.22	41	137	07	Clay, Jacob, wife of
Conner	Joseph	7.31	1866			46	3.25	47	137	08	
Conner	Thomas M.	1.13	1859				3.01	1	137	09	Conner, J. & C., child of
Conner	John D.	3.10	1859				4.28	1	137	10	Conner, J. & C., child of
Conner	Clara E.	12.10	1860				8.01	1	137	11	
Cornman	Alexander	12.04	1878			69	11.23	70	137	12	

Frankford - Lutheran and Reformed Stone Church Graveyard

Surname	Given Name	Death Mo/Dy	Death Year	Birth Mo/Dy	Birth Year	Att. Age Yr	Age Mo/Dy	Cm Ag	Pg	No	Other Information
Cornman	Catharine	3.27	1866			55	6.09	56	137	13	Cornman, Alexander, wife of
Dar	John						3.19	1	137	14	
Deitch	William H.	1.19	1864			7	1.00	8	137	19	Deitch, David & Catharine, son of
Diehner	John H.	3.17	1897			52	5.15	53	137	17	
Diener	Catharine	6.18	1865			56	7.21	57	137	18	Diener, Philip, wife of
Drawbaugh	Sarah A.	5.26	1885	8.24	1854			31	137	15	Drawbaugh, G. L., wife of
Drawbaugh	Mary Ellen	3.22	1883				10.20	1	137	16	Drawbaugh, G. L. & Sarah A., daughter of
Dumma	Absalom	10.01	1849	6.08	1825			25	137	20	see Thumma
Eberts	Manolia A.	12.02	1899			9	10.10	10	137	21	
Erford	Susanna	11.29	1857			44	0.24	45	137	22	Erford, Jacob, wife of
Ernest	Jacob	10.08	1831			68	2.17	69	137	23	German
Ernst	Conrad	5.05	1847			49	4.24	50	137	24	
Ernst	Elizabeth	12.06	1843			48	2.09	49	137	25	Ernst, Conrad, wife of; brown sand hdstn
Failer	Catharine D.	2.13	1835			4	8.13	5	137	26	
Failor	John	10.29	1888			82	8.26	83	137	27	
Failor	Catharine	10.11	1875			67	10.25	68	137	28	Failor, John, wife of
Failer	Anna	4.15	1839			33	9.17	34	137	29	
Failer	Sarah E.	3.25	1845	9.14	1844			1	137	30	
Finkenbinder	Sarah Ann	7.12	1864			36	3.07	37	137	34	Finkenbinder, Adam, wife of
Finkenbinder	Rebecca M.	4.27	1864	4.27	1831			34	137	35	
Finkenbinder	Amanda C.	5.10	1864	9.30	1852			12	137	36	Finkenbinder, Jeremiah & Rebecca, dau. of
Finkenbinder	Jonathan	12.30	1891			68	0.24	69	137	37	
Finkenbinder	Nancy	2.21	1895			71	7.00	72	138	01	
Finkenbinder	George	7.08	1859			38	3.03	39	138	02	
Finkenbinder	Catharine A.	3.03	1851	11.16	1845			6	138	03	Finkenbinder, George & Sarah, dau. of
Finkenbinder	Elizabeth	2.05	1871	2.17	1847			24	138	04	Finkenbinder, George & Elizabeth, dau. of
Fralich	George A.	6.19	1834			75	4.12	76	137	31	
Fralich	Juliann	12.07	1826			62		63	137	32	Fralich, Geo., wife of; brown sand hdstn
Fralich	George	7.18	1831				1.25	1	137	33	aged 8 weeks; brown sand headstone
Garland	Maud Elva	2.05	1902						138	05	Garland, J. W. & V. B., daughter of
Garman	John	1.12	1888	5.29	1813			75	138	06	
Garman	Sarah A.	2.02	1901			76		77	138	07	Garman, John, wife of
Garman	Mary E.	12.29	1896	3.18	1862			35	138	08	Garman, William H., wife of
Gilbert	Frederick	10.20	1830			44	1.12	45	138	14	German; red sand headstone
Gillough	Barbara	11.05	1881						138	15	aged about 75 years
Gillough	Albert	9.23	1874			81	0.11	82	138	16	
Gillough	Jacob C.	11.15	1877				11.19	1	138	17	
Gillough	Adam K.	1.12	1888				2.12	1	138	18	
Gillough	infant son	3.21	1880				0.07	1	138	19	
Graton	Edward	9.18	1871			82		83	138	09	
Graton	Susan	10.03	1855			52		53	138	10	Graton, Edward, wife of
Graton	Mary	6.18	1852			22		23	138	11	
Graton	Ellen	4.00	1855			16		17	138	12	
Graton	Josiah	3.17	1876			38		39	138	13	
Grissinger	Alexander L.	7.28	1873	8.02	1832			41	138	20	
Hall	Jonathan	12.21	1868	1.06	1794			75	138	21	
Hall	Eliza	10.16	1890	5.10	1811			80	138	22	
Hiser	Adam	2.18	1868	6.21	1789			79	138	23	
Hiser	Catharine	11.22	1868			75	0.12	76	138	24	Hiser, Adam, wife of
Hoover	Jacob	11.08	1866			49	11.27	50	138	26	

Frankford - Lutheran and Reformed Stone Church Graveyard

Surname	Given Name	Death Mo/Dy	Year	Birth Mo/Dy	Year	Att. Age Yr	Cm Mo/Dy	Ag	Pg	No	Other Information
Hoover	Anna C.	12.17	1900			71	10.27	72	138	27	
Hoover	John	3.24	1875			63	6.28	64	138	28	
Hoover	John	12.02	1868	10.18	1787			82	138	29	
Hoover	Juliana	10.19	1872			84	10.00	85	138	30	
Hoover	Margaret	1.14	1864			35	7.29	36	138	31	Hoover, John & Juliana, daughter of
Hoover	Jacob B.	1.29	1838				6.19	1	138	32	Hoover, D. P. & S., daughter of
Hoover	Savilla Ann	12.15	1896			51	4.02	52	138	33	Hoover, Jacob, wife of
Hoover	Susan	10.14	1843			36	10.14	37	138	34	Hoover, Daniel, wife of
Hoover	Elmirah Agnes	2.28	1864			15	9.19	16	138	35	Hoover, D. P. & S., daughter of
Hoover	Caroline S.	5.17	1863	3.04	1861			3	138	36	Hoover, John & Elizabeth, daughter of
Hoover	Mervin S.	7.12	1883				2.18	1	138	37	Hoover, Elias E. & Mary E., son of
Hoover	Rosy I.					4	0.06	5	138	38	Hoover, S. W. & M. E., daughter of
Hoover	Elizabeth	9.29	1895			77	8.17	78	138	39	Hoover, John, wife of
Hosfeld	Mary E.	4.26	1884	3.03	1808			77	138	25	Hosfeld, Sabastian [sic], wife of;
Hughes	Polly	8.30	1854			51	6.07	52	139	03	
Hurley	Samuel	2.28	1847	4.08	1816			31	139	01	
Hurley	Nancy	6.11	1889			31	3.06	32	139	02	Hurley, Samuel, wife of
Jackson	Barbara A.	9.23	1863			3	7.23	41	139	04	Jackson, James & Sarah A., daughter of
Jackson	Sarah A.	5.17	1883			43	10.22	44	139	05	Jackson, James wife of
Jackson	Henrietta E.	8.10	1882			18	5.04	19	139	06	Jackson, James & Sarah A., daughter of
Jumper	Sarah A.	8.00	1860			21		22	139	07	
Kast	George	11.23	1798	9.15	1726	79	2.08	73	139	08	German; red sand headstone
Kast	John Philip	10.18	1804	12.22	1765	38	9.26	39	139	09	German; slate headstone
Kast	Michael	5.25	1804	3.26	1768	36	1.29	37	139	10	German; slate headstone
Kash	Sarah A.	8.17	1850			9	9.17	10	139	11	
Kast	Elizabeth	10.21	1805	3.08	1793	12	6.13	13	139	12	German, slate headstone; see Kosh
Kell	Agnes	12.11	1893			51	7.25	52	139	13	Kell, W. S., wife of
Keihl	Philip	4.02	1885			80	10.28	81	139	14	
Keihl	Mary	1.30	1899			83	9.28	84	139	15	
Keihl	John	9.03	1831			33	6.09	34	139	16	
Kiahl	Elizabeth M.	4.12	1835			61	5.05	62	139	17	[Kiahl ?]
Kiehl	George	1.17	1850	9.04	1772			78	139	18	
Kiehl	Catharine	7.27	1838			24	4.15	25	139	19	Kiehl, Philip, wife of
Kiehl	John F.	2.20	1899			55	6.24	56	139	20	
Kiehl	Anna C.	8.08	1901			56	0.28	57	139	21	
Kiehl	Abraham	11.01	1891			80		81	139	22	
Kiehl	Frances	12.15	1860			47	9.01	48	139	23	Kiehl, Abraham, wife of
Kennedy	Amanda	11.21	1857			5	10.26	6	139	24	Kennedy, Andrew & S., daughter of
Kennedy	Josiah	12.16	1862	7.12	1836			27	139	25	
Kennedy	Evoline	9.27	1861	12.23	1858			3	139	26	Kennedy, Josiah & Maria, child of
Kennedy	Andrew Martin	5.07	1863	10.01	1862			1	139	27	Kennedy, Josiah & Maria, child of
Kennedy	Mary	3.24	1882			55	8.27	56	139	28	
Kiner	John J.	8.12	1856				6.02	1	140	03	Kiner, John & Sarah, son of
Kinert	Christian	12.31	1863			76	7.05	77	139	29	
Kinert	Mary	3.23	1863			79	0.08	80	140	01	
Kinert	Mary Catharine	12.05	1850			7	10.08	8	140	02	Kinert, William & Sarah, daughter of
Kitch	David	12.21	1889			52	6.09	53	140	04	
Kitch	John	10.09	1884			72	9.15	73	140	05	
Kitch	Eliza C.	2.16	1893			79	2.09	80	140	06	
Kitch	Susannah	6.05	1880			33		34	140	07	Kitch, John & Eliza C., daughter of

Frankford - Lutheran and Reformed Stone Church Graveyard

Surname	Given Name	Death Mo/Dy	Year	Birth Mo/Dy	Year	Att. Age Yr	Mo/Dy	Cm Ag	Pg	No	Other Information
Knisely	Catharine	5.18	1892			68	7.00	69	140	08	
Kolb	David D.	5.21	1866			80	11.20	81	140	10	
Kolb	Catharine	11.29	1868			86	2.20	87	140	11	Kolb, David, wife of
Kosh	Elizabeth	11.18	1835			35	5.08	36	140	12	Kosh, George, wife of; see Kash and Kast
Kost	George	7.26	1859			63	7.25	64	140	13	
Kost	Mary	11.10	1897			84	10.22	85	140	14	[spelling varies]
Kosht	Charles	11.04	1862			5	0.17	6	140	15	Kosht, George & Mary, youngest son of
Kosht	Elizabeth	11.17	1850			2	0.24	3	140	16	Kosht, William & Catharine, daughter of; see Kast and Kash
Kriner	John	2.25	1871			56	6.11	57	140	09	
Landis	Luther E.	5.21	1898	5.13	1898			1	140	17	
Laurich	Nicholas	5.27	1838			87	0.13	88	140	18	
Lehn	John	3.12	1851	4.25	1780			71	140	19	Esq.
Lahn	Soloma	11.17	1842			60	8.14	61	140	20	Lahn, John, Esq., wife of
Lehn	Peter	1.25	1850	10.11	1806			44	140	21	
Lehn	Levi	10.27	1847			5	3.08	6	140	22	Lehn, Peter & Elizabeth, son of
Lehn	David	5.19	1852	4.13	1848			5	140	23	Lehn, Peter & Elizabeth, son of
Lehn	John	12.27	1887			66	10.19	67	140	24	
Lehn	Barbara Ann	3.26	1867			44	5.05	45	140	25	Lehn, John, wife of
Lehn	Lucetta E.	4.03	1850	3.16	1849			2	140	26	Lehn, John & Barbara Ann, daughter of
Lehn	Sarah A. P.	11.17	1851			34	4.25	35	140	27	Lehn, Jonathan, Esq., wife of
Lehn	Sarah	5.20	1852	11.20	1818			34	140	28	
Lehn	Dessie E.	10.20	1886			5	11.28	6	140	29	Lehn, John H. & Ellen, child of
Lehn	Lottie E.	10.25	1886			8	2.24	9	140	30	Lehn, John H. & Ellen, child of
Leichty	Thomas							0	140	31	Co. F, 209 Pa. Infantry [no dates given]
Leidich	Elizabeth B.	9.29	1883			5	4.13	6	140	32	Leidich, W. H. & S. E., dau. of [1883?]
Lipert	John	12.15	1836			61	10.15	62	140	33	brown sand head stone
Logan	John	5.30	1869			75	1.02	76	141	01	
Ludt	John	8.25	1890	10.28	1817			73	141	02	
Ludt	Sophia	1.22	1883	4.25	1829			54	141	03	Ludt, John, wife of
Ludt	Minnie A.	6.01	1896			27	4.09	28	141	04	
Ludt	Caroline	8.10	1866			2	3.03	3	141	05	Ludt, John & S., daughter of
Mell	Jane	5.16	1853			80		81	141	06	
Mell	Catharine	1.24	1842			31		32	141	07	Mell, W., wife of; brown sand headstone
Mellinger	John	6.21	1864			87	11.00	88	141	08	
Mellinger	John, Jr.	12.05	1896			85	11.11	86	141	09	
Mellinger	Mary	3.10	1873			67	6.10	68	141	10	
Mentzer	John	1.21	1885			55		56	141	11	
Mentzer	John H.	1.04	1877	4.16	1858			19	141	12	Mentzer, John J. & Anna, son of
Miller	Samuel	9.29	1850	12.23	1819			31	141	13	
Miller	Daniel	10.07	1892	3.12	1814			79	141	14	
Miller	Lizzie Jane	4.01	1889			27	0.26	28	141	15	Miller, Daniel & E., daughter of
Minich	Leonard	10.16	1866	8.08	1778			89	141	16	
Minich	Christina	1.05	1867	6.00	1788			79	141	17	Minich, Leonard, wife of
Minnich	Leonard	4.08	1855	1.17	1821			35	141	18	
Minnich	Sarah A.	12.06	1891			65	6.03	66	141	19	Minnich, Leonard, widow of; Kiehl, Abraham, wife of
Minich	Emanuel	1.05	1862			8	6.05	9	141	20	Minich, Leonard & S. A., son of
Minich	Catharine Sylvania	7.01	1894			17	8.11	18	141	21	Minich, J. H. & E., daughter of
Minnich	John P.	9.21	1889	8.03	1806			84	141	22	

Frankford - Lutheran and Reformed Stone Church Graveyard

Surname	Given Name	Death Mo/Dy	Year	Birth Mo/Dy	Year	Att. Age Yr	Mo/Dy	Cm Ag	Pg	No	Other Information
Minnich	Elizabeth	11.24	1884	1.21	1809			76	141	23	Minnich, John P., wife of
Minnich	Leonard F.	12.28	1904	4.30	1848			57	141	24	
Minich	Mary Ann					1	6.00	2	141	25	Minich, B. & B., daughter of
Minich	Mary Ann	2.20	1857			26	9.11	27	141	26	Minich, Barnet, wife of; Hosler, John & Catharine, daughter of
Minnich	Michael								141	27	Co. I, 49th Pa. Infantry: [no dates]
Minich	Barnet	9.10	1897			68	5.25	69	141	28	
Minich	Caroline	6.02	1853	12.27	1851			2	141	29	
Mordorf	Conrad	6.27	1867			86		87	142	10	
Mordorf	Elizabeth	1.27	1861	6.01	1784			77	142	11	Mordorf, Conrad, Sr., wife of
Mordorf	Conrad	8.12	1854			28	4.08	29	142	12	killed by lightning
Mordorf	Amos Cramer	11.12	1858			6	1.12	7	142	13	Mordorf, C. & M., son of
Mordorf	John	6.08	1886	11.25	1811			75	142	14	
Mordorf	Mary A.	2.28	1888	7.06	1816			72	142	15	
Mordorf	Cyrus	12.21	1841			1	11.28	2	142	16	
Mordorf	John	12.20	1843			1	2.09	2	142	17	
Mordorf	Mary	10.20	1848			6	0.09	7	142	18	
Mordorf	John	7.27	1856			3	0.28	4	142	19	Mordorf, Levi & Susanna, son of
Mountz	Martin	9.18	1845			59	9.00	60	141	30	sand headstone
Mountz	Ann Mary	3.27	1858			70	2.21	71	141	31	Mountz, Martin, wife of
Mountz	Martin	1.15	1860			34	9.05	35	141	32	
Mountz	Sarah J.	1.16	1862			5	3.12	6	141	33	Mountz, M. & S., daughter of
Mountz	Margaret S.	9.06	1859				9.06	1	141	34	Mountz, M. & S., daughter of
Mountz	Sarah Jane	3.30	1850	11.13	1838			12	141	35	Mountz, John & Susanna, daughter of
Mountz	Daniel	6.01	1866			56	2.07	57	141	36	
Mountz	Elizabeth	11.06	1888			77	10.28	78	141	37	
Mountz	John H.	12.13	1876	11.28	1846			31	141	38	Mountz, John & Susanna, son of
Mountz	John	9.16	1879			67	4.01	68	141	39	
Mountz	Susanna Knisely	3.21	1890			75	11.21	76	141	40	
Mountz	infant son	1.30	1869				0.27	1	142	01	Mountz, W. H. & Sarah A., child of
Mountz	infant daughter	10.15	1871				0.07	1	142	02	Mountz, W. H. & Sarah A., child of
Mountz	Ivy Bertha	8.24	1876			1	7.20	2	142	03	Mountz, W. H. & Sarah A., child of
Mountz	Jacob	4.02	1881	7.29	1818			63	142	04	
Mountz	Matilda Q.	2.19	1856	10.28	1815			41	142	05	Mountz, Jacob, wife of
Mountz	Abraham Joshua	10.18	1857				7.02	1	142	06	Mountz, Jacob & Margaret, son of
Mountz	Hannah	8.27	1840			13	3.04	14	142	07	Mountz, Mary & Martin, twin child of
Mountz	Deanna	3.13	1842			1	8.17	2	142	08	Mountz, Daniel & Elizabeth, daughter of
Mountz	infant daughter	3.31	1844				0.11	1	142	09	Mountz, John & Susanna, daughter of
Musselman	Jacob	12.21	1875						142	20	aged about 65 years
Myers	William	3.09	1894			63	6.06	64	142	21	
Myers	Eliza E.	7.05	1891			17	9.14	18	142	22	Myers, William & Mary E., daughter of
Myers	William E.	10.27	1874			5	7.00	6	142	23	Myers, William & Mary E., daughter of
Myers	Annie M.	5.15	1884			18	7.29	19	142	24	Myers, William & Mary E., daughter of
Nailor	David	5.06	1862			61	0.11	62	142	25	
Nailor	Elizabeth	7.12	1881			77	9.06	78	142	26	Nailor, David, wife of
Nailor	Herman Andrew	12.18	1902				3.18	1	142	27	Nailor, D. A. & Ada E., son of
Nickey	Abraham	2.02	1860			38	7.18	39	142	28	
Nickey	David	10.07	1847	9.07	1782			66	142	29	
Nickey	Mary Ann	8.05	1835	6.08	1789			47	142	30	Nickey, David, wife of
Nickey	Abraham	12.19	1884			85		86	142	31	

Frankford - Lutheran and Reformed Stone Church Graveyard

Surname	Given Name	Death Mo/Dy	Death Year	Birth Mo/Dy	Birth Year	Att. Age Yr	Age Mo/Dy	Cm Ag	Pg	No	Other Information
Nickey	Elizabeth	7.25	1876			73	0.01	74	142	32	Nickey, Abraham, wife of
Nickey	George	8.27	1839			93		94	142	33	
Nickey	George	2.04	1858			35	7.20	36	142	34	
Nickey	George	4.25	1870	8.22	1867			3	142	35	
Nickey	Jacob B.	1.11	1864	6.22	1823			41	142	36	soldier
Nickey	Mary Ann	5.16	1850	1.29	1823			28	142	37	Nickey, Jacob B., wife of
Nickey	Margaret J.	1.26	1866			38	0.27	39	142	38	Nickey, Jacob B., wife of
Nickey	Solomon W.	9.14	1877			33	4.19	34	143	01	
Nickey	David F.	6.14	1879	9.09	1876			3	143	02	
Nickey	Israel	7.31	1899			73	6.04	74	143	03	
Nickey	Elizabeth	1.10	1902			75	2.03	76	143	04	
Nickey	Benjamin		1897		1827			71	143	05	
Nickey	Jacob	10.09	1877	10.17	1806			71	143	06	
Nickey	John G.	10.11	1878			55	10.03	56	143	07	
Nickey	Elizabeth	3.31	1894			74	2.16	75	143	08	
Nickey	Sarah A.	3.16	1872			20	1.15	21	143	09	Nickey, John G. & S., daughter of
Nickey	Harry E.						2.10	1	143	10	[two identical adjacent entries]
Nickey	John C.	1.03	1889			30	6.22	31	143	11	[middle initial may be G]
Nickey	Caroline A.	7.27	1856	2.22	1855			2	143	12	Nickey, John G. & Elizabeth, daughter of
Nickey	Lizzie F.	4.03	1897			35	6.10	36	143	13	
Nickey	Emma G.	9.29	1895	9.19	1882			14	143	14	
Nickey	Sarah Ann	10.27	1852	4.07	1851			2	143	15	Nickey, Benjamin & Sarah, daughter of
Nickey	Catharine Ann	8.15	1857	4.19	1857			1	143	16	Nickey, John & Susanna, twin child of
Orris	Christopher	3.02	1853	4.07	1785			68	143	17	
Orris	Ann M.	12.02	1878	12.20	1789			89	143	18	Orris, Christopher, wife of
Orris	George B.	12.07	1889			66	0.28	67	143	19	
Orris	Barbara	9.30	1864			32	0.09	33	143	20	Orris, George B., wife of; Shambaugh, Philip & Anna M., daughter of
Orris	Elizabeth	9.26	1888			61	3.09	62	143	21	Orris, George B., wife of
Orris	Christopher	12.28	1850	9.15	1848			3	143	22	Orris, Christopher, & Martha, child of
Orris	Maria	4.17	1854				3.04	1	143	23	Orris, Christopher, & Martha, child of
Quigley	Sarah Agness	6.28	1853	9.17	1824			29	143	27	
Quigley	Peres W.	2.02	1899			78	11.15	79	143	28	
Quigley	Margaret	6.14	1896			75	5.03	76	143	29	Quigley, P. W., wife of
Quigley	James B.	8.05	1895			42	8.03	43	143	30	
Reese	Martin	4.29	1878	9.22	1792			86	143	24	
Ruff	John F.	5.08	1845	1.22	1778			68	143	25	
Ruff	Elizabeth Barbara	1.26	1854			75	11.22	76	143	26	Ruff, John Frederick, consort of
Seitz	John	3.24	1839				3.21	1	144	20	Seitz, John & Liza, son of; brown sand
Sells	George W.	3.20	1874			44	6.00	45	144	14	
Sell	Catharine	11.12	1864			30	2.23	31	144	15	Sell, George W., wife of [sp. varies]
Sells	Theodore	10.28	1878						144	16	Sells, G. W. & C., son of
Sells	Andrew J.	2.13	1884			54	4.24	55	144	17	
Sells	Elizabeth	4.05	1890			59	4.25	60	144	18	Sells, Andrew J., wife of
Sells	George	9.12	1877			13	4.20	14	144	19	Sells, Andrew J. & E., son of
Sentman	John P.	9.15	1841			4	10.25	5	144	21	
Sentman	George W.	2.21	1833				0.23	1	144	22	
Sentman	Sylvester Lehn	12.14	1835			2	8.25	3	144	23	Lehn, John, Esq., grandson of
Shambaugh	George	7.04	1859	11.14	1802			57	143	31	
Shambaugh	Mary	4.20	1879	1.07	1811			69	143	32	Shambaugh, George, wife of

Frankford - Lutheran and Reformed Stone Church Graveyard

Surname	Given Name	Death Mo/Dy	Year	Birth Mo/Dy	Year	Att. Age Yr	Cm Mo/Dy	Ag	Pg	No	Other Information
Shambaugh	Susannah	3.11	1880			28	4.05	29	143	33	Shambaugh, George, wife of
Shambaugh	Philip	9.24	1845			83	6.02	84	143	34	
Shambaugh	Hannah	3.19	1855			89	9.04	90	143	35	
Shambaugh	Philip	4.15	1846	10.08	1789			57	143	36	
Shambaugh	Margaret	9.07	1825	6.11	1788			38	143	37	German
Shambaugh	Elvina	10.03	1850	1.03	1834			17	143	38	Shambaugh, Philip & Ann. M., daughter of
Shambaugh	Samuel W.	8.06	1895			56	5.03	57	144	01	
Shambaugh	Jane E.	9.11	1893			52	7.09	53	144	02	Shambaugh, S. W., wife of
Shambaugh	Caroline	4.26	1883			42	7.25	43	144	03	Shambaugh, Henry, wife of
Shambaugh	Sallie Ann	9.06	1880				6.02	1	144	04	
Shambaugh	Charles Albert	9.12	1880				6.08	1	144	05	
Shambaugh	Emma J.	2.24	1875			2	11.19	3	144	06	
Shambaugh	Levi E.	3.17	1870			3	3.11	4	144	07	Shambaugh, S. W. & J. E., child of
Shambaugh	Jacob T.	2.02	1870			6	6.06	7	144	08	Shambaugh, S. W. & J. E., child of
Shambaugh	Russell L.	9.06	1901				5.00	1	144	09	Shambaugh, S. A. & Maud, son of
Shambaugh	Rosey M.	8.03	1892	6.15	1892			1	144	10	
Shambaugh	Bertha L.	9.01	1893	7.16	1893			1	144	11	
Shanabrough	Mary M.	11.07	1895	3.26	1881			15	144	12	Shanabrough, Joseph & Elizabeth
Shatto	Mary A. Beecher	9.23	1882			31	2.19	32	144	13	Shatto, Benjamin L., wife of
Shearer	John	8.18	1875			74	7.12	75	144	24	
Shibley	David	3.30	1876	8.30	1805			71	145	08	
Shibley	Elizabeth	9.03	1854	8.17	1805			50	145	09	Shibley, David, wife of
Shively	Christiana M.	4.15	1880			44	4.20	45	145	10	
Shively	John P.	8.01	1899	6.23	1830			70	145	11	
Shopp	Christian	12.11	1894			70	4.08	71	146	01	
Shopp	Susan	12.22	1902			74	4.01	75	146	02	
Shopp	Mary E.	11.08	1870			14	0.23	15	146	03	Shopp, C. K. & Susan, daughter of
Shopp	Samuel M.	4.01	1863			3	10.22	4	146	04	Shopp, Christian & Susan, daughter of
Shopp	Catharine	1.04	1863				0.20	1	146	05	Shopp, Christian & Susan, daughter of
Shughart	John P.	1.02	1893			75	5.29	76	146	11	
Shughart	Catharine	2.18	1892			74	3.29	75	146	12	Shughart, John P., wife of
Shughart	Franklin	3.20	1899			61	6.05	62	146	13	
Shughart	Anna	8.03	1880			43	10.15	44	146	14	Shughart, F., wife of
Shughart	Wilson	1.27	1867	2.04	1852			15	146	15	Shughart, John P. & Catharine, child of
Shughart	Sarah A.	4.06	1852	6.06	1842			10	146	16	Shughart, John P. & Catharine, child of
Shughart	John	4.08	1852	3.29	1847			6	146	17	Shughart, John P. & Catharine, child of
Shughart	Joseph Z.	4.28	1860	10.11	1858			2	146	18	Shughart, John P. & Catharine, child of
Shughart	Jonas	2.02	1882			57	8.07	58	146	19	
Shughart	John R.	10.18	1885			3	2.08	4	146	20	Shughart, George W. & Bell, son of
Shughart	Chester F.	4.13	1895	6.23	1894			1	146	21	Shughart, Joseph B. & Catharine, son of
Shughart	Maria	8.20	1856				8.15	1	146	22	Shughart, A. & A., daughter of
Shughart	Joseph Benjamin		1899		1881			19	146	23	Shughart, G. & S. B., son of
Shuman	Simon	2.21	1828			31	9.20	32	146	10	German; pale sand headstone
Sipe	Peter	3.09	1901			83	5.06	84	145	01	
Sipe	Sarah	2.25	1898			82	11.20	83	145	02	Sipe, Peter, wife of
Sipe	Jacob L.	3.20	1852	10.02	1848			4	145	03	Sipe, Peter & Sarah, child of
Sipe	Samuel H.	3.27	1852	2.09	1844			9	145	04	Sipe, Peter & Sarah, child of
Sipe	Samuel H.		1901		1868			34	145	05	
Sipe	Emma C.	11.12	1902	2.25	1866			37	145	06	Sipe, P. J., wife of
Sites	John	6.21	1856	2.21	1776			81	145	07	

Frankford - Lutheran and Reformed Stone Church Graveyard

Surname	Given Name	Death Mo/Dy	Death Year	Birth Mo/Dy	Birth Year	Att. Age Yr	Age Mo/Dy	Cm Ag	Pg	No	Other Information
Snider	Susanna	2.05	1853	12.20	1779			74	145	12	
Schneider	-----	4.20	1814	4.21	1787			27	145	13	German; red sand headstone
Snyder	Catharine	7.09	1843			3	3.03	4	145	14	Snyder, J. D. & B., daughter of
Snider	Henry	7.10	1871			69	6.13	70	145	15	
Snider	Elizabeth	10.25	1844			42		43	145	16	Snider, Henry, wife of
Snider	Elizabeth	6.23	1881	9.20	1818			63	145	17	Snider, Henry, wife of
Snyder	John	9.13	1855	4.09	1777			79	145	18	
Snyder	Margaret	3.10	1863			85	2.21	86	145	19	Snyder, John, wife of
Snyder	George	2.04	1879	11.24	1853			26	145	20	
Snider	Simon	10.20	1844			14	0.12	15	145	21	Snider, Henry, child of
Snider	Mary Margaret	10.26	1844			7	11.04	8	145	22	Snider, Henry, ch. of; brown sand hdstn.
Snider	Susana	12.22	1844			20	0.15	21	145	23	Snider, Henry, child of;
Snider	Elizabeth	1.11	1845			19	0.16	20	145	24	Snider, Henry, child of
Snyder	John	1.05	1848				4.20	1	145	25	Snyder, Henry & Elizabeth, son of
Snyder	Wilson	1.29	1853				6.12	1	145	26	
Snider	Alfred	1.07	1863			3	5.07	4	145	27	Snider, Henry & Elizabeth, son of
Snyder	Nancy	12.15	1897	3.26	1820			78	145	28	Snyder, John C., wife of
Snyder	Samuel	9.08	1885			77	7.07	78	145	29	
Snyder	Elizabeth	10.23	1880			71	8.24	72	145	30	Snyder, Samuel, wife of
Snyder	Harry K.	8.29	1890			1	10.24	2	145	31	Snyder, Albert H. & Eliza A., son of
Snyder	Romaine E.	4.13	1899				3.04	1	145	32	
Snyder	John C.	2.20	1869	7.15	1802			67	145	33	
Snyder	Henry	1.25	1900			56	9.19	57	145	34	
Snyder	Solomon	1.06	1898	4.22	1832			66	145	35	
Snyder	Sadie J.	1.26	1895	12.03	1854			41	145	36	
Snyder	Mary Ellen		1900		1880			21	145	37	Snyder, S. & E. J., daughter of
Snyder	Barbara	9.04	1889	5.06	1818			72	145	38	Snyder, J. D., wife of
Snyder	Barbara A.	5.17	1883			1	10.00	2	145	39	Snyder, G. W. & E., daughter of
Sowers	Mary Ann	2.02	1854			5	10.26	6	145	41	Sowers, Jacob & Eve, daughter of
Stine	Jacob	2.17	1837			40	1.27	41	145	40	
Stone	John	1.11	1869	12.11	1825			44	146	06	
Stone	Mary A.	5.29	1884	12.01	1824			60	146	07	Stone, John, wife of
Strohm	William	2.06	1892			72	11.29	73	146	08	
Strohm	Eliza	9.01	1886			63	6.05	64	146	09	Strohm, William, wife of
Stump	Henry	9.13	1865			79	10.01	80	146	24	
Stump	Margaret	12.26	1881			84	5.00	85	146	25	
Stump	John	2.06	1879	9.08	1802			77	146	26	
Stump	Elizabeth	8.01	1885	10.01	1811			74	146	27	
Swigert	John George	4.12	1862			73	8.03	74	144	25	
Swiger	William	4.19	1875	1.21	1809			67	144	26	
Swiger	Eve	12.29	1896			82	0.06	83	144	27	
Swigert	Margaret	7.26	1896		1818	82	0.06	83	144	28	
Swigert	Amos E.	7.28	1878	9.16	1853			25	144	29	
Swigert	Leonard	3.18	1887	1.14	1845			43	144	30	
Swigert	Mary	3.23	1828			37	0.12	38	144	31	
Swigert	Margaretta	9.21	1829			39	8.21	40	144	32	
Swigert	John	8.24	1824	8.20	1823			2	144	33	
Swigert	Mary Ann	1.14	1844			8		9	144	34	Swigert, G. & Barbara, daughter of
Swigert	William	8.25	1834	7.15	1825			10	144	35	brown sand headstone
Swigert	Barbara	7.27	1838			41	5.21	42	144	36	

Frankford - Lutheran and Reformed Stone Church Graveyard

Surname	Given Name	Death Mo/Dy	Year	Birth Mo/Dy	Year	Att. Age Yr	Mo/Dy	Cm Ag	Pg	No	Other Information
Swiger	Wilson	7.24	1856	4.24	1856			1	144	37	
Swiger	Amelia	10.04	1854	4.04	1854			1	144	38	
Swiger	William Franklin	3.04	1853	1.17	1843			11	144	39	Swiger, W. F. & Eve, child of
Swiger	Elizabeth M.	7.20	1849				6.02	1	144	40	Swiger, W. F. & Eve, child of
Thomas	John C.	7.31	1851	2.26	1849			3	146	28	Thomas, George & Mary A., son of
Throne	Amos A.	4.19	1878				7.17	1	146	29	Throne, Conrad & Christian [sic], son of
Thumma	Peter	10.29	1892			81	11.09	82	146	30	
Thumma	Eliza S.	12.01	1869			54	10.18	55	146	31	Thumma, Peter, wife of
Thumma	Christopher		1904		1826			79	146	32	
Thumma	Sarah Ann		1904		1829			76	146	33	Thumma, Christopher, wife of
Thumma	Henry	8.02	1842	7.10	1820			23	146	34	
Thumma	Susanna	10.05	1865			78	11.24	79	146	35	Thumma, Jacob, wife of
Thumma	Jacob S.	12.14	1850	12.27	1847			3	146	36	Thumma, Abraham & Elizabeth, son of
Thumma	Lottie	9.13	1899	9.13	1898			2	146	37	Thumma, D. A. & A. R.[?], daughter of
Waggoner	Abraham, Sr.	6.02	1849	1.19	1784			66	147	01	
Waggoner	Mary Magdalena	3.01	1843	1.23	1792			52	147	02	Waggoner, Abraham, Sr., wife of
Waggoner	Maria								147	03	[no dates given]
Waggoner	Abraham	2.13	1851	2.22	1813			38	147	04	
Waggoner	Anna M.	3.10	1884	2.14	1814			71	147	05	Waggoner, Abraham, widow of; Mounts, Jacob, wife of
Waggoner	Henry W.	5.04	1874	9.03	1807			67	147	06	
Waggoner	Elizabeth	6.04	1875	6.14	1811			64	147	07	Waggoner, Henry, wife of
Waggoner	John W.	6.20	1901			66	6.13	67	147	08	Private, Co. C, 158 Regt., Pa. Infantry; discharged August 12, 1863
Waggoner	Charles F.	3.15	1891			18	0.20	19	147	09	
Waggoner	Anna Christina	5.03	1843	11.17	1780			63	147	10	Waggoner, Jacob, wife of
Waggoner	Charlotte C.	12.26	1889			41	10.07	42	147	11	Waggoner, B., wife of
Waggoner	Laura M.	8.18	1889			5	1.07	6	147	12	Waggoner, B. L. & C. C., daughter of
Walker	Peter B.	12.15	1896			72	8.12	73	147	13	served in Co. C, 158th Regt., and in Co. H, 202d Regt., Pennsylvania Infantry
Walker	Catharine	10.04	1886			73	1.02	74	147	14	Walker, Peter B., wife of
Walker	Alcinda A.	8.19	1863	2.09	1828			36	147	15	
Walker	Nancy	1.03	1863			62	11.29	63	147	16	Walker, Richard, wife of
Warner	John A.	8.09	1883			1	0.24	2	147	17	Warner, T. K. & S. E., son of
Weary	David			12.11	1844				147	18	d. --
Weary	Margaret R.	2.03	1896	8.20	1851			45	147	19	
Weary	Grace E.	3.31	1889	6.06	1888			1	147	20	
Wert	John	10.11	1872	4.12	1803			70	147	21	
Wert	Mary M.	4.23	1884	11.28	1801			83	147	22	Wert, John, wife of
Wert	Susan	10.05	1895			53	5.08	54	147	23	Wert, William, wife of
Wert	J. William	9.15	1899			2	9.29	3	147	24	Wert, George & Lillie B., son of
Wert	Annie M.	12.10	1862				7.18	1	147	25	Wert, William & Susanna, child of
Wert	Henry S.	2.25	1881				11.16	1	147	26	Wert, William & Susanna, child of
Wert	William W.	3.08	1875			1	6.04	2	147	27	Wert, William & Susanna, child of
Wetzel	Robert G. C.	1.21	1892			6	8.00	7	147	28	Wetzel, J. W.[?] & M.[?] C., son of
Wetzel	Joseph	1.10	1891	11.11	1812			79	147	29	
Wetzel	Sarah	1.05	1880	2.07	1814			66	147	30	Wetzel, Joseph, wife of
Wetzel	John Z.	4.11	1842			4	0.11	5	147	31	
Wetzel	Henry	6.01	1859	5.04	1840			20	147	32	Wetzel, Joseph & Sarah, child of
Wetzel	Rebecca	2.04	1852	6.23	1846			6	147	33	Wetzel, Joseph & Sarah, child of

Frankford - Lutheran and Reformed Stone Church Graveyard

Surname	Given Name	Death Mo/Dy	Year	Birth Mo/Dy	Year	Att. Yr	Age Mo/Dy	Cm Ag	Pg	No	Other Information
Wetzel	David	1.31	1852	6.30	1844			8	147	34	Wetzel, Joseph & Sarah, child of
Wickard	Rebecca	3.20	1870			22	3.15	23	147	35	Wickard, Calvin, wife of; ----, William & E., daughter of
Williams	Elizabeth	1.04	1865			51	5.16	52	147	36	Williams, Josiah, wife of; [aged 1<u>6</u> dys?
Wire	John	7.09	1895			86	5.24	87	147	37	
Wire	Peter	1.09	1903			63	2.19	64	148	01	Co. C, 158th Regt., Pa. Infantry
Wirt	John P.	3.29	1833			1	5.10	2	148	02	
Wolf	Jacob	4.13	1863	3.24	1805			59	148	03	
Wolf	Christina	1.06	1862			47	8.03	48	148	04	
Wolf	Catharine	9.16	1866			59	5.27	60	148	05	
Wolf	Christian	12.10	1853			71	4.28	72	148	06	
Wolf	Charlotte Eve	8.18	1860			76	1.04	77	148	07	Wolf, Christian, wife of
Wolf	Sarah	4.10	1833				1.18	1	148	08	Wolf, Jacob & Leah, daughter of
Wynkoop	John M.	10.02	1857			2	0.01	3	148	09	Wynkoop, M. & S., son of
Wynekoop	Susanna	12.23	1876			63	8.06	64	148	10	Wynekoop, Matthew, wife of
Yoter	Samuel B.		1885		1845			41	148	11	
Yoter	Ellen				1846				148	12	Yoter, Samuel B., wife of
Yoter	Caroline	12.12	1873			26	0.18	27	148	13	Yoter, Joseph L., wife of
Young	Henry L.	8.13	1855			24	4.11	25	148	14	
Young	Marietta Catharine	6.20	1855			1	4.22	2	148	15	
Zeigler	Anna M.	6.09	1871			69	2.09	70	148	16	Shambaugh, Philip, former wife of
Zeigler	William P.	11.27	1890			65	7.04	66	148	17	
Zeigler	Rebecca								148	18	Zeigler, William P., wife of

Frankford - Lutheran Brick Church Graveyard

LUTHERAN BRICK CHURCH GRAVEYARD

Surname	Given Name	Death Mo/Dy	Year	Birth Mo/Dy	Year	Att. Age Yr	Mo/Dy	Ag	Cm	Pg	No	Other Information
Alexander	James	2.13	1872	7.28	1797			75	156	05	soldier
Alexander	Elizabeth	1.23	1862			66	3.19	67	156	06	(b. 1796)
Alexander	Mary	2.24	1851			24	6.23	25	156	07	Alexander, J. & E., daughter of
Alexander	John	11.18	1863				7.18	1	156	08	Alexander, J. & Christianna, son of
Allen	Samuel			11.15	1833				156	01	
Allen	Elizabeth	2.07	1904	6.09	1832			72	156	02	
Allen	Harvey A.	2.14	1872	12.12	1866			6	156	03	Allen, Samuel & Elizabeth, son of
Allen	Reuben	2.11	1863			7	4.09	8	156	04	Allen, Samuel & Elizabeth, son of
Anthony	Michael	10.05	1859		1791	68	3.13	69	156	09	
Anthony	John	6.02	1838	9.00	1824			14	156	10	Anthony, Eve & Michael, son of
Anthony	Eve	1.15	1864		1793	71	7.14	72	156	11	Anthony, Michael, wife of
Anthony	Michael F.	5.06	1895			69	4.04	70	156	12	
Anthony	Sarah	12.24	1869			38	8.09	39	156	13	Anthony, Michael F., wife of
Armold	Samuel	8.07	1861			62		63	156	14	(b. 1799)
Armold	Elizabeth	5.17	1847			50	1.13	51	156	15	Armold, Henry, wife of
Armolt	Joseph E.	11.08	1901			67	3.09	68	156	16	
Armold	Sarah	12.11	1902	9.02	1835			68	156	17	
Baltozer	Elizabeth	1.02	1891			84	9.03	85	156	18	
Baldoser	George	3.15	1858			11	0.11	12	156	19	Baldoser, George & Mary, son of
Barrick	David			3.10	1825				156	20	
Barrick	Catharine	1.15	1902	1.27	1822			80	156	21	Barrick, David, wife of
Barrick	F. Albert	12.25	1889				2.19	1	156	22	Barrick, M. L. & Ellen, son of
Barrick	Levi H.				1844				156	23	
Barrick	Anna M.				1850				156	24	Barrick, Levi, wife of
Barrick	Joseph A.		1875		1871			5	156	25	
Batrum	Samuel	5.03	1870			38	5.14	39	156	26	
Beltzhoover	George M.	3.14	1875				11.14	1	156	27	Beltzhoover, George & Jane M., son of
Benner	John	12.01	1827		1761	66	10.12	67	157	16	slate headstone
Berry	Thomas	1.00	1829			62	6.24	63	156	28	(b. 1767)
Berry	Samuel	11.20	1874			72		73	156	29	
Berry	Elizabeth	10.06	1855			37	11.03	38	156	30	Berry, Samuel, wife of
Billman	Annie Maud	4.17	1885			1	10.22	2	156	31	Billman, Adam E. & Eliza, daughter of
Bixler	Annie C.	7.09	1876	10.05	1874			2	156	32	
Bloser	Peter	3.10	1839			93		94	157	31	gray sandstone; lettering almost obliterated
Bloser	Elizabeth	9.14	1807			51		52	157	32	Bloser, Peter, wife of; aged 51 years, - months, 28 days
Bloser	Peter	2.19	1830			45	11.03	46	157	33	
Bloser	Anna	8.12	1857			67		68	157	34	Bloser, Peter, wife of
Bloser	Peter	3.31	1885	9.05	1815			70	157	35	
Bloser	Solomon	7.29	1861	2.07	1830			32	157	36	
Bloser	John P.		1902		1822			81	157	37	
Bloser	Elizabeth		1904		1826			79	157	38	Bloser, John P., wife of
Bloser	John	8.26	1860			79	10.1	80	157	39	
Bloser	Catharine	3.19	1853	4.17	1781			72	157	40	Bloser, John, wife of
Bloser	Mary					5		6	157	41	Bloser, John & Catharine, daughter of
Bloser	William	6.30	1871			89	3.15	90	158	01	
Bloser	Martha	6.21	1835			36	1.18	37	158	02	Bloser, William, wife of

Surname	Given Name	Death Mo/Dy	Year	Birth Mo/Dy	Year	Att. Age Yr	Mo/Dy	Ag	Cm	Pg	No	Other Information
Bloser	Elizabeth	11.12	1866	9.09	1817			50		158	03	Bloser, William, daughter of
Bloser	J. William	8.22	1889	2.16	1865			25		158	04	
Bloser	Catharine	8.14	1895	3.06	1824			72		158	05	
Bloser	William B.	6.10	1896	12.18	1821			75		158	06	
Bloser	Ella Mary	9.01	1875				5.05		1	158	07	Bloser, M. B. & Mary E., daughter of
Bloser	Catharine	4.09	1865	5.15	1823			42		158	08	Bloser, David, wife of
Bloser	Mary	3.28	1867	11.03	1828			39		158	09	Bloser, Benjamin, wife of
Bloser	Lavina	3.27	1849			19	8.27	20		158	10	
Bloser	Jamima	3.07	1851			17	7.00	18		158	11	
Bloser	Margaret	10.16	1835			58		59		158	12	Bloser, H., wife of
Bloser	Rebecca	4.11	1900			75	2.25	76		158	13	
Bloser	Catharine	9.06	1858			28	9.18	29		158	14	Bloser, S. D., wife of
Bloser	Norman A.	2.02	1885				5.17		1	158	15	Bloser, James O. & F. C., son of
Bloser	Laura Faith	7.16	1897			1	1.27		2	158	16	Bloser, S. B. & S. A., daughter of
Bloser	Hazel E.	10.26	1899							158	17	Bloser, S. P. & A. E., daughter of
Boldosser	George	4.00	1847			40	4.00	41		157	02	date of death is given is April 31
Boldosser	John E.	5.02	1876	10.15	1867				9	157	03	Boldosser, W. H. & Elizabeth, son of
Boldosser	Samuel E.			3.15	1875					157	04	Boldosser, I. B. and C. B., child of
Boldosser	Charles A.			3.15	1875					157	05	Baldosser, I. B. & C. B., child of
Boldosser	Clark S.	8.06	1880	4.09	1880				1	157	06	Baldosser, I. B. & C. B., child of
Boldosser	Robert C.	12.11	1884	4.27	1884				1	157	07	Boldosser, I. B. & C. B., child of
Boll	Philip				1838					157	08	
Boll	Mary W.		1898		1851			48		157	09	Boll, Philip, wife of
Boll	Catharine		1873		1839			35		157	10	Boll, Philip, wife of
Boll	Hiram A.	1.08	1873				6.20		1	157	11	Boll, P. A. & C., child of
Boll	Salome A.	7.10	1870			1	9.14		2	157	12	Boll, P. A. & C., child of
Boll	Sarah Rena	11.13	1877			2	2.26		3	157	13	Boll, P. A. & M. W., child of
Boll	Ira David	7.27	1878				3.08		1	157	14	Boll, P. A. & M. W., child of
Boll	Albert Edmund	5.17	1884	7.07	1879				5	157	15	Boll, P. A. & M. W., child of
Boughman	M. Angella	3.14	1897			2	7.21		3	157	17	Boughman, S. P. & M. A., daughter of
Bower	Benjamin	9.13	1884			53	11.19	54		157	27	
Bower	Anna Mary	12.25	1883			41	6.29	42		157	28	Bower, Benjamin, wife of
Bower	Maggie E.	8.28	1878				0.28		1	157	29	Bower, Benjamin & Anna Mary, child of
Bower	Benjamin S.	10.03	1881				3.21		1	157	30	Bower, Benjamin & Anna Mary, child of;
Bowman	Willie M.	8.16	1871				11.04		1	157	18	Bowman, J. H. & S. L., child of
Bowman	Walter M.	8.08	1869				4.23		1	157	19	Bowman, J. H. & S. L., child of
Bowman	Charlie	6.12	1894			10	8.06	11		157	20	Bowman, J. H. & Susan L., son of
Bowman	Clarence F.	3.14	1887				1.00		1	157	21	Bowman, J. H. & Susan L., son of
Bowman	Abraham, Jr.	9.14	1843	12.16	1824			19		157	22	
Bowman	Samuel	2.24	1872			54	5.03	55		157	23	
Bowman	Christian	5.02	1882			42		43		157	24	
Bowman	Elizabeth									157	25	Bowman, Christian, wife of
Bowman	Harry	4.09	1899			25		26		157	26	Bowman, C. & E., son of
Bricker	David	4.08	1833		1755	78	2.05	79		156	34	(b. 1755)
Bricker	Molly	4.28	1838		1762	75		76		156	35	Bricker, David, wife of; (b. 1762)
Bricker	David	12.16	1831	9.10	1786			46		156	36	
Bricker	Mary	2.29	1860		1788	72	11.04	73		156	37	Bricker, David, wife of; (b. 1788)
Bricker	Isamiah	3.18	1851	1.16	1841			11		157	01	Bricker, Joel and Susan, daughter of
Brim	Catharine A.	7.14	1859	3.27	1858			2		156	33	Brim, J. & R., daughter of
Brownsbarger	Joseph	9.27	1823			24	11.11	25		158	18	red sand headstone

Frankford - Lutheran Brick Church Graveyard

Surname	Given Name	Death Mo/Dy	Year	Birth Mo/Dy	Year	Att. Age Yr	Cm Mo/Dy	Ag	Pg	No	Other Information
Brownsbarger	John	4.28	1832			1	1.18	2	158	19	Brownsbarger, John, son of
Buckwalter	Israel	11.19	1902	7.02	1846			57	158	20	
Buckwalter	Annie E.			1.05	1849				158	21	
Burkhart	John	3.14	1903			56	11.28	57	158	22	
Burkholder	James C.				1842				158	23	
Burkholder	Annie B.				1848				158	24	Burkholder, James C., wife of
Burkholder	Daisie Ola		1904		1889			16	158	25	
Burtnett	Jacob M.	5.11	1884			60	4.11	61	158	26	
Burtnett	Susan H. [?]	11.26	1895	4.29	1826			70	158	27	Burtnett, Jacob M., wife of
Carbaugh	Elizabeth	6.04	1887	7.10	1815			72	158	28	Carbaugh, Theodore, wife of
Carl	Elizabeth	11.03	1892	5.03	1836			57	158	29	Carl, Alfred, wife of
Carl	Charlotte T.	6.19	1864	9.20	1863			1	158	30	
Carl	Margaret L.	3.05	1865	1.13	1859			7	158	31	
Carl	Maurice R.	10.01	1881	9.22	1881			1	158	32	
Clouse	Nancy	2.12	1895			60		61	158	36	Clouse, David, wife of
Clouse	John	4.29	1902			65	8.18	66	158	37	
Clouse	Mary	4.29	1904			77	4.29	78	158	38	
Clouse	John	11.19	1870				0.17	1	158	39	
Clouse	Lydia	12.04	1872			4	10.29	5	158	40	
Clouse	Levi	2.17	1865				1.12	1	158	41	
Comrey	Andrew	4.16	1875	11.05	1805			70	158	33	
Comrey	Catharine A.	4.16	1881	3.10	1814			68	158	34	Comrey, Andrew, wife of
Comrey	Elizabeth	8.01	1838			1	6.00	2	158	35	Comrey, Andrew & Ann Catharine, dau. of
Cornman	Martin	11.28	1902			70	9.22	71	158	42	
Cornman	Susan	7.18	1897			64	8.11	65	158	43	
Dare	Peter, Sr.					69		70	159	01	slate headstone
Dare	Mary					59		60	159	02	slate headstone
Dare	Peter					16		17	159	03	slate headstone
Darr	Sarah	12.28	1828			15	5.05	16	159	04	slate headstone
Dare	Moses						0.05	1	159	05	
Dare	Elias	4.24	1824				0.08	1	159	06	sand stone headstone
Darr	Catharine	1.21	1835			24		25	159	07	
Darr	Henry	6.11	1843			60	4.26	61	159	08	slate headstone
Darr	Maria Magdalena	2.01	1827			44	6.00	45	159	09	German
Darr	Henry	4.27	1853			27	3.27	28	159	10	
Dell	Jacob	9.13	1825			39	3.08	40	159	36	
Deihl	Elizabeth	6.02	1868			83	2.21	84	159	37	
Deihl	Michael	8.10	1840	9.26	1777			63	159	38	
Deihl	Susanna	6.08	1876			89	3.00	90	159	39	
Derr	John Amos	3.29	1876	4.17	1824			52	159	40	
Derr	Elizabeth	6.04	1905	7.18	1818			87	159	41	
Dill	Catharina	12.25	1810		1745	65	3.05	66	159	42	(b. 1745); German; slate headstone
Diel	Michael	12.15	1831			21	8.00	22	159	43	
Doner	Abraham	2.23	1861			55	3.26	56	160	01	
Doner	Catharine	3.29	1870	12.26	1811			59	160	02	Doner, Abraham, wife of
Drawbaugh	William	6.20	1817			49		50	159	11	
Drawbaugh	Catharine	4.07	1839			65		66	159	12	
Drawbaugh	John	10.07	1882			58	10.11	59	159	13	
Drawbaugh	Nancy	10.09	1893			74	2.14	75	159	14	
Drawbaugh	George A.	11.06	1882			25	4.04	26	159	15	Drawbaugh, John & Nancy, son of

Frankford - Lutheran Brick Church Graveyard

Surname	Given Name	Death Mo/Dy	Year	Birth Mo/Dy	Year	Att. Age Yr	Mo/Dy	Cm Ag	Pg	No	Other Information
Drawbaugh	J. Freeman	10.04	1882			22	7.21	23	159	16	Drawbaugh, John & Nancy, son of
Drawbaugh	S. Wilson	10.09	1882			29	9.21	30	159	17	Drawbaugh, John & Nancy, son of
Drawbaugh	John	12.09	1878			90		91	159	18	soldier
Drawbaugh	Leah	11.01	1869			77		78	159	19	D----, John, wife of
Drawbaugh	John	7.19	1838	5.00	1837			2	159	20	
Drawbaugh	Maggie M.	6.11	1879				3.04	1	159	21	Drawbaugh, Joseph & E., child of
Drawbaugh	Mattie E	10.01	1884			16	7.20	17	159	22	Drawbaugh, Joseph & E., child of
Drawbaugh	Joseph	11.30	1899			61	0.17	62	159	23	
Drawbaugh	William	10.28	1884	3.01	1807			78	159	24	
Drawbaugh	Catharine	1.27	1892	9.24	1815			77	159	25	
Drawbaugh	William B.	4.22	1881			14	6.04	15	159	26	Drawbaugh, Joseph & E., son of
Drawbaugh	James A.	4.00	1857			8	5.10	9	159	27	Drawbaugh, W. & M., son of; died Apr. 3<u>1</u>, 1857
Drawbaugh	David P.	5.23	1861			22	1.23	23	159	28	Drawbaugh, George & Barbara, son of
Drawbaugh	Catharine Agnes	12.06	1864			15	1.08	16	159	29	Drawbaugh, John & Nancy, daughter of
Drawbaugh	Margaret	3.19	1879			57	4.18	58	159	30	Drawbaugh, William, wife of
Drawbaugh	Eliza Ellen	4.15	1860			26	7.16	27	159	31	Drawbaugh, H. F., wife of
Drawbaugh	Clarence King	12.13	1861			5	2.20	6	159	32	
Drawbaugh	Blanche M.	5.11	1892				0.07	1	159	33	Drawbaugh, J. P. & J. L., child of
Drawbaugh	J. Harry	4.14	1891				6.24	1	159	34	Drawbaugh, J. P. & J. L., child of
Drawbaugh	Harminta C.	10.21	1904	10.02	1897			8	159	35	Drawbaugh, J. P. & J. L., child of
Ebrite	Ludwig	4.00	1825						160	03	age about 60 years
Ebrite	Elizabeth	6.20	1864			77	6.24	78	160	04	Ebrite, Ludwig, wife of
Eckart	George	10.25	1848	9.01	1767			82	160	05	
Eckert	Margaret	3.14	1847	10.26	1771			76	160	06	Eckert, George, wife of; [sp. varies]
Elicker	Catharine	8.22	1842			72	1.24	73	160	07	
Ensminger	Lewis	12.26	1867						160	08	Ensminger, Joseph & Mary, child of
Ensminger	Elvy May	6.03	1881						160	09	Ensminger, Joseph & Mary, child of
Ernst	John	8.12	1838			83		84	160	10	
Ernst	Christian	9.23	1823			50	10.00	51	160	11	
Ernst	Catharine								160	12	d. Sep.
Ernst	Samuel	9.00	1834			26		27	160	13	
Ernst	John	9.05	1892			63	5.28	64	160	14	
Ernst	Catharine	1.24	1842			25	10.08	26	160	15	Ernst, John, wife of
Ernst	David C.	4.12	1883			23	5.26	24	160	16	Ernst, John & Jane M., child of
Ernst	John S.	10.10	1881			0	7.07	1	160	17	Ernst, John & Jane M., child of
Ernst	David	6.06	1867			65	6.05	66	160	18	
Ernst	Sarah	2.02	1869			70	8.12	71	160	19	
Ernst	Levi B.	5.22	1834			7	0.08	8	160	20	Ernst, D., son of
Failor	John H.	1.24	1857			0	7.04	1	160	21	
Failor	Henry E.	9.09	1852			0	1.03	1	160	22	
Failor	Eliza J.	5.13	1881			38	6.02	39	160	23	Failor, J. W., wife of
Failor	Elizabeth M.	3.21	1881			13	0.08	14	160	24	Failor, J. W. & E. J., daughter of
Failor	John P.	8.17	1872			2	5.00	3	160	25	Failor, James & Eliza, son of
Failor	Christian	11.29	1868			68	11.17	69	160	26	
Failor	Margaret	5.01	1881			70	4.00	71	160	27	Failor, Christian, wife of
Fahler	William	6.30	1851	11.01	1818			33	160	28	
Fenton	William B.	8.06	1860			0	3.16	1	160	29	Fenton, J. & A. M., son of
Fickes	Abram A.	2.25	1889			42	1.19	43	160	34	
Finkenbinder	John	2.14	1885			72		73	160	35	

Frankford - Lutheran Brick Church Graveyard

Surname	Given Name	Death Mo/Dy	Year	Birth Mo/Dy	Year	Att. Age Yr	Mo/Dy	Cm Ag	Pg	No	Other Information
Finkenbinder	Susan	3.26	1870			54	10.03	55	160	36	Finkenbinder, Samuel, wife of
Finkenbinder	Philip	2.25	1887			77	3.10	78	160	37	
Finkenbinder	Elizabeth	9.05	1876			68	11.18	69	160	38	Finkenbinder, Philip, wife of
Finkenbinder	Elizabeth			4.16	1841	0	0.03		160	39	[d. date not given]
Finkenbinder	George	4.08	1857			71	6.00	72	161	01	
Finkenbinder	Catharine	6.16	1861			70	7.23	71	161	02	Finkenbinder, George, wife of
Freet	Benjamin	8.06	1873			64	11.28	65	160	30	
Freet	Elizabeth	3.29	1875			88	1.01	89	160	31	
Freet	Elizabeth	7.31	1888			74	4.08	75	160	32	
Freet	Catharine E.	8.02	1879			28	4.13	29	160	33	
Fry	Samuel, Sr.	2.26	1873			70	10.21	71	161	06	
Fry	Sarah	7.01	1866			64	3.20	65	161	07	Fry, Samuel, Sr., wife of
Fry	Isaac	3.24	1889	7.17	1838			51	161	08	
Fry	Samuel	3.23	1893			65	7.17	66	161	09	
Fry	Mary Ann	12.07	1893			71	0.23	72	161	10	Fry, George, wife of
Fry	John	7.17	1900			65	7.04	66	161	11	
Fry	James W.	12.05	1864			0	2.19	1	161	12	Fry, J. & M., son of
Fry	Emma J.	9.05	1867			0	11.23	1	161	13	
Fry	Ann S.	11.02	1874			0	0.26	1	161	14	
Fry	Thurman A.	8.05	1889			0	1.09	1	161	15	Fry, S. A. & S. B., son of
Funk	John	7.27	1884	6.25	1826			59	161	03	
Funk	Mary M.	5.20	1877	4.12	1807			71	161	04	
Funk	Jacob	5.28	1882	4.03	1803			80	161	05	
Gayman	Annie H. [?]	8.09	1882			24	4.28	25	161	16	Gayman, John H., wife of
Gayman	Samuel	9.04	1900	6.28	1843			58	161	17	
Gayman	Sophia J.			2.11	1845				161	18	Gayman, Samuel, wife of
Gayman	Bertha M.	1.25	1898	4.18	1895			3	161	19	Gayman, M. H. & A. G., daughter of
Gebhart	Minnie Alice	9.06	1871	7.15	1871			1	161	23	Gebhart, Jacob & Elizabeth, child of
Gebhart	Wanda	12.21	1871	12.30	1864			7	161	24	Gebhart, Jacob & Elizabeth, child of
Gebhart	Albert	8.08	1866			0	5.11	1	161	25	Gebhart, Jacob & Elizabeth, child of
Gebhart	Susannah	1.13	1864	10.03	1863			1	161	26	Gebhart, Jacob & Elizabeth, child of
Gebhart	Emaline	10.30	1868	8.03	1868			1	161	27	Gebhart, Jacob & Elizabeth, child of
Gebhart	Simon			5.09	1867				161	28	Gebhart, Jacob & Elizabeth, son of; d. Dec. 28, 187-
Gebhart	Eli	9.02	1879			19	5.00	20	161	29	Gebhart, Jacob & Elizabeth, son of
Gettys	Mary	6.23	1867			74	2.23	75	161	30	
Gettys	Elizabeth	3.01	1884			46	9.28	47	161	31	
Givler	Henry J.	5.21	1897			66		67	161	37	
Graham	Edwin C.	1.31	1881			0	6.05	1	161	20	Graham, James M. & Annie C., child of
Graham	Annie McFarlane	8.18	1887	6.03	1883			5	161	21	Graham. James M. & Annie C., child of
Graham	Laura May	8.26	1887	5.14	1886			2	161	22	Graham. James M. & Annie C., child of
Green	John	1.03	1881			55	9.03	56	161	33	
Green	Susan	1.06	1885	8.09	1833			52	161	34	Green, John & Susan, child of
Green	John Rankin	9.11	1878			14	2.05	15	161	35	Green, John & Susan, child of
Green	Lizzie J.	4.17	1875			3	10.06	4	161	36	Green, John & Susan, child of
Greider	Frances I.	9.15	1901	6.17	1901			1	161	32	Greider, J. & L., daughter of
Haines	Sarah Ann	1.17	1892			61	8.15	62	161	38	Haines, William A., wife of
Haines	William A.	6.14	1898			70	0.26	71	161	39	
Haines	Fanny A.	12.19	1882			19	7.12	20	161	40	Haines, W. A. & Sarah, daughter of
Haines	Abner C.	3.11	1868			10	2.20	11	162	01	

Surname	Given Name	Death Mo/Dy	Year	Birth Mo/Dy	Year	Att. Age Yr	Mo/Dy	Ag	Cm	Pg	No	Other Information
Haines	Mary, Mrs.	2.06	1885			71	3.02	72		162	02	formerly Boldosser
Hale	Christiana	3.23	1866			74		75		162	03	Hale, Mikel, wife of
Harmon	Catharine	6.09	1851			3	7.00	4		162	04	Harmon, Thomas & Mary, daughter of
Heberlig	John	1.15	1821			23	2.17	24		162	05	slate headstone
Heberlig	Magdalena	8.20	1821			57	11.20	58		162	06	
Heberlig	Johannes		1824			14	6.11	15		162	07	d. --- 25, 1824; slate; German
Heberlig	Jacob	6.05	1824			6	0.07	7		162	08	slate; German
Heberlig	John	11.18	1827			67	11.18	68		162	09	slate
Heberlig	Mable G.	2.04	1892			0	0.07	1		162	10	Heberlig, J. E. & Ida J., daughter of
Hefflefinger	John	11.05	1867	6.09	1792			76		162	11	
Hefflefinger	Elizabeth	3.09	1856			60	2.11	61		162	12	Hefflefinger, John, wife of
Hefflefinger	Ellen	1.09	1857			13	10.16	14		162	13	Hefflefinger, J. & E., daughter of
Hefflefinger	William	9.07	1827			30	4.15	31		162	14	slate headstone
Hefflefinger	Mary Ann	4.01	1848			19	11.16	20		162	15	Hefflefinger, Wm. and Elizabeth, dau. of
Hefflefinger	David	5.04	1854	2.20	1832			23		162	16	
Hefflefinger	Philip	5.05	1860			56	9.22	57		162	17	
Hefflefinger	Catharine	5.03	1874			74		75		162	18	Hefflefinger, Philip, wife of
Hefflefinger	Benjamin	2.03	1885	5.02	1836			49		162	19	soldier
Hefflefinger	Henry E.	12.17	1868			12	0.14	13		162	20	Hefflefinger, Benjamin & Sarah, child of
Hefflefinger	Minnie A.					0	6.16	1		162	21	Hefflefinger, Benjamin & Sarah, child of
Hefflefinger	Maggie J.	12.24	1891			29	10.05	30		162	22	
Hefflefinger	David	6.14	1878			38	8.16	39		162	23	soldier
Hefflefinger	Margaret A.	12.13	1865			39	5.06	40		162	24	Hefflefinger, John P., wife of
Hefflefinger	Samuel K>	11.26	1862			8	0.03	9		162	25	Hefflefinger, John P. & M. A., son of
Heffleman	William Henry	2.23	1823			0	8.09	1		162	26	
Heffleman	Mary Ann	12.14	1833			22	0.26	23		162	27	Heffleman, John, consort of
Hemminger	John	5.21	1871			68	10.17	69		162	28	
Hemminger	Martha	12.13	1893			78	4.00	79		162	29	
Hemminger	Sue M.	1.31	1899			60	2.17	61		162	30	
Hemminger	Maria C.	2.25	1875			30	7.05	31		162	31	Hemminger, J. D., wife aof
Hemminger	Sallie B.	6.12	1871			2		3		162	32	Hemminger, J. D. & M. C., child of
Hemminger	Clara Maria	4.16	1875			0	1.26	1		162	33	Hemminger, J. D. & M. C., child of
Hoffman	Jacob S.	1.31	1864			7	10.07	8		162	34	Hoffman, Jonathan & Barbara, son of
Hoon	Elizabeth	4.11	1901			60	7.21	61		162	35	
Hoover	George	12.24	1868	1.19	1817			52		162	36	
Hoover	Nancy Gants	5.09	1855	10.23	1815			40		162	37	Hoover, George, wife of
Hoover	Catharine J.	12.19	1871			51	11.02	52		163	01	Hoover, George, wife of
Hoover	William	4.07	1897	9.28	1824			73		163	02	
Hoover	Elizabeth	4.11	1897	1.08	1830			68		163	03	Hoover, William, wife of
Hoover	G. B. McClellan	1.03	1864			1	1.07	2		163	04	
Hoover	Edward	4.30	1869			1	4.17	2		163	05	
Hoover	Henry H.	11.08	1882			29	11.02	30		163	06	
Hoover	Lovina J.	2.26	1890	9.17	1854			36		163	07	Hoover, John, wife of
Hoover	George B.	9.06	1875			16	6.26	17		163	08	
Hoover	William	12.28	1863			4	11.22	5		163	09	
Hoover	Susanna	9.05	1880			23	2.29	24		163	10	
Hoover	Samuel	7.27	1826			0	1.06	1		163	11	
Hoover	William A.	2.06	1902			21	1.03	22		163	12	Hoover, W. A. & M. E., son of
Hoover	Annie Kate	3.07	1875			3		4		163	13	Hoover, W. M. & S. A., daughter of
Hoover	William F.	10.13	1832			4	2.06	5		163	14	

Frankford - Lutheran Brick Church Graveyard

Surname	Given Name	Death Mo/Dy	Year	Birth Mo/Dy	Year	Att. Age Yr	Mo/Dy	Cm Ag	Pg	No	Other Information
Hoover	George	10.09	1832			3	1.12	4	163	15	
Hoover	John	10.05	1832			5	5.02	6	163	16	
Hoover	Max M.	8.24	1894			0	11.24	1	163	17	Hoover, Joseph F. & Nannie C., son of
Hoover	Rebecca E.	11.02	1859			3	1.11	4	163	18	Hoover, G. K. & M., child of
Hoover	John Ellsworth	12.04	1863			1	11.08	2	163	19	Hoover, G. K. & M., child of
Hoover	Oliver D.	6.05	1868			1	4.13	2	163	20	Hoover, G. K. & M., child of
Hoover	Robert H.	3.01	1872			1	3.29	2	163	21	Hoover, G. K. & M., child of
Ickes	Irvin A.	11.02	1904			0	0.02	1	163	22	Ickes, W. H. & A. M., child of
Ickes	Charles W.	3.07	1903			0	10.00	1	163	23	Ickes, W. H. & A. M., son of; aged 10 mos.-10 mos. ?
Kammerer	Jacob	10.04	1830	9.28	1803			28	163	24	German
Kamarer	Mathias	10.04	1870			62	5.23	63	163	25	
Kammerer	Susan	9.06	1870			69	6.00	70	163	26	
Kammerer	Alvinda P.	6.28	1900			43	1.05	44	163	27	
Kamarer	Mathias	8.11	1885			43	10.09	44	163	28	[spelling varies]
Kamarer	Sarah	1.19	1890			74	4.18	75	163	29	Kamarer, Mathias, wife of
Kammerer	Zacharias	2.10	1851	4.17	1848			3	163	30	Kammerar, Mathias & Sarah, child of
Kammerer	Jacob Abraham	2.11	1851	2.08	1850			2	163	31	Kammerer, Mathias & Sarah, child of
Kammerer	Leah Emily	2.15	1851	11.01	1847			4	163	32	Kammerer, Mathias & Sarah, child of
Kammerer	Elizabeth Ann	4.15	1857			14	2.00	15	163	33	Kammerer, Mathias & Sarah, child of
Kammerer	Joshua C.	11.05	1874			23	7.00	24	163	34	Kammerer, Mathias & Sarah, child of
Kammerer	Eugene P.	6.09	1886			26	4.22	27	163	35	Kammerer, Mathias & Sarah, child of
Kammerer	John D.	2.01	1894			42	9.23	43	163	36	
Keck	Harry	5.16	1886			32	4.00	33	163	38	
Keefauver	Frederick	9.16	1865			60		61	163	39	buried at Centerville
Keefauver	Sarah Yeats	4.13	1892			91	4.23	92	163	40	Keefauver, Frederick, wife of
Keihl	Philip		1902		1838			65	164	01	
Keihl	Alice C.		1885		1873			13	164	02	
Kendig	Henry	1.09	1858			74	8.09	75	164	03	
Kinch	John	9.07	1836			57	1.00	58	164	05	
Kinch	Jacob	12.04	1840			26	6.19	27	164	06	
King	John	7.19	1847	6.15	1766			82	164	07	
King	Catharine Elizabeth	9.01	1819			39		40	164	08	King, John, wife of; aged 39 years, 19 [?] months
King	David					0	6.00	1	164	09	King, John & Catharine E., son of
King	Henry	10.16	1834			28		29	164	10	
King	George	2.08	1836			29	5.21	30	164	11	
King	Elizabeth	6.10	1826			15		16	164	12	
Kleber	Elizabeth	1.20	1805	4.27	1787			18	164	04	Kleber, Martin & Catharine, daughter of
Knouse	George W.	9.15	1887			71		72	164	25	
Knouse	Elizabeth	8.22	1895			85		86	164	26	Knouse, George W., wife of
Koch	John					63		64	164	13	
Koch	Mary					88		89	164	14	Koch, John, wife of
Koch	John	12.09	1888			67	8.09	68	164	15	
Koch	Elizabeth	1.05	1872			44	11.20	45	164	16	Koch, John, wife of
Koch	Leah	2.06	1876			18	11.04	19	164	17	
Koch	Frankie T.	5.02	1877			0	6.18	1	164	18	Koch, Jacob & Margaret, son of
Koser	Israel	6.05	1898			73	6.22	74	164	19	both h. and w. age given as same
Koser	Rebecca	1.19	1891			73	6.22	74	164	20	Koser, Israel, wife of
Kosht	William	5.22	1875			52	11.09	53	164	21	

Frankford - Lutheran Brick Church Graveyard

Surname	Given Name	Death Mo/Dy	Death Year	Birth Mo/Dy	Birth Year	Att. Age Yr	Age Mo/Dy	Age	Cm	Pg	No	Other Information
Kosht	Catharine	6.13	1877			54	3.21	55	164	22		Kosht, William, wife of
Kosht	Emma	10.06	1878			10	2.18	11	164	23		Kosht, John & Mary, child of
Kosht	George	2.16	1867			0	9.02	1	164	24		Kosht, John & Mary, child of
Kramer	Samuel A.	11.15	1884			2	3.04	3	163	37		
Leas	Mary E.	8.25	1868			0	0.18	1	164	27		Leas, C. & S., child of
Leas	Margaret J.	9.09	1869			0	1.29	1	164	28		Leas, C. & S., child of
Lehman	Jacob	3.20	1848			69		70	164	29		
Lehman	Catharine	1.31	1860			70		71	164	30		Lehman, Jacob, wife of
Lehman	Mary Jane	5.16	1855			25	8.19	26	164	31		Lehman, Jacob & Catharine, daughter of
Lehman	William	6.25	1848	11.01	1787			61	164	32		
Lehman	Elizabeth	10.09	1880	4.09	1796			85	164	33		
Lehman	Elizabeth	9.12	1892	3.27	1800			93	164	34		
Lehman	Jacob	11.23	1884	10.17	1813			72	164	35		
Lehman	Florence B.	10.08	1886			4	6.26	5	164	36		
Lehman	William	11.13	1872			66		67	164	37		
Lehman	Harriet	5.02	1887			74	2.24	75	164	38		
Lehman	John	5.24	1877			26	3.09	27	164	39		
Lehman	Jacob	2.22	1872			22	6.02	23	164	40		Lehman, William & Harriet, son of
Lehman	William H.	6.05	1860			17	9.15	18	164	41		Lehman, William & Harriet, son of
Lehman	William A.	3.04	1890	3.24	1826			64	164	42		
Lehman	Anna L.	9.15	1902	8.04	1832			71	164	43		Lehman, William A., wife of
Lehman	Levi	10.03	1879	10.18	1835			44	164	44		
Lehman	James C.	11.07	1889			24	0.26	25	165	01		
Lehman	W. C. Leroy	9.22	1887			0	1.22	1	165	02		Lehman, S. P. & Annie, son of [d. 1887?]
Lehman	George F.				1863				165	03		
Lehman	Martha		1904		1866			39	165	04		Lehman, George F., wife of
Lehman	D. Smiley	12.05	1888			0	0.03	1	165	05		Lehman, G. F. & K. M., son of
Lehman	Myrtle G.		1893		1892			2	165	06		
Lehman	William H.		1903		1861			43	165	07		
Lehman	Mary Susan	4.01	1851	5.01	1849			2	165	08		Lehman, David & M., daughter of
Leib	Annie C.	12.23	1890			30	1.09	31	165	09		Leib, C. H., wife of
Leib	William C.	11.28	1886						165	13		
Little	Susan	2.28	1878			82		83	165	10		
Lutz	Martin	6.03	1827	6.02	1768			60	165	11		German
Lutz	Elizabeth	9.17	1850	5.09	1771			80	165	12		Lutz, Martin, wife of
Mayberry	Ruth Enola		1901		1900			2	165	14		Mayberry, C. E. & Annie, daughter of
McCoy	Jane M.	10.15	1899			4	0.02	5	166	37		McCoy, H. & E. S., daughter of
Mell	John	11.03	1840	4.25	1771			70	165	15		
Mell	Adam	10.16	1768	10.16	1745			24	165	16		German; slate headstone
Mell	Maria Barbara	5.00	1800			54	6.03	55	165	17		German; slate headstone
Mentzer	John	2.05	1861			80	1.21	81	165	18		
Mentzer	Elizabeth	7.06	1880	3.14	1793			88	165	19		
Mentzer	Simon		1888		1830			59	165	20		
Mentzer	Barbara		1903		1844			60	165	21		
Mentzer	Henry S.		1890		1874			17	165	22		
Mentzer	George E.		1900		1873			28	165	23		
Mentzer	John	3.28	1879			62	4.07	63	165	24		
Mentzer	Eve Ann	7.17	1893			72		73	165	25		Mentzer, John, wife of
Mentzer	Ida Jane	8.23	1866			0	10.21	1	165	26		Mentzer, John & Annie, daughter of
Mentzer	Frederick	7.06	1874			60	10.06	61	165	27		

Frankford - Lutheran Brick Church Graveyard

Surname	Given Name	Death Mo/Dy	Year	Birth Mo/Dy	Year	Att. Age Yr	Mo/Dy	Cm Ag	Pg	No	Other Information
Mentzer	Martha	7.29	1883	10.22	1815			68	165	28	
Mentzer	Mary	11.11	1881			41	8.13	42	165	29	Mentzer, Francis, wife of
Mentzer	William H.	7.18	1870			0	1.27	1	165	30	Mentzer, F. & M., son of
Mentzer	John	3.18	1884			41	9.09	42	165	31	
Mentzer	Mamie	5.04	1885			0	11.25	1	165	32	
Mentzer	David		1903		1832			72	165	33	
Mentzer	Henry		1895		1820			76	165	34	
Mentzer	Mary		1895		1820			76	165	35	
Mentzer	George				1835				165	36	
Mentzer	Harriet Oiler		1895		1846			50	165	37	Mentzer, George, wife of
Mentzer	Sally B.	11.02	1875			3	8.21	4	165	38	Mentzer, George & Harriet, child of
Mentzer	Franky	2.21	1878			1	2.20	2	165	39	Mentzer, George & Harriet, child of
Mentzer	Myrtle Viola	9.11	1896	4.20	1893			4	165	40	
Miller	Anna	5.04	1844			22	0.27	23	165	41	
Miller	Jeremiah D.		1904		1861			44	165	42	
Miller	Annie G.	5.06	1884			1	5.14	2	165	43	
Miller	Mary J.	7.22	1884			4	4.16	5	166	01	
Miller	Charles B.	4.28	1900	3.10	1899			2	166	02	Miller, G. G. & I. F., son of
Miller	Charles F.	11.26	1886			4	2.22	5	166	03	Miller, James A. & Ellen C., child of
Miller	Catharine E.	6.04	1897			16	1.06	17	166	04	Miller, James A. & Ellen C., child of
Miller	Edward V.	9.21	1887			18	0.21	19	166	05	Miller, Adam & Elizabeth, child of
Miller	Nannie J.	1.03	1891			19	3.07	20	166	06	Miller, Adam & Elizabeth, child of
Miller	Martha M.	6.21	1893			19	6.09	20	166	07	Miller, Adam & Elizabeth, child of
Mitten	Edward C.	4.06	1884	3.21	1884			1	166	08	Mitten, F. I. & Katie E., son of
Mitten	Elizabeth	11.04	1887	3.27	1802			86	166	09	
Mitten	Elizabeth	1.20	1899			78	10.00	79	166	10	Mitten, David, wife of
Mitten	Katie E.	6.03	1890			33		34	166	11	Mitten, Frank, wife of
Mitten	William V.		1905		1850			56	166	12	
Mitten	David	3.24	1885			0	3.04	1	166	13	Mitter, David & Elizabeth, son of
Mohler	Peter	7.23	1899	5.07	1821			79	166	14	
Mohler	Anna	3.24	1886			71	8.17	72	166	15	Mohler, Peter, wife of
Mohler	Elizabeth		1901		1849			53	166	16	
Mordorf	Levi	12.18	1894	12.13	1844			51	166	17	
Mowery	Elmer K		1904		1872			33	166	18	
Musser	Susanna	4.01	1864			84	0.24	85	166	19	
Musser	Abram R.	4.09	1898			75		76	166	20	
Musser	Mary Ann	9.29	1875			51	6.08	52	166	21	Musser, A. R., wife of
Musser	Susan C.	4.23	1905			53		54	166	22	
Myers	Peter	6.19	1884	12.19	1800			84	166	23	
Myers	Conrad	11.11	1876	2.14	1804			73	166	24	
Myers	Margaret	9.02	1879	3.06	1805			75	166	25	Myers, Conrad, wife of
Myers	William E. [?]	3.16	1904			39	0.26	40	166	26	
Myers	Ralph E.	11.23	1897			5	6.16	6	166	27	
Myers	Christian	10.16	1834			57	6.02	58	166	28	
Myers	John		1902		1834			69	166	29	
Myers	Maria				1828				166	30	
Myers	James Edmond	2.09	1878			20	0.09	21	166	31	Myers, John & Maria, child of
Myers	Sarah Ann	2.13	1864			0	4.13	1	166	32	
Myers	Elizabeth	6.10	1833			51		52	166	33	Myers, John, wife of
Myers	Margaret	11.11	1881	6.30	1802			80	166	34	

Frankford - Lutheran Brick Church Graveyard

Surname	Given Name	Death Mo/Dy	Year	Birth Mo/Dy	Year	Att. Age Yr	Mo/Dy	Cm Ag	Pg	No	Other Information
Myers	Barnet	2.13	1890			65	2.20	66	166	35	
Myers	Nancy	6.23	1901			68	0.02	69	166	36	
Nehf	Henry	7.07	1856	9.10	1782			74	166	38	
Neff	Eve Matilda	1.10	1864			18	6.04	19	166	39	Neff, Henry & A. C., child of
Neff	William F. [?]	8.07	1863			3	0.18	4	166	40	Neff, Henry & A. C., child of
Oiler	George	3.06	1886			76	3.03	77	167	01	
Oiler	Sarah Heckman	2.11	1889			72	2.25	73	167	02	Oiler, George, wife of
Oiler	Andrew	4.09	1882			79	2.22	80	167	03	
Oiler	Polly	11.01	1899			89	5.21	90	167	04	Oiler, Andrew, wife of
Oiler	Lucy Ann	8.23	1845			0	11.10	1	167	05	Oiler, Andrew & M., dau. of; slate hdstn
Oiler	John	7.05	1872			60	1.11	61	167	06	
Oiler	Catharine	12.30	1890			75	0.21	76	167	07	Oiler, John, wife of
Orris	John	12.04	1892	8.15	1809			84	167	08	
Orris	Elizabeth	5.17	1879			64	3.06	65	167	09	Orris, John, wife of
Orris	John A.	6.20	1844			1	6.00	2	167	10	Orris, John & Elizabeth, child of
Orris	Sylvester J.	11.07	1864			20	0.19	21	167	11	Orris, John & Elizabeth, son of; Co. H, 202d Regt., Pa. Vols.; d. Alexandria
Orris	Martha M.	1.13	1886			0	0.07	1	167	12	Orris, W. L. & H. J., daughter of
Peffer	Mary M.	5.12	1895			60	6.25	61	167	13	Peffer, George W., wife of
Ployer	Jacob	5.17	1897			77	1.07	78	167	14	
Ployer	Sophia	6.08	1896			73	7.17	74	167	15	Ployer, Jacob, wife of
Ployer	William A.	8.16	1858			3	11.25	4	167	16	Ployer, Jacob & Sophia, child of
Ployer	William H.	3.16	1871			3	4.23	4	167	17	
Raudabaugh	Polly	5.04	1854			38	1.12	39	167	18	Raudabaugh, Samuel, wife of
Reep	Jacob Frederick	9.04	1865			63	11.21	64	167	20	
Reep	Mary Charlotte	5.30	1869			67	7.10	68	167	21	Reep, Jacob F., wife of
Reifsnyder	Abraham	11.06	1823			47	6.19	48	167	19	
Ressler	Eve	10.13	1864			74	9.23	75	167	22	Ressler, Samuel, wife of
Rex	Rachel Kremer	5.07	1850	6.14	1830			20	167	23	Rex, Jeremiah, wife of
Rex	Joseph	8.08	1849			0	1.18	1	167	24	Rex, Jeremiah & Rachel, son of
Rex	Catharine Minnich	4.17	1857			70	9.14	71	167	25	Rex, Daniel, wife of
Rhoads	John	10.31	1869			34	5.19	35	167	28	
Rhoads	Elizabeth E.	1.16	1860			2	0.26	3	167	29	Rhoads, John & Margaret, daughter of
Rice	Benjamin	5.29	1885	4.24	1815			71	167	26	
Rice	Anna M.	5.09	1886	10.05	1821			65	167	27	
Rupp	Benjamin R.	1.11	1892			56	11.13	57	167	30	
Salisbury	Benjamin	8.12	1857			50	11.02	51	167	31	
Salisbury	Salome	12.01	1896			83	2.23	84	167	32	Salisbury, Benjamin, wife of
Salsburg	Catharine	11.18	1864			22	1.24	23	167	33	
Salsburg	William	9.29	1879	7.27	1851			29	168	01	Salsburg, Benjamin & Salome, child of
Salsburg	Andrew	12.24	1871	12.22	1846			26	168	02	Salsburg, Benjamin & Salome, child of
Salsburg	Susannah	9.14	1871	11.14	1853			18	168	03	Salsburg, Benjamin & Salome, child of
Salsburg	Elias	1.21	1869	5.05	1849			20	168	04	Salsburg, Benjamin & Salome, child of
Sanderson	William	5.25	1901			63	7.28	64	168	05	
Sanderson	Anna	10.15	1874			72	6.12	73	168	06	Sanderson, William, wife of
Sanderson	Samuel	7.23	1850			20	3.13	21	168	07	Sanderson, William & Anna, child of
Sanderson	Andrew	2.04	1833			1	3.25	2	168	08	Sanderson, William & Anna, child of
Sanderson	Mary J.	2.15	1833			5	9.23	6	168	09	Sanderson, William & Anna, child of
Sanderson	Eliza J.	8.12	1859			20	0.05	21	168	10	Sanderson, William & Anna, child of
Sanderson	William	5.01	1860			59	1.27	60	168	11	

Frankford - Lutheran Brick Church Graveyard

Surname	Given Name	Death Mo/Dy	Year	Birth Mo/Dy	Year	Att. Age Yr	Mo/Dy	Ag	Cm	Pg	No	Other Information
Sanderson	George	1.25	1866			1	4.20	2		168	12	Sanderson, William & S. J., son of
Sanderson	Anna M.					2	0.23	3		168	13	Sanderson, William & S. J., daughter of; d. Dec. 3, 186-
Schneider	Henry	9.27	1825			64		65		168	34	
Snyder	Mary M.	4.08	1824			59		60		168	35	
Sell	John	12.14	1875			85	8.24	86		168	23	
Sell	Sussana Kesler	1.11	1871			75	0.01	76		168	24	Sell, John, wife of
Sell	John		1904		1837			68		168	25	
Sell	Catharine		1905		1821			85		168	26	
Sell	Catharine	12.21	1860			61	0.27	62		168	27	Sell, Henry, wife of
Sell	John A.	6.03	1842			0	4.05	1		168	28	Sell, Daniel & Frances M., son of
Shambaugh	Elizabeth	6.15	1879			82		83		168	14	Shambaugh, Philip, wife of
Shambaugh	Michael	12.06	1900			75		76		168	15	
Shambaugh	Mary	3.15	1892			60		61		168	16	Shambaugh, Michael, wife of
Shambaugh	Clara E.	5.24	1881	2.14	1880			2		168	17	Shambaugh, L. J. & M. E., daughter of
Shanabrough	Charles Earl	7.14	1883			1	6.15	2		168	18	Shanabrough, John T. & Minnie, son of
Shanabrough	Raymond Roy	3.13	1887			1	8.02	2		168	19	Shanabrough, John T. & Minnie, son of
Sharp	Rebecca J.	9.16	1887			20	11.28	21		168	20	Sharp, W. B., wife of
Sharp	Charley H.	10.24	1886	2.28	1886			1		168	21	
Shimp	William	6.03	1877			68	10.18	69		169	01	
Shimp	Nancy	1.10	1883			71	10.27	72		169	02	
Shimp	Daniel	12.08	1863			20	5.19	21		169	03	Shimp, William & Nancy, child of
Shimp	Elizabeth	3.11	1847			13	1.20	14		169	04	Shimp, William & Nancy, child of
Shimp	William	2.02	1857			17	8.22	18		169	05	
Sipe	John	8.18	1826			53		54		168	30	
Sipe	Leah	9.00	1830			13	2.20	14		168	31	
Sipe	William Henry	11.15	1836			0	2.23	1		168	32	Sipe, Henry, son of
Sipe	Martha Ellen	12.21	1838			1	3.11	2		168	33	Sipe, H. & Margaret, daughter of
Sleabaugh	Sarah	8.05	1830			37		38		168	29	Warner, Burkhart, daughter of
Smith	Henry A.		1905		1839			67		168	36	
Smith	Rebecca				1842					168	37	Smith, Henry A., wife of
Smith	John A.		1876		1871			6		168	38	
Snider	Jonathan	6.25	1894			81		82		168	39	
Snider	Sarah	5.02	1896			76		77		168	40	Snider, Jonathan, wife of
Snyder	Henry	3.29	1847			61	6.07	62		169	35	
Snyder	Elizabeth	12.14	1868			83	5.22	84		169	36	
Snyder	Catharine	12.01	1859			54		55		169	37	Snyder, Jonathan, wife of
Snyder	John		1902		1833			70		169	38	
Snyder	Catharine				1833					169	39	Snyder, John, wife of
Snyder	Joseph	7.09	1838	5.07	1835			4		169	40	
Souder	John	11.06	1890			78	9.08	79		169	13	
Souder	Elizabeth	1.23	1896			78	2.03	79		169	14	Souder, John, wife of
Souder	David	8.05	1860			39	7.13	40		169	15	
Souder	Samuel	9.20	1860			37	10.21	38		169	16	
Souder	Susanna	10.04	1860			19	0.27	20		169	17	Souder, John & E., daughter of
Stichler	John H.	10.03	1862			22	10.04	23		169	06	Corp., Co. E, 130 Regt. PV; d. of wounds received at the Battle of Antietam
Stickler	Elizabeth	12.14	1875			48	3.12	49		169	07	
Stickler	John	3.20	1873			70	9.15	71		169	08	
Stichler	Margaret	10.25	1861			54	5.24	55		169	09	Stichler, John, wife of; [sp. varies]

Frankford - Lutheran Brick Church Graveyard

Surname	Given Name	Death Mo/Dy	Year	Birth Mo/Dy	Year	Att. Age Yr	Age Mo/Dy	Cm Ag	Pg	No	Other Information
Stickler	Sarah	2.20	1873			42	3.00	43	169	10	
Stine	John	4.13	1891	9.25	1827			64	169	11	
Stine	Ann	4.03	1898	1.26	1826			73	169	12	
Stoner	David	6.02	1838			42	5.15	43	169	18	
Stover	Harry W.	12.05	1887			0	2.11	1	169	19	Stover, W. H. & N. A., child of
Stover	Clyde	4.03	1892			0	0.29	1	169	20	Stover, W. H. & N. A., child of
Stover	Amanda	1.17	1901			48	1.19	49	169	21	
Stover	Alice R.	4.10	1890			3	0.23	4	169	22	
Stover	Jacob	9.29	1902			73	7.04	74	169	23	
Stover	Catharine	10.19	1892			63	7.06	64	169	24	Stover, Jacob, wife of
Stover	Bertha E.	1.15	1895	3.02	1891			4	169	25	
Stum	Henry		1901		1830			72	169	27	
Stum	Mary A. Sell		1898		1831			68	169	28	Stum, Henry, wife of
Stum	Daniel	2.28	1865			37	0.08	38	169	29	
Stum	Elizabeth C.	1.08	1904			70		71	169	30	Stum, Daniel, wife of
Stum	Morris A.	8.04	1883			23		24	169	31	
Stum	James M.	1.09	1891			36		37	169	32	
Stum	Rebecca E.	10.22	1893			29	8.29	30	169	33	Stum, John A., wife of
Stum	Samuel H.	7.22	1885			2	0.22	3	169	34	Stum, E. H. & Lucy, son of
Swartz	Jesse Z.	8.25	1865			26	10.13	27	168	22	soldier
Swords	Susannah J.	1.13	1892			74	3.19	75	169	26	
Taylor	George	7.06	1901						169	41	Private, Co. K, 1st Regt., N. H. Inftry.
Throne	George	12.25	1890			37	4.04	38	169	42	
Thumma	Ellen A.		1895		1848			48	169	43	[b. 1848 ?]
Thumma	Ella May	1.23	1878			2	10.23	3	169	44	Thumma, W. S. & E. A., daughter of
Utley	Peter	2.03	1830			55	6.15	56	170	01	
Utly	Elizabeth	5.20	1836			21	3.25	22	170	02	
Utley	Samuel	11.21	1844			32	2.20	33	170	03	
Wagner	Elizabeth	8.08	1897	2.12	1826			72	170	04	
Waigal	Magdalen A.	10.19	1831			54		55	170	05	Waigal, Henry, wife of
Weise	Lizzie C.	12.13	1874			17	8.12	18	170	06	Weise, John F. & Sophia, daughter of
Wolf	Myrtle L.	3.04	1890			4	6.07	5	170	07	Wolf. T. & A. C., daughter of
Wolf	Samuel	8.01	1892			78	3.00	79	170	08	
Wolf	Susan	9.30	1884			62	9.09	63	170	09	Wolf, Samuel, Sr., wife of
Wolf	Charles E.	5.23	1900	7.23	1870			30	170	10	
Wolf	David		1895		1844			52	170	11	
Wolf	John		1903		1838			66	170	12	
Worst	Benjamin				1835				170	13	
Worst	Mary	4.15	1901			61	0.13	62	170	14	
Worst	Daniel	4.06	1849	8.23	1799			50	170	15	
Worst	Susan	9.28	1884			80	4.20	81	170	16	
Zeigler	Johannes	4.17	1828	1.16	1793			36	170	19	German inscription
Zeigler	Catharine	10.22	1820	3.17	1795			26	170	20	German inscription
Zeigler	Margaret	3.26	1850			40		41	170	21	Zeigler, William, wife of
Zeigler	Susan	10.11	1857			58	0.02	59	170	22	Zeigler, William, relict of
Zeigler	Charles	10.05	1823	9.16	1798			26	170	23	
Zeigler	Frederick	9.17	1866	6.13	1787			80	170	24	
Zeigler	Barbara	10.01	1830	2.10	1793			38	170	25	
Zeigler	Philip	11.19	1846	6.17	1766			81	170	26	

Frankford - Lutheran Brick Church Graveyard
Possum Hill Church Graveyard

LUTHERAN BRICK CHURCH GRAVEYARD (continued)

Surname	Given Name	Death Mo/Dy/Year	Birth Mo/Dy/Year	Att. Age Yr/Mo/Dy	Cm Ag	Pg	No	Other Information
Zeigler	Catharine	2.14/1833	9.08/1763		70	170	27	Zeigler, Philip, wife of
Zeigler	Catharine	3.20/1835	8.08/1817		18	170	28	Zeigler, Frederick & Elizabeth, child of
Zeigler	Elizabeth	5.26/1835	9.29/1818		17	170	29	Zeigler, Frederick & Elizabeth, child of
Zeigler	William	4.30/1846		55	56	170	30	
Zalar	Mary	2.12/1834		89/11.19	90	170	18	
Zoller	Nicholas	1.23/1814	12.07/1774		40	170	17	German

POSSUM HILL CHURCH GRAVEYARD

Surname	Given Name	Death Mo/Dy/Year	Birth Mo/Dy/Year	Att. Age Yr/Mo/Dy	Cm Ag	Pg	No	Other Information
Barrick	Leah E.	10.10/1855		16/ 8.17	17	149	01	
Barrick	Andrew	11.03/1862		53/ 7.23	54	149	02	
Bricker	Elias	10.19/1891		73/10.27	74	149	03	
Bricker	Sarah	10.05/1895		78/ 7.01	79	149	04	Bricker, Elias, wife of
Clay	Mathias H.	3.20/1904	2.09/1842		63	149	05	
Clay	John	4.25/1888	12.03/1814		74	149	06	
Clay	Susanna	5.19/1874		64/ 9.16	65	149	07	Clay, John, wife of
Diller	Levi F.	3.29/1870		19/ 1.13	20	149	08	Diller, Francis & N., son of
Finkenbinder	Daniel	4.07/1854		65/ 1.16	66	149	09	
Finkenbinder	Margaret			68/ 3.19	69	149	10	Finkenbinder, Daniel, wife of
Hefflefinger	Simon	1.12/1863		2/ 6.08	3	149	19	Hefflefinger, Thomas & Rebecca, child of
Hefflefinger	Mary E.	6.30/1864		1/ 8.19	2	149	20	Hefflefinger, Thomas & Rebecca, child of
Hefflefinger	Thomas					149	21	Co. H, 202d Regt., Pa. Infantry
Heiser	Peter	5.29/1888		78/ 6.23	79	149	11	
Heiser	Lizzie A.	3.31/1894		36/ 8.30	37	149	17	Heiser, E. W., wife of
Hiser	Mary Ann	1.13/1860		22/ 4.18	23	149	18	Hiser, William, wife of
Jumper	Benjamin	3.21/1874		64/11.15	65	149	12	
Jumper	Mary	4.14/1880		68/ 3.11	69	149	13	Jumper, Benjamin, wife of
Jumper	Simon	3.22/1900		67/ 2.05	68	149	14	
Jumper	Elizabeth J.	11.26/1890		55/ 6.04	56	149	15	Jumper, Simon, wife of
Jumper	Barnet	11.05/1898	1.00/1835		64	149	16	Private, Co. H, 149th Regiment, Pennsylvania Volunteer Infantry
Kennedy	Andrew	6.01/1896		67/ 5.00	68	149	22	
Kennedy	Susan	2.12/1903		73	74	149	23	
Mayberry	Leah E.	5.25/1865		12/10.04	13	149	24	Mayberry, Joseph, Sarah A., & Mariah,
Mayberry	Mary C.	5.25/1865		10/ 8.00	11	149	25	children of; all seven lost their
Mayberry	Isabella	5.25/1865		6/ 5.25	7	149	26	lives by fire May 25, 1865
Mayberry	Jeremiah	5.25/1865		5/ 4.22	6	149	27	see above
Mayberry	Elizabeth	5.25/1865		3/ 7.25	4	149	28	see above
Mayberry	Joseph	5.25/1865		2/ 5.05	3	149	29	see above
Mayberry	David	5.25/1865		/10.08	1	149	30	see above
Minich	Henry	4.06/1897		66/ 6.17	67	150	01	

Frankford - Possum Hill Church Graveyard

Surname	Given Name	Death Mo/Dy	Death Year	Birth Mo/Dy	Birth Year	Att. Age Yr	Mo/Dy	Cm Ag	Pg	No	Other Information
Minich	Caroline	4.03	1901			65	8.11	66	150	02	
Morrison	Martha J.	10.10	1859			11	7.05	12	150	12	Radabaugh, S. & H., adopted daughter to
Mountz	Adam	2.14	1860			37	7.04	38	150	03	
Mountz	Anna Mary	4.30	1855			71	3.17	72	150	04	Mountz, Adam, wife of
Mountz	Adam, Sr.	2.19	1863			83	11.16	84	150	05	
Mountz	Levi J.	1.31	1890			44	11.19	45	150	06	
Mountz	William H.	1.01	1901	4.21	1842			59	150	07	
Mountz	Ira F.	5.11	1904	3.10	1877			28	150	08	Prof.
Mountz	Adeline Kennedy	3.16	1890			35	8.12	36	150	09	Mountz, L. J., wife of
Mountz	Omi D.	2.18	1887				3.22	1	150	10	
Mountz	Oscar J.	1.25	1890				4.10	1	150	11	
Oiler	Daniel	1.31	1882			66	7.11	67	150	13	
Oiler	Mary	5.13	1890	12.16	1814			76	150	14	Oiler, Daniel, wife of
Raudabaugh	Emma F.	5.12	1878			14	7.18	15	150	15	Raudabaugh, S. & M. E., child of
Raudabaugh	Edward S.	3.09	1875	3.20	1865			10	150	16	
Sipe	John P.	2.23	1886			7	1.26	8	150	17	
Sipe	Lottie V.	4.09	1900				0.01	1	150	18	
Thumma	Nancy E.	4.09	1879			19	0.28	20	150	19	Thumma, S. & H. [?], daughter of
Thumma	Samuel	6.19	1892			68	7.09	69	150	20	Corporal, Co. F, 209th Pa. Infantry
Thumma	Nancy	6.29	1892			68	2.27	69	150	21	
Walter	Jacob	4.30	1903	3.28	1817			87	150	22	
Walter	Jacob	12.31	1900	4.29	1816			85	150	23	
Walters	Carrie M.	2.14	1905	11.26	1881			24	150	24	Walters, J. C., wife of
Walters	Mary E.	5.06	1877				0.01	1	150	25	Walters, William R. & Mary E., child of
Walters	George E.	4.17	1875				0.07	1	150	26	Walters, William R. & Mary E., child of
Weigle	Floyd Edgar	1.03	1903				8.25	1	150	27	Weigle, William & Leah, son of
Wolf	Juliann	3.24	1864			62	3.13	63	150	28	Wolf, George, wife of
Wolf	Lizza	4.18	1864			10	8.22	11	150	29	Wolf, William & Eliza, daughter of
Yorlets	Sarah A.	2.21	1884			58	0.12	59	150	30	

Hopewell - Hanna Graveyard

HOPEWELL TOWNSHIP

HANNA GRAVEYARD

Surname	Given Name	Death Mo/Dy	Year	Birth Mo/Dy	Year	Att. Yr	Age Mo/Dy	Cm Ag	Pg	No	Other Information
Barr	John L.	12.01	1864			1	1.00	2	177	01	Barr, Robert L. & Mary A., child of
Barr	William A.	6.13	1865			6	0.21	7	177	02	Barr, Robert L. & Mary A., child of
Barr	Maggie B.	2.11	1870			3	7.20	4	177	03	Barr, Robert L. & Mary A., child of
Beaty	Elizabeth E.	11.25	1863	1.04	1809			55	177	04	
Beaty	Elizabeth	10.19	1815		1777	38		39	177	05	Beaty, John, wife of; Wherry, Samuel, daughter of; (b. 1777)
Cooper	Samuel K.		1836			25		26	177	06	
Cooper	Jane Nicholson		1835			28		29	177	07	Smith, John M., wife of; [see Smith, Jane Nicholson Cooper (179:13)]
Diehl	Esther	6.05	1866		1778	88	1.00	89	177	08	Diehl, Peter, wife of; (b. 1778)
Elliott	John	2.15	1871	12.28	1797			74	177	09	
Elliott	Elizabeth	4.02	1867			58		59	177	10	Elliott, John, Esq., wife of
Faughender	Mary H. H.	8.27	1866	3.09	1835			32	177	11	Faughender, William H., wife of
Hanna	William	7.07	1861			58	2.21	59	177	12	
Hanna	Martha	1.30	1846	1.07	1810			37	177	13	Hanna, William, wife of
Hanna	Jane	4.14	1877	3.01	1808			70	177	14	Hanna, William, wife of
Hanna	Samuel	8.21	1850	10.27	1833			17	177	15	
Hanna	John	12.13	1846			1	3.23	2	177	16	
Hanna	Martha E.	12.05	1846	1.19	1840			7	177	17	
Hanna	John	10.11	1823			57		58	177	18	Big Spring Presb. [noted after entry]
Hanna	Samuel	2.08	1825			53		54	177	19	Big Spring Presb. [noted after entry]
Hanna	Elsie	2.10	1850			78		79	177	20	Hanna, Samuel, wife of; BSPC [noted...]
Hanna	Eliza	3.17	1885	9.15	1808			77	177	21	Big Spring Presb. [noted after entry]
Holmes	Susan	2.14	1850	12.17	1779			71	177	22	
Kerr	Paul	11.28	1846		1767	79		80	177	23	
Laughlin	Robert B.	8.08	1868	2.25	1803			66	177	24	
Laughlin	Maria	11.17	1879	3.05	1802			78	177	25	Laughlin, Robert B., wife of
Laughlin	John	6.07	1859	11.13	1772			87	177	26	
Laughlin	Mary	7.07	1832	6.02	1782			51	177	27	Laughlin, John, consort of
Laughlin	Margaret	2.07	1888	4.12	1811			77	177	28	
Martin	Ann	3.02	1863	4.01	1782			81	178	01	
McElhinny	James	2.15	1870	8.16	1791			79	178	22	
McElhinny	Elizabeth	11.16	1881	4.15	1802			80	178	23	McElhinny, James, wife of
McElwain	William B.	8.08	1874		1794	80	1.07	81	178	16	
McAlwain	Susanna	5.02	1839			42	2.30	43	178	17	McAlwain, W. B., wife of [sp. varies]
McElwain	Elizabeth	5.26	1853		1810	43	9.02	44	178	18	McElwain, William B., wife of
McElwain	Ellen	12.23	1860	2.06	1823			38	178	19	McElwain, William B. & Susanna, dau. of
McElwain	William G.	8.13	1870	7.03	1813			58	178	20	
McElwain	Margaret	3.13	1859			38	0.02	39	178	21	
McKinney	David, Sr.	3.19	1849			73		74	178	24	
McKinney	Jennet Smith	4.11	1843			90	0.06	91	178	25	McKinney, David, wife of
McKinny	William Reynolds	1.01	1836			4	11.19	5	178	26	McKinney, Abraham S. & Margaret R., son
Miller	Henry G.	5.02	1871	8.15	1813			58	178	02	
Miller	Elizabeth J.	9.00	1874			55	5.00	56	178	03	Miller, Henry G., wife of
Mitchell	William	9.29	1854		1776	77		78	178	04	
Mitchell	Mary	8.28	1877	12.24	1801			76	178	05	Mitchell, William, wife of

Hopewell - Hanna Graveyard

Surname	Given Name	Death Mo/Dy	Death Year	Birth Mo/Dy	Birth Year	Att. Age Yr	Age Mo/Dy	Cm Ag	Pg	No	Other Information
Mitchell	Mary	5.21	1897			70	1.14	71	178	06	
Mitchell	John	1.17	1894	1.25	1825			69	178	07	
Mitchell	William Clarence	1.10	1894	11.18	1892			2	178	08	Mitchell, John & Clementina, son of
Montgomery	Ellen	12.15	1864	6.11	1789			76	178	09	
Morrett	Mary J.	2.17	1892			63	10.16	64	178	10	Morrett, William, wife of
Mowery	David	1.27	1862	4.13	1824			38	178	11	
Mowery	Jane M.	3.26	1888			60	0.18	61	178	12	
Mowery	Clarissa	6.24	1853			1	0.24	2	178	13	Mowery, David & Mary J., child of
Mowery	Joseph E.	10.11	1862			5	5.17	6	178	14	Mowery, David & Mary J., child of
Myers	Wilhelmina E.	4.25	1897			62	8.15	63	178	15	
Newcomer	Sarah Elliott	5.20	1874			34	6.28	35	178	27	Newcomer, Benjamin, wife of
Peebles	William	10.22	1830			49	0.20	50	178	28	
Peebles	Eleanor	9.14	1859			70	11.10	71	178	29	Peebles, William, wife of
Peebles	William D.	4.13	1837			15	10.29	16	178	30	Peebles, William & Eleanor, son of
Peebles	Benjamin A.	7.04	1877	10.28	1825			52	178	31	
Peebles	Martha Barr	8.01	1874	12.04	1823			51	178	32	Peebles, B. A., wife of
Peebles	William A.	4.06	1858				10.00	1	178	33	Peebles, B. A. & Martha, child of
Peebles	Martha Ellen	12.22	1863			4	8.16	5	178	34	Peebles, B. A. & Martha, child of
Peebles	Hugh Barr	10.01	1865			3	5.06	4	178	35	Peebles, B. A. & Martha, child of
Peebles	Sarah Ellen	8.01	1864			36	2.05	37	178	36	Peebles, Robert, wife of
Peebles	Hugh B.		1862						178	37	Peebles, Robert & Sarah Ellen, child of
Peebles	Martha Bell		1863						179	01	Peebles, Robert & Sarah Ellen, child of
Peebles	William		1864						179	02	Peebles, Robert & Sarah Ellen, child of
Pislee	Peter	3.28	1853			52	2.00	53	179	03	
Pislee	Elizabeth	12.10	1847			44	1.16	45	179	04	Pislee, Peter, wife of [date]
Pislee	Horace B.			2.12	1856				179	05	Pislee, C. R. & B. H., ch. of [no death
Pislee	Franklin	8.03	1853	5.27	1853			1	179	06	Pislee, C. R. & B. H., child of
Reinhardt	Augusta Louisa	11.29	1864	7.15	1829			36	179	07	
Reinhardt	Ernst Edward	2.17	1872	10.21	1831			41	179	08	
Reinhardt	Sophia H.	10.15	1879			54	8.23	55	179	09	
Smith	Jacob	5.26	1825			62		63	179	10	
Smith	Eleanor	7.07	1833			51		52	179	11	Smith, Jacob, wife of
Smith	Abraham W.	1.20	1848			42	0.12	43	179	12	
Smith	Jane Nicholson Cooper		1835						179	13	Smith, John M., wife of; [see Cooper, Jane Nicholson (177:07)]
Smith	D. R.	5.07	1864			52		53	179	14	(M. D.); "Sacred to the memory of the beloved physician"; committed suicide
Smith	D. Harvey					17		18	179	15	Smith, Dr., son of; "Died at the Columbia Classical Institute"
Wagoner	William	5.16	1859			61	2.13	62	179	16	
Wherry	Samuel	1.21	1826		1746			81	179	17	aged upward of 80 years
Wherry	John	4.14	1828			51		52	179	18	(b. 1776)
Wherry	Margaret	6.26	1837		1774	62		63	179	19	Wherry, John, wife of
Wherry	John M.	3.14	1835			29		30	179	20	

Hopewell - Hoover Farm Graveyard
　　　　　Mt. Tabor Church Graveyard

HOOVER FARM GRAVEYARD

Surname	Given Name	Death Mo/Dy	Year	Birth Mo/Dy	Year	Att. Age Yr	Mo/Dy	Ag	Cm	Pg	No	Other Information
Bert	John H.	5.23	1884			41	8.00	42	195	01		Rev.
Bert	Annie M.					25	5.18	26	195	02		(no date of death)
Burkhart	Rebecca E.	3.28	1896	9.07	1848			48	195	18		
Chronister	Jacob W.	7.25	1896			43	2.12	44	195	03		
Hoover	David	5.14	1869	4.24	1811			59	195	04		
Hoover	Anna Mary	10.14	1814		1743	71	9.22	72	195	05		
Hoover	Martin	6.07	1868		1851	17	4.02	18	195	06		Hoover, Christian & Anna, son of
Hoover	Martin	10.12	1841		1775	66	9.25	67	195	07		(b. 1775)
Hoover	Mary	6.02	1854		1782	72	2.19	73	195	08		Hoover, Martin, wife of; (b. 1782)
Hoover	Anna	4.30	1893			69	6.10	70	195	09		
Hoover	Christian	2.10	1884			78	4.27	79	195	10		
Hoover	John	2.11	1877	3.01	1804			73	195	11		Rev.
Hoover	Catharine	3.08	1873			69	4.14	70	195	12		Hoover, John, wife of
Hoover	Joel	4.22	1889			65	10.00	66	195	13		
Hoover	Fannie	4.02	1883			68		69	195	14		
Hoover	Maria	10.06	1891	11.10	1818			73	195	15		[varies]
Martin	John	3.25	1845			1	7.21	2	195	16		Hoover, David & Mary, son of [name
Wengert	Nancy G.					57	5.15	58	195	17		d. Aug. 20; [no year given]

MT. TABOR CHURCH GRAVEYARD

Surname	Given Name	Death Mo/Dy	Year	Birth Mo/Dy	Year	Att. Age Yr	Mo/Dy	Ag	Cm	Pg	No	Other Information
Barrick	Rebecca	4.29	1896			76	6.09	77	196	01		Barrick, Andrew, wife of
Hefflefinger	Maggie	2.09	1890			49	3.23	50	196	02		
McCoy	Frank W.	1.24	1901	6.08	1877			24	196	03		
McCoy	Laura A.	11.09	1885			30	7.27	31	196	04		
McCoy	Willie Orton	9.17	1880			1	10.00	2	196	05		McCoy, D. D. & J. E. [?], son of
McCoy	Daniel M.	11.16	1878				2.16	1	196	06		son of "Archible"
McCoy	Louisa E.	8.25	1899			37	0.28	38	196	07		
Watson	Mary B.	2.21	1894			68	11.04	69	196	08		
Watson	James W.	9.14	1894			74	0.12	75	196	09		

Hopewell - Newburg Church of God Graveyard

NEWBURG CHURCH OF GOD GRAVEYARD

Surname	Given Name	Death Mo/Dy	Death Year	Birth Mo/Dy	Birth Year	Att. Age Yr	Mo/Dy	Cm Ag	Pg	No	Other Information
Baker	Catharine E.	12.21	1868			26	10.10	27	188	01	Baker, David H., wife of; Strohm, H. & Susan, daughter of
Baker	Annie Martha	1.10	1868			0	7.15	1	188	02	Baker, D. H. & C. E., child of
Baker	infant son	3.02	1862						188	03	Baker, D. H. & C. E., child of
Bitner	John F.	6.10	1864			44	2.07	45	188	05	
Boblitz	Henry		1896		1826			71	188	14	
Boblitz	Nancy		1896		1819			78	188	15	
Booth	John C.	11.16	1847	12.27	1815			32	188	16	Rev.
Brechbill	infant	11.22	1871						188	04	Brechbill, J. & M. C., daughter of
Bricker	Godfrey	4.25	1891			79	10.27	80	188	06	
Bricker	Elizabeth	6.24	1890			84	4.13	85	188	07	
Bricker	Jineye E.	8.08	1868			1	7.08	2	188	08	Bricker, Jerry & Mary E., child of
Bricker	infant	11.12	1865			0	0.04	1	188	09	Bricker, Jerry & Mary E., child of
Bricker	infant	11.03	1864						188	10	Bricker, Jerry & Mary E., child of
Bricker	Mary	2.17	1894			10	0.11	11	188	11	Bricker, Jerry & Mary E., child of
Bricker	Mary E.	8.30	1893			53	4.26	54	188	12	Bricker, J. wife of
Bricker	William C.	8.09	1863			0	3.28	1	188	13	
Burkhart	Samuel G.	9.27	1881			0	9.09	1	188	17	Burkhart, G. G. & Anna M., son of
Carmony	Jacob M.	3.27	1851			0	7.16	1	188	18	Carmony, J. H. & C. A., son of
Charlton	James	7.05	1865			56		57	188	19	Rev. " His 2 sons sleep by his side"
Charlton	Catharine	5.15	1878	4.29	1806			73	188	20	
Clippinger	Elizabeth	11.23	1862	7.04	1832			31	188	25	Clippinger, John, wife of
Clippinger	John R.	8.20	1887	11.12	1862			25	188	26	Clippinger, John & Elizabeth, son of
Clippinger	Susanna	9.15	1856			1	7.25	2	188	27	Clippinger, John & Elizabeth, dau. of
Clippinger	Solomon	2.23	1891	4.21	1815			76	188	28	
Clippinger	Eva	3.17	1893	2.08	1819			75	188	29	
Clippinger	Josiah	10.19	1849	12.21	1847			2	188	30	Clippinger, Solomon & Eve, child of
Clippinger	Mary Elizabeth	11.25	1849	12.04	1845			4	188	31	Clippinger, Solomon & Eve, child of
Clippinger	Solomon	8.17	1862	3.16	1860			3	188	32	Clippinger, Solomon & Eve, child of
Clippinger	Elizabeth	3.31	1856			31	11.13	32	188	33	Clippinger, Elder Peter, wife of; Cope, John & Sarah, daughter of
Clippinger	John	4.06	1855			0	5.02	1	189	01	Clippinger, Elder Peter & Elizabeth, son
Coover	Samuel A.	6.25	1863			0	5.10	1	189	02	Coover, Adam & Sophia, [son] of
Coover	Rachel M.	2.16	1865			0	7.07	1	189	03	Coover, Adam & Sophia, [daughter] of
Creamer	Susanna	2.20	1897	7.21	1821			76	188	21	
Creamer	Samuel	9.24	1890	9.07	1821			70	188	22	
Creamer	Mary A. M.	10.03	1883	2.27	1883			1	188	23	Creamer, George M. & Myra E., dau. of
Creamer	Clarence E.	12.30	1850			0	11.26	1	188	24	Creamer, George M. & Myra E., son of
Davor	Leah	3.21	1869			64	3.01	65	189	04	Davor, B. M., wife of
Devor	Catharine M. D.	3.00	1844			1	8.08	2	189	05	Devor, Richard M. & Leah, daughter of
Diehl	Catharine	9.07	1856			85	0.08	86	189	06	Diehl, George, wife of
Diehl	Levi Hamsher	8.15	1857			13	11.15	14	189	07	Diehl, Levi & Magdalene, son of
Deihl	Susannah	11.26	1844			3	5.19	4	189	08	Deihl, Simon & Susannah, daughter of
Eisenhower	J. F.	3.24	1863			48	10.19	49	189	09	
Eisenhower	Carolina	2.16	1859	8.28	1833			26	189	10	Eisenhower, J. W., wife of
Eisenhower	Edward Thomas	9.05	1854	6.01	1853			2	189	11	Eisenhower, J. F. & Catharine J. son of
Eisenhower	Edwin E.	5.23	1863			6	4.07	7	189	12	Eisenhower, J. F. & C. J., son of
Elliott	Wilbur S.	6.23	1891			11	11.23	12	189	13	Elliott, John & Sadie M., son of

Hopewill - Newburg Church of God Graveyard

Surname	Given Name	Death Mo/Dy	Year	Birth Mo/Dy	Year	Att. Age Yr	Mo/Dy	Cm Ag	Pg	No	Other Information
Fickes	Carl J.	11.22	1880			0	2.19	1	189	18	Fickes, C. M. & M. J., son of
Fields	John B.	3.23	1890	3.29	1865			25	189	19	Hawk, Abbie O., son of
Finkenbinder	Carrie M.	3.15	1889			13	8.04	14	189	20	
Finkenbinder	infant daughter	1.14	1877			0	0.08	1	189	21	-----, daughter of
Fisher	Henry S.	5.29	1875			60	3.16	61	189	22	
Fisher	Catharine	9.09	1875			55	0.21	56	189	23	Fisher, Henry S., wife of
Ford	Oscar L.	4.08	1858			2	0.02	3	189	24	Ford, John & Susanna, son of
Forehope	Nancy	1.01	1888	9.05	1810			78	189	25	Hefflebower, Henry, former wife of
Franklin	Effie M.	1.23	1892			1	0.29	2	189	14	
Franklin	infant son	2.10	1881						189	15	
Franklin	infant daughter	11.28	1882						189	16	
Franklin	infant son	10.15	1883						189	17	
Fyler	Nancy A.	2.24	1894			66	1.01	67	189	26	
Gamber	Joseph S.	10.15	1866	6.09	1831			36	189	27	
Gamber	Martha E.	12.05	1875			20	0.27	21	189	28	
Gamber	William	12.14	1866	8.28	1800			67	189	29	
Gamber	Agnes	3.27	1864			55	1.04	56	189	30	Gamber, William, wife of
Gamber	Mary A.	1.24	1866			5	11.24	6	189	31	Gamber, Joseph & Eliza, child of
Gamber	Alfred H.	9.13	1866			0	10.15	1	190	01	Gamber, Joseph & Eliza, child of
Gamber	William A.	4.23	1872			18	2.18	19	190	02	Gamber, Joseph & Eliza, child of
Gamber	Margaret	6.09	1860			16		17	190	03	Gamber, William & Agnes, child of
Gamber	John	7.04	1857			23	4.03	24	190	04	Gamber, William & Agnes, child of
Gamber	William Ross	9.15	1861			1	5.24	2	190	05	Gamber, G. A. & Lavinia, son of
Gilbert	George M.	1.25	1900			70	10.19	71	190	06	
Gilbert	Elizabeth C.	2.07	1883			53	3.29	54	190	07	Gilbert, G. M., wife of
Gilbert	Florence Virginia	9.01	1863			6	7.10	7	190	08	Gilbert, George M. & E. C., child of
Gilbert	John William	9.06	1863			4	10.08	5	190	09	Gilbert, George M. & E. C., child of
Gilbert	Mary Ellen	8.30	1862			8	2.02	9	190	10	Gilbert, George M. & E. C., child of
Gross	Andrew	8.16	1890	7.27	1807			84	190	11	
Gross	Amanda C. B.	6.21	1894	7.11	1825			69	190	12	Gross, Andrew, wife of
Gross	Sarah	8.08	1863	8.02	1811			53	190	13	Gross, A., wife of
Gross	Jacob								190	14	Gross, Andrew & Sarah, child of
Gross	Daniel								190	15	Gross, Andrew & Sarah, child of
Gross	Amanda Caroline Blythe		1894		1825			70	190	16	
Hamsher	Eli		1847			2	3.00	3	190	17	Hamsher, Adam, & Mary Ann, son of
Hardy	Eliza S.	12.04	1890			75		76	190	18	
Harzok	Susan N.	1.01	1854			26	0.08	27	190	19	Harzok, John, wife of
Hefflebower	Henry	7.31	1872	4.01	1801			72	190	20	
Hefflebower	William D.	4.11	1898	10.11	1835			63	190	21	Co. K, 158th Regt., Pennsylvania Inf.
Hefflefinger	John P.	7.06	1882	5.01	1822			61	190	22	
Hoffman	Mary J.	9.29	1896			57	7.19	58	190	23	Hoffman, C. H., wife of
Hoffman	infant son	5.22	1875			0	0.02	1	190	24	Hoffmen, C. H. & M. J., son [1] of
Hoffman	infant son	5.22	1875			0	0.02	1	190	25	Hoffmen, C. H. & M. J., son [2] of
Hoover	Charles W.	3.30	1870	5.10	1869			1	190	26	
Hutchison	Emma					3	7.00	4	190	27	Hutchison, N. R. & S. V., child of
Hutchison	Carrie					4	5.18	5	190	28	Hutchison, N. R. & S. V., child of
Kauffman	H. B.	1.23	1891			61		62	190	29	
Kauffman	Willie	1.28	1882			11	8.20	12	190	30	Kauffman, H. B. & M. E., son of; shot himself on being teased by playmates
Keefer	Carrie E.	7.15	1866				0.05	1	190	32	Keefer, H. C. & E. R., daughter of

Hopewell - Newburg Church of God Graveyard

Surname	Given Name	Death Mo/Dy	Year	Birth Mo/Dy	Year	Att. Age Yr	Mo/Dy	Cm Ag	Pg	No	Other Information
Kindig	Mary	1.17	1852	12.29	1769			83	190	33	Kindig, Tobias, wife of
Kunkle	Margaret			4.15	1856	0	5.25	1	190	31	Kunkle, Martin & Agnes, dau. of; [d. ?]
Kunkle	Thomas E.	2.28	1866			2	3.21	3	190	34	Kunkle, Martin & Agnes, [son] of
Landis	Ellen	4.27	1878			27	7.22	28	191	01	Landis, Harry, wife of
Lindsey	Joseph G.	2.18	1879			76	7.21	77	191	02	
Lindsey	Elizabeth	1.11	1842			32	3.27	33	191	03	Lindsey, Joseph G., wife of
Long	Sidney H.	2.28	1878			6	7		191	04	
McCleaf	Eliza		1900		1828			75	191	29	[b. 1828 ?]
McCleaf	Elizabeth M.	3.01	1854	10.31	1853			1	191	30	McCleaf, Calvin & Ann M., child of
McCleaf	Jane L.	3.15	1855	2.22	1855			1	191	31	McCleaf, Calvin & Ann M., child of
McClure	J. F.								192	05	Co. F., 209th Pennsylvania Infantry
McClure	Elenor	5.08	1864			73	5.20	74	192	06	McClure, James, wife of
McCoy	Sarah A.	2.17	1845	9.07	1844			1	192	01	
McCoy	Susanna G.	8.11	1853	2.11	1852			2	192	02	
McCoy	J. Edward	11.23	1881			27	1.22	28	192	03	Dr.
McCoy	Daniel	5.10	1884			73	10.06	74	192	04	
McGaw	Frank L.	10.19	1887	10.03	1869			19	192	07	McGaw, W. S. & S. A., son of
Miller	Michael	3.08	1839			46	3.06	47	191	05	
Miller	Elizabeth	11.11	1877			79	9.27	80	191	06	(b. 1798)
Miller	Libbie	4.23	1884	3.20	1835			50	191	07	
Miller	John M.	5.28	1872			52	5.10	53	191	08	
Miller	Fanny Miller [sic]	6.18	1888	8.30	1814			74	191	09	Gamber, William, former wife of
Miller	John E.	9.04	1865			8	10.24	9	191	10	Miller, John M. & Fannie, child of
Miller	Mary F.	8.19	1865			4	9.09	5	191	11	Miller, John M. & Fannie, child of
Miller	J. A.	12.06	1868			23	8.15	24	191	12	Miller, J. P. & Jemima, child of
Miller	Harper G.	5.13	1868			0	8.19	1	191	13	Miller, J. P. & Jemima, child of
Miller	Burdon S.	6.04	1869			0	2.12	1	191	14	Miller, J. P. & Jemima, child of
Miller	infant son								191	15	Miller, Albert H. & B. C., son of
Miller	Lulu Clare	1.29	1890			1	7.27	2	191	16	Miller, S. F. & K. M., daughter of
Morrow	Floyd	8.13	1893			2	2.00	3	191	23	Morrow, J. W. & L. B., child of
Morrow	infant son								191	24	Morrow, J. W. & L. B., child of
Mowery	Adam		1899		1819			81	191	17	
Mowery	Mary		1854		1823			32	191	18	Mowery, Adam, wife of
Mowery	Solomon C.	9.17	1865			20	3.07	21	191	19	Mowery, Adam & Mary, son of
Mowery	William	9.06	1854			0	5.03	1	191	20	Mowery, Adam & Mary, son of
Mowery	Annie E.	4.17	1873			7	1.07	8	191	21	Mowery, Adam & Sarah, daughter of
Mowery	Mattie N.	12.10	1892			18	8.16	19	191	22	Mowery, G. & C. J., daughter of
Myers	Lucy Ann	6.19	1873			49	9.19	50	191	25	Myers, Abraham, wife of
Myers	Mary Ann	8.18	1850	10.06	1832			18	191	26	Myers, Jacob & Mary, daughter of
Myers	David	2.19	1845			6	10.06	7	191	27	Myers, Jacob & Mary, son of
Myers	Leah	1.01	1845			4	6.25	5	191	28	Myers, Jacob & Susannah, daughter of
Ober	Jacob	8.15	1854			61	1.15	62	192	08	
Ober	Jacob M.	9.11	1855			30	5.14	31	192	09	
Ober	Catharine	4.20	1875			76	4.09	77	192	10	Ober, Jacob, wife of
Ober	Mary Ann	3.27	1892			66	1.14	67	192	11	Ober, J. J., wife of
Ober	Ephraim B.	6.19	1863			29	7.27	30	192	12	
Phelebaum	Samuel								192	13	Co. F, 207th Pennsylvania Infantry
Pislee	John	4.25	1873			43	4.25	44	192	14	
Pislee	Cora I.	4.11	1871			0	0.16	1	192	15	Pislee, John & Sarah, daughter of
Pislee	Emma E.	8.31	1862			0	5.16	1	192	16	Pislee, John & Sarah, daughter of

Hopewell - Newburg Church of God Graveyard

Surname	Given Name	Death Mo/Dy	Year	Birth Mo/Dy	Year	Att. Age Yr	Mo/Dy	Cm/Ag	Pg	No	Other Information
Ramp	Joseph	8.20	1856	11.27	1827			29	192	17	
Rea	Rodella	8.19	1869	2.27	1869			1	192	18	Rea, Mary E., daughter of
Rea	James Alonza	7.25	1869			15	0.02	16	192	19	Rea, J. A. & E. M., child of
Rea	Samantha J.	6.02	1850			0	8.15	1	192	20	Rea, J. A. & E. M., child of
Sanlino	Antony	2.11	1885		1856	29		30	192	21	Natyvo in Italia; Morto in Newburg
Seilhamer	Anna Mary	8.25	1866			2	2.00	3	193	06	Seilhamer, G. W. & Harriet, daughter of
Shanabrook	Nettie J.	2.18	1883			8	6.18	9	192	22	Shanabrook, John & Amanda, daughter of
Shoemaker	Elizabeth	1.01	1893			62		63	193	11	Shoemaker, G., wife of
Shoemaker	Nora					0	0.06	1	193	12	Shoemaker, G. & E., infant daughter of
Shoemaker	Catharine J.	1.25	1889	10.27	1817			72	193	13	Eisenhower, John F., former wife of
Skelly	Margaret V.	5.13	1891			43	5.05	44	193	07	
Skelly	Samuel C.	4.09	1879			32	4.15	33	193	08	
Skelly	Charles	8.21	1868			2	1.25	3	193	09	Skelly, Samuel & Maggie, son of
Stake	John A.	6.25	1885	9.08	1879			6	192	24	Stake, Robert H. & Anna M., son of
Stake	Lottie B.	3.26	1888	4.05	1881			7	192	25	
Stake	Carrie F.	6.29	1888	6.18	1882			7	192	26	
Staub	Julian Ruth					3	3.02	4	192	23	Staub, J. A., Rev. & M. C., daughter of
Stevens	Mary Ellen	10.29	1868	1.10	1863			6	192	27	
Stevick	Samuel	9.21	1839			26	4.24	27	192	28	
Stevick	Barbara Lindsey	4.10	1885			68		69	192	29	Stevick, Samuel, former wife of
Stevick	Harry S.	6.24	1881			23		24	192	30	
Stevick	Isabella	11.20	1894			68	9.03	69	192	31	Stevick, C. C., wife of
Stevick	Charles C.	12.24	1862	1.24	1861			2	192	32	Stevick, Christian & Isabella, child of
Stevick	Sarah B.	7.09	1861	1.24	1861			1	192	33	Stevick, Christian & Isabella, child of
Stevick	William H.	1.28	1845			1	4.23	2	192	34	Stevick, John & Mary, child of
Stevick	Lylly B.	7.12	1859			0	4.00	1	193	01	Stevick, John & Mary, child of
Stevick	Susan A.	6.30	1863			2	11.20	3	193	02	Stevick, John & Mary, child of
Stevick	Emma P.	11.22	1893	10.14	1856			38	193	03	
Stevick	Judith Ellen	7.05	1896			35	11.06	36	193	04	
Stewig	John H.	8.17	1865			8	9.02	9	193	05	Stewig, Felix & Mary A., son of
Stouffer	Mary	9.04	1875			67	11.29	68	193	14	Stouffer, John, relict of
Stouffer	Isaac	8.15	1857			11	0.09	12	193	15	Stouffer, John & Polly, child of
Stouffer	Josiah	8.27	1857			8	3.26	9	193	16	Stouffer, John & Polly, child of
Stouffer	Mary A.	5.20	1864			19		20	193	17	Stouffer, John & Polly, child of
Stouffer	Clarence F.	11.11	1863			0	5.10	1	193	18	Stouffer, Josephus & R., son of
Stouffer	Christian C.	10.05	1898			67	11.18	68	193	19	
Stouffer	Margaret D.	12.23	1882			78	9.26	79	193	20	Stouffer, Christian, relict of
Stouffer	Barbara	1.24	1887	2.28	1805			82	193	21	
Stouffer	Clara					1	4.00	2	193	22	Stouffer, C. C. & M., daughter of
Stouffer	Jennie B.	4.14	1895	12.30	1870			25	193	23	Stouffer, F. E.?, wife of
Stouffer	Emma M.	7.06	1884			0	2.05	1	193	24	Stouffer, D. C. & C. J., daughter of
Stouffer	Anna C.	1.01	1895			70	6.07	71	193	25	Stouffer, D. K., wife of
Stouffer	Rachel Isabella	12.29	1857			7	3.08	8	193	26	Stouffer, David K. & Ann C., daughter of
Stouffer	Katie E.	12.29	1870	3.17	1858			13	193	27	Stouffer, A. J. & Mary E., daughter of
Strike	Matilda A. Gamber	4.21	1870			29	8.04	30	193	10	Strike, Solomon, wife of
Strohm	John E.	4.22	1884	7.16	1850			34	193	28	
Strohm	Henry	8.14	1887	4.01	1809			79	193	29	
Strohm	Jane Elliott	5.04	1900	12.30	1848			52	193	30	Strohm, John R., wife of
Strohm	Susan	2.05	1814		1743	71	3.23	72	193	31	Strohm, Henry, wife of
Strohm	Nora Alina	11.22	1882			2	10.20	3	194	01	Strohm, Alexander, daughter of

NEWBURG CHURCH OF GOD GRAVEYARD (continued)

Surname	Given Name	Death Mo/Dy	Death Year	Birth Mo/Dy	Birth Year	Att. Age Yr	Age Mo/Dy	Cm Ag	Pg	No	Other Information
Stroman	Martha J.	8.05	1861	7.16	1859			3	194	02	Stroman, Emanuel & Agnes, daughter of
Stroman	Susanna	10.18	1851	8.04	1846			6	194	03	Stroman, Emanuel & Angelina, daughter of
Wagner	Eve	12.30	1862			39	3.27	40	194	04	Wagner, Michael, wife of
Wagner	Israel	2.22	1867	2.22	1833			35	194	05	
Wallace	Catharine	10.24	1864			37	10.04	38	194	06	Wallace, Thomas, wife of
Watson	J. R.								194	07	Co. F, 207th Pennsylvania Infantry
Weirich	Mary Ann	4.14	1849			27	1.26	28	194	08	Weirich, George, wife of
Weist	John L.	8.10	1889			53	11.28	54	194	09	
Weist	Kassiah J.	3.01	1896			57	4.20	58	194	10	
Weist	Lizzie A.	9.26	1880			15	3.05	16	194	11	Weist, J. L. & Kassiah, daughter of
Whisler	Mary	2.10	1870			80		81	194	12	

STOUFFER FARM GRAVEYARD

Surname	Given Name	Death Mo/Dy	Death Year	Birth Mo/Dy	Birth Year	Att. Age Yr	Age Mo/Dy	Cm Ag	Pg	No	Other Information
Byers	Benjamin	3.19	1886	7.15	1810			76	197	01	
Byers	Elizabeth Stouffer	12.30	1890	2.06	1810			81	197	02	Byers, Benjamin, wife of
Henry	Francis	11.06	1874		1827	47	11.01	48	197	03	Henry, George W., wife of [Francis (sic)
Rone	Peter B.	1.10	1889	5.14	1869			20	197	04	
Stouffer	Peter	11.22	1856		1803	53	0.18	54	197	05	
Stouffer	Drusilla	11.14	1848		1806	42	5.22	43	197	06	Stouffer, Peter, wife of
Stouffer	John, Sr.	9.25	1857		1798	59	7.30	60	197	07	
Stouffer	Mary	7.02	1840			38	8.28	39	197	08	Stouffer, John, Sr., wife of
Stouffer	Jacob, Sr.	4.28	1845		1769	76		77	197	09	
Stouffer	Elizabeth	8.29	1834		1771	62		63	197	10	Stouffer, Jacob, Sr., wife of
Stouffer	Jacob	12.04	1887		1793	93		94	197	11	
Stouffer	Jacob	3.26	1874		1805	69		70	197	12	

Hopewell - Zion Reformed Church Graveyard

ZION REFORMED CHURCH GRAVEYARD

Surname	Given Name	Death Mo/Dy|Year	Birth Mo/Dy|Year	Att. Age Yr	Cm Mo/Dy	Ag	Pg	No	Other Information
Au	Christopher	9.30|1855		77	10.05	78	180	01	
Au	Magdalena	6.17|1850	12.23|1776			74	180	02	Au, Christopher, consort of
Au	John	12.23|1837	1.17|1817			21	180	03	Au, Christopher & Magdalena, son of
Au	Elizabeth	6.30|1837	7.15|1803			34	180	04	Au, Christopher & Magdalena, daughter of
Au	Eliza J.	6.08|1883		36	2.25	37	180	05	
Au	Jacob	1.18|1877		75	1.26	76	180	06	
Au	William L.	3.31|1899		48	4.05	49	180	07	
Baker	Henry	4.29|1872		62		63	180	08	
Baker	Maggie	5.12|1871		21	2.08	22	180	09	Baker, H. & Sarah, daughter of
Bistline	Andrew	6.16|1900	1.23|1830			71	180	10	
Bistline	Catharine	1.06|1871		37	4.21	38	180	11	Bistline, Andrew, wife of
Book	Florence Grace	8.28|1900		1	9.08	1	180	12	Book, A. C. & A. J., dau. of: [21 mo.]
Bowers	Frank W.	10.12|1900	|1872	27		28	180	13	(b. 1872)
Bowers	-----	1.14|1892		0	2.27	1	180	14	Bowers, S. & E. A., son of;
Boyd	Florence Lytle	8.11|1896		0	1.20	1	180	15	Boyd, J. R. [?] & S. B., daughter of
Boyd	Elizabeth	9.09|1881		78	8.28	79	180	16	Boyd, Robert, wife of
Boyd	Sarah Jane	1.24|1860		11	4.02	12	180	17	Boyd, Robert & Elizabeth, daughter of
Boyd	Elizabeth	1.27|1860		15	2.15	16	180	18	Boyd, Robert & Elizabeth, child of
Boyd	Jeremiah	2.23|1845		3	11.03	4	180	19	Boyd, Robert & Elizabeth, child of
Carbaugh	Rebecca	6.14|1851		32	10.14	33	180	20	Carbaugh, Michael, wife of
Carbaugh	William L.	11.15|1854		1	0.25	2	180	21	Carbaugh, T. M. & Elizabeth, son of
Carson	John	2.28|1877	1.17|1794			84	180	22	Capt.
Carson	Elizabeth	7.07|1881		77	11.19	78	180	23	
Conner	George	5.14|1840	1.04|1804			37	180	24	
Conner	Mary	10.02|1883		75	3.00	76	180	25	Conner, George, wife of
Conner	Catharine	3.06|1840	12.01|1836			4	180	26	Conner, George & Mary, daughter of
Conner	Mary A.	9.02|1885		44	9.17	45	180	27	
Conner	Moses	10.01|1872		44	3.01	45	180	28	
Conner	Sarah	10.14|1860	9.04|1822			39	180	29	Conner, Moses, wife of
Conner	infant son	10.11|1860					180	30	Conner, Moses & Sarah, son of
Conner	infant daughter	10.11|1860					180	31	Conner, Moses & Sarah, daughter of
Diehl	Joanna	11.23|1879	11.11|1825			55	180	34	
Diehl	Joseph	10.10|1896		67	6.09	68	181	01	
Diehl	George Adam	9.13|1868		2	10.27	3	181	02	Diehl, Joseph & M., son of
Diller	Francis	3.10|1857		71	8.26	72	181	03	Rev.
Diller	Maria	2.07|1871		73	11.20	74	181	04	Diller, Francis, wife of
Drewart	Ellen	9.08|1852		31	8.29	32	180	32	Drewart, Richard & Sarah, daughter of
Drewett	Thomas M.	2.14|1863		0	3.26	1	180	33	Drewett, James & Obadiah [sic], son of
Driver	Laura Alice	7.04|1882		1	2.15	2	181	05	Driver, F. A. & S. H., daughter of
Dunlap	James M.	3.12|1891	6.18|1826			65	181	06	
Dunlap	Eliza J.	10.28|1898	9.23|1840			59	181	07	Dunlap, James, wife of
Dunlap	Laura S. E.	10.16|1869	|1854			16	181	08	Dunlap, James M. & Elizabeth, dau. of; b. 12, 1854 [sic]
Dunlap	Charlie S.	3.30|1872	2.14|1871			2	181	09	Dunlap, J. M. & Jennie, child of
Dunlap	Martha E.	9.12|1881	7.15|1880			2	181	10	Dunlap, J. M. & Jennie, child of
Eichelberger	Franklin	4.05|1896		64	0.25	65	181	11	
Eichelberger	Louisa Elsie Idelia	2.05|1885	9.09|1874			11	181	12	Eichelberger, Franklin & Louisa, daughter of

Hopewell - Zion Reformed Church Graveyard

Surname	Given Name	Death Mo/Dy	Year	Birth Mo/Dy	Year	Att. Age Yr	Cm Mo/Dy	Ag	Pg	No	Other Information
Etter	Arabella D.	10.02	1879			7	7.10	8	181	13	
Etter	Margaret E.	10.10	1879			15	5.27	16	181	14	
Etter	Samuel J.	10.30	1863			6	8.10	7	181	15	Etter, J. & S. A., son of
Etter	Jonathan	5.21	1898			69	0.13	70	181	16	
Failor	Andrew	2.17	1880	8.07	1819			61	181	17	
Failor	Susan	3.05	1898	6.15	1815			83	181	18	
Fyler	Delia E.	3.14	1881						181	19	Fyler, Ira M. & M. A., daughter of
Garman	Daniel C.	8.01	1891			61	5.25	62	181	20	
Gebhart	Martha	1.24	1860	2.10	1830			30	181	21	Gebhart, Isaac, wife of
Gebhart	Eve Ann	2.12	1861	2.17	1840			21	181	22	Gebhart, Isaac, wife of
Gebhart	Mary A.	2.09	1860	9.05	1852			8	181	23	Gebhart, Isaac & Martha, daughter of
Geese	Susan	1.04	1889	1.10	1823			66	181	29	
Geese	John	1.30	1888	9.26	1819			69	181	30	
Gelwicks	John	12.12	1887			76	8.03	77	181	24	
Gelwicks	Magdalene	6.01	1894			81	7.01	82	181	25	Gelwicks, John, wife of
Gelwicks	John	1.15	1853	9.08	1774			79	181	26	
Gelwicks	Annie E.	2.15	1848	10.19	1839			9	181	27	Gelwicks, John & M., daughter of
Gelwicks	Jeremiah	6.06	1859	3.30	1848			12	181	28	Gelwicks, John & M., son of
Gilbert	Henry	5.12	1857	12.12	1790			67	181	31	
Gilbert	Margaret Rebecca	10.18	1867			76	9.27	77	181	32	Gilbert, Henry, wife of
Gilbert	Maria	6.13	1878			56	9.00	57	181	33	
Gilbert	John	7.16	1880			57		58	181	34	
Gilbert	Margaret E.	3.22	1870			16	10.12	17	181	35	Gilbert, John S. & Catharine, dau. of
Gilbert	Henry	1.12	1881			59	0.18	60	182	01	
Gilbert	Susanna	4.03	1897			78	8.19	79	182	02	Gilbert, Henry, wife of
Gochenauer	John	6.23	1885	6.29	1828			57	182	03	
Gochenauer	Elizabeth			5.21	1831				182	04	
Gross	Viola May	7.26	1884			0	1.16	1	182	05	Gross, C. P. & M. E., daughter of
Hagey	Josiah C.	12.01	1876			1	2.09	2	182	22	Hagey, A. S. & Mollie J., son of
Harman	Samuel	3.05	1887			66	9.18	67	182	06	Co. K, 158 Regt., Pennsylvania Militia
Harman	Peter	2.01	1877			63	8.24	64	182	07	
Harmon	Elizabeth	6.26	1873		1779	94	4.00	95	182	08	
Harmon	Margaret	10.17	1875			58	11.09	59	182	09	Harmon, John, wife of
Harmon	John	12.28	1879			18	8.07	19	182	10	Hermon, Peter & Hannah, son of [sic]
Harmon	David	4.08	1857	4.01	1857			1	182	11	Harmon, George & Maria S., son of
Harmon	Maria Sabina	4.05	1857	4.08	1834			23	182	12	Harmon, George, wife of
Harman	Bertha B.	5.24	1896			2	7.07	3	182	13	Harman, William & Ada B., daughter of
Haun	David	11.03	1876			75	1.03	76	182	14	
Haun	Eliza	9.02	1893			77	8.27	78	182	15	Haun, David, wife of
Haun	Philip	9.02	1863			64		65	182	16	
Haun	Jane	8.07	1847			54		55	182	17	
Haun	Jacob	11.09	1834	8.14	1764			71	182	18	slate
Haun	Mary	11.02	1838			75	2.03	76	182	19	Haun, Jacob, wife of
Haun	John	11.25	1827	1.30	1805			23	182	20	Haun, Jacob, son of; slate carved
Haun	Michael	7.06	1819			11	5.00	12	182	21	Haun, Jacob, son of
Heberlig	Benjamin	10.24	1850	5.08	1807			44	182	23	
Heberlig	Mary A.	9.22	1884			43		44	182	24	Heberlig, Jacob, wife of
Heberlig	Maggie E.	5.13	1863			1	2.18	2	182	25	Heberlig, Jacob & Mary A., dau. [E.?]
Heberlig	William Henry	2.08	1870			1	1.19	2	182	26	Heberlig, B. F. & H. L., son of
Heberlig	John	5.12	1889			94	2.19	95	182	27	

Hopewell - Zion Reformed Church Graveyard

Surname	Given Name	Death Mo/Dy	Year	Birth Mo/Dy	Year	Att. Age Yr	Mo/Dy	Cm Ag	Pg	No	Other Information
Heberlig	Margaret	12.17	1867			64	6.24	65	182	28	Heberlig, John, Sr., wife of
Heberlig	Elizabeth	3.18	1889			49	11.26	50	182	29	Heberlig, Adam, wife of
Heberlig	Margaret J.	11.19	1861	5.22	1857			5	182	30	Heberlig, Adam & Elizabeth, daughter of
Heberlig	Samuel	7.03	1876			77	7.13	78	182	31	
Heberlig	Hannah	7.16	1895			87	11.26	88	182	32	
Heberlig	Samuel A.	12.16	1862			7		8	182	33	
Heberlig	Catharine A.	3.21	1896	8.10	1826			70	182	34	Heberlig, Joseph F., wife of
Heberlig	Mary A.	12.11	1865			1	11.00	2	183	01	Heberlig, J. F. & C. A., daughter of
Heberlig	Jeremiah	4.13	1862			0	0.28	1	183	02	Heberlig, J. F. & C. A., son of
Heberlig	Peter H.	2.19	1860	5.03	1858			2	183	03	Heberlig, J. F. & Catharine A., son of
Heberlig	Joseph	7.10	1855	10.24	1833			22	183	04	Heberlig, Samuel & Hanna, son of [1855?]
Heberlig	Benjamin	3.23	1843			4	3.17	5	183	05	Heberlig, Samuel & Hannah, son of
Heberlig	Caroline	12.21	1842			2	7.27	3	183	06	Heberlig, Samuel & Hannah, daughter of
Heberlig	Elijah	3.06	1849			4	4.16	5	183	07	Heberlig, Samuel & Hannah, son of
Heberlig	William	10.28	1898			59	0.06	60	183	08	
Heberlig	Martha H.	1.13	1883			0	2.25	1	183	09	Heberlig, S. B. & M. J., daughter of
Heberlig	Clarence B.	1.27	1879			1	10.11	2	183	10	Heberlig, William & Mary C., child of
Heberlig	John W.	1.24	1875			0	1.03	1	183	11	Heberlig, William & Mary C., child of
Hefflefinger	James	12.24	1899			56	7.13	57	183	12	
Hefflefinger	Jacob	1.02	1900						183	13	Private, Co. K, 201st Regt., Pa. Vols.
Hefflefinger	Sarah E.	9.15	1860			28	3.00	29	183	14	Hefflefinger, David & Elizabeth, dau. of
Hefflefinger	Thomas	5.08	1878			73	9.16	74	183	15	
Hefflefinger	Agnes	9.17	1868			65	0.17	66	183	16	Hefflefinger, Thomas, wife of
Hefflefinger	Thomas	6.16	1831		1766	65	3.19	66	183	17	
Hefflefinger	Mary E.	11.15	1865			30	6.23	31	183	18	Hefflefinger, Thomas, wife of; Brickley, William & Margaret, dau. of
Hefflefinger	Maggie	12.20	1865			5	3.28	6	183	19	Hefflefinger, Thomas & Mary B., dau. of
Hefflefinger	Mary E. A.	2.04	1863			4	6.15	5	183	20	Hefflefinger, Thomas & Mary B., dau. of
Hefflefinger	infant son	11.22	1861			0	1.29	1	183	21	Hefflefinger, David & Eliza P., son of
Hefflefinger	William	12.01	1856			28	4.09	29	183	22	Hefflefinger, Thomas & Agnes, child of
Hefflefinger	Alexander	6.28	1851			18	6.04	19	183	23	Hefflefinger, Thomas & Agnes, child of
Hefflefinger	Catharine	9.02	1847		1761	86	5.14	87	183	24	Hefflefinger, Philip, wife of
Hefflefinger	Philip	12.13	1839		1757	82	4.00	83	183	25	(b. 1757); was a drummer boy in the Rev.
Hefflefinger	John	1.01	1878			39	11.24	40	183	26	
Hefflefinger	Alberta E.	4.24	1873			2	3.15	3	183	27	Hefflefinger, John & S. C., daughter of
Hefflefinger	infant daughter	10.21	1876						183	28	Hefflefinger, John & S. C., daughter of
Hefflefinger	infant daughter	5.22	1868						183	29	Hefflefinger, John & S. C., daughter of
Hefflefinger	Frank Hays	3.29	1882			14	6.23	15	183	30	Hefflefinger, David & E. Jane, son of
Hefflefinger	infant son			8.06	1877				184	01	Hefflefinger, John & S. C., son of
Hefflefinger	Samuel	1.18	1895	3.27	1806			89	184	02	
Hefflefinger	David Calvin	6.13	1886			21	6.16	22	184	03	Hefflefinger, David & Elizabeth J., son
Hefflefinger	Benjamin	4.29	1875			35	2.02	36	184	04	
High	Mary High (?)	4.27	1869	8.13	1814			55	184	05	
Holby	Henry	8.30	1883	8.30	1813			71	184	06	
Holby	Catharine					67	6.28	68	184	07	Holby, Henry, wife of
Holby	Hannah M.	12.12	1877			24	7.25	25	184	08	Holby, Hiram, wife of
Holby	Hiram C.	4.02	1869			18	3.26	19	184	09	Heberlig, S. & H., dau. [sic] of [?]
Holby	Mary	1.22	1881			0	2.08	1	184	11	Holby, J. F. & Lucy, daughter of
Holler	John	5.09	1864			34	9.23	35	184	10	
Humbarger	Jacob	4.01	1874			68	10.09	69	184	12	

Hopewell - Zion Reformed Church Graveyard

Surname	Given Name	Death Mo/Dy	Death Year	Birth Mo/Dy	Birth Year	Att. Age Yr	Age Mo/Dy	Cm Ag	Pg	No	Other Information
Humbarger	Benjamin	1.03	1873			66		67	184	13	
Keesaman	Josephine	4.04	1855			0	11.16	1	184	14	Keesaman, William & Sara, child of
Keesaman	David Carson	2.27	1860			3	4.03	4	184	15	Keesaman, William & Sara, child of
Keesaman	Sarah E.	11.03	1864			1	6.12	2	184	16	Keesaman, William & Sara, child of
Ketron	John	5.03	1855						184	17	
Koser	Jonathan	11.10	1862	3.02	1797			66	184	18	
Koser	Culbertson	7.16	1863	9.12	1831			32	184	19	
Lay	Mary E.	2.12	1898			0	0.15	1	184	23	Lay, L. D. & I. C., daughter of
Lehman	John	5.31	1883			65	2.21	66	184	20	Rev.
Lehner	Lewis	12.24	1880			68	9.26	69	184	21	
Lehner	Nancie	4.12	1890			66	1.26	67	184	22	Lehner, Lewis, wife of
Long	John	5.12	1855			75	10.14	76	184	24	
Long	Susannah	4.05	1865			29	0.03	30	184	25	Long, Andrew, wife of
Lusk	Fannie Ellen	5.12	1872	9.26	1834			38	184	26	
Lusk	Elizabeth	10.15	1877			87		88	184	27	
Marshall	James Oliver	11.13	1872	6.22	1872			1	184	28	Marshall, Robert & Jennie, son of
McCausland	Carrie	12.10	1878			27	6.19	28	185	26	McCausland, Asbury, wife of
McCausland	Sadie E.	11.28	1877			1	4.04	2	185	27	McCausland, Asbury & Carrie, daughter of
McCausland	Samuel B.					70		71	185	28	
McCausland	Eve	12.12	1886			74	7.28	75	185	29	
McCausland	William								185	30	Co. G, 2d. Pa. H. A.; [Co. C?]
McCavitt	Mary C.	3.23	1851						185	25	McCavitt, John, wife of
McCoy	Joshua W.	3.25	1874	1.19	1804			71	185	31	
McCoy	Sarah A.	8.19	1872			58	8.06	59	185	32	McCoy, J. W., wife of
McElwain	Joseph	1.18	1888			80	2.00	81	185	33	
McElwain	John E.	8.25	1869			0	0.03	1	185	34	McElwain, Joseph & Elizabeth, child of
McElwain	Elizabeth	2.29	1860	10.27	1855			5	185	35	McElwain, Joseph & Elizabeth, child of
McKee	Samuel	3.26	1894	6.28	1806			88	185	36	
McKee	Thomas	5.29	1878	10.12	1794			84	185	37	
McLaughlin	David	3.20	1884			76	3.01	77	186	01	
McLaughlin	Martha M.	5.20	1885			75	3.08	76	186	02	
Miller	Ludwig	1.26	1836		1755	80		81	184	29	a soldier of the Revolution
Miller	Anna Barbara	9.25	1823	2.25	1761			63	184	30	Miller, Ludwick, consort of
Miller	Lewis	7.31	1816	6.22	1783			34	184	31	Miller, Ludwick & Anna Barbara, son of
Miller	Caroline Jane	4.09	1873			24	9.01	25	184	32	
Miller	Jane Hull	12.16	1880			67		68	184	33	Miller, James, wife of; [Hull ?]
Miller	Philip	11.14	1895			64	5.22	65	184	34	
Miller	Samuel	12.21	1893			75	4.06	76	184	35	Private, Co. A, 101 Regt. Pa. Vol. Inft.
Miller	Mary E.	3.23	1877			38		39	184	36	Miller, Samuel, wife of
Miller	Samuel	2.19	1872			78	6.02	79	184	37	a soldier of the War of 1812
Miller	Catharine	12.29	1875			83	11.17	84	184	38	
Morrett	Jacob	10.03	1837			29		30	185	15	
Morrett	Nicholas	4.01	1836		1751	85		86	185	16	
Morrett	Mary	8.25	1853		1768	84		85	185	17	Morrett, Nicholas, wife of
Mowery	Joseph H.	5.24	1894			24		25	185	01	
Mowery	Catharine	11.18	1871	10.13	1792			80	185	02	
Mowery	Solomon	12.16	1870			80	4.17	81	185	03	
Mowery	Mary E.	4.13	1885			22	5.18	23	185	04	Mowery, John & Rosanna, daughter of
Mowery	Andrew	8.13	1887			58		59	185	05	
Mowery	Harry E. M.	1.16	1890			9	2.06	10	185	06	Mowery, Andrew, son of

Hopewell - Zion Reformed Church Graveyard

Surname	Given Name	Death Mo/Dy	Year	Birth Mo/Dy	Year	Att. Age Yr	Mo/Dy	Ag	Cm	Pg	No	Other Information
Mowery	John Calvin	10.23	1876			27	2.06	28		185	07	Mowery, John & Rosanna, son of
Mowery	Margaret J.	3.29	1869			22	9.22	23		185	08	Mowery, John & Rosanna, daughter of
Mowery	Laura Ann May					1	2.14	2		185	09	Mowery, John & Sarah J., daughter of
Mowery	Hanna C.			9.22	1858	6	3.00	6		185	10	Mowery, Samuel & Sarah R., daughter of
Mowery	John	2.18	1885	10.26	1815			70		185	11	
Mowery	Rosanna	10.01	1864			38	1.19	39		185	12	Mowery, John, wife of
Mowery	Mary C.	5.12	1852			4	6.00	5		185	13	Mowery, John & Rosanna, daughter of
Mowery	Mary	11.22	1839	4.06	1801			39		185	14	Mowery, Adam, wife of
Myers	W. Erle	3.26	1899			1	4.12	2		185	18	Myers, D. P. & J. M., son of
Myers	Parker R.	3.06	1897			14		15		185	19	Myers, A. & E., son of
Myers	Mary A.	9.01	1899			71	8.16	72		185	20	[A.?]
Myers	Henry	2.03	1851			25	3.16	26		185	21	
Myers	Mary A.	12.24	1876			26	1.15	27		185	22	Myers, Henry & Mary A., daughter of
Myers	Mary A. Keesaman	1.23	1862	12.10	1789			73		185	23	Myers, Jacob, wife of
Myers	Mary C.	5.16	1899			54		55		185	24	Myers, Abram, wife of
Neidigh	Sarah C.	9.22	1896			62	7.07	63		186	05	Neidigh, Michael, wife of
Nickey	Eve	6.04	1847	11.22	1796			51		186	03	Nickey, Jacob, wife of
Nickey	Elizabeth Springer	9.18	1867	12.10	1819			48		186	04	Nickey, George, wife of
Pilgrim	Maria	6.20	1876			51	3.17	52		186	06	
Ramp	John	2.09	1892	1.20	1817			76		186	07	
Ramp	Elizabeth	7.24	1889	3.08	1821			69		186	08	Ramp, John, wife of
Ramp	Jacob Rupley	2.15	1861	7.02	1860			1		186	09	Ramp, John & Lacy R., son of
Ramp	Jacob, Sr.	12.03	1875			74	6.11	75		186	10	
Ramp	Eve	5.27	1884			78	11.14	79		186	11	Ramp, Jacob, Sr., wife of
Ramp	Anna Mary Heberlig	3.03	1872			82	5.00	83		186	12	Ramp, William, wife of
Reader	Abraham									186	13	Co. F., 8th Maryland Infantry
Reader	Annie Bell	8.29	1883			21	8.29	22		186	14	Reeder, Jacob & Sarah, daughter of
Reinhardt	Mary R.	1.11	1882			25	3.03	26		186	15	Reinhardt, Max H., wife of
Reinhardt	-----	4.11	1880			1	3.11	2		186	16	Reinhardt, Max H. & Mary, son of
Reinhardt	Carl Ferdinand	5.18	1896			69	6.18	70		186	17	
Reinhardt	Minnie Sophia	12.08	1895			21	6.05	22		186	18	Reinhart, C. Ferdinand & Mary J., dau.
Reinhardt	Mary Elizabeth	6.21	1897			17	2.26	18		186	19	Reinhart, Ferdinand & Mary J., dau. of
Ruth	William	10.26	1882	9.04	1816			67		186	20	
Ruth	Elizabeth Conner	8.31	1898	8.22	1831			66		186	21	Ruth, William, wife of
Ruth	William M.	4.30	1893	11.1	1869			24		186	22	Ruth, William & Elizabeth, son of
Shoap	Linda A.	12.07	1889			31	9.13	32		186	31	Shoap, John H., wife of
Shoap	Harry B.	4.22	1887			2	10.00	3		186	32	Shoap, John & Linda A., son of
Shriner	Mary A.	7.04	1852							186	25	aged about 75 years
Shriner	Elias	3.15	1844			76		77		186	26	
Shriner	Elizabeth H.	6.16	1849					0		186	27	aged about 26 years
Shulenberger	Benjamin	4.03	1892	4.06	1832			60		187	02	
Shulenberger	Anna	9.15	1894	9.29	1829			65		187	03	
Shulenberger	Stella H.	2.20	1889			0	6.02	1		187	04	Shulenberger, J. C. & Sarah C., child of
Shulenberger	Thompson S.	9.25	1868			3	10.05	4		187	05	Shulenberger, J. C. & Sarah C., child of
Shulenberger	Emerson B.	4.27	1874			8	0.28	9		187	06	Shulenberger, J. B. & Martha S., ch. of
Shulenberger	William B.	8.22	1875			11	4.02	12		187	07	Shulenberger, J. B. & Martha S., ch. of
Shulenberger	Samuel Kirk	2.21	1885			3	1.00	4		187	08	Shulenberger, J. B. & Martha S., ch. of
Shulenberger	J. Emmett	4.02	1889			14	8.12	15		187	09	Shulenberger, J. B. & Martha S., son of
Shulenberger	Theodore R.	9.08	1860			0	5.02	1		187	10	Shulenberger, J. & C., child of
Shulenberger	Amanda J.	8.02	1863							187	11	Shulenberger, J. & C., child of

Hopewell - Zion Reformed Church Graveyard

Surname	Given Name	Death Mo/Dy	Year	Birth Mo/Dy	Year	Att. Age Yr	Mo/Dy	Ag	Cm	Pg	No	Other Information
Shulenberger	John	1.08	1875			67	2.11	68		187	12	
Shulenberger	Janet	3.26	1857			53	3.15	54		187	13	Shulenberger, John, wife of
Shulenberger	Catharine	5.20	1887	1.07	1825			63		187	14	Shulenberger, John, wife of
Shulenberger	Anthony S.	8.20	1845			4	5.16	5		187	15	
Shulenberger	Mary J.	2.16	1859	7.15	1858			1		187	16	Shulenberger, Benjamin & Ann, child of
Shulenberger	Sarah E.	8.25	1860	1.28	1860			1		187	17	Shulenberger, Benjamin & Ann, child of
Smith	Mary	5.15	1891			58	5.08	59		186	28	Smith, Michael, wife of
Smith	Anna J.	8.18	1865			1	7.26	2		186	29	
Smith	Susan	8.15	1871			1	1.23	2		186	30	
Stephens	Elinor [?] E.	4.18	1884			22	1.15	23		186	24	
Stover	Lydia May	9.01	1892			0	3.06	1		187	01	
Stump	-----	3.09	1900			8	10.16	9		187	18	Stump, W. A. & L. B., son of
Swartz	Esamiah	10.23	1880			29	4.00	30		186	23	Swartz, Samuel, wife of
Thrush	Richard	9.19	1892			78	1.00	79		187	19	Private, Co. D, 77th Regt., Pa. Vols.
Thrush	Elizabeth	10.26	1897			81	10.22	82		187	20	
Watson	William	7.02	1823			41	9.00	42		187	21	
Watson	Susanna	6.16	1866			84	2.27	85		187	22	Watson, William, wife of
Weaver	Peter	8.10	1845			77		78		187	23	
Weaver	Margaret			8.20	1770					187	24	Weaver, Peter, wife of; d. Apr. 8, 1885 [death year is probably in error]
Weaver	John	8.12	1876			78		79		187	25	
Weaver	Catharine	10.01	1868			62		63		187	26	Weaver, John, wife of
Whisler	Clara B. E.	6.19	1876			1	9.17	2		187	27	Whisler, W. H. & Margaret, daughter of
Whisler	infant	8.22	1877							187	28	Whisler, W. H. & Margaret, son of
Wolf	John	4.15	1866	1.24	1785			82		187	29	

Lower Allen - Eberly's Mill Graveyard

LOWER ALLEN TOWNSHIP

EBERLY'S MILL GRAVEYARD

Surname	Given Name	Death Mo/Dy	Year	Birth Mo/Dy	Year	Att. Age Yr	Mo/Dy	Cm Ag	Pg	No	Other Information
Adams	George H.	2.27	1865	11.25	1848			17	125	01	Adams, William & Agnes, son of
Bailey	infant son	5.06	1846	3.02	1846			1	125	03	Bailey, John & Frances, infant son of
Balsley	John	11.02	1872			70	2.22	71	125	02	
Black	Mary Jane	11.18	1842			3	9.20	4	125	04	Black, Samuel & Sarah, daughter of
Black	Sarah J.	6.07	1847			3	8.08	4	125	05	Black, Samuel & Sarah, daughter of
Brenner	Bertha V.	1.19	1873			1	11.27	2	125	06	
Brownfelter	Amos		1885		1835			51	125	07	
Brownfelter	Susan		1886		1834			53	125	08	Brownfelter, Amos B., wife of
Bubb	William Urich	9.24	1852	10.10	1851			1	125	09	Bubb, Frank & Margaret, son of
Bubb	Charlie	11.15	1860	12.10	1857			3	125	10	Bubb, Frank & Margaret, son of
Chapman	William	11.17	1864			31	0.17	32	125	11	Co. L, 99 Pa. Regt.; killed in Fort Sedgwick near Petersburg, VA
Crist	David W.	5.24	1842	10.01	1841			1	125	12	
Darr	John	9.25	1864	10.05	1812			52	125	13	
Darr	Nancy	12.18	1840			29	11.07	30	125	14	Darr, John, wife of
Darr	Elena Jane	4.15	1851			1	0.20	2	125	15	Darr, John & R. Darr, daughter of
Darr	Mary Ellen	5.10	1851			5	9.09	6	125	16	Darr, John & R. Darr, daughter of
Davis	Leah Jane	8.23	1858				5.07	1	125	17	Davis, James & Lydia A., daughter of
Davis	George Ellsworth	9.29	1862	9.06	1862			1	125	18	Davis, James & Lydia A., son of
Dey	Benjamin F.	9.17	1855			1	9.11	2	125	23	[Dey (sic)]
Drawbaugh	Dovane T.	8.04	1855				3.12	1	125	19	Drawbaugh, Daniel & Elsetta J., son of [mother Elesetta in this entry]
Drawbaugh	Naomi E.	5.21	1863			2	0.27	3	125	20	Drawbaugh, Daniel & Elsetta J., dau. of
Drawbaugh	Ida May	11.14	1871			7	11.20	8	125	21	Drawbaugh, Daniel & Elsetta J., dau. of
Drawbaugh	Emma C.	11.18	1871			15	2.07	16	125	22	Drawbaugh, Daniel & Elsetta J., dau. of
Frownfelter	A.								125	24	Co. I, 149th Pennsylvania Infantry
Gardner	John C.	11.27	1871	6.10	1870			2	125	25	
Gillen	Anderson	6.02	1857				5.17	1	125	28	Gillen, Samuel & Rebecca, son of
Gillen	Jeanette J.	8.31	1862	11.14	1861			1	125	29	
Gonter	Mary	3.08	1831		1761	69	9.00	70	125	30	Gontner, John, wife of; (b. 1761) [spelling varies]
Good	Elizabeth E.	5.27	1869	4.06	1865			5	125	31	Good, E. & L., daughter of
Good	William Grant	8.19	1870	5.13	1867			4	125	32	Good, E. & L., daughter of
Greenawalt	Daniel	1.19	1838	10.27	1802			36	125	26	
Greenawalt	Elizabeth	11.15	1864	9.04	1833			32	125	27	
Hains	George	12.01	1865			53	2.18	54	126	02	
Haines	Isaac E.	12.31	1856			30	6.25	31	126	03	
Hambright	Mary	8.31	1831			35		36	126	01	
Harper	Daniel	11.07	1855			53	6.07	54	126	04	
Hart	Daniel L.	7.20	1883			66	10.04	67	126	05	
Hart	John L. R.	4.16	1861			19	7.17	20	126	06	Hart, Daniel & Lizzie, son of
Hart	Harvey Glen	12.09	1888				3.07	1	126	07	Hart, C. & M., son of
Hart	Willie L.	11.29	1889			18		19	126	08	Hart, Calvin & Martha H., son of; d. aged 18 yrs. ----
Heck	John, Sr.	7.02	1795		1731	63		64	126	09	(b. 1731)
Heck	John, Sr.	3.30	1847						126	10	aged about 77 years

Lower Allen - Eberly's Mill Graveyard

Surname	Given Name	Death Mo/Dy	Year	Birth Mo/Dy	Year	Att. Age Yr	Mo/Dy	Ag	Cm	Pg	No	Other Information
Heck	Christina	5.31	1834			45	7.17	46		126	11	Heck, John, consort of; Gontner, John & Mary, daughter of
Heck	Mary	8.21	1823			8	4.08	9		126	12	Heck, John & Christina, daughter of
Heck	William	2.10	1837			63		64		126	13	
Heck	William	1.26	1901			81	3.20	82		126	14	
Heck	Esther	11.02	1848	4.01	1822			27		126	15	Heck, William, wife of; Steel, John & Catharine, daughter of
Heck	Ester Jane	6.19	1874			25	7.23	26		126	16	Heck, W. & E., daughter of
Heck	infant son			5.01	1852					126	17	Heck, William & Anna Mary, son of
Heck	infant daughter			3.24	1853					126	18	Heck, William & Anna Mary, daughter of
Heck	infant son	11.07	1858	10.27	1858				1	126	18	Heck, William & A. M., son of
Heck	Rebecca	3.04	1848	3.04	1823				26	126	20	Heck, Jacob, wife of; Drawbaugh, John & Leah, daughter of
Heck	Sarah Jane	11.08	1847	11.02	1847				1	126	21	Heck, Jacob & Rebecca, daughter of
Heck	Elizabeth	11.19	1872			19	4.02	20		126	22	Heck, George, wife of
Long	Barbara	3.01	1856							126	23	aged about 56 years
Miller	infant daughter	9.23	1858				0.03	1		126	24	Miller, George & Nancy, daughter of
Nailor	Jacob	12.22	1865			51	7.04	52		126	25	
Nailor	Catharine	4.07	1847			30	4.29	31		126	26	Nailor, Jacob, wife of
Nailor	Sophia C.	8.24	1863			22	10.27	23		126	27	Nailor, J. & C., daughter of
Noell	Elizabeth	8.10	1860			72	7.03	73		126	28	
Ogden	Robert		1906		1865			42		126	29	
Peterman	Elt. D.	5.20	1863	4.07	1862				2	126	30	Peterman, Jacob & Lydia A., son of
Price	Catharine	4.04	1832			29	5.25	30		126	31	Price, Abraham, wife of
Price	Catharine	2.21	1854			41	4.08	42		126	32	Price, Abraham, wife of; Heck, John & Christiana, daughter of
Price	Mary	8.30	1832			8	7.06	9		127	01	Price, Abraham & Catharine, daughter of
Row	Peter M.	3.14	1903			86	10.13	87		127	02	
Row	Anna	6.10	1875			53	7.14	54		127	03	Row, Peter M., wife of
Row	Amanda	2.25	1848				0.12	1		127	04	Row, P. M. & A., daughter of
Row	Mary M.	5.19	1851			9	9.06	10		127	04	Row, P. M. & A., daughter of
Row	Amos	9.16	1853				0.12	1		127	05	Row, P. M. & A., son of
Row	Joseph L.	4.18	1862				1.14	1		127	06	Row, P. M. & A., son of
Saylor	Elizabeth	5.20	1834			25	1.15	26		127	08	Saylor, George, Jr., consort of
Sellers	Solomon	5.21	1843			8	10.01	9		127	10	Sellers, Solomon & Christiana, son of
Sellers	Christiann	5.07	1842			44	6.25	45		127	11	Sellers, Solomon, wife of; Comp, Stephen & Ann, daughter of
Sellers	Henry	3.10	1841				8.27	1		127	12	Sellers, Solomon & Christiann, son of
Shadel	Jacob T.	4.14	1861	11.29	1858				3	127	09	Shadel, Uriah H. & Sarah, son of
Sipe	Mary	1.30	1867			68		69		127	16	Sipe, Martin, wife of; aged 68 years -- 13 days
Sipe	William H.	2.19	1867				9.20	1		127	17	
Smith	Elizabeth C.	2.02	1858	3.11	1855				3	127	18	
Snyder	Elizabeth Row	2.03	1878	5.27	1852				26	127	19	Snyder, J. L., wife of; Row, Peter M. & Anna, daughter of
Stephen	Henry	1.18	1865							127	13	aged about 68 years
Stephen	Elizabeth	4.08	1848	9.25	1790			58		127	14	Stephen, Henry, wife of
Stephen	Susan	4.29	1858			40	8.19	41		127	15	Stephen, Henry, wife of
Tyson	Sophia	3.21	1854			61		62		127	20	
Urich	infant son	5.28	1845						0	127	21	Urich, Samuel & Elizabeth, son of

Lower Allen - Eberly's Mill Graveyard

Surname	Given Name	Death Mo/Dy	Year	Birth Mo/Dy	Year	Att. Age Yr	Cm Mo/Dy	Ag	Pg	No	Other Information
Whitmer	Isaac	7.07	1860			26	3.09	27	127	24	Whitmer, John & Lydia, son of
Wills	Samuel	9.02	1847			57		58	127	22	native of Parish Donaugh, County Monaghan, Ireland
Wills	Mary	7.15	1850			68		69	127	23	Wills, Samuel, wife of; native of Parish Donagh [sic], County Monaghan, Ireland

Lower Allen - Lisburn Cemetery

LISBURN CEMETERY

Surname	Given Name	Death Mo/Dy	Year	Birth Mo/Dy	Year	Att. Age Yr	Mo/Dy	Cm Ag	Pg	No	Other Information
Bailey	Leah E.	1.23	1884			90		91	130	01	
Barton	John	7.12	1802			47	11.24	48	130	02	
Barton	Isaac	9.26	1868			70	8.23	71	130	03	
Barton	David D.	5.13	1894	6.01	1834			60	130	04	Co. F, 1st Regt., Pennsylvania Vols.
Barton	infant daughter								130	05	Barton, David D. & Susan, daughter of
Barton	twin children								130	06	Barton, David D. & Susan, children of
Bricker	Henry J.					62		63	130	07	
Bricker	Mary A.	8.04	1889			76	3.16	77	130	08	
Bricker	Russel					1	9.00	2	130	09	Bricker, George, son of;
Bricker	Clara E.					5	10.25	6	130	10	Bricker, George, daughter of;
Bricker	Nomie						9.04	1	130	11	Bricker, D. & H., daughter of
Byers	Joseph	4.10	1829			75	5.10	76	130	12	
Byers	Eliza	6.15	1878			61	10.21	62	130	13	Byers, Joseph, wife of
Byers	George	12.13	1843				7.13	1	130	14	Byers, Joseph & Eliza, child of
Byers	Joseph	9.27	1854			1	1.05	2	130	15	Byers, Joseph & Eliza, child of
Byers	George W.	10.25	1871			27	0.16	28	130	16	Byers, Joseph & Eliza, child of
Byers	Elizabeth	5.18	1846						130	17	Byers, Frederick & Mary, daughter of; d. aged -- years, 10 months, 7 days
Cain	Rebekah	2.08	1833			32	11.00	33	130	18	
Drorbaugh	infant son	3.31	1846	3.31	1846			1	130	19	Drorbaugh, William & Maria, child of
Drorbaugh	Christiann	9.22	1852			15	11.04	16	130	20	Drorbaugh, William & Maria, child of
Drorbaugh	Sarah	8.06	1863			24	3.04	25	130	21	Drorbaugh, William & Maria, child of
Dunlap	Rebecca	9.27	1840			65	4.00	66	130	22	
Edmondson	Mary	4.19	1895	6.20	1880			15	130	23	[b. 1880 ?]
Finney	Rebecca Lloyd	2.12	1900			78	4.17	79	130	24	Finney, James, wife of
Gher	Ephraim	5.11	1845			19	0.28	20	130	25	Gher, Andrew & Catharine, son of
Gher	Melissa	6.30	1845			1	11.06	2	130	26	Gher, Andrew & Jane, daughter of
Gher	Mary	12.29	1859			44		45	130	27	Gher, Paul & Elizabeth, daughter of
Gher	Emma J.	8.10	1885			17	9.06	18	130	28	
Gher	S. A.	10.12	1889	3.29	1889			1	130	29	[text reads "March 29, Oct. 12, 1889"]
Gher	Blanche B.	4.26	1863			2	1.16	3	130	30	
Grove	Emma Jane	2.01	1851				10.21	1	130	31	Grove, Samuel & Catharine, daughter of
Hall	George W.	10.16	1870			77	10.08	78	131	01	
Hall	Mary	8.03	1861			45	9.04	46	131	02	Hall, George W., wife of
Hart	Barbara A.	3.11	1884	1.11	1823			62	131	03	
Hart	John M.	2.01	1889			76	3.15	77	131	04	
Hart	Michael	5.14	1891	4.03	1815			77	131	05	
Hart	Mary Ellen	1.17	1892			62	3.25	63	131	06	Hart, John M., wife of; Lloyd, William & Amanda Anderson, daughter of
Hart	Charles								131	07	Hart, Michael & B. A., infant of
Hart	Martha								131	08	Hart, Michael & B. A., infant of
Heck	Jane Umberger	9.29	1907			88		89	131	09	b. Feb. 18 ----, aged 88 years & --
Heck	Mary Ellen	7.25	1872			32	10.20	33	131	10	Heck, John G. & Jane, daughter of
Hickernell	Margaret	9.14	1826						131	11	
Hickernell	Jacob	4.18	1832						131	12	
Hickernell	Jacob	4.23	1900	9.29	1810			90	131	13	
Hickernell	Mary A. Miller	10.22	1833			21	4.02	22	131	14	Hickernell, J., wife of
Hickernell	Sarah A. Moore	1.22	1858			43	3.26	44	131	15	Hickernell, J., wife of

Lower Allen - Lisburn Cemetery

Surname	Given Name	Death Mo/Dy	Year	Birth Mo/Dy	Year	Att. Age Yr	Mo/Dy	Cm Ag	Pg	No	Other Information
Hickernell	Mary Weber	9.04	1891			65	2.27	66	131	16	Hickernell, J., wife of
Hickernell	Thomas F.	1.10	1862			28	2.19	29	131	17	
Hicks	Philemon H.	1.23	1862				0.12	1	131	21	Hicks, Philemon & Elizabeth A., son of; Starr, J. & E., grandson of
Howerter	Lida J.		1887		1857			31	131	18	
Howerter	Sarah		1888		1837			52	131	19	Howerter, Samuel, wife of
Howerter	Eliza	10.05	1851			19	6.27	20	131	20	Howerter, Jacob & Susan, daughter of
Hull	Robert P.	11.26	1879			38	8.01	39	131	22	
Hull	infant son	1.09	1867				0.18	1	131	23	Hull, R. P. & M. J., son of
Jameson	Elizabeth	10.01	1839			20		21	131	24	
Jameson	Amelia	5.23	1848	5.10	1788			61	131	25	Jameson, Charles, wife of
Kann	Daniel H.	2.21	1900			57	10.14	58	131	26	
Kann	Matilda C.	10.31	1885			44	1.03	45	131	27	Kann, Daniel H., wife of
Kleier	Jacob	9.10	1845	2.18	1807			39	131	36	inscription in German; first letter of name is uncertain
Konn	Catharine	8.09	1853			47	9.04	48	131	33	Konn, Henry, daughter of
Konn	Daniel	9.22	1846			20	2.10	21	131	34	Konn, Henry & Catharine, son of
Konn	Elmira	12.22	1850			6	4.27	7	131	35	Konn, Henry & Catharine, daughter of
Krall	Martha	4.03	1862			75		76	131	28	Krall, Henry, wife of
Krall	William	7.30	1887			62	2.22	63	131	29	
Krall	Christianna	3.29	1905			77	6.02	78	131	30	
Krall	William H.	5.30	1881			1	10.10	2	131	31	Krall, J. H. & Rebecca, son of
Krall	Lizzie Ann	6.30	1907			57		58	131	32	
Lemer	Lerew	2.17	1877			70	5.23	71	132	05	M. D.
Lemer	Sarah Ann	4.21	1862			38	11.01	39	132	06	Lemer, L., Dr., wife of
Lemer	George McL.	4.22	1863			1	7.13	2	132	07	Lemer, L., Dr. & S. A., son of
Lloyd	William	6.14	1860			64		65	132	01	
Lloyd	Amanda A.	8.26	1853			46		47	132	02	
Lloyd	Carolina	4.14	1849			11	2.00	12	132	03	Lloyd, William & Amanda, daughter of
Loyd	William	12.24	1831			16	4.02	17	132	04	
McCafery	William	1.03	1829			31	5.00	32	132	13	
McCaffrey	Jesse	5.04	1834			30	0.16	31	132	14	
Meckley	Maud	10.29	1884			3	4.29	4	132	08	Meckley, S. R. & S. J., daughter of
Meckley	Howard	7.21	1887			1	2.12	2	132	09	Meckley, S. R. & S. J., son of
Meckley	Paul	9.23	1890						132	10	Meckley, S. R. & S. J., son of; [date is not specified as that of death]
Metzler	Thomas		1843		1767			77	132	11	
Moore	Elizabeth	4.06	1863			73	1.14	74	132	12	Moore, Mordica, wife of [Mordica (sic)]
Naylor	William	8.24	1876			82	9.26	83	132	15	
Naylor	Lydia	4.27	1888			81		82	132	16	
Naylor	Andrew J.	8.16	1849			9	7.18	10	132	17	
Naylor	John B.	12.31	1862			24	6.28	25	132	18	fell at the Battle of Stone River, Tenn.
Naylor	Isaac N.	5.20	1884			39	6.12	40	132	19	
Nebinger	Charles K.	7.18	1858			1	6.10	2	132	20	Nebinger, Edwin & Sarah, son of
Nebinger	Mary	8.09	1860			1	4.26	2	132	21	Nebinger, Edwin & Sarah, daughter of
Neel	Elizabeth	4.04	1832			39	11.00	40	132	23	
Nelson	D. W.								132	22	Co. H, 130th Pa. Infantry; [no dates]
Orth	Joseph	12.23	1862	8.04	1859			4	132	24	Orth, Hiram C. & Agnes, son of
Paul	Peter	3.20	1860	3.17	1787			74	132	25	
Paul	Susan C.	2.15	1864	2.07	1788			77	132	26	

Lower Allen - Lisburn Cemetery

Surname	Given Name	Death Mo/Dy	Death Year	Birth Mo/Dy	Birth Year	Att. Age Yr	Att. Age Mo/Dy	Age Ag	Cm	Pg	No	Other Information
Paul	Mary J.	5.30	1863			3	7.30	4		132	27	Paul, Peter & Elizabeth, child of
Paul	Sarah E.	1.28	1864			1	3.30	2		132	28	Paul, Peter & Elizabeth, child of
Paul	infant son	7.25	1853				4.00	1		132	29	Paul, Peter & Elizabeth, child of
Paul	infant	1.19	1858				0.02	1		132	29	Paul, Peter & Elizabeth, child of
Pipher	Celia	9.30	1863			2	0.01	3		132	31	Pipher, S. C. & E. J., daughter of
Shaw	Lydia	8.18	1825			76		77		132	32	
Shaw	John		1894		1819			76		132	33	
Shaw	Henrietta		1907		1821			87		132	34	
Shaw	Martha A.	12.17	1850			2	1.17	3		132	35	Shaw, Philip & Rebecca, daughter of
Shaw	John	12.17	1850			4	10.09	5		133	01	Shaw, Philip & Rebecca, child of
Shaw	Philip	1.07	1851			3	6.08	4		133	02	Shaw, Philip & Rebecca, child of
Shaw	George W.	6.16	1897			15	3.06	16		133	03	
Sidle	George B. McClellan	10.09	1863				2.18	1		133	14	Sidle, Peter & Elizabeth, child of
Sidle	Susan C.	10.12	1866			1	10.27	2		133	15	Sidle, Peter & Elizabeth, child of
Smyser	Michael P.	7.02	1903	6.05	1830			74		133	16	Co. I, 149th Pennsylvania Volunteers
Smyser	Mary A.	10.03	1904	7.08	1827			78		133	17	
Sprenkle	John	12.08	1884			66	7.14	67		133	12	
Sprenkle	Leah	11.11	1885			69	9.03	70		133	13	Sprenkle, J., wife of
Starr	Samuel	6.10	1815			60	1.16	61		133	04	
Starr	Mary	5.03	1845			43	7.17	44		133	05	Starr, Samuel, wife of
Starr	James	5.30	1876	6.06	1798			78		133	06	
Starr	Elizabeth	1.29	1883	11.25	1804			79		133	07	Starr, James, wife of
Starr	George B.	7.09	1845			4	0.28	5		133	08	Starr, James & Elizabeth, child of
Starr	John L.	1.01	1852			12	6.24	13		133	09	Starr, James & Elizabeth, child of
Starr	Dollie	8.13	1861			1	9.24	2		133	10	Starr, W. H. & M. J., child of
Starr	infant daughter	2.14	1870			1	2.22	2		133	11	Starr, W. H. & M. J., child of
Umberger	David	8.26	1854			79		80		133	18	
Umberger	Dorothy	6.27	1863			81	4.28	82		133	19	was lying a corpse while the Rebels were in Lisburn
Wiley	Ira J.	3.07	1888			20	10.13	21		133	20	Wiley, W. J. & C. M., son of
Young	Martha					72		73		133	21	d. Jan. 15, 188-

Lower Allen - Monroe Woods Farm Graveyard

MONROE WOODS FARM GRAVEYARD

Surname	Given Name	Death Mo/Dy	Death Year	Birth Mo/Dy	Birth Year	Att. Age Yr	Att. Age Mo/Dy	Cm Ag	Pg	No	Other Information
Cramer	Elizabeth		1835			13		14	129	01	Cramer, George & Elizabeth, daughter of
Cramer	George	2.05	1853			63		64	129	02	
Gher	Paul	3.07	1895			48	8.10	49	129	03	
Gher	Elizabeth	12.21	1851			61	7.13	62	129	04	Gher, Paul, wife of
Gher	Gideon		1825		1825			1	129	05	Gher, P. & E., son of
Gher	John	4.20	1830			16	4.00	17	129	06	Gher, Paul & Elizabeth, son of
Gher	Levi		1831		1831	16	4.00	17	129	07	Gher, P. & E., son of
Gher	-----	3.00	1840			22		23	129	08	Gher, P. & E., son of
Gher	Paul	5.00	1840			21		22	129	09	Gher, P. & E., son of; d. May - 1840
Walker	Isaac	10.12	1839			49	3.21	50	129	10	
Walker	John	11.03	1847			20	1.15	21	129	11	

Middlesex - Carlisle Springs Church Graveyard

MIDDLESEX TOWNSHIP

CARLISLE SPRINGS CHURCH GRAVEYARD

Surname	Given Name	Death Mo/Dy	Death Year	Birth Mo/Dy	Birth Year	Att. Age Yr	Att. Age Mo/Dy	Cm Ag	Pg	No	Other Information
Albright	Solomon			4.22	1819				101	01	
Albright	Caroline	2.05	1897	4.06	1820			77	101	02	Albright, Solomon, wife of
Albright	George A.	5.17	1864			9	5.23	10	101	03	Albright, Solomon & Catharine, son of
Albright	Wilbur Charles						11.19	1	101	04	Albright, O. T. & E. C., son of
Barnhill	John	11.22	1865	12.13	1808			57	101	05	
Barnhill	Jane	7.12	1859	9.03	1808			51	101	06	Barnhill, David, wife of
Barnhill	Margaret	7.29	1889			60	5.24	61	101	07	Barnhill, David, wife of
Barnhill	Sarah	8.21	1855	10.20	1853			2	101	08	Barnhill, William & Mary Ann, dau. of
Bauchman	Absalom	6.21	1880	8.11	1806			74	101	09	
Baughman	Fanny	7.03	1888			81	10.21	82	101	10	
Berntheisle	Annie M.	7.28	1892			18	1.00	19	101	16	
Bistline	Josiah H.	2.12	1849	8.27	1844			5	101	18	Bistline, John & Catharine, son of
Bistline	Elmira	3.23	1851	9.18	1850			1	101	19	Bistline, Baltzer & Mary, daughter of
Bistline	Mary Ann J. C.	1.26	1851	1.12	1851			1	101	20	
Bistline	Samuel	7.17	1892			89	9.10	90	101	32	
Bistline	Sarah	6.07	1876	12.04	1806			70	101	33	Bistline, Samuel, wife of
Braught	Moses	11.06	1869			48		49	101	11	
Braught	Amanda	12.05	1893			62		63	101	12	
Braught	Catharine	2.20	1868	11.23	1852			16	101	13	Braught, Moses & Amanda, daughter of
Braught	Mary Jane	12.08	1862				9.08	1	101	14	Braught, Moses & Amanda, child of
Braught	Susanna	8.04	1856			1	2.14	2	101	15	Braught, Moses & Amanda, child of
Breneizer	Samuel F.	2.28	1888			2	2.04	3	101	17	Breneizer, I. & S. C., son of
Brindle	George	7.08	1867	6.21	1791			77	101	21	
Brindle	Elizabeth	1.30	1864	2.12	1797			67	101	22	Brindle, George, wife of
Brindle	Samuel J.	1.19	1892	6.26	1861			31	101	23	
Brindle	David P.			9.30	1832				101	24	
Brindle	Sarah Baer			3.04	1836				101	25	
Brindle	J. P.						2.00	1	101	26	Brindle, J. P. & A. R., infant son of
Brindle	Andrew J.	10.16	1838			5	7.25	6	101	27	
Brindle	William D.	6.16	1831			1	1.04	2	101	28	
Brindle	Anna M.	1.08	1862		1859			4	101	29	Brindle, John P. & Amanda R., child of; b. September 3<u>1</u>, 1859
Brindle	Charles W.	10.09	1862			11	11.22	12	101	30	Brindle, John P. & Amanda R., child of
Brindle	Mary E.	2.20	1860	4.25	1852			8	101	31	Brindle, John P. & Amanda R., child of
Brown	Levering	2.01	1869			58	5.03	59	101	34	
Brown	Sarah J.	2.12	1872			52	9.14	53	101	35	Brown, Levering, wife of
Brown	Johnnie	3.03	1890				1.12	1	102	01	Brown, J. S. & M. J., child of
Brown	Charlie	2.06	1895				2.20	1	102	02	Brown, J. S. & M. J., child of
Brown	Carrie M.	9.25	1898				3.10	1	102	03	Brown, J. S. & M. J., child of
Brownawell	Henry	7.24	1846		1778	68		69	102	04	(b. 1778)
Brownawell	Elizabeth	8.01	1873	7.09	1780			94	102	05	Brownawell, Henry, wife of
Brownawell	Elizabeth	1.11	1885	2.15	1814			71	102	06	
Brownawell	Elias	2.03	1875	2.22	1810			65	102	07	
Brownawell	Catharine	2.05	1869	4.29	1815			54	102	08	Brownawell, Elias, wife of
Brownawell	Levi	3.09	1853	1.15	1853			1	102	09	Brownawell, Elias & Catharine, child of

Middlesex - Carlisle Springs Church Graveyard

Surname	Given Name	Death Mo/Dy/Year	Birth Mo/Dy/Year	Att. Age Yr/Mo/Dy	Cm Ag	Pg	No	Other Information
Brownawell	infant son		3.07/1857			102	10	Brownawell, Elias & Catharine, child of
Brownawell	Elias	3.15/1852	2.26/1852		1	102	11	Brownawell, Elias & Catharine, child of
Brownawell	Barbara Jane	10.19/1855	9.29/1855		1	102	12	Brownawell, David & Lydia, daughter of
Brownawell	Charles Franklin	3.23/1863	9.20/1860		3	102	13	Brownawell, Oliver J. F. & Mary A., son
Burgett	John	7.13/1900		65/0.11	66	102	14	
Burgett	Anna A.	9.12/1902		58/5.00	59	102	15	
Burkhart	Martin	4.30/1862	2.02/1794		69	102	16	
Burkhart	Catharine	7.25/1875	9.23/1793		82	102	17	Burket, Martin, wife of [Burket (sic)]
Burkhart	Mary Elsie	9.16/1863	3.22/1863		1	102	18	Burkhart, John & Anna A., daughter of
Buttorf	Frederick	7.08/1859	12.07/1784		75	102	19	
Casey	Christopher	1.19/1846		74/10.16	75	102	20	
Casey	Mary C.	2.25/1860		61/1.21	62	102	21	
Chandler	Catharine	8.09/1857	10.13/1836		21	102	22	Chandler, Hezekiah, wife of; Brindle, George & Elizabeth, daughter of
Chorpenning	Maggie F.	5.03/1886		9/6.12	10	103	16	
Christlieb	Elizabeth	6.25/1870		81/0.19	82	102	29	Christlieb, George, wife of
Clendenin	James	11.18/1885	4.13/1823		63	102	26	
Clendenin	Ann Barbara	12.16/1880	6.03/1826		55	102	27	
Clendenin	Willie R. Brindle	2.11/1889		5/0.05	6	102	28	
Clouser	Elizabeth	4.08/1878		50/11.23	51	103	17	Clouser, John, wife of
Clouser	Harry H.		11.14/1883	10.11		103	18	[no date of death given]
Clouser	Harvey J.	6.23/1894		15/8.09	16	103	19	Clouser, George & Katie, child of
Clouser	infant					103	20	Clouser, George & Katie, child of
Clouser	Florence M.	2.22/1887		1/1.00	2	103	21	Clouser, C. & M., child of
Clouser	Charles H.	1.13/1890		1/0.13	2	103	22	Clouser, C. & M., child of
Coleman	John Henry B.	4.29/1864		2.11	1	102	33	Coleman, John & Jane, son of
Coleman	Anna Maria	3.08/1858	12.06/1854		4	102	34	Coleman, John & Jane, son of
Cornman	Henry	9.12/1830	1776		55	102	35	
Cornman	Mary Norris	12.11/1841	1778	63/10.00	64	102	36	Cornman, Henry, wife of
Cornman	William	1.08/1883		79/6.19	80	102	37	
Cornman	Sarah (Spahr)	6.18/1832		19/7.11	20	102	38	Cornman, William, wife of
Cornman	Catharine (Kuhns)	5.23/1843		30/5.27	31	102	39	
Cornman	Elizabeth (Maloon)	2.13/1861		54/0.05	55	103	01	(4th wife Anna Lyons)
Cornman	Mary Ann	3.23/1842		17/11.04	18	103	02	Cornman, William & Catharine, child of
Cornman	Samuel	4.01/1842		7/11.13	8	103	03	Cornman, William & Catharine, child of
Cornman	Elizabeth	3.31/1842		3/5.00	4	103	04	Cornman, William & Catharine, child of
Cornman	Rebecca Jane	6.22/1851		5/3.01	6	103	05	Cornman, William & Elizabeth, child of
Cornman	Henry	4.01/1842		6		7	103	06	
Cornman	Mary C. L.	2.13/1857				103	07	Cornman, Ephraim & Harriet, child of; b. January 23, ---
Cornman	William Parker	12.18/1868		5/3.01	6	103	08	Cornman, Ephraim & Harriet, child of
Cornman	John	2.02/1875	12.01/1803		72	103	09	
Cornman	Jane	8.29/1893		82/2.29	83	103	10	
Cornman	William A.	8.28/1850	4.09/1828		23	103	11	Cornman, John & Jane, son of
Cornman	David	2.02/1883	10.05/1813		70	103	12	
Cornman	Elizabeth	5.21/1897		78/5.06	79	103	13	
Cornman	John	3.27/1882	2.23/1800		83	103	14	(wagonmaker)
Cornman	Sarah (Wolf)	1.28/1868	1803	64/7.22	65	103	15	Cornman, John, wife of
Crammer	John	10.01/1853		19/1.23	20	102	23	b. Jan. 8, 183-
Cramer	John	2.22/1832	10.20/1775		57	102	24	

Middlesex - Carlisle Springs Church Graveyard

Surname	Given Name	Death Mo/Dy	Death Year	Birth Mo/Dy	Birth Year	Att. Age Yr	Att. Age Mo/Dy	Cm Ag	Pg	No	Other Information
Cramer	Anna Mary	4.19	1867	1.18	1782			86	102	25	Cramer, John, wife of
Criswell	David	3.00	1894						102	30	
Criswell	Catharine	12.27	1896						102	31	
Criswell	Arthur J.	5.11	1861	11.07	1860			1	102	32	
Darr	Mary E.	1.31	1861			3	1.03	4	103	23	
Diller	Elizabeth	5.02	1857			52	5.22	53	103	24	Diller, Benjamin & Catharine, dau. of
Diller	Michael	4.16	1880	9.17	1810			70	103	25	
Diller	Leah	2.12	1868	3.05	1817			51	103	26	Diller, Michael, wife of
Diller	Mary E.	1.05	1894			59	4.00	60	103	27	Diller, Adam, wife of
Diller	Thomas A.	11.03	1873			7	8.25	8	103	28	Diller, Adam & M. E., son of
Donnelly	William	11.05	1863	4.11	1801			63	103	29	
Donnelly	Ann M.	2.05	1888			85		86	103	30	[aged 85 ?]
Donnelly	Sarah Emma	8.18	1866	10.02	1865			1	103	31	Donnelly, Washington & Catharine, ch. of
Donnelly	Washington	1.26	1886			21	11.12	22	103	32	Donnelly, Washington & Catharine, ch. of
Duey	Johnnie A.		1885				10.23	1	103	33	[d. February 29, 1885]
Feister	John	11.10	1872			65	0.17	66	103	34	
Feister	Agnes	12.16	1884			74	2.06	75	103	35	
Fiester	Barbara	2.22	1843	6.16	1775			68	104	01	Fiester, Casper, wife of
Fiester	Sarah A. C.	9.25	1838	5.05	1833			6	104	02	Fiester, John & Agnes, daughter of
Fetzer	John Henry	5.02	1856	4.27	1856			1	104	03	Fetzer, John & Mary Ann, son of
Garland	Sarah A.	11.19	1892			59	10.05	60	104	04	Garland, S. A., wife of
Garland	S. Eddie	4.29	1879			6	4.06	7	104	05	Garland, S. A. & Sarah, child of
Garland	Katie O.	8.04	1894			23	0.04	24	104	06	Garland, S. A. & Sarah, child of
Garman	Susan	4.30	1903	7.07	1857			46	104	07	
Garver	Francis	9.27	1880						104	08	born in Kilsheim, Germany
Garver	Susanna	5.15	1889			66	5.05	67	104	09	
Geiling	Adam	1.17	1895	9.15	1818			77	104	10	
Geiling	Sophia Barbara	7.26	1875	6.14	1823			53	104	11	Geiling, Adam, wife of
Gutshall	Jacob	12.17	1857	10.13	1782			76	104	12	
Gutshall	Susan	5.17	1886	12.11	1786			100	104	13	
Gutshall	Jacob	4.21	1893	6.24	1819			74	104	14	
Gutshall	Eliza			4.14	1827				104	15	d. ----
Gutshall	George	11.18	1887	5.21	1814			74	104	16	
Gutshall	Sarah E.	6.16	1889	11.02	1816			73	104	17	
Gutshall	John N.	10.31	1888			40	11.16	41	104	18	
Gutshall	Mary E.	5.29	1887			56	10.29	57	104	19	
Gutshall	F. A.			12.25	1850				104	20	d. ----
Gutshall	Sarah F.	7.25	1901	10.05	1857			44	104	21	
Gutshall	John	1.27	1882			68		69	104	22	
Gutshall	Viola	8.15	1887				5.23	1	104	23	Gutshall, Amos & M. B., child of
Gutshall	infant son	3.00	1890						104	24	Gutshall, Amos & M. B., child of
Gutshall	Catharine	8.15	1838			1	3.00	2	104	25	Gutshall, George & Sarah, child of; [(Gootschall) note on entries 25-28]
Gutshall	William F.	4.11	1852	7.19	1850			2	104	26	Gutshall, George & Sarah, child of
Gutshall	David	12.20	1857	4.22	1853			5	104	27	Gutshall, George & Sarah, child of
Gootschall	James A.	4.25	1859	1.17	1856			4	104	28	Gutshall, George & Sarah, child of
Gutshall	Anna M..	6.18	1859	5.15	1854			6	104	29	Gutshall, Jacob & Eliza, child of
Gutshall	Harry P.	3.01	1872				11.01	1	104	30	Gutshall, Jacob & Eliza, child of
Gutshall	George R.	4.30	1892			22	9.25	23	104	31	Gutshall, Jacob & Eliza, child of [R. ?]
Haas	Peter	3.13	1848					0	104	32	aged about 75 years

Middlesex - Carlisle Springs Church Graveyard

Surname	Given Name	Death Mo/Dy	Year	Birth Mo/Dy	Year	Att. Age Yr	Cm Mo/Dy	Ag	Pg	No	Other Information
Haas	Mary	2.04	1848	4.05	1779			69	104	33	Haas, Peter, wife of
Haas	Adam	4.02	1842	9.05	1819			23	104	34	
Haas	Peter	2.07	1889			75	7.03	76	104	35	
Haas	Catharine	2.05	1900	6.02	1822			78	104	36	
Hall	Moses	6.12	1849	8.10	1801			48	104	37	
Hare	Peter	2.05	1865	3.04	1811			54	104	38	
Hare	Sarah	11.23	1871			68	0.05	69	104	39	Hare, Peter, wife of
Hare	Susanna	7.14	1860			19	4.04	20	104	40	Hare, Peter & Sarah, daughter of
Honich	Adam R.	5.04	1888			46	2.12	47	105	01	
Hoy	Charles A.	3.30	1887				0.07	1	105	02	Hoy, J. Wes. & S. J., son of
Humer	Jacob	12.19	1850	2.20	1817			34	105	03	
Humer	Mary	6.15	1848			53	4.03	54	105	04	
Humer	Mary C.	1.16	1850	6.11	1848			2	105	05	
Humer	Sarah	3.29	1893	2.04	1818			76	105	06	
Humer	Jacob	5.11	1836	4.30	1788			49	105	07	
Humer	George	2.15	1833				0.09	1	105	08	Humer, Jacob, son of
Jacobs	Henry	2.09	1865	5.03	1788			77	105	09	
Jacobs	Jane	11.08	1850	4.05	1797			54	105	10	Jacobs, Henry, wife of; Wolf, John, & Elizabeth, daughter of
Jacobs	Abraham	3.09	1851			32	10.10	33	105	11	
Jacobs	Henry J.	4.08	1833	5.05	1830			3	105	12	
Jacobs	John	3.20	1872	2.11	1792			81	105	13	
Jacobs	Catharine	11.10	1873	1.06	1791			83	105	14	Jacobs, John, wife of
Jacobs	David	2.17	1881			57	5.28	58	105	15	(removed to Old Graveyard, Carlisle)
Jacobs	John W.	2.22	1886	10.13	1857			29	105	16	
Jacobs	Samuel A.			1.29	1834				105	17	d. ---
Jacobs	Elizabeth Bistline			1.11	1840				105	18	d. ---
Jacobs	Charles M.	2.03	1899	7.15	1861			38	105	19	
Jacobs	Jeremiah	1.29	1834						105	20	aged about 3 years
Jacobs	Jonas	11.05	1835			9	9.10	10	105	21	
Jacobs	Mary	5.19	1892			65		66	105	22	
Jacobs	Josie Wetzel	3.17	1874				10.12	1	105	23	Jacobs, George & Phebe Wetzel, son of [sic]
Jacobs	Albert Roy	11.16	1892						105	24	Jacobs, Charles S. & A. C., inf. son of
Jones	Bertie Ann	6.14	1878	10.31	1876			2	105	25	Jones, Theodore & Sarah, daughter of
Keihl	George	9.21	1873			73	3.17	74	105	26	
Keihl	Mary	5.30	1879			81	5.13	82	105	27	Kiehl, George, wife of; [spelling varies
Kell	Harry	3.15	1893			39	2.00	40	105	28	
Kell	Alta May	2.19	1878				2.24	1	105	29	Kell, H. & A. E, daughter of
Keller	Washington	1.04	1897			55	6.14	56	105	30	
Keller	Alto May	12.01	1897			9	7.09	10	105	31	Keller, W. & E., daughter of
Kitch	Elizabeth	10.14	1849	6.26	1775			75	105	32	Kitch, Martin & Catharine, daughter of
Kitch	Lewis W.	8.29	1870	8.22	1853			18	105	33	Kitch, John & Eliza, son of
Kitch	John H.	2.01	1885			15	4.06	16	105	34	
Kitner	Minnie J.	5.09	1885			2	8.15	3	105	35	Kitner, S. M. & E. E., daughter of
Kunkle	George	2.28	1888			84	5.14	85	105	36	
Kunkle	Alfred H.	9.16	1896			38	3.09	39	105	37	
Kutz	Joseph			1.08	1821				105	38	d. ---
Kutz	Elizabeth	8.03	1891	5.07	1826			66	105	39	
Kutz	William	3.04	1866				6.27	1	105	40	Kutz, Joseph & Elizabeth, son of

Middlesex - Carlisle Springs Church Graveyard

Surname	Given Name	Death Mo/Dy	Year	Birth Mo/Dy	Year	Att. Age Yr	Mo/Dy	Age	Cm	Pg	No	Other Information
Leephart	Margaret	4.12	1849			32	10.25	33		106	01	Leephart, Daniel, wife of
Loophart	Catharine	8.17	1838			51	7.18	52		106	02	Loophart, Jacob, wife of
Lesher	John W.	5.14	1873	12.24	1871			2		106	03	
Lesher	Harry B.	10.18	1884	10.08	1884			1		106	04	
Lesher	John M.	11.08	1894	5.11	1811			84		106	05	
Lesher	Mary Ann	10.23	1892			82	5.00	83		106	06	Lesher, John M., wife of
Lesher	Charles R.	10.02	1886	7.06	1886			1		106	07	
Lesher	Laura C.	12.03	1887	12.14	1868			19		106	08	[middle name is given as "Co."]
Lesher	John Walter	5.14	1873	12.24	1871			2		106	09	Lesher, Jacob & Mary Ann, son of
Lesher	infant son			7.22	1866					106	10	Lesher, David & Eliza, son of
Lesher	infant son			8.15	1867					106	11	Lesher, David & Eliza, son of
Line	John	5.24	1862	3.01	1862			1		106	12	Line, Leonard & Catherine, child of
Line	Leonard	10.09	1868	8.09	1868			1		106	13	Line, Leonard & Catherine, child of
Lipe	Henry	3.11	1835				6.00	1		106	14	
Lipe	John	6.15	1831				1.22	1		106	15	d. aged 7 weeks & 3 days
Low	Peter	4.18	1866	2.13	1778			89		106	16	
Low	Peter	8.28	1888			76		77		106	17	
Low	Elizabeth	8.00	1866	7.00	1776			91		106	18	Low, Peter, wife of
Low	Jennie	1.17	1882			74		75		106	19	Low, Peter, wife of; Jennie, Our Mother insane in later years; d. at poorhouse
Low	Fanny Lissy	5.30	1868	7.28	1867			1		106	20	Low, David & Catharine, child of
Low	Samuel E. F.	4.08	1873		1872			2		106	21	Low, David & Catharine, ch. of; b. ---- 21, 1872
Mentzer	Fossie	3.18	1886			3	9.15	4		106	22	Mentzer, F. & E., daughter of
Myers	Michael	4.29	1886			72	7.07	73		106	23	d. 1886 [?]
Myers	Theodore	3.24	1868	4.04	1852			16		106	24	
Myers	John B.	11.02	1901	7.05	1847			55		106	25	
Myers	Emma			11.02	1849					106	26	
Myers	Susan	5.21	1862	10.03	1793			69		106	27	
Myers	Martha Ellen	9.04	1854	2.17	1854			1		106	28	Myers, Michael & Elizabeth, daughter of
O'Hara	Charles	12.19	1876	4.18	1874			3		106	29	O'Hara, George & Annie, son of
Railing	William	4.18	1874			58	10.15	59		106	30	
Railing	Mary A.	11.27	1881			68	1.22	69		106	31	
Railing	Samuel A.	3.13	1890	1.16	1840			51		106	32	
Railing	Annie M.	9.17	1888			11		12		106	33	Railing, S. A. & V., daughter of
Reed	Sarah Hair	3.31	1876	2.19	1849			28		106	34	Reed, J. H., wife of
Rinehart	Joseph	8.26	1881	8.15	1816			66		106	35	
Rinehart	Susan	2.02	1879	2.12	1810			69		106	36	Rinehart, Joseph, wife of
Rodgers	M. B.	11.27	1882	4.18	1811			72		106	37	Dr.
Rodgers	Amanda B.	5.25	1899	12.08	1819			80		107	01	
Rodgers	Eliza	6.29	1855	11.26	1854			1		107	02	
Rodgers	Alexander	6.13	1869	1.04	1839			31		107	03	Co. G, 130th Pennsylvania Infantry
Saylor	Jacob	1.11	1838			64	2.00	65		107	04	
Saylor	Christina	2.11	1844		1781	63	0.18	64		107	05	
Schwartz	John	12.11	1872	6.21	1797			76		107	06	
Schwartz	Catharine	6.20	1875	5.04	1797			79		107	07	
Schwartz	Sophia	5.31	1895	3.22	1826			70		107	08	
Schwartz	John B.	10.24	1850	9.24	1848			3		107	09	Schwartz, Michael & Elizabeth, son of; b. 1848 [? possibly 1846]
Seiler	Jarome	9.07	1887			69		70		107	18	[Jarome (sic)]

Middlesex - Carlisle Springs Church Graveyard

Surname	Given Name	Death Mo/Dy	Year	Birth Mo/Dy	Year	Att. Age Yr	Mo/Dy	Cm Ag	Pg	No	Other Information
Seiler	Sophia R.	12.17	1898			76		77	107	19	
Siler	Juliana	3.03	1868	9.20	1852			16	107	20	Siler, Jerome, daughter of [sp. varies]
Senk	Fannie	12.25	1881			12	2.22	13	107	16	
Shambaugh	Wilbert A.	10.05	1889				0.11	1	107	10	Shambaugh, H. A. & L. J., son of
Shatto	Ellie Bernhill	11.25	1897	1.23	1863			35	107	11	Shatto, M., wife of
Sheaffer	John	7.10	1856	9.30	1774			82	107	17	
Shufman	Margaret	2.16	1867			36		37	108	04	Shufman, Peter, wife of
Shuler	Sarah A.	2.05	1887			32	0.19	33	108	05	Shuler, John W., wife of
Shuler	Charles Elmer	3.29	1893			16	7.24	17	108	06	Shuler, Sylvester & Martha, son of
Shuler	infant daughter			3.12	1882				108	07	Shuler, S. & Anna M. daughter of
Smith	George	9.07	1871			57	3.26	58	107	21	
Smith	Mary	7.22	1894			83	1.14	84	107	22	
Smith	George Washington	4.19	1862	1.29	1841			22	107	23	Smith, George & Mary, son of
Smith	Jacob	5.04	1856	9.06	1782			74	107	24	
Smith	Catharine								107	25	Smith, Jacob, wife of; born Aug. 7, 17--
Smith	Isaac	2.28	1898	6.12	1817			81	107	26	
Smith	Margaret	8.07	1881			68	4.19	69	107	27	
Smith	Henry Oliver	3.01	1851	5.04	1841			10	107	28	Smith, Isaac & Margaret, son of
Smith	Amanda Elizabeth	5.01	1851	7.03	1850			1	107	29	Smith, Isaac & Elizabeth, daughter of
Smith	George Elmer	7.04	1863				0.06	1	107	30	Smith, Isaac R. & Catharine E., son of
Smith	William J.	4.16	1880			45	6.06	46	107	31	
Snyder	Susan	3.23	1893			53	10.07	54	108	08	Snyder, James P., wife of
Spahr	Benjamin	2.12	1851			45	6.26	46	107	12	b. July 18, 18-5
Spahr	David	3.07	1868	12.04	1778			90	107	13	
Spahr	Mary C.	5.16	1879		1791	88	2.26	89	107	14	
Spahr	William Brainard	1.20	1864			14	6.24	15	107	15	Spahr, John H. & Mary E., son of
Stauffer	Mathias	7.00	1836			21		22	107	33	
Stouffer	Mary	8.02	1846	2.12	1767			80	107	34	
Stouffer	Jacob	8.05	1879			66	5.07	67	107	35	
Stouffer	Anna	5.31	1886			66	2.07	67	107	36	Stouffer, Jacob, wife of
Stone	Lizzie	4.08	1868				0.02	1	107	37	
Stone	Albert W.	5.09	1897			7	0.12	8	107	38	Stone, J. S. & Annie M., son of
Stone	infant daughter			9.27	1892				107	39	Stone, John & Annie, daughter of
Stone	John	4.01	1893			9	0.18	10	107	40	Stone, Peter & Mary, son of
Stone	Dessie M.	12.14	1898				3.18	1	108	01	Stone, Peter & Mary, daughter of
Stoner	Catharine E.					33	7.12	34	108	02	
Stoner	Elizabeth								108	03	[no dates given]
Swigert	Felix	9.10	1852			35	11.04	36	107	32	
Thoman	Adam	4.24	1886	10.07	1805			81	108	09	
Thoman	Nancy	4.10	1850	1.15	1811			40	108	10	
Thoman	Margaret	1.14	1892	12.27	1814			78	108	11	
Trostle	Peter	8.18	1877			65	2.00	66	108	12	
Trostle	Caroline E.					18	10.20	19	108	13	
Trostle	Daniel	9.16	1884			67	0.15	68	108	14	
Ward	Jacob	2.20	1866	7.03	1802			64	108	15	
Ward	Mary	2.21	1866	2.09	1800			67	108	16	Ward, Jacob, wife of
Ward	Jane Ann	10.28	1875	3.16	1826			50	108	17	
Ward	Mary E.	6.02	1878			22	5.15	23	108	18	Ward, John & Jane A., daughter of
Weary	Jacob, Sr.	9.01	1864	11.14	1785			79	108	19	
Weary	George	11.27	1868	1.14	1815			54	108	20	

Middlesex - Carlisle Springs Church Graveyard

Surname	Given Name	Death Mo/Dy	Year	Birth Mo/Dy	Year	Att. Age Yr	Mo/Dy	Age Cm	Pg	No	Other Information
Weary	John	4.10	1850	9.25	1848			2	108	21	Weary, John & Elizabeth, son of
Weary	Catharine	4.21	1852	4.02	1785			68	108	22	Weary, Jacob, Sr., wife of
Weary	Angelo	2.17	1853				0.17	1	108	23	Weary, J. & S., child of
Weary	Susan E.	10.28	1857						108	24	Weary, J. & S., child of
Weary	Samuel	3.26	1852	3.28	1851			1	108	25	Weary, John & Elizabeth, son of
Weary	Samuel	11.00	1856	1.11	1853			4	108	26	Weary, George & Susan, son of
Weary	Aaron	4.02	1849	5.22	1848			1	108	27	Weary, Jacob & Susanna, child of
Weary	Martha A.	4.08	1851	3.22	1851			1	108	28	Weary, Jacob & Susanna, child of
Weary	Mary Jane	6.09	1851	1.14	1846			6	108	29	Weary, Jacob & Susanna, child of
Weary	Harvey M.	4.02	1885			1	0.22	2	108	30	Weary, J. A. & B. K., child of
Weary	Lizzie M.	9.02	1888				6.19	1	108	31	Weary, J. A. & B. K., child of
Weary	William Henry	7.07	1860				0.06	1	108	32	Weary, J. & S., son of f
Weaver	Margaret	1.31	1867	3.03	1778			89	109	08	Weaver, Philip, wife of
Weibley	Esther	9.14	1831			28	10.14	29	109	09	Weibley, John, wife of
Wert	J. Peter	8.28	1844	3.21	1766			79	108	33	
Wert	Elizabeth	10.26	1843	2.14	1771			73	108	34	Wert, Peter, wife of
Wert	Jacob	10.13	1891			84	4.00	85	108	35	
Wert	Margaret	4.13	1893						108	36	Wert, Jacob, wife of; aged 7 years, 1 month, 3 days (some mistake)
Wert	Joseph	12.31	1874			77	1.15	78	108	37	
Wert	Phebe	3.12	1891			83	2.01	84	108	38	Wert, Joseph, wife of
Wert	Anna B.	9.01	1902	5.11	1837			66	108	39	
Wert	Willis P.	3.25	1869	2.08	1869			1	108	40	Wert, Emil & M. A., child of
Wert	infant daughter	9.23	1886						108	41	Wert, Emil & M. A., child of
Wert	Alvin H.	2.11	1892			20	8.27	21	109	01	
Wert	Peter	8.18	1831	3.11	1829			3	109	02	Wert, Martin & Anna. S., child of
Wert	Martin	2.23	1833	1.22	1833			1	109	03	Wert, Martin & Anna. S., child of
Wert	Sally Ann	4.19	1840	3.04	1835			6	109	04	Wert, Martin & Anna. S., child of
Wert	William	2.26	1887			5	0.24	6	109	05	Wert, D. J. P. & L. A., child of
Wert	George	5.05	1885			7	10.16	8	109	06	Wert, D. J. P. & L. A., child of
Wert	Elmer S.	12.24	1871				0.15	1	109	07	Wert, D. J. P. & L. A., child of
Wetzel	John	5.26	1842			39	0.23	40	109	10	
Wetzel	Catharine	10.05	1881			77	8.10	78	109	11	
Wetzel	Joseph			11.11	1842				109	12	
Wetzel	Elizabeth J.	5.02	1898	2.16	1832			67	109	13	
Wickard	George	5.06	1863			81	8.24	82	109	14	
Wickert	Jane	9.16	1833			48	9.03	49	109	15	
Wolf	John	7.24	1824	4.27	1770			55	109	16	
Wolf	Margaret	3.04	1806	11.24	1803			3	109	17	Wolf, John, daughter of
Wolf	Jacob	1.01	1864			64	8.26	65	109	18	
Wolf	Mary	11.11	1832			31	1.01	32	109	19	Wolf, Jacob, wife of
Wolf	Frederick	6.15	1846			15	7.08	16	109	20	Wolf, Jacob, son of
Wolf	David	2.24	1879			69	1.19	70	109	21	
Wolf	Anna	4.17	1873			61	10.01	62	109	22	
Wolf	Margaretta	10.15	1862	9.28	1835			28	109	23	Wolf, John, wife of
Wolf	Joseph Parker					10	1.15	11	109	24	Wolf, John & Margaretta, son of
Wolf	Susannah	9.06	1848						109	25	Wolf, David & Ann, child of
Wolf	Henry						0.06	1	109	26	Wolf, David & Ann, ch. of; d. 8.11, 184-
Wolf	Elizabeth A.	5.14	1897	12.29	1839			58	109	27	Wolf, Joseph, wife of
Wolf	Josie	2.15	1897	8.17	1896			1	109	28	Wolf, A. P. & Susie, son of

Middlesex - Carlisle Springs Church Graveyard
         Dunker Church Graveyard

CARLISLE SPRINGS CHURCH GRAVEYARD (continued)

Surname	Given Name	Death Mo/Dy/Year	Birth Mo/Dy/Year	Att. Age Yr/Mo/Dy	Cm Ag	Pg	No	Other Information
Wolf	Emanuel	11.13/1844	1.14/1842		3	109	29	Wolf, John & Mary, child of
Wolf	Daniel	7.13/1845	5.10/1831		15	109	30	Wolf, John & Mary, child of
Wolf	Henry David	9.07/1838	11.27/1837		1	109	31	
Zeigler	John	11.09/1863	11.16/1787		76	109	32	
Zeigler	Barbara	3.13/1838		43	44	109	33	
Zeigler	John J.	9.04/1879		87/ 7.14	88	109	34	
Zeigler	Margaret	6.26/1845		46/10.11	47	109	35	Zeigler, John J., first wife of
Zeigler	Susan	5.02/1878		72/ 4.05	73	109	36	Zeigler, J. J., wife of
Zeigler	Mary Ann	4.23/1846	9.18/1828		18	109	37	Zeigler, J. Jacob & Margaret, dau. of
Zeigler	Andrew	5.18/1891		74/ 8.26	75	109	38	
Zeigler	Mary	5.13/1869		47/ 5.19	48	109	39	Zeigler, Andrew, wife of
Zeigler	Susan	6.07/1894	1.28/1823		72	109	40	
Zeigler	Jonathan	5.12/1883	8.28/1817		66	109	41	
Zeigler	Elizabeth	4.19/1895	9.05/1819		76	109	42	Zeigler, Jonathan, wife of
Zeigler	Anna Jane	2.13/1851	4.16/1850		1	109	43	Zeigler, Jonathan & Elizabeth, dau. of

DUNKER CHURCH GRAVEYARD

Surname	Given Name	Death Mo/Dy/Year	Birth Mo/Dy/Year	Att. Age Yr/Mo/Dy	Cm Ag	Pg	No	Other Information
Adams	David	3.16/1887	1.28/1834		54	112	01	
Adams	Barbara N.	5.20/1892		52/11.16	53	112	02	Adams, David, wife of
Bear	Samuel	8.21/1879	/1798	81/10.20	82	112	03	(b. 1798)
Bear	Catharine	8.18/1894		80/ 8.04	81	112	04	Bear, Samuel, wife of
Bear	Alfred G.	8.14/1869		4/ 4.11	5	112	05	Bear, Eli & C., son of
Bear	Martha	11.13/1882		14/ 8.17	15	112	06	Bear, Eli & Catharine, daughter of
Bigham	William H.	12.19/1863		/ 4.06	1	112	07	
Bigham	John	5.24/1864		49/ 4.09	50	112	08	
Bigham	Alfred Joseph H.	6.20/1862		3/10.24	4	112	09	
Buffington	Elizabeth	3.25/1860	10.16/1779		81	112	10	
Buffington	Anna	2.02/1871	12.31/1808		63	112	11	
Carmichael	Joseph	3.03/1880	10.18/1800		80	112	12	
Carmichael	Susannah	11.25/1892	6.22/1810		83	112	13	Carmichael, Joseph, wife of
Curtis	Isaac L.	4.27/1889	4.14/1841		49	112	14	
Dewalt	William	3.27/1875	/1821	54/ 8.25	55	112	15	(b. 1821)
Dice	Fanny M.	9.24/1894		/11.19	1	112	16	Dice, J. W. & M. L., daughter of
Fair	Catharine	5.30/1862		22/ 8.21	23	112	17	Knaub, J. & C., daughter of; from this inscription it cannot be determined if if Fair is a middle or a married name
Knaub	Ella Catharine	12.20/1894		76/ 2.20	77	112	18	Knaub, Jacob, wife of
Kreider	Mary Edna	12.26/1891		/ 5.24	1	112	19	Kreider, Emanuel & Lizzie, daughter of

Middlesex - Dunker Church Graveyard

Surname	Given Name	Death Mo/Dy	Death Year	Birth Mo/Dy	Birth Year	Att. Age Yr	Att. Age Mo/Dy	Cm Ag	Pg	No	Other Information
Leib	Jonas		1875		1803			73	112	20	
Leib	Rebecca		1866		1813			54	112	21	
Lesher	Mary Elizabeth	1.23	1864	10.09	1841			23	112	22	Lesher, John, wife of
Miller	Joseph	7.03	1886	2.09	1812			75	112	23	
Miller	Susannah	5.23	1855			40	11.02	41	112	24	Miller, Joseph, wife of
Miller	Catharine	10.11	1861	3.14	1814			48	112	25	Miller, Joseph, wife of
Miller	Amos B.	9.16	1849	10.05	1847			2	112	26	Miller, Joseph & S., child of
Miller	Sussanah	7.03	1855	5.12	1855			1	112	27	Miller, Joseph & S., child of
Miller	Mary E.	11.28	1862			10	5.20	11	112	28	Miller, Joseph & Susannah, daughter of
Miller	Jacob					44	10.02	45	112	29	
Miller	Harry H.	10.14	1888	9.25	1888			1	113	01	
Miller	George	4.03	1892	12.29	1891			1	113	02	
Myers	Katie E.	6.03	1873	3.21	1863			11	113	03	Myers, Alfred & Mary Jane, daughter of
Neiswanger	Daniel	10.01	1858	5.23	1858			1	113	04	Neiswanger, John & Sarah, son of
Nickey	Elizabeth	2.22	1897		1814	83	10.12	84	113	05	(b. 1814)
Nickey	B. F.	4.18	1889			60	7.16	61	113	06	Rev.
Nickey	Catharine	2.27	1875			44	11.00	45	113	07	Nickey, B. F., wife of
Nickey	George	5.05	1861	8.12	1791			70	113	08	
Nickey	Sarah	11.27	1863	7.27	1797			67	113	09	Nickey, George., wife of
Nickey	Mary Ann	3.21	1867			33	4.00	34	113	10	
Nickey	Jacob	1.27	1864	2.02	1835			29	113	11	
Nickey	Fanny	4.01	1861	7.28	1859			2	113	12	Nickey, Jacob & Esther, child of
Nickey	Joseph E.	10.28	1861	6.30	1861			1	113	13	Nickey, Jacob & Esther, child of
Nickey	Annie J.	7.27	1887			17	5.11	18	113	14	[d. 1887?]
Nickey	David	2.23	1863	7.23	1861			2	113	15	Nickey, Benjamin F. & C., child of
Nickey	Susanna	5.08	1869				7.25	1	113	16	Nickey, Benjamin F. & C., child of
Rebert	John	1.05	1894			90	4.24	91	113	17	[Rebert ?]
Rebert	Christena	10.20	1891			90	3.00	91	113	18	[Christena (sic)] [Rebert ?]
Shatto	Samuel	12.22	1896			88	2.01	89	113	19	
Shatto	Anna M.	9.15	1875			69	9.03	70	113	20	
Strayer	Catharine	10.18	1879	5.03	1827			53	113	21	Strayer, Hiram, wife of
Swords	Benjamin	10.09	1892			63	1.28	64	113	22	
Wilson	Earl McKinley	11.25	1891				2.28	1	113	23	Wilson, John & Annie, son of

Middlesex - Letort Spring Church Graveyard

LETORT SPRING CHURCH GRAVEYARD

Surname	Given Name	Death Mo/Dy	Year	Birth Mo/Dy	Year	Att. Age Yr	Mo/Dy	Cm Ag	Pg	No	Other Information
Albright	Peter	11.04	1871	8.12	1809			63	030	01	
Albright	Hannah	6.01	1892		1792	80	4.09	81	030	02	(b. 1792) [dates and age do not agree]
Albright	Anna	8.04	1865			14	0.06	15	030	03	Albright, Peter & Hannah, daughter of
Albright	Samuel	1.17	1881	3.08	1856			25	030	04	
Albright	Jacob	1.12	1886	6.15	1804			82	030	05	
Albright	Mary	2.22	1885	7.27	1806			79	030	06	Albright, Jacob, wife of
Albright	Jonas	3.15	1897	5.06	1832			65	030	07	
Albright	Mary Shambaugh	8.18	1901	9.13	1834			67	030	08	Albright, Jonas, wife of
Albright	Jacob	2.19	1882	7.22	1836			46	030	09	
Albright	Mary E.	4.23	1878				9.11	1	030	10	Albright, Sophia & ----, child of
Albright	Anna M.	8.24	1878			6	7.12	7	030	11	Albright, Sophia & ----, child of
Albright	Maria Ilgenfritz	7.01	1858			22	0.10	23	030	12	Albright, Jacob & M., daughter of
Albright	Johnny Paul	1.12	1866	9.08	1862			4	030	13	Albright, Jacob & Henrietta, son of
Albright	Emma	4.07	1866				10.14	1	030	14	Albright, Jonas & Mary J., daughter of
Albright	Chester W.	12.20	1884	10.08	1881			4	030	15	Albright, George A. & Sadie E., son of
Allen	Samuel	3.09	1878			74	6.00	75	030	16	
Ashenfelter	Samuel	9.06	1890			69	4.00	70	030	17	
Ashenfelter	Louisa	5.28	1896			74	10.14	75	030	18	
Bair	Elizabeth	3.11	1869		1779	90	10.04	91	030	19	
Basehore	David	4.10	1868	1.16	1795			74	030	20	
Basehore	Sarah	9.19	1850	4.01	1801			50	030	21	Basehore, David, wife of
Bashore	John S.	11.19	1869			41	7.25	42	030	22	
Berkheimer	Harvey	8.11	1887			18	2.10	19	030	24	
Berkheimer	infant son	5.20	1876						030	25	Berkheimer, G. & S. A., son of
Bierbrower	Dora	9.15	1881			5	7.06	6	030	33	
Bierbrower	Elizabeth	4.19	1888			80	6.16	81	030	34	
Blosser	Benjamin	5.22	1882			87	8.22	88	031	10	
Blosser	Margaret	9.29	1902				4.11	1	031	11	
Blosser	Helen M.	3.09	1900				2.11	1	031	12	Blosser, A. C. & Laura, daughter of
Boas	Jacob	4.04	1884	11.05	1815			69	031	02	Rev.
Boas	Franklin Goodman	10.22	1865	12.15	1863			2	031	03	Boas, Jacob & Rebecca, child of
Boas	Henry Goodman	1.10	1851	6.09	1849			2	031	04	Boas, Jacob & Rebecca, child of
Boas	Wesley Augustus	3.02	1852	2.21	1852			1	031	05	Boas, Jacob & Rebecca, child of
Boas	Emma Elizabeth	6.02	1845	4.28	1845			1	031	06	Boas, Jacob & Rebecca, child of
Bolen	Carrie Ruth	12.05	1891				3.00	1	031	07	Bolen, William & Lydia A., daughter of
Bowers	Wilson G.	9.15	1854			4	0.17	5	031	08	Bowers, William & Caroline, child of
Bowers	Alfred S.	9.13	1854				9.26	1	031	09	Bowers, William & Caroline, child of
Braught	Edward A.	7.03	1901			30	1.26	31	030	23	
Breckenmaker	Philip	2.11	1879			91	8.01	92	030	26	
Breckenmaker	Catharine	5.09	1861			75	3.00	76	030	27	Breckenmaker, Philip, wife of
Breckenmaker	Philip	8.06	1896			82	1.08	83	030	28	
Breckenmaker	Lydia	3.03	1901			84	1.12	85	030	29	Breckenmaker, Philip, wife of
Breckenmaker	Susan	7.10	1866	10.11	1819			47	030	30	Breckenmaker, Philip, wife of
Breckenmaker	Andrew	4.20	1858			14	7.16	15	030	31	Breckenmaker, Philip & Susan, son of
Breckenmaker	Magdalene	12.22	1864			19	4.10	20	030	32	Breckenmaker, P. & S., daughter of
Bricker	Sallie G.	12.13	1886				5.20	1	031	01	Bricker, Benjamin & Kate, infant dau. of
Buttorf	John	8.31	1884			67	7.22	68	031	13	
Buttorf	Elizabeth	11.13	1871	3.17	1819			53	031	14	Buttorf, John, wife of

Middlesex - Letort Spring Church Graveyard

Surname	Given Name	Death Mo/Dy	Year	Birth Mo/Dy	Year	Att. Age Yr	Mo/Dy	Cm Ag	Pg	No	Other Information
Coleman	John	9.14	1896			66		67	031	16	
Coleman	Jane								031	17	[no dates given]
Collins	Margaret	1.29	1874			33	7.29	34	031	18	Collins, Amos, wife of
Cornman	Mary					73		74	031	19	
Cornman	William K.	8.12	1887			76	2.15	77	031	20	
Cornman	Elizabeth	11.29	1889			70	3.11	71	031	21	
Cornman	John A.	10.06	1871			15	6.16	16	031	22	Cornman, William & Elizabeth, child of
Cornman	William C.			10.05	1845	5	2.20	6	031	23	Cornman, William & Elizabeth, child of
Cornman	Charles B.	9.05	1872			4	11.17	5	031	24	Cornman, H. P. & E. C., child of
Cornman	Harry A.	7.30	1870				6.11	1	031	25	Cornman, H. P. & E. C., child of
Cramer	John	8.26	1867			29	3.20	30	031	15	Cramer, Jacob & Eliza, son of
Crotzer	Elizabeth	6.30	1870	4.16	1781			90	031	26	
Darr	Samuel	7.12	1871	11.25	1870			1	031	27	Darr, H. & C., son of
Deitch	George W.	2.04	1882			7	4.22	8	031	28	Deitch, Christ & Mary A., son of
Dewalt	Annie E.	4.10	1877			1	6.06	1	031	29	Dewalt, W. C. & J. E., daughter of
Dull	John	4.09	1874	2.24	1802			73	031	30	
Ebersol	John	1.16	1868			85	7.04	86	031	31	
Ebersol	Elizabeth	12.09	1842			50	4.19	51	031	32	Ebersole, Johannes, wife of
Ebersol	John	6.29	1852	10.13	1817			35	031	33	Ebersole, John & Elizabeth, son of
Eppley	Martin Luther		1901		1839			63	031	34	
Eppley	Mary E. Kutz				1846				031	35	Eppley, M. L., wife of
Eppley	Daniel K.		1879		1877			3	031	36	
Eppley	Ella E.		1881		1881			1	031	37	
Eppley	Sarah E.		1887		1885			3	031	38	
Farenbaugh	George	3.30	1901	3.02	1817			85	032	01	
Farenbaugh	Jane			2.02	1820				032	02	Farenbaugh, George, wife of
Farenbaugh	Rebecca Shreiner	2.23	1875			34		35	032	03	Farenbaugh, George & Elizabeth, dau. of
Felgner	Henry	3.02	1858			45	6.08	46	032	05	
Firestine	Ida	1.19	1893			4	10.07	5	032	06	
Fortenbaugh	Sarah E.	9.29	1892			24	0.15	25	032	07	Fortenbaugh, David H., wife of
Fortenbaugh	Setta V.	3.16	1858			2	4.18	3	032	08	Fortenbaugh, D. H. & S. E., daughter of
Fought	Peter	2.11	1852	5.04	1776			76	032	09	
Fought	Elizabeth	12.13	1866	8.05	1804			63	032	10	
Franklin	John G.	3.22	1891			41	0.24	42	032	04	
Fuget	Andrew Clarence	2.07	1882			4	3.01	5	032	11	Fuget, W. A. & A. S., son of
Garber	George W.	3.09	1893				8.20	1	032	12	Garber, H. & J., son of
Gill	Thomas	2.09	1875			77	3.01	78	032	21	
Gill	John C.	4.12	1866			47	4.29	48	032	22	
Gill	B. W.								032	23	Co. F, 17th Pa. Cavalry [no dates given]
Gladfelter	Moses	7.07	1891	2.01	1816			76	032	13	
Gladfelter	Elizabeth	1.15	1901	1.08	1819			83	032	14	
Gladfelter	John	7.23	1896	10.16	1813			83	032	15	
Gladfelter	Susan	11.27	1896	8.28	1805			92	032	16	
Gladfelter	Sarah	6.23	1886	3.15	1850			37	032	17	Gladfelter, Jeremiah, widow of
Gladfelter	Harry M.	8.20	1889			4	9.18	5	032	18	Gladfelter, W. F. & S. J., son of
Green	J. B.								032	19	Lieutenant, Co. F, 17 Pa. Cavalry
Greybill	Dephen	2.10	1881	1.04	1881			1	032	20	Greybill, John & B., son of; [Dephen ?]
Grubb	John	10.14	1880			68	2.06	69	032	24	
Grubb	Elizabeth	4.03	1889			76	0.06	77	032	25	
Grubb	David	1.26	1843	3.16	1842			1	032	26	Grubb, John & Elizabeth, child of

Middlesex - Letort Spring Church Graveyard

Surname	Given Name	Death Mo/Dy	Year	Birth Mo/Dy	Year	Att. Age Yr	Mo/Dy	Cm Ag	Pg	No	Other Information
Grubb	John	6.10	1848	10.20	1847			1	032	27	Grubb, John & Elizabeth, child of
Grubb	William H.	11.28	1850	1.28	1844			7	032	28	Grubb, John & Elizabeth, child of
Grubb	Joseph	11.27	1850	1.13	1849			2	032	29	Grubb, John & Elizabeth, child of
Grubb	Jacob	1.19	1843	9.18	1839			4	032	30	Grubb, John & Elizabeth, child of
Grubb	Christian	12.07	1850	12.19	1848			2	032	31	Grubb, Jacob & Mary, son of
Hach	George N.	11.16	1884			82	5.02	83	032	33	(or Hagh)
Hach	Elizabeth	4.24	1833			72	5.09	73	032	34	(or Hagh)
Hackenberger	Samuel	3.08	1892	10.07	1824			68	032	32	
Hanshaw	Mary E. Braught	4.14	1890	3.04	1860			31	032	35	Hanshaw, Harry, wife of
Hartman	Sarah Melhorn	8.07	1901	4.27	1818			84	032	36	
Hartman	Jacob	12.24	1869	12.31	1804			65	032	37	
Hartman	Isaac	4.22	1864			28	2.00	29	032	38	Hartman, Jacob & Catharine, son of
Hartman	Clara	6.01	1854	3.02	1853			2	032	39	Hartman, Jacob & Sarah, daughter of
Hartman	Harmon	4.03	1860				2.19	1	032	40	Hartman, Jacob & Sarah, daughter of
Heagy	Earl	9.17	1894				0.06	1	033	01	Heagy, G. W. & Ida E., son of
Heiser	Lydia A. Minnich	12.11	1889			52	3.04	53	033	02	
Hemp	Harry E.	4.24	1877			13	6.10	14	033	03	Hemp, J. & L., child of
Hemp	Annie L.	6.02	1876			3	3.20	6	033	04	
Hertzler	Magdalena Witmer	2.26	1874	1.19	1817			58	033	05	Hertzler, A., wife of
Hoerner	Andrew	11.22	1901			81	5.09	82	033	06	
Hoerner	Elizabeth	10.30	1898			71	7.23	72	033	07	
Hoerner	Abraham Goodman	9.01	1859				0.19	1	033	08	Hoerner, Andrew & Elizabeth, child of
Hoerner	Mary Ann	9.04	1849				3.18	1	033	09	Hoerner, Andrew & Elizabeth, child of
Hoffman	Catharine Helen						3.17	1	033	10	
Hosler	Elizabeth					72	5.00	73	033	11	Hosler, John, wife of
Ilgenfritz	Frederick	9.22	1891			75	0.04	76	033	12	
Ilgenfritz	Sarah	10.01	1891			63	9.02	64	033	13	
Ilgenfritz	William			8.22	1831				033	14	[no death date given]
Ilgenfritz	Caroline	4.02	1902	4.23	1836			66	033	15	
Ilgenfritz	Noah	11.23	1858	11.09	1858			1	033	16	
Ilgenfritz	Wesley	2.02	1860	1.31	1860			1	033	17	
Ilgenfritz	Daniel								033	18	[no dates given]
Ilgenfritz	Minnie S. Dunkleberger	3.24	1897			25	5.01	26	033	19	Ilgenfritz, Daniel, wife of
Ilgenfritz	Mary	6.27	1860			59	2.06	60	033	20	Ilgenfritz, Frederick, wife of
Ilgenfritz	Henry	12.02	1850	11.21	1839			12	033	21	Ilgenfritz, Frederick & Mary, son of
Ilgenfritz	Catharine	5.21	1867			41	2.05	42	033	22	Ilgenfritz, William, wife of
Ilgenfritz	Harvey E.	11.16	1874			18	2.21	19	033	23	Ilgenfritz, William & Caroline, son of
Ilgenfritz	Katie E.	11.16	1894			25	5.17	26	033	24	Ilgenfritz, William & Caroline, dau. of
Ilgenfritz	Solomon	1.10	1844	2.22	1829			15	033	25	Ilgenfritz, Jacob & Catharine, son of
Ilgenfritz	Catharine	4.09	1850			55	11.29	56	033	26	Ilgenfritz, Jacob, wife of
Kauffman	Daniel	8.05	1895			75	1.12	76	033	27	
Kauffman	Laura L.	12.21	1870				7.07	1	033	28	
Kauffman	Amanda	3.03	1874			38	11.00	39	033	29	
Keene	Mary	4.01	1831			27	2.20	28	033	33	Keene, M., wife of
Keiser	Mary Ann					62	3.06	63	033	30	Keiser, David, wife of
Kline	Washington	6.20	1900			74	3.28	75	033	31	
Kline	Sarah A.	11.05	1891	8.31	1836			56	033	32	Kline, Washington, wife of
Kuntz	William H.	4.08	1884			57	2.24	58	033	34	
Kuntz	Nancy	5.04	1892			66	1.02	67	033	35	

Middlesex - Letort Spring Church Graveyard

Surname	Given Name	Death Mo/Dy	Year	Birth Mo/Dy	Year	Att. Age Yr	Mo/Dy	Cm Ag	Pg	No	Other Information
Kuntz	Michael	4.18	1872			75		76	033	36	[4/18?/1872]
Kutz	Jacob	5.31	1875	5.18	1796			80	033	37	
Kutz	Sarah	7.07	1883	5.26	1808			76	033	38	Kuts, Jacob, wife of
Kutz	Benjamin D.	7.22	1879	2.24	1834			46	033	39	
Kutz	David	12.15	1871			78	2.25	79	034	01	
Kutz	Lydia Bear	1.09	1889	2.06	1800			89	034	02	Kutz, David, wife of
Kutz	Mary	4.28	1853	11.24	1831			22	034	03	Kutz, David, wife of
Kutz	Henry	3.04	1841			18	4.16	19	034	04	Kutz, David & Lydia, son of
Kutz	George	1.27	1889			59	3.24	60	034	05	
Kutz	Sarah	2.24	1890			64	10.13	65	034	06	Kutz, George, wife of
Kutz	Margaret C.	1.10	1889			34	10.15	35	034	07	Kutz, F. J., wife of
Kutz	Daniel	10.15	1892	12.13	1831			61	034	08	
Kutz	Catharine Witmer	6.27	1899	4.09	1830			70	034	09	Kutz, Daniel, wife of
Kutz	Gideon	2.25	1875			77	7.04	78	034	10	
Kutz	Ann Mary	12.22	1881			81	5.24	82	034	11	
Kutz	Elizabeth	3.29	1857			84	2.07	85	034	12	
Kutz	Benjamin	5.26	1849	8.07	1808			41	034	13	Kutz, Dewalt & Elizabeth, son of
Kutz	Rebecca	11.05	1850	8.13	1846			5	034	14	Kutz, Jacob & Sarah, daughter of
Kutz	William Alfred	11.10	1854	1.26	1853			2	034	15	Kutz, George & Sarah, son of
Kutz	Levi	1.06	1865			22	0.20	23	034	16	Kutz, Jacob & Sarah E., son of; Co. A, 101st Regt., Pennsylvania Volunteers; d. at Roanoke Island, NC
Kutz	Sarah J.	3.01	1888			48	1.21	49	034	17	
Kutz	Harvey A.	3.17	1879	2.19	1852			28	034	18	
Kutz	Eve	6.17	1851	6.12	1814			38	034	19	Kutz, Isaiah, wife of
Kutz	Elizabeth	8.02	1872			41	4.08	42	034	20	Kutz, Daniel, wife of
Kutz	Anna Mary	1.30	1854	1.22	1801			54	034	21	Kutz, Samuel, wife of
Kutz	Fanny M. Ilgenfritz	8.15	1888			20	6.14	21	034	22	Kutz, William M., wife of
Kutz	Sarah	6.15	1875	5.18	1853			23	034	23	Kutz, Charles, wife of
Kutz	Catharine	6.13	1870			44	7.11	45	034	24	Kutz, John, wife of
Kutz	Lizzie	5.18	1872			16	5.21	17	034	25	Kutz, John & C., daughter of
Kutz	Manda E.	3.13	1851	7.28	1844			7	034	26	Kutz, John & Catharine, daughter of
Kutz	D. Webster	6.16	1893			2	1.18	3	034	27	Kutz, William M. & Mary E., son of
Low	Michael	1.00	1881	8.00	1800			81	034	28	
Low	Susan	12.17	1893	2.14	1811			83	034	29	Low, Michael, wife of
Low	Solomon	10.09	1864			24	0.22	25	034	30	Sergeant, Co. F, 17th Pennsylvania Cavalry; wounded in Shenandoah Valley, August 25, 1864
Lyter	Jacob								034	31	Co. F, 17th Pa. Cavalry [no dates given]
Lyter	Robert	9.22	1850	10.11	1847			3	034	32	Lyter, Jacob & Rebecca, son of
Lyter	Joseph	3.21	1850	3.27	1837			13	034	33	Lyter, Joseph & Barbara, son of
Lyter	John	9.07	1859			4	4.04	5	034	34	Lyter, John & Elizabeth, son of
Lyter	Joseph	12.31	1850	6.01	1845			6	034	35	Lyter, John & Elizabeth, son of
Manning	Sadie C.	5.31	1878			21	8.19	22	034	36	Manning, Christian S., wife of; Wise, Isaac & M. J., daughter of
Martin	David	12.11	1890	12.08	1817			74	035	01	
Martin	Margaret			12.25	1825				035	02	
Martin	Sallie E.	1.21	1886			8	0.05	9	035	03	
Martin	Mervin F.	2.13	1890	7.09	1886			4	035	04	Martin, J. A. & M. E., son of
Martin	Minnie A.	7.25	1872				7.19	1	035	05	Martin, W. & C., daughter of

Middlesex - Letort Spring Church Graveyard

Surname	Given Name	Death Mo/Dy	Year	Birth Mo/Dy	Year	Att. Age Yr	Cm Mo/Dy	Pg Ag	No	Other Information
Martin	Samuel E.	9.06	1899				4.22	1	035 06	Martin, J. W. & E. [?] M., [son] of [text says daughter of]
Mathias	Harry E.	5.11	1899			13	5.23	14	035 07	Martin, J. C. & A. M., son of; [last name uncertain, but probably Mathias]
McBride	Annie C.	7.13	1885	1.27	1841			45	035 15	McBride, J. C., wife of; Breckenmaker, P. & S., daughter of
McBride	John C.	5.23	1888	10.04	1842			46	035 16	
McBride	Abram B.	7.04	1889	7.28	1870			19	035 17	McBride, J. C. & A. C., son of
Meals	Angeline E.	9.11	1860				1.02	1	035 08	Meals, George W. & M. E., daughter of
Melester	Alexander	9.22	1887			65	0.28	66	035 09	
Mohler	Samuel	3.31	1883			53	1.18	54	035 10	
Mohler	Jacob R.	2.09	1871						035 11	Mohler, S. & E., son of; aged 3 years, 17 months, 18 days
Mohler	Mary C.	1.31	1859				0.28	1	035 12	Mohler, S. & E., daughter of
Mohler	Albert H.	5.24	1858			3	6.27	4	035 13	
Mohler	Clara A.	5.25	1858			5	7.26	6	035 14	
Nailor	Daniel	1.14	1878			62	11.04	63	035 18	
Nailor	Catharine	2.17	1876			57	3.01	58	035 19	Nailor, Daniel, wife of
Nailor	Amanda	11.20	1897			57	6.25	58	035 20	
Neff	Susan	9.30	1900	12.11	1819			81	035 21	
Neisley	Jesse W.	8.21	1899			27	4.03	28	035 23	
Neisley	Elizabeth	3.02	1889			39	5.23	40	035 24	Neisley, Jacob B., wife of; Wolgemuth, J. M., daughter of
Niesley	Jacob	4.05	1879	7.01	1810			69	035 25	
Niesley	Eli W.	6.04	1877	9.06	1868			9	035 26	Niesley, Jacob B. & Elizabeth, son of
Niesley	Fanny	2.14	1895	1.04	1811			85	035 27	
Nevel	Jacob	11.00	1851	1.10	1796			56	035 22	d. Nov 31, 1851
Paul	Jacob	3.07	1861			75		76	035 28	
Paul	Barbara	12.17	1864			78	9.11	79	035 29	Paul, Jacob, wife of
Paul	Jacob	8.25	1877			56	11.11	57	035 30	
Paul	Sarah J.	10.24	1858			15	8.28	16	035 31	Paul, Jacob & E., child of
Paul	Henrietta	3.14	1864			10	2.21	11	035 32	Paul, Jacob & E., child of
Paul	Catharine E.	12.24	1869				8.29	1	035 33	Paul, Henry & Lydia A., daughter of
Porter	Joseph F.	6.15	1889			61	11.21	62	035 34	
Porter	Ellis F.	8.30	1863			3	7.03	4	035 35	Porter, M. & J. F., son of [3?/07.03]
Pyke	-----	3.24	1900				0.10	1	035 36	Pyke, J. H. & S. E., son of
Railing	John	3.02	1901			60	0.10	61	036 01	
Railing	Catharine Ann	5.15	1884			38	6.25	39	036 02	
Reaghert	John M.	2.06	1893			49	4.03	50	036 03	
Reaghert	Mary Smeagh	7.02	1872	5.30	1845			28	036 04	
Reaghert	Magdalene	7.25	1892			78	3.18	79	036 05	
Reemer	John	1.12	1848	12.25	1799			49	036 06	
Reemer	Elizabeth	12.30	1856	7.12	1799			58	036 07	Reemer, John, wife of
Rinehart	Emma M.	6.28	1888			28	0.02	29	036 08	Rinehart, J. C., wife of
Ruch	Samuel	4.10	1847	8.10	1807			40	036 15	
Ruhl	Jesse	10.07	1891	3.05	1812			80	036 09	
Ruhl	Emma A.	10.15	1892	4.02	1850			43	036 10	
Ruhl	Mary A.	1.12	1897	6.29	1820			77	036 11	
Ruhl	Christian	12.18	1851	1.14	1787			65	036 12	
Ruhl	Moses	3.05	1841	11.11	1838			3	036 13	Ruhl, Jesse & Mary, son of

Middlesex - Letort Spring Church Graveyard

Surname	Given Name	Death Mo/Dy	Year	Birth Mo/Dy	Year	Att. Age Yr	Mo/Dy	Ag	Cm	Pg	No	Other Information
Ruhl	Christian	10.26	1824	11.10	1815			9	036	14		
Ryder	Charles E.	12.05	1876	9.03	1866			11	036	16		Ryder, S. C. & J. C., son of
Ryder	Lucetta	6.07	1876	2.10	1869			8	036	17		Ryder, S. G. & J. C., daughter of
Saretell	Maria	1.00	1879	7.12	1829			50	036	18		Low, M. & S., daughter of
Seitz	Lucetta M.	10.12	1858			1	11.27	2	036	26		Seitz, S. W. & M. A., child of
Seitz	Minnie E.	8.16	1863	4.16	1862			2	036	27		Seitz, S. W. & M. A., child of
Sites	Rebecca	12.13	1900			50	10.03	51	036	28		
Shetron	Lizzie	9.30	1897	8.18	1866			32	036	23		Shetron, D. N., wife of
Shetron	Maudie	6.21	1902	4.07	1894			9	036	24		
Shreiner	Rebecca	2.23	1875			34		35	036	22		Farenbaugh, George & Elizabeth, dau. of
Shuff	Delilah	3.11	1864			40	10.20	41	037	07		[text reads "Dlilah"]
Shuff	Anna A.	8.16	1865			8	9.04	9	037	08		Shuff, James & E., daughter of
Smec [?]	George P.	8.15	1898			1	10.02	2	036	25		Smec [?], H. A. & A. M., son of
Smith	James	10.09	1902	5.15	1835			68	036	29		
Smith	Elizabeth Kutz			9.06	1831				036	30		Smith, James, wife of
Smith	Susanna	7.18	1856	12.15	1855			1	036	31		Smith, Jacob A. & Anna, child of
Smith	Anna E.	2.09	1855	9.20	1854			1	036	32		Smith, Jacob A. & Anna, child of
Snyder	Henry	1.24	1885	7.16	1812			73	037	09		
Snyder	Elizabeth	7.28	1886	7.12	1809			78	037	10		
Snyder	Amanda	3.03	1862			7	3.22	8	037	11		Snyder, Henry & E., daughter of
Snyder	Harry	1.17	1871			3	5.21	4	037	12		Snyder, J. N. & M., son of
Sowers	B. F.		1899		1876			24	036	40		
Sowers	Minnie B.		1900		1874			27	036	41		Sowers, B. F., wife of
Sowers	Nellie G.		1899		1897			3	036	42		
Stickle	Jacob	9.06	1867			67		68	036	33		
Stickle	Jacob	4.06	1883			38	7.25	39	036	34		
Stickle	Catharine	1.13	1885			84	3.14	85	036	35		
Stickle	Peter	11.30	1857	10.14	1856			2	036	36		Stickle, J. & C., son of
Stickle	Daniel A.	11.07	1895			21	11.27	22	036	37		
Stickle	Mervin	10.28	1894				4.20	1	036	38		
Stone	Harriet I.	6.07	1893			41	1.17	42	037	01		Stone, George W., wife of
Stone	Harry E.	1.20	1875				0.14	1	037	02		Stone, G. W. & H., child of
Stone	George W.	10.28	1873				0.01	1	037	03		Stone, G. W. & H., child of
Stone	John	4.25	1876	3.04	1871			6	037	04		Stone, Henry & Anna, child of
Stone	Sarah Ellen	2.14	1875	5.28	1874			1	037	05		Stone, Henry & Anna, child of
Stone	Lizzie A.	9.13	1867			1	5.25	2	037	06		Stone, Israel & Jane, daughter of
Strausbaugh	Elminah Ashenfelter	6.10	1875			31	0.21	32	036	19		Strausbaugh, William, wife of; Ashenfelter, S. & L., daughter of
Strickler	Mary G.	2.18	1866				1.09	1	036	39		Strickler, John H. & Kate, daughter of
Swanger	Lizzie	1.14	1887			25	10.12	26	036	20		
Swanger	Elizabeth	2.27	1899			77	2.17	78	036	21		
Tobias	Simon	10.15	1860			48		49	037	14		
Trego	Rebecca	7.18	1884	4.06	1846			39	037	13		Trego, Parker M., wife of; Stickle, J. & C., daughter of
Troup	Samuel S.	3.17	1894	10.20	1822			72	037	15		
Troup	Elizabeth			8.27	1823				037	16		
Troup	George W.	2.08	1895	1.08	1852			44	037	17		
Troup	Mary E. Sidesinger	2.24	1895	12.22	1857			38	037	18		Troup, George W., wife of
Ulrich	Christiann	2.25	1865			58		59	037	19		Ulrich, John, wife of
Ulrich	Susan Mountz	4.19	1876			51	6.01	52	037	20		Ulrich, John, wife of

Middlesex - Letort Spring Church Graveyard

Surname	Given Name	Death Mo/Dy	Year	Birth Mo/Dy	Year	Att. Age Yr	Mo/Dy	Cm Ag	Pg	No	Other Information
Waidly	Susanna	2.12	1857			36	11.08	37	037	21	Waidly, Amos, consort of
Waidly	William H.	2.16	1858			18	1.23	19	037	22	Waidly, Amos S., child of
Waidly	Eleanora					6	8.02	7	037	23	Waidly, Amos S., child of
Wanbaugh	Mary E.	9.10	1896	8.15	1849			48	037	24	
Weary	Samuel	8.02	1885	4.16	1812			74	037	25	
Weary	Maria	2.04	1898	2.02	1818			81	037	26	
Weary	Sarah E.	12.27	1846			1	5.02	2	037	27	Weary, Samuel & Maria, child of
Weary	Oliver F.	5.16	1848	8.25	1843			5	037	28	Weary, Samuel & Maria, child of
Weary	Paul B.	11.24	1901	11.13	1896			6	037	29	
Weary	Keller A.	7.19	1898	2.13	1898			1	037	30	
Weitzel	Mary	8.07	1900			57	6.01	58	037	35	
Westfall	Henry	1.20	1891	3.09	1817			74	037	31	
Westfall	Jeremiah	4.25	1872	12.02	1844			28	037	32	
Westfall	Catharine	11.12	1861	11.16	1852			9	037	33	
Westfall	William	1.11	1857	7.11	1855			2	037	34	
Wink	Daniel	5.03	1896	5.09	1807			89	037	36	
Wink	Catharine	11.13	1874	12.09	1808			66	037	37	Wink, Daniel, wife of
Wink	Rebecca	7.24	1854	12.04	1832			22	037	38	Wink, Daniel & Catharine, daughter of
Wise	Anna M.	4.26	1884	2.04	1863			22	038	01	Jackson, Samuel H., wife of [name ?]
Witmer	Samuel	12.14	1893	3.04	1825			69	038	02	
Witmer	Clarissa Williams	3.14	1898	1.22	1833			66	038	03	Witmer, Samuel, wife of
Witmer	Joseph	8.27	1853	2.10	1785			69	038	04	
Witmer	Catharine Eberly	4.29	1876	6.08	1792			84	038	05	Witmer, Joseph, wife of
Witmer	Rebecca	3.12	1830	9.10	1827			3	038	06	
Witmer	Benjamin E.	7.29	1853	8.17	1832			21	038	07	
Witmer	Benjamin		1872		1871			2	038	08	
Witmer	Lizzie		1875		1864			12	038	09	
Witmer	Samuel		1880		1873			8	038	10	
Witmer	John	11.23	1837	9.08	1820			18	038	11	
Wonders	-----	1.21	1887			2	5.03	3	038	12	Wonders, Daniel & Sarah, son of
Zeigler	Gertie M. Kutz	1.30	1901			21	11.20	22	038	14	
Zettler	Elizabeth	2.12	1869	5.07	1780			89	038	13	Zettler, George, wife of

Middlesex - Mennonite Graveyard at Balfour
Old Hoffer Farm Graveyard
Peter Albright Farm Graveyard

MENNONITE GRAVEYARD AT BALFOUR

Surname	Given Name	Death Mo/Dy	Death Year	Birth Mo/Dy	Birth Year	Att. Age Yr	Att. Age Mo/Dy	Cm Ag	Pg	No	Other Information
Gingrich	Peter	8.23	1888	4.13	1799			90	111	01	
Gingrich	Elizabeth	6.10	1869	11.18	1798			71	111	02	Gingrich, Peter, wife of
Grosz	Margaret	9.18	1863			6	1.16	7	111	03	
Grosz	Emma F.	1.26	1886			11	3.18	12	111	04	
Grosz	Christian	3.03	1891			46	11.20	47	111	05	
Grosz	John	11.12	1890		1812	78	2.27	79	111	06	(b. 1812)
Grosz	Catharine	4.16	1891		1818	73	2.22	74	111	07	(b. 1818)
Hastings	Mary	10.05	1838			1	1.02	2	111	08	Hastings, William S. & Fanny, dau. of
Hastings	William S.	1.31	1840			30	1.27	31	111	09	[middle initial S ?]
Hastings	Frances	12.13	1846			29	4.15	30	111	10	Hastings, William S., wife of
Jackson	Martha	7.28	1863		1808	55	7.12	56	111	11	Jackson, Joseph, wife of; (b. 1808)
Miller	Jacob	12.11	1844		1775	68		69	111	12	(b. 1775)
Miller	Sarah G.	8.05	1852			2	11.10	3	111	13	Miller, Samuel & M. I., daughter of
Miller	David	11.28	1863	12.24	1790			73	111	14	
Miller	Mary	9.21	1883			92	6.06	93	111	15	
Railing	Andrew	1.24	1886			42	11.01	43	111	16	
Railing	Rebecca	12.13	1889		1851	38	4.09	39	111	17	(b. 1851)
Stouffer	Jennie E.	2.26	1872				3.00	1	111	18	Stouffer, B. R. & J. H., daughter of
Weitzel	Jacob	4.05	1872	11.20	1804			67	111	19	
Weitzel	Ida L.	5.09	1876						111	20	Weitzel, J. & M., daughter of

OLD HOFFER FARM GRAVEYARD

Surname	Given Name	Death Mo/Dy	Death Year	Birth Mo/Dy	Birth Year	Att. Age Yr	Att. Age Mo/Dy	Cm Ag	Pg	No	Other Information
Miller	John	1.10	1812			66		67	114	01	General
Miller	Matthew, Sr.	8.28	1790			72		73	114	02	

PETER ALBRIGHT FARM GRAVEYARD

Surname	Given Name	Death Mo/Dy	Death Year	Birth Mo/Dy	Birth Year	Att. Age Yr	Att. Age Mo/Dy	Cm Ag	Pg	No	Other Information
Cornprobst	Sarah	10.15	1831			27		28	110	01	Cornprobst, Joseph, wife of

MIFFLIN TOWNSHIP

BETHANY CHURCH GRAVEYARD

Surname	Given Name	Death Mo/Dy	Death Year	Birth Mo/Dy	Birth Year	Att. Age Yr	Age Mo/Dy	Cm Ag	Pg	No	Other Information
Barrack	Andrew	8.29	1892			75	3.21	76	272	01	
Barrack	Hannah G.	5.31	1860			1	2.19	2	272	02	Barrick, Andrew & Rebecca, child of [spelling varies in entries 01-06]
Barrack	Daniel	6.26	1864			19	5.02	20	272	03	Barrick, Andrew & Rebecca, child of
Barrack	Caroline A.	7.31	1868			11	8.15	12	272	04	Barrick, Andrew & Rebecca, child of
Barrick	David L.	2.15	1900			67	2.27	68	272	05	
Barrick	Malachi	11.11	1858				0.06	1	272	06	Barrack, David & Margaret, son of
Barrick	Martin W.	10.15	1874				5.04	1	272	07	
Barrick	Clara B.	4.05	1871				3.00	1	272	08	
Barrick	Simon J.	12.19	1875				3.13	1	272	09	
Barrick	John A.	3.02	1859				5.09	1	272	10	Barrick, Jonathan A. & Nancy, child of
Barrick	James A.	8.18	1864				10.11	1	272	11	Barrick, Jonathan A. & Nancy, child of
Barrick	David H.	9.26	1867				8.09	1	272	12	Barrick, Jonathan A. & Nancy, child of
Barrick	Calvin	11.09	1868				0.13	1	272	13	Barrick, Jonathan A. & Nancy, child of
Barrick	Samuel W.	9.16	1873				2.21	1	272	14	Barrick, Jonathan A. & Nancy, child of
Barrick	Henry E.	12.30	1876				0.01	1	272	15	Barrick, Jonathan A. & Nancy, child of
Carothers	Elizabeth E.	12.16	1857			2	2.21	3	272	16	Carothers, A. & Catharine, daughter of
Christlieb	Charles G.	3.13	1867			35	1.00	36	272	17	
Christlieb	Edgar H.	9.16	1861				6.13	1	272	18	Christlieb, C. G. & Mary J., son of
Clinepeter	Adaline C.	4.24	1866			23	6.24	24	272	19	
Conner	Ralph S.	10.19	1892				1.07	1	272	20	
Conner	Emma M.	11.04	1890				5.27	1	272	21	
Deardorff	John A.			7.22	1846				272	22	
Deardorff	Jennie E.			7.04	1850				272	23	Deardorf, John A., wife of
Deardorff	Jacobi L.	5.03	1894	5.13	1892			2	272	24	[Jacobi (sic)]
Dickson	John A.	3.27	1859			4	2.25	5	272	25	Dickson, J. E. & S. A., son of
Dunlap	Malinda	9.18	1871			29	0.18	30	272	26	Dunlap, Hugh T., wife of
Evig	Mary Magdalene	5.09	1874		1791	83	11.09	84	272	27	(b. 1791)
Gilmore	John H.	2.24	1875			49	6.09	50	272	28	
Gilmore	Margaret Jane	4.29	1864			36	2.12	37	272	29	Gilmore, John H., wife of
Hoon	George	9.02	1866			64	11.21	65	272	30	
Hoon	Elizabeth	5.02	1885			84		85	272	31	Hoon, George, wife of
Hoon	W. Alexander S.	11.23	1863			3	11.20	4	272	32	Hoon, G. & E., son of
Humberger	Joseph	6.03	1864			33		34	272	33	[text reads "in her 34th year"]
Hurley	Jane Mary	3.29	1883	4.04	1849			34	272	34	Hurley, James, wife of
Hurley	Maggie E.	2.25	1879			1	10.23	2	272	35	Hurley, James & J. M., daughter of
Hurley	John M.	11.03	1899			23	9.09	24	273	01	Hurley, George & Sarah, son of
Martin	Lewis H.	8.02	1881				0.19	1	273	02	Martin, S. O. & Annie, son of
Mixell	Solomon	1.16	1872				7.23	1	273	03	Mixell, John G. & S. J., son of
Phreaner	Samuel R.	11.24	1859			5	1.02	6	273	04	Phreaner, Charles & Rebecca, son of
Piper	George M.	2.12	1864			1	6.07	2	273	05	Piper, George & Agness, son of
Reed	Philip	5.11	1873			42	11.11	43	273	06	
Reed	John E.	6.12	1875			3	8.17	4	273	07	Reed, P. & A., son of
Snoke	Emanuel	2.14	1891			73	7.06	74	273	08	[aged 6? days]
Snoke	Leah	10.28	1893			75	8.23	76	273	09	

Mifflin - Bethany Church Graveyard

Surname	Given Name	Death Mo/Dy	Year	Birth Mo/Dy	Year	Att. Age Yr	Mo/Dy	Cm Ag	Pg	No	Other Information
Snoke	Aaron	12.06	1863			6	0.06	7	273	10	
Snoke	Edwin H.	1.17	1883			4	0.10	5	273	11	Snoke, S. C. & Anna M., son of
Thomas	Nancy	12.18	1887			37	2.20	38	273	12	Thomas, G. W., wife of
Walters	Carrie I.	3.17	1868				8.14	1	273	13	Walters, J. C. & M. C., dau. of [186<u>8</u> ?]
Weaver	Charley H.	12.12	1875			7	7.12	8	273	14	
Whisler	William	5.04	1867			30	0.17	31	273	15	
Whisler	Abram	5.08	1886	1.12	1834			53	273	16	
Whisler	Solomon	1.01	1880			2	11.26	3	273	17	Whisler, Abraham & Sarah, child of
Whisler	Levi	5.07	1871			4	1.10	5	273	18	Whisler, Abraham & Sarah, child of
Whisler	John	12.03	1864				0.12	1	273	19	Whisler, Abraham & Sarah, child of
Whisler	Jeremiah	1.04	1880			7	5.11	8	273	20	
Whistler	Daniel	4.25	1880			73	2.13	74	273	21	
Whistler	David	6.29	1884	10.04	1809			75	273	22	
Whistler	Nancy	6.24	1876			64	4.10	65	273	23	Whistler, David L., wife of

Mifflin - Bethel Church Graveyard

BETHEL CHURCH GRAVEYARD

Surname	Given Name	Death Mo/Dy	Death Year	Birth Mo/Dy	Birth Year	Att. Age Yr	Cm Mo/Dy	Ag	Pg	No	Other Information
Armold	John	1.14	1887			65	2.24	66	263	01	Co. L, 9th Regt., Pa. V. C.
Baker	Peter	5.20	1864			74	9.11	75	263	02	
Baker	Leah	6.09	1883	7.31	1797			86	263	03	
Barrick	Daniel	12.07	1873			73	9.27	74	263	04	
Barrick	Elizabeth	5.11	1887	6.20	1795			92	263	05	
Barrick	Mary Ellen	10.27	1863			3	5.08	4	263	06	Barrick, John & Mary J, child of
Barrick	Charles F.	7.15	1878			0	11.08	1	263	07	Barrick, John & Mary J, child of
Barrick	John A.				1833				263	08	
Barrick	Mary		1905		1839			67	263	09	Barrick, John A., wife of
Barrick	Mary E.		1863		1860			4	263	10	
Barrick	Charles Y.		1878		1877			2	263	11	
Dunbar	Clara B.	12.22	1900			27		28	263	12	Dunbar, E. H., wife of
Fahnestock	John	2.22	1864			22	4.16	23	263	13	a soldier
Fahnestock	Christina	1.22	1871			67		68	263	14	Fahnestock, John, wife of
Fahnestock	John	8.01	1874			69	10.17	70	263	15	
Fahnestock	Maggie L.	8.01	1880	6.09	1880			1	263	16	Fahnestock, George & S., daughter of
Foose	Gertrude May	9.19	1900			11	4.12	12	263	17	Foose, J. W. & Louisa, daughter of
Fry	Frederick		1901		1820			82	263	18	
Fry	Elizabeth		1889		1817			73	263	19	
Gottschall	Solomon	2.08	1856			35	11.05	56	263	20	
Heckman	Philip	4.30	1864			87	7.06	58	263	21	
Heckman	Sussannah	2.15	1876			90	6.00	61	263	22	Heckman, Philip, wife of
Hurley	Alexander	10.16	1901			81		82	263	23	Private, Co. I, 101st Regt.
Hurley	Sarah	6.29	1900	5.05	1826			75	263	24	Hurley, Alexander, wife of
Hurley	James	2.08	1867			89	1.17	90	263	25	a soldier
Hurley	Leah	8.02	1894			68	10.19	69	263	26	Hurley, George, wife of
Hurley	Adam M.	1.28	1871			8	6.26	9	263	27	Hurley, George & Leah, son of
Ickes	Miller			4.28	1842				263	28	
Ickes	Emeline	3.17	1885	6.18	1844			41	263	29	Ickes, Miller, wife of
Ickes	John W.	7.02	1876	10.16	1875			1	263	30	Ickes, Miller, child of
Ickes	Stacy G.	2.02	1891	5.01	1889			2	263	31	Ickes, Miller, child of
Kennedy	Alexander	3.16	1904			67		68	263	32	Private, Co. D, 187th Regt.
Kesnel	John	12.08	1900						263	33	Private, Co. K, 158th Regt., Pennsylvania Volunteer Infantry
Miller	Adam	11.17	1880			78	10.22	76	263	34	
Miller	Barbara E.	2.08	1877			72	6.14	73	264	01	Miller, Adam, wife of
Mitchell	William	4.15	1864			45		46	264	02	
Moffitt	Rosetta E.	2.06	1904				10.01	1	264	03	Moffitt, D. A. & L. E., daughter of
Neideigh	David	9.28	1887			59	0.04	60	264	04	
Spangler	Annie B.		1898		1867			32	264	05	
Stum	John								264	06	Co. H, 202nd Pennsylvania Infantry
Stum	Arthur N.	2.11	1905	9.28	1904			1	264	07	Stum, W. A. & M. E., child of
Stum	Ola R.	9.23	1881	8.13	1881			1	264	08	Stum, W. A. & M. E., child of
Stum	Edward D.	9.30	1901	4.30	1898			4	264	09	Stum, W. A. & M. E., child of
Yost	Etthal I.	9.03	1892			1	5.00	2	264	10	Yost, W. D. & S. A., daughter of [Etthal (sic)]
Zeigler	Frances					36	8.00	37	264	11	Zeigler, John L., wife of; d. Dec. 9, 186-

Mifflin - Center Church Graveyard

CENTER CHURCH GRAVEYARD

Surname	Given Name	Death Mo/Dy	Death Year	Birth Mo/Dy	Birth Year	Att. Age Yr	Age Mo/Dy	Cm Ag	Pg	No	Other Information
Bear	Benjamin								265	01	[no dates given]
Bear	Lavina A.	4.23	1901			35		36	265	02	Bear, Francis, wife of
Bower	Nancy	8.27	1873			68	4.17	69	265	03	Bower, David, wife of
Clouse	Jacob M.	11.26	1877			38	7.06	39	265	10	
Clouse	Mary E.	10.08	1879	4.02	1849			31	265	11	
Cohick	Christian F.	1.07	1901			79		80	265	04	soldier
Cohic	Sarah Ann	1.13	1897			71		72	265	05	Cohic, C. F., wife of [spelling varies]
Cohic	George W.	9.02	1871			16	5.17	17	265	06	Cohic, C. F. & Sarah Ann, child of
Cohick	Anna C.	3.11	1886			24	10.00	25	265	07	Cohic, C. F. & Sarah Ann, child of [spelling varies]
Cohick	Laura F.	9.24	1889			22	11.16	23	265	08	
Cohic	Barney	11.15	1892			28		29	265	09	
Daelhousen	Henry Daniel	5.02	1853			86	7.18	87	265	12	
Daelhousen	Ann Catharine	12.11	1846			72	7.24	73	265	13	Daelhousen, Henry, wife of; gray sand head stone
Daelhousen	Daniel	2.04	1880			79	8.15	80	265	14	
Daelhousen	Barbara	2.08	1875			73	3.23	74	265	15	Daelhousen, Daniel, wife of
Dewalt	Jeremiah	5.24	1902	5.26	1824			78	265	16	
Dewalt	Rebecca	2.25	1897			69	5.04	70	265	17	Dewalt, Jeremiah, wife of
Dewalt	Elizabeth Ellen	2.05	1875			20	7.17	21	265	18	Dewalt, J. & R., daughter of
Dull	Joseph	2.08	1880	6.16	1816			64	265	19	
Dull	Leah	12.28	1858	7.04	1824			35	265	20	Dull, Joseph, wife of
Ensminger	Jacob	7.20	1837	10.31	1759			78	265	21	b. in Lebanon Co.; d. in Mifflin twp.
Ensminger	Magdalana	8.21	1836			69	0.25	70	265	22	Ensminger, Jacob, wife of
Ensminger	Jacob	4.10	1861			62	6.01	63	265	23	
Ensminger	Mary A.	9.29	1890			87	5.25	88	265	24	Ensminger, Jacob, wife of
Ensminger	Daniel	2.05	1851	5.17	1849			2	265	25	Ensminger, Jacob & Mary A., son of
Ensminger	Mary Ann	3.03	1881			33	5.17	34	265	26	
Ensminger	Molly	1.04	1838				11.25	1	265	27	
Ensminger	Joseph	1.12	1847			3	3.16	4	265	28	
Ensminger	Hannah S.	9.14	1883			28	6.04	29	265	29	Ensminger, Francis A., wife of; [S.?]
Ensminger	George	11.10	1892			85	2.22	86	265	30	
Ensminger	Rebecca	3.28	1858			45	1.28	46	265	31	Ensminger, George, wife of [3/28?/1858]
Ensminger	David	1.16	1847			8	3.16	9	265	32	Ensminger, George & Rebecca, child of
Ensminger	Washington	1.31	1847			5	10.00	6	266	01	Ensminger, George & Rebecca, child of
Ensminger	Jacob H. [?]	12.23	1856			22	9.15	23	266	02	
Finkenbinder	David	8.31	1867	12.20	1791			76	266	26	
Finkenbinder	Elizabeth	4.15	1870	12.19	1796			74	266	27	
Fry	Sarah	1.25	1873	8.25	1852			21	266	28	
Fry	William A.	2.14	1898	11.18	1870			28	266	29	
Fry	Frederick G.		1905		1904			2	266	30	
Gayman	Jonas	12.04	1891			73	1.08	74	266	03	
Gayman	Elizabeth	11.30	1901			81	5.10	82	266	04	
Gees	Jacob	3.03	1885			73	8.14	74	266	05	
Gees	Nancy	1.24	1894			81	6.17	82	266	06	
Greeger	John A.	12.29	1850			22	3.16	23	266	07	
Greeger	George	8.01	1878			74	9.19	75	266	08	
Greeger	Victor Roy	11.11	1889				11.20	1	266	09	Greeger, G. W. & I. J., son of

Mifflin - Center Church Graveyard

Surname	Given Name	Death Mo/Dy	Death Year	Birth Mo/Dy	Birth Year	Att. Age Yr	Att. Age Mo/Dy	Cm Ag	Pg	No	Other Information
Gutshall	John	11.26	1901			80	1.00	81	266	10	
Gutshall	Mary	3.09	1902			78	6.06	79	266	11	
Gutshall	Oliver Jacob	8.21	1877			16	7.06	17	266	12	Gutshall, John & Mary, son of
Gutshall	Daniel	8.04	1899			83		84	266	13	
Gutshall	Mary	9.21	1895			76		77	266	14	
Gutshall	William	5.23	1901	1.15	1824			78	266	15	
Gutshall	Maria	7.22	1899	3.09	1822			78	266	16	
Gutshall	Isaac		1902		1854			49	266	17	
Gutshall	Mary Alice		1902		1899			4	266	18	
Gutshall	David W.		1902		1845			58	266	19	
Gutshall	George W.		1878		1878			1	266	20	
Gutshall	Mervin M.		1887		1872			16	266	21	
Gutshall	John H.	9.03	1873				3.10	1	266	22	
Gutshall	Arthur E.	9.27	1878				9.19	1	266	23	
Gutshall	Lizzie	10.09	1890			43	1.00	44	266	24	Gutshall, J. D., wife of
Gutshall	Simon	12.08	1899			51	3.03	52	266	25	
Hamilton	W. H.	10.05	1880			45	11.24	46	266	31	
Hamilton	Margaret A.	12.21	1894	8.29	1827			68	266	32	
Hamilton	Maggie M.	2.18	1881				7.10	1	266	33	Hamilton, Thomas M. & M. J., dau. of
Heckendorn	Lulu Blanche	4.26	1893			4	6.20	5	266	34	Heckendorn, Charles & Hettie, dau. of
Henry	George	10.20	1874	3.31	1817			58	266	35	
Henry	Sarah	6.17	1904	10.18	1820			84	266	36	
Henry	John	1.23	1851			3	9.26	4	266	37	Henry, George & Sarah, child of
Henry	David W.	1.31	1851			1	4.27	2	266	38	Henry, George & Sarah, child of
Henry	John	8.24	1878			65	11.24	66	266	39	
Henry	Nancy	2.16	1878			65	1.03	66	266	40	Henry, John, wife of
Henry	William	12.03	1888			77	5.18	78	266	41	
Henry	Elizabeth	4.13	1894			83	7.11	84	266	42	Henry, J. W., wife of
Henry	Joseph M.	7.16	1884				8.03	1	266	43	Henry, George H. & J. E., son of [8.03?]
Henry	Joseph			4.24	1823				266	44	[death date not given]
Henry	Anna E.	4.07	1900	6.07	1820			80	267	01	
Henry	Elmina	10.05	1862			1	9.10	2	267	02	Henry, T. M. & R., child of
Henry	Carrie Jarine	9.24	1866				0.05	1	267	03	Henry, T. M. & R., child of
Henry	John M.	2.04	1870			7	7.00	8	267	05	Henry, T. M. & R., child of
Hershey	Isaac	5.23	1886	2.21	1824			63	267	05	
Hershey	Elizabeth	3.30	1893	8.10	1827			66	267	06	Hershey, Isaac, wife of
Hershey	Samuel S.	8.12	1862	12.02	1847			15	267	07	Hershey, Isaac & Elizabeth, child of
Hershey	Harvey B.	10.25	1870	5.16	1866			5	267	08	Hershey, Isaac & Elizabeth, child of
Hershey	Catharine L.	11.12	1854	9.07	1853			2	267	09	Hershey, Isaac & Elizabeth, child of
Hershey	Jemima	12.10	1861	9.17	1855			7	267	10	Hershey, Isaac & Elizabeth, child of
Hershey	Mary	1.21	1845						267	11	Hershey, John, wife of; age near 64 yrs.
Hoover	Lizzie D.	2.05	1875			20	8.17	21	267	12	Hoover, John, wife of
Jacoby	Catharine		1903		1818			86	267	13	
Jacoby	Mary	3.22	1876			74	6.24	75	267	14	
Jumper	John	5.07	1851			44		45	267	15	
Jumper	Clark Victor	3.13	1893			1	4.04	2	267	16	Jumper, Theodore & Laura, son of
Knettle	George	10.12	1816			76		77	267	17	
Knettle	Elizabeth C.	12.28	1817			70		71	267	18	Knettle, George, consort of
Knettle	Isaac	8.08	1826			41	8.25	42	267	19	
Landis	Henry	5.31	1890			81	6.16	82	267	20	

Mifflin - Center Church Graveyard

Surname	Given Name	Death Mo/Dy	Year	Birth Mo/Dy	Year	Att. Age Yr	Mo/Dy	Cm Ag	Pg	No	Other Information
Landis	Elizabeth	1.02	1891			68	10.15	69	267	21	Landis, Henry, wife of
Landis	Rosanna	10.19	1862			8	2.24	9	267	22	Landis, Henry E., daughter of
Landis	Charles S.	10.19	1881			5	11.18	6	267	23	
Landis	Myrtle Z.	10.14	1889				1.08	1	267	24	
Lay	Catharine	2.11	1853			24	4.17	25	267	25	Lay, George, wife of
Lay	John	6.26	1865	10.20	1819			46	267	26	
Lay	Elizabeth	3.01	1875			54	5.00	55	267	27	Lay, John, wife of
Lehman	George	6.10	1880			64		65	267	28	
Lehman	Nancy	12.27	1895			72	8.25	73	267	29	
Lehman	William C.	3.09	1883			19	1.02	20	267	30	Lehman, George & Nancy, child of
Lehman	Joseph	10.27	1862			9	7.22	10	267	31	Lehman, George & Nancy, child of
Lehman	Simon	11.08	1862			12	1.22	13	267	32	Lehman, George & Nancy, child of
Lehman	Annie Florence	3.30	1887				9.17	1	267	33	Lehman, G. W. & Maggie, daughter of
McCallister	Elizabeth	2.15	1896			42		43	268	07	McCallister, John, wife of
McGlin	John M.	8.20	1861				0.17	1	268	08	McGlin, S. & E., son of
Miller	Juleyann	1.28	1832			36	11.00	37	267	34	
Miller	Henry	8.22	1848			56	5.06	57	267	35	
Miller	John	6.24	1849			68	2.18	69	267	36	
Miller	Rachel	7.03	1853			66	8.22	67	267	37	
Miller	John	2.27	1871			54	11.00	55	267	38	Miller, John & Rachel, son of
Miller	John M.	5.22	1862	10.23	1803			59	268	01	
Miller	Bertha K.	2.26	1897	2.22	1896			2	268	02	Miller, S. & A., daughter of
Miller	Lucinda	11.20	1900			60		61	268	03	
Moffitt	William	7.15	1887			59	11.15	60	268	04	Co. A, 87th Regt., Pennsylvania Vols.
Mohler	George Perkins	3.21	1886	3.05	1886			1	268	05	
Mumper	Mary	1.26	1880			28	8.27	29	268	06	Mumper, Arnold R., wife of
North	George	9.06	1835						268	09	aged 23 yrs. & 1 mo. (or 33 yrs.)
North	Jacob	10.08	1850			55	3.24	56	268	10	
Oiler	Peter	5.04	1874			53	11.28	54	268	11	[aged 2_8_ days (?)]
Oiler	Susan	11.30	1893			76	8.13	77	268	12	Oiler, Peter, wife of
Oiler	George H.	4.08	1896	6.11	1866			30	268	13	killed by the explosion of an engine
Over	Mabel V.	5.02	1895			4	3.23	5	268	14	
Railing	George	7.26	1860	7.12	1794			67	268	15	
Railing	Ann Barbara	9.23	1886	4.22	1805			82	268	16	Railing, George, wife of
Railing	Henry	12.28	1863			75	4.17	76	268	17	
Railing	Catharine	3.09	1846			58	4.00	59	268	18	Railing, Henry, wife of
Railing	Samuel	2.21	1893			76	2.29	77	268	19	
Railing	Rosanna	7.25	1892			72	9.02	73	268	20	Railing, Samuel, wife of
Railing	Mary C.	9.15	1846				1.23	1	268	21	Railing, Samuel & Rosanna, child of
Railing	Jacob H.	1.25	1852			2	2.10	3	268	22	Railing, Samuel & Rosanna, child of
Railing	Emma S.	1.15	1858				2.08	1	268	23	
Railing	Sarah	1.23	1894			43	6.01	44	268	24	Railing, Levi A., wife of
Reeder	Anna	10.08	1887			6	11.20	7	268	25	Reeder, E. & Sarah J., daughter of
Rider	Emanuel	10.20	1852			13	9.21	14	268	26	Rider, William & Anna M., son of
Rynard	Susannah	10.22	1886	4.28	1818			69	268	27	Rynard, Cyrus A., wife of
Rynard	George W.	12.10	1886	6.03	1846			41	268	28	
Salter	David	3.19	1893	8.19	1827			66	268	29	
Salter	Elizabeth	5.18	1866			34	2.02	35	268	30	Salter, David, wife of; Show--, Henry & Mary, daughter of; (or Skow--)
Smith	George	11.27	1901			79	8.22	80	268	31	

Mifflin - Center Church Graveyard

Surname	Given Name	Death Mo/Dy	Death Year	Birth Mo/Dy	Birth Year	Att. Age Yr	Att. Age Mo/Dy	Cm Ag	Pg	No	Other Information
Smith	Mary	9.28	1897			78	8.25	79	268	32	
Smith	Effie	10.23	1898			15	0.25	16	268	33	[d. 10.23 ?]
Smith	Leffery	4.27	1902			55	10.13	56	269	01	
Sollenberger	John A.	11.11	1893			46	5.10	47	269	02	
Stum	Jacob	8.19	1872			55	9.25	56	269	03	
Stum	Lydia	4.23	1887			46	1.07	47	269	04	
Stum	Michael	4.08	1899			72	0.27	73	269	05	
Stum	Mary Catharine	8.01	1885			23	4.06	24	269	06	
Thomas	John	9.16	1896	5.24	1819			78	269	07	
Thomas	Mary	4.09	1890			66	7.29	67	269	08	Thomas, John, wife of
Thomas	Samuel G.			3.22	1880				269	09	
Whistler	Christian	12.28	1814			39	1.00	40	269	14	
Whistler	Catharine	7.01	1868			89	2.21	90	269	15	Whistler, Christian, wife of
Whistler	Abraham	12.25	1856			71	10.02	72	269	16	
Whistler	Susanna E.	2.13	1845			56	4.02	57	269	17	Whistler, Abraham, wife of
Whisler	Susan	2.15	1845						269	18	
Whistler	Isaac	12.23	1874			63	5.17	64	269	19	
Whistler	Sophia	8.28	1899			88		89	269	20	Whistler, Isaac, wife of
Whistler	John	7.14	1874			79	0.28	80	269	21	
Whistler	Easter	3.04	1876			78	6.17	79	269	22	
Whistler	Mary	4.17	1877			60		61	269	23	
Whistler	Joseph	10.04	1900	10.25	1831			69	269	24	
Whistler	Samuel E.	10.03	1904	5.04	1839			66	269	25	
Whistler	Mary A.	4.22	1902	9.25	1847			55	269	26	
Whistler	Elizabeth Ann	12.31	1852	2.12	1851			2	269	27	Whistler, John & Nancy, daughter of
Whistler	Alfred S.		1903		1867			37	269	28	
Whistler	Nancy	6.16	1804			47	11.17	48	269	29	Whistler, Daniel, wife of
Whistler	Sarah	1.16	1853			30		31	269	30	Whistler, David A., wife of
Whistler	Gillen	8.28	1852			2	11.01	3	269	31	Whistler, Elias & Mary, child of
Whistler	Mary E.	5.27	1855				3.02	1	269	32	Whistler, Elias & Mary, child of
Whistler	Emmie S.	3.02	1875				2.18	1	269	33	Whistler, George & Elizabeth, child of
Whistler	Samuel Ira	12.30	1883				5.26	1	269	34	Whistler, George & Elizabeth, child of
Widders	Sarah Ann	4.27	1863			35	5.30	36	269	10	Widders, Samuel, wife of
Wise	Samuel	7.15	1830			38		39	269	11	
Wise	Elizabeth	4.19	1843			51	9.19	52	269	12	Wise, Samuel, wife of
Wise	Abraham	1.08	1832			64		65	269	13	
Wolf	David	2.04	1851			1	11.04	2	269	35	Wolf, Samuel & S., son of
Wolf	Sarah Anna	11.08	1862			6	2.00	7	269	36	Wolf, Samuel & S., son of

Mifflin - Mount Hope Cemetery

MOUNT HOPE CEMETERY

Surname	Given Name	Death Mo/Dy	Year	Birth Mo/Dy	Year	Att. Yr	Age Mo/Dy	Cm Ag	Pg	No	Other Information
Barrick	Bruce Sherden	11.17	1904			2	5.08	3	271	01	
Hosler	George	11.19	1886			67	0.10	68	271	02	
Hosler	Mary	9.23	1870			46	0.02	47	271	03	Hosler, George, wife of [death and age identical for 03 and 04]
Hosler	Catharine	9.23	1870			46	0.02	47	271	04	Hosler, George, wife of [see above]
Hosler	Catharine	4.07	1885			42	8.07	43	271	05	Hosler, George, wife of
Hosler	Joseph		1900		1821			80	271	06	
Hosler	Elizabeth	11.22	1863			5	8.00	6	271	07	
Hosler	Bertie C.	4.14	1888			12		13	271	08	
Hosler	John Earl	3.23	1856			2	0.01	3	271	09	Hosler, L. E. & J. D., son of
Jumper	Charles Wilmer		1904		1884			21	271	10	
Lay	Jacob	6.23	1884		1805	79	3.17	80	271	11	(b. 1805)
Stump	Michael M.	2.08	1905			72		73	271	12	Private, Co. C, 138th Pa. Vols., Inf.
Thomas	John Loyd	9.19	1882			1	6.05	2	271	13	Thomas, J. A., & Sue, son of
Whistler	Paul Basom	1.04	1902				0.02	1	271	14	Whistler, G. T. & A. Rebecca, son of

Mifflin - Snoke Graveyard

SNOKE GRAVEYARD

Surname	Given Name	Death Mo/Dy	Death Year	Birth Mo/Dy	Birth Year	Att. Age Yr	Cm Mo/Dy	Cm Ag	Pg	No	Other Information
Bistline	Lydia	1.10	1881			42	8.10	43	270	01	Bistline, Andrew, wife of
Bistline	Sarah C.	10.22	1880			8	8.25	9	270	02	Bistline, Andrew & Lydia, child of
Bistline	Mary E.	10.30	1867				2.12	1	270	03	Bistline, Andrew & Lydia, child of
Bowman	Samuel	5.05	1877			67	7.16	68	270	04	
Bowman	Margaret	4.06	1860			48	6.23	49	270	05	Bowman, Samuel, wife of
Bowman	Sarah Ann	7.09	1872			25	7.11	26	270	06	Bowman, Samuel & Margaret, daughter of
Bowman	Henry W.	12.17	1900			57	9.28	58	270	07	
Bowman	George G.	6.23	1878			2	1.29	3	270	08	Bowman, Henry & Susan, child of
Bowman	William H.	10.21	1870				4.15	1	270	09	Bowman, Henry & Susan, child of
Bowman	Manerva Jane	9.02	1868				9.25	1	270	10	Bowman, Henry & Susan, child of
Bowman	Joseph	1.06	1875	2.17	1838			37	270	11	Bowman, Maria, husband of
Bowman	Jane E.	2.17	1875			38	0.01	39	270	12	Bowman, Benjamin F., wife of
Bowman	John W.	8.18	1873				3.04	1	270	13	
Bowman	George A.	1.21	1873			1	7.25	2	270	14	
Bowman	Benjamin F.	5.30	1873				0.16	1	270	15	
Burkhart	John	7.24	1900	12.19	1837			63	270	16	
Burkhart	Rebecca	2.24	1879	3.03	1844			35	270	17	Burkhart, John, wife of
Burkhart	Martin	8.03	1885	2.01	1864			22	270	18	[d. 1885 ?]
Burkhart	Jesse	1.19	1893	9.06	1874			19	270	19	
Burkhart	Charlie	11.24	1889				4.24	1	270	20	
Burkhart	Leah Fanny	1.09	1871				0.02	1	270	21	Burkhart, John & Rebecca, daughter of
Hollar	John	9.00	1865	11.11	1799			66	270	22	
Hollar	Rosanna	9.20	1865	11.14	1813			52	270	23	Hollar, John, wife of
Lambert	Catharine	7.17	1854			70		71	270	24	
Snoke	John	7.13	1866			81	5.17	82	270	26	Rev.
Snoke	Hannah	7.30	1867			81	4.26	82	270	27	
Steerick	Hannah	4.25	1853			28	3.13	29	270	25	
Whisler	John	6.21	1859			38	6.06	39	270	28	
Whisler	John	2.06	1861		1781	80	0.15	81	270	29	(b. 1781)
Whisler	Joseph	11.25	1883			77	3.12	78	270	30	
Whisler	Moses	9.21	1850			41	0.08	42	270	31	
Whisler	Maria A.	3.15	1889	10.09	1811			78	270	32	Whisler, Moses, wife of
Whisler	Elizabeth	10.15	1838			1	6.25	2	270	33	Whisler, Moses & M., child of
Whisler	Joseph	4.06	1839			5	11.04	6	270	34	Whisler, Moses & M., child of
Whisler	Susan	11.08	1846			4	7.28	5	270	35	Whisler, Moses & M., child of

Mifflin - Zeigler's Church Graveyard

ZEIGLER'S CHURCH GRAVEYARD

Surname	Given Name	Death Mo/Dy	Year	Birth Mo/Dy	Year	Att. Yr	Age Mo/Dy	Ag	Cm Pg	No	Other Information
Allman	Christopher	5.02	1806		1742			65	228	01	
Asper	George	11.13	1865	6.00	1787			79	228	02	
Asper	Salome	10.28	1871	1.01	1797			75	228	03	
Christlieb	Solomon	5.11	1850	2.18	1797			54	228	04	[2/18?/1797]
Christlieb	Isaac	5.22	1858	3.27	1791			68	228	05	
Christlieb	George	1.06	1846	5.29	1784			62	228	06	
Christlieb	Catharine	10.30	1837		1744			94	228	07	
Christlieb	Charles	6.27	1837	6.01	1750			88	228	08	
Diehl	Joseph	10.09	1859	1.16	1796			64	228	09	
Diehl	Susannah	5.27	1847	4.14	1793			55	228	10	Diehl, Joseph, wife of
Diel	Elizabeth				1775				228	11	d. 1845?
Diel	Peter		1812		1753			60	228	12	
Dunlap	Anna	3.15	1855		1794			62	228	13	Dunlap, Thomas, wife of
Failor	Christian	1.16	1845	7.14	1772			73	229	01	
Failor	Christina	4.23	1862	1.15	1779			84	229	02	Failor, Christian, wife of
Gilmore	John	8.13	1826	4.00	1798			29	229	03	
Giveler	Henry	3.31	1835	1.22	1773			63	229	04	
Heberlig	Barbara	11.11	1827	10.00	1801			27	229	05	Heberlig, John, wife of
Hemminger	Jacob	4.01	1830	10.09	1765			65	229	06	
Hemminger	Susan	5.23	1863	8.14	1778			85	229	07	Hemminger, Jacob, wife of
McDermond	Henry	3.13	1857		1792			66	229	13	
McDermond	Mary	5.09	1862		1796			67	229	14	McDermond, Henry, wife of
Mentzer	Frederick	9.03	1864		1790			75	229	08	
Mentzer	Catharine	7.02	1860	4.18	1777			84	229	09	Mentzer, Frederick, wife of
Myers	Jacob	8.28	1838	8.19	1761			78	229	10	
Myers	Margaret	10.28	1834						229	11	Myers, Jacob, wife of; b. 175-
Myers	John	9.14	1823	11.09	1781			42	229	12	
Ramp	Samuel	4.20	1868	9.00	1793			75	229	15	
Ramp	Elizabeth	3.23	1868	12.03	1794			74	229	16	
Ramp	Philip	10.31	1843	8.10	1760			84	229	17	
Ramp	Elizabeth	12.20	1835	12.24	1758			77	229	18	
Roush	Jacob	3.25	1861		1788			74	229	19	
Roush	Elizabeth	3.25	1861	4.10	1784			77	229	20	Roush, Jacob, wife of
Stoneberger	Elizabeth	8.10	1837		1767			71	229	21	
Wise	Elizabeth	8.15	1840		1772			69	229	22	
Zeigler	John	4.29	1863	6.00	1787			76	229	23	
Zeigler	Catharine	10.14	1856	3.00	1787			70	229	24	

Newton - Irishtown Church Graveyard

NEWTON TOWNSHIP

IRISHTOWN CHURCH GRAVEYARD

Surname	Given Name	Death Mo/Dy	Year	Birth Mo/Dy	Year	Att. Age Yr	Mo/Dy	Cm Ag	Pg	No	Other Information
Aby	John H.	10.23	1880			7	2.04	8	275	01	Aby, John W. & M. E., son of
Barrick	Daniel	12.25	1898			80	7.27	81	275	02	
Barrick	Mary J.	10.03	1872			34	5.08	35	275	03	Barrick, G. W., wife of
Barrick	Susan E.	12.11	1903			62	8.13	63	275	04	
Beaston	John								275	05	Co. F, 207th Pennsylvania Infantry
Bitner	J. Clyde	10.20	1891			1	2.26	2	275	06	Bitner, J. L. & Clara, child of
Bitner	Grace V.	12.11	1895			3	0.17	4	275	07	Bitner, J. L. & Clara, child of
Bitner	John Bosler	8.31	1902	7.01	1900			3	275	08	Bitner, J. L. & Clara, child of
Bitner	infant son								275	09	[no information given]
Clody	Emily	2.29	1856			1	1.21	2	275	11	Clody, David & Mary, daughter of
Conner	Catharine	10.15	1873	11.07	1824			49	275	10	
Diven	Thomas	2.28	1879			47	4.12	48	275	13	
Diven	Sarah Jane	1.19	1864			2	4.12	3	275	14	Diven, Thomas & Susan, daughter of
Diven	Ida E.	8.28	1881			7	6.19	8	275	15	
Diven	Jacob	11.10	1883			74	11.22	75	275	16	
Diven	Margaret	6.02	1882			66		67	275	17	Diven, Jacob, wife of
Diven	Margaret A.	3.01	1899			51		52	275	18	
Dovener	James	5.17	1898			80	10.02	81	275	12	Private, Co. E, 3rd Reg., U. S. Arty.
Failor	Elenora	7.04	1897	1.24	1848			55	275	19	Failor, Israel, wife of
Finkenbinder	Catharine	12.24	1857	12.14	1852			6	275	20	Finkenbinder, John & Margaret, dau. of
Finkenbinder	Susan	3.10	1883			25	3.10	26	275	21	
Finkenbinder	William								275	22	Co. E, 130th Pennsylvania Infantry
Finkenbinder	William S.	11.30	1874				10.08	1	275	23	Finkenbinder, William & S. E., son of
Finkenbinder	William	7.12	1887	11.24	1803			84	275	24	
Finkenbinder	Nancy A.	8.24	1873			54	3.09	55	275	25	Finkenbinder, William F., wife of
Finkenbinder	Mary C.	1.21	1858			2	1.00	3	275	26	Finkenbinder, W. & Nancy, daughter of
Finkenbinder	John	2.05	1858			4	3.20	5	276	01	Finkenbinder, William & Nancy, son of
Finkenbinder	John	1.17	1885	12.09	1807			78	276	02	
Finkenbinder	Margaret	1.28	1900			81	6.00	82	276	03	
Forehope	Eve	9.21	1872			87		88	276	04	
Forehope	Rosannah	5.20	1877			66	7.07	67	276	05	
Forehope	Jacob	9.08	1890			77	8.12	78	276	06	
Forehope	Catharine	2.19	1873			57	9.25	58	276	07	Forehope, Jacob, wife of
Forehope	John Winebrenner	2.22	1846				1.22	1	276	08	Forehope, Jacob & Catharine, son of
Forehope	Samuel M.	6.21	1857			22	6.23	23	276	09	
Fosnaught	John	7.18	1883			64	10.03	65	276	10	
Fosnaught	Eliza	7.02	1893	6.13	1824			70	276	11	
Fosnaught	Jane A.	3.06	1864	3.07	1853			11	276	12	Fosnaught, John & Eliza, child of
Fosnaught	John E.	6.11	1866			11	8.15	12	276	13	Fosnaught, John & Eliza, child of
Fosnot	John E.	3.14	1880				2.14	1	276	14	Fosnot, J. J. & Kate, son of
Gardner	William W.		1901		1855			47	276	15	
Getter	Frederick J.	3.14	1860			8	3.02	9	276	16	Getter, G. & M., child of
Getter	William W. W.	2.16	1860			1	5.00	2	276	17	Getter, G. & M., child of; [W. W. (sic)]
Gilbert	Eve	5.12	1881	11.19	1826			55	276	18	Gilbert, William, wife of
Harvey	Mary Jane	3.10	1891			36	1.10	37	276	19	
Hefflebower	Samuel B.	4.07	1872			2	3.17	3	276	20	Hefflebower, H. W. & S. A., son of

Newton - Irishtown Church Graveyard

Surname	Given Name	Death Mo/Dy	Year	Birth Mo/Dy	Year	Att. Age Yr	Mo/Dy	Cm Ag	Pg	No	Other Information
Hoover	Henry H.	8.15	1877			47	10.03	48	276	21	
Householder	Flossy Byrl	8.31	1886				8.00	1	276	22	
Jacoby	Eugene A.	2.01	1873			2	1.21	3	276	23	
Jacoby	William	10.03	1873			28	10.26	29	276	24	
Kendig	Daniel	5.14	1809		1727	82	11.08	83	276	25	(b. 1727)
Kendig	Susannah	4.18	1872			66	8.19	67	276	26	Kendig, Daniel, wife of
Kendig	Daniel Bowman	2.16	1861			20	7.16	21	276	27	Kendig, Daniel & Susannah, son of
Kendig	Henry	5.17	1875			79	2.19	80	276	28	
Kendig	Catharine	5.09	1861			62	11.15	63	276	29	Kendig, Henry, wife of
Kendig	Michael S.	5.12	1863			20	9.15	21	276	30	Kendig, Henry & Cath., son of; soldier
Kendig	Emanuel H.	1.05	1884			29	5.06	30	276	31	
Kendig	Rudolph	1.23	1881	7.04	1798			83	276	32	
Kendig	Eliza A.	2.09	1886			85	10.05	86	276	33	Kendig, Rudolph, wife of
Kendig	Henry R.	5.25	1858			32	5.25	33	276	34	
Kendig	Tobias B.	12.30	1880			24	1.09	25	276	35	[mid. init. B ?]
Kendig	Jacob W.	7.07	1860				7.00	1	276	36	
Kendig	Henry T.	9.27	1860				10.00	1	276	37	
Kendig	Mary	9.02	1861			1	10.09	2	277	01	Kendig, Samuel & Sarah, daughter of
Kendig	Arlington	12.18	1858			4	5.00	5	277	02	Kendig, Samuel & Sarah, son of
Kough	David E.	8.29	1892			53	8.16	54	277	03	
Kough	Mary C.	5.06	1870			3	5.25	4	277	04	Kough, D. E. & Sarah A., child of
Kough	Norissa L.	5.07	1881			3	11.10	4	277	05	Kough, D. E. & Sarah A., child of
Kough	Sarah E.	3.00	1876				1.02	1	277	06	Kough, D. E. & Sarah A., child of
Kough	S. S.	4.24	1881			11	4.04	12	277	07	Kough, B. F. & Margaret, child of
Kough	Philip N.	11.06	1873			11	2.07	12	277	08	Kough, B. F. & Margaret, ch. of; killed
Kuhn	Isaac	12.29	1889			9	3.19	10	277	09	
Kuhn	Sarah	11.27	1884			65	8.15	66	277	10	Kuhn, Isaac, wife of
Lutz	Lydia	2.22	1866			46	1.07	47	277	11	Lutz, John S., wife of
Lytle	Robert A.			10.21	1860				277	12	
Lytle	Emma T.	10.15	1904	9.09	1861			44	277	13	Lytle, Robert A., wife of
Marquart	William W.	8.27	1900	10.07	1855			45	277	14	
Miller	Margaret M.	2.20	1859			37	11.20	38	277	15	Miller, Samuel, Jr., wife of
Miller	David	8.24	1893			65		66	277	16	
Miller	Elizabeth	2.29	1860			4		5	277	17	Miller, D. & M., daughter of
Miller	Addie K.		1863				1.05	1	277	18	Miller, D. & M., dau. of; d. 2/29 1863 [possibly a confusion of month and day with the entry above]
Mixel	John	6.23	1874			86		87	277	19	
Mixel	Eva	12.26	1877			84	3.00	85	277	20	
Rowe	Peter	7.12	1877			81	1.05	82	277	21	
Rowe	Elizabeth	10.07	1890			89	7.17	90	277	22	Rowe, Peter, wife of
Rowe	Tobias C.			4.02	1829				277	23	
Rowe	Sarah A.			3.25	1837				277	24	Rowe, Tobias, wife of
Rowe	Emma Jane	1.27	1858			1	5.00	2	277	25	
Rowe	infant son	11.02	1867						277	26	Rowe, Peter & Mary E., son of
Row	Harry Eugene	12.23	1866				7.15	1	277	27	Row, W. & L., son of
Rushmyer	John	12.12	1885			67		68	277	28	Co. I, 10th Regt., V. R. C.; transferred from Co. I, 7th Regt., M. V.
Ruth	Henry	5.24	1853	9.18	1829			24	277	29	
Ruth	John	2.27	1846			68	6.21	69	277	30	

Newton - Irishtown Church Graveyard

Surname	Given Name	Death Mo/Dy	Year	Birth Mo/Dy	Year	Att. Age Yr	Mo/Dy	Cm Ag	Pg	No	Other Information
Snoke	M. Jane	6.06	1892			49	7.07	50	277	35	
Snoke	John	12.06	1904			64	9.29	65	277	36	
Spangler	William	9.05	1888			64	10.20	65	277	31	a soldier
Spangler	Minnie A.	3.28	1882			16	10.23	17	277	32	
Spangler	Elvina								277	33	[no dates given]
Speck	Mary M.	3.20	1860			39		40	277	34	
Stover	Elmer E.	4.28	1884			34	3.16	35	277	37	[aged 34 ?]
Wagner	Samuel	3.05	1855			46	7.16	47	277	38	
Wagner	Nancy	2.19	1890			79		80	277	39	Wagner, Samuel, wife of
Waggoner	Henry Alexander	2.12	1858				6.15	1	277	40	Waggoner, J. & L., son of
Waggoner	Nancy Ellen	1.14	1858			4	5.12	5	278	01	Waggoner, S. & N., daughter of
Wagner	Nancy E.		1862		1856				7	278	02	
Walker	Mary E.	11.30	1869			23	7.03	24	278	03	Walker, Ezekiel & Harriet, child of
Walker	James Milton	3.08	1849				0.26	1	278	04	Walker, Ezekiel & Harriet, child of
Walker	Peter Row	8.07	1852						278	05	d. aged ? yrs. 6 mos. 4 days
Weaver	Jacob	5.06	1879			69	1.14	70	278	06	
Weaver	Barbara A.	5.18	1877			64	4.24	65	278	07	Weaver, Jacob, wife of
Weaver	George	2.28	1850	11.26	1849			1	278	08	Weaver, Jacob & Barbara, son of
Wickline	Elizabeth Brigen	12.25	1855		1848			8	278	09	Wickline, John & Mary Ann, daughter of b. September 31, 1848
Wickline	John Thompson	12.15	1855	10.24	1845			11	278	10	Wickline, John & Mary Ann, son of
Wilson	Charles A.	2.18	1884			7	1.00	8	278	11	Wilson, R. H. & M. E., son of
Wolf	Sarah E.	4.25	1864			3	0.12	4	278	12	Wolf, David S. & S., daughter of
Yarlets	Dazzie May	10.05	1886				2.02	1	278	13	Yarlets, David & Mary, daughter of

OAKVILLE U. B. CEMETERY

Surname	Given Name	Death Mo/Dy	Year	Birth Mo/Dy	Year	Att. Yr	Age Mo/Dy	Ag	Cm	Pg	No	Other Information
Bowers	Mary E.	1.05	1873	3.08	1840			33	279	07		Bowers, David H., wife of
Brandt	Jane	12.11	1888			51	4.05	52	279	01		Brandt, Joseph, wife of
Brandt	Joseph	2.02	1899			65	7.26	66	279	02		
Brandt	Lizzie M.	5.03	1888			17	10.15	18	279	03		
Brewster	Charles	3.04	1885	2.16	1824			62	279	04		
Brewster	Judith C.	7.26	1891			64		65	279	05		
Brewster	Elizabeth R.	10.22	1862	2.01	1857			6	279	06		
Crider	Jacob	1.31	1888			77	3.07	78	279	08		
Eckman	Joseph	12.07	1883			61	6.21	62	279	09		
Forney	Rebecca	4.11	1884			75		76	279	10		
Gelvin	Miles	2.18	1873	2.07	1811			63	279	11		
Gelvin	Catharine	2.24	1894			81	0.23	82	279	12		
Gelvin	Mary E.	6.10	1861	10.16	1840			21	279	13		Gelvin, James & Mary, daughter of
Harmony	John F.	12.05	1886			54	3.19	55	279	14		
Husler	Sarah Jane	3.11	1879			17	1.00	18	279	15		
Lehman	Henry	8.07	1889			70	8.19	71	279	16		
Lehman	Mary A.	11.17	1862			47	11.17	48	279	17		Lehman, H., wife of
Lehman	Jacob A.	9.11	1877				9.00	1	279	18		Lehman, William & Susan, child of
Lehman	George	8.09	1885				0.04	1	279	19		Lehman, William & Susan, child of
Livingston	Frank C.	9.13	1865				1.25	1	279	20		Livingston, John & Elizabeth, child of
Livingston	Annie M.	12.25	1864				7.00	1	279	21		Livingston, John & Elizabeth, child of
Long	David L.	11.05	1860			27		28	279	22		
Long	Benjamin T.						9.00	1	279	23		Long, D. L. & M., son of
Long	Mary Jane	6.29	1875			37		38	279	24		Long, Aaron D., wife of; d. aged 37 years, ? months, 14 days
Miller	David A.	4.05	1894			46		47	279	25		
Miller	George Mervin	4.09	1900	3.29	1881			20	279	26		
Owen	Alexander	12.03	1861	10.22	1820			42	279	27		Rev.
Quigley	Mary	10.11	1874			1	1.09	2	279	28		Quigley, J. K. & L. S., daughter of
Sheets	Elizabeth	3.01	1864			76	6.27	77	279	29		Sheets, David, wife of
Shriner	William	4.11	1890			77	11.15	78	280	05		
Smith	Belser	7.04	1831			86		87	279	30		brown sand headstone broken and held together by wires
Smith	Magdalena	7.04	1831			86		87	280	01		Smith, B., wife of
Smith	William	4.22	1899			92		93	280	02		
Smith	Susanna	2.01	1879			67	11.22	68	280	03		Smith, William, wife of
Smith	Samuel	6.06	1899			68		69	280	04		
Varner	Elizabeth	8.15	1889			74	3.10	75	280	06		
Waggoner	Joseph	2.16	1863			68		69	280	07		
Waggoner	Hannah	10.15	1868			63	9.15	64	280	08		
Whistler	Elizabeth	2.21	1901	8.26	1824			77	280	09		
Whistler	Joseph	9.27	1892	10.13	1817			75	280	10		
Whistler	Sarah	5.14	1875			58	5.06	59	280	11		Whistler, Joseph, wife of
Whistler	Jacob M.	4.09	1873	8.26	1848			25	280	12		Whistler, Joseph & Sarah, son of
Zinn	T. R.								280	13		Co. F., 130th Pennsylvania Infantry
Zinn	Jenette B.	3.07	1859	6.03	1853			6	280	14		Zinn, A. B. & M. A., daughter of

Newton - Old Roads Graveyard

OLD ROADS GRAVEYARD

Surname	Given Name	Death Mo/Dy	Year	Birth Mo/Dy	Year	Att. Age Yr	Age Mo/Dy	Cm Ag	Pg	No	Other Information
Bet	Maria								281	01	b. Sept. 16 --; d. Sept. 30, --; marker is red sand stone & broken; inscription is in German and almost entirely illegible; information doubtful
Conner	Laura Bell	3.28	1851	11.13	1849			2	281	02	
Flickinger	Elizabeth	5.31	1847			49	0.13	50	281	03	
Hiskey	Margaret	10.28	1830			12	5.09	13	281	04	
Kenage	Catharine	3.19	1819			61	4.01	62	281	05	Kenage, Joseph, wife of
Kenage	Rachel	8.30	1824				11.12	1	281	06	Kenage, Joseph & Elizabeth, daughter of
Kenage	Henry	3.27	1849			61	6.01	62	281	07	
Rhodes	Philip		1824						281	08	d. ---- -- 1824
Rhodes	Jacob		1824			29		30	281	09	
Rhodes	Barbara		1824			75		76	281	10	
Roads	Jacob	3.04	1837			87	5.02	88	281	11	a soldier of the Revolution

STOUGHSTOWN LUTHERAN CHURCH GRAVEYARD

Surname	Given Name	Death Mo/Dy	Death Year	Birth Mo/Dy	Birth Year	Att. Age Yr	Mo/Dy	Cm Ag	Pg	No	Other Information
Cope	Sarah E.	6.12	1863	5.31	1860			4	262	01	Cope, Samuel & Rebecca, daughter of
Farner	Lydia	3.28	1870						262	02	Farner, Conrad, wife of
Goodhart	Ezemiah R.	4.10	1863			10	0.23	11	262	03	Goodhart, William & S., daughter of
Goodhart	Anna P.	3.05	1876			1	11.24	2	262	04	Goodhart, C. A. & A. E., daughter of
Hettrick	William H.	10.29	1866			20	1.04	21	262	05	
Mellinger	Christopher	6.07	1871			57	7.27	58	262	06	
Mellinger	Christopher	9.12	1853	11.29	1849			4	262	07	Mellinger, Christopher & Nancy, son of
Miller	Savilla G.	12.25	1869			4	10.21	5	262	08	Miller, G. B. & H., child of
Miller	John H.	8.17	1870				5.14	1	262	09	Miller, G. B. & H., child of
Miller	Rebecca L.	3.09	1879			7	10.04	8	262	10	Miller, G. B. & H., child of
Muck	William	3.10	1897			79	4.24	80	262	11	
Muck	Margaret	10.05	1893			72	1.27	73	262	12	Muck, William, wife of
Much	John H.	9.29	1893			53		54	262	13	Co. D, 187th Regt., Pa. Vols. [Much ?]
Muck	Harriet	1.03	1881			28	3.28	29	262	14	Muck, William & Margaret, daughter of
Muck	Martha Jane	8.29	1852	6.01	1846			7	262	15	Muck, William & Margaret, daughter of
Null	William F.	9.16	1866				2.18	1	262	16	Null, Abram & Rachel, child of
Null	John E.	5.13	1862				6.06	1	262	17	Null, Abram & Rachel, child of
Null	Fanny G.	7.28	1872			1	8.19	2	262	18	Null, Abram & Rachel, child of
Null	Eva F.	9.17	1877			2	8.05	3	262	19	Null, Abram & Rachel, child of
Rife	Mary	6.29	1870			79	0.25	80	262	20	Rife, Daniel, wife of
Sipe	Catharine Amanda	2.10	1851	11.30	1844			7	262	21	
Sipe	Sarah Isabella								262	22	b. Jan. 5, 184-; d. Feb. 23, 185-

Newville - Big Spring Presbyterian Graveyard

NEWVILLE BOROUGH

BIG SPRING PRESBYTERIAN GRAVEYARD

Surname	Given Name	Death Mo/Dy	Year	Birth Mo/Dy	Year	Att. Age Yr	Cm Mo/Dy	Ag	Pg	No	Other Information
Adams	Robert	5.14	1874	10.02	1798			76	202	01	
Adams	Anna B.	2.25	1892	1.26	1801			92	202	02	
Adams	Ephraim	12.14	1893	1.21	1806			88	202	03	
Adams	Elizabeth Barr	1.20	1879	4.19	1819			60	202	04	Adams, Ephraim, wife of
Adams	Margaret Jane	12.12	1893		1834	59	9.00	60	202	05	
Adams	Anna J.	11.04	1855	7.24	1849			7	202	06	
Adams	Adaline	3.03	1862	11.07	1856			6	202	07	
Adams	Anna M.	8.23	1879						202	08	Adams, R. A. & J. E., daughter of; aged ? years, 9 months, 28 days
Ahl	Alexander								202	09	Dr. [no dates given]
Ahl	Elizabeth Williams								202	10	[no dates given]
Ahl	Serrod	6.25	1868	2.21	1846			23	202	11	
Ahl	Elizabeth	9.28	1869	1.26	1850			20	202	12	
Ahl	Laura	8.25	1871	12.20	1852			19	202	13	
Ahl	Emma	11.27	1855	4.20	1854			2	202	14	
Ahl	Augustus	11.25	1859	4.24	1859			10	202	15	
Ahl	Abraham	4.17	1849	2.24	1849			1	202	16	
Allen	James Williams	7.19	1869		1789	80	0.24	81	202	17	(b. 1789)
Allen	Janes	11.30	1903			80		81	202	18	[Janes (sic)]
Allen	John	2.10	1817						202	19	
Allen	Jesse K.	4.09	1865			23	11.00	24	202	20	Co. B, 1st Rifle, Pennsylvania Volunteers; died a prisoner at Saulsbury, N. C., and is buried there with the unknown dead
Arbegast	Rebecca	10.25	1880			65	11.27	66	202	21	Arbegast, Joseph, wife of
Auxer	Elizabeth	4.11	1815	10.02	1796			19	202	22	Auxer, George, wife of
Barr	Alexander	9.04	1831			66		67	202	23	(b. 1764)
Barr	Margaret	2.27	1808			7	7.20	8	202	24	Barr, Alexander & Margaret, daughter of
Barr	Hugh, Sr.		1852		1792			61	202	25	
Barr	Martha		1866		1800			67	202	26	
Barr	Sarah, Mrs.	1.27	1838			35		36	202	27	Geddes, John, Dr. & Elizabeth, dau. of
Bear	Mary	5.04	1869			73		74	203	03	
Binnen	Mary E.	8.00	1853			81		82	203	07	
Blair	James	4.19	1862	2.05	1826			37	202	28	
Boyd	William	2.02	1846	1.05	1778			69	203	08	
Boyd	Martha	4.08	1848	12.14	1779			69	203	09	Boyd, William, wife of
Boyd	Abigail	3.28	1849			77		78	203	10	Boyd, William, relict of
Boyd	Elizabeth	1.02	1865			67	1.00	68	203	11	
Boyd	William Y.	4.23	1878	7.23	1802			76	203	12	
Boyd	M. B.	8.03	1899	11.01	1816			83	203	13	
Boyd	Mary	3.18	1856	10.01	1819			37	203	14	Boyd, Matthew, wife of
Boyd	Hanna E.	1.27	1896	6.24	1836			60	203	15	Boyd, M. B., wife of
Boyd	Martha A.	4.10	1904	6.09	1821			83	203	16	
Boyd	Mary	4.19	1904	1.14	1819			86	203	17	
Boyd	James	3.07	1864			64		65	203	18	
Boyd	Jane	4.19	1869			69	7.24	70	203	19	Boyd, James, wife of

Newville - Big Spring Presbyterian Graveyard

Surname	Given Name	Death Mo/Dy	Death Year	Birth Mo/Dy	Birth Year	Att. Age Yr	Age Mo/Dy	Cm Ag	Pg	No	Other Information
Boyd	Rebecca Mary	4.20	1875	6.08	1842			33	203	20	
Boyles	Elsie J.	6.16	1883	10.19	1882			1	203	21	Boyles, John & Mary, child of
Boyles	Daisy R.	6.05	1884	6.18	1877			7	203	22	Boyles, John & Mary, child of
Bracken	William	1.16	1803		1753	49		50	202	31	Capt.
Brandon	Mary Eleanor	4.19	1876			61		62	202	29	
Brandon	Ellie Martha	11.29	1870			9	4.00	10	202	30	Brandon, W. B. & Mary E., daughter of
Brannan	Thomas								202	32	Co. H, 22d Regt., U.S.C.T. (colored)
Brattan	Adam	6.06	1820		1744			77	202	33	aged about 76 years
Brattan	Anna	12.26	1840		1752	87		88	202	34	Brattan, Adam, wife of
Brattan	William	3.11	1862		1791	70		71	202	35	
Brattan	Samuel	8.16	1864			67		68	202	36	
Brattan	George	9.13	1860			75		76	202	37	
Brattan	Mary	7.23	1837			70		71	202	38	
Brattan	Martha Weakley	10.01	1857			78		79	203	01	
Brattan	William	9.18	1790						203	02	Brattan, Adam, infant son of
Brewster	William	6.25	1879			72		73	203	04	Dr.
Brewster	James R.		1893		1809			85	203	05	
Brewster	Nancy J.		1889		1822			68	203	06	
Brown	John	6.10	1842	9.19	1752			90	203	23	a soldier of the Revolution
Brown	Margaret	9.17	1836			88		89	203	24	Brown, John, wife of
Brown	James	10.11	1822	12.31	1778			44	203	25	
Brown	Martha	2.07	1852	8.10	1792			60	203	26	Brown, James, wife of
Brown	John	5.27	1870	6.16	1787			83	203	27	
Brown	Mary	3.02	1864			61		62	203	28	Brown, John, wife of
Brown	Joseph	7.19	1863			38		39	203	29	Brown, John & Mary, son of
Brown	Mary	9.23	1807						203	30	Brown, John, Sr., daughter of; aged about 43 years
Brown	John	6.20	1889			79	5.11	80	203	31	
Brown	Catharine G.	6.04	1878			63	9.10	64	203	32	Brown, John, wife of
Brown	John	5.08	1865			85		86	203	33	
Brown	Eleanor	4.24	1838			59		60	203	34	
Brown	Mary	9.16	1862	4.15	1788			75	203	35	
Brown	Eliza J.	9.16	1830	5.01	1816			15	203	36	
Brown	Joseph	7.31	1862			85		86	203	37	
Brown	Nancy	10.15	1835			35	3.10	36	203	38	Brown, Joseph, wife of
Brown	William	5.13	1864			67		68	203	39	
Brown	Jane	3.10	1877			74	5.29	75	203	40	
Brown	Rachel	3.24	1805			36		37	203	41	
Brown	James	2.15	1845			51		52	203	42	
Brown	Elizabeth M.	6.14	1848			29		30	203	43	Brown, James, wife of
Brown	J. Culbertson	5.20	1863	11.04	1814			49	203	44	
Brown	Ellen Q.	5.28	1858	2.05	1818			41	203	45	Brown, John C., consort of
Brown	James Brackenridge	10.25	1895	8.16	1822			74	203	46	
Brown	Ellen Martin	3.30	1891	8.21	1822			69	203	46	
Brown	Nathaniel G.	12.02	1864			46		47	203	48	d. in her 47th year
Brown	Catharine	1.23	1869			53		54	204	01	Brown, Nathaniel, wife of
Brown	Martha B.		1897		1854			44	204	02	
Brown	George								204	03	Co. E, 187th Pennsylvania Infantry; [no dates given]
Bryson	William	1.13	1800		1728	72		73	204	14	(b. 1728); has a slate tombstone

Newville - Big Spring Presbyterian Graveyard

Surname	Given Name	Death Mo/Dy	Year	Birth Mo/Dy	Year	Att. Age Yr	Cm Mo/Dy	Pg Ag	No	Other Information
Buchanan	Thomas	10.13	1823		1747	75		76	204	04	General; soldier of the Revolution; Captain in Col. Edward Hand's Regt.; Sheriff of Cumberland County, 1789
Buchanan	William	7.07	1843						204	05	
Buchanan	Ezekiel	8.31	1831						204	06	
Buchanan	Mary	10.16	1823			59		60	204	07	
Buchanan	Robert	5.03	1833						204	08	
Buchanan	Elizabeth	8.25	1863						204	09	
Butler	Elliott								204	10	Corp., Co. A, 127th U.S.C.T. (colored)
Butler	Samuel	4.27	1859	2.02	1788			72	204	11	(colored)
Butler	Sallie	3.15	1881	4.04	1793			88	204	12	(colored)
Byers	Daniel	9.28	1870			68	2.29	69	204	13	
Campbell	William	4.01	1864	10.26	1789			75	204	15	
Carnahan	Mary	9.07	1823						204	16	Carnahan, William, consort of; aged about 30 years; slate tombstone
Carnahan	Judath	5.21	1835			71		72	204	17	Carnahan, Robert, wife of
Carson	Priscilla	8.16	1864			72		73	204	18	
Carson	Hannah	4.05	1844			69		70	204	19	
Carter	Eva Alice								204	20	Carter, W. R. & Alice A., daughter of
Carter	Alice	6.22	1887			38		39	204	21	
Carter	Charles W.	10.00	1896	1.00	1896			1	204	22	
Chestnut	Lucy B.	1.24	1902			29		30	204	28	
Chestnut	Alta C.	7.31	1901		1898	2		3	204	29	(b. 1898)
Cobean	William S.	8.06	1859			64		65	204	30	
Cobean	Mary McFarlane	8.04	1855			50		51	204	31	Cobean, William S., wife of
Cook	Samuel	7.18	1841						204	32	
Cook	Jane	8.31	1843			48		49	204	34	
Cornog	Belle E.	11.17	1868	11.10	1844			25	204	35	
Cox	Mary	12.03	1866			65		66	204	36	
Coyle	Scott	8.31	1875	12.10	1809			66	204	37	
Coyle	Nancy	2.19	1843			26	8.00	27	204	38	Coyle, Scott, consort of
Coyle	William Huston						10.00	1	204	39	Coyle, Scott & Nancy Huston, child of
Coyle	Anna					4		5	204	40	Coyle, Scott & Nancy, child of
Cratzer	Joseph E.					11		12	204	23	
Cratzer	John H.	10.30	1858			1		2	204	24	Cratzer, William & Elizabeth, son of
Crawford	William	8.15	1860			61		62	204	25	
Crawford	Sarah, Mrs.	10.23	1845			44		45	204	26	Crawford, William, wife of
Crawford	G. W.								204	33	Sergeant, Co. G, 45th U. S. C. Infantry; (colored)
Cremer	Martha Jane	7.10	1846	2.01	1825			22	204	27	Cremer, Theodore H., wife of; Graham, Robert & Elizabeth M., daughter of
Daugherty	Rachel		1856		1789			68	204	41	Daugherty, George, wife of; also "Our Father"; see Dougherty
Daugherty	father					82		83	204	42	[this entry is part of previous entry]
Davidson	John	3.08	1823			80		81	204	43	
Davidson	Leacy	4.08	1823			75		76	205	01	
Davidson	John	1.09	1840	12.15	1786			54	205	02	
Davidson	Eleanor	1.09	1877	4.05	1797			80	205	03	
Davidson	John M.	1.23	1875			63	3.24	64	205	04	
Davidson	Charles E.	7.25	1875			9	2.13	10	205	05	

Newville - Big Spring Presbyterian Graveyard

Surname	Given Name	Death Mo/Dy	Year	Birth Mo/Dy	Year	Att. Age Yr	Mo/Dy	Age	Cm	Pg	No	Other Information
Davidson	Margaret	11.21	1883			56	6.07	57	205	06		Davidson, John H., wife of
Davidson	John		1900		1831			70	205	07		
Davidson	Jennie				1835				205	08		Davidson, John, wife of
Davidson	George		1859						205	09		son [no further reference]
Davidson	John S.		1901		1829			73	205	10		
Davidson	Alexander	10.19	1865			78	4.05	79	205	11		
Davidson	Jane	8.19	1879			88	8.20	89	205	12		
Davidson	Margaret E.		1904		1836			69	205	13		
Davidson	Alexander L.		1852		1831			22	205	14		
Davidson	Catharine		1860		1807			54	205	15		
Davidson	Samuel		1880		1804			77	205	16		
Davidson	John Y.		1840		1802			39	205	17		
Davidson	George	6.12	1856	10.27	1777			79	205	18		
Davidson	Jane	12.06	1863	3.13	1779			85	205	19		Davidson, George, wife of
Davidson	George G.	3.27	1886			69	7.29	70	205	20		
Davidson	Jane E.	1.09	1856	10.24	1820			36	205	21		Davidson, George G., wife of
Davidson	Margaret	11.10	1864			53	11.16	54	205	22		Davidson, George G., wife of
Davidson	Jane E.	12.13	1855				11.15	1	205	23		Davidson, George G. & Jane E., child of
Davidson	George E.	7.28	1848				11.00	1	205	23		Davidson, George G. & Jane E., child of
Davidson	Mary M.	8.03	1851			1	11.08	2	205	24		Davidson, George G. & Jane E., child of
Davidson	James	9.27	1858			68		69	205	26		
Davidson	Annie	9.17	1867			75		76	205	27		Davidson, James, wife of
Davidson	Ann	6.08	1827			33	0.06	34	205	28		Davidson, James, consort of
Davidson	James A.		1904		1827			78	205	29		
Davidson	Nancy C.				1830				205	30		Davidson, James A., wife of
Davidson	William	8.25	1843			54	8.02	55	205	31		
Davidson	Mary	4.03	1843			51	4.15	52	205	32		Davidson, William, wife of
Davidson	Eleanor	9.02	1838			19	11.00	20	205	33		Davidson, William & Mary, daughter of; aged 19 years, 11 months, -- days
Davidson	William M.	3.08	1863			12	3.19	13	205	34		
Davidson	Margaret E.	10.17	1889			65	7.18	66	205	35		Davidson, William M., wife of
Davidson	William G.	9.15	1864			54	1.08	55	205	36		
Davidson	Mary W.	4.20	1850			38		39	205	37		
Davidson	William	1.25	1882			71	5.13	72	205	38		
Davidson	Rosanna H. McF.	8.02	1845			35		36	205	39		
Davidson	Jane Ann	4.21	1833			3	7.00	4	205	40		Davidson, John & Eliza, daughter of
Davidson	John L.	2.08	1837			20	3.00	21	205	41		
Davidson	Ann	2.17	1866			77	3.00	78	205	42		
Davidson	Lacy L.	8.09	1877			59	0.29	60	206	01		
Davidson	Matilda	1.14	1891						206	02		
Davidson	Mary A.	12.20	1854						206	03		
Deckard	Johnson Ellsworth	1.06	1870			6	1.16	7	206	04		Deckard, Jacob R. & Sue B., child of
Deckard	Ada Sue	2.27	1864			2	11.23	3	206	05		Deckard, Jacob R. & Sue B., child of
Denning	William		1830		1737			94	206	06		The patriotic blacksmith and forger of wrought iron cannons during the Revolution; erected by the State of Penn.
Diener	John	5.18	1897	7.25	1810			87	206	07		
Diller	Harry	1.02	1877			9	2.16	10	206	08		Diller, B. P. & A. L., child of
Diller	Lacy K.	1.11	1877			6	3.00	7	206	09		Diller, B. P. & A. L., child of
Diller	Lewis E.	1.19	1877			4	6.00	5	206	10		Diller, B. P. & A. L., child of

Newville - Big Spring Presbyterian Graveyard

Surname	Given Name	Death Mo/Dy	Year	Birth Mo/Dy	Year	Att. Age Yr	Mo/Dy	Cm Ag	Pg	No	Other Information
Diller	Frank H.	10.17	1869				4.12	1	206	11	Diller, B. P. & A. L., child of
Dougherty	Mary J.	11.12	1890			54		55	206	12	Dougherty, J. S., wife of [see Daugherty
Duey	Conrad	10.15	1833			63		64	206	33	
Duey	Rachel	2.22	1854			84		85	206	34	Duey, Conrad, wife of
Dunbar	John	10.18	1829			61		62	206	13	[text reads "in her 62d year"]
Dunbar	Robert H.	10.15	1834			23		24	206	14	
Dunbar	Isabella	9.25	1824			24		25	206	15	
Dunbar	William McFarlan	1.06	1835			26	0.17	27	206	16	[McFarlan (sic)]
Dunbar	Mary	1.30	1830			57		58	206	17	
Duncan	Eliza Smith	8.07	1863	6.18	1789			75	206	18	
Duncan	David D. G.	8.30	1895	2.14	1817			79	206	19	
Duncan	Grizelda P. Linn	9.11	1900	7.22	1824			77	206	20	
Duncan	Theresa A.	10.05	1867	2.06	1865			3	206	21	
Duncan	Flora G.	12.05	1891	4.02	1867			25	206	22	
Duncan	Arabella	1.15	1872			25		26	206	23	
Duncan	David M.	5.15	1872				6.00	1	206	24	Duncan, Linn & Arabella, son of
Duncan	M. B. Boyd					2	6.08	3	206	25	Duncan, W. L. & Lydia Bell, son of
Dunfee	Hannah	12.14	1840			71	1.28	72	206	26	
Dunlap	Daniel Scott		1893		1811			83	206	27	
Dunlap	Fannie	1.25	1872			51	9.13	52	206	28	
Dunlap	Elizabeth	4.15	1841			23		24	206	29	Heffleman, Michael & Mary, daughter of
Dunlap	Anna	9.20	1852			6	2.00	7	206	30	
Dunlap	Ralph	9.05	1863			1	6.00	2	206	31	
Dunlap	Johnny M.	8.04	1877			4	7.07	5	206	32	Dunlap, N. B. & E. M., son of
Ege	Michael Peter	3.29	1853						206	35	
Ege	Jane Louisa McKinney	11.09	1853						206	36	
Ege	Jane Elmira	5.26	1850			57	1.21	58	206	37	Ege, Joseph A., wife of
Ege	Mary Ann	2.18	1842	8.27	1830			12	206	38	
Ege	Mary Ellen	7.30	1850				3.13	1	206	39	
Elliott	Nancy	4.16	1798			46		47	206	40	slate tombstone
Elliott	Thomas	3.19	1849			62		63	206	41	
Elliott	Elizabeth, Mrs.	2.19	1859			64	7.06	65	206	42	
Elliott	Alexander	7.12	1866			47	7.23	48	206	43	
Elliott	Robert Fullerton	12.13	1859			4	0.10	5	207	01	Elliott, James L. & Catharine A., son of
Elliott	Bessie C.	12.23	1881			4	9.17	5	207	02	Elliott, John A. & Emma J., daughter of
Erskine	Ebenezer		1901		1821			81	207	03	D. D.
Erskine	Florence Trainer		1879		1878			2	207	04	
Ewing	Elizabeth, Mrs.	1.16	1846			55		56	207	05	Gillespie, George & Sarah, daughter of
Ewing	Margaret Hays		1901		1900			2	207	06	
Fenton	Samuel T.		1892		1820			73	207	07	
Ferguson	William	4.23	1834						207	08	aged about 76 years; a soldier of the Revolution
Ferguson	George	2.22	1874			57	10.23	58	207	09	
Fickes	Andrew	12.12	1882			60	6.18	61	207	12	[aged 6 (?) mos.]
Fickes	Anna	4.25	1882			54	3.17	55	207	13	Fickes, Andrew, wife of
Fields	Rosa M.	2.16	1886			38	8.01	39	207	11	Fields, J. L., wife of; (colored)
Frownfelter	Catharine	6.15	1849			44	8.02	45	207	14	Frownfelter, John, wife of
Frownfelter	Mary Ann	6.03	1847			17	3.15	18	207	15	Frownfelter, John & Catharine, dau. of
Frownfelter	Lydia J.		1900		1832			69	207	16	
Frownfelter	Samuel	4.12	1896			50	5.19	51	207	17	

Newville - Big Spring Presbyterian Graveyard

Surname	Given Name	Death Mo/Dy	Year	Birth Mo/Dy	Year	Att. Age Yr	Mo/Dy	Cm Ag	Pg	No	Other Information
Fry	Jesse R.		1893		1832			62	207	10	Captain, Co. D, 77th Regt., Pa. Vols.
Fulton	Francis	10.16	1843			78		79	207	18	
Fulton	Sarah	8.04	1834			65		66	207	19	Fulton, Francis, consort of
Fulton	F. Huston	6.01	1855			48		49	207	20	
Fultin	Sarah Ann	8.29	1842			27	4.23	28	207	21	Fultin, Francis H., consort of [sic]
Fulton	Samuel H.	1.25	1838			1	8.16	2	207	22	
Fulton	Sarah Isabella	8.14	1853			14	9.24	15	207	23	
Fulton	James	8.17	1860			64	10.07	65	207	24	
Fulton	Grizzella Blean	6.12	1875			70	4.30	71	207	25	Fulton, James, wife of
Fulton	David Blean	2.20	1876			39	11.10	40	207	26	
Fulton	Robert	8.16	1891		1838			54	207	27	a soldier
Fulton	Jennie Bell	9.19	1868				8.28	1	207	28	Fulton, Robert & Minnie, daughter of
Furman	Ella	4.01	1896			28		29	207	29	Furman, Charles E., wife of
Furman	Flesta Bell	1.27	1897			1	9.15	2	207	30	Furman, Charles E. & Ella, daughter of
Galbreath	William	11.00	1815			83		84	207	31	
Galbreath	Sarah	2.22	1827			78	3.18	79	207	32	Galbreath, William, consort of
Galbreath	John	6.03	1845			40		41	207	33	
Galbreath	Leah		1838			34		35	207	34	Galbreath, John, wife of
Galbreath	Julian		1841			5		6	207	35	d. in her 6th year [female ?]
Gebhart	Elizabeth	6.19	1869			34	11.27	35	208	26	Gebhart, Samuel C., wife of
Gebhart	Elmer G.	12.15	1868				4.03	1	208	27	Gebhart, S. C. & E. C., son of
Geddes	John	12.05	1840	8.16	1766			75	208	28	(M. D.)
Geddes	Elizabeth Peebles	5.20	1839	2.08	1772			68	208	29	
Geddes	John P.	12.08	1837	10.10	1799			39	208	30	(M. D.)
Geddes	Jane		1889		1805			85	208	31	
Geddes	Martha F.		1897		1808			90	208	32	
Gettys	Rebecca	3.17	1897	11.15	1827			70	208	33	Gettys, James, wife of; b. in Newville; d. in Washington, D. C.
Geese	Christian	3.12	1816	1.17	1788			29	208	34	
George	C. S.							0	208	35	Co. E, 127th Pa. Infantry [no dates]
Gillelen	Margaret	5.07	1852	6.25	1828			24	209	05	
Gillespie	George	7.24	1887			78		79	209	06	
Gillespie	Lucinda B. Stewart	7.05	1875			55	4.00	56	209	07	Gillespie, George, wife of
Gillespie	Robert E.	4.13	1845				7.00	1	209	08	
Gillespie	Samuel B.	4.27	1881			27		28	209	09	
Gillespie	Nathaniel	8.16	1824			75		76	209	10	
Gillespie	Ann	11.16	1827			44		45	209	11	
Gillespie	Alfred E.	11.08	1851			12	0.26	13	209	12	Gillespie, Samuel & Elizabeth, son of
Gillespie	Nancy	8.21	1835			48		49	209	13	
Gillespie	Martha	6.25	1819			72	4.05	73	209	14	
Gillespie	Mary E.	10.06	1863			6		7	209	15	
Gillespie	James G.	10.17	1863			12		13	209	16	
Glauser	Shaeffer M.		1900		1822			79	207	36	[Shaeffer (sic)]
Glauser	Catharine		1903		1824			80	207	37	
Glenn	Alexander	11.13	1835	2.22	1787			49	208	36	
Glenn	William Mills	6.15	1884	6.28	1817			67	208	37	
Glenn	Mary Jane	3.03	1879			56	9.21	57	208	38	Glenn, William M., wife of
Glenn	Maria	5.28	1841	5.17	1792			50	208	39	Glenn, Alexander, wife of
Glenn	Anna Maria	2.07	1852	3.23	1848			4	208	40	Glenn, William M. & Mary J., daughter of
Graham	James	9.25	1807		1725	82		83	207	38	

Newville - Big Spring Presbyterian Graveyard

Surname	Given Name	Death Mo/Dy	Year	Birth Mo/Dy	Year	Att. Age Yr	Cm Mo/Dy	Ag	Pg	No	Other Information
Graham	Martha	7.22	1779			48		49	208	01	
Graham	Isaiah	8.27	1835			66	3.00	67	208	02	
Graham	Nancy (Lindsey)	2.17	1841			68	6.00	69	208	03	(Graham, Isaiah, wife of)
Graham	Nancy	1.19	1863			64	7.02	65	208	04	Graham, Isaiah & Nancy, daughter of
Graham	Samuel	4.27	1869			73	4.17	74	208	05	
Graham	Robert M.	1.24	1873			73		74	208	06	
Graham	Robert M.	12.06	1855			56		57	208	07	
Graham	William	11.21	1868			61	0.21	62	208	08	
Graham	Nancy (Davidson)	12.10	1876			68	8.04	69	208	09	Graham, William, wife of
Graham	William Findley		1904		1843			62	208	10	
Graham	Alfred M.	2.19	1882	11.15	1849			33	208	11	
Graham	James	11.11	1874			71	1.16	72	208	12	
Graham	David C.	12.10	1856						208	13	
Graham	Emma B.	7.17	1883			40	11.14	41	208	14	Graham, John B., wife of
Graham	Maggie D.	2.03	1892			11	8.20	12	208	15	
Graham	George M.	3.27	1870	12.24	1802			68	208	16	
Graham	Eliza (Alter)	2.26	1870	1.16	1805			66	208	17	Graham, George M., wife of
Graham	George W.	5.24	1839				3.14	1	208	18	Graham, George & Eliza Alter, child of
Graham	Jane	3.14	1846				9.05	1	208	19	Graham, George & Eliza Alter, child of
Graham	Elizabeth	6.10	1847			11	5.22	12	208	20	Graham, George & Eliza Alter, child of
Graham	Mary	2.17	1852			17	7.08	18	208	21	Graham, George & Eliza Alter, child of
Graham	George W.	5.16	1863			22	5.10	23	208	22	Sergeant; killed in a skirmish with the Rebels near Piedmont Station, Virginia
Graham	John			8.04	1843				208	23	[death date not given]
Graham	Harriet McKee	10.04	1871			25	11.15	26	208	24	
Graham	Isabel Sterrett	10.06	1896	11.13	1840			56	208	25	
Green	John, Sr.	2.25	1846			76	6.00	77	208	41	
Green	Samuel	3.27	1892			73		74	209	01	
Green	Mary	12.09	1902			82		83	209	02	
Green	William	7.17	1889	9.15	1805			84	209	03	
Green	Jane Duncan	5.24	1893	1.28	1809			85	209	04	Green, William, wife of
Gumpert	Miriam	1.24	1901	8.19	1849			52	209	17	
Gutshall	Jeremiah		1904		1825			80	209	18	
Gutshall	Nancy A.		1901		1828			74	209	19	Gutshall, Jeremiah, wife of
Hackett	Henry G.	12.07	1845			53	10.05	54	209	20	
Hackett	Mary	9.28	1854			59	9.04	60	209	21	Hackett, Henry G. H., wife of
Hackett	Mary Ellen	11.26	1870	8.05	1846			25	209	22	Hackett, Robert & Margaret, daughter of
Hackett	Minerva B.	11.09	1881	2.17	1857			25	209	23	Hackett, Frank D., wife of
Hackett	Frank L.	3.11	1897	8.16	1895			2	209	24	Hackett, F. D. & L. M., son of
Hackett	Robert Coulter	3.15	1851			2	1.19	3	209	25	Hackett, Robert & Margaret, wife of
Hamill	Mary	10.13	1811			24		25	209	26	Hamill, William, wife of
Hanna	John	10.11	1823			57		58	209	27	
Hanna	Samuel	2.08	1825			53		54	209	28	
Hanna	Else	2.10	1850			78		79	209	29	Hanna, Samuel, wife of
Hanna	Eliza	3.17	1885	9.15	1808			77	209	30	
Hard	James H.	10.10	1862	9.20	1856			7	209	31	
Hard	William G.	5.04	1868	6.05	1866			2	209	32	
Harder	Samuel	6.00	1841			37		38	209	33	
Harder	Mary E.	3.00	1852			50		51	209	34	
Harlan	James	6.21	1832			40		41	209	35	

Newville - Big Spring Presbyterian Graveyard

Surname	Given Name	Death Mo/Dy	Death Year	Birth Mo/Dy	Birth Year	Att. Age Yr	Att. Age Mo/Dy	Ag	Cm	Pg	No	Other Information
Harlan	Ruth	2.02	1854	11.15	1792			62		209	36	
Harlan	George	3.11	1892	1.12	1794			99		209	37	was a great checker player
Harlan	Elizabeth	8.09	1858	4.09	1811			48		209	38	
Harlan	James M.	5.15	1894			74	5.00	75		209	39	
Harlan	Ruth E.	5.08	1896			70	3.00	71		209	40	
Harlan	Matthew R.	9.18	1868			8	3.16	9		209	41	Harlan, J. M. & R. E., son of
Harlan	Mary Ruth	1.26	1860			3	2.21	4		209	42	Harlan, J. M. & R. E., daughter of
Harlan	Robert	11.19	1802			32		33		209	43	slate tombstone
Harper	Samuel	4.15	1802			27		28		210	01	slate tombstone
Harper	John	9.25	1804			73		74		210	02	slate tombstone
Harper	Jean	3.16	1808			73		74		210	03	Harper, John, relict of; slate tombstn.
Harper	James	2.13	1816							210	04	aged near 59 years
Harper	Mary	2.08	1852	12.02	1762			90		210	05	
Harper	Margaret	8.08	1817			19		20		210	06	Harper, James & Mary, daughter of
Harper	William	5.18	1824			63		64		210	07	
Harper	Esther	4.13	1827							210	08	Harper, William, relict of; aged about 63 years
Harper	Andrew	1.19	1827			28	2.13	29		210	09	
Harper	Elizabeth	10.10	1827			21	3.00	22		210	10	
Harper	John	10.11	1846	11.29	1793			53		210	11	Major
Harper	Mary, Mrs.	8.03	1865			67		68		210	12	Harper, John, Major, wife of; Lewis, Diana, daughter of
Harper	Dianna L.	8.07	1829			6	8.00	7		210	13	Harper, John & Mary L., daughter of
Harper	Margaret	2.13	1871			64		65		210	14	Harper, William & Esther, daughter of
Harper	John	6.05	1847	6.22	1795			52		210	15	
Harper	Elizabeth	3.27	1813			40		41		210	16	Harper, John H., wife of
Harper	Margaret	5.21	1830			25		26		210	17	Harper, John, Jr., wife of; Harper, John, of Adams County, daughter of
Harper	Sarah	3.16	1848			79		80		210	18	Harper, Samuel, wife of
Harper	David	6.03	1801			27		28		210	19	slate head stone
Hartzell	Jane E. Boyd	11.01	1886	10.12	1838			49		210	20	Hartzell, Charles D., wife of
Hays	Patrick	7.28	1856			89		90		210	21	
Hays	Margaret	1.23	1857			66		67		210	22	Hays, Patrick, wife of
Hays	Jane	11.30	1842			19		20		210	23	Hays, Patrick & Margaret, daughter of
Hays	John E.	3.29	1877		1842	34		35		210	24	Sergeant, 130th Regt., Pa. Volunteers
Hays	Robert M.	3.04	1889			75	9.09	76		210	25	
Hays	Hannah Sharp	5.11	1889			70	2.17	71		210	26	Hays, Robert M., wife of
Heagy	Eliza	10.01	1888			62		63		210	27	
Heap	John									210	28	[no dates given]
Heffelman	Michael	7.24	1845	3.09	1780			66		210	29	
Heffleman	Mary	2.02	1837	12.22	1785			52		210	30	Heffleman, Michael, wife of [sp. varies]
Herron	James	4.03	1846			41	6.00	42		210	31	
Hood	Joseph	9.13	1868	2.10	1829			40		210	32	
Hood	Sarah	3.18	1852			57	5.20	58		210	33	Hood, Joseph, consort of
Hood	Josiah	10.02	1873	8.11	1794			80		210	34	soldier of War of 1812
Hood	Mary Jane	2.28	1831			12	8.08	13		210	35	Hood, Josiah, daughter of
Hood	Elizabeth	8.24	1842			18		19		210	36	Hood, Josiah, daughter of
Hood	Mary Elizabeth	9.30	1843			1	2.07	2		210	37	
Hood	Robert	11.22	1902			77		78		210	38	Private, Co. C, 158th Regt., Pa. Vols., Infantry; discharged August 12, 1863

Newville - Big Spring Presbyterian Graveyard

Surname	Given Name	Death Mo/Dy	Death Year	Birth Mo/Dy	Birth Year	Att. Age Yr	Age Mo/Dy	Ag	Cm	Pg	No	Other Information
Horn	Simon Buser	4.19	1862	8.07	1846			16		211	07	Horn, Henry & Elizabeth Buser, son of
House	John	11.00	1872		1782	90		91		210	39	soldier of War of 1812
House	Elizabeth	8.00	1863			79		80		210	40	House, John, wife of
House	Ruhannah J.		1904		1818			87		210	41	
House	John, Jr.		1835			22		23		210	42	
House	William		1836			12		13		211	01	
House	Jane	10.00	1812				8.00	1		211	02	
House	Michael		1823			7		8		211	03	
House	George		1824			1		2		211	04	
House	Jacob		1832			25		26		211	05	
Householder	Florie H.	12.18	1867			2		3		211	06	Householder, Frank & Dessie, daughter of
Howard	Nicholas	11.18	1847							211	08	soldier of War of 1812
Hudson	William	3.08	1828			1	7.00	2		211	09	aged 19 months
Hume	Anna M.	9.04	1852			6	6.00	7		211	10	Hume, William D. & Hetty G., daughter of
Hunter	Joseph	6.28	1835			59		60		211	11	
Hunter	Rebecca	11.25	1851			71		72		211	12	Hunter, Joseph H., wife of
Hursh	William Ray	5.30	1865				3.00	1		211	13	
Huston	James	6.17	1825			41		42		211	14	
Ickes	Charles	1.23	1873	3.12	1811			62		211	15	
Ickes	Lucinda	2.12	1881			71		72		211	16	Ickes, Charles, wife of
Ickes	Henry	11.08	1861			16	0.29	17		211	17	Ickes, Charles & Lucinda, child of
Ickes	Charles	10.01	1878			22	8.20	23		211	18	
Irvine	Samuel	3.09	1806			58		59		211	19	Esq.; Lt. Colonel, 3d Battalion, Pennsylvania Infantry, 1776-17--
Irvine	Mary	10.28	1819			74		75		211	20	Irvine, Samuel, Esq., relict of
Irwin	James	2.22	1854			77		78		211	21	
Irwin	Prudence	10.20	1818			33		34		211	22	Irwin, James, wife of
Irvine	Ruth, Miss	12.21	1859			82	5.00	83		211	23	
Irwin	Isabella	4.20	1881	5.10	1808			73		211	24	
Irwin	Elizabeth J.	1.27	1880	10.20	1813			67		211	25	
Irvine	Samuel	5.10	1849			64		65		211	26	
Irvine	Rosanna	4.04	1834			36		37		211	27	Irvine, Samuel, consort of
Irvine	Isabella	7.12	1839			36	4.07	37		211	28	Irvine, Samuel, consort of
Irvine	Margaret R. McClelland	9.02	1886	9.21	1803			83		211	29	Irvine, Samuel, wife of
Irvine	Mary	1.07	1833			2		3		211	30	
Irvine	Margaretta	2.13	1878			37	7.15	38		211	31	Irvine, Samuel I., wife of
Irvine	Annie Wagner	3.01	1897							211	32	Irvine, Samuel I., wife of
Irvine	R. Hays	12.09	1886			24	9.28	25		211	33	Irvine, S. I. & Margaretta, son of
Irvine	Bruce Kilgore	11.11	1877			2	7.03	3		211	34	Irvine, S. I. & Margaretta, son of
Irvine	Mary					19	3.18	20		211	35	
Irvine	Mary Ellen						3.00	1		211	36	Irvine, Mary, only child of
Irvine	Sarahbella									211	37	[no dates given]
Irvine	James Davidson									211	38	[no dates given]
Jacob	Joseph	10.08	1861			81		82		211	39	
Jacob	Lydia	12.20	1849			63		64		212	01	Jacob, Joseph, wife of
Jacob	Joseph A.	1.28	1870			39		40		212	02	
Jacob	Lydia	4.29	1893	11.21	1820			73		212	03	
Jacobs	Adam		1872		1787			86		212	04	
Jacobs	Sarah Lenney	8.30	1834			46		47		212	05	Jacobs, Adam, wife of
Jacobs	Margery		1865		1795			71		212	06	

Newville - Big Spring Presbyterian Graveyard

Surname	Given Name	Death Mo/Dy	Death Year	Birth Mo/Dy	Birth Year	Att. Age Yr	Age Mo/Dy	Cm Ag	Pg	No	Other Information
Jacobs	William L.				1837				212	07	
Jacobs	John		1888		1814			75	212	08	
James	Harry Marshall	3.07	1882			1	9.09	2	212	09	
Jenkins	George								212	10	Co. B, 23d U. S. C. T. (colored)
Johnson	James W.	8.31	1823	10.31	1822			1	212	11	[W. ?]
Johnson	Elizabeth	3.02	1817			58		59	212	12	
Johnson	John	9.08	1841			60		61	212	13	
Johnson	William H.	7.16	1869			23		24	212	14	
Johnson	William B.					33		34	212	15	
Johnson	Robert C. Geddes					3		4	212	16	Johnson, William B., son of
Johnson	N. H.	7.16	1869						212	17	U. S. Navy
Karlskint	Peter	1.01	1900						212	18	Private, Co. D, 69th Regt., N. Y. Vols.
Keiffer	Cora V.	5.11	1885			12	5.11	13	212	19	Keiffer, A. & M., daughter of; (colored)
Kelley	John Jackson	2.17	1857	9.17	1827			30	212	20	
Kelly	John	3.01	1864			73		74	212	21	[spelling varies]
Kelly	Grizzella	3.23	1864			63	1.08	64	212	22	[spelling varies]
Kelley	George Samuel	9.14	1850			8	10.12	9	212	23	Kelley, John & Grizzella, son of; [sp.?]
Kelly	C. V.	2.23	1895	11.26	1822			73	212	24	
Kelly	Agnes A.			8.14	1832				212	25	
Kelley	John A.	3.14	1864			1	3.00	2	212	26	Kelly, John & Elizabeth, son of; [sp. ?]
Kelley	Maggie A.	12.15	1869	1.23	1869			1	212	27	
Kennedy	Thomas	3.09	1831			86		87	212	28	
Kennedy	Margaretta	1.16	1826			66		67	212	29	Kennedy, Thomas, consort of
Kennedy	Alexander	7.17	1878			52	6.16	53	212	30	
Kennedy	Willie	8.13	1875	9.16	1873			2	212	31	Kennedy, W. S. & M. son of
Ker	William	10.08	1854	1.01	1753			102	212	32	
Ker	William	9.20	1874	10.30	1791			83	212	33	
Ker	Elizabeth Bell	12.24	1844	9.16	1806			39	212	34	Ker, William, wife of
Ker	Lizzie J.	6.22	1879	10.14	1840			39	212	35	Ker, William & Eliza B., daughter of
Ker	Mary Bell	8.08	1881	11.29	1837			44	212	36	
Ker	Mary	9.21	1828				4.22	1	212	37	Ker, William & Eliza, daughter of
Ker	Thomas Orr	3.18	1897	12.05	1895			2	212	38	Ker, W. O. & Jane, son of
Kerr	Sarah	6.29	1838			53		54	212	39	Kerr, Alexander M., consort of
Kerr	William G.		1817			1		2	212	40	Kerr, Alexander M. & Sarah, child of
Kerr	Sarah		1824			6		7	212	41	Kerr, Alexander M. & Sarah, child of
Ker	Elizabeth J.	1.29	1840	3.07	1835			5	212	42	
Kilgore	William	10.11	1823			67		68	213	07	
Kilgore	Isabella	2.18	1820			64	4.00	65	213	08	Kilgore, William, consort of
Kilgore	Jesse	8.19	1823			59	8.06	60	213	09	
Kilgore	Jane	12.05	1834			62	8.15	63	213	10	
Kilgore	Margery	1.12	1824			9	2.27	10	213	11	
Kilgore	James	2.11	1877			75	9.09	76	213	12	
Kinsly	J. R.								213	13	Co. H, 3d Pennsylvania Cavalry
Kinsly	John	12.13	1851			70		71	213	14	
Klink	George	1.30	1869			76	8.07	77	213	15	
Klink	Elizabeth	3.24	1875			80		81	213	16	Klink, George, wife of
Knettle	William	9.05	1833			78		79	212	43	"in her 79th year"; [d. 9.05 ?]
Knettle	Lacy H.	5.24	1890			82		83	212	44	
Knettle	Hannah E.	3.26	1841			12	3.13	13	213	01	Knettle, William & Lacy, daughter of
Knettle	Henry	7.05	1843			70		71	213	02	

Newville - Big Spring Presbyterian Graveyard

Surname	Given Name	Death Mo/Dy	Year	Birth Mo/Dy	Year	Att. Age Yr	Cm Mo/Dy	Ag	Pg	No	Other Information
Knettle	Hannah G.	10.27	1854						213	03	Knettle, Henry, wife of; about 76 years
Knettle	Matilda	7.27	1898			55	7.21	56	213	04	
Knettle	Laura Bell	6.12	1862				11.29	1	213	05	Knettle, Joseph L. & Matilda, child of
Knettle	William Green	8.01	1863				8.22	1	213	06	Knettle, Joseph L. & Matilda, child of
Knight	Thomas H.	4.30	1852			56	6.22	57	213	17	
Knight	Elizabeth	4.17	1863			58	1.06	59	213	18	Knight, Thomas H., wife of
Knight	Jeremiah	5.01	1852			23	6.11	24	213	19	Knight, Thomas H. & Elizabeth, son of
Knight	Alexander	12.22	1829			4	2.16	5	213	20	
Knight	James								213	21	U. S. Navy [no dates given]
Koons	Isaac	11.19	1874			82	2.00	83	213	22	
Koons	Jane	8.11	1866			70	8.28	71	213	23	Koons, Isaac, wife of
Koons	Thomas	10.10	1850			19	3.03	20	213	24	
Koons	Jane E.	11.07	1877	11.10	1833			44	213	25	
Koons	Mary J.	2.15	1888			66	5.24	67	213	26	Koons, William C., wife of
Koons	Willie C.	6.24	1875			17	6.00	18	213	27	Koons, William C. & Mary J., son of
Koons	Joseph T.	7.28	1870			1	5.13	2	213	28	Koons, James & Mary E., child of
Koons	Mary B.	8.18	1873			1	5.14	2	213	29	
Koser	Alexander	4.12	1875			58	11.29	59	213	30	
Koser	Lavina C.	3.03	1905			81	9.21	82	213	31	
Koser	Howard M.	2.12	1901	6.19	1857			44	213	32	
Kulp	Eve	10.04	1857			82		83	213	33	
Kulp	Mary A.	2.17	1882			67	11.03	68	213	34	
Kyle	J. House					4		5	213	35	
Laird	Hugh	9.30	1815			28		29	213	36	
Laird	Thomas	4.19	1830			36		37	213	37	
Laird	James	10.19	1834			81		82	213	38	
Laird	Robert	1.15	1848			57		58	213	39	
Laird	Catharine	6.19	1850			85	7.00	86	213	40	Laird, Mary & John, mother of
Laughlin	Atcheson	1.11	1825			68		69	213	41	
Laughlin	William R.	2.12	1838	2.06	1784			55	213	42	[R. ?]
Laughlin	Mary	10.22	1842			81		82	213	43	
Laughlin	Atcheson	7.07	1876			76		77	214	01	died in her 77th year
Laughlin	James	2.11	1851	9.14	1785			66	214	02	
Laughlin	John A.	5.14	1893	3.24	1816			78	214	03	
Laughlin	Jane S.	8.26	1897	5.08	1831			67	214	04	
Laughlin	Eliza	2.21	1864			67		68	214	05	
Laughlin	Nancy	8.18	1871			77		78	214	06	
Laughlin	Isabella O.	4.02	1891	10.01	1813			78	214	07	
Laughlin	William L.	12.13	1862			41		42	214	08	killed in the Battle of Fredericksburg
Laughlin	Walter	11.24	1859	3.27	1859			1	214	09	
Laughlin	Edgar M.	2.05	1871	12.31	1862			9	214	10	
Lawrence	Anna Manda	11.06	1832			23	6.00	24	214	11	red sand headstone
Leckey	Daniel	3.03	1854			70	6.00	71	214	12	
Leckey	Ann	9.25	1843			65	5.19	66	214	13	Leckey, Daniel, wife of
Leckey	Daniel A.	9.13	1824			7	2.20	8	214	14	
Leckey	Serabella	10.06	1823	9.01	1789			35	214	15	
Leckey	William Alexander	12.03	1894			84	5.19	85	214	16	
Leckey	Matthew D.		1886		1814			73	214	17	
Leckey	Sarah		1887		1815			73	214	18	
Leckey	James B.	4.10	1875			55	4.22	56	214	19	

Newville - Big Spring Presbyterian Graveyard

Surname	Given Name	Death Mo/Dy	Year	Birth Mo/Dy	Year	Att. Age Yr	Age Mo/Dy	Cm Ag	Pg	No	Other Information
Leckey	Mary E.	10.22	1881			59	10.08	60	214	20	
Lemon	Diana, Mrs.	12.00	1837			75		76	214	21	
Lenney	William	10.20	1823			41		42	214	22	
Lenney	Sarah	3.17	1862			72		73	214	23	Lenney, William, wife of
Lenney	Mary Blair		1883		1821			63	214	24	
Lenney	William		1898		1822			77	214	25	
Lenney	Catharine Elliott		1902		1827			76	214	26	
Lenney	Isaac	8.14	1848			54		55	214	27	
Lenny	Hannah	8.16	1869			71		72	214	28	Lenny, Isaac, wife of; [spelling varies]
Lenney	Elizabeth	1.17	1847			64		65	214	29	
Lenney	Eleanor	1.22	1863			48	7.29	49	214	30	
Lewis	James W.	9.12	1872			11	8.13	12	214	31	Lewis, Jacob T. & S. J., son of
Lindsey	William	1.23	1838	7.06	1793			45	214	33	
Lindsey	Mary Forbes	10.26	1842	4.27	1786			57	214	34	Lindsey, William, wife of
Lindsey	William E.	1.06	1859	2.21	1822			37	214	35	
Lindsey	Sophia	9.24	1860	9.19	1829			32	214	36	Lindsey, William E., wife of
Lindsey	Peter Wilt	12.08	1866			15	7.00	16	214	37	Lindsey, Peter & Sarah, son of
Lindsey	Jane	5.04	1837			78	7.00	79	214	38	
Lindsey	John F.	2.14	1888	9.02	1819			69	214	39	
Lindsey	Rachel W.	11.18	1894	3.06	1821			74	214	40	Lindsey, John F., wife of
Linn	Maggie A.	2.22	1869	12.14	1833			36	214	32	Linn, W. H., wife of
Logan	James	10.26	1828			45		46	214	41	
Logan	Alexander		1870		1795			76	214	42	
Logan	Martha Mc.		1873		1797			77	214	43	
Logan	Robert Laird		1842		1841			2	214	44	
Logan	Mary Elliott		1902		1870			33	214	45	
Logan	William Alexander		1900		1839			62	215	01	
Long	Louise Hulme	8.23	1877			1	1.00	2	215	02	Long, H. D. & L. M., daughter of
Loy	Clarence B.	2.05	1901			16		17	215	03	
Manning	Harry		1899		1834			66	215	04	
Manning	Margaretta Beistline								215	05	[no dates given]
Manning	George B. McC.		1865		1862			4	215	06	
Manning	Edna I.	8.24	1878	8.07	1878			1	215	07	Manning, J. & Ella, daughter of
Martin	John M.	8.29	1871			66	1.21	67	215	08	
Martin	Ruhama	7.08	1879			70	4.28	71	215	09	Martin, J. M., wife of [7/8?/1879]
Mathers	Andrew T.	11.00	1889	7.00	1805			85	215	10	
Mathers	Nancy	8.19	1882	8.26	1802			80	215	11	Mathers, Andrew, wife of
Mathers	William	10.18	1850			89		90	215	12	
McCachran	Isabella	1.08	1851	1.08	1765			87	216	08	b. at Abington; d. near Philadelphia
McCachran	Robert	2.25	1885	9.24	1798			87	216	09	Rev.
McCachran	Jane (Laughlin)	11.27	1871			69	3.24	70	216	10	McCachran, Robert, Rev., wife of
McCachran	James	8.25	1885	1.01	1797			89	216	11	
McCachran	Rachel	9.22	1859			36	10.00	37	216	12	McCachran, James, wife of
McCachran	Isabella	11.05	1891	4.29	1807			85	216	13	
McCachran	John	6.08	1850			15	3.00	16	216	14	
McCachran	Robert	11.29	1881	11.28	1881			1	216	15	McCachran, Robert & Martha, child of
McCachran	William C.	8.11	1890	3.01	1890			1	216	16	McCachran, Robert & Martha, child of
McCaleb	James	5.25	1855			30	2.08	31	216	17	
McCandlish	William	4.09	1827			58		59	216	18	
McCandlish	Jane	8.04	1827			45		46	216	19	McCandlish, William, relict of

Newville - Big Spring Presbyterian Church

Surname	Given Name	Death Mo/Dy/Year	Birth Mo/Dy/Year	Att. Age Yr/Mo/Dy	Cm Ag	Pg	No	Other Information
McCandlish	Thomas	8.17/1876		58	59	216	20	
McCandlish	Mary G.	5.09/1852		28	29	216	21	McCandlish, T. M., wife of
McCandlish	Mamie	9.11/1874		22	23	216	22	McCandlish, Thomas & Mary, daughter of
McCandlish	James	4.14/1882		62/11.21	63	216	23	
McCandlish	Julia	11.12/1871		49/11.17	50	216	24	McCandlish, James, wife of
McCandlish	John M.	/1903	/1861		43	216	25	
McCandlish	Maria	10.01/1827		24	25	216	26	McCandlish, John, consort of
McCandlish	Julia	3.30/1869		21	22	216	27	
McCandlish	J. Morris	3.23/1871		18/9.00	19	216	28	
McCandlish	J. Walter	11.30/1877		16/9.21	17	216	29	
McCandlish	Alice	9.28/1878		32/7.22	33	216	30	
McCandlish	Mary	4.20/1852		48	49	216	31	
McCandlish	Jane R.	1.15/1869		61	62	216	32	
McCandlish	Elizabeth	3.27/1882		69	70	216	33	
McCandlish	Margaret M.	7.17/1888		64/2.02	65	216	34	
McCandlish	W. Morris			2	3	216	35	[the name appears as "Mc. W. Morris"
McCandlish	John	5.29/1859		3/7.21	4	216	36	McCandlish, J. & J. A., child of
McCandlish	Freddie	4.28/1859		1/3.10	2	216	37	McCandlish, J. & J. A., child of
McClure	Isabel E.	7.30/1871		20/7.12	21	220	17	McClure, Jacob W. & Mary, daughter of
McCormick	Thomas	1.16/1835		68/7.18	69	218	47	
McCormick	Elizabeth	2.20/1824		58/11.00	59	218	48	McCormick, Thomas, consort of
McCormick	William	6.00/1835				218	49	
McCormick	Margaret	12.11/1831		22	23	218	50	
McCormick	Jane	8.00/1857	10.00/1785		72	218	51	
McCoy	John F.	/1840	3.24/1832		8	218	52	
McCoy	George J.	5.25/1835	7.07/1834		1	219	01	
McCrea	William	/1837	/1759		79	217	40	
McCrea	Margaret	/1822	/1759		64	217	41	McCrea, William, wife of
McCrea	John	3.15/1879	5.28/1803		76	217	42	
McCrea	William	10.25/1886	7.21/1800		87	217	43	
McCrea	Mary Jane	2.25/1855	6.01/1816		39	217	44	McCrea, William, wife of
McCrea	Margaret	4.16/1842	9.01/1839		3	218	01	McCrea, William & Mary Jane, child of
McCrea	William H.	5.19/1853	10.14/1840		13	218	02	McCrea, William & Mary Jane, child of
McCrea	Florence W.	5.25/1867	10.05/1846		21	218	03	McCrea, William & Mary Jane, child of
McCrea	Alexander L.	/1898	/1848		51	218	04	
McCullough	John	3.10/1808		67	68	219	20	
McCullough	Elizabeth Huston	/1813				219	21	McCullough, John, wife of; aged about 73 years
McCullough	James	8.13/1825		64	65	219	22	McCullough, John & E. H., son of
McCullough	William	11.08/1824		45	46	219	23	
McCullough	Sarah	4.04/1834		51	52	219	24	McCullough, William, relict of
McCullough	John	2.05/1847		75	76	219	25	
McCullough	Mary	9.05/1862		89	90	219	26	McCullough, John, wife of
McCullough	David W.	11.22/1859		60/11.06	61	219	27	
McCullough	Betsey	12.28/1882	9.03/1804		79	219	28	McCullough, David W., wife of; Coyle, David & Martha Linn, daughter of
McCullough	Jane E.	10.01/1855		10/11.00	11	219	29	McCullough, David W. & E., daughter of
McCullough	Jane Dunbar	3.07/1838		33	34	219	30	McCullough, John, consort of
McCullough	Sarah Evaline	2.16/1845		8/6.04	9	219	31	McCullough, John & Jane Dunbar, dau. of
McCullough	James	11.01/1850		48	49	219	32	

Newville - Big Spring Presbyterian Church

Surname	Given Name	Death Mo/Dy	Year	Birth Mo/Dy	Year	Att. Yr	Age Mo/Dy	Cm Ag	Pg	No	Other Information
McCullough	M. Harriet	2.25	1876			28		29	219	33	
McCullough	Mary Henderson	6.24	1847			74		75	219	34	McCullough, James, wife of
McCullough	Annie E.	5.01	1866			40		41	219	35	McCullough, W. Linn, wife of
McCullough	Leonidas	4.27	1881	5.27	1842			39	219	36	
McCullough	Sarah Bella	12.26	1870			3	10.15	4	219	37	McCullough, Leo & Emma, child of
McCullough	Mary Ellen	12.27	1870			1	3.16	2	219	38	McCullough, Leo & Emma, child of
McCullough	Margaretta M.	4.02	1842			29		30	219	39	McCullough, James, wife of
McCullough	Mary Jane	7.28	1850			28		29	219	40	
McCullough	Berdilla	2.27	1862			18		19	220	01	
McCullough	Jane A.	3.02	1851			2		3	220	02	
McCullough	Jane Hays	4.28	1866	12.09	1819			47	220	03	
McCullough	Samuel	11.10	1881			66		67	220	04	
McCullough	James	11.29	1892			81		82	220	05	
McCullough	William J.		1902		1836			67	220	06	
McCullough	William A.		1904		1834			71	220	07	
McCullough	Martha								220	08	McCullough, William A., wife of
McCune	William	2.11	1879	1.23	1807			73	220	09	
McCune	Margaretta	12.31	1850	7.05	1849	1	5.25	2	220	10	McCune, William & Margaretta A., dau. of [two entries: (1) b. 7.05 1849, d. 12.31 1850 (2) d. 12.31 1851, aged 1 year, 5 months, 25 days]
McCune	Jennie	7.21	1887	2.05	1849			39	220	11	McCune, John K., wife of
McCune	John Brady	9.08	1883	5.10	1881			3	220	12	McCune, John K. & J. A., child of
McCune	Mary Bell	5.25	1888	9.14	1872			16	220	13	McCune, John K. & J. A., child of
McCune	Margaret J.	12.13	1900	9.24	1826			75	220	14	
McCune	J. A.							0	220	15	Co. M, 7th Pennsylvania Cavalry
McCune	Ruth Jennings	3.05	1898			5	1.02	6	220	16	McCune, S. A. & Anne I., daughter of
McDannell	Daniel	3.27	1789	11.11	1722			67	216	38	b. in the Kingdom of Ireland; slate headstone
McDannel	Jane	6.28	1798	1.01	1726			73	216	39	b. in County Tyrone, Ireland; slate headstone
McDannel	John	1.01	1800			71	1.15	72	217	01	
McDannell	Daniel	6.26	1811			59	11.08	60	217	02	
McDannell	Jane	2.18	1842			77		78	217	03	
McDannell	Daniel	11.13	1825			33	7.20	34	217	04	McDannell, Daniel, son of
McDannell	Margaret	5.08	1809			12	2.02	13	217	05	
McDannell	William S.	8.23	1896			73		74	217	06	
McDannell	Mary	1.23	1902			79		80	217	07	
McDannell	John Martin	8.10	1856			9	4.00	10	217	08	McDannell, W. S. & Mary, son of
McDannell	Elizabeth, Mrs.	5.25	1866			75	7.07	76	217	09	
McDermond	Joseph		1869		1796			74	218	05	
McDermond	Nancy		1868		1792			77	218	06	
McDermond	Elizabeth		1901		1824			78	218	07	
McDermond	Isabella		1831		1820			12	218	08	
McDermond	Mary Agnes	3.11	1879			30	5.05	31	218	09	McDermond, John & Catharine, daughter of
McDonald	Margaret	11.10	1831						219	05	aged about 57 years
McDowell	John	6.09	1829			51		52	219	02	
McDowell	Margaret	5.30	1855			64	5.11	65	219	03	
McDowell	Samuel	4.24	1830			63		64	219	04	

Newville - Big Spring Presbyterian Graveyard

Surname	Given Name	Death Mo/Dy	Year	Birth Mo/Dy	Year	Att. Age Yr	Mo/Dy	Cm Ag	Pg	No	Other Information
McDowell	Mary	12.24	1834			65		66	219	06	
McDowell	William J.	12.18	1834	7.27	1808			27	219	07	
McDowell	Elizabeth	6.08	1851	11.16	1797			54	219	08	
McDowell	Margaret	6.09	1851	12.30	1792			59	219	09	
McDowell	Samuel K.	12.08	1862	11.03	1805			58	219	10	
McDowell	Mary	4.28	1863	9.18	1794			69	219	11	
McDowell	John	7.27	1857			31	7.27	32	219	12	
McDowell	Agnes E.	3.09	1864	10.17	1819			45	219	13	
McDowell	Mary I.	2.12	1865	3.07	1836			29	219	14	McDowell, James L., wife of
McDowell	Maggie L.	4.07	1884	7.29	1863			21	219	15	McDowell, James L. & Mary I., dau. of
McDowell	Rachel	10.03	1893	8.03	1803			91	219	16	
McDowell	John	7.31	1878	11.11	1801			77	219	17	
McElhenny	Margaret	4.22	1835			42		43	218	10	McElhenny, Robert, wife of
McElwain	Andrew, Jr.	8.21	1840			55	3.21	56	217	10	
McElwain	Mary	10.27	1868			70	3.11	71	217	11	McElwain, Andrew, Jr. wife of
McElwain	Robert	1.18	1853			72		73	217	12	
McElwain	Jane	5.12	1869			79		80	217	13	
McFarlane	Esther	2.18	1789			19		20	217	14	
McFarlane	Patrick	3.16	1792			65		66	217	15	a large granite slab
McFarlane	Rosanna	11.26	1812			77		78	217	16	on slab of Patrick McFarlane
McFarlane	William	1.29	1802			45		46	217	17	granite slab, 2nd one
McFarlane	William	1.07	1806			2		3	217	18	granite slab, 2nd one
McFarlane	James	1.26	1812			4		5	217	19	granite slab, 2nd one
McFarlane	James	12.16	1807			49		50	217	20	
McFarlane	Elizabeth	3.26	1814			49		50	217	21	McFarlane, James, consort of
McFarlane	William	4.05	1811			66		67	217	22	
McFarlane	Eleaner	10.19	1814			37		38	217	23	
McFarlane	Elizabeth	3.06	1816			48		49	217	24	
McFarlane	Robert	4.24	1838	11.15	1784			54	217	25	
McFarlane	Clemens	4.30	1869	3.20	1798			72	217	26	interred in Spring Hill Cemetery at Shippensburg; see Spring Hill Cemetery
McFarlane	Lydia	3.29	1846			46	7.00	47	217	27	McFarlane, Clemens, wife of
McFarlane	Thomas	6.24	1832			26		27	217	28	
McFarlane	Robert	9.14	1847	10.23	1776			71	217	29	
McFarlane	Jane	3.11	1833			45		46	217	30	McFarlane, Robert, wife of
McFarlane	Jane M.	2.01	1882	11.21	1799			83	217	31	McFarlane, Robert, wife of
McFarlane	Robert W.	4.16	1845			27		28	217	32	
McGaw	Thomas Edgar	9.02	1867			1	8.01	2	217	33	
McGlen	Jennett	1.15	1879						218	11	
McIntire	John	8.16	1830			85		86	218	35	
McIntire	Margaret	9.17	1830			74		75	218	36	McIntire, John, wife of
McIntire	Mary	6.13	1853			45		46	218	37	
McKeehan	George	11.30	1884		1810			75	218	12	
McKeehan	Benjamin	10.23	1814			63	2.21	64	218	13	
McKeehan	Tabitha	1.21	1824			21	8.03	22	218	14	McKeehan, John, consort of
McKeehan	William Smith					40	9.02	41	218	15	
McKeehan	Robert	4.26	1863			78	6.13	79	218	16	
McKeehan	Mary	2.28	1854			71	11.04	72	218	17	McKeehan, Robert, wife of
McKeehan	Samuel	12.12	1870			84		85	218	18	
McKeehan	Deborah McBride	4.30	1867			78		79	218	19	McKeehan, Samuel, wife of

Newville - Big Spring Presbyterian Graveyard

Surname	Given Name	Death Mo/Dy	Year	Birth Mo/Dy	Year	Att. Age Yr	Mo/Dy	Cm Ag	Pg	No	Other Information
McKeehan	Benjamin		1885		1819			67	218	20	
McKeehan	Jane Mary		1887		1821			67	218	21	
McKeehan	Rebecca E.	4.28	1891	6.20	1819			72	218	22	
McKeehan	Jane E. Davidson		1903		1854			50	218	23	McKeehan, Oliver, wife of
McKibben	Joseph	11.13	1836			42	5.00	43	218	24	
McKibben	Tabitha	6.05	1826			24	0.12	25	218	25	
McKibben	Thomas A.	3.02	1881	10.12	1803			78	218	26	
McKinny	Jane R.	10.13	1889	10.25	1821			8	218	27	
McKinny	David A.	9.01	1880	8.19	1850			31	218	28	
McKinny	Mary R.	4.05	1876	11.05	1852			24	218	29	
McKinny	Leonidas Coyle	2.07	1864				2.00	1	218	30	McKinny, S. D. & H. A., son of
McKinstry	James	1.30	1846			41	0.09	42	218	31	
McKinstry	Jane	3.22	1845			72		73	218	32	McKinstry, James, wife of
McKinstry	James	10.23	1825	11.22	1776			49	218	33	
McKinstry	William H.	8.14	1874			66	0.06	67	218	34	
McLaughlin	Thomas	5.19	1878			88		89	217	34	
McLaughlin	Elizabeth	1.01	1866			76		77	217	35	McLaughlin, Thomas, wife of
McLaughlin	Elizabeth	3.21	1878	12.25	1828			50	217	36	
McLaughlin	Jane	1.12	1893			40	1.10	41	217	37	McLaughlin, Daniel, wife of
McLaughlin	Samuel Harper	9.02	1878						217	38	McLaughlin, Daniel H. & J. A., son of; aged -- months, 27 days
McLaughlin	Charles Bruce	11.14	1892			2	1.13	3	217	39	
McMonigal	Agnes	5.19	1812						219	18	aged --- years; slate head stone
McMonigal	William	7.14	1813			47		48	219	19	slate head stone
McMullen	William	6.23	1882			77	4.21	78	220	18	
McMullen	Elizabeth C.	2.20	1853			50	1.00	51	220	19	McMullen, William, wife of
McWilliams	John								218	38	[38-44 one entry in text; no dates]
McWilliams	Sallie D.								218	39	McWilliams, John, wife of
McWilliams	Mary								218	40	McWilliams, John & Sallie D., child of
McWilliams	James								218	41	McWilliams, John & Sallie D., child of
McWilliams	Tiry								218	42	McWilliams, John & Sallie D., child of
McWilliams	Jane								218	43	McWilliams, John & Sallie D., child of
McWilliams	John								218	44	McWilliams, John & Sallie D., child of
McWilliams	Hetty Rose								218	45	McWilliams, John & Sallie D., child of
McWilliams	Robert	3.10	1813			27		28	218	46	
Megaw	Joseph	7.22	1811			2		3	215	13	
Megaw	James	3.26	1838			63		64	215	14	
Megaw	Sarah	5.24	1840			70		71	215	15	
Megaw	Samuel	4.15	1878			70	11.28	71	215	16	
Megaw	Elizabeth	8.17	1872			66	10.23	67	215	17	Megaw, Samuel, wife of
Mickey	Robert			1.14	1823				215	18	[date of death not given]
Mickey	Elizabeth	9.21	1893	2.18	1827			67	215	19	Mickey, R., consort of
Mickey	James Ira	3.19	1887			28	0.05	29	215	20	
Mickey	Robert, Sr.								215	21	died at an advanced age
Mickey	Agnes								215	22	Mickey, Robert, wife of; died at an advanced age
Mickey	Robert, Jr.	12.03	1827			80	11.12	81	215	23	
Mickey	Ezemiah	12.08	1830			75		76	215	24	Mickey, Robert, Jr., wife of
Mickey	Ezemiah	4.15	1858			1	1.30	2	215	25	Mickey, R. & --, daughter of
Mickey	James		1835			40		41	215	26	

Newville - Big Spring Presbyterian Graveyard

Surname	Given Name	Death Mo/Dy	Year	Birth Mo/Dy	Year	Att. Age Yr	Mo/Dy	Ag	Cm	Pg	No	Other Information
Mickey	Lucetta		1862			60	7.09	61		215	27	Mickey, James, wife of
Mickey	Mildred A.	3.17	1863			2	4.21	3		215	28	Mickey, H. & E. D., daughter of
Mickey	Laura A.	12.27	1859			9	6.22	10		215	29	
Mickey	Charles C.	12.11	1877			9	0.03	10		215	30	
Miller	Henry	1.23	1838			61	0.22	62		215	31	
Miller	John F.	9.16	1849	5.10	1808					42	215	32	
Miller	Mary	2.25	1889	7.06	1803					86	215	33	
Miller	Martha Ann		1902		1834					69	215	34	
Mixell	George	4.29	1905			68				69	215	35	Private, Co. A, 202d Regt.
Moffitt	Robert E.	9.14	1856			76	4.08	77		215	36	
Moffitt	David S.	5.08	1888	9.18	1818					70	215	37	
Moffitt	Sarah	4.30	1887	12.18	1821					66	215	38	
Moffitt	Robert	3.14	1860			2	5.06	3		215	39	Moffitt, David & Sarah, son of
Montgomery	John W.	10.08	1870			19				20	215	40	
Moore	William	7.11	1864			72	11.06	73		215	41	
Moore	Jane	5.02	1838			49				50	215	42	Moore, William, wife of
Morrow	Rachel Talbot	1.03	1900	1.15	1812					88	215	43	
Morrow	John Stevenson	4.18	1865	7.26	1788					77	215	44	
Morrow	John Benton		1900		1838					68	215	45	
Mowrer	Mary	11.29	1889			71	3.02	72		216	01	
Mull	Anna M.	9.05	1865			10	3.05	11		216	02	
Mull	Sarah Bella P.	11.17	1859			2	5.03	3		216	03	
Myers	Catharine Rhoads	1.12	1838			21	5.11	22		216	04	Myers, Henry, wife of
Myers	Margaret E.	10.30	1862			3	11.23	4		216	05	Myers, M. & E., child of
Myers	George W.	9.20	1838			2	0.17	3		216	06	Myers, M. & E., child of
Myers	Mary J.	3.01	1895	6.20	1819					76	216	07	
Neal	James, Sr.	2.27	1793								220	20	inscription on an elevated marble slab [with the six following inscriptions]
Neal	Sarah	9.13	1814								220	21	Neal, James, wife of;
Neal	John	9.22	1814								220	22	Neal, James, Sr. & Sarah, son of
Neal	Sarah	2.08	1818								220	23	Neal, James, Sr. & Sarah, dau. of
Neal	Mary Ann	9.19	1831								220	24	Neal, James, Sr. & Sarah, dau. of
Neal	Margaret	2.22	1835								220	25	
Neal	James	3.25	1838								220	26	Colonel; [see Neal, James, Sr.
Neff	George H.	7.11	1890			47	8.23	48		220	27	Co. I, 12th Regt., Pennsylvania Volunteer Reserve Corps; also Co. D, 190th Regt., Pennsylvania Volunteers
Newman	Genny Hunt					1	5.02	2		220	28	Newman, Albert & Annie, daughter of
Nicholson	Richard	12.18	1792		1713	79				80	220	29	(b. 1713); granite slab
Nicholson	Mary	1.05	1793		1710	83				84	220	30	(b. 1710); granite slab
Nickey	Jacob	1.01	1886			88	11.27	89		220	31	
Nickey	Fanny	3.16	1878	5.13	1802					76	220	32	Nickey, Jacob, wife of
Noel	Elizabeth Elliott	10.09	1873			53	2.10	54		220	33	Noel, Jacob, wife of
Noel	Martha E.	12.31	1868			2	4.19	3		220	34	Noel, Jacob & Elizabeth, daughter of
North	Mary	5.09	1867			31	10.00	32		220	35	
North	Rebecca	1.28	1870			74	4.19	75		220	36	
Oliver	Mary	4.11	1875	4.02	1837					39	220	37	Oliver, James, wife of; McCachran, Robert, Rev. & Jane, daughter of
Over	Keziah	7.28	1861			60	10.05	61		220	38	Over, Samuel, wife of
Over	Adaline	9.19	1849			11	3.23	12		220	39	Over, Samuel & Keziah, daughter of

Newville - Big Spring Presbyterian Graveyard

Surname	Given Name	Death Mo/Dy	Death Year	Birth Mo/Dy	Birth Year	Att. Age Yr	Age Mo/Dy	Cm Ag	Pg	No	Other Information
Palm	Margaret		1841		1828			14	221	01	
Patterson	Andrew	11.10	1792			62		63	221	02	
Patterson	Mary	3.15	1807			73		74	221	03	Patterson, Andrew, consort of
Patterson	Thomas	12.10	1822			48		49	221	04	Patterson, Andrew & Mary, son of
Patterson	Elizabeth	3.08	1798			26		27	221	05	slate head stone
Patterson	Obadiah	3.10	1804			42		43	221	06	Patterson, Robert & Sarah, son of
Patterson	Ann	3.05	1840			72		73	221	07	Patterson, Obadiah, wife of
Patton	Elizabeth, Mrs.	2.04	1870	1.03	1797			74	221	08	
Peebles	William		1776						221	09	Captain; killed at the Battle of Flatbush, Long Island
Peebles	Robert	1.07	1830			54	8.28	55	221	10	Captain
Peirce	Paul	6.07	1794			78		79	221	12	[Peirce (sic)]
Pierce	Joseph	8.30	1806			49		50	221	13	
Pierce	Jane	2.23	1827			58	2.00	59	221	14	Pierce, Joseph, wife of
Perry	Abraham								221	11	Co. K, 25th U. S. C. Infantry; (colored)
Philips	Edward	12.25	1857			60		61	221	15	
Philips	Jane	12.22	1870			77		78	221	16	Philips, Edward, wife of
Philips	James A.	4.26	1847			20	11.00	21	221	17	Philips, Edward & Jane, child of
Philips	Nancy I.	9.22	1853			21		22	221	18	Philips, Edward & Jane, child of
Philips	William D.	1.03	1857			28		29	221	19	Philips, Edward & Jane, child of
Pollock	Mary	8.00	1858			79		80	221	20	Pollock, Joseph, relict of
Ralston	David	3.08	1849			65	5.00	66	221	21	
Ralston	Lacy	1.28	1863			72		73	221	22	Ralston, David, wife of
Ralston	Mary	2.13	1852			72		73	221	23	
Ralston	Jane E.	2.26	1857	2.07	1833			25	221	24	Ralston, Andrew, wife of
Ralston	James McA.		1903		1823			81	221	25	
Ralston	James Dunlap	8.19	1871				9.00	1	221	26	Ralston, James M. & Margaret J., ch. of
Ralston	William Wallace	11.13	1876			4		5	221	27	Ralston, James M. & Margaret J., ch. of
Randall	Lawrence H.		1900		1810			91	221	28	
Randall	Jane Dunlap		1887		1813			75	221	29	
Randall	W. Graham		1843		1842			2	221	30	
Randall	Florence	10.23	1871	1.04	1848			24	221	31	
Randall	Ralph W.	11.12	1870	12.24	1868			2	221	32	Randall, R. S. & P., child of
Randall	Ira L.	2.12	1871	1.17	1870			2	221	33	Randall, R. S. & P., child of
Randall	Earnest Hawkins	2.21	1897	10.18	1883			14	221	34	Randall, R. S. & M. A., child of; [R. ?]
Randall	Lawrence Edmund	11.08	1890	6.12	1885			6	221	35	Randall, R. S. & M. A., child of; [R. ?]
Randolph	Paul	6.13	1861			58		59	221	36	
Randolph	Emily	8.12	1869			68		69	221	37	Randolph, Paul, wife of
Randolph	Mary	12.12	1841			39		40	221	38	Randolph, John, consort of; Knettle, Henry & Hannah, daughter of
Rankin	Mary J.	11.02	1845			27	3.23	28	221	39	Rankin, Archibald, Dr., consort of
Reed	Hugh		1823		1783			41	221	40	
Reed	Jane		1861		1788			74	221	41	
Reed	James	5.12	1842			52		53	221	42	
Reed	James	2.10	1855			35	6.26	36	221	43	
Reed	Rebecca	12.03	1839			5	4.02	6	222	01	Reed, J. & E., daughter of
Reed	William	11.14	1862	1.08	1821			42	222	02	
Rhoads	John P.	10.06	1823			36	5.21	37	222	16	
Rhoads	Barbara	3.18	1874			85	5.09	86	222	17	
Richards	Eliza K.	6.22	1861			3	5.18	4	222	03	

Newville - Big Spring Presbyterian Graveyard

Surname	Given Name	Death Mo/Dy	Year	Birth Mo/Dy	Year	Att. Age Yr	Mo/Dy	Ag	Cm	Pg	No	Other Information
Richardson	J. H.									222	04	Corporal, Co. B, 5th Massachusetts Cavalry; (colored)
Richardson	Jennie B.	2.26	1896			17	0.25	18		222	05	Richardson, James & Bella, daughter of
Richey	William	2.03	1830							222	06	Esq.; aged about 70 years
Rippey	Elizabeth Finley	9.16	1832							222	07	
Ritner	Mary Jane	6.05	1845			22			23	222	08	Ritner, Peter, wife of; Davidson, William & Mary, daughter of
Ritner	Amelia Jane	10.18	1870	8.06	1823			48		222	09	Ritner, Peter, wife of
Ritner	Jane Woodburn	3.23	1860	6.01	1858			2		222	10	Ritner, Peter & A. J., child of
Ritner	Susan	1.24	1861	1.06	1861			1		222	11	Ritner, Peter & A. J., child of
Ritner	Margaret Sharp	2.22	1865	8.28	1864			2		222	12	Ritner, Peter & A. J., daughter of
Roberts	Robert G.	1.18	1836			1	1.00	2		222	13	Roberts, Andrew & Catharine, child of
Roberts	Nancy	11.16	1839				8.07	1		222	14	Roberts, Andrew & Catharine, child of
Robinson	Mittie	6.19	1880	8.23	1872			8		222	15	Robinson, R. E. & A. M., daughter of
Russell	James F.		1883		1806			78		222	18	
Russell	Mary Jane		1886		1810			77		222	19	Russell, James F., wife of
Scouller	Eleanor	6.27	1858	5.07	1816			43		224	03	Scouller, William M., wife of
Sellers	Susanna	4.17	1875			63	2.20	64		222	28	Deckard, J. B., mother of
Sharp	James	1.28	1823	1.17	1774			50		222	26	
Sharp	John Wilson	2.25	1823	7.20	1807			16		222	27	
Sheriff	Margaret	4.27	1867			27	3.16	28		222	29	
Sheriff	Miles A.	12.12	1866			6	6.07	7		222	30	
Shullenberger	Maggie S.	1.25	1875			1	4.25	2		224	15	
Smith	Hugh	3.17	1823			73		74		223	29	
Smith	Elizabeth McCormick	5.22	1822			58		59		223	30	Smith, Hugh, wife of
Smith	David D.	8.07	1823				7.28	1		223	31	Smith, Samuel & Ruth, child of
Smith	Samuel	8.07	1839				1.18	1		223	32	Smith, Samuel & Ruth, child of
Smith	Mary	8.31	1840			7	4.08	8		223	33	Smith, Samuel & Ruth, child of
Smith	Joseph	1.26	1869			67	8.26	68		223	34	Smith, Hugh & Elizabeth, son of
Smith	Rebecca Duncan	12.21	1894	10.12	1811			84		223	35	Smith, Joseph, wife of
Smith	Susan	3.18	1870			63	0.06	64		223	36	[d. 3.15 ?]
Smith	James		1874		1810			65		223	37	
Smith	Matilda Palm		1875		1812			64		223	38	Smith, James, wife of
Smith	Margaret J.		1844		1840			5		223	39	Smith, J. & M., child of
Smith	Alexander G.		1844		1843			2		223	40	Smith, J. & M., child of
Smith	James H.		1847		1845			3		223	41	Smith, J. & M., child of
Smith	Margaretta M.		1855		1851			5		223	42	Smith, J. & M., child of
Smith	Frances A.		1858		1857			2		223	43	Smith, J. & M., child of
Smith	James H.				1848					223	44	[no death date given]
Smith	Anna M.		1854							226	01	[year not specified as that of death]
Snodgrass	Nancy Buchanan	4.23	1859							224	08	Snodgrass, B., wife of
Snowden	James H.	10.21	1889	10.06	1839			51		224	09	Co. A, 24th U. S. C. T.; (colored)
Snowden	Samuel									224	10	Sergt., Co. G, 8th U.S.C. Inf. (colored)
Sollenberger	Michael		1855		1811			45		224	04	
Sollenberger	William H.		1856		1854			3		224	05	
Sollenberger	Julia A. Mahon		1896		1816			81		224	06	Sollenberger, Michael, wife of
Sollenberger	Sarah A.		1871		1851			21		224	07	
Spencer	George W.	4.10	1873				8.06	1		222	31	Spencer, D. W. & S. C., son of
Spottswood	M., Mrs.		1833			23		24		224	11	
Spottswood	Lizzie	7.17	1889			58		59		224	12	

Newville - Big Spring Presbyterian Graveyard

Surname	Given Name	Death Mo/Dy	Year	Birth Mo/Dy	Year	Att. Age Yr	Age Mo/Dy	Cm Ag	Pg	No	Other Information
Stanton	Perry	8.12	1889			74		75	222	20	Rev. (colored)
Stanton	Mary	4.16	1876			68		69	222	21	Stanton, P., Rev., wife of
Stanton	Grace E.	8.29	1871				11.17	1	222	22	Stanton, John T. & M. A., daughter of
Starrett	James Milford T.	6.18	1812			53	11.00	54	222	23	
Starrett	Martha		1858	7.23	1801	57		57	222	24	Starrett, Robert, wife of;
											-----, Thomas W., daughter of;
											b. Lancaster County; see Sterrett
Stawart	Jane	1.06	1835			52		53	222	25	Stawart, James, consort of; see Stewart
Steel	Robert	8.17	1836			70		71	222	32	
Steel	Mary	8.19	1859			83	6.19	84	222	33	Steel, Robert, wife of
Sterrett	David	11.02	1790						222	34	aged about 53 years
Sterrett	Alexander M.	2.10	1809			6	5.00	7	222	35	
Sterrett	David	7.26	1825			58	3.00	59	222	36	
Sterrett	Rachel	12.28	1823			27		28	222	37	Sterrett, David, Jr., wife of
Sterrett	David D.	12.17	1874			32	0.14	33	222	38	
Sterrett	Isabella	2.16	1850						222	39	Sterrett, David, consort of
Sterrett	David	5.06	1864			64	1.06	65	222	40	
Sterrett	Rebecca E.	3.07	1865			62	6.26	63	223	01	Sterrett, David, wife of
Sterrett	David	11.28	1832	2.24	1828			5	223	02	Sterrett, David & Rebecca, child of
Sterrett	Thomas	12.02	1832	10.23	1831			2	223	03	Sterrett, David & Rebecca, child of
Sterrett	Martha M.	10.08	1869			24	0.09	25	223	04	Sterrett, David W., wife of
Sterrett	Rebecca Ellen	5.08	1869			1	2.11	2	223	05	Sterrett, D. W. & M. M., daughter of
Sterrett	A. W.	6.30	1880	12.09	1814			66	223	06	
Sterrett	Ezemiah E.	7.08	1837	1.01	1816			22	223	07	Sterrett, A. W., wife of
Sterrett	Marion Sharp		1904		1879			26	223	08	Sterrett, A. W., wife of
Sterrett	Brice Innes	3.07	1873			62		63	223	09	
Sterrett	Elizabeth	3.14	1858			41		42	223	10	Sterrett, Brice Innes, wife of
Sterrett	Jane	9.21	1832			23	1.07	24	223	11	see Starrett
Stevenson	James								223	12	[no dates given]
Stevenson	John	8.19	1777			38		39	223	13	Stevenson, James, son of above [223:12]
Stevenson	Rachel	4.30	1780			34		35	223	14	Stevenson, John, wife of; Scroggs,
											Alexander, daughter of
Stevenson	William	12.01	1817			76		77	223	15	
Stevenson	Jane	5.27	1818			66		67	223	16	
Stevenson	Margaret	4.01	1821						223	17	
Stevenson	John	1.01	1835			55		56	223	18	
Stevenson	Jane	2.14	1835			40		41	223	19	
Stevenson	Mary	2.11	1837			54		55	223	20	
Stevenson	William	11.27	1848			56	2.05	57	223	21	
Stewart	John M.	1.20	1884			72	11.00	73	223	22	
Stewart	Rebecca M.	4.02	1897			82		83	223	23	
Stewart	Mary E.	4.25	1881			35		36	223	24	Stewart, John & Rebecca, daughter of
Stewart	William Graham	4.12	1899	4.15	1841			58	223	25	M. D.
Stewart	Samuel P.		1890		1818			73	223	26	
Stewart	Margaretta McDannell		1895		1823			73	223	27	Stewart, Samuel P., wife of
Stewart	William M.		1869		1858			12	223	28	see Stuart
Stover	Amos	9.09	1858	10.18	1835			23	224	13	
Stuart	Thomas M.	6.16	1852						224	16	
Swiler	Prudence H. Davidson	4.23	1847			33		34	224	02	Swiler, James, wife of
Swoyer	Juliann	4.08	1828			29	8.29	30	224	14	Swoyer, Jacob, consort of

Newville - Big Spring Presbyterian Graveyard

Surname	Given Name	Death Mo/Dy	Death Year	Birth Mo/Dy	Birth Year	Att. Age Yr	Att. Age Mo/Dy	Cm Ag	Pg	No	Other Information
Thompson	Mathew	10.13	1823			68		69	224	26	red sand headstone
Thompson	Matthew	5.27	1882	8.01	1804			78	224	27	
Thompson	Elizabeth	3.14	1869	7.22	1818			51	224	28	Thompson, Matthew, wife of
Thompson	Susannah	7.04	1830			25		26	224	29	
Thompson	Joseph	11.05	1832			46		47	224	30	
Thompson	Joseph J.	7.26	1867			12	8.21	13	224	31	
Thompson	Lydia E.	8.08	1841			3	2.19	4	224	32	
Thompson	Ruth R.	1.30	1841				0.16	1	224	33	
Thompson	Mary Ann	4.27	1869			59	2.29	60	224	34	
Thompson	Easter	12.13	1873			75	0.02	76	224	35	
Trego	Rebecca	10.07	1823			71		72	224	17	Trego, Moses, wife of
Tritt	Peter	2.24	1839	3.05	1755			84	224	18	
Tritt	Elizabeth	2.07	1835			74	2.00	75	224	19	Tritt, Peter, consort of
Tritt	Samuel	2.22	1873			69	5.08	70	224	20	
Tritt	Ann Eliza	9.23	1843			33	3.29	34	224	21	Tritt, Samuel, wife of
Tritt	Julia Ann	11.26	1875			53	7.04	54	224	22	Tritt, Samuel, wife of
Tritt	William Henderson	2.28	1860			5	1.23	6	224	23	Tritt, Samuel & J. A., son of
Tritt	Robert F.	3.09	1898			5		6	224	24	Tritt, E. G. & E. B., son of
Tritt	Frances Charlotte	2.28	1899	3.16	1818			81	224	25	
Vanard	William Harry	11.04	1859				9.24	1	225	07	Vanard, William & Eliza, son of
Vanard	Sarah A. Melstead	2.20	1840			33	9.09	34	225	08	Vanard, John, wife of; [Melsted ?]
Vanard	Robert	4.14	1859			19	3.03	20	225	09	Vanard, John & Sarah A., son of
Vanderbilt	Jacob, Sr.	4.11	1804						224	36	[age is given as 10 years]
Vanderbilt	Elizabeth	11.21	1822						224	37	Vanderbilt, Jacob, Sr., wife of
Vanderbilt	Cornelius	12.09	1851	10.11	1775			77	224	38	
Vanderbelt	Mary	12.28	1829	6.18	1776			54	224	39	Vanderbilt, Cornelius, wife of; [spelling varies]
Vanderbelt	Cornelius L.	10.16	1854			45	9.11	46	224	40	
Vanderbelt	Mahala	8.05	1883	6.27	1819			65	224	41	Vanderbelt, Cornelius, wife of
Vanderbilt	Cornelius H.	6.29	1862	8.03	1841			21	225	01	Vanderbilt, Cornelius L. & M., son of; killed and buried at Willis Church near Charles City Cross Roads, Va.; Co. H, 3rd Regt., Pennsylvania Cavalry
Vanderbilt	Jane E.	11.24	1846			6	10.01	7	225	02	Vanderbelt, L. & Mahala, child of
Vanderbilt	Joshua Steel	8.04	1852			1	3.16	2	225	03	Vanderbilt, L. & Mahala, child of
Vanderbilt	John Wilson	8.23	1850			5	10.23	6	225	04	Vanderbilt, Joshua & Catharine, child of
Vanderbilt	William Cass	1.11	1851			2	2.02	3	225	05	Vanderbilt, Joshua & Catharine, child of
Vanderbilt	Cornelius Hays	8.24	1852			1	9.00	2	225	06	
Wagner	John	3.30	1889	4.30	1808			81	225	10	
Waggoner	George A.	3.22	1843	4.19	1837			6	225	11	Waggoner, John & Jane, son of
Wagner	Jacob A.	12.16	1874	11.08	1852			23	225	12	
Wagner	Mary E.	7.12	1877	1.12	1839			39	225	13	
Wagner	Eva F.	8.27	1882	9.10	1857			25	225	14	
Wagner	John A.	8.01	1876				4.00	1	225	15	Wagner, S. C. & Laura, son of
Wallace	John	12.12	1814			70		71	225	16	
Wallace	Agnes	5.28	1827			60		61	225	17	
Wallace	John H.					19		20	225	18	
Wallace	Thomas	9.30	1832			39	10.03	40	225	19	
Wallace	Mary	4.13	1838			41	4.21	42	225	20	Wallace, Thomas, consort of
Wallace	Margaret	4.02	1855			63		64	225	21	

Newville - Big Spring Presbyterian Graveyard

Surname	Given Name	Death Mo/Dy	Death Year	Birth Mo/Dy	Birth Year	Att. Age Yr	Age Mo/Dy	Cm Ag	Pg	No	Other Information
Wallace	John		1876		1798			79	225	22	
Wallace	Mary		1887		1801			87	225	23	Wallace, John, wife of
Weakley	Samuel	2.10	1829			73		74	225	24	
Weakley	Hetty	10.01	1819			63		64	225	25	
Weakley	John	11.22	1826			47		48	225	26	Weakley, Samuel & Hetty, son of
Weast	Leonard	11.12	1882			75	10.03	76	225	27	
Weast	Jane Elliott M.	8.16	1863			59	6.12	60	225	28	Weast, Leonard, wife of
Weiss	Lavinia Catharine	3.28	1849			2	5.00	3	225	29	Weiss, J. S., Rev. & E., daughter of
Whiteside	Jane A.	2.03	1876			76		77	226	26	Whiteside, Thomas, Dr., relict of
Whitley	Andrew	12.07	1848			79		80	226	25	
Williams	Joshua	8.21	1838			70		71	225	30	Rev.; D.D.; Pastor, Big Spring Presbyterian Church, 1801-1829
Williams	Eleanor	4.28	1856			76		77	225	31	Williams, Joshua, Rev., wife of
Williams	James Campbell		1822			21		22	225	32	Williams, Joshua, Rev., son of
Williams	Tabitha P.	7.05	1866	1.08	1812			55	225	33	Williams, L. H., wife of
Williams	Jane Whiteside		1839			3	4.00	4	226	01	Williams, L. H. & Tabitha, child of
Williams	Margaretta		1844			6	8.00	7	226	02	Williams, L. H. & Tabitha, child of
Williams	Eliza Ker		1848				11.00	1	226	03	Williams, L. H. & Tabitha, child of
Williams	Samuel Lewis		1851			1	9.00	2	226	04	Williams, L. H. & Tabitha, child of
Williams	Catharine	3.14	1862	8.05	1780			82	226	05	Williams, George, (of Bellefonte), relict of; born near Ickesburg, Perry Co.; died near Newville; Elliott, Thomas & Jane, daughter of
Williams	William K.	12.11	1864			1	2.06	2	226	06	Williams, D. W. & Jane A., son of
Williamson	Tamar	3.23	1819			50		51	226	07	Williamson, David, wife of
Williamson	Williamson	4.24	1837			46		47	226	08	[Williamson Williamson (sic)]
Wilson	Samuel	3.01	1799			44		45	226	09	Rev.; d. in the 15th year of ministry
Wilson	Jane	5.29	1835			74		75	226	10	Wilson, Samuel, Rev., wife of
Wilson	John	1.30	1809			16	2.10	17	226	11	Wilson, Samuel, Rev., son of; on the same slab is the name "John Heap"
Wilson	Mathew	6.06	1824			77		78	226	12	
Wilson	Samuel	4.03	1837			88		89	226	13	
Wilson	Joseph		1883		1816			68	226	14	
Wilson	Esther Butler		1900		1825			76	226	15	Wilson, Joseph, wife of
Wilt	Peter		1842		1775			68	226	16	
Wilt	Susanna		1900		1818			83	226	17	
Wilt	Peter, Jr.		1813		1813			1	226	18	
Wilt	Kittyanne		1822		1810			13	226	19	
Wilt	Eleanora		1865		1802			64	226	20	
Wilt	Hannah H.	9.05	1887			75		76	226	21	Wilt, A., wife of
Wilt	Thomas								226	22	"In memory of" [no other information]
Wilt	Mary								226	23	"In memory of" [same entry as 226:22]
Wimer	Martha E.	12.27	1875			50		51	226	24	
Wolf	Anna	2.08	1889			68	10.10	69	226	27	
Woodburn	Julia A.	4.23	1863			37		38	226	36	
Woodburn	John M.			4.06	1833				226	37	[no death date given]
Woodburn	Lucy Stewart	9.26	1896	10.18	1825			71	226	38	
Woodburn	Charles E.	2.06	1886	2.21	1865			21	226	39	
Woodburn	Thomas A.	9.14	1886						226	40	[date is not specified as that of death]
Woodburn	John M.	4.10	1865			57		58	226	41	

Newville - Big Spring Presbyterian Church

Surname	Given Name	Death Mo/Dy	Year	Birth Mo/Dy	Year	Att. Age Yr	Mo/Dy	Cm Ag	Pg	No	Other Information
Woodburn	Elmira Louisa	1.12	1845			6	3.16	7	226	42	Woodburn, J. M. & A. D., daughter of
Woodburn	Ann Jane	9.12	1835						226	43	Woodburn, J. M. & A. D., child of
Woods	N. J. Ramsey	1.28	1866			57	0.28	58	226	28	[57/0.28 (?)]
Woods	Charlotte Holmes	10.21	1904			85	5.14	86	226	29	Woods, N. J. Ramsey, wife of
Woods	Lizzie M.	12.06	1862			13	3.00	14	226	30	Woods, N. J. R. & C. H., child of
Woods	Jonathan	11.10	1867			20	10.20	21	226	31	Woods, N. J. R. & C. H., child of
Woods	Nathan C.	12.09	1869	9.20	1844			26	226	32	Woods, N. J. R. & C. H., child of
Woods	Jennie A.	1.26	1878	9.27	1851			27	226	33	Woods, N. J. R. & C. H., child of
Woods	William	12.10	1867			85		86	226	34	
Woods	Margaret	2.23	1868			72		73	226	35	

NEWVILLE CEMETERY

Surname	Given Name	Death Mo/Dy	Death Year	Birth Mo/Dy	Birth Year	Att. Age Yr	Age Mo/Dy	Cm Ag	Pg	No	Other Information
Abrahims	Jacob		1900		1822			79	245	01	
Abrahims	Emma C.		1851		1851			1	245	02	
Abrahims	Martha A.		1856		1854			3	245	03	
Abrahims	Sarah J.		1862		1859			4	245	04	
Allin	Mary Isabel	1.10	1899	5.29	1866			33	245	05	
Askin	Robert Y.	12.22	1894	12.27	1838			56	245	06	
Askin	Caroline	6.09	1889	12.31	1841			48	245	07	
Askin	Martha R.	3.16	1881				4.13	1	245	08	
Baker	Van.	4.21	1904			84	4.01	85	245	09	
Baker	Hannah	8.11	1885			57	1.14	58	245	10	Baker, Van., wife of
Baltimore	Lewis	12.10	1900						245	11	Pvt., Co. D, 6th Regt., Cav.; (colored)
Bartley	Herbert D.	5.26	1901			50		51	245	12	Bartley, Marie Dubois, husband of
Beam	George P.	3.12	1905	6.20	1833			72	245	20	
Beam	G. Franklin	4.30	1876	10.18	1862			14	245	21	
Beam	Elizabeth	7.06	1898	1.01	1855			44	245	22	
Bear	Magdalene R.	12.08	1859			41	5.13	42	245	23	Bear, Samuel, wife of
Bear	Joshua E.	11.06	1854				5.20	1	245	24	Bear, Samuel & Magdalene, son of
Bell	Margaret	12.27	1870			55		56	245	29	[aged 55 ?]
Beltshoover	Eliza Jane	9.18	1844	1.19	1840			5	245	27	Beltshoover, Jacob & Louisa, daughter of
Beltshoover	Joseph	3.02	1844	7.05	1841			3	245	28	Beltshoover, Jacob & Louisa, son of
Bentz	Adam	4.11	1883			33	11.02	34	245	25	
Bentz	Susan C.	4.10	1868			23	2.18	24	245	26	Bentz, Samuel, wife of; Brown, Henry & Leah, daughter of
Bigham	James		1846		1794			53	246	11	
Bigham	Susan E.		1840		1808			33	246	12	
Bishop	William	8.16	1887			66	1.14	67	246	13	
Black	Isaac	8.03	1889			55	10.08	56	245	13	
Black	Armstrong C.	8.30	1885	12.20	1807			78	245	14	
Black	Anna Shellabarger	4.11	1895	1.23	1813			83	245	15	Black, Armstrong C., wife of
Black	Christian	5.13	1835	2.23	1835			1	245	16	Black, Armstrong & Ann, child of
Black	John	9.24	1839	7.07	1836			4	245	17	Black, Armstrong & Ann, child of
Black	Ann Eliza	11.19	1845	7.02	1842			4	245	18	Black, Armstrong & Ann, daughter of
Blean	David		1804		1725			80	245	30	
Blean	Isabella		1822		1739			84	245	31	Blean, David, wife of
Blean	Robert		1848		1770			79	245	32	Blean, David & Isabella, son of
Blean	Mary Craig		1835		1770			66	245	33	Blean, Robert, wife of
Blean	William		1872		1798			75	245	34	Blean, Robert & Mary, son of
Blean	Robert, Jr.	7.07	1864			61	4.28	62	245	35	
Blean	Margaret	1.05	1890			78	10.00	79	245	36	Blean, Robert, wife of
Blean	Jane	7.14	1855			22		23	245	37	Blean, Robert & Margaret, daughter of
Blean	Martha E.	2.12	1845						245	38	
Blean	William	3.25	1846			16	8.00	17	245	39	Blean, John & Elizabeth, son of
Blean	John					1	4.00	2	245	40	aged 16 months
Bower	Daniel	12.03	1846			50		51	246	14	
Bower	Margaret	3.12	1883			80	2.11	81	246	15	Bower, Daniel, wife of
Bower	Adam		1899		1834			66	246	16	
Bower	Lucretia H.		1884		1883			2	246	17	
Boyles	Bertha	12.12	1902			27	10.06	28	246	18	Boyles, Jesse, wife of

Newville - Newville Cemetery

Surname	Given Name	Death Mo/Dy	Death Year	Birth Mo/Dy	Birth Year	Att. Age Yr	Att. Age Mo/Dy	Cm Ag	Pg	No	Other Information
Brattan	Samuel W.		1899		1835			65	245	19	
Brehm	John D.	10.24	1880	2.19	1815			66	246	01	
Brahm	Henry	8.01	1859			78		79	246	02	
Brahm	Elizabeth	8.28	1854			67	3.00	68	246	03	Brahm, Henry, wife of
Brehm	Joseph J.	3.28	1869			41		42	246	04	
Brehm	Elizabeth	4.07	1899			82		83	246	05	
Brehm	Nelson Dale	4.19	1900	5.22	1879			21	246	06	
Brehm	Sarah E.	3.25	1902			54	6.19	55	246	07	Brehm, R. H., wife of
Brehm	Daisy Luella	11.27	1882			4	8.10	5	246	08	Brehm, R. H. & S. E., daughter of
Brehm	Elizabeth M.	12.04	1854			5		6	246	09	
Brehm	Augustus	1.17	1881	12.09	1880			1	246	10	
Broce	David	3.15	1899			47		48	246	19	
Brown	William	1.03	1855			67		68	246	20	
Brown	Rebecca	3.09	1879			91		92	246	21	
Brown	Henry	6.22	1899	5.06	1810			90	246	22	
Brown	Leah	12.15	1870	2.18	1819			52	246	23	Brown, Henry, wife of
Brown	William		1862		1824			39	246	24	
Brown	Hannah C.		1859		1829			31	246	25	Brown, William, wife of
Brown	John C.	11.27	1878			19	9.15	20	246	26	
Brown	Thomas	10.13	1875			48	10.23	49	246	27	
Brown	Susan	7.13	1890			61	10.15	62	246	28	Brown, Thomas, wife of
Brown	Anna Mary	10.22	1870	2.18	1855			16	246	29	Brown, T. & S., daughter of
Butler	Francis	2.25	1901		1829			73	246	30	born in Maryland
Chisnell	Jacob H.	9.25	1887			78	4.18	77	247	02	Captain
Chisnell	Anna M. Goodhart	12.23	1888			76	4.19	77	247	03	Chisnell, J. H., wife of
Chisnell	Mary	12.20	1838						247	04	Chisnell, J. H. & A. M., child of
Chisnell	John	9.28	1842						247	05	Chisnell, J. H. & A. M., child of
Chisnell	Abraham G.	1.14	1856			11	2.18	12	247	06	Chisnell, J. H. & A. M., son of
Clandy	John C.	2.19	1897	6.14	1839			58	246	31	Dr.
Clandy	Father	7.04	1844	5.20	1802			43	246	32	inscription on Clandy monument [246:31]
Clandy	Mother	4.09	1890	6.07	1811			79	246	33	inscription on Clandy monument [246:31]
Clandy	Margeret E.	3.18	1849	7.15	1844			5	246	34	
Clandy	Elizabeth	10.18	1858	3.06	1834			25	246	35	
Cole	Warren Frederick	7.05	1901						246	38	(colored)
Coleman	Orid H.	3.13	1893						246	39	Sergeant, Co. M, 17th Regt., Pa. Cavalry
Cope	Benjamin	10.21	1870	9.10	1788			83	246	40	
Cope	Sarah	4.18	1870	10.12	1800			70	246	41	
Cornprobst	John H.	7.23	1895	2.22	1894			5	246	42	[189<u>5</u> ?]
Cornprobst	Margaret		1904		1831			74	246	43	
Cornprobst	Mary E.		1860		1859			2	246	44	
Cornprobst	Lillie F.		1873		1873			1	247	01	
Craig	John		1794		1744			51	246	36	Rev.; buried the day he was to have been installed pastor of Big Spring U.B. Ch.
Craig	Grissell		1824		1768			57	246	37	Craig, John, Rev., wife of
Dales	Mary B.	4.05	1874			8	10.09	9	247	07	Dales, J. & A. B., daughter of
Davidson	Coyle M.	8.12	1894				5.23	1	247	08	Davidson, J. C. & A. M., son of
Davidson	Margaret J.	6.19	1885			49	11.01	50	247	09	
Davidson	John Y.	1.29	1890			51	7.11	52	247	10	
Davidson	Nancy	6.17	1874			51	6.00	52	247	11	
Davidson	Andrew	7.02	1877			90	10.10	91	247	12	

Newville - Newville Cemetery

Surname	Given Name	Death Mo/Dy	Year	Birth Mo/Dy	Year	Att. Age Yr	Mo/Dy	Cm Ag	Pg	No	Other Information
Davidson	Elizabeth	10.31	1893			73	1.23	74	247	13	
Davidson	Jane Ann	4.13	1894			68	3.11	69	247	14	
Davidson	Barbara	11.27	1863			69	1.26	70	247	15	
Delancy	Samuel Rhoads	11.09	1903			17	9.14	18	247	16	Delancy, John C. & Priscilla, son of
Derrick	Peter		1902		1832			71	247	17	
Derrick	Leah		1887		1839			49	247	18	Derrick, Peter D., wife of
Diehl	Thomas H.	2.28	1862			1	10.13	2	247	19	Diehl, E. & S., child of
Diehl	Alfred L.	12.14	1881			3	1.23	4	247	20	Diehl, E. & S., child of
Dobbs	Joseph	5.17	1877			45	1.07	46	247	21	
Dunlap	William	5.04	1808			50		51	247	22	
Dunlap	Sarah	11.17	1852			88		89	247	23	Dunlap, William, wife of
Dunlap	William	10.20	1826			45		46	247	24	
Dunlap	Elizabeth	5.30	1839			54		55	247	25	Dunlap, William, consort of
Dunlap	Samuel	1.25	1835			31		32	247	26	
Dunlap	James	9.16	1840			42		43	247	27	
Dunlap	Jane		1848			58		59	247	28	
Dunlap	Mary		1852			38		39	247	29	
Dunlap	Mary	11.16	1863			73		74	247	30	
Dunlap	Catharine	9.08	1864	10.16	1798			66	247	31	
Dunlap	John	9.12	1864			64		65	247	32	
Dunlap	William	1.14	1871			68		69	247	33	
Dunlap	Julia	12.30	1870			70		71	247	34	Dunlap, William, wife of; aged 7- years (70)
Dunlap	John S.	5.03	1874	11.28	1810			64	247	35	
Dunlap	Mary	6.01	1895	12.20	1812			83	247	36	
Dunlap	Lizzie S.	1.18	1859			19	0.16	20	247	37	Dunlap, J. S. & M., child of
Dunlap	Theodore M.	6.13	1861			7	0.02	8	247	38	Dunlap, J. S. & M., child of
Dunlap	J. Armstrong	11.23	1851				6.21	1	247	39	Dunlap, J. S. & M., child of
Dunlap	Sarah	7.30	1882			90		91	247	40	[1882 ?]
Dunlap	Nancy	12.14	1870			62	5.00	63	247	41	
Dunlap	Sarah A.		1891			77		78	247	42	
Dunlap	Nancy E.		1905		1826			80	247	43	
Dunlap	Eugene E.	6.16	1881			3		4	247	44	Dunlap, J. & L., child of
Dunlap	Flora G.					4		5	247	45	Dunlap, J. & L., child of
Eichelberger	Angenora	8.04	1900			42	6.04	43	248	01	Eichelberger, R. D., wife of
Eichelberger	Elsie E.	2.14	1895			0	0.06	1	248	02	
Elliott	James	8.24	1849			70		71	248	03	
Elliott	Nancy	7.19	1852			72		73	248	04	
Elliott	John	8.20	1864			59	10.19	60	248	05	
Elliott	Maria	4.25	1893			72	4.04	73	248	06	
Elliott	W. L.	9.28	1900	5.20	1825			76	248	07	
Elliott	Nancy	1.23	1884			54		55	248	08	Elliott, W. L., wife of
Failor	Jacob	1.31	1875			74	8.21	75	248	09	
Failor	Elizabeth	6.13	1872			67	7.04	68	248	10	Failor, Jacob, wife of
Failor	Sarah	8.30	1898			63	7.08	64	248	11	
Failor	Levi	3.04	1904	6.08	1840			64	248	12	
Felix	Leah M.	5.25	1880			51	8.12	52	248	13	Felix, Robert, wife of
Felix	George W.	10.14	1875			25	1.21	26	248	14	Felix, Robert & Leah M., son of
Felix	Anna Verle	2.13	1893	2.16	1886			7	248	15	Felix, Jacob & Iva, daughter of
Fenton	Martha	12.30	1903			51	0.04	52	248	16	Fenton, R. J. S., wife of

Newville - Newville Cemetery

Surname	Given Name	Death Mo/Dy	Year	Birth Mo/Dy	Year	Att. Age Yr	Cm Mo/Dy	Ag	Pg	No	Other Information
Ferree	Jonathan E.				1826				248	17	Co. D, 187th Regt., Pa. Vol. Infantry
Ferree	Letitia Vanard				1831				248	18	Ferree, Jonathan E., wife of
Ferree	Mary Ellen		1872		1854			19	248	19	
Ferree	Susannah		1862		1859			4	248	20	
Fickes	Andrew	6.12	1863	8.11	1831			32	248	21	Co. F., 158th Pennsylvania Infantry
Finkenbinder	Isaac	5.30	1893			60	7.26	61	248	22	
Finkenbinder	Isabella	12.09	1883			59		60	248	23	Finkenbinder, Isaac, wife of
Fosnot	Edu. W.		1899		1841			59	248	24	[Edu. (sic)]
Fry	Frederick	8.30	1884			74	3.21	75	248	25	
Fry	Rosanna	5.08	1883			70	4.13	71	248	26	Fry, Frederick, wife of
Fry	Elizabeth Mary	12.24	1883			44	5.06	45	248	27	Fry, F. & R., daughter of
Fry	Margaret Ellen	2.03	1901	5.12	1847			54	248	28	
Garber	Walter Forman	12.10	1902	10.16	1902			1	248	29	Garber, F. T. & Alice E., son of
Gayman	John S.	4.05	1900	2.07	1899			2	248	30	Gayman, John & Clemmie, son of
Getter	Philip	10.01	1883			64	7.29	65	249	09	
Getter	Sarah Virginia Arlington	11.06	1884			35	9.05	36	249	10	Getter, P. & H., daughter of
Getter	Daniel C.	1.25	1864			9	3.01	10	249	11	Getter, P. & H., son of
Gill	Eleanor	9.17	1895			76	0.05	77	249	12	Gill, James, wife of
Gill	Grace Thompson	3.19	1897			18	1.18	19	249	13	Gill, Thomas & Lydia B., child of
Gill	Thomas M.					0	2.15	1	249	14	Gill, Thomas & Lydia B., child of
Gilmore	John H.	10.04	1869	6.26	1866			4	249	15	
Glauser	Robert Mateer	1.18	1871			1		2	248	31	
Glauser	Mary Belle	12.03	1900			28		29	248	32	Glauser, Stacy G. & Kate D., daughter of
Glauser	Kate D.	11.15	1890			47		48	248	33	
Glauser	Thomas Baer		1901		1896			6	248	34	
Goodhart	John	3.30	1883			60	1.27	61	249	16	
Goodhart	Margaret Huston	12.15	1895	2.11	1825			71	249	17	Goodhart, John, wife of
Goodhart	Emma G.	9.27	1884			27	11.03	28	249	18	Goodhart, John & M. H., child of
Goodhart	W. -----	1.07	1867			8	10.00	9	249	19	Goodhart, John & M. H., child of
Goodhart	Jennie Huston	3.15	1891	5.27	1867			24	249	20	
Goodhart	Rebecca Riley	3.04	1892	2.21	1860			33	249	21	
Goodhart	William	6.25	1897	2.23	1820			78	249	22	
Goodhart	Florence B.	1.25	1891	12.25	1890			1	249	23	Goodhart, O. & C. B. [?], daughter of
Goodlink	Agnes J.	2.13	1898			75		76	249	24	(colored)
Gracey	William		1845		1782			64	248	35	
Gracey	Priscilla Graham		1842		1778			66	248	36	Gracey, William, wife of
Gracey	Robert		1871		1811			61	248	37	Rev., D. D.: pastor Chambersburg, 1837; Pittsburg, 1853; released 1867
Gracey	Jane Kelso		1876		1813			64	248	38	Gracey, Robert, Rev., wife of
Gracey	John		1880		1817			64	248	39	
Gracey	Isabella O. Sharpe		1887		1821			67	249	01	Gracey, John, wife of
Gracey	Jennie M.		1883		1852			32	249	02	[b. 1852 ?]
Gracey	William	4.06	1880			66		67	249	03	
Gracey	Sarah A. Dunlap	7.03	1845			28	3.25	29	249	04	Gracey, William, wife of
Gracey	Rachel Woodburn	9.07	1890	7.24	1827			64	249	05	Gracey, William, wife of
Gracey	Mary Belle	8.24	1887	9.25	1852			35	249	06	
Greaver	William Franklin	10.16	1857			31	6.03	32	249	07	Rev.; died in Williamsport, MD
Greaver	William F.	5.30	1858			1	3.26	2	249	08	Greaver, W. F., Rev. & A. A., son of
Gross	Rebecca	4.24	1867			22	10.26	23	249	30	Gross, Oliver, wife of
Grove	George	9.14	1892			81	1.07	82	249	25	Dr.

Newville - Newville Cemetery

Surname	Given Name	Death Mo/Dy	Year	Birth Mo/Dy	Year	Att. Age Yr	Mo/Dy	Cm Ag	Pg	No	Other Information
Grove	Louisa, Mrs.	10.27	1847			31	7.02	32	249	26	Grove, George, Dr., wife of
Grove	George	3.08	1865			17	4.14	18	249	27	Grove, George, Dr. & Louisa, child of
Grove	Elizabeth H.	11.03	1881			39	8.00	40	249	28	Grove, George, Dr. & Louisa, child of
Grove	Mary	3.18	1894			76		77	249	29	Grove, Jacob, wife of
Hartzell	Ethel Jacobs		1898		1890			9	249	31	Hartzell, Walter E. & Mary C., dau. of
Harvey	William T.		1902		1840			63	249	36	
Harvey	Elizabeth J.		1915		1841			75	249	37	d. 1915; [handwritten addition]
Hastings	William R.		1900		1814			87	249	32	
Hastings	Mary A.		1890		1818			73	249	33	Hastings, William R., wife of
Hastings	John W.	12.17	1859			18	1.02	19	249	34	Hastings, William & M. A., son of
Hastings	John H. A.		1859		1841			19	249	35	Hastings, William R. & M. A., son of
Heberlig	Daniel	6.22	1897			85	0.23	86	250	01	
Heberlig	Sarah	4.09	1863						250	02	Heberlig, Daniel, wife of
Heberlig	Margaret	1.03	1897			54	4.09	55	250	03	Heberlig, D. & S., daughter of
Heberlig	Annie M.	11.24	1902			48	10.10	49	250	04	
Heberlig	Daniel	2.06	1857			0	6.16	1	250	05	
Heberlig	Sarah Bell	12.14	1857			6	0.12	7	250	06	
Heberlig	Nancy E.	5.26	1861			2	9.19	3	250	07	
Heberlig	Alice E.	8.19	1860			0	5.06	1	250	08	Heberlig, S. & J., child of
Heberlig	George B.	5.30	1867			3	6.00	4	250	09	Heberlig, S. & J., child of
Heberlig	Joseph	12.14	1810			73	8.17	74	250	10	
Heberlig	Mary	1.15	1883	4.28	1810			73	250	11	Heberlig, Joseph, wife of
Heberlig	Mary Etta	3.25	1896			1	5.08	2	250	12	Heberlig, H. A. & Elva, daughter of
Heckman	John A.	5.22	1866			15	2.24	16	250	13	Heckman, Samuel & Rachel, child of
Heckman	James Albert	2.03	1871			12	8.11	13	250	14	Heckman, Samuel & Rachel, child of
Heckman	George H.	7.07	1864			0	1.07	1	250	15	Heckman, Samuel & Rachel, child of
Hefflebower	Samuel	11.11	1893	7.13	1821			73	250	16	
Hefflebower	G. Thompson		1899		1838			62	250	17	
Hefflebower	Mary C.		1868		1840			29	250	18	Hefflebower, G. Thompson, wife of
Hefflebower	George Duncan	1.08	1888			4	2.16	5	250	19	Hefflebower, G. T. & M. E., son of
Hefflebower	George	3.17	1858			64	0.11	65	250	20	
Hefflebower	Catharine	4.02	1877			76	10.14	77	250	21	Hefflebower, George, wife of
Hefflefinger	Earl G.		1900		1890			11	250	22	
Helman	Adam				1832				250	23	
Helman	Mary		1905		1827			79	250	24	
Hemminger	Jacob	2.27	1898	3.16	1810			88	250	25	
Hemminger	Mary	12.07	1857	2.23	1823			35	250	26	Hemminger, Jacob, wife of
Hemminger	Susan	2.28	1898	6.06	1846			52	250	27	Hemminger, Jacob & Mary, daughter of
High	Margaret	9.27	1889			77	4.02	78	250	28	
Hildebrand	Margaret Ann	10.27	1894			53	3.01	54	250	29	
Hoch	Samuel	11.20	1889			51		52	250	30	
Hoch	Cletie Hocker								250	31	[no dates given]
Hoch	John Landis								250	32	[no dates given]
Hoch	Joseph Clarence								250	33	[no dates given]
Hoch	George Eber								250	34	[no dates given]
Hoover	William C.	8.25	1838			4	10.06	5	250	35	
Hoover	John	4.30	1876			86		87	250	36	
Hoover	Anna	6.23	1874			72	8.18	73	250	37	Hoover, John, wife of
Hoover	Ann Catharine	12.31	1850	11.11	1836			15	250	38	Hoover, John & Anna, child of
Hoover	Henry	1.31	1851	5.18	1834			17	250	39	Hoover, John & Anna, child of

Newville - Newville Cemetery

Surname	Given Name	Death Mo/Dy	Year	Birth Mo/Dy	Year	Att. Age Yr	Mo/Dy	Cm Ag	Pg	No	Other Information
Huntsberger	Mirene	9.07	1863			0	9.28	1	250	40	Huntsberger, F. & R. E., daughter of
Huntsberger	J. Otto	12.25	1885	12.02	1885			1	251	01	
Hursh	Annie E.	4.20	1886			26	7.17	27	251	02	Hursh, James H., wife of
Hursh	John L.	1.01	1860			2	7.21	3	251	03	Hursh, John & Sarah, son of
Huston	Samuel	7.24	1883	6.05	1797			87	251	04	
Huston	Ann Fulton	4.12	1880			80	2.15	81	251	05	Huston, Samuel, wife of
Huston	Alfred	5.01	1893	1.06	1841			53	251	06	
Huston	Mary E.	12.10	1877	4.04	1835			40	251	07	Huston, Alfred, wife of
Huston	Keziah I.	9.04	1888			49	7.21	50	251	08	
Huston	Anna E.	4.17	1889			45	0.05	46	251	09	
Huston	Jane A.	10.30	1884	5.02	1835			50	251	10	
Huston	S. Henderson	4.09	1867			34	3.27	35	251	11	
Huston	Margaretta	3.02	1870			33		34	251	12	
Huston	F. Fulton	4.07	1852			24		25	251	13	
Huston	John R.	9.27	1890			29	11.03	30	251	14	
Huston	Joseph B.	1.01	1883			28	2.08	29	251	15	
Huston	James S.	1.21	1863			32	11.21	33	251	16	
Huston	Laura	4.24	1863			0	6.00	1	251	17	Huston, James S. & Mary J., daughter of
Huston	Maggie	7.17	1894	11.24	1866			28	251	18	Huston, W. J., wife of
Jackson	Robert	12.10	1880			71		72	251	19	
Jackson	Elizabeth	6.06	1883			72		73	251	20	[d. 6.0_6_ ?]
Jackson	Isabella	11.12	1889			50		51	251	21	
Jackson	Emma	9.18	1883	10.01	1849			34	251	22	Jackson, J. D., wife of
Jacoby	Jacob	5.24	1869			68	9.18	69	251	23	
Jacoby	Christian	9.10	1890	3.07	1838			53	251	24	
Jacoby	Susie Ellen	10.22	1881			19	0.22	20	251	25	Jacoby, Christian & Wilhelmina
Jacoby	William		1905		1833			73	251	26	
Jacoby	Susanna				1834				251	27	Jacoby, William, wife of
Jacoby	Mary	12.21	1889			80	4.14	81	251	28	
James	Edwin	4.19	1889			55	5.27	56	251	29	
James	Anna A.	3.25	1890			56	10.17	57	251	30	James, Edwin, wife of
Jones	Benjamin	4.13	1881	3.09	1809			73	251	31	
Jones	Mary	11.05	1894	12.13	1813			81	251	32	
Jones	Mary C.	12.03	1889	7.06	1846			44	251	33	
Jones	Jane S.	2.17	1860			5	8.15	6	251	34	
Jones	James D.	5.05	1853			0	9.00	1	251	35	
Keiffer	Emma	5.06	1900			30	10.03	31	251	36	Keiffer, B. F., wife of
Keiffer	Paul Raymon					0	0.15	1	251	37	Keiffer, B. F. & Emma, son of; 2 w. 1 d.
Killian	John	2.23	1865			85	5.00	86	251	38	
Killian	Elizabeth	7.23	1866			80	1.07	81	251	39	Killian, John, wife of
Killian	Charles	4.22	1877	7.09	1811			66	251	40	
Killian	Margaret	12.29	1884	12.19	1822			63	251	41	
Killian	Henry	1.30	1896	11.02	1813			83	251	42	
Killian	Ann Eliza	2.15	1891	12.10	1818			73	251	43	Killian, Henry, wife of
Killian	Ann Eliza	12.23	1855	5.28	1847			9	252	01	
Killian	Samuel J.	12.09	1894	3.20	1842			53	252	02	Private, Co. D, 21 Regt., Pa. Cavalry
Kirkpatrick	Jennie W.		1893		1892			2	252	03	Kirkpatrick, J. & Ella, daughter of
Kissinger	George C.	4.06	1872			21	3.22	22	252	04	
Kissinger	James M.	3.08	1872			23	5.21	24	252	05	
Kissinger	Jane Mary	8.12	1863			0	0.18	1	252	06	

Newville - Newville Cemetery

Surname	Given Name	Death Mo/Dy	Year	Birth Mo/Dy	Year	Att. Yr	Age Mo/Dy	Cm Ag	Pg	No	Other Information
Kissinger	Joseph	2.09	1886	2.15	1827			59	252	07	
Kissinger	Margaret	3.01	1900	10.13	1826			74	252	08	Kissinger, Joseph, wife of
Kissinger	J. Luther	11.16	1891			2	2.07	3	252	09	Kissinger, W. J. & M. G., son of
Kling	Moses	12.08	1894			87	9.13	88	252	10	
Kling	Julia Ann	7.16	1884			69	5.23	70	252	11	Kling, Moses, wife of
Koons	Mary E.	8.25	1901			0	10.07	1	252	12	Koons, B. L. & E. Z., daughter of
Kyle	James	5.14	1871			74		75	252	13	
Kyle	Sarah					65		66	252	14	Kyle, James, wife of
Kyle	S. Maud					1	6.00	2	252	15	Kyle, J. M. & L. M., eldest daughter of
Lamb	Sarah	1.01	1827			34		35	252	16	
Landis	George		1899		1826			74	252	17	
Landis	Mary Bell		1860		1858			3	252	18	
Landis	Sarah A. Piper		1903		1855			49	252	19	Landis, C. R., wife of
Landis	Jacob	12.07	1892						252	20	Private, Co. H, 202 Regt., Pa. Vols.
Landis	Margaret	2.17	1892			71		72	252	21	Landis, Jacob, wife of
Landis	Mary								252	22	[no dates given]
Lay	John	7.14	1869			22	10.11	23	252	23	
Lay	Melvin	8.02	1901	5.29	1891			11	252	24	
Lay	Eliza Jane	11.14	1901			83	8.28	84	252	25	
Layburn	Charles A.	1.09	1883			19	5.08	20	252	26	Layburn, John & Frances, ch. of (colored
Layburn	John E.	12.30	1883			17	3.02	18	252	27	Layburn, John & Frances, ch. of (colored
Lehman	Louisa Zinn		1904		1823			82	252	28	
Leidigh	Henry, Sr.		1890		1811			80	252	29	
Leidigh	Martha M.		1896		1812			85	252	30	Leidigh, Henry, wife of
Leidigh	Henry, Jr.		1849		1845			5	252	31	
Leidigh	George W.		1863		1834			30	252	32	
Leidigh	George F.								252	33	Leidigh, J. H. & S. S., son of
Line	George	7.06	1894	7.06	1826			69	252	34	
Line	Isabella W. Huston	10.07	1898	11.21	1823			75	252	35	Line, George, wife of
Line	George Arthur	2.03	1897	5.06	1895			2	252	36	
Line	David Alexander	11.25	1856			5	10.11	6	252	37	
Line	Wilberforce Scott	2.07	1861			1	8.06	2	252	38	
Line	Sarah Frances	2.26	1855			7	7.22	8	252	39	
Line	Jennie Clair	1.15	1859			3	9.07	4	252	40	
Lininger	Peter		1863		1820			44	252	41	
Lininger	Martha		1904		1824			81	252	42	Lininger, Peter, wife of
Livingston	Michael	3.05	1877	8.03	1818			59	252	43	
Livingston	Henry		1870		1831			40	252	44	
Livingston	Henry B.		1862		1861			2	252	45	
Livingston	Lucy E.		1870		1869			2	253	01	
Long	Abbia D.	12.22	1872			5	6.03	6	253	02	Long, Samuel & Sarah M., daughter of
Luck	Charles	5.02	1900	6.03	1861			39	253	03	
Luck	John	9.26	1903	1.11	1827			77	253	04	G.A.R.
Madison	Joseph	10.11	1900						253	05	
Madison	Fanny	4.19	1903						253	06	
McCaleb	Bert A.	3.29	1895			24		25	253	32	
McCulloch	William	7.10	1886			87	3.10	88	253	33	
McCulloch	Jane C.	2.23	1877			69	8.10	70	253	34	McCulloch, William, wife of
McCulloch	Jane	2.22	1900			52		53	253	35	
McCulloch	Mary E.	8.23	1867			26		27	253	36	McCulloch, W. H., wife of

Newville - Newville Cemetery

Surname	Given Name	Death Mo/Dy	Year	Birth Mo/Dy	Year	Att. Age Yr	Mo/Dy	Cm Ag	Pg	No	Other Information
McCulloch	Sarah Belle	11.12	1867			0	7.04	1	253	37	
McCulloch	James		1901		1824			78	253	38	
McCulloch	Martha Brown		1854		1827			28	253	39	McCulloch, James, wife of
McCulloch	Thomas	2.16	1868			70	10.14	71	253	40	
McCulloch	Isabella	3.16	1863			61	10.09	62	253	41	McCulloch, Thomas, wife of
McCulloch	Isabella	3.01	1839	6.04	1837			2	254	01	McCulloch, Thomas & Isabella, child of
McCulloch	John Craig	8.24	1850			20	9.26	21	254	02	McCulloch, Thomas & Isabella, child of
McCulloch	J. Harrold	9.05	1890	5.07	1889			2	254	03	McCulloch, J. H. & H. E., son of
McCullough	Samuel	12.06	1894			38		39	254	04	
McCullough	Annie M.	1.17	1896			37		38	254	05	
McCullough	Anna M. McKee	2.25	1888			42		43	254	06	McCulloch, Cyrus, wife of
McElwain	Andrew	1.02	1855	2.24	1810			45	254	07	
McElwain	Elsie J. Gilmor	12.31	1893	4.22	1823			71	254	08	McElwain, Andrew, wife of
McElwain	Mary H.	2.22	1905	1.12	1846			60	254	09	
McElwain	Andrew	2.15	1860	10.09	1852			8	254	10	
McKee	David Jackson	9.03	1863	5.05	1815			49	254	11	
McKee	Margaret Ann	1.02	1897			79	5.16	80	254	12	McKee, David Jackson., wife of
McKee	Joseph M.	9.00	1850			32		33	254	13	
McKee	Mary S.	12.00	1864			42		43	254	14	
McKee	Mary Ann	8.05	1881	4.06	1812			70	254	15	
McKee	Joseph	11.19	1840			74		75	254	16	
McKee	Mary					88		89	254	17	
McKee	Lizzie W.					10		11	254	18	
McKeehan	Benjamin	10.16	1873	11.24	1785			88	254	19	
McKeehan	Margaret	1.03	1848			31	3.19	32	254	20	McKeehan, James, wife of; Sharp, John & Jane, daughter of; d. Baltimore
McKeehan	Eleanor Hackett	10.08	1873			46		47	254	21	McKeehan, James, wife of
McKeehan	James	9.16	1893			68	10.00	69	254	22	
McKeehan	Benjamin		1873		1785			89	254	23	possibly a duplicate of #19
McKeehan	Mary		1872		1787			86	254	24	McKeehan, Benjamin, wife of
McKeehan	Margaret M. B.		1903		1827			77	254	25	
McKeehan	J. A.	5.18	1895	5.07	1817			79	254	26	
McKeehan	Rebecca	3.29	1851			32		33	254	27	McKeehan, J. A., wife of
McKeehan	Mary Ann	1.22	1884	5.03	1830			54	254	28	McKeehan, J. A., wife of
McKeehan	William		1871		1793			79	254	29	
McKeehan	Rebecca		1896		1805			92	254	30	McKeehan, William, wife of
McKeehan	Thaddeus Stevens	9.17	1862			24		25	254	31	Co. K, 130th Penn. Infantry; killed at Antietam, MD; body not recovered
McLaughlin	Jane Donaldson	9.06	1890	8.06	1812			79	254	32	
McLaughlin	Robert								254	33	"Family; Father; Mother" [six persons are listed, 254:33-38
McLaughlin	G. Tidings								254	34	listed with Robert McLaughlin family
McLaughlin	Mary J.								254	35	listed with Robert McLaughlin family
McLaughlin	Susan								254	36	listed with Robert McLaughlin family
McLaughlin	Belle E.								254	37	listed with Robert McLaughlin family
McLaughlin	-----								254	38	McLaughlin, Robert, wife of;
Mell	Mary E.		1846		1845			2	253	07	
Mell	David		1891		1816			76	253	08	
Mellinger	Christina Hoover	8.07	1886			79	7.07	80	253	09	Mellinger, John W., wife of
Mentzer	Henry	4.16	1893			70		71	253	10	

Newville - Newville Cemetery

Surname	Given Name	Death Mo/Dy	Year	Birth Mo/Dy	Year	Att. Age Yr	Mo/Dy	Age	Cm	Pg	No	Other Information
Montgomery	Robert	4.11	1879			64	6.28	65	253	11		
Montgomery	Rachel M.	10.20	1862			48		49	253	12		
Myers	David	9.12	1876			59	1.25	60	253	13		
Myers	Elizabeth	3.08	1874			55	4.24	56	253	14		Myers, David, wife of
Myers	Susan	2.21	1884			37	2.08	38	253	15		
Myers	Alma R.	1.14	1886			2	9.19	3	253	16		Myers, John & Annie A., daughter of
Myers	Catharine Matilda	9.02	1872	10.29	1838			34	253	17		Myers, Samuel, wife of
Myers	Thomas Reese	8.16	1895	1.09	1890			6	253	18		Myers, T. E. & E. J., child of
Myers	Elizabeth	2.25	1888			2	0.23	3	253	19		Myers, T. E. & E. J., child of
Myers	Paul Sheaffer	8.05	1896	1.24	1896			1	253	20		Myers, Charles C. & Elizabeth M., son of
Myers	Catharine	2.06	1897	3.03	1817			80	253	21		
Myers	Jacob	8.21	1869			48	0.07	49	253	22		
Myers	John B.	5.21	1884	9.12	1828			56	253	23		
Myers	Emily W.		1903		1849			55	253	24		
Myers	John B.	10.21	1881	6.08	1881			1	253	25		
Myers	Maggie Y.	5.10	1889	4.05	1883			7	253	26		
Myers	Sarah	3.27	1882			60	1.09	61	253	27		
Myers	John	2.08	1860			61	3.04	62	253	28		
Myers	Eve	5.22	1873			82	7.06	83	253	29		Myers, John, wife of
Myers	William A.	8.15	1901	8.18	1839			62	253	30		
Myers	Margaretta Y. McKee	1.20	1882			35	3.17	36	253	31		Myers, William A., wife of
Negly	Elizabeth	5.04	1870	10.03	1793			77	254	39		
Orris	Levan H.	12.16	1903			69	2.06	70	254	40		
Orris	John Sylvester	11.15	1895			30	0.20	31	254	41		Orris, Levan H., & Nancy A., son of: interred in Spring Hill Cemetery, Shippensburg
Otto	Joseph S.	12.13	1859			54	8.20	55	255	01		
Otto	Rachel	2.10	1882			72	1.00	73	255	02		Otto, Joseph S., wife of
Otto	Mary M.	11.25	1843			6	10.15	7	255	03		
Otto	Samuel B.	1.08	1844			10	2.28	11	255	04		
Otto	Anna M.	7.05	1873			0	1.14	1	255	05		Otto, H. B. & Alice E., daughter of
Patton	James	8.30	1835			27		28	255	06		
Patton	Richard	6.08	1851			88		89	255	07		
Patton	Sarah	10.11	1856	10.22	1776			80	255	08		Patton, Richard, wife of
Patton	Mary E.	12.23	1861			43	10.01	44	255	09		Patton, William, wife of
Patton	Mary J.	3.21	1865	4.04	1824			41	255	10		Patton, William, wife of
Peiffer	William	4.08	1899	3.06	1842			58	255	11		Peiffer, William, wife of
Peiffer	Rebecca	7.16	1898	12.31	1843			55	255	12		Peiffer, William, wife of
Perlet	Dorothea	6.11	1860			24	7.28	25	255	13		Perlet, John, wife of
Piper	Samuel	3.07	1869			81		82	255	14		
Piper	Mary Jane McCullough	3.00	1889	10.25	1810			79	255	15		Piper, Samuel, wife of; d. Mar. 2-, 1889
Piper	James	1.01	1846			69		70	255	16		Capt.
Piper	Catharine	7.07	1844			63		64	255	17		Piper, James, Capt., wife of
Piper	Margaret	10.30	1849			66		67	255	18		Miss
Piper	Nancy	4.25	1851			35		36	255	19		Piper, John, wife of
Piper	James		1770		1698			73	255	20		b. Ireland; d. near head of Big Spring
Piper	Margaret Cleland								255	21		Piper, James, wife of; died near same time
Piper	Samuel		1822		1739			84	255	22		
Piper	Jane Elder		1839			90		91	255	23		Piper, Samuel, wife of

Newville - Newville Cemetery

Surname	Given Name	Death Mo/Dy	Year	Birth Mo/Dy	Year	Att. Yr	Age Mo/Dy	Ag	Cm	Pg	No	Other Information
Piper	James		1802			24			25	255	24	
Piper	Elder D.		1820			23			24	255	25	A. B.
Piper	William		1810			18			19	255	26	
Piper	Martha		1843			58			59	255	27	
Piper	Jane		1823			37			38	255	28	
Piper	Samuel Elder		1901		1826				76	255	29	
Piper	Jane W.		1893		1833				61	255	30	Piper, S. E., wife of
Piper	Margaret J.		1855		1851				5	255	31	
Piper	Mary L.		1863		1857				7	255	32	
Piper	Margaret McC.		1863		1862				2	255	33	
Piper	Jane I.		1874		1860				15	255	34	
Piper	J. Elder		1899		1882				18	255	35	Piper, J. M. & Ada, son of; Piper, John, family of
Piper	Maria		1831		1801				31	255	36	Piper, John, family of
Piper	Ann		1837		1798				40	255	37	Piper, John, family of
Piper	Jane		1847		1824				24	255	38	Piper, John, family of
Piper	Sarah Sankey		1861		1826				36	255	39	Piper, John, family of
Piper	John		1866		1789				78	255	40	
Piper	Sarah		1870		1802				69	255	41	
Pleyer	Philip A.	8.13	1888			38	1.10	39	255	42		
Rea	Margaret Pipes		1851			76			77	255	43	
Rhoads	H.	4.01	1883			74	9.02	75	255	45		
Rhoads	Sarah A.	8.10	1887			79	3.00	80	255	46		
Rideout	Emma	6.25	1891			31	2.24	32	255	44		(colored)
Scouller	John		1823		1776				48	256	20	
Scouller	Jane		1868		1782				87	256	21	Scouler, John, wife of
Scouller	John B.		1815		1810				6	256	22	
Scouller	James Y.		1815		1812				4	256	23	
Scouller	Thomas C.		1900		1818				83	256	24	
Scouller	James B.	9.11	1899	7.12	1820				80	256	25	Rev.
Scouller	Helen I.	5.08	1895	5.06	1821				75	256	26	
Scouller	James F.	9.02	1877	11.07	1876				1	256	27	Scouler, J. B. & A. E., son of
Scouller	John Brown	2.09	1878	5.07	1842				36	256	28	
Seitz	Henry H.	7.11	1884	5.20	1831				54	256	12	
Seitz	Lydia A.	12.21	1903	2.13	1837				67	256	13	Seitz, Henry H., wife of
Shaffer	Sarah B.	3.23	1890			83	1.23	84	256	01		
Shaffer	Susannah	9.18	1884			58	9.20	59	256	02		Shaffer, W. B., wife of
Sharpe	Andrew J.	9.08	1858	3.14	1837				22	256	04	
Sharpe	Samuel M.	4.19	1889	1.28	1823				67	256	05	
Sharp	Annie	4.11	1873			3	6.23	4	256	06		Sharp, S. McK. & M. A., daughter of
Sharp	Andrew	3.16	1837	3.12	1794				44	256	07	
Sharpe	Rosanna Barr	11.13	1882	8.21	1806				77	256	08	
Sharpe	Mary McCulloch	9.26	1881	6.21	1852				30	256	09	Sharpe, John C., wife of
Sheaffer	Emma E.	9.02	1890			0	9.27	1	256	10		Sheaffer, Reuben & Amanda, daughter of
Shenk	Jane S.		1903		1849				55	256	11	
Shively	Simon		1896		1833				64	256	14	
Shoemaker	Mary Ellen	2.17	1868			40	6.20	41	256	29		Shoemaker, William B., Dr., wife of
Shoemaker	Robbie	1.05	1866			9	7.25	10	256	30		Shoemaker, William B., Dr. & M. E., son
Shoemaker	Maggie E.	7.16	1868			0	7.11	1	256	31		Shoemaker, William B., Dr. & M. E., child of

Newville - Newville Cemetery

Surname	Given Name	Death Mo/Dy	Year	Birth Mo/Dy	Year	Att. Yr	Age Mo/Dy	Cm Ag	Pg	No	Other Information
Shoemaker	Minnie B.	7.14	1868			0	7.09	1	256	32	Shoemaker, William B., Dr., & M. E., child of
Skinner	Maria B.	9.10	1887			82	6.20	83	256	16	Skinner, John S., wife of
Skiner	Harry Uhler	12.03	1876			0	1.10	1	256	17	Skiner, S. M. & Elizabeth, son of
Smith	Mary C.	10.03	1898	6.19	1843			56	256	15	
Snyder	Peter L.	8.29	1892			54		55	257	02	
Spangler	Esther Susanna	8.21	1892			1	9.27	2	256	03	Spangler, William I. & Elizabeth C., daughter of
Stough	Margaret S.		1894		1833			62	256	33	
Stough	Thomas		1892		1824			69	256	34	
Swigert	Christiana E.	2.09	1857			21	11.27	22	256	18	Swigert, George, wife of
Swigert	Jennie	8.03	1865			1	10.00	2	256	19	Swigert, G. W. & E. T., daughter of; d. 1 year, 10 months, --days
Swoyer	Jacob	4.02	1864						256	35	Ensign & Lieutenant, 5th U. S. Infantry, 1812-1815
Swoyer	Sarah M., Mrs.	4.26	1870			74	3.14	75	256	36	
Swoyer	Judith	2.02	1859			63		64	256	37	
Swoyer	George	1.04	1863	12.04	1833			30	257	01	b. Newville; d. Sommerville, TN; Captain, Co. B, 7th Kansas Cavalry
Thomas	Mary Linn Elliott	8.31	1887	3.06	1851			37	257	12	Thomas, F. H., wife of
Thompson	Alexander S.	12.04	1878	4.28	1834			45	257	13	Rev.; pastor Worthington & Slade Run Churches, Armstrong County, Nov. 20, 1867; d. in 11th year of ministry
Thompson	Alexander C.	1.22	1876			5		6	257	14	Thompson, Alexander S. & Bell D., ch. of
Thompson	John Dunlap	10.09	1882			4		5	257	15	Thompson, Alexander S. & Bell D., ch. of
Throne	John	4.17	1898			71	10.18	72	257	16	
Throne	Conrad	2.16	1872			75	2.01	76	257	17	
Throne	Elizabeth	5.06	1869			72	0.18	73	257	18	Throne, Conrad, wife of
Throne	David	2.07	1843	1.11	1838			6	257	19	Throne, Conrad & Elizabeth, son of
Thrush	William G.		1904		1835			70	257	20	
Thrush	Mary J.				1829				257	21	
Thrush	Barnebas	11.28	1888			84	11.26	85	257	22	
Thrush	Elizabeth	7.14	1882			79	7.25	80	257	23	Thrush, Barnebas, wife of
Thrush	John H.	12.11	1897			55		56	257	24	
Trego	John	12.08	1862	1.18	1807			56	257	03	Trego, Eli & Esther, son of
Trego	Louisa	12.18	1867			58	7.26	59	257	04	Trego, John, wife of
Trego	Rebecca Eleanor	2.15	1857	12.28	1831			26	257	05	Trego, John & Louisa, eldest daughter of
Trego	Edward A.	11.08	1865	9.17	1844			22	257	06	Trego, John & Louisa, son of
Trego	Eddie	11.01	1870				8.10	1	257	07	Trego, J. K. & C. S., son of
Trimmer	Richard			4.00	1834				257	08	
Trimmer	Matilda	10.00	1900	9.00	1833			68	257	09	Trimmer, Richard, wife of
Tritt	Anna Dora	6.06	1879	3.14	1860			20	257	10	
Tritt	Harrie F.	5.13	1875			7	2.17	8	257	11	Tritt, B. F. & A. R., son of
Utley	Maggie Jane	7.26	1871				6.14	1	257	25	
Waggoner	Abraham	3.08	1868			48	9.13	49	257	26	
Waggoner	Mary Bell	7.18	1858				5.18	1	257	27	Waggoner, A. & M., daughter of
Wallace	Henderson	10.12	1886			40		41	257	30	Co. H. [?], 3 Regt., U. S. C. I. (colored)

Newville - Newville Cemetery

Surname	Given Name	Death Mo/Dy	Death Year	Birth Mo/Dy	Birth Year	Att. Age Yr	Mo/Dy	Cm Ag	Pg	No	Other Information
Wallace	William		1874		1800			75	257	31	Wallace inscriptions obtained at Charles Eby's marble office in Newville for Wallace's brought here from other cems.
Wallace	Mary J.		1882		1807			76	257	32	[see note for William Wallace]
Wallace	Margaret L.		1850		1837			14	257	33	[see note for William Wallace]
Wallace	John W.		1856		1833			24	257	34	[see note for William Wallace]
Wallace	James M.		1870		1834			37	258	01	[see note for William Wallace]
Wallace	Annie M.		1872		1845			28	258	02	[see note for William Wallace]
Wallace	Ada		1872		1849			24	258	03	[see note for William Wallace]
Wallace	Elizabeth G.		1884		1843			42	258	04	[see note for William Wallace]
Wallace	Agnes S.		1890		1841			50	258	05	[see note for William Wallace]
Wallace	Laura M.		1905		1849			57	258	06	[see note for William Wallace]
Wallace	William Jackson		1886		1839			48	258	07	[see note for William Wallace]
Wallace	Mary G.		1896		1843			54	258	08	Wallace, William, wife of; [see note for William Wallace]
Wallace	James		1852		1789			64	258	09	[see note for William Wallace]
Wallace	Sarah								258	10	Wallace, James, wife of; [see note for William Wallace
Wastafer	Lacy Ellen	7.24	1891			54	10.05	55	257	28	Wastafer, William, wife of
Wastafer	Lissie Lindsey	3.14	1871			5	2.15	6	257	29	Wastafer, William & L. E., daughter of
Westafer	Samuel	9.08	1872			79	0.06	80	258	12	
Westafer	Susan	5.11	1883	4.06	1799			85	258	13	Westafer, Samuel, wife of
Wells	Catharine E.	5.30	1905			59		60	258	11	
Whistler	Catharine A.		1900		1832			69	258	23	
Wild	Samuel	10.24	1842			42	3.00	43	258	14	
Wild	Anna B.	1.16	1880			83	8.26	84	258	15	Wild, Samuel, wife of
Wilkinson	Enos	9.03	1879			55	8.09	56	258	16	
Wilkinson	Caroline	12.25	1895			78	9.22	79	258	17	Wilkinson, Enos, wife of
Williams	Edith		1887		1885			3	258	18	(colored)
Wise	Rebecca		1872		1802			71	258	19	
Wise	John		1834		1803			32	258	20	
Wise	Catharine E.	3.05	1860	5.10	1853			7	258	21	Wise, Harriet, daughter of
Wise	Jacob	12.24	1850	2.03	1831			20	258	22	Wise, John & Rebecca, son of
Wolf	Susan E.		1897		1837			61	258	31	Wolf, Joseph, wife of
Woodburn	B. W.	5.31	1895						258	25	
Woodburn	Elizabeth	7.10	1894			72		73	258	26	Woodburn, B. W., wife of
Woodburn	Skiles	7.08	1878			83		84	258	27	
Woodburn	Margaret McKeehan	12.07	1878			80		81	258	28	Woodburn, Skiles, wife of
Woodburn	A. Sharpe	11.29	1889	9.10	1832			58	258	29	
Woodburn	Rebecca M.	1.31	1867	11.16	1866			1	258	30	Woodburn, A. & B. S., daughter of
Woods	James T.	5.25	1894	9.25	1835			59	258	24	

PROSPECT HILL CEMETERY

Surname	Given Name	Death Mo/Dy	Year	Birth Mo/Dy	Year	Att. Age Yr	Mo/Dy	Cm Ag	Pg	No	Other Information
Ahl	John	4.09	1844			68		69	232	01	M. D.
Ahl	Nancy Vaughn	5.27	1851			79		80	232	02	Ahl, John, Dr., wife of
Ahl	Peter	3.20	1897	12.16	1815			82	232	03	
Ahl	Daniel V.	9.16	1896	2.20	1826			71	232	04	
Ahl	Samuel S.	1.22	1851			41		42	232	05	
Ahl	Martha J.	1.09	1881	2.22	1807			74	232	06	
Ahl	Mary E.	3.29	1882	11.07	1818			64	232	07	
Ahl	Eleanor G.					0	0.28	1	232	08	Ahl, David & Mary E., dau. of; age 4 wk.
Alexander	Rosann	12.02	1867			31	4.20	32	232	11	Alexander, Elias, wife of
Alexander	Elias	1.28	1872			39	0.28	40	232	12	
Alexander	Samuel		1896		1830			67	232	13	
Allen	Samuel R.	4.24	1891			76	3.10	77	232	09	
Allen	Jane	1.25	1893			76	8.29	77	232	10	
Arbegast	James E.		1904		1862			43	232	14	
Arbegast	Katie B.		1861						232	15	Arbegast, James E., wife of; [1861 is not specified as death date]
Arbegast	George J.	12.31	1894			88	1.02	89	232	16	
Arbegast	Anna M.	10.27	1883			72	4.14	73	232	17	
Baker	George	4.15	1883			82	3.14	83	232	18	
Baker	Martha	3.21	1889			74	9.05	75	232	19	
Baker	Henry	3.13	1854			78	3.00	79	232	20	
Baker	Catharine	3.13	1852			72	3.16	73	232	21	Baker, Henry, wife of
Baker	William	5.12	1851			28	3.00	29	232	22	Baker, Henry & Catharine, son of
Baker	Frank	3.27	1888			44	4.18	45	232	23	Dr.
Baker	Annie S.		1903		1836			68	232	24	
Baker	Mary Savilla	1.21	1902			37		38	232	25	Baker, J. E., wife of
Baker	Mary M.	8.24	1860			0	4.06	1	232	26	Baker, H. & J., daughter of
Barrick	Mary Belle Margaret	7.08	1903	6.18	1903			1	232	33	
Barto	Mary Melinda	8.29	1856	5.09	1853			4	232	34	Barto, Jonathan & Rebecca, child of
Barto	Melinda Elizabeth	2.14	1852	8.04	1850			2	232	35	Barto, Jonathan & Rebecca, child of
Barto	Anna Maria	1.29	1852	5.18	1848			4	232	36	
Baum	Wilmer	12.18	1888			1	3.19	2	232	27	Baum, J. A. & M. E., son of
Beetem	Abram C.	2.10	1901			17	4.14	18	232	37	"The Evangelist:
Bender	George A.	7.07	1902			0	0.11	1	232	38	Bender, G. W. & M. J., son of
Berrier	Thomas	3.28	1900			69		70	232	39	
Berrier	Franklin P.	1.15	1885			17	4.07	18	233	01	
Berrier	Sarah Luella	2.12	1902	9.26	1870			32	233	02	Berrier, Thomas & Susan, daughter of
Boldosser	J. Reed		1903		1895			9	233	10	
Boldosser	Catharine	8.04	1904	5.09	1879			26	233	11	Boldosser, G. E., wife of
Bower	John J.		1867		1827			41	233	13	
Bower	Hannah M.		1895		1834			62	233	14	Bower, John J., wife of
Bower	William A.		1871		1851			21	233	15	
Bower	Annie E.		1884		1854			31	233	16	
Bower	Louisa A.		1859		1856			4	233	17	
Bower	John		1859		1858			2	233	18	
Bowman	John	10.22	1894			60	11.17	61	233	12	
Boyd	John Calvin	4.08	1896	1.16	1877			20	233	19	killed by the explosion of an engine at a portable saw mill

Newville - Prospect Hill Cemetery

Surname	Given Name	Death Mo/Dy	Year	Birth Mo/Dy	Year	Att. Age Yr	Mo/Dy	Cm Ag	Pg	No	Other Information
Boyd	Luther Aden [?]	4.26	1898	12.19	1895			3	233	20	
Brandt	David	9.06	1861			63		64	232	28	These remains were brought from a private graveyard in Mifflin township
Brandt	-----	1.19	1882			80	0.29	81	232	29	Brandt, David wife of; remains brought from a private graveyard in Mifflin twp
Brandt	Sally	9.25	1871			0	10.24	1	232	30	Brandt, Samuel & Anna, daughter of
Brandt	Luetta	11.04	1902	4.17	1901			2	232	31	
Brandt	Carrie May	8.15	1878	1.15	1878			1	232	32	Brandt, Aquilla & Vinnie, daughter of
Bricker	John	4.22	1868			71	11.14	72	233	03	
Bricker	Eliza	2.16	1893	2.22	1805			88	233	04	
Bricker	Jacob Erb	3.13	1842			1	10.00	2	233	05	
Bricker	Ruth					0	9.00	1	233	06	Bricker, J. H. & Julia V., daughter of
Bricker	John H.	12.31	1900			64	9.18	65	233	07	
Bricker	Kate E.	2.18	1875			35		36	233	08	Bricker, John H., wife of
Bricker	W. Albert	8.25	1890	2.19	1887			4	233	09	Bricker, W. C. & E. C., son of
Burns	Tressa	2.28	1903	7.10	1871			32	233	21	
Byers	Samuel	9.08	1883			51	3.19	52	233	22	
Byers	Nancy E.	3.04	1897	4.12	1834			63	233	23	
Byers	Malinda			4.12	1858				233	24	Byers, Samuel & Nancy E., child of
Byers	John A.	12.21	1859			0	3.20	1	233	25	Byers, Samuel & Nancy E., child of
Byers	Emma D.	4.16	1876			19	10.16	20	233	26	Byers, Samuel & Nancy E., child of
Carl	George	11.28	1888			79	8.20	80	233	38	[11/28?/1883]
Carl	Margaret	1.08	1891			83	11.09	84	233	39	
Carl	Mary A.	7.29	1887			50	11.01	51	233	40	
Carothers	William W.		1892		1820			73	233	27	
Carothers	Catharine		1894		1828			67	233	28	Carothers, William W., wife of
Carothers	William Ward	8.24	1872	4.20	1872			1	233	29	Carothers, W. W. & E. A., son of
Carothers	John B.		1850		1845			6	233	30	
Carothers	Mary		1854		1853			2	233	31	
Carothers	John B.	3.29	1851			4	5.04	5	233	32	Carothers, William B. & Catharine, son
Carothers	Martin J.	3.18	1897	8.14	1825			72	233	33	Rev.
Carothers	Elizabeth E.			1.16	1827				233	34	
Carothers	James M.		1899		1829			71	233	35	
Carothers	Isabella J.		1902		1842			61	233	36	
Carothers	Jane Clark	6.06	1899	2.14	1819			81	233	37	
Chambers	James	7.06	1883			53		54	233	41	Lieutenant, Co. E., 49th Pa. Infantry
Chisolm	Mollie E. Middleton	9.05	1881	3.08	1859			23	233	42	Chisolm, H. C., wife of
Christlieb	Jacob	5.09	1884	3.27	1791			94	234	01	
Christlieb	Julian	9.28	1854			50		51	234	02	
Cooper	Levina	2.16	1896			36		37	234	03	Cooper, Samuel, wife of
Davidson	Hannah		1894		1823			72	234	04	
Davidson	George H.		1899		1859			41	234	05	
DeHaven	David S.	6.04	1896	4.11	1842			55	234	06	
Derr	Barbara E.	4.06	1888	3.11	1809			80	234	07	
Derr	Daniel	9.02	1876	3.31	1796			81	234	08	
Derr	Elizabeth	2.06	1858	4.17	1797			61	234	09	Derr, Daniel, wife of
Derr	Eliza Jane	9.18	1892	4.27	1827			66	234	10	Derr, Daniel, wife of
Derr	Ferdinand	1.19	1904	11.07	1828			76	234	11	
Derr	Mary	11.21	1872	9.23	1824			49	234	12	Derr, Ferdinand, wife of
Derr	Frances	12.11	1868	10.01	1845			24	234	13	Derr, Isaac, wife of

Newville - Prospect Hill Cemetery

Surname	Given Name	Death Mo/Dy	Year	Birth Mo/Dy	Year	Att. Age Yr	Mo/Dy	Cm Ag	Pg	No	Other Information
Duck	Philip	7.15	1830			72	11.13	73	234	14	"A patriot of the Rev. War"; Corporal, Capt. Decker's Co., Col. Magaw;s Bn.
Dock	Elizabeth	2.07	1848			84	5.11	85	234	15	Dock, Philip, relict of
Dock	Philip	12.03	1860			72		73	234	16	one of the volunteers who distinguished themselves on the battlefields of Chippewa & Lundy's Lane in War of 1812
Dock	Mary	7.04	1881			81	10.10	82	234	17	
Dock	Mary	2.18	1848	4.29	1792			56	234	18	
Duck	Peter	12.15	1841	8.15	1796			46	234	19	
Dock	Amelia	12.16	1844			53	2.02	54	234	20	
Duck	Jesse	10.12	1840			45	10.05	46	234	21	all Ducks and Docks are buried on same lot and are of the same family
Duffey	James A.	4.06	1901			64		65	234	22	
Dunkleberger	Catharine	9.13	1898			56	7.20	57	234	23	Dunkleberger, Nathaniel, wife of
Dunkleberger	J. W.	3.28	1898	2.15	1863			36	234	24	
Dunkleberger	Edith M.	11.02	1889	10.21	1889			1	234	25	
Dunkleberger	John	2.25	1901	1.24	1838			64	234	26	
Dunkleberger	Margaret A.								234	27	[no dates given]
Dunlap	W. S.		1875		1839			37	234	28	
Eckman	John Milton	9.25	1861			0	1.05	1	234	29	Eckman, T. Alexander & Mary, child of
Eckman	Anna Mary	9.09	1855			0	10.22	1	234	30	Eckman, T. Alexander & Mary, child of
Eisenhower	Jacob	1.19	1892			84	10.09	85	234	31	
Eisenhower	Jane M.	9.17	1882			74	5.26	75	234	32	
Elliott	Robert E.	2.11	1897	5.03	1829			68	234	33	Elliot, R. E. & Elizabeth, child of
Elliott	Emma	2.04	1884	8.13	1861			23	234	34	Elliot, R. E. & Elizabeth, child of
Elliott	Annie E.	3.14	1886	5.15	1864			22	234	35	Elliot, R. E. & Elizabeth, child of
Elliott	James S.	3.06	1892	11.06	1856			24	234	36	Elliot, R. E. & Elizabeth, child of
Emerich	Willis Irvin	4.07	1876	1.13	1853			14	234	37	Emerich, George & Eliza, son of
Ernst	Samuel Wilson	12.00	1861	10.00	1858			4	234	38	
Ernst	Naomi Frances	9.00	1883	4.00	1866			18	234	39	
Evelhock	George	3.24	1856			56	7.00	57	234	40	
Evelhock	Rebecca	9.03	1865			58	3.04	59	234	41	
Fahnestock	Benjamin	3.28	1905			73	6.07	74	235	01	
Faust	Catharine Warden	4.05	1892	9.09	1862			30	235	02	Faust, W. G., wife of
Faust	George C.	4.18	1899	10.15	1882			17	235	03	a son [presumbly of Catherine Faust]
Finkenbinder	Lulu B.	2.23	1897			12	3.17	13	235	04	Finkenbinder, W. H. & Emma, daughter of
Fishburn	J. Kenyon	12.05	1890			27	2.12	28	235	05	killed at Mifflintown Pa. by an engine
Fosnot	Bessie I.	2.16	1877			2	4.07	3	235	06	Fosnot, L. C. & L. B., child of
Fosnot	Maud L.	2.14	1879			6	6.21	7	235	07	Fosnot, L. C. & L. B., child of
Fosnot	J. M.	6.20	1863			6	10.20	7	235	08	Fosnot, J. C. & E., eldest daughter of
Fosnaught	Mary	7.03	1871			66	10.27	67	235	09	Fosnaught, Jacob, wife of
Fosnot	Margarete	10.23	1888			0	4.03	1	235	10	Fosnot, G. B. M. & A. K., daughter of
Frymier	Isaac		1895		1813			83	235	12	
Frymier	Catharine Trexler		1845		1814			32	235	13	Frymier, Isaac, wife of
Frymier	Catharine Jones		1893		1811			83	235	14	Frymier, Isaac, wife of
Frymier	Anna Boyle		1886		1853			34	235	15	
Funk	John	5.26	1891			59		60	235	11	
Gamber	George A.				1836				235	16	
Gamber	Lavinia		1896		1838			59	235	17	Gamber, George A., wife of
Gamber	Robert Z.		1890		1865			26	235	18	Gamber, George A. & Lavinia A., son of

Newville - Prospect Hill Cemetery

Surname	Given Name	Death Mo/Dy	Year	Birth Mo/Dy	Year	Att. Age Yr	Mo/Dy	Cm Ag	Pg	No	Other Information
Getter	Cora A.	1.01	1900			32		33	235	19	
Getter	May	3.02	1898			0	0.14	1	235	20	Getter, Cora A., daughter of
Getter	Eliza A.	9.29	1904			60		61	235	21	
Getter	Lovie	10.03	1872			2		3	235	22	Getter, G. F. & L. A., daughter of
Gill	John H.	10.29	1896			56		57	235	27	
Gilmore	James	10.23	1852			54		55	235	28	
Gilmore	Eleanor	3.29	1885	6.25	1806			79	235	29	Gilmore, James, wife of
Ginter	Jacob	1.19	1874			75	10.26	76	235	30	
Ginter	David G.	12.28	1863			5	3.07	6	235	31	Ginter, Jacob & Mary, child of
Ginter	Jacob S.	12.11	1863			12	4.17	13	235	32	Ginter, Jacob & Mary, child of
Ginter	Catharine	4.21	1866			29	11.05	30	235	33	Ginter, Jacob & Elizabeth, daughter of
Greagor	Maudie M.	6.24	1884			0	1.00	1	235	23	[spelling uncertain; Greagor]
Green	John	2.20	1849			40		41	235	24	
Green	Jane M.	2.11	1842			1		2	235	25	
Green	Elizabeth	9.02	1850			2		3	235	26	
Griffin	William H.	8.14	1880	7.18	1880			1	235	34	
Gross	Henry	6.16	1893			60	0.02	61	235	35	
Grove	Harry M.	4.02	1892			6	1.07	7	235	36	Grove, S. & Sarah, son of
Gussman	Alice R.	9.06	1877	2.26	1850			28	235	37	Gussman, George L., wife of
Hamaker	David	2.17	1879			65	1.25	66	236	05	
Hamaker	Elizabeth	12.01	1877			67	9.08	68	236	06	Hamaker, David, wife of
Hammer	Susan Ann	9.18	1864			34	0.24	35	235	38	Hammer, G. B., Captain, wife of
Hammer	John P.	9.16	1884			80	9.15	81	235	39	
Hammer	Catharine	1.16	1873			70	4.16	71	236	01	Hammer, John P., wife of
Hammer	Susan A.		1901		1846			56	236	02	
Hammer	Catharine R.		1904		1830			75	236	03	
Hammer	Ida M.								236	04	Hammer, William A. & Margaret, infant daughter of
Handshew	Caddie E.	8.30	1879			38	5.16	39	236	07	Handshew, J. W., wife of
Harlan	John F.		1896		1831			66	236	08	
Heberlig	Susan	2.20	1885			70	4.18	71	236	09	
Heberlig	Catharine	3.10	1875			64	1.17	65	236	10	
Heberlig	Rudolph	11.07	1863	4.01	1785			79	236	11	
Heberlig	Susan					71	5.27	72	236	12	Heberlig, Rudolph, wife of
Heberlig	Margaret	3.22	1865			54	0.18	55	236	13	Heberlig, Rudolph, wife of
Heberlig	Martha E.	1.19	1857			4	9.09	5	236	14	Heberlig, Rudolph & Margaret, dau. of
Heberlig	Millard F.	4.08	1888			0	4.19	1	236	15	Heberlig, W. E. & M. H., son of
Heckman	Daniel	7.29	1889			63	7.04	64	236	16	
Heckman	Harriet	1.12	1893			64	4.27	65	236	17	
Hefflefinger	Nancy	8.28	1845			39	6.18	40	236	18	Hefflefinger, B., wife of
Hefflefinger	Mary E.	7.12	1889			0	5.29	1	236	19	Hefflefinger, P. L. & R. J., daughter of
Heiser	Catharine	12.26	1904			29	10.18	30	236	20	Heiser, C. S., wife of
Heiser	Anna M.	9.27	1898	9.25	1880			19	236	21	
Heller	Elizabeth	6.01	1903			62	0.05	63	236	22	
Hemminger	William		1874		1831			44	236	24	
Hemminger	Elizabeth		1903		1835			69	236	25	Hemminger, William, wife of
Hemminger	Willie B.		1879		1873			7	236	26	
Hench	R. Alexander			3.06	1829				236	23	on the Brandt lot; probably a relative; d. July 11, 184-
Henneberger	C. A.		1887		1836			52	236	27	

Newville - Prospect Hill Cemetery

Surname	Given Name	Death Mo/Dy	Year	Birth Mo/Dy	Year	Att. Yr	Age Mo/Dy	Cm Ag	Pg	No	Other Information
Henry	Sarah B.	6.16	1898			29	10.06	30	236	28	Henry, Andrew D., wife of
Henry	Abraham	8.03	1904			65	4.19	66	236	29	Private, Co. D. 187th Regiment, Pennsylvania Volunteers
Henry	Jacob	5.31	1891	5.11	1811			81	236	30	
Henry	Joseph E.	8.07	1893	10.22	1863			30	236	31	
Hess	Catharine E.	5.17	1897			22	10.12	23	236	32	Hess, Drurill, daughter of
Hiltibidle	Terry	1.14	1881			59	8.29	60	236	33	Hiltibidle, Henry, wife of
Hoch	Sarah	4.16	1899			65	10.13	66	236	34	Hoch, Aaron, wife of
Hoch	William Oren	11.06	1855	10.10	1855			1	236	35	Hoch, A. B. & A. M., son of
Hoch	Ethel	4.19	1894			4	4.01	5	236	36	Hoch, F. K. & Jennie, child of
Hoch	Clair	9.03	1888			0	3.14	1	237	01	Hoch, F. K. & Jennie, child of
Hollenbaugh	Samuel	1.13	1888			63	3.18	64	237	03	
Hollenbaugh	John E.	3.31	1875			6	8.12	7	237	04	
Hollenbaugh	Cora V.	3.24	1977			0	5.19	1	237	05	
Hollenbaugh	Solomon	10.07	1859						237	06	
Hollenbaugh	David T.	12.21	1863			4	2.14	5	237	07	Hollenbaugh, Samuel & Catharine, ch. of
Hollenbaugh	Carson S.	12.07	1863			6	2.00	7	237	08	Hollenbaugh, Samuel & Catharine, ch. of
Holt	Thomas B.	10.30	1899			56	5.00	57	237	09	Co. E, 33rd Regt., Ohio Vol. Infantry
Hood	Elizabeth	12.02	1891			81		82	237	02	
Hoover	Joseph F.	5.04	1872			43	6.17	44	237	10	
Hoover	David H.	2.05	1899	10.00	1826			73	237	11	
Hoover	Christian F.	10.14	1898	8.15	1856			43	237	12	
Huntsberger	Daniel	6.23	1902	8.18	1832			70	237	13	
Huntsberger	Rebecca J.	1.29	1895	5.04	1835			60	237	14	
Huntsberger	Frances A.	10.14	1859	3.19	1856			4	237	15	Huntsberger, Daniel & Rebecca, child of
Huntsberger	William E.	10.29	1860	8.10	1860			1	237	16	Huntsberger, Daniel & Rebecca, child of
Huntsberger	Elizabeth	8.14	1871	2.07	1871			1	237	17	Huntsberger, Daniel & Rebecca, child of
Huntsberger	Emma F.	7.14	1886	11.13	1864			22	237	18	Huntsberger, A. G., wife of
Huntsberger	Samuel	9.17	1896			53		54	237	19	
Huntsberger	Peter	6.28	1851	9.07	1807			44	237	20	
Huntsberger	Elizabeth	2.01	1893	7.09	1810			83	237	21	Huntsberger, Peter, wife of
Huntsberger	Nancy	10.20	1849			8	2.02	9	237	22	Huntsberger, Peter & Elizabeth, dau. of
Huntsberger	Peter	1.16	1865	6.27	1836			29	237	23	Huntsberger, Peter & Elizabeth H., son; captured at Wyatts Farm, VA, Sept. 29, 1864; d. Salisbury, NC and buried there
Huntsberger	Jonas D.	4.19	1889			54		55	237	24	
Huntsberger	Mary E.	9.03	1900			60		61	237	25	
Huntsberger	J. Walter		1878			1		2	237	26	Huntsberger, J. D. & M. E., son of
Huntsberger	Elizabeth	10.21	1849			10	7.03	11	237	27	Huntsberger, Peter & Elizabeth, dau. of
Jacoby	Peter	1.22	1861			45	3.18	46	237	28	
Jacoby	Mary J.	4.08	1862			29	8.16	30	237	29	
Jacoby	George	4.01	1893			66	8.06	67	237	30	
Jones	Peter	5.03	1893						237	31	Private, Co. D, 107th Regt., Pa. Vols.
Kelly	Samuel K.	6.28	1891			59	4.15	60	237	33	
Kendig	Elizabeth Jacoby	2.17	1892			68		69	237	35	Kendig, Daniel, wife of
Kennedy	Mary A. Moorhead	8.24	1896			84	3.29	65	237	34	
Kern	Charles B.	5.29	1901	10.15	1893			8	237	36	
Kershaw	Elizabeth Elliot Middleton	9.11	1897	3.12	1850			38	237	37	Kershaw, Joshua D., wife of;
Killian	Abraham		1890		1816			75	237	38	

Newville - Prospect Hill Cemetery

Surname	Given Name	Death Mo/Dy	Year	Birth Mo/Dy	Year	Att. Age Yr	Mo/Dy	Cm Ag	Pg	No	Other Information
Killian	Susan		1902		1822			81	238	01	Killian, Abraham, wife of
Killian	Henry F.		1850		1843			8	238	02	
Killian	Martha E.		1884		1845			40	238	03	
Killian	Mary J.		1850		1849			2	238	04	
Killian	J. B.	11.00	1891	8.00	1880			12	238	05	
Killian	S. W.	11.00	1891	1.00	1887			5	238	06	
Killian	R. C.		1892	11.00	1889			3	238	07	
Killian	F. DeH.	1.00	1904	12.00	1878			26	238	08	
Killian	Robert C.	5.30	1871			0	11.25	1	238	09	Killian, J. W. & I. J., son of
Krall	Mary Lindsey		1897		1896			2	237	32	
Kunkle	George B.	7.20	1901			78	5.02	79	238	10	
Kutz	Ira J.	3.26	1864			5	7.18	6	238	11	Kutz, A. J. & S., child of
Kutz	Parker B.	1.21	1863			1	6.10	2	238	12	Kutz, A. J. & S., child of
Leidig	M. E.		1902		1841			62	238	13	
Leidig	Mary A.	10.02	1880			50	3.16	51	238	14	Leidig, J. B., wife of
Leidig	Amand C.	5.02	1878			21	5.07	22	238	15	[Amand (sic)]
Lewis	George P.	1.19	1848			2	4.18	3	238	16	
Lewis	Lydia B.	2.07	1853			0	6.19	1	238	17	
Lewis	David C.	10.31	1889			30	0.12	31	238	18	
Lewis	James	7.27	1875			73	7.00	74	238	19	
Lewis	Lydia	10.12	1896			76	7.22	77	238	20	
Lewis	Mary E.	6.06	1856			6	4.17	7	238	21	Lewis, James & Lydia, daughter of
Lewis	Flora May	3.03	1875			1	7.25	2	238	22	Lewis, Samuel W. & N., daughter of
Lindsay	Joseph A.		1903		1846			58	238	23	
Loy	Martha J.	8.06	1885			55	8.11	56	238	24	Loy, Jacob, wife of
Martz	John C.		1898		1855			44	238	25	
Martz	Anna M.		1880		1879			2	238	26	
Martz	Anna May	1.29	1880			0	5.00	1	238	27	Martz, J. C. & Mary C., daughter of
Martz	David		1896		1824			73	238	28	
Martz	Susan	1.18	1873	4.12	1825			48	238	29	Martz, David, wife of
Martz	David Henry	1.01	1861			10	8.04	11	238	30	Martz, David & Susanna, son of
Maurice	Herman W.	10.31	1896			5	11.03	6	238	31	Maurice, J. J. & A. F., child of
Maurice	Carrie	11.03	1896			3	10.10	4	238	32	Maurice, J. J. & A. F., child of
Maurice	Mary E.	11.20	1896			2	4.20	3	238	33	Maurice, J. J. & A. F., child of
McClure	Rachel	6.13	1894			48		49	239	45	McClure, W. C., wife of; d. in his 49 yr
McClure	Emma J.	5.13	1875			2		3	240	01	McClure, W. C. & R. M., daughter of
McCoy	P. G.		1895		1829			65	239	43	
McCoy	Margaret		1895		1835			61	239	44	McCoy, P. G., wife of
McDermond	Joseph	8.16	1893			65	3.11	66	240	02	
McDermond	Sarah A.	7.01	1897			64	5.16	65	240	03	
McDermond	Clara J.	7.02	1862			3	8.07	4	240	04	McDermond, J. & S. A., daughter of
McIvor	David Y.		1902		1838			65	240	05	
McIvor	Susan C.		1882		1841			42	240	06	
McKeehan	William Parker	6.18	1893			28		29	240	07	
McKeehan	Anne M.		1896		1862			35	240	08	
McWilliams	Adalbert	10.02	1871	12.05	1842			29	240	09	
Mentzer	Virginia Pearl	1.08	1903			0	10.08	1	238	34	Mentzer, S. & A. J., daughter of
Middleton	Andrew	6.22	1812			46		47	238	35	red sand stone head stone
Middleton	Margery Gillelen	5.24	1834			67		68	238	36	Middleton, Andrew, wife of; red sand stone head stone

Newville - Prospect Hill Cemetery

Surname	Given Name	Death Mo/Dy	Year	Birth Mo/Dy	Year	Att. Age Yr	Mo/Dy	Cm Ag	Pg	No	Other Information
Middleton	Margaret	3.22	1831			23		24	238	37	Middleton Robert, consort of; red sand stone headstone
Middleton	Andrew M.	6.30	1871	7.26	1804			67	238	38	[7/26?/1804]
Middleton	Nancy E.	3.03	1881	4.03	1817			64	238	39	
Middleton	William Arbuckle	1.17	1899	9.23	1830			69	238	40	
Middleton	Jennie D.	10.11	1874			0	2.27	1	238	41	Middleton, W. A. & Mary E., child of
Middleton	Catharine E.	9.09	1857			0	8.27	1	239	01	Middleton, W. A. & Mary E., child of
Middleton	Robert	3.05	1858			70	4.26	71	239	02	Esq.
Miller	Willis U.	6.19	1890	9.30	1856			34	239	03	M. D.
Miller	Jacob P.	4.15	1900	5.01	1822			78	239	04	
Miller	Jemima			2.08	1829				239	05	
Miller	Spangler G.	2.03	1904			35	4.27	36	239	06	
Miller	Jerrie A.	3.04	1892						239	07	
Miller	Mary M.	7.30	1893			0	2.15	1	239	08	
Miller	Paul B.	7.24	1899			0	8.21	1	239	09	
Miller	Esther C.	2.21	1901			0	3.07	1	239	10	
Miller	Susie J.	2.03	1888			9	2.11	10	239	11	Miller, Jacob & Jane, daughter of
Miller	Agness E.	1.04	1899	3.20	1863			36	239	12	Miller, John A., wife of
Miller	Aletta								239	13	Miller, R. & S. M., infant daughter of
Miller	James D.	4.22	1889			61	11.00	62	239	14	
Minnich	Adam	2.02	1893	1.07	1831			63	239	15	
Minnich	Ellas [?]	12.21	1875			0	6.07	1	239	16	Minnich, Adam & Emma, daughter of
Minnich	John	10.17	1850			23	2.02	24	239	17	
Minnich	William	10.08	1850			17	10.27	18	239	18	
Mitchell	Sydney C.	12.29	1901	12.13	1878			24	239	19	Co. G, 19th U. S. Infantry; killed at Naga, Cebu Island, Philippine Islands
Mitchell	Alice B.	9.30	1898	8.05	1878			21	239	20	Mitchell, Sydney C., wife of; Carothers, W. W. & E. A., daughter of
Mitten	William A.	11.27	1896			64	8.13	65	239	21	Co. D, 187th Regt., Pa. Volunteers
Mitten	Catharine	9.09	1904	11.26	1827			77	239	22	Mitten, W. A., wife of
Mitten	David J.	7.16	1859			0	11.16	1	239	23	
Mowery	David A.		1893		1857			37	239	24	
Murphy	George	3.12	1892			78	1.10	79	239	25	
Murphy	Harriet	3.16	1892			77	9.29	78	239	26	[5 children below named in this entry]
Murphy	John								239	27	Murphy, George & Harriet, child of
Murphy	Sharpe								239	28	Murphy, George & Harriet, child of
Murphy	James								239	29	Murphy, George & Harriet, child of
Murphy	Mary								239	30	Murphy, George & Harriet, child of
Murphy	Charlotte								239	31	Murphy, George & Harriet, child of
Murphy	Mary Matilda Robinson								239	32	Murphy, Emma, daughter of
Myers	Benjamin	4.14	1887	4.08	1816			72	239	33	
Myers	Alfred	2.01	1889	8.14	1850			39	239	34	
Myers	Howard	1.05	1897			2	4.03	3	239	35	Myers, Abram & Louella, child of
Myers	Cordia A.	5.21	1897			6	1.13	7	239	36	
Myers	Joel		1899		1838			62	239	37	
Myers	Walter Fosnot	2.26	1884			0	6.01	1	239	38	Myers, Abram J., & Lou Ella, child of
Myers	John Herman	9.20	1888			1	6.27	2	239	39	Myers, Abram J., & Lou Ella, child of
Myers	Sophia	2.03	1879			30	5.23	31	239	40	Myers, John B., wife of
Myers	John		1879		1810			70	239	41	
Myers	Elizabeth								239	42	Myers, John, wife of

Newville - Prospect Hill Cemetery

Surname	Given Name	Death Mo/Dy	Year	Birth Mo/Dy	Year	Att. Age Yr	Mo/Dy	Ag Cm	Pg	No	Other Information
Negley	Rebecca Jane	8.17	1878			1	6.17	2	240	18	Negley, Jacob & Mary P., daughter of
Nehf	Henry	11.05	1902			78	8.22	79	240	19	
Nehf	Anna C.	1.06	1901			79	7.05	80	240	20	
Nehf	Clara J.	5.10	1898			41	8.27	42	240	21	Nehf, John A., wife of
Neibert	N. S.			9.16	1864				240	10	[d. date not given]
Neibert	Sallie C.			12.23	1864				240	11	[d. date not given]
Neibert	Carrie May	3.22	1889	8.26	1887			2	240	12	Neibert, N. S. & S. C., child of
Neibert	Roy V.	1.08	1898	12.11	1895			3	240	13	Neibert, N. S. & S. C., child of
Neidich	Catharine F.	1.30	1871			20	3.15	21	240	14	Neidich, Levi, wife of
Neidich	Catharine	8.10	1871			0	7.01	1	240	15	Neidich, Levi & Catharine E., dau. of
Neidigh	Sarah J.	7.19	1903			58		59	240	16	
Neidigh	Libby May	8.04	1871			0	2.28	1	240	17	
O'Donnel	Frank	7.07	1894			53		54	240	22	
Preisler	Catharine		1898		1816			83	240	23	
Prosser	Pearl L.	1.08	1900			3	7.00	4	240	24	Prosser, W. A. & Alice, daughter of
Railing	Pearl J.		1905		1904			2	240	25	
Rea	Cora G.	8.15	1887	3.03	1867			21	240	26	Rea, Charles E., wife of
Rebok	Bessie B.	8.16	1893			11	4.14	12	240	27	
Rebok	Frank	9.28	1887			0	6.00	1	240	28	
Rhoads	Mathias	5.16	1905			65		66	240	34	Prins. [?], Co. A, 21st Regt., Pennsylvania Cavalry
Rhoads	Sarah	12.05	1895			58	6.04	59	240	35	
Rhoads	Sarah J.	10.17	1900			65		64	240	36	
Ritner	Peter	3.03	1889			70	6.00	71	240	29	
Ritner	Jane M.	7.09	1900			65	2.26	69	240	30	Ritner, Peter, wife of
Ritner	Mary Davidson	12.07	1898	12.01	1849			50	240	31	
Ritter	Elizabeth	5.06	1892			65	6.28	66	240	32	
Ritter	Daniel	4.17	1893			71	8.24	72	240	33	
Sener	John				1840				242	03	[no death date given]
Sener	Catharine				1836				242	04	[no death date given]
Sensebaugh	Mary	1.02	1862			4	4.21	5	240	37	Sensebaugh, J. D. & Matilda, daughter of
Sensebaugh	John	5.22	1886			27	2.18	28	240	38	
Sensebaugh	John	8.05	1849	8.25	1763			86	242	05	
Sensebaugh	Rachel	8.04	1848	2.26	1766				242	06	Sensebaugh, John, wife of; [text gives birth date as 1866, an obvious error]
Sensebaugh	Mary	1.20	1874			80	4.03	81	242	07	
Sensebaugh	Margaret	8.02	1881			78	1.08	79	242	08	
Sensebaugh	John D.	7.07	1873			72	2.05	73	242	09	
Sharp	Robert B.	3.29	1874			49	4.20	50	241	34	
Sharp	George G.	9.28	1886			20	11.28	21	241	35	
Sharp	James H.	11.20	1886			19	6.23	20	241	36	
Shellebarger	Jacob	9.02	1855	12.11	1804			51	241	01	
Shellebarger	Eliza Reichert	7.10	1888	8.18	1813			55	241	02	Shellebarger, Jacob, wife of
Shellebarger	Isaac	5.05	1852	6.30	1849			3	241	03	
Sheriff	John	7.01	1849			39	4.19	40	241	04	
Sherf	Mary	3.13	1864			57		58	241	05	
Sharf	Sarah	9.16	1880			51	5.12	52	241	06	Sharf, Jacob, wife of
Shipley	-----	12.03	1863			51		52	241	16	Shipley. Benjamin, wife of
Shoap	T. Edward	9.17	1890	12.10	1863			27	241	17	
Shopwell	John	2.07	1900						241	18	Private, Co. H, 202nd Regt., Pa. Vols.

Newville - Prospect Hill Cemetery

Surname	Given Name	Death Mo/Dy	Death Year	Birth Mo/Dy	Birth Year	Att. Age Yr	Age Mo/Dy	Cm Ag	Pg	No	Other Information
Shopwell	Carrol Walz					0	0.21	1	241	19	Shopwell, David & Mary, son of; age 3 wk
Shreffler	Henry	12.12	1904			68		69	241	07	1st Lieutenant., Co. F, 208th Regt., Pennsylvania Volunteers
Shreffler	Salome G.	5.01	1868			1	3.06	2	241	08	Shreffler, H. & M. E., daughter of
Shulenberger	B. F.		1901		1840			62	241	27	
Shulenberger	Samuel	1.05	1845			31	3.05	32	241	28	
Shulenberger	Margaret White	6.19	1885			70	9.01	71	241	29	Shulenberger, Samuel, consort of
Shulenberger	Elizabeth	2.09	1845			7	7.16	8	241	30	
Shulenberger	Ralph	9.11	1877			3	0.16	4	241	31	
Smith	Sebastian Boner	2.19	1885	12.18	1810			75	241	09	b. Stadtsteinnach, K. of Bavaria, Germ.
Smith	Mary	2.03	1846	8.01	1816			30	241	10	Smith, Sebastian, B., wife of
Smith	Mary	3.07	1851	2.06	1820			32	241	11	Smith, Sebastian, B., wife of
Smith	Anna E.	7.11	1889	7.04	1811			79	241	12	Smith, Sebastian, B., wife of
Smith	Doratha	3.02	1847			1	7.00	2	241	13	Smith, Sebastian, B., daughter of
Smith	Harvey O.	10.30	1898			3	3.22	4	241	14	
Smith	Mervin I.	4.02	1879			28		29	241	15	Smith, M. & M. C., son of
Snyder	Henry F.	12.31	1895	4.12	1834			62	241	33	
Spangler	William W.	10.31	1892			51	8.12	52	241	37	[51/08?.12]
Spangler	Catharine	3.08	1887			48	9.28	49	241	38	Spangler, William W., wife of
Spangler	Earl S.	3.05	1885			0	1.14	1	241	39	Spangler, P. M. & H. J., son of
Spangler	Elizabeth	10.10	1898	10.05	1826			73	241	40	
Spangler	Yost	5.17	1878	8.29	1800			78	241	41	
Spangler	Rebecca	3.29	1870	4.05	1803			65	241	42	Spangler, Yost, wife of
Sponsler	George	12.04	1898	8.20	1810			89	241	20	
Sponsler	Sarah E.	3.03	1899	3.07	1815			84	241	21	
Sprout	Levi B.	7.14	1899	11.04	1837			62	241	22	
Sprout	Sarah E.	1.23	1894	7.27	1842			52	241	23	Sprout, Levi B., wife of
Sprout	Willie	9.28	1882						241	24	Sprout, R. N. & Kate C., infant son of
Staver	Sarah Jane	7.01	1891			54	3.01	55	241	43	Staver, Levi, wife of
Staver	Henry F.	9.26	1880			13	9.25	14	242	01	
Stough	James K. P.	11.11	1899			54	10.10	55	241	25	
Strohm	Minnie S.	7.01	1901			32		33	241	26	Strohm, Edwin D., wife of
Stum	Henry		1903		1836			68	241	32	
Swartz	Ira Abram	9.16	1897			1	10.23	2	242	02	
Talhelm	John		1898		1830			69	242	10	
Talhelm	George E.	5.14	1877			17	11.01	18	242	11	Talhelm, John & Elizabeth, son of
Tanner	Flora Belle		1903		1867			37	242	12	Tanner, Sheridan, C., wife of
Taylor	Anna E.	8.19	1887			38	2.05	39	242	13	Talhelm, John & Elizabeth, daughter of
Thomas	William H.	9.13	1861			0	9.26	1	242	15	Thomas, D. W. & E. A., child of
Thomas	David A.	5.05	1864			1	0.11	2	242	16	Thomas, D. W. & E. A., child of
Thomas	George B. Mc.	9.06	1864			2	7.10	3	242	17	Thomas, D. W. & E. A., child of
Thomas	Flora May	8.27	1878						242	18	Thomas, D. W. & E. A., child of
Thomas	Ralph K. T.	8.02	1902	1.02	1880			23	242	19	Thomas, D. W. & E. A., child of
Thomas	Elia	11.26	1898			14	11.22	15	242	20	Thomas, D. W. & E. A., child of
Thomas	Martha D.	4.15	1858			62	8.05	63	242	21	Thomas, Josiah, wife of
Thomas	Martha Jane	3.04	1858			22	5.15	23	242	22	Thomas, Josiah & Martha D., child of
Thomas	George Davidson	7.09	1855			22	0.20	23	242	23	Thomas, Josiah & Martha D., child of
Thrush	David T.	5.05	1890						242	30	
Tritt	Christian	1.05	1879	3.21	1841			38	242	14	
Trough	H. A.	7.08	1893			63		64	242	24	

Newville - Prospect Hill Cemetery

Surname	Given Name	Death Mo/Dy	Year	Birth Mo/Dy	Year	Att. Age Yr	Mo/Dy	Cm Ag	Pg	No	Other Information
Trough	T. M. Grath	8.29	1866			0	7.28	1	242	25	Trough, H. A. & J. C., child of
Through	Harry McClane	2.03	1873			2	2.18	3	242	26	Trough, H. A. & J. C., child of; [sp. ?]
Trough	J. Luther	2.08	1887			31	0.01	32	242	27	
Trough	Mary Victoria Goodhart	7.06	1888			33	7.20	34	242	28	Trough, J. L., wife of
Trough	Sallie Grizzella	4.18	1878			0	8.09	1	242	29	
Wagner	Isaac	10.28	1895	8.25	1821			75	242	31	Corporal, Co. F, 158th Regt., Pennsylvania Volunteers, Infantry
Wagner	Walter	5.24	1888	9.26	1873			15	242	32	
Wagner	J. M.	3.01	1875			51	0.16	52	242	33	
Wagner	Mary J.	11.24	1886			57	10.22	58	242	34	Wagner, J. M., wife of
Walker	Willie Sanderson	11.21	1871			4	10.23	5	242	35	Walker, M. & M. A., son of
Warden	Joseph B.		1889		1815			75	242	36	
Warden	Mary A.		1883		1820			64	242	37	
Weast	Leonard		1892		1807			86	243	01	
Weast	Catharine A.		1850		1819			32	243	02	
Weast	Rebecca		1864		1842			23	243	03	
Weast	Abraham		1868		1846			23	243	04	
Weast	William B.		1890		1868			23	243	05	
Weast	James O.	7.21	1894	10.12	1876			18	243	06	
Weast	George	4.06	1899	10.01	1848			51	243	07	
Weaver	Jacob R.		1899		1830			70	243	08	
Weiser	Reuben								243	09	Co. K., 126th Pennsylvania Volunteers
Westafer	Mary	10.19	1864			42	6.18	43	243	10	Westafer, John, wife of
Westfall	Oliver C.		1901		1841			61	243	11	
Westfall	Rebecca				1848			0	243	12	Westfall, Oliver, wife of
Westfall	Flora M.		1898		1882			17	243	13	
Westfall	Maud E.		1884		1884			1	243	14	
Westfall	William G.		1885		1885			1	243	15	
Whaler	John Elmer Ellsworth	8.11	1862			1	3.23	2	242	38	Whaler, John & Elizabeth, son of
Wheler	John D.		1871		1836			36	243	16	
Wheler	Ellsworth		1862		1861			2	243	17	
Wheler	Elizabeth		1905		1837			69	243	18	
Wheler	D. W.	7.28	1898			66	5.05	67	243	19	Sergeant., Co. H, 3rd Penna. Cavalry
Wheler	Sue Thornton	8.08	1873	9.09	1831			42	243	20	Wheler, D. W., wife of
Wheler	Annie L.								243	21	Wheler, D. W. & S. T., child of
Wheler	Maria A.								243	22	Wheler, D. W. & S. T., child of
Wheler	Nannie Bell								243	23	Wheler, D. W. & S. T., child of
Wheler	Arthur T.								243	24	Wheler, D. W. & S. T., child of
Wheler	John	3.11	1864			57	5.28	58	243	25	
Wheler	Elizabeth	4.09	1860			49	11.20	50	243	26	Wheler, John, wife of
Wheler	Phoebe		1903		1838			66	243	27	his wife; [presumably John, 243:25]
Wheler	Mamie E.		1880		1875			6	243	28	
Wheler	Jacob W.		1892		1834			59	243	29	
Wheler	Ada F.		1866		1861			6	243	30	
Wheler	Charles C.		1874		1873			2	243	31	
Wheeler	Williard W.		1900		1897			4	243	32	Wheeler, H. B. & C. A., son of
Whistler	Daniel	10.21	1903			60	9.08	61	243	44	
Whistler	Elizabeth								243	45	Whistler, Daniel, wife of; [no dates]
White	Mary Middleton	6.05	1891	11.06	1843			48	243	43	White, E. Norton, wife of; buried at Duncannon, Pennsylvania

Newville - Prospect Hill Cemetery

Surname	Given Name	Death Mo/Dy	Death Year	Birth Mo/Dy	Birth Year	Att. Age Yr	Att. Age Mo/Dy	Cm Ag	Pg	No	Other Information
Wichlein	George	3.13	1854			76	5.13	77	243	33	
Williams	John		1897		1808			90	243	34	
Williams	Susanna		1892		1813			80	243	35	Williams, John, wife of
Williams	Benjamin	4.23	1893	9.10	1822			71	243	36	
Williams	Catharine	10.18	1897	7.16	1825			73	243	37	Williams, Benjamin, wife of
Williams	C. Elizabeth	5.28	1869	8.24	1853			16	243	38	Williams, B. & C., daughter of
Wilson	William H.	7.09	1896	4.15	1825			74	243	39	
Wilson	Lazarus K.					48	9.13	49	243	40	Seaman "Great Western"; U. S. N.
Wilson	Elizabeth	8.03	1896			45		46	243	41	Wilson, Lazarus, wife of
Wilson	Mary A.	10.23	1902	5.21	1872			31	243	42	
Worst	Samuel	1.02	1864			7	11.20	8	243	46	Worst, Joseph & Mary, son of
Worst	Annie M.	10.13	1868			11	11.06	12	244	01	Worst, Levi & Rachel, daughter of
Wyke	Christopher		1817		1740	77		78	244	02	(b. 1740)
Wyke	Susannah		1787			40		41	244	03	Wyke, Christopher, wife of
Wyke	Margaret	9.00	1823		1733	90		91	244	04	Wyke, Christopher, 2nd wife; (b. 1733)
Wyke	George	12.17	1825			44		45	244	05	Wyke, Christopher, son of
Wyke	Sarah	10.11	1826			16		17	244	06	Wyke, Sarah, daughter of
Wyke	William M.	12.17	1845			2		3	244	07	Wyke, William & Hannah, son of
Wyke	Joseph	4.04	1848				10.00	1	244	08	
Young	Mary C.	11.28	1853			49	3.13	50	244	09	
Zeigler	Nancy	10.24	1862			41	11.00	42	244	10	
Zeigler	Jacob	2.14	1857			68		69	244	11	
Zeigler	Barbara	1.20	1855			69	6.00	70	244	12	Zeigler, Jacob, wife of
Zeigler	John J.		1889		1826			64	244	13	
Zeigler	Nancy		1898		1834			65	244	14	Zeigler, John J., wife of
Zeigler	Franklin								244	15	Zeigler, John J. & Nancy, infant son of
Zeigler	Jacob A.								244	16	Zeigler, John J. & Nancy, infant son of

Newville - United Presbyterian Church Graveyard

UNITED PRESBYTERIAN CHURCH GRAVEYARD

Surname	Given Name	Death Mo/Dy	Death Year	Birth Mo/Dy	Birth Year	Att. Age Yr	Cm Mo/Dy	Cm Ag	Pg	No	Other Information
Beaty	Agnes	1.07	1807		1729	78		79	198	01	
Beaty	William	11.01	1809			78		79	198	02	
Chism	David								198	04	[listed on line with David]
Chism	John								198	05	[listed on line with John]
Chism	Thomas								198	06	[listed on line with Margaret]
Chism	Margaret								198	07	[listed on line with Thomas]
Chism	Sen.								198	08	[Sr. (?)]
Chism	Margaret								198	09	Chism, Sen., wife of
Chism	Jane	10.29	1857						198	10	
Craig	John		1794						198	03	Rev.; aged about 50
French	James	5.24	1851			4	7.05	5	198	11	
French	Samuel	11.05	1881		1817	64	2.11	65	198	12	
French	Elizabeth Zeigler	3.26	1862			40	9.07	41	198	13	French, Samuel, wife of
French	Margaret E.	8.13	1845			1	4.19	2	198	14	
Gracey	Sarah A.	7.03	1845			28	3.25	29	198	15	Gracey, William, wife of
Hannon	Jameson	2.00	1853	3.00	1805			48	198	16	
Hannon	Margaret R.	8.20	1870	5.06	1815			56	198	17	
Hannon	Margaret Williamson	11.00	1848	12.00	1840			8	198	19	Hannon, Jameson, & M. R., daughter of
Hannon	Josephine	3.15	1875						198	19	Hannon, Jameson, & Margaret R., dau. of
Heannan	Sarah	3.26	1831			21	0.12	22	198	20	
Heannan	William, Jr.	2.05	1831			22	9.00	23	198	21	
Heannan	William, Sr.	10.25	1825		1766	59		60	198	22	
Heannan	Mary	1.19	1832			27		28	198	23	
Heannan	Rebecca	8.29	1834			16		17	198	24	
Hoon	Elizabeth	2.23	1860	4.20	1829			31	198	25	Hoon, William, wife of
Huston	William	2.06	1821			68		69	198	26	
Huston	Mary	5.04	1822						198	27	
Huston	Sarah								198	28	Huston, James, wife of
Huston	James	6.05	1824			41		42	198	29	Huston, William & Mary, son of
Huston	Eleanor	1.30	1815			30	7.05	31	198	30	Huston, William & Mary, child of
Huston	Martha	1.24	1818			17	4.23	18	198	31	Huston, William & Mary, child of
Huston	Eliza	5.09	1818			20	2.27	21	198	32	Huston, William & Mary, child of
Huston	Mary	12.11	1820			33	9.01	34	198	33	Huston, William & Mary, child of
Huston	Margaret	5.28	1819			23	0.03	24	198	34	Huston, William & Mary, child of
Irwin	Alfred L.	9.03	1869	8.27	1844			26	198	35	
Jackson	Robert	12.10	1880			71		72	198	36	
Jackson	Elizabeth	6.08	1883			72		73	198	37	
Jackson	Emma	9.18	1883	10.01	1849			34	198	38	Jackson, J. D., wife of
Jackson	Isabella	11.12	1889			50		81	198	39	
Johnson	Jane	6.18	1819			28		29	199	02	Johnson, John wife of; Huston, William & Mary, daughter of
Jones	William H.	12.11	1861	11.23	1856			4	199	01	Jones, J. M. & P. E., son of
Kyle	Matthew	11.27	1855		1778			77	199	03	d. in his 97th year; [ages do not agree]
Laird	Andrew M.	9.17	1854	1.14	1827			28	199	04	
Mathers	Agnes	2.24	1817		1791	26	6.30	27	199	05	Huston, William & Mary, child of
McCulloch	Elizabeth	6.25	1845		1797	47		48	199	14	McCulloch, John, wife of
McCulloch	Mary E.	8.23	1867			26		27	199	15	McCulloch, W. H., wife of
McCulloch	Sarah Bell	11.12	1867			0	7.04	1	199	16	"Little" preceeds given name

Newville - United Presbyterian Church Graveyard

Surname	Given Name	Death Mo/Dy	Year	Birth Mo/Dy	Year	Att. Age Yr	Mo/Dy	Age Cm	Pg	No	Other Information
McElwain	Martha Jane	6.15	1884			28	6.16	29	199	13	McElwain, William, wife of
McMoor	Rachel					73		74	199	17	
McNeal	Samuel	6.20	1860		1778	82	7.05	83	199	18	
Montgomery	James	11.29	1861		1787	74	0.09	75	199	08	
Montgomery	Elizabeth	7.19	1859		1777	82		83	199	09	
Montgomery	Robert	4.11	1879		1815	64	6.28	65	199	10	
Montgomery	Rachel M.	10.20	1862		1813	48		49	199	11	
Montgomery	infant son								199	12	Montgomery, Robert & Rachel M., son of
Moore	John					75		76	199	06	
Moore	David					21		22	199	07	
Rea	John	12.15	1867			23	5.18	24	199	19	
Rea	George	9.22	1867			25	7.05	26	199	20	
Rea	Isabella	4.19	1869			64		65	199	21	Rea, George, wife of
Rea	George	9.23	1865			59		60	199	22	
Rea	Mary Jane	7.27	1850			17	5.10	18	199	23	Rea, George, & Isabella, child of
Rea	Nancy Elizabeth	5.05	1850			12	7.23	13	199	24	Rea, George, & Isabella, child of
Rea	Sarah Ann	5.03	1844			13	3.15	14	199	25	Rea, George, & Isabella, child of
Rea	William	5.20	1857			21		22	199	26	
Rea	Annie H.	3.14	1883			37	1.16	38	199	27	Rea, J. D., wife of
Rea	Elizabeth L.	5.20	1871			32	1.10	33	199	28	Rea, J. D., wife of
Rea	Effa Jane	9.27	1865	8.27	1865			1	199	29	Rea, James & Elizabeth, daughter of
Rea	Ella Bell	11.05	1886	9.27	1866			21	199	30	Rea, James & Elizabeth, daughter of
Reed	Agness								199	31	Reed, J. H., wife of: Huston, James & Sarah, daughter of
Scott	John	8.27	1876			42		43	200	24	
Scroggs	Sarah	12.11	1855		1783	72		73	200	25	(b. 1783)
Sharp	Robert	9.12	1815			67		68	199	32	
Sharp	Margaret McDowell	8.13	1810						199	33	Sharp, Alexander, consort of
Sharp	Alexander	12.08	1824		1756	68		69	199	34	
Sharp	Isabella Oliver	6.07	1843	7.16	1771			72	199	35	Sharp, Alexander, wife of
Sharp	Margaret	9.18	1815						199	36	Sharp, Robert, of Newton, consort of; aged about 80 years; slate
Sharp	Andrew	11.13	1865			45	7.24	46	199	37	
Sharp	Andrew	1.20	1868			46	8.04	47	199	38	
Sharp	John	7.12	1863		1783	80	6.18	81	199	39	
Sharp	Martha (Huston)	12.29	1862		1792	70		71	200	01	Sharp, John, wife of
Sharp	Martha	9.27	1861			38		39	200	02	Sharp, John & Martha, daughter of
Sharp	Margaret	1.27	1870			51	9.10	52	200	03	
Sharp	Thomas	8.15	1888	5.29	1827			62	200	04	
Sharp	Margaret	4.02	1873			47	0.25	48	200	05	Sharp, Thomas, wife of; was Margaret Jane Jacobs, of Mifflin Twp.
Sharp	Margaret McDowell	8.15	1810			50		51	200	06	Sharp, Alexander, consort of
Sharp	Margaret	12.00	1797						200	07	Sharp, Alexander & Margaret, daughter of
Sharp	Elder	3.00	1805	3.27	1786			19	200	08	
Sharp	Alexander	12.13	1860			34		35	200	09	
Sharp	Alexander	1.28	1857		1796	60		61	200	10	Rev.
Sharp	Elizabeth Bryson	1.27	1870	9.11	1797			73	200	11	Sharp, Alexander, Rev., D. D, wife of
Sharpe	Jane E.	10.22	1861	12.17	1826			35	200	12	Sharp, Alexander & Elizabeth, dau. of
Sharp	Jane W.	6.27	1876		1795	81		82	200	13	
Sharp	William H. B.	7.31	1849			21		22	200	14	

Newville - United Presbyterian Church Graveyard

Surname	Given Name	Death Mo/Dy	Death Year	Birth Mo/Dy	Birth Year	Att. Age Yr	Att. Age Mo/Dy	Cm Ag	Pg	No	Other Information
Sharp	Thomas	6.15	1830			29	4.00	30	200	15	unmarried
Sharp	William M.	8.20	1835		1798	37		38	200	16	(b. 1798)
Sharp	Joshua W.	4.07	1881	5.24	1831			50	200	17	Capt.; d. in Jaffa, Palestine
Sharp	Lewis W.	2.06	1875	12.08	1854			21	200	18	
Sharp	Eliza Ann	1.04	1858	3.31	1819			39	200	19	Sharp, S. W. wife of; McKeehan, Samuel & Deborah, daughter of
Sharp	Alexander	2.13	1868	4.26	1849			19	200	20	Sharp, S. W. & Eliza A., son of
Sharp	John R.	8.01	1875	7.15	1830			46	200	21	
Sharp	Martha T. W.	2.29	1884	3.02	1834			50	200	22	
Sharp	Martha J. W.	12.20	1882	7.07	1863			20	200	23	Sharp, John R. & Martha T. W., dau. of
Vance	John	6.16	1849		1773	75		76	200	26	
Vance	Jane	11.09	1837		1781	55		56	200	27	Vance, John, consort of
White	John G.	8.12	1848	4.11	1818			31	200	28	White, Crawford & E., son of; b. New Castle, Lawrence Co. Pennsylvania; d. Cumberland County
Woodburn	John	1.11	1846		1754	92		93	200	31	
Woodburn	Mary	1.16	1836		1764	72		73	200	32	Woodburn, John, consort of
Woodburn	Samuel	11.13	1834		1765	68		69	200	33	
Woodburn	James	8.20	1863		1788	75	1.20	76	200	34	
Woodburn	Elizabeth	9.28	1851		1792	59	1.15	60	200	35	Woodburn, James, wife of
Woodburn	Thomas Smith	10.14	1839	8.20	1807			33	200	36	
Woods	William P.	11.02	1862			20	1.18	21	200	29	Woods, J. P. & J. P., son of; Private, Co. E., 130th Regt., Penn. Volunteers; Captain Laughlin - Colonel Zinn
Woods	Margaret	2.28	1865			15	11.01	16	200	30	

Newville - Zion Lutheran Church Graveyard

ZION LUTHERAN CHURCH GRAVEYARD

Surname	Given Name	Death Mo/Dy	Year	Birth Mo/Dy	Year	Att. Yr	Age Mo/Dy	Cm Ag	Pg	No	Other Information
Bear	Magdalena R.	12.08	1859			1	5.13	2	230	01	
Bower	John J.	2.26	1868	7.22	1827			41	230	05	also 4 infant Bower children
Bowermaster	Elizabeth					27		28	230	06	Bowermaster, Christian, wife of
Bricker	Martha L.	9.02	1856			37	6.00	38	230	02	Bricker, Archibald, wife of
Bricker	Ann Eliza			7.19	1856				230	03	Bricker, Archibald & Martha L., child of [no date of death]
Bricker	John	7.30	1856						230	04	Bricker, Archibald & Martha L., child of
Clouse	Loyd	3.13	1873			0	10.18	1	230	07	
Clouse	Franklin	3.18	1873			0	10.23	1	230	08	Clouse, J. M. & E., son of
Davidson	George A.	11.26	1859						230	09	Davidson, J. & S., son of
Dinnar	Sophia	8.18	1846			8		9	230	10	(perhaps Diunar)
Finkenbinder	Ann Margaret	7.03	1853						230	11	
Finkenbinder	George Edward	8.22	1853						230	12	Finkenbinder, Adam & Sarah Ann, infant child of
Gilmor	William H.	1.13	1860			7	4.12	8	230	13	Gilmore, J. H. & M. J., son of
Haldeman	infant son					0	0.20	1	230	17	Haldeman, George & A., child of
Haldeman	John Milton					1	4.00	2	230	18	Haldeman, George & A., child of [aged 16 months]
Hale	Margaret Catharine	9.25	1850	3.04	1836			15	230	14	Hale, Mary M., daughter of
Hale	John	9.16	1854	10.06	1775			79	230	15	
Hale	Mary M.	10.06	1858	9.05	1781			78	230	16	
Henry	William L.	7.03	1867			0	1.05	1	230	19	Henry, William & Anna, son of
Holby	Morris L.	11.06	1868			0	3.02	1	230	20	Holby, William & K., child of
Holby	infant son	9.16	1867			0	0.16	1	230	21	Holby, William & K., child of
Hower	Catharine	7.08	1850	12.25	1780			70	230	22	
Hower	Jacob	5.15	1837			24	5.00	25	230	23	
Hower	Jacob, Sr.	11.00	1837			55		56	230	24	
Kesler	Jacob	5.28	1853	6.26	1823			30	230	25	
King	Jacob	12.15	1855	4.02	1812			44	230	26	
Langry	William	11.14	1862			21	8.01	22	230	28	Langry, John & Rebecca, son of; d. from wounds received at Battle of Antietam
Latshaw	Susanna	4.14	1861			32	0.09	33	230	27	Latshaw, Samuel, wife of
Lehman	William	11.21	1845			0	5.08	1	230	29	Lehman, William & Jane, child of
Lehman	John Edward	1.03	1850			3	1.03	4	230	30	Lehman, William & Jane, child of
Lechtner	George	3.14	1853			59		60	230	31	
Long	George	10.25	1850	9.25	1837			14	231	01	Long, Jacob & Mary, child of
Long	Mary M.	8.23	1855			1	6.00	2	231	02	Long, Jacob & Mary, child of; [M. ?]
Lontz	James H.	10.07	1851			7	4.08	8	231	03	Lontz, Jonas & Hannah, son of
Martin	Leah M.	9.00	1871			11	10.04	12	231	04	Martin, Henry H. & Jane, son?; d. 9.31
Mayberry	Mary G.	9.10	1858			35		36	231	05	Mayberry, John, wife of
McMullen	Mary	3.16	1878			61	11.23	62	231	08	[b. date also given as Mar. 16, 1878; probable transcription error]
Moore	Sarah	3.04	1868			72		73	231	06	
Mull	J.								231	07	Corporal, Co. I, 165th Pa. Infantry
Ruth	Anna	9.04	1840	5.16	1839			2	231	09	Ruth, Isaac & Mary, daughter of
Ruth	Uriah D.	3.26	1841			4		5	231	10	Ruth, R. & S., son of
Slaybaugh	Hannah	10.03	1868			65		66	231	11	Slaybaugh, Henry, wife of
Slaybaugh	Anna F.	12.08	1880			31	11.07	32	231	12	

Newville - Zion Lutheran Church Graveyard

Surname	Given Name	Death Mo/Dy	Year	Birth Mo/Dy	Year	Att. Age Yr	Mo/Dy	Cm Ag	Pg	No	Other Information
Snevely	Elizabeth	8.22	1840			42		43	231	13	Snevely, John, wife of
Spidel	I.								231	14	[no dates given]
Stitzel	Anna E.	10.21	1862			6	7.00	7	231	15	Stitzel, William & Catharine, dau. of
Strohm	Barbara Ellen	12.12	1880			47	10.07	48	231	16	Strohm, Solomon, wife of
Strohm	Clara Bell	9.22	1880			15	07.27	16	231	17	Strohm, Solomon & Barbara, daughter of
Waggoner	Michael M.	3.09	1853			36	0.22	37	231	18	Waggoner, Michael & Nancy, son of
Yeager	Anna E.	2.03	1851			8	1.11	9	231	19	
Yeager	Emma J.	2.11	1851			1	0.01	2	231	20	
Young	Jane	2.24	1862	4.01	1834			28	231	21	Young, Robert, wife of

North Middleton - Bethel Church Graveyard

NORTH MIDDLETON TOWNSHIP

BETHEL CHURCH GRAVEYARD

Surname	Given Name	Death Mo/Dy	Death Year	Birth Mo/Dy	Birth Year	Att. Age Yr	Cm Mo/Dy	Ag	Pg	No	Other Information
Dewalt	Susan	1.14	1890			54	8.26	55	135	01	
Dewalt	Lucinda								135	02	Dewalt, J. E., wife of [no dates given]
Dick	Eve Ann	10.03	1885			65	10.21	66	135	03	Dick, Jacob, wife of
Fry	William G.		1898		1852			47	135	04	
Kriner	Grace M.	10.22	1897			10	7.02	11	135	05	Kriner, P. J. & L. B., daughter of
Lightner	John S.	2.15	1888			81	2.12	82	135	06	
Lightner	Julia	10.12	1888			71		72	135	07	
Lightner	Thomas E.	3.10	1896	6.12	1840			56	135	08	
Mellinger	Levi	6.28	1897			77	9.11	78	135	09	
Reiber	Margaret	5.24	1900			58	4.00	59	135	10	Reiber, David, wife of
Sheffer	Joseph H.	1.22	1894			11		12	135	12	Sheffer, S. & Susan, son of
Smeigh	John	7.28	1887			43		44	135	13	Sergeant, Co. D, 19th Penn. Cavalry; [d. 1887 ?]
Swarner	Hannah	12.04	1888			81	2.29	82	135	11	Swarner, George, wife of
Swiger	Wilbur Dale	2.02	1888			1	0.29	2	135	14	

North Middleton - Wagner's Church Graveyard

WAGNER'S CHURCH GRAVEYARD

Surname	Given Name	Death Mo/Dy	Death Year	Birth Mo/Dy	Birth Year	Att. Age Yr	Cm Mo/Dy	Ag	Pg	No	Other Information
Allen	George W.	7.21	1865			38	9.14	39	039	01	
Allen	William H.	11.25	1880			19	4.00	20	039	02	
Barley	John G.	2.27	1883			76	1.05	77	039	03	
Barley	John F.	8.02	1903			68	9.28	69	039	04	
Barley	Mary	3.26	1873			68	11.26	69	039	05	Barley, John G., wife of
Barley	William B.	1.04	1882	12.25	1841			41	039	06	
Barley	James B.	11.14	1877				7.05	1	039	07	Barley, William & Catharine, child of
Barley	Jacob P.	3.16	1867	2.15	1866			2	039	08	Barley, William & Catharine, child of
Barley	Gertie P.	9.20	1880			1	11.23	2	039	09	Barley, William & Catharine, child of
Barley	Anna M.	3.28	1879			2	2.10	3	039	10	Barley, Abraham & A. C., child of
Barley	Susanna P.	4.11	1879				6.02	1	039	11	Barley, Abraham & A. C., child of
Barley	David E.	6.24	1866			1	6.11	2	039	12	Barley, Jacob & Sarah A., son of
Barley	Sarah A.	12.10	1866	2.27	1840			27	039	13	Barley, Jacob, wife of
Barrick	John	1.11	1889			67	0.04	68	039	14	
Barrick	Susan	4.03	1893			34	11.28	35	039	15	
Barrick	Levi	4.24	1891						039	16	
Barrick	Gordon L.	4.22	1885			1	0.27	2	039	17	Barrick, Levi & Anna, child of
Barrick	Chester C.	4.11	1893			2	4.17	3	039	18	Barrick, Levi & Anna, child of
Braught	George	5.02	1890	11.10	1810			80	039	19	
Braught	Susannah	3.07	1884			73	6.10	74	039	20	Braught, George, wife of
Briner	Catharine	9.24	1861	2.17	1791			71	039	21	Briner, Peter, wife of
Carbaugh	Batch S.	11.15	1881			4	8.12	5	039	22	Carbaugh, Zachariah & Annie, son of
Dewalt	Harvey W.	2.18	1888	8.20	1887			1	039	23	Dewalt, E. & S. A., infant son of
Diller	Francis Renfew					19	5.01	20	039	24	[Renfew (sic)]
Duey	Elizabeth A.	11.03	1865				2.29	1	039	25	Duey, William & Elizabeth, daughter of
Duey	Alice	5.18	1872	3.26	1872			1	039	26	Duey, Samuel & Minnie C., daughter of
Duey	William D.	3.22	1882			18	11.01	19	039	27	Duey, William & Elizabeth, son of
Dunlap	Mary Ann	5.17	1851		1781	70	5.25	71	039	28	Dunlap, John, wife of; (b. 1781)
Earnest	Conrad	11.16	1892	2.00	1827			66	039	29	[birth date given as Feb. 29, 1827]
Earnest	Mary E.	5.07	1876			19	9.17	20	039	30	Earnest, Conrad & Mary, daughter of
Greider	John	1.08	1894			54		55	040	01	
Gruver	William E.	1.03	1863			1	2.15	2	040	02	Gruver, John & Angeline, son of
Hollenbaugh	Joseph	2.23	1897			73		74	040	03	[text reads "aged 74th year"]
Hollenbaugh	Charles A.	7.14	1900			11	11.05	12	040	04	
Hollenbaugh	Mary B.	11.13	1889			32	7.11	33	040	05	
Jackson	Hannah	8.13	1882			69	2.23	70	040	06	
Jackson	Annie E.	11.26	1863			15	1.26	16	040	07	
Jackson	Richard C.	6.12	1863			26	8.22	27	040	08	
Jones	John	1.24	1865			65	3.05	66	040	09	
Kell	Peter	3.21	1894			81	3.00	82	040	10	
Kell	Eliza	5.21	1874			51	4.29	52	040	11	
King	Park Elmer	1.19	1887			16	4.07	17	040	12	King, Christian & Susan, child of
King	Minnie	11.16	1877				0.24	1	040	13	King, Christian & Susan, child of
King	Andrew	11.30	1861						040	14	King, Christian & Susan, child of
Lenhart	Rebecca	2.15	1870			73	7.25	74	040	15	Lenhart, Jacob, wife of
Lepperd	George S.	4.28	1892	9.05	1832			60	040	16	
Lepperd	Mary A.	4.30	1898	8.02	1837			61	040	17	Lepperd, George S., wife of
Lepperd	Minnie	2.23	1889	4.06	1865			24	040	18	Lepperd, George S. & Mary A., dau. of

North Middleton - Wagner's Church Graveyard

Surname	Given Name	Death Mo/Dy	Year	Birth Mo/Dy	Year	Att. Age Yr	Cm Mo/Dy	Pg Ag	No	Other Information
Nailor	David	4.15	1903			75	8.12	76	040	19	
Nailor	Catharine	5.10	1882			57	3.21	58	040	20	Nailor, David, wife of
Nailor	Effie F.						5.10	1	040	21	Nailor, William G. & A., child of
Nailor	George P.					1	8.05	2	040	22	Nailor, William G. & A., child of
Naylor	Lydia	10.24	1855			40	2.18	41	040	23	Naylor, Barnard, wife of
Nickey	Mary E.	9.13	1856					1	040	24	Nickey, B. F. & C., daughter of; [birth given as March 11, 1865; possible transposition of digits in year]
Reed	Kennedy	11.22	1894	3.17	1844			51	040	25	
Shaw	Susanna	4.15	1869			81	7.19	82	040	26	Shaw, William, Rev., wife of
Sheaffer	William R.	3.01	1898			73	6.27	74	040	28	
Sheaffer	Catharine	12.15	1882			54	8.22	55	040	29	Sheaffer, William, wife of
Shearer	Emanuel	3.11	1897			63	1.08	64	040	30	
Shearer	Elizabeth	9.10	1900			63	5.12	64	040	31	
Shearer	Amos	12.06	1886			19	4.26	20	040	32	Shearer, Emanuel & Elizabeth, son of
Shearer	Sarah E.	11.19	1892			25	5.11	26	040	33	Shearer, Rhoddy, wife of
Shearer	Emma M.	6.19	1991			32	4.17	33	040	34	
Shearer	Elsie May					1	6.00	2	041	01	Shearer, J. & E. M., daughter of
Sheriff	John H.	7.25	1887			27	6.12	28	041	02	
Shetron	Elgie M.	8.22	1896				7.00	1	041	03	Shetron, Allen & E. S., daughter of
Shughart	Anthony	5.11	1885			58	2.22	59	041	04	
Shughart	William	2.25	1872			74	10.21	75	041	05	
Shughart	Mary	12.28	1882			81	1.16	82	041	06	Shughart, William, wife of
Shughart	Anthony E.	5.04	1873			2	4.04	3	041	07	Shughart, E. & S., son of
Shughart	Emma R.	9.15	1878			11	9.19	12	041	08	Shughart, W. & E., daughter of
Shughart	William	8.06	1900			74	10.28	75	041	09	
Shughart	Elizabeth	9.01	1896			68	8.16	69	041	10	Shughart, William, wife of
Shughart	Dessie M.	2.06	1895			5	10.01	6	041	11	Shughart, P. K. & A. M., daughter of
Shughart	Elmer E.	4.17	1876			1	2.24	2	041	12	Shughart, P. & K., child of
Strohm	George	6.06	1861		1780	81	9.13	82	042	29	(b. 1780)
Strohm	Anna Mary	2.05	1866			74	1.18	75	042	30	Strohm, George, wife of
Stutsman	Catharine	1.20	1889			65		66	041	13	
Swartz	Elmer E.	3.10	1863				7.19	1	040	27	Swartz, L. & M., son of
Thomas	George E.	8.26	1881			25	10.24	26	041	14	
Thomas	George	10.08	1887			64	3.10	65	041	15	
Thomas	Shearden						0.22	1	041	16	Thomas, G. & May, son of
Thomas	George W.	7.22	1893			1	5.00	2	041	17	Thomas, Albert & Emma, son of
Thumma	Abraham	10.04	1896			80	8.10	81	041	18	
Thumma	Elizabeth J.	6.16	1872	8.14	1859			13	041	19	Thumma, A. & E., daughter of
Thumma	Mary	6.28	1876			54	5.26	55	041	20	Thumma, J. & S., daughter of
Waggoner	John	9.25	1874			56	2.28	57	041	21	
Waggoner	Elizabeth	12.02	1889			68	2.13	69	041	22	Waggoner, John, wife of
Wagoner	John Elmer	10.02	1882			18	8.28	19	041	23	[Wagoner (sic)]
Waggoner	Jacob	10.30	1878	11.15	1815			63	041	24	
Waggoner	Mary	2.21	1895	2.05	1817			79	041	25	
Waggoner	Dessie J. Saxton	7.18	1875	4.12	1849			27	041	26	Waggoner, Jacob C., wife of
Waggoner	Sarah I. Armstrong	3.22	1892	7.05	1864			28	041	27	Waggoner, Jacob C., wife of
Waggoner	Wilson K.								041	28	[no dates given]
Waggoner	Jennie E. Armstrong	2.25	1898			39	6.27	40	041	29	Armstrong, W. K., wife of; [unexplained last name difference]

North Middleton - Wagner's Church Graveyard

Surname	Given Name	Death Mo/Dy	Year	Birth Mo/Dy	Year	Att. Age Yr	Mo/Dy	Ag	Cm	Pg	No	Other Information
Waggoner	Laura C.	10.03	1894			37	4.14	38		041	30	
Waggoner	John S.	4.16	1893			38	4.14	39		041	31	
Walker	Minnie May	9.12	1882			1	0.17	2		041	32	Walker, F. & A., daughter of
Wert	Martin	1.05	1852	6.03	1800				52	041	33	
Wert	Anna S.	7.23	1875			76	6.21	77		041	34	Wert, Martin, wife of
Wert	Samuel	12.26	1885	11.26	1827				59	042	01	
Wert	Samuel G.	3.02	1873	9.27	1872				1	042	02	Wert, Samuel & Lydia Ann, son of
Wert	Sarah J.	2.20	1860				7.22		1	042	03	Wert, John & M., daughter of
Wert	Daniel Barley	2.04	1863	3.16	1860				3	042	04	Wert, Samuel & Lydia Ann, son of
Wetzel	Moses	4.17	1872			73	5.15	74		042	05	
Wetzel	Mary R.	7.13	1875			74	7.26	75		042	06	Wetzel, Moses, wife of
Wetzel	Jacob	3.31	1863			66	8.06	67		042	07	
Wetzel	Anna	10.12	1898	2.23	1827				72	042	08	
Wetzel	Parker	9.12	1862			1	4.23	2		042	09	Wetzel, William & M. M., son of
Wetzel	Sarah E. C. Wickard	7.10	1882	4.12	1857				26	042	10	Wetzell, George M., wife of
Wetzel	infant son									042	11	Wetzel, G. M. & S. E. C., son of
Wickard	David	12.21	1886			68	11.13	69		042	12	
Wickard	Martha	12.27	1890			67	11.13	68		042	13	Wickard, David, wife of
Wickard	Harvey D.	12.13	1877			1	1.14	2		042	14	Wickard, C. J. & S. C., son of
Wolf	infant son	7.18	1880							042	15	Wolf, P. R. & F. M., son of
Yarlets	Lucetta C. Barnhill	11.28	1879			28	4.08	29		042	16	Yarletts, Joseph R., wife of [spelling varies]
Yarlets	Henry	6.22	1852	12.01	1826				26	042	17	
Yorlets	John S.	1.12	1883			58	3.24	59		042	18	
Yorlets	Rebecca J.	7.04	1864			38	3.05	39		042	19	Yorlet, John S., wife of; also their five children; [spelling varies]
Yorlets	Lucetta	11.12	1883			70	8.07	71		042	20	
Yorlets	Jonas	10.11	1878	8.10	1797				80	042	21	[d. 1878 (?)]
Yorlets	Elizabeth	9.03	1892	10.08	1826				66	042	22	Yorlets, Jacob, wife of
Yorlets	William Proope	7.26	1887	2.25	1886				2	042	23	Yorlets, Henry & Minnie W., inf. son of
Zimmerman	George	6.25	1899			61	9.28	62		042	25	
Zimmerman	Mary M.	9.29	1881			42		43		042	26	Zimmerman, George, wife of
Zimmerman	Raymond L.	2.19	1899			25	4.24	26		042	27	
Zimmerman	Leo Edward	3.05	1886				0.05	1		042	28	Zimmerman, Charles & Eleetta, son of

South Middleton - Flint Ridge Chapel Graveyard
Garber Graveyard

SOUTH MIDDLETON TOWNSHIP

FLINT RIDGE CHAPEL GRAVEYARD

Surname	Given Name	Death Mo/Dy	Year	Birth Mo/Dy	Year	Att. Age Yr	Mo/Dy	Ag	Cm	Pg	No	Other Information
Davis	Clarence A.	1.29	1891				7.29	1	118	01		Davis, James S., & A. C., son of
Frost	Mary A.	4.10	1895			37	9.12	38	118	02		Frost, George, wife of
Glass	Catharine	4.22	1903			76	7.12	77	118	03		Glass, Daniel, wife of
Mortorff	James F.	2.02	1901			50	9.05	51	118	04		
Shuff	Thomas	10.13	1890			65	1.27	66	118	05		
Winand	Charles E.	11.01	1903	8.23	1888			16	118	06		
Yesler	John	7.03	1867			20	10.19	21	118	07		Yesler, Henry & Catharine, son of
Yesler	Lydia Ann	4.01	1891			33	11.11	34	118	08		Yesler, Henry & Catharine, daughter of
Yesler	Henry	11.26	1896			75	11.16	76	118	09		
Yesler	Catharine	7.27	1897			76	11.07	77	118	10		Yesler, Henry, wife of

GARBER GRAVEYARD

Surname	Given Name	Death Mo/Dy	Year	Birth Mo/Dy	Year	Att. Age Yr	Mo/Dy	Ag	Cm	Pg	No	Other Information
Garber	Jacob, Sr.	6.08	1849			75	8.17	76	116	01		
Garber	Susanna	12.25	1863	1.27	1789			75	116	02		
Garber	Mary Ann	2.27	1849			22	5.15	23	116	03		Garber, Jacob & Susannah, daughter of; [first name spelling varies]
Garber	Jacob	12.07	1839			23	1.16	24	116	04		German
Garber	Sarah Ann	11.26	1850	11.11	1839			12	116	05		Garber, George & Lydia A., daughter of
Garber	Catharine	11.22	1850	11.17	1847			4	116	06		Garber, George & Lydia, daughter of

South Middleton - Mount Victory Graveyard
   Strickler Graveyard

MOUNT VICTORY GRAVEYARD

Surname	Given Name	Death Mo/Dy	Year	Birth Mo/Dy	Year	Att. Age Yr	Mo/Dy	Cm Ag	Pg	No	Other Information
Chronister	Alice J.	7.25	1894			45	6.21	46	117	03	Chronister, Jacob H., wife of
Chronister	Harry J. A.	9.06	1895				8.21	1	117	04	Chronister, Lank & Julia A., son of
Coulson	Jacob F.	1.10	1896			69	7.05	70	117	01	Private, Co. F, 99th Regt., Pennsylvania Volunteers
Coulson	Calvin	9.19	1901			45	4.00	46	117	02	
Gardner	Barnhart	8.21	1900			65	5.04	66	117	05	
Marsh	Samuel	2.15	1892			23	3.18	24	117	06	
Marsh	Alpheus	1.14	1893			62	11.11	63	117	07	

STRICKLER GRAVEYARD

Surname	Given Name	Death Mo/Dy	Year	Birth Mo/Dy	Year	Att. Age Yr	Mo/Dy	Cm Ag	Pg	No	Other Information
Hartzler	Abraham	9.09	1861			87	5.08	88	115	01	
Hartzler	Catharine	4.26	1864			80	0.08	81	115	02	
Hoffer	John	2.13	1871			7	1.20	8	115	03	Hoffer, D. & E., son of
Hoffer	Alfred H.	11.13	1876			26	2.08	27	115	04	(M. D.)
Hoffer	Daniel	11.20	1901			80	11.00	81	115	05	
Strickler	Ulrich	6.15	1871			70	8.09	71	115	06	
Strickler	Catharine Hertzler	8.26	1838	12.24	1810			28	115	07	Strickler, Ulrich, consort of; died leaving two children, Abraham and John
Strickler	Abraham	9.02	1887			53	1.17	54	115	08	
Strickler	Barbara M.	5.17	1899			61	6.09	62	115	09	Strickler, Abraham, wife of
Strickler	Frankie H.	8.31	1875				9.19	1	115	10	Strickler, Abraham & Barbara, son of
Strickler	Sammy Herr	8.19	1872				4.20	1	115	11	
Strickler	Lizzie Hulda	3.29	1892			22	1.01	23	115	12	Strickler, J. Edwin, wife of
Strickler	Barbara May	3.29	1892			2	0.24	3	115	13	Strickler, J. E. & L. H., daughter of
Strickler	Jacob D.	12.30	1898	11.14	1898			1	115	14	Strickler, J. K. & J. E., son of

Penn - Centerville Lutheran Church Graveyard

PENN TOWNSHIP

CENTERVILLE LUTHERAN CHURCH GRAVEYARD

Surname	Given Name	Death Mo/Dy	Death Year	Birth Mo/Dy	Birth Year	Att. Age Yr	Cm Mo/Dy	Pg Ag	No	Other Information
Armagast	Catharine E.	2.26	1839				8.00	1	093 01	Armagast, George & Mary, daughter of
Auld	William	11.20	1833			76	5.23	77	093 02	
Auld	Christiana	8.12	1830			73	2.23	74	093 03	Auld, William, wife of
Auld	John	6.25	1859			62	8.27	63	093 04	
Auld	Mary W.	11.02	1866			68	10.15	69	093 05	Auld, John, wife of
Baldwin	Mary Ann	1.31	1837	1.27	1835			3	093 06	Baldwin, James & Elizabeth, daughter of
Baugher	J. A.								093 07	Co. F, 207th Pa. Infantry; [no dates]
Baugher	William H.	9.22	1866				0.17	1	093 08	
Baugher	Margaret Elizabeth	10.24	1838			6	6.25	7	093 09	Baugher, Henry & Annie, daughter of
Baugher	Mary E.	7.22	1870			1	5.11	2	093 10	
Beecher	Mary Ann	11.07	1850			24	6.02	25	093 12	Beecher, Jesse, wife of; Clandy, M. & E., daughter of; (perhaps Claudy)
Beetem	Samuel, Sr.	7.08	1856	6.22	1767			90	093 13	Esq.
Beetem	Mary	2.11	1834			72	0.23	73	093 14	Beetem, Samuel, consort of
Beetem	Nancy	5.02	1862			85		86	093 15	Beetem, Samuel, wife of
Beetem	Jacob, Sr.	3.24	1853			65	2.05	66	093 16	
Bishop	Martin	11.11	1891			29	11.10	30	093 17	
Bishop	Katie D.	11.23	1880	12.05	1856			24	093 18	Bishop, James & Ann C., daughter of
Bitzer	Lucia	10.21	1837	3.02	1813			25	093 19	Bitzer, Samuel, wife of; Balmer, Christian, daughter of
Blair	Margaret	6.17	1847			32		33	093 11	Blair, Henry, wife of
Blyler	Elizabeth	3.30	1850			49		50	093 27	
Botdorf	Jonathan Calvin	4.02	1862				3.12	1	093 25	Botdorf, Jonathan & Susan, son of
Brindle	Solomon	9.09	1889	3.31	1803			87	093 21	
Brindle	Sarah Ann Smith	6.12	1898	1.18	1816			83	093 22	Brindle, Solomon, wife of
Brindle	Elizabeth	4.10	1857	7.14	1843			14	093 23	Brindle, S. & S. A., daughter of
Brindle	Mary Ann	3.07	1830	5.09	1813			17	093 24	
Brinn	Mary	8.26	1872			70		71	093 20	
Bushman	Mary M.	12.07	1850	2.16	1776			75	093 26	
Carmany	Jacob	1.25	1859			20		21	093 28	
Cashman	Margaret Ann	7.05	1873			43	9.29	44	093 29	Cashman, John P., wife of
Cashman	John Elmer	9.29	1873				3.01	1	093 30	Cashman, J. P. & M. A., son of
Chesnell	John	1.12	1854			72		73	094 09	
Chisnell	Elizabeth	1.22	1855			69	1.15	70	094 10	[Chesnell], John, wife of; [sp. varies]
Clandy	Martin	1.01	1859			58	10.19	59	093 31	(perhaps Claudy)
Clandy	Elizabeth	5.28	1831			34	0.07	35	093 32	Clandy, Martin, 1st wife of
Clandy	Mary A.	8.27	1873			70	8.21	71	093 33	Clandy, Martin, wife of
Clandy	Catharine F.	12.03	1832			4	4.03	5	094 01	Clandy, Martin & Elizabeth, daughter of
Clandy	Ann Elizabeth	2.23	1839			3	4.14	4	094 02	Clandy, Martin & Mary, child of
Clandy	William Martin	1.14	1839			1	1.11	2	094 03	Clandy, Martin & Mary, child of
Clandy	Martha Ellen	3.15	1857			14	11.12	15	094 04	Clandy, Martin & Mary, child of
Clandy	Jacob	12.27	1854			59	1.13	60	094 05	
Clandy	John	10.10	1857			55	6.10	56	094 06	
Clandy	Clara M.	8.17	1865				3.03	1	094 07	Clandy, L. & A. M., daughter of
Clandy	Abraham	7.17	1875			71	4.19	72	094 08	
Coover	Deitrich	4.23	1865			46	4.29	47	094 14	Dr.

Penn - Centerville Lutheran Church Graveyard

Surname	Given Name	Death Mo/Dy	Year	Birth Mo/Dy	Year	Att. Age Yr	Cm Mo/Dy	Ag	Pg	No	Other Information
Coover	Sarah E.	1.12	1860			31	8.30	32	094	15	Coover, D., Dr., wife of
Coover	Elmirah M.	2.17	1850	4.15	1848			2	094	16	Coover, Deitrich, Dr. & Sarah E., dau.of
Coover	Alie L.	1.23	1859			2	5.15	3	094	17	Coover, Deitrich, Dr. & Sarah E., dau.of
Coover	William	2.26	1860				1.24	1	094	18	Coover, Deitrich, Dr. & Sarah E., son of
Coover	Sarah Frances	9.03	1856			2	5.20	3	094	19	Coover, Adam E., daughter of
Creamer	Emma L.	6.17	1864			4	7.02	5	094	11	Creamer, Christian & Mary, daughter of
Creamer	Margaret Ann	5.11	1857	6.11	1853			4	094	12	Creamer, Christian & Mary, daughter of
Creglow	Susanna	8.10	1840			45	6.30	46	094	13	Creglow, William, wife of
Cully	Mary E.	11.11	1859	7.04	1837			23	094	20	Cully, David, wife of; Wolf, David & M., daughter of
Culley	Mary E.	12.29	1860			1	1.21	2	094	21	Cully, David & M. E., daughter of; [spelling varies]
Deem	Eleanor M.	4.01	1891			72	4.11	73	094	22	
Donor	John	6.05	1895			86	7.04	87	094	23	
Donor	Anna	12.22	1891			76	3.11	77	094	24	Doner, John, wife of
Donor	Samuel A.	7.24	1873	9.14	1843			30	094	25	soldier
Donor	Isaac Lefever	10.07	1838			1	11.27	2	094	26	Doner, J. & Ann, son of
Eberts	Rosella Jane	11.27	1867			1	6.05	2	094	27	Eberts, Samuel & E., daughter of
Eckert	John	8.18	1856	12.25	1801			55	094	28	
Eckert	Sarah Ellen	8.29	1852			3	11.00	4	094	29	
Faust	Peter	3.17	1882			57	7.06	58	094	30	
Faust	Catharine	3.05	1871			49	1.09	50	094	31	Faust, Peter, wife of
Fickes	George	8.16	1844	12.01	1805			39	094	33	
Fickes	Valentine	9.02	1830	2.25	1808			23	095	01	
Fickes	Elizabeth	1.29	1839			21	3.26	22	095	02	
Fisher	Samuel	2.07	1871			42	0.27	43	095	03	
Ford	Rebecca K.	1.30	1862			25	7.08	26	095	04	
Ford	Susanna May	8.11	1862				6.17	1	095	05	
Frantz	Samuel	12.10	1856			54		55	094	32	
Gilbert	Catharine	12.05	1861			35		36	095	06	Gilbert, John, wife of
Givler	Elizabeth	12.07	1873			57	11.19	58	095	07	Givler, Henry, wife of
Goodhart	Isaac	4.06	1873			80	5.21	81	095	08	
Goodhart	Mary M.	1.20	1878			82	8.21	83	095	09	
Goodhart	Frederick	11.02	1880			71	4.11	72	095	10	
Goodhart	Cyrus A.	5.08	1883			51	7.07	52	095	11	
Goodhart	A. Eliza	7.27	1889	3.10	1852			38	095	12	Goodhart, Cyrus A., wife of
Guldon	Mella	6.10	1884			1		2	095	13	Guldon, G. W. & J. V., daughter of
Hall	John	11.23	1879			58	7.23	59	095	14	
Hall	Alice	6.12	1867			12	8.12	13	095	15	Hall, John & E., only daughter of
Heagy	Sarah G.	8.12	1868			28	0.04	29	095	16	Heagy, John C., wife of; John, William & Anna, daughter of
Heagy	Lillie F.	2.25	1864				4.06	1	095	17	Heagy, John & Sarah, daughter of
Hemminger	Jacob	9.22	1874			77	9.09	78	095	18	
Hemminger	Frances	2.15	1874			73		74	095	19	Hemminger, Jacob, wife of
Hemminger	Frances	4.11	1852			30	4.18	31	095	20	
Henry	James L.	9.23	1887	8.16	1813			75	095	21	
Henry	William M.	7.05	1855			4	10.12	5	095	22	Henry, J. L. & C. M., child of
Henry	Ellie G.	3.18	1871			13	3.09	14	095	23	Henry, J. L. & C. M., child of
Henry	Carl	5.19	1878				3.14	1	095	24	Henry, J. L. & E. L., son of
Himes	Clarence Jacob	9.07	1888				5.14	1	095	25	Himes, J. H. & C., son of

Penn - Centerville Lutheran Church Graveyard

Surname	Given Name	Death Mo/Dy	Year	Birth Mo/Dy	Year	Att. Age Yr	Mo/Dy	Ag	Cm	Pg	No	Other Information
Hocker	George P.	10.25	1859			20	7.20	21		095	26	Hocker, John & Elizabeth, son of
Hocker	Ephraim	9.20	1838	5.19	1834			5		095	27	Hocker, John & Elizabeth, son of
Hocker	Anna Margarette	10.01	1826			22	2.22	23		095	28	Hocker, Peter, consort of
Hoover	Mary Magdalena	6.16	1833			38	5.06	39		095	29	Hoover, David, wife of
Hoover	Anna Catharine	1.22	1850	3.04	1844			6		095	30	
Hoover	Mary E.	10.27	1852	8.07	1851			2		095	31	
John	William	4.02	1888	5.09	1814			74		095	32	
John	Anna	8.25	1880			65	9.14	66		095	33	John, William, wife of
Karns	Sarah Ellen	11.29	1845							095	34	Karns, David H. & Elizabeth, dau. of; born in Washington County, MD
Kechler	C. A.									096	01	Co. A, 188 Pa. Infantry; [no dates]
Keefouver	Frederick	9.19	1865			60		61		096	02	
Keefourer	Augustus	8.09	1840			6	11.06	7		096	03	Keefourer, F. & S., son of; [Keefourer (sic)]
Keihl	Sarah R.	5.12	1871			32	3.00	33		096	04	Kiehl, John, wife of; Doner, John & Ann, daughter of; [spelling varies]
Kelly	John	8.25	1867			62		63		096	05	
King	John	2.06	1876			71	9.20	72		096	06	
King	Catharine	5.08	1882			80	2.09	81		096	07	King, John, wife of
Kissinger	Adam	4.20	1850			87		88		096	08	
Kissinger	John	6.18	1862			83	3.00	84		096	09	
Kissinger	Adam	11.15	1843	2.18	1778			66		096	10	soldier
Kissinger	William G.	10.07	1859			2	10.00	3		096	11	Kissinger, George & Maria, son of
Kunkle	Harry E.	3.06	1873			1	11.24	2		096	12	Kunkle, Joseph & Sarah J., son of
Lesher	Lydia B.	8.03	1886			1	10.24	2		096	13	Lesher, P. H. & S. J., daughter of
Lindsay	Willie Carl	1.13	1881				10.14	1		096	14	Lindsay, J. B. & A. M., son of
Lockard	Hannah	2.07	1879			64		65		096	15	
Lockard	Catharine	1.11	1876							096	16	Lockard, Samuel, wife of
Lockard	William	11.17	1854			32	0.29	33		096	17	
Lockard	Sarah	2.25	1852			39	3.00	40		096	18	
Logan	George W.	1.26	1875			25	10.10	26		096	19	
Long	Rosannah	2.01	1851	2.14	1787			64		096	20	Long, Samuel, wife of
Low	Jacob	2.27	1880			32	11.22	33		096	21	
Machon	Joseph	9.07	1872			56		57		096	22	
Meals	Daniel	10.25	1864			70	9.13	71		096	23	soldier
Messinger	Daniel	12.17	1871	11.08	1806			66		096	24	
Messinger	Elizabeth	2.17	1879	8.17	1800			79		096	25	Messinger, Daniel, wife of
Miller	Michael	11.08	1822	9.08	1752			71		096	26	German; pale sand headstone
Mixell	Jacob	8.24	1889			66		67		096	27	
Mixell	John	9.24	1856				5.00	1		096	28	Mixell, Jacob & Elizabeth, child of
Mixell	Amanda M.	2.22	1858			3	8.03	4		096	29	Mixell, Jacob & Elizabeth, child of
Mixell	Martha J.	8.20	1858			1	0.02	2		096	30	Mixell, Jacob & Elizabeth, child of
Morrison	Anna M. E.	4.05	1870			6	8.08	7		096	31	Morrison, Samuel & N. A., daughter of
Morrison	Samuel J.	4.12	1870			1	4.10	2		096	32	Morrison, Samuel & N. A., son of
Myers	Ephraim		1838							096	33	d. - 8, 1838
Myers	Mary Agnes	10.30	1843	4.26	1843			1		096	34	pale sand headstone
Neff	Michael	3.09	1865	3.08	1814			52		096	35	
Nerons	J. R.									096	36	Co. F, 207th Pa. Infantry; [no dates]
Noggle	George	1.13	1849	5.26	1788			61		096	37	
Noggle	Susan	6.26	1849	5.26	1790			60		096	38	Noggle, George, wife of

Penn - Centerville Lutheran Church Graveyard

Surname	Given Name	Death Mo/Dy	Year	Birth Mo/Dy	Year	Att. Age Yr	Mo/Dy	Cm Ag	Pg	No	Other Information
Noggle	Elizabeth	1.15	1851			1	7.28	2	097	01	Noggle, Jacob & Sarah, daughter of
Noggle	Reuben Luther	2.09	1850			1	2.26	2	097	02	
Owen	Lizzie May	9.09	1865			1	4.20	2	097	03	Owen, S. W., Rev., & Cordelia, dau. of
Palm	Leander E.	4.14	1873	10.09	1843			30	097	04	soldier
Palm	David	10.06	1841	11.25	1785			56	097	05	
Palm	Jane	11.29	1884			82	10.04	83	097	06	Palm, David, wife of
Palm	Jacob, Sr.	11.27	1835			80		81	097	07	a soldier of the Revolution
Palm	Elizabeth	10.17	1831	6.18	1784			48	097	08	Palm, David, wife of
Palm	Elizabeth Weise	12.28	1839			21	0.03	22	097	09	Palm, Peter, married Oct. 8, 1839
Palm	Catharine	6.13	1850	8.22	1821			29	097	10	Palm, Peter, wife of
Pecher	Daniel	4.04	1860			5	4.24	6	097	11	Vance, Anna, son of
Pechart	Isaac	7.21	1892			74	8.20	75	097	12	
Pechart	Jane	3.27	1885			62	3.29	63	097	13	Pechart, Isaac, Capt., wife of
Pechart	Minnie A.	3.26	1864			1	6.04	2	097	14	Pechart, John L. & Jane, child of
Pechart	Calvin Kyle	10.15	1870	10.02	1870			1	097	15	Pechart, John L. & Jane, child of
Peffer	John	9.07	1872			84		85	097	16	
Peffer	Elizabeth	4.01	1875			83		84	097	17	Peffer, John, wife of [d. in his 84th yr
Phillips	Joseph	11.12	1827	4.06	1826			2	097	18	
Reigle	Jacob	5.26	1885	5.17	1801			85	097	19	
Reigle	Susan	8.05	1870			69	6.07	70	097	20	Reigle, Jacob, wife of
Rife	Daniel	4.22	1894			73		74	097	21	
Rife	Susan	9.24	1900			82	1.24	83	097	22	
Rupert	Caroline	3.05	1879	11.30	1824			55	097	23	Rupert, Howard, wife of
Saltzgiver	Michael	9.08	1877			57	8.20	58	097	24	
Saltzgiver	Maggie	12.28	1877			33	10.19	34	097	25	Saltzgiver, J. C., wife of
Sellers	Samuel		1896		1820			77	097	30	
Sellers	Eleanor Steel		1892		1820			73	097	31	Sellers, Samuel, wife of
Sellers	Evaline F.	6.15	1864			7	7.23	8	097	32	
Sellers	Martha	3.28	1864			10	4.00	11	097	33	
Sellers	Ida B.	8.22	1862			2	0.27	3	097	34	
Sellers	Joshua	5.18	1852			54	10.22	55	097	35	
Sellers	Henry M.	10.30	1850	7.02	1828			23	098	01	
Sellers	Altivesta A.	3.08	1860			1	8.08	2	098	02	Sellers, Samuel & Ellenor, child of
Sellers	Charles Klink	8.25	1853			2	4.03	3	098	03	Sellers, Samuel & Ellenor, child of
Sellers	William Henry	9.02	1853			10	6.28	11	098	04	Sellers, Samuel & Ellenor, child of
Sellers	Jane Ann	9.03	1853			4	6.25	5	098	05	Sellers, Samuel & Ellenor, child of
Sennet	Grover C.	3.04	1885				3.07	1	098	06	Sennet, John & H., son of
Sheaffer	Samuel	3.10	1849	2.16	1794			56	097	27	
Sheffler	Elizabeth	5.27	1871	12.31	1800			71	097	28	
Sheffler	Adam	6.27	1869	3.03	1804			66	097	29	
Shoemaker	Henry Carey	5.20	1863				1.08	1	098	27	Shoemaker, David & Sarah, son of
Shriver	William	1.26	1861			82	6.06	83	098	15	
Shriver	Sarah	8.05	1870	11.09	1783			87	098	16	
Shriver	Isaac Edgar	1.07	1843				5.08	1	098	17	
Shroyer	J. O.								098	28	Co. F, 17th Pa. Cavalry; [no dates]
Slusser	Lizzie C.	9.09	1887			18	5.25	19	099	01	Slusser, J. B. & Kate, daughter of
Slusser	Ida R.					1	9.00	2	099	02	
Smith	Henry	10.16	1868			68		69	098	18	
Smith	Barbara	3.25	1885			84	9.07	85	098	19	Smith, Henry, wife of
Smith	Ellen A. McClay	11.12	1891			73	9.24	74	098	20	Smith, Benjamin W., wife of

Penn - Centerville Lutheran Church Graveyard

Surname	Given Name	Death Mo/Dy	Year	Birth Mo/Dy	Year	Att. Age Yr	Mo/Dy	Cm Ag	Pg	No	Other Information
Smith	Benjamin W.	6.10	1890			81	4.07	82	098	21	
Smith	Reuben C.	7.14	1850	10.04	1849			1	098	22	Smith, Benjamin & Catharine, son of
Smith	Wilson H.	9.19	1865			25	8.12	26	098	23	soldier
Smith	John L.	2.03	1896			74	5.02	75	098	24	
Smith	Elizabeth	4.15	1857			11	4.20	12	098	25	Smith, L. & J., daughter of
Snoke	Amanda	5.03	1868			19	3.00	20	098	29	Snoke, George, wife of
Snyder	George W.	8.16	1867				3.12	1	099	03	Snyder, Henry A. & C., son of [1867 ?]
Sowers	William								098	26	Co. B., 165th Pa. Infantry; [no dates]
Spangler	Nancy	7.15	1878			59	10.00	60	097	26	Spangler, William L., wife of
Spence	Matilda	11.25	1870			31	2.06	32	098	07	Spence, David, wife of
Spence	John	2.09	1887			83	5.03	84	098	08	
Spence	Catharine	8.06	1875	11.15	1799			76	098	09	Spence, John, wife of
Spence	Joseph	1.15	1876	10.07	1810			66	098	10	
Spence	Isabella Jane	7.24	1856			19	8.24	20	098	11	Spence, John & Catharine, daughter of
Spence	Clarence J.	7.29	1864				9.24	1	098	12	Spence, D. A. & M., child of
Spence	John A.	8.22	1868				2.14	1	098	13	Spence, D. A. & M., child of
Spence	William S.	6.29	1883				7.28	1	098	14	Spence, D. A. & E., child of
Stoner	Philip	10.11	1885	12.00	1813			72	098	30	
Swords	Abraham	1.08	1890			69	5.19	70	098	31	
Sword	David	5.11	1852			41		42	098	32	
Sword	Philip J.	12.23	1855			77		78	098	33	
Sword	Susan M.	12.29	1870			17	6.21	18	098	34	
Sword	Mary Susanna	8.07	1872			88	9.10	89	098	35	
Sword	John	7.11	1877			64	8.21	65	098	36	
Sword	Elizabeth	4.14	1878			66	0.28	67	098	37	
Thomas	Anna	8.01	1822	7.02	1821			2	099	21	
Throne	Margaret E.	3.06	1881			28	7.26	29	099	22	
Throne	William	6.20	1883			53	7.21	54	099	23	
Throne	Jacob	11.29	1896			76	8.22	77	099	24	
Throne	Susanna	11.09	1887			67	10.24	68	099	25	Throne, Jacob, wife of
Throne	Jane Mary	7.26	1867			11	7.16	12	099	26	Throne, Jacob & Susanna, daughter of
Tritt	Peter	1.02	1860			78		79	099	04	
Tritt	Sarah	11.14	1861			78	8.15	79	099	05	Tritt, Peter, wife of
Tritt	Christian	1.10	1871			74		75	099	06	
Tritt	Lydia	6.09	1849			46	8.04	47	099	07	Tritt, Christian, wife of
Tritt	William K.		1851		1807			45	099	08	
Tritt	Catharine		1902		1813			90	099	09	Tritt, William K., wife of
Tritt	John S.	5.21	1882			49	11.23	50	099	10	
Tritt	Isabella C.	12.13	1861			1	7.11	2	099	11	Tritt, J. S. & S. J., child of
Tritt	John G.	12.18	1861			2	11.17	3	099	12	Tritt, J. S. & S. J., child of
Tritt	Ida L.	12.14	1872			7	1.11	8	099	13	Tritt, J. S. & S. J., child of
Tritt	Mary L.	4.27	1874				6.05	1	099	14	Tritt, J. S. & S. J., child of
Tritt	Christian	8.12	1846				0.05	1	099	15	Tritt, P. N. & N., child of
Tritt	Maggie T.	11.09	1864			7	6.19	8	099	16	Tritt, P. N. & N., child of
Tritt	Sarah E.	2.25	1869			7	2.29	8	099	17	Tritt, Jacob M. & S. A., child of
Tritt	Ida G.	12.02	1872			5	6.07	6	099	18	Tritt, Jacob M. & S. A., child of
Tritt	Mary Ellen	2.06	1862			23	10.17	24	099	19	Tritt, David P., wife of
Tritt	Martin Luther	5.12	1838				7.13	1	099	20	
Umholtz	Ellen G. H.	3.26	1881			34	0.11	35	099	27	Umholtz, D. V., wife of
Underwood	Clara Bell					5	9.00	6	099	28	

Penn - Centerville Lutheran Church Graveyard

Surname	Given Name	Death Mo/Dy	Year	Birth Mo/Dy	Year	Att. Age Yr	Mo/Dy	Ag	Cm	Pg	No	Other Information
Utley	William H.	7.13	1863				3.16	1		099	29	Utley, John & C., son of
Vanasdal	Jacob	5.26	1861			50	11.01	51		099	30	
Vanasdal	W. T.									099	31	Co. E [?], 20th Pa. Cavalry; [no dates]
Walt	Mary C.	1.20	1839			1	2.01	2		099	32	Walt, C. & S. A., daughter of
Walt	Isaac	12.09	1891			81	1.21	82		099	33	
Walt	Eleanor Ann	4.19	1860	5.16	1827			33		099	34	Walt, Isaac, wife of; Spence, John & C., daughter of
Walt	Martha J.	1.24	1839			2	5.25	3		100	01	Walt, C. & S. A., child of
Walt	Joseph W.	1.25	1839			5	3.14	6		100	02	Walt, C. & S. A., child of
Weakley	James	8.21	1873			87	5.09	88		100	03	
Weakley	Elizabeth	8.29	1856			52		53		100	04	
Weekline	McKinley	8.04	1889			79		80		100	05	
White	Maria	4.10	1890			73		74		100	06	
Whitmer	George	1.31	1858	1.21	1825			34		100	07	
Whitmer	Samuel G.	7.15	1866			22	9.03	23		100	08	Weekline, Lucretia, only son of; Co. F, 17th Pennsylvania Cavalry
Williamson	Margaret A.	8.12	1858			1	11.20	2		100	09	Williamson, F. G. & A. B., daughter of
Wolf	Sarah	12.04	1863			66	1.26	67		100	10	Wolf, David, wife of
Wolf	Mary	9.03	1869	3.22	1808			62		100	11	Wolf, David, wife of
Wolf	John S.	7.28	1885			72	9.25	73		100	12	
Wolf	Mary	8.16	1890			76		77		100	13	Wolf, J. S., wife of
Yhost	Solomon	10.07	1868	1.16	1824			45		100	15	
Yhost	Eliza	6.01	1859	2.03	1832			28		100	16	Yhost, Solomon, wife of
Young	Annie F.	10.03	1875	3.15	1875			1		100	14	Young, J. L. & M. M., daughter of
Zinn	Isaac	8.17	1857			58	4.19	59		100	17	
Zinn	Catharine Spatz	7.10	1882	1.24	1808			75		100	18	Zinn, Isaac, wife of
Zinn	Peter	9.20	1872	7.31	1807			66		100	19	
Zinn	Elizabeth	7.10	1886			74	6.02	75		100	20	Zinn, Peter, wife of
Zinn	Amos	8.09	1845	2.10	1834			12		100	21	Zinn, Peter & Elizabeth, son of
Zinn	Florence E.	5.15	1864			1	4.14	2		100	22	Zinn, J. H. & S. A., daughter of
Zinn	Mary R. Spangler	9.06	1885			46	11.24	47		100	23	Zinn, John, wife of
Zinn	John W.	9.28	1869				6.08	1		100	24	Zinn, J. & M. R., son of
Zinn	Minnie C.	1.22	1873			2	5.20	3		100	25	Zinn, G. & L. A., daughter of
Zinn	Hannah	3.20	1839	2.28	1836			4		100	26	Zinn, Isaac & Catharine, daughter of

Penn - Cummingstown Cambellite Church Graveyard

CUMMINGSTOWN CAMBELLITE CHURCH GRAVEYARD

Surname	Given Name	Death Mo/Dy	Year	Birth Mo/Dy	Year	Att. Age Yr	Cm Mo/Dy	Ag	Pg	No	Other Information
Lefever	Isaac	9.19	1881			80	9.03	81	092	01	
Lefever	Elizabeth R.	3.27	1881			79	4.05	80	092	02	Lefever, Isaac, wife of
Lefever	Rebecca	12.17	1875		1798	77	11.01	78	092	03	(b. 1798)
Lefever	Matilda	1.08	1885			62	11.10	63	092	04	Lefever, David, wife of [b. 18<u>8</u>5 ?]
Stout	Adam M.	6.26	1891	11.15	1866			25	092	05	

Penn - Dickinson Presbyterian Church Graveyard

DICKINSON PRESBYTERIAN CHURCH GRAVEYARD

Surname	Given Name	Death Mo/Dy	Death Year	Birth Mo/Dy	Birth Year	Att. Age Yr	Age Mo/Dy	Ag	Cm	Pg	No	Other Information
Adair	James	5.23	1864	8.05	1781			83		086	01	
Adair	Abigail	8.05	1865	9.09	1789			76		086	02	Adair, James, wife of
Black	Thomas W.	12.20	1861			71	3.00	72		086	03	
Black	Catharine	11.18	1864			69	9.00	70		086	04	Black, Thomas W., wife of
Black	Jacob C.	12.13	1856	12.30	1823			33		086	05	Dr.
Black	Henry	6.14	1883			68	11.24	69		086	06	
Black	Margaret	5.31	1864			44	6.29	45		086	07	Black, Henry, wife of
Black	John W.	8.28	1848				9.00	1		086	08	Black, Henry & Margaret, child of
Black	Jacob C.	12.08	1851			2	1.05	3		086	09	Black, Henry & Margaret, child of
Black	Frances C.	2.11	1859			15	3.09	16		086	10	Black, Henry & Margaret, child of
Black	Alice	8.30	1864			3		4		086	11	Black, Henry & Margaret, child of
Brandt	Neola		1899		1885			15		086	12	Brandt, W. H. & Agnes H. [?], dau. of
Brown	William A.		1905		1829			77		086	13	
Brown	Isabella H. Harper		1904		1828			77		086	14	Brown, William A., wife of
Brown	Hulda P.		1867		1865			3		086	15	
Brown	Joseph		1869		1869			1		086	16	
Brown	Willie		1872		1872			1		086	17	
Brown	Philip									086	18	Co. B, 107th Pa. Infantry; [no dates]
Brown	Elizabeth S.		1897		1897			1		086	19	Brown, J. Harper & Mima, daughter of
Caldwell	David A.	6.12	1890	1.27	1813			78		086	20	
Caldwell	Sarah H.	12.23	1898			81	6.19	82		086	21	Caldwell, D. A., wife of
Caldwell	John Stuart	7.02	1856				5.23	1		086	22	Caldwell, David & Sarah H., son of
Caldwell	Jane	2.01	1865			41	9.00	42		086	23	
Carl	Eliza		1902		1817			86		086	24	
Carothers	John R.	7.30	1835			43		44		086	25	
Carothers	Jane	2.27	1867			67	6.10	68		086	26	
Carothers	Samuel	4.14	1858	8.11	1776			82		086	27	
Carothers	Samuel Woods	5.12	1864			24	6.04	25		086	28	
Carothers	Samuel	5.04	1897	3.10	1839			59		086	29	
Carothers	George	9.17	1899			71	0.23	72		086	30	
Carothers	Jane					61		62		086	31	86:31-32 one entry in text
Carothers	Margaret									086	32	Carothers, Jane, daughter of
Coffey	Agnes	1.02	1872			43		44		086	33	Coffey, W. A., wife of
Coffey	Carl Seymour	3.27	1874			11	6.05	12		086	34	Coffey, W. A. & A., child of
Coffey	Almodin K.	9.01	1867			2	7.00	22		086	35	Coffey, W. A. & A., child of
Cummins	John	4.26	1838		1772	66		67		086	36	
Cummins	Elizabeth, 2d	5.14	1839			4	10.01	5		086	37	Cummins, C. P., Rev. & M., child of
Cummins	Charles S., 4th						7.00	1		086	38	Cummins, C. P., Rev. & M., child of; d. May 28, ----
Donaldson	Robert	2.12	1867			86		87		087	26	
Donaldson	Jane	7.31	1872			87	6.06	88		087	27	Donaldson, Robert, wife of
Eckels	Charles C.	10.11	1854			1	2.18	2		087	28	Eckels, Robert & Amanda, son of
Ege	Peter, Sr.	1.29	1847			71	0.29	72		087	29	of Pine Grove
Etter	Daniel	11.26	1862			33	1.02	34		088	01	
Ewing	George	5.29	1849			52		53		088	02	
Ewing	Jane	12.31	1852			23	9.00	24		088	03	
Ewing	Frances	1.12	1853			20	2.05	21		088	04	
Ewing	Jane	11.00	1855			57		58		088	05	Miss

Penn - Dickinson Presbyterian Church Graveyard

Surname	Given Name	Death Mo/Dy	Year	Birth Mo/Dy	Year	Att. Age Yr	Age Mo/Dy	Cm Ag	Pg	No	Other Information
Ewing	William Wise	3.04	1862			21		22	088	06	3d Pa. Cavalry, U. S. Army; killed
Ewing	Eleanor	8.27	1892			81	10.00	82	088	07	Ewing, George, wife of
Ferguson	David	7.30	1872			74	10.11	75	088	24	
Ferguson	Mary Ann	3.29	1875			81	9.19	82	088	25	Ferguson, David, wife of
Fickes	John C.	9.13	1866			24		25	088	26	
Fickes	Benjamin	5.02	1873			63	7.24	64	088	27	
Fickes	Mary A.	5.29	1877			59	0.02	60	088	28	
Forbes	Acquilla A. Reese	9.26	1856			1	2.14	2	088	29	Forbes, William & M., son of
Foster	James	2.14	1834		1759	74		75	088	30	(b. 1759)
Frownfelter	Margaret	11.17	1872			66		67	088	31	
Galbraith	Joseph S.	6.21	1837		1761	75		76	087	01	(b. 1761)
Galbraith	Sarah	3.27	1857			76		77	087	02	Galbraith, Joseph S., wife of
Galbraith	William	5.04	1876			69		70	087	03	
Galbraith	Jane	10.14	1893			89		90	087	04	
Galbraith	Joseph	5.29	1885			69		70	087	05	
Galbraith	Mary J.	8.01	1864			46	9.29	47	087	06	Galbraith, J., wife of
Galbraith	William	1.28	1845	9.23	1842			3	087	07	Galbraith, Joseph & Mary Jane, child of
Galbraith	Margaret	7.03	1851	12.15	1849			2	087	08	Galbraith, Joseph & Mary Jane, child of
Galbraith	William	7.03	1856	6.02	1854			3	087	09	
Galbraith	John	12.27	1893			21		22	087	10	
Galbraith	Lizzie M. C.	11.03	1896			20	11.11	21	087	11	Galbraith, John, wife of
Goodhart	Lewis	6.18	1891	4.15	1822			70	087	18	
Goodhart	Charlotte	11.15	1892	6.15	1827			66	087	19	Goodhart, Lewis, wife of
Goodhart	Frances R.	7.08	1860	4.11	1846			15	087	20	Goodhart, Lewis & Charlotte, child of; [R. ?]
Goodhart	George G.	6.26	1872	7.21	1865			7	087	21	Goodhart, Lewis & Charlotte, child of
Goodhart	Mary A.	2.08	1884			59	2.18	60	087	22	Goodhart, A., wife of
Goodhart	James A.	8.19	1879			26	0.28	27	087	23	Goodhart, A., son of
Goodhart	Savilla J.	3.29	1885			29	8.28	30	087	24	Goodhart, F. H. wife of
Goodhart	M. Esther	3.12	1896	4.25	1893			3	087	25	Goodhart, T. & M. A., daughter of
Green	John T.	10.24	1884	10.11	1806			79	087	12	
Green	Bathsheba McCune	12.19	1876	7.02	1813			64	087	13	Green, John T., wife of
Green	O. M.	11.17	1882	6.22	1845			38	087	14	Rev.; a missionary in Japan for 7 years
Green	William	2.05	1868			49		50	087	15	
Green	William H.	5.25	1888			21	4.06	22	087	16	Green, Joseph & Martha J., son of
Green	Mary Jane	10.09	1851			30		31	087	17	Green, James, wife of; Kelso, James & Mary, daughter of; adjacent overturned stone probably that of husband James
Hance	Ella J.	8.31	1887			1	1.04	2	088	08	Hance, J. M. & B., daughter of
Harper	William	3.04	1873	8.18	1801			72	088	09	
Harper	Isabella	3.13	1863						088	10	Harper, William, Hon., wife of
Hays	David S.	11.30	1836			33	1.16	34	088	11	Dr.
Hays	Sarah	8.29	1830			10		11	088	12	Hays, David & Mary, daughter of
Hays	David S.	6.24	1879			43	7.16	44	088	13	
Hayes	Helen Elizabeth	4.02	1903	9.26	1901			2	088	14	Hayes, R. Bruce & Helen, daughter of; a life lost by drowning
Hayes	Jane E.	8.22	1903			88	9.09	87	088	15	
Hemminger	Joseph	2.08	1882			48	8.12	49	088	16	
Hemminger	Caroline C.	4.18	1897			61	11.13	62	088	17	Hemminger, Joseph, wife of
Hemminger	Frank Elmer	11.10	1873			1	5.10	2	088	18	Hemminger, J. & C. C., son of

Penn - Dickinson Presbyterian Church Graveyard

Surname	Given Name	Death Mo/Dy	Year	Birth Mo/Dy	Year	Att. Age Yr	Cm Mo/Dy	Ag	Pg	No	Other Information
Henry	Hannah E.	6.15	1855	7.20	1831			24	088	19	
Henry	Agnes M.	5.14	1859	10.04	1829			30	088	20	
Huston	John	4.02	1869			73		74	088	21	
Huston	Eliza W.	2.04	1851			58		59	088	22	[text reads "in his 59th year; this and the following entry may be confused]
Huston	Sidney W.	4.08	1869			43		44	088	23	[text reads "daughter of John Huston"; see previous entry]
Irvine	Joseph	10.11	1851			67		68	088	32	
Kelso	John S.	1.29	1875	1.17	1825			51	088	33	
Kelso	James K.	1.22	1864			44	2.13	45	088	34	
Kenyon	Samuel M.	9.12	1869	7.27	1801			69	088	35	
Kenyon	Eliza Jane	9.26	1856	3.14	1806			51	088	36	
Kincaid	Mary	9.12	1866			94		95	088	37	Kinkaid, John, wife of
Kyle	John	3.23	1876	10.16	1802			74	089	01	
Kyle	Mary E. Hambright	7.28	1897						089	02	Kyle, John, wife of
Kyle	Linda J.	4.28	1891	11.13	1858			33	089	03	Kyle, John & Mary E., daughter of
Lee	Mary	11.19	1836			29	0.02	30	089	04	
Lefever	D. Frank	1.11	1890			11	7.28	12	089	05	Lefever, H. R. & N. J., son of
Lindsay	Elizabeth	10.19	1875	3.17	1802			74	089	06	Lindsey, Alexander, wife of; [sp. varies
Logan	John H.	12.24	1864			27	2.23	28	089	07	
Logan	Sarah	9.08	1863			23	0.07	24	089	08	Logan, John H., wife of
Logan	Mary Nannette	8.14	1864			1	0.22	2	089	09	Logan, J. H. & S. J., daughter of
Martz	Mary	4.08	1875			58	6.15	59	089	10	
McCaslin	Jane, Mrs.	9.30	1862			77		78	089	36	
McClean	Sophia	1.26	1850				5.00		089	34	aged nearly 6 mos.
McCune	Bathsheba	1.11	1892			51		52	089	35	McCune, John T., wife of
McLaughlin	James Thomas	10.31	1854			4	6.11	5	089	37	McLaughlin, William & Eliza Ann, son of
Mehaffie	John A.	4.08	1862			24	3.08	25	089	11	
Mehaffie	Samuel	12.29	1863			31	2.21	32	089	12	
Mehaffie	John	11.02	1854			53		54	089	13	
Mehaffie	Elizabeth	8.21	1881	3.07	1803			79	089	14	Mehaffie, John, wife of
Mahaffie	Rebecca	6.03	1901			66	8.28	67	089	15	Mahaffie (sic)
Mehaffie	Martha	10.13	1887			56	4.14	57	089	16	
Miller	Elizabeth A.	9.08	1859			22	11.19	23	089	17	Miller, William E., Capt., wife of
Miller	Mary E.	2.16	1839	4.17	1838			1	089	18	
Mitten	Mary E.	11.13	1892	1.06	1851			42	089	19	Mitten, Alexander, wife of
Moore	James		1899		1805			95	089	20	
Moore	Elizabeth Ripton		1836		1808			29	089	21	Moore, James, wife of
Moore	Jane		1853		1814			40	089	22	Moore, James, wife of
Moore	Elizabeth		1849		1831			19	089	23	
Moore	William		1840		1839			2	089	24	
Moore	John		1847		1843			5	089	25	
Moore	Martha M.		1853		1849			5	089	26	
Moore	David	8.12	1864			17	1.00	18	089	27	Co. H, 194th Pennsylvania Volunteers; d. at Camp Mankins, Baltimore, MD
Moore	Ella	5.04	1905			59		60	089	28	Moore, Samuel, wife of
Moore	Harry	9.15	1873			4	0.25	5	089	29	Moore, S. & E., son of
Myers	Benjamin	5.03	1848			45	6.25	46	089	30	
Myers	Mary	5.08	1847			63		64	089	31	
Myers	Abraham	4.01	1858			70		71	089	32	Myers, Benjamin, brother of [89:30]

Penn - Dickinson Presbyterian Church Graveyard

Surname	Given Name	Death Mo/Dy	Year	Birth Mo/Dy	Year	Att. Age Yr	Mo/Dy	Cm Ag	Pg	No	Other Information
Myers	Nancy	3.11	1845			56	3.10	57	089	33	Myers, Abraham, wife of
Palm	Edward G.	1.05	1862			6	1.03	7	089	38	Palm, William & M. A., son of
Parks	William	8.17	1857			87		88	089	39	
Parks	Eliza					74		75	090	01	
Parks	Sarah A.	7.23	1889			68		69	090	02	
Parks	George	11.07	1848			11		12	090	03	
Parks	Samuel	12.24	1862			35		36	090	04	
Parks	Elizabeth	3.13	1862			72		73	090	05	
Patterson	Frances Hays	1.00	1851			81		82	090	06	Patterson, R., wife of
Peffer	Henry W.		1899		1852			48	090	07	
Piper	Samuel	6.01	1900	8.12	1819			81	090	08	
Reed	Martha	2.04	1899				8.02	1	090	09	Reed, D. E. & M. E., child of
Reed	Florence	4.29	1900				5.23	1	090	10	
Rinker	Mary A.	9.24	1879	6.27	1827			53	090	11	Rinker, Henry, Rev., wife of
Robinson	Jane Ann	6.04	1852	4.30	1818			35	090	12	Robinson, A. S., wife of
Robinson	William Woods	9.27	1842			2	0.06	3	090	13	Robinson, Allen S. & Jane Ann, son of
Ross	Mary G.	4.17	1893			42	7.16	43	090	14	
Russell	Mary Jane	3.16	1861						090	15	Russell, William, wife of; Harper, William & I., daughter of
Russell	William N.	12.03	1879	2.27	1806			74	090	16	
Sands	Julia Ann	7.31	1856			66		67	090	17	
Seavers	Elizabeth	3.13	1877			49	3.08	50	090	22	Seavers, Michael, wife of
Seavers	Josephine	1.12	1860				3.12	1	090	23	Seavers, M. & E., daughter of
Shaw	Joseph	8.12	1838			65		66	090	18	
Shaw	Joseph A.	8.19	1864			23	4.06	24	090	19	Co. D., 187th Regt., Pennsylvania Volunteers; killed at Weldon Railroad
Shaw	James R.	4.16	1888			79	3.20	80	090	20	
Shaw	Catharine	6.28	1883			71	0.03	72	090	21	Shaw, James R., wife of
Shenk	Herman H.		1902		1873			30	090	24	
Shenk	Merle A.		1902		1900			3	090	25	Shenk, H. H. & Lillie, son of
Spriggs	Mary Elizabeth	11.06	1851			4	9.17	5	090	26	Spriggs, James H. & Eleanor J., child of
Spriggs	Helen Margaret	11.20	1851			3	2.00	4	090	27	Spriggs, James H. & Eleanor J., child of
Stuart	Samuel	1.31	1874			84	10.20	85	090	28	
Stuart	Nancy	6.22	1866			79	2.26	80	090	29	
Stuart	Samuel	5.02	1873	8.15	1818			55	090	30	
Stuart	Samuel Carson	2.09	1860			5	0.28	6	090	31	
Stuart	Robert Donaldson	3.12	1860			8	7.00	9	090	32	
Stuart	Huston Kennedy	3.08	1860			1	0.22	2	090	33	
Stuart	James Alexander	8.26	1862			12	9.17	13	090	34	
Stuart	Elmer	10.06	1867			5	8.20	6	090	35	
Stuart	Jennie N.	10.30	1895	10.17	1876			20	090	36	Stuart, W. & J., child of
Stuart	Hays	3.04	1897	11.21	1874			23	090	37	Stuart, W. & J., child of
Thompson	Mary Magdalene	6.30	1873			36	8.26	37	091	09	Thompson, John C., wife of
Thompson	Mary Magdalene	7.02	1873				0.04	1	091	10	Thompson, J. C. & M. M., daughter of
Thrush	John	4.20	1871			76		77	091	11	
Thrush	Sarah	3.15	1871			73		74	091	12	
Trego	John	8.10	1863			77	1.25	78	090	38	
Trego	Catharine	5.17	1850			68		69	091	01	Trego, John, wife of
Trego	Rebecca	10.12	1838	2.11	1813			26	091	02	Trego, John & Catharine, daughter of
Trego	Levi	7.23	1872	5.23	1810			63	091	03	

Penn - Dickinson Presbyterian Church Graveyard

Surname	Given Name	Death Mo/Dy	Death Year	Birth Mo/Dy	Birth Year	Att. Age Yr	Att. Age Mo/Dy	Cm Ag	Pg	No	Other Information
Trego	Mary	3.17	1883			64	3.05	65	091	04	Trego, Levi, wife of
Trego	Louisa	10.15	1873	3.15	1860			14	091	05	Trego, L. & M., daughter of
Trego	Jennie	4.03	1871			1	6.25	2	091	06	Trego, J. E. & M. J., daughter of
Trego	Elizabeth	4.20	1874			54	10.08	55	091	07	Trego, Jacob, wife of
Trego	Edith Jane	6.13	1879			38	8.07	39	091	08	Trego, Jacob & Elizabeth, daughter of
Walker	Tobias	9.05	1831			8		9	091	13	
Walmsley	William G.	8.28	1866			78		79	091	14	
Weakley	James	4.03	1863	7.27	1787			76	091	15	soldier
Weakley	Eliza	8.20	1849			52		53	091	16	Weakley, James, wife of; Geddes, John, Dr., daughter of
Weakley	Elizabeth	8.01	1840			12		13	091	17	Weakley, James & Eliza, daughter of
Weakley	William	11.10	1836			54	9.08	55	091	18	
Weakley	James Wilson	5.12	1894			22	8.22	23	091	19	Weakley, H. H. & J. P., only son of
Williamson	Johnston	9.08	1859			70	0.07	71	091	20	
Williamson	Albert	7.30	1870			25	2.08	26	091	21	Co. I, 9th Pennsylvania Cavalry, 1st Brigade, 1st Division
Williamson	John A.	12.27	1892			32	10.13	33	091	22	
Williamson	Harry R.						1.21	1	091	23	Williamson, J. A. & M. P., son of
Williamson	Mary	9.29	1870			70	5.15	71	091	24	Williamson, William, wife of
Williamson	Margaret	12.21	1879			86	1.04	87	091	25	
Woodburn	J. S.	12.09	1892			55	8.00	56	091	30	
Woodburn	Tillie	10.10	1869			23	7.20	24	091	31	Woodburn, J. S., wife of
Woods	Mary S.	12.22	1858	5.13	1804			55	091	26	Woods, A., Sr. of Salem, Columbiana County, Ohio, wife of; Galbraith, S. & Sarah, daughter of
Woods	Samuel A.					4	9.00	5	091	27	Woods, George D. & Elizabeth, son of
Woods	William					64		65	091	28	
Woods	Martha Mary	12.30	1853			4	2.17	5	091	29	

Penn - Hisner Graveyard

HISNER GRAVEYARD

Surname	Given Name	Death Mo/Dy	Year	Birth Mo/Dy	Year	Att. Age Yr	Mo/Dy	Age	Cm	Pg	No	Other Information
Bishop	Jacob G.	1.05	1903	11.25	1828			75		274	01	
Bishop	Elizabeth	5.16	1882			82	11.14	83		274	02	Bishop, Jacob, wife of
Bishop	Jacob	8.21	1866			67	8.00	68		274	03	
Goodhart	Jacob	10.03	1827			62	6.01	63		274	04	
Goodhart	Mary Magdalene	1.31	1816			42	8.12	43		274	05	
Goodhart	Jacob	10.01	1840	4.09	1805			36		274	06	
Goodhart	Elizabeth	12.09	1832			12	8.01	13		274	07	
Goodhart	Abraham	2.04	1864			73	1.03	74		274	08	
Goodhart	Mary	9.25	1872			82	4.09	83		274	09	
Goodhart	W. A.	12.26	1839	1.20	1839			1		274	10	Goodhart, M. & E., son of
Hisner	John	3.29	1859	3.16	1791			69		274	11	
Hisner	Mary	2.06	1887			91	11.03	92		274	12	Hisner, John, wife of
Hisner	John	8.20	1838	2.02	1824			15		274	13	Hisner, John & Mary, child of
Hisner	Catharine	9.01	1838	8.24	1816			23		274	14	Hisner, John & Mary, child of
Hisner	Sophia	9.28	1841	12.14	1825			16		274	15	Hisner, John & Mary, child of
Hisner	Samuel	1.11	1846	12.27	1819			27		274	16	Hisner, John & Mary, child of
Hisner	John	11.23	1833			69		70		274	17	
Hisner	Sophia	4.09	1850	8.28	1762			88		274	18	Hisner, John, Sr., wife of

Penn - Huntsdale Dunker Cemetery

HUNTSDALE DUNKER CEMETERY

Surname	Given Name	Death Mo/Dy	Death Year	Birth Mo/Dy	Birth Year	Att. Age Yr	Att. Age Mo/Dy	Cm Ag	Pg	No	Other Information
Baker	William H.		1900		1842			59	074	01	
Beecher	William P.	7.03	1901	2.06	1827			75	074	06	
Beecher	Mary A.	4.30	1869			44		45	074	07	Beecher, William, wife of
Beecher	Maud C.	3.22	1874			1	7.00	2	074	08	Beecher, M. C. & Walker, A. A., daughter of; aged 1 year, 7 months, - days
Bender	Mary	1.23	1878			29	8.06	30	074	09	Bender, Levi, wife of
Bender	Mary E.	10.19	1879			5	2.04	6	074	10	Bender, L. & M., daughter of
Black	Mary E.	3.27	1888			3	10.25	4	074	02	Black, C. F. & M. C., daughter of
Bobb	Daniel	7.27	1887		1819	68	11.22	69	074	13	(b. 1819)
Bobb	Elizabeth	12.11	1893			72	8.06	73	074	14	Bobb, Daniel, wife of
Bobb	Daniel H.	5.15	1862			2	9.26	3	074	15	Bobb, C. & J., son of
Bobb	Sarah Jane	7.22	1877				0.07	1	074	16	Bobb, D. M. & E., son of
Bobb	Jonnie M.	7.09	1881			2	6.02	3	074	17	Bobb, A. M. & L. A., son of
Brandt	William	11.09	1901	8.29	1832			70	074	03	
Brandt	Mary E.	12.12	1861			3	9.25	4	074	04	Brandt, William & C., daughter of [E.?]
Brandt	Katie V.	1.24	1892	5.08	1869			23	074	05	Brandt, William & C., daughter of
Brindle	George Frederick	8.17	1856			1	0.04	2	074	11	Brindle, Cyrus & Rosanna, son of
Brindle	Sarah E.	1.24	1889			37	0.16	38	074	12	Brindle, William, wife of; [E. ?]
Cash	John P.	2.27	1899	3.06	1820			79	074	18	
Chronister	Cornelius	12.02	1901			55	11.10	56	075	11	
Cockley	Samuel	6.07	1875	6.29	1785			90	074	20	
Cockley	Susanna	6.12	1871	11.05	1789			82	074	21	Cockley, Samuel, wife of
Cockley	Magdalene	7.03	1873	12.29	1828			45	074	22	Cockley, Henry, wife of
Cockley	Benjamin	11.27	1872	2.04	1867			6	074	23	Cockley, Henry & Magdalene, child of
Cockley	Samuel	12.26	1872	11.08	1869			4	074	24	Cockley, Henry & Magdalene, child of
Cockley	John	10.08	1878	5.14	1858			21	074	25	Cockley, Henry & Magdalene, child of
Cockley	Anna	8.23	1879	4.14	1873			7	074	26	Cockley, Henry & Magdalene, child of
Cockley	Sarah	2.10	1885			51	0.21	52	074	27	Cockley, Noah, wife of
Cockley	Emma Eve	3.29	1882			1	4.01	2	074	28	Cockley, N. B. & M. A., child of
Cockley	Sarah E.	9.10	1879				4.01	1	074	29	Cockley, N. B. & M. A., child of
Cockley	Emma Catharine	8.01	1869			3	2.02	4	074	30	Cockley, Samuel & Catharine, child of
Cockley	Susan Ellen			4.04	1871	1	6.21	2	074	31	Cockley, Samuel & Catharine, child of
Cockley	Clar Irene	2.13	1881			2	1.25	3	074	32	Cockley, Samuel & Catharine, child of; [Clar (sic)]
Coover	Christian	8.24	1837			54	3.07	55	074	33	
Coover	Sarah	4.16	1860			74		75	075	01	Coover, Christian, wife of
Coover	Abraham	5.10	1851	8.30	1813			38	075	02	
Coover	Hannah	5.14	1884			72	4.01	73	075	03	
Coover	David	2.19	1901			83	11.26	64	075	04	
Coover	Elizabeth	11.12	1893			70	0.07	71	075	05	Coover, David, wife of
Coover	John	7.15	1856			75	8.29	76	075	06	
Coover	Sarah	3.27	1872			80	9.17	81	075	07	Coover, John, wife of
Coover	Mary C.	8.24	1856			1	5.01	2	075	08	
Coover	Susannah M.	3.30	1857			4	1.25	5	075	09	Coover, D. & E., child of
Coover	John G.	11.01	1878			18	11.23	19	075	10	Coover, D. & E., child of
Crim	Jacob	5.27	1838	1.26	1784			55	074	19	
Damuth	Eve M.	3.31	1831			89		90	075	12	coarse slate
Danz	G. Herman	11.06	1888	8.29	1824			65	075	13	German inscription

Penn - Huntsdale Dunker Cemetery

Surname	Given Name	Death Mo/Dy	Death Year	Birth Mo/Dy	Birth Year	Att. Age Yr	Age Mo/Dy	Cm Ag	Pg	No	Other Information
Danz	Elizabeth	12.23	1900	4.06	1824			77	075	14	Danz, G. Herman, wife of; German inscr.
Deitzel	Harry J.	7.10	1901	12.08	1899			2	075	23	
Dellinger	Susanah	4.08	1853	4.20	1770			83	075	24	
Dellinger	George	11.28	1858			57		58	075	25	
Dellinger	Leah	12.24	1880			73	3.20	74	075	26	Dellinger, George, wife of
Dellinger	Sarah J.	9.12	1856			9	0.29	10	075	27	Dellinger, George & Leah, daughter of
Dellinger	Georgie Elmer	11.27	1873			2	1.18	3	075	28	Dellinger, Henry & Elizabeth, son of
Demuth	Samuel	8.26	1844			73	9.18	74	075	15	
Demuth	Barbara	4.05	1842			60	11.04	61	075	16	Demuth, Samuel, wife of
Demuth	David	4.27	1863			41	10.13	42	075	17	
Demuth	Maria	8.10	1883			56	8.05	57	075	18	Demuth, David, wife of
Demuth	Mary E.	5.24	1892			38	6.28	39	075	19	Demuth, D. & M., child of
Demuth	Samuel	6.09	1847				1.03	1	075	20	Demuth, D. & M., child of
Demuth	David Charles	1.19	1864			7	8.20	8	075	21	Demuth, D. & M., child of
Demuth	Joseph	7.09	1899			39	1.25	40	075	22	
Eberly	Isabella R.	8.09	1879				2.00	1	075	29	Eberly, Amos & Dessie E., daughter of
Ecker	David P.	11.10	1857			65	5.23	66	075	30	Dr.
Ecker	Maria	2.14	1857			19	2.20	20	075	31	Ecker, David P., wife of
Ecker	Samuel D. G.	4.28	1868			11	2.26	12	075	32	Ecker, David R. & Maria S., only ch. of
Ecker	Allettee	6.30	1856			62	10.10	63	075	33	[spelling of first name varies]
Ecker	Juliann C.	5.11	1849			22	0.15	23	075	34	Ecker, David & Alleytee, daughter of
Ecker	William P. G.	9.24	1853			33	8.20	34	076	01	Ecker, David & Alleytee, eldest son of
Ecker	Samuel H.	8.24	1884	8.18	1833			52	076	02	Dr.; b. in Gettysburg, Pennsylvania; d. at Walnut Bottom
Ecker	M. J. C.	4.12	1895			71	8.09	72	076	03	Ecker, David & Alleytee, daughter of
Ecker	M. A C.	2.15	1896			74	0.15	75	076	04	Ecker, David & Alleytee, daughter of
Ecker	David	1.29	1902			72	3.17	73	076	05	
Eckert	William		1905		1830			76	076	06	
Eckert	Catharine				1836				076	07	Eckert, William, wife of
Eckert	John A.	9.05	1872			10	10.05	11	076	08	Eckert, William & Catharine, son of
Ernst	J. Calvin	2.26	1884			42	4.24	43	076	09	
Ernst	Nora Evelyn	7.22	1870			1	1.01	2	076	10	Ernst, J. C., & S. F., child of
Ernst	Elsie Maud						8.12	1	076	11	Ernst, J. C., & S. F., child of
Etter	Sarah	5.07	1885			55	5.09	56	076	12	Etter, John, wife of
Etter	S. Lawrence	10.29	1904	2.19	1904			1	076	13	Etter, A. & M. E., son of
Evans	Owen	7.31	1830			54		55	076	14	red sand headstone
Fagan	Mary A.	2.08	1884	7.14	1832			52	076	15	Fagan, John B., wife of
Finkey	Mathew T.	2.09	1905	10.13	1898			7	076	18	Finkey, M. & M., son of
Foust	Philip	8.30	1897			69	11.23	70	076	19	
Foust	Catharine	7.21	1901			71	10.05	72	076	20	Foust, Philip, wife of
Foust	Anna M.	1.26	1884			25	8.20	26	076	21	Foust, P. & C., daughter of
Frantz	Joseph	6.29	1892			51		52	076	16	
Frantz	Sallie	5.17	1878			12	4.14	13	076	17	Frantz, Joseph & Jane, daughter of
Furst	John	9.29	1857			13	11.01	14	076	22	Furst, Joseph & Juliann, son of
Furst	Moses	8.25	1872			56	5.20	57	076	23	
Garber	Charles	5.30	1850	7.05	1786			64	076	24	
Garber	Susanna	10.19	1865	9.29	1798			68	076	25	Garber, Charles, wife of
Garber	Charles	9.15	1891			70	1.25	71	076	26	
Garber	Peter	3.20	1868			43	8.27	44	076	27	
Garber	Sarah	1.07	1882			52	8.00	53	076	28	Garber, Peter, wife of

Penn - Huntsdale Dunker Cemetery

Surname	Given Name	Death Mo/Dy/Year	Birth Mo/Dy/Year	Att. Age Yr/Mo/Dy	Cm Ag	Pg	No	Other Information
Garber	Charles D.	8.10/1857		1/10.10	2	076	29	Garber, Peter & Sarah, child of
Garber	Idilla	12.03/1864		/3.03	1	076	30	Garber, Peter & Sarah, child of
Gelbaugh	Anna C. E.	2.06/1896	8.19/1859		37	076	31	Gelbaugh, G. W., wife of
Gelbaugh	Earl E.	7.19/1892	3.14/1891		2	076	32	
Gibble	Henry	12.07/1895	6.28/1814		82	076	33	
Gibble	Catharine	3.25/1894	4.18/1815		79	076	34	
Gibble	Solomon	7.01/1902		65/7.26	66	076	35	
Gibble	Elizabeth	11.20/1893		55/2.27	56	076	36	Gibble, Solomon, wife of
Gibble	Emeline	10.23/1861		/0.11	1	077	01	Gibble, Solomon & E., child of
Gibble	William H.	11.29/1872		2/4.17	3	077	02	Gibble, Solomon & E., child of
Gibble	Harvey S.	4.21/1897		/2.23	1	077	03	Gibble, S. & P. E., son of
Goodyear	Bertie M.	12.08/1884		/10.05	1	077	04	Goodyear, D. A. & R., daughter of
Harbold	George S.	3.24/1894		73/7.04	74	077	05	
Harbold	Mary	7.07/1890		67/1.00	68	077	06	Harbold, G. S., wife of
Harbold	Elizabeth	3.19/1878	5.18/1817		61	077	07	Harbold, John, wife of
Harlacher	Charles B.	5.01/1884	8.13/1845		39	077	08	
Harlacher	Ella J.	7.08/1870		/8.12	1	077	09	Harlacher, C. B. & M. A., daughter of
Hastings	W. F.	2.17/1899		44/7.29	45	077	10	
Hastings	Mabel	5.25/1883		1/0.25	2	077	11	Hastings, W. F. & K., daughter of
Hastings	John E.	7.00/1872		4/6.07	5	077	12	
Hastings	Mary C.	8.23/1883		18/10.18	19	077	13	
Hastings	Henry	9.05/1888		/10.19	1	077	14	
Hastings	George W.	10.16/1889		57	58	077	15	
Hastings	William Oscar	12.30/1893		7/6.07	8	077	16	
Hastings	Laura J.	3.15/1895		34/0.29	35	077	17	
Hastings	Clarence	9.25/1896		/1.26	1	077	18	Hastings, W. H. & A. M., son of
Heagy	Mary	11.11/1893		48/0.29	49	077	19	Heagy, Henry, wife of
Heagy	Samuel E.	12.04/1879		2/9.11	3	077	20	Heagy, Henry & Mary, child of
Heagy	Lizzie K.	6.30/1884		13/1.29	14	077	21	Heagy, Henry & Mary, child of
Heagy	Annie Priscilla	5.03/1894	7.29/1884		10	077	22	Heagy, Henry & Mary, child of
Heagy	Fanny	2.27/1873		1/11.26	2	077	23	Heagy, Levi & Eliza, child of
Heagy	Mary Jane	9.15/1876	2.05/1873		4	077	24	Heagy, Levi & Eliza, child of
Hefflefinger	Bruce E.	1.18/1891		/4.04	1	077	25	Hefflefinger, J. B. & L. R., son of
Heller	Elizabeth Ch.	1.14/1878	8.20/1824		54	077	26	Heller, Christoph, wife of
Heller	George L.	7.18/1889		81/9.29	82	077	27	
Highlands	William E.	5.28/1872		39	40	077	28	
Highlands	Catharine	3.26/1863		39/10.23	40	077	29	Highlands, William E., wife of
Himes	Lavina E.	9.20/1881		31/6.18	32	077	30	Himes, J. E., wife of
Hollinger	George	5.10/1861		42/10.04	43	077	31	
Hollinger	Daniel	10.08/1859		64/5.15	65	077	32	
Hollinger	Catharine	5.17/1872		76/1.00	77	077	33	Hollinger, Daniel, wife of
Hollinger	Henry	/1833	/1825		9	077	34	Hollinger, D. & C., child of
Hollinger	Joseph	/1838	/1838		1	077	35	Hollinger, D. & C., child of
Hollinger	Daniel	/1856	/1856		1	077	36	Hollinger, J. & M. A., child of
Hollinger	Catharine	/1860	/1859		2	077	37	Hollinger, J. & M. A., child of
Hollinger	Jennie A.	8.14/1891	7.05/1854		38	078	01	Hollinger, A., wife of
Hollinger	Leah					078	02	Hollinger, Daniel, wife of; [no dates]
Hollinger	Mary L.	11.16/1862		3/0.16	4	078	03	Hollinger, D. & L., daughter of
Hollinger	Jacob					078	04	[no dates given]
Hollinger	Mary A.	6.20/1891		63/3.27	64	078	05	Hollinger, Jacob, wife of

Penn - Huntsdale Dunker Cemetery

Surname	Given Name	Death Mo/Dy	Year	Birth Mo/Dy	Year	Att. Yr	Age Mo/Dy	Cm Ag	Pg	No	Other Information
Hollinger	Anna Eliza	7.02	1862	4.03	1861			2	078	06	Hollinger, Samuel & S. A., child of
Hollinger	Samuel A.	6.15	1872	11.04	1849			23	078	07	Hollinger, Samuel & S. A., child of
Hollinger	Jacob H.	3.26	1891	7.13	1877			14	078	08	Hollinger, G. W. & A. E., son of
Hollinger	William L.	12.13	1884	10.08	1883			2	078	09	Hollinger, A. & K., son of
Hoover	Fanny	11.06	1875			34	1.27	35	078	13	Hoover, Jacob, wife of
Hosfeld	Christiana Elizabeth	4.21	1867			70	11.14	71	078	10	
Hosfelt	Jonas	12.17	1873			12	2.03	13	078	11	
Hosfelt	Emma	12.17	1873			4	6.05	5	078	12	
Hurting	Nicholas	10.09	1830	3.26	1780			51	078	14	
Hutchison	John G.	5.30	1872	9.30	1805			67	078	15	
Hutchison	Mary	12.05	1841			28	6.24	29	078	16	Hutchison, John G., wife of
Hutchison	Mary	2.05	1882			79	4.00	80	078	17	Hutchison, J. G., wife of
Hutchison	Catharine	4.12	1842			3	10.22	4	078	18	Hutchison, J. & M., child of
Hutchison	John F.	8.22	1854	5.15	1853			2	078	19	Hutchison, William & Elizabeth, son of
Hutchison	Catharine Ann	7.06	1860			1	5.06	2	078	20	Hutchison, William & E., daughter of
Hutchison	Agnes Caroline	4.21	1869			2	8.12	3	078	21	Hutchison, W. A. & Elizabeth, dau. of
Jacobs	Daniel		1902		1820			83	078	22	
Johnson	Conrad	10.15	1873	6.17	1807			67	078	23	
Johnson	Mary A.	2.25	1888	10.01	1809			79	078	24	
Johnson	Elizabeth	6.04	1852			40	0.17	41	078	25	Johnson, Samuel, wife of
Jones	William	1.01	1900						078	26	Private, Co. E., 130th Pa. Vol. Infantry
Jones	John	5.06	1905						078	27	Private, Co. G., 21st Regt., Pa. Cavalry
Kampher	Philip	5.29	1869			76	5.04	77	078	28	
Kampher	Susannah	7.15	1900			87	6.12	88	078	29	Kampher, Philip, wife of
Kechler	Cora B.	12.16	1884			5	5.05	6	078	30	Kechler, F. G. & S. E., daughter of
Keeny	Michael H.	8.01	1900			74	3.09	75	079	04	
Keeny	Lamiah	7.03	1887			60	4.24	61	079	05	Keeny, M. H., wife of
Keller	Elder Daniel	8.29	1897	9.23	1813			84	078	31	
Keller	Catharine	3.18	1898	11.04	1813			85	079	01	Keller, Elder Daniel, wife of
Keller	Mary F.	1.03	1860			2	11.13	3	079	02	Keller, D. & C., daughter of
Keller	Bertie M.	8.14	1873	4.21	1872			2	079	03	Keller, E. & C., daughter of
Kiehl	Abraham	4.29	1886	8.11	1810			76	079	06	
Kiehl	Lavina	4.11	1876			66	10.09	67	079	07	Kiehl, Abraham, wife of
Kissinger	Simpson	6.06	1875			71		72	079	12	
Kissinger	Dothorah	7.10	1878			69	6.04	70	079	13	Kissinger, Simpson, wife of; [Dothorah (sic)]
Kissinger	Levi		1901		1840			62	079	14	
Kissinger	Catharine		1901		1838			64	079	15	Kissinger, Levi, wife of
Kissinger	John Lee	6.10	1864				7.17	1	079	16	Kissinger, L. & C., son of
Kissinger	William	7.17	1895	1.23	1870			26	079	17	killed in the railroad accident near Morristown, Pennsylvania
Kline	John C.	4.26	1858			33		34	079	18	
Kneisly	George	2.20	1816			64	6.18	65	079	08	German; red sand headstone
Knisely	Ann	8.03	1825			33	6.10	34	079	10	Knisely, Samuel, Sr., wife of; red sand
Knisely	Mary	5.01	1816			49		50	079	11	red sand headstone
Kough	Margaret	3.16	1901	12.04	1832			69	079	19	Kough, B. F., wife of
Kough	Samuel Franklin	5.29	1899				10.23	1	079	20	Kough, W. H. & E. M., son of
Kough	Eva C.					1	5.00	2	079	21	Kough, Ira J. & S. Edna, dau. of; d.2.27
Kreider	Paul Emanuel	1.02	1904				7.17	1	079	09	Kreider, E. & E. S., son of
Kurtz	Abraham	3.16	1863			83	3.12	84	079	22	

Penn - Huntsdale Dunker Cemetery

Surname	Given Name	Death Mo/Dy	Year	Birth Mo/Dy	Year	Att. Age Yr	Mo/Dy	Cm Ag	Pg	No	Other Information
Kurtz	Maria	8.14	1868			48	10.02	49	079	23	Kurtz, Israel, wife of
Kurtz	Delilah	8.26	1868			32	7.16	33	079	24	Kurtz, Noah, wife of
Latshaw	Samuel G.	10.02	1900			44	1.12	45	079	25	
Latshaw	Elizabeth	2.03	1872	4.09	1788			84	079	26	
Leicey	William B.	1.22	1857				11.22	1	079	27	Leicey, John & Sarah, son of
Line	Esther Janette	6.26	1902	11.05	1900			2	079	28	Line, G. L. & Nettie E., daughter of
Linn	Henry H.	11.19	1858			4	1.29	5	079	29	Linn, A. & C., child of
Linn	Silas D. F.	2.24	1863				6.00	1	079	30	Linn, A. & C., child of
Linn	Amanda M. T.	1.31	1864			15	8.20	16	079	31	Linn, A. & C., child of
Mahaffey	Susannah	2.13	1886			40	0.01	41	080	01	Mahaffey, S. W., wife of
March	Peter	2.01	1888			87	1.10	88	080	04	
March	Elizabeth	12.28	1893			85	11.22	86	080	05	
Martin	George H.	6.15	1873			14	0.05	15	080	06	Martin, John & Rebecca, child of
Martin	Jacob C.	7.20	1876			9	8.06	10	080	07	
Mater	John	12.02	1868	11.28	1789			80	080	02	
Mater	Daniel	3.15	1896			55		56	080	03	d. in her 56th year
Mellinger	John	12.22	1881			82	4.23	83	080	08	
Mellinger	Anthony F.	4.17	1883			35	8.16	36	080	09	
Messinger	Sallie J. Fulton	3.24	1850			25	0.01	26	080	10	Messinger, James, wife of
Miller	Henry	3.18	1859						080	11	aged about 64 years
Miller	Annie	3.26	1873						080	12	aged about 60 years
Miller	Hetty	11.24	1834			42	8.23	43	080	13	
Miller	Nancy	11.10	1899	1.20	1836			64	080	14	Miller, Joseph, wife of
Miller	Andrew	3.06	1901	2.17	1867			35	080	15	
Miller	Elizabeth	1.19	1890	12.07	1845			45	080	16	Miller, D. H., wife of
Miller	Dortha	1.09	1874			3	6.09	4	080	17	Miller, Henry H. & Catharine, child of
Miller	Alice A.	10.08	1880			11	11.08	12	080	18	Miller, Henry H. & Catharine, child of
Miller	Margaret Ann	11.25	1869			2	8.13	3	080	19	Miller, J. C. & M. J., daughter of
Miller	Emma R.	4.02	1903	4.05	1902			1	080	20	Miller, W. L. & E. B., daughter of
Mohler	Sarah	6.01	1891			66	5.26	67	080	21	Mohler, Israel, wife of
Morrow	Sarah A.	7.08	1904	8.20	1853			51	080	22	Morrow, William A., wife of
Mowery	Benjamin	8.08	1901			63	4.03	64	080	23	
Musser	Susanna	11.27	1857	10.23	1816			42	080	24	
Musser	Mary	5.21	1878			63	4.20	64	080	25	
Myers	Jacob	7.03	1895	5.13	1823			73	080	26	
Myers	Eliza E.	2.07	1882	3.24	1825			57	080	27	Myers, J., wife of
Myers	Jacob F.	11.11	1871	9.04	1852			20	080	28	Myers, J. & E. E., son of
Myers	John T.	3.10	1896			48	7.00	49	080	29	
Myers	William O.	6.16	1883			1	4.11	2	080	30	Myers, J. T. & M. E., son of
Myers	Helen E. L.	7.24	1882	6.26	1882			1	080	31	Myers, W. A. & S. K., daughter of
Naugle	Nancy	8.05	1885			69	10.20	70	080	32	see Noggle
Newcomer	John	4.19	1854			58	10.27	59	080	33	
Newcomer	Catharine E.	8.09	1856			2	2.03	3	080	34	Newcomer, John & Susanna, child of
Newcomer	Simon	1.14	1860	11.04	1857			3	080	35	Newcomer, John & Susanna, child of
Newcomer	Levi	6.21	1855			20	4.18	21	080	36	
Newcomer	Mary C.	2.02	1863				6.00	1	080	37	Newcomer, C. & M., daughter of
Newcomer	George M.	11.27	1871			6	9.26	7	080	38	Newcomer, Samuel & Mary, only son of
Newcomer	Mary	4.27	1872			74	5.13	75	080	39	
Newcomer	Sophia	7.27	1894			64	6.28	65	081	01	
Nickey	Samuel	7.05	1875	10.10	1789			86	081	02	b. in Lancaster Co.

Penn - Huntsdale Dunker Cemetery

Surname	Given Name	Death Mo/Dy	Year	Birth Mo/Dy	Year	Att. Age Yr	Mo/Dy	Cm Ag	Pg	No	Other Information
Noggle	Michael	3.16	1892			87		88	081	03	see Naugle
Ocker	Christopher C.	10.12	1863			34	10.08	35	081	04	
Ocker	Mary Catharine	4.13	1857			5	5.23	6	081	05	Ocker, Christopher & Elizabeth, child of
Ocker	George W. S.	3.14	1833				2.02	1	081	06	Ocker, Christopher & Elizabeth, child of
Ott	Elder McClellan	4.17	1863	2.25	1863			1	081	07	Ott, S. & M., son of
Otto	John		1903		1835			69	081	08	Citizen Soldier; Co. A, 7th Regt., Pa. R. V. C., 1861-1865; prisoner of war in Libby, Andersonville, and Florence
Otto	John L.		1887		1873			15	081	09	Otto, J. & M. E., son of
Otto	Warren P. S.	11.13	1898	6.19	1896			3	081	10	Otto, W. P. S. & S. M., son of
Paxton	Sarah Ann Beecher	12.21	1874			72	3.17	73	081	11	Paxton, John, wife of
Pechert	Katie	5.17	1896			66	1.00	69	081	12	
Plough	Samuel	2.21	1888			78	3.26	79	081	13	
Plough	Catharine	10.24	1887			76	6.05	77	081	14	
Plough	Samuel S., Jr.	1.23	1874			31	9.17	32	081	15	
Plough	John S.	1.21	1872			35	1.24	36	081	16	
Plough	Annie	1.17	1872				5.24	1	081	17	Plough, John S. & M. A., daughter of
Plough	Catiann	4.04	1878	6.08	1877			1	081	18	Plough, H. E. & Rebecca, daughter of
Railing	Martha J.	3.28	1903			48	4.16	49	081	19	Railing, John M., wife of
Railing	Lizzie A.	7.27	1876				11.27	1	081	20	Railing, J. M. & M. J., child of
Railing	Bertie May	2.06	1883				0.17	1	081	21	Railing, J. M. & M. J., child of
Reddig	Willie H.	9.15	1880			2	4.05	3	081	22	Reddig, C. F. & K. A., son of
Reighter	William R. [?]		1901		1845			57	081	23	
Robinson	David	11.02	1887			70	4.22	71	081	24	Co. K, 68th Pennsylvania Cavalry
Rockey	Samuel	10.10	1876	4.01	1811			66	081	25	
Royer	John	2.02	1871			69	0.04	70	081	26	
Schweitzer	Sarah Alice	10.06	1886			27	2.20	28	083	10	Schweitzer, Peter G., wife of
Shank	Henry	12.17	1839			74	8.24	75	082	24	[spelling varies]
Shenk	Elizabeth	4.02	1854	10.13	1783			71	082	25	Shenk, Henry, wife of
Shenk	Henry	2.14	1880	6.07	1829			51	082	26	
Shenk	Henry	10.31	1861			70	9.14	71	082	27	
Shenk	Catharine	2.04	1845			45	7.05	46	082	28	Shenk, Henry, wife of
Shenk	Elias	11.17	1860			34	10.21	35	082	29	
Shenk	Catharine	3.09	1868			34	8.27	35	082	30	Shenk, Elias, wife of
Shenk	George W.	2.18	1895			49	4.18	50	082	31	
Shank	Annie N.	7.24	1880	9.24	1875			5	082	32	Shank, G. W. & A. M., daughter of; [spelling varies]
Shenk	Daniel	5.24	1885	1.21	1823			63	082	33	
Shenk	Susan	1.21	1889	12.17	1822			67	082	34	
Shenk	Harry W.	1.14	1897			48	4.00	49	082	35	
Shenk	Susannah	11.22	1881			3	2.19	4	082	36	Shenk, H. W. & H. M, child of
Shenk	Hetty Lizzie	5.20	1873				6.21	1	082	37	Shenk, H. W. & H. M, child of
Shenk	Sarah Ann	1.29	1860			2	7.07	3	082	38	Shenk, Daniel & S., daughter of
Shenk	Harvey	7.18	1873				0.18	1	083	01	Shenk, Daniel M. & S. A., child of
Shenk	Anna Mary	8.02	1872			1	9.24	2	083	02	Shenk, Daniel M. & S. A., child of
Shenk	Martin	2.25	1898			78	5.16	79	083	03	
Shenk	Susanna	8.18	1896			71	6.02	72	083	04	Shenk, Martin, wife of
Shenk	David W.	10.07	1898	3.01	1847			52	083	05	
Shenk	Hetty M.	11.17	1902	5.08	1847			56	083	06	Shenk, D. W., wife of
Shenk	William Clarence	8.16	1883	9.10	1881			2	083	07	Shenk, Samuel E. & Jane S., child of

Penn - Huntsdale Dunker Cemetery

Surname	Given Name	Death Mo/Dy	Year	Birth Mo/Dy	Year	Att. Age Yr	Mo/Dy	Ag	Cm/Pg	No	Other Information
Shenk	Della Maud	6.11	1875	7.12	1871			4	083	08	Shenk, Samuel E. & Jane S., child of
Shenk	Caroline	4.19	1898			70	3.20	71	083	09	Shenk, John, wife of
Sheaffer	David	8.20	1850	10.31	1785			65	082	01	
Sheaffer	Susanna	5.12	1870			82	8.11	83	082	02	Sheaffer, David, wife of
Sheaffer	Hetty	1.15	1852	2.02	1816			36	082	03	Sheaffer, David & Susan, child of
Sheaffer	Susannah Swonger	7.11	1856	3.07	1820			37	082	04	Sheaffer, David & Susan, child of
Sheaffer	Henry	11.29	1870	9.19	1809			62	082	05	
Sheaffer	Margaret	5.22	1904	10.03	1814			90	082	06	
Sheaffer	Joel	11.21	1884			73	1.17	74	082	07	[confusion of dates with spouse ?]
Sheaffer	Catharine	11.21	1884			73	1.17	74	082	08	Sheaffer, Joel, wife of; [see 82:30]
Sheaffer	Sabina E.	7.09	1877			33	2.07	34	082	09	
Sheaffer	William	8.20	1890			58	1.17	59	082	10	
Sheaffer	Mary Gibble	11.26	1903	9.16	1844			60	082	11	Sheaffer, William H., wife of
Sheaffer	Mahala C. Brindle	7.15	1881			40	1.24	41	082	12	Sheaffer, George W., wife of
Sheaffer	George E.	4.25	1872				9.18	1	082	13	Sheaffer, G. W. & M. C., child of
Sheaffer	Harvey C.	8.01	1880	11.27	1879			1	082	14	Sheaffer, G. W. & M. C., child of
Shafer	Alfred N.	12.08	1869			2	7.15	3	082	15	Shafer, L. S. & A. E., son of
Sheaffer	Bertie F.						1.07	1	082	16	Sheaffer, J. M. & L. J., daughter of
Sheaffer	Mary C.	8.07	1867			2	0.15	3	082	17	Sheaffer, John & C. M., child of
Sheaffer	Dolly F.	10.30	1872				7.17	1	082	18	Sheaffer, John & C. M., child of
Sheaffer	Harvey M.	3.12	1876	2.27	1876			1	082	19	Sheaffer, John & C. M., child of
Sheller	George	12.10	1892			67	2.00	68	082	20	
Sheller	Mary	11.02	1901			75	6.27	76	082	21	
Sheller	Samuel Good	8.24	1868	7.07	1867			2	082	22	Sheller, George & Mary, son of
Sheller	John B.	5.07	1897			20	5.22	21	082	23	
Shipp	Thomas	12.04	1863			66	2.07	67	083	11	
Shipp	Mary	4.03	1874			73	4.09	74	083	12	
Shoedler	Peter	8.09	1877			77	11.27	78	083	22	
Shoemaker	Samuel	4.27	1880			21	1.19	22	083	23	
Short	Frances B.	3.29	1887			70	4.13	71	083	24	
Snoke	Samuel	1.14	1871	8.24	1809			62	083	25	
Snoke	Rebecca	1.30	1878	5.26	1808			70	083	26	Snoke, Samuel, wife of
Sollenberger	Joseph	9.24	1882	3.15	1798			85	083	15	
Sollenberger	Mary M.	3.12	1842	11.26	1805			37	083	16	Sollenberger, Joseph, wife of
Sollenberger	Mary Ann	3.05	1844	4.26	1837			7	083	17	Sollenberger, Joseph & Mary M., dau. of
Sollenberger	Joseph M.	7.13	1890	2.20	1828			63	083	18	
Sollenberger	Anna Mary	10.15	1902	1.19	1818			85	083	19	
Sollenberger	Catharine	5.16	1874			87	10.13	88	083	20	Sollenberger, John, wife of
Souders	Mary A.	1.29	1898			16	4.27	17	083	21	
Spangler	Catharine E.	6.14	1866			25	2.01	26	081	27	Spangler, Thomas J., wife of
Spidle	Mary E.	9.08	1889			55		56	083	13	
Stamy	Elder J. F.								081	28	[Elder is probably a title]
Stamy	Emily C.	5.05	1901			71	5.05	72	081	29	Stamy, J. F., wife of
Stamy	John F.	3.05	1900			35	7.08	36	081	30	
Stamy	Elmer Knox	11.09	1895			5	7.04	6	081	31	
Stamy	John F.	10.26	1888	8.27	1887			2	081	32	
Stoner	Catharine	3.18	1888			34	5.09	35	083	27	
Stoner	Willie S.	10.26	1885			6	9.23	7	083	28	
Stover	Elizabeth S.	8.07	1887	7.05	1828			60	083	29	Stover, Adam, wife of
Straw	Frances E.	4.30	1867				3.07	1	081	33	Straw, Joseph & Isabella, daughter of

Penn - Huntsdale Dunker Cemetery

Surname	Given Name	Death Mo/Dy	Year	Birth Mo/Dy	Year	Att. Age Yr	Mo/Dy	Cm Ag	Pg	No	Other Information
Sumerland	John	9.07	1871			62	5.13	63	083	30	
Sumerland	Elizabeth	3.31	1876			64	11.00	65	083	31	Sumerland, John, wife of
Sumerland	Thomas	7.04	1854				8.16	1	083	32	
Sumerland	Jacob R.	12.13	1858			3	3.00	4	083	33	aged 3 years, 3 months, --
Swigert	Annie J. Young	3.08	1883			23	5.02	24	083	14	Swigert, G. W., wife of
Throne	William O.	9.07	1871				7.04	1	084	04	Throne, David & Mary, son of
Thrush	Bertha S. Sollenberger	12.23	1901			23	11.03	24	084	05	Thrush, J. A., wife of
Trine	John	9.13	1884			71		72	083	34	
Tritt	P. Stough	6.03	1896			36	4.08	37	083	35	
Tritt	Alice Bell	9.20	1881			2	1.08	3	083	36	Tritt, P. S. & A. M., daughter of
Tritt	Clarence S.	9.11	1881				0.02	1	083	37	Tritt, J. A. & J. E., son of
Tritt	Charles Zigler	4.30	1884			7	5.08	8	084	01	Tritt, S. J. & Mary C., son of
Tritt	Peter N.	3.16	1887			65	8.22	66	084	02	
Tritt	Nancy	3.25	1891			71	5.23	72	084	03	Tritt, Peter N., wife of
Utz	Daniel	6.06	1851			82	1.01	83	084	06	
Utz	Eve	10.04	1858			82	10.28	83	084	07	Utz, Daniel, wife of
Utz	Eve	4.05	1847			1	1.02	2	084	08	Utz, H. & M., daughter of
Vance	Daniel	12.24	1901			77	10.00	78	084	09	Private, Co. F, 207th Regt., Pennsylvania Volunteer Infantry
Vance	Daniel W. Williams	9.07	1868	8.08	1867			2	084	10	
Wade	Mary M.	3.28	1887			58	9.09	59	084	11	
Wagner	Jacob	11.27	1872			42	8.00	43	084	12	
Walker	B. W.								084	13	Sergeant, Co. F, 17th Pa. Infantry
Walker	Mervin S. C.	3.29	1899			1	7.27	2	084	14	Walker, S. K. & M. E., son of
Walters	Rebecca E.	7.10	1883			34	2.01	35	084	15	Walters, J. T., wife of
Walters	Clara B.	2.12	1881	7.11	1879			2	084	16	Walters, J. T. & R. E., daughter of
Weaver	Bennuwell	9.13	1890			74	8.13	75	084	17	
Weaver	Nancy	10.07	1881			65	0.21	66	084	18	Weaver, Bennuwell, wife of
Wentz	Anna M.	3.18	1901				5.19	1	084	19	Wentz, J. T. & Elma, daughter of
Widder	George	1.06	1855	3.15	1790			65	084	20	
Widder	Mary	11.26	1864	9.24	1789			76	084	21	Widder, George, wife of
Widder	Catharine Whisler	5.11	1898			71	3.13	72	084	22	Widder, David, wife of
Widder	Cyrus	9.27	1832				0.13	1	084	23	
Widder	Francis Marion	12.20	1861			4	3.03	5	084	24	
Widder	Elizabeth Jane	8.08	1862				2.03	1	084	25	
Widder	Mary Hetty	2.04	1863			7	4.14	8	084	26	Widder, David & C., child of
Widder	Ida C.	5.22	1863				11.16	1	084	27	Widder, David & C., child of
Witmer	Susanna K.	10.05	1879			5	2.01	6	084	28	Witmer, Daniel, & Lydia, child of
Witmer	Nancy S.	10.15	1879			2	2.06	3	084	29	Witmer, Daniel, & Lydia, child of
Wolf	Henry K.	7.29	1864			1	11.20	2	084	32	
Wolf	John A.	8.01	1855				11.03	1	084	33	
Wolfe	William E.	1.10	1891			16	10.00	17	084	34	Wolfe, Daniel & Susan, son of
Wolf	Eliza G.	9.06	1872			1	8.17	2	085	01	Wolf, D. & S., daughter of
Wolf	Cora E.	8.01	1873				5.03	1	085	02	Wolf, D. & S., child of
Wolf	Mary M.	8.24	1877				3.02	1	085	03	Wolf, D. & S., child of
Wolf	David D.	8.15	1875				2.13	1	085	04	Wolf, D. & S., child of
Wolf	Oscar	8.24	1880				5.11	1	085	05	Wolf, D. & S., child of
Woods	Nicholas	7.09	1891			54		55	084	30	
Woods	Elizabeth	2.04	1890			52	1.26	53	084	31	Woods, Nicholas, wife of
Worst	George T.	7.29	1894			28	8.26	29	085	06	

Penn - Huntsdale Dunker Cemetery

Surname	Given Name	Death Mo/Dy	Year	Birth Mo/Dy	Year	Att. Age Yr	Mo/Dy	Ag	Cm	Pg	No	Other Information
Yeingst	Albert	4.19	1868			1	8.09	2		085	07	Yeingst, William & Maria A., son of
Yetter	John	5.27	1847	11.13	1785			62		085	09	pale sand headstone
Yost	Alice E.	9.29	1896			11	8.27	12		085	08	Yost, W. D. & S. A., daughter of
Young	Maria	5.30	1885			51	2.16	52		085	10	Young, J. A., wife of
Young	Willie	4.04	1875			1	0.18	2		085	11	Young, J. A. & M., son of
Zell	James									085	12	Private, Co. K, 17th Regt., Pennsylvania Cavalry
Zug	David	1.01	1901	8.08	1827			74		085	13	
Zug	Lucetta	5.04	1884			55	5.15	56		085	14	Zug, David, wife of; Bitner, Adam & Fanny, daughter of

Upper Allen - Lantz's School House Cemetery

UPPER ALLEN TOWHSHIP

LANTZ'S SCHOOL HOUSE CEMETERY

Surname	Given Name	Death Mo/Dy	Death Year	Birth Mo/Dy	Birth Year	Att. Age Yr	Age Mo/Dy	Ag	Cm	Pg	No	Other Information
Eichelberger	M. Ella		1908		1870			39	134	01		
Krall	Joseph		1859		1809			51	134	02		
Krall	Barbara		1889		1814			76	134	03	Krall, Joseph, wife of
Krall	Mary A.		1852		1838			15	134	04	Krall, J. & B., child of
Krall	John		1854		1842			13	134	05	Krall, J. & B., child of
Krall	Mathias		1859		1848			12	134	06	Krall, J. & B., child of
Krall	Ira		1868		1854			15	134	07	Krall, J. & B., child of
Krall	Joseph		1876		1844			33	134	08	Krall, J. & B., child of; veteran of the war of '61 - '65
Krall	Anna S.	3.13	1859	3.31	1792			67	134	09	Krall, Christian, wife of
Krall	George W.		1904		1849			56	134	10	
Lambert	Michael	2.09	1852						134	11	aged about 66 years
Lambert	Mary	1.15	1861			42	9.22	43	134	12	
Lambert	William	3.31	1870			28	4.03	29	134	13	
Lambert	John	4.10	1876			28	3.28	29	134	14	[d. 187<u>6</u> ?]
Lambert	William	6.04	1890			78	4.05	79	134	15	
Lambert	Anna	11.16	1857			42	2.01	43	134	16	Lambert, William, wife of; Scherich, Christian & Anna, daughter of
Lambert	Mary Jane	11.17	1850			7	1.19	8	134	17	Lambert, William & Anna, child of
Lambert	George Washington	10.16	1850			1	10.29	2	134	18	Lambert, William & Anna, child of
Lambert	Sarah Ann	10.21	1850			10	7.03	11	134	19	Lambert, William & Anna, child of
Lambert	Ann Eliza	10.23	1850			3	10.29	4	134	20	
Lantz	Levi	4.11	1891	3.07	1834			58	134	21	
Lantz	Margaret D.	10.02	1903	9.01	1844			60	134	22	
Lantz	Harry L.								134	23	[no dates given]
Lantz	George W.								134	24	[no dates given]
Lantz	Carrie R.								134	25	[no dates given]
Lantz	Charles								134	26	[no dates given]
Lantz	Maggie								134	27	[no dates given]
Lantz	Annie								134	28	[no dates given]
Lantz	George P.	9.15	1856	2.06	1786			71	134	29	
Lantz	Elizabeth	12.25	1866			78	8.05	79	134	30	Lantz, George, wife of
Lantz	George	4.20	1811			22	8.24	23	134	31	Lantz, George & Elizabeth, child of
Lantz	Jacob	6.02	1848			21	10.27	22	134	32	Lantz, George & Elizabeth, child of
Lantz	Catharine	2.25	1890	1.26	1811			79	134	33	
Miller	George	3.12	1854				3.24	1	134	34	Miller, Samuel & Elizabeth, child of
Miller	Robert L.	2.26	1863			3	8.00	4	134	35	Miller, Samuel & Elizabeth, child of
Miller	George W.	6.09	1880			3	2.24	4	134	36	Miller, J. A. & Rebecca S., son of
Snyder	Lilly May	9.14	1860				10.00	1	134	37	Snyder, P. & M., daughter of
Snyder	Edward	11.06	1860				0.04	1	134	38	
Snyder	Catharine K.	2.03	1862				3.19	1	134	39	Snyder, P. & M., daughter of

West Pennsboro - Bear Graveyard

WEST PENNSBORO TOWNSHIP

BEAR GRAVEYARD

Surname	Given Name	Death Mo/Dy	Death Year	Birth Mo/Dy	Birth Year	Att. Age Yr	Att. Age Mo/Dy	Cm Ag	Pg	No	Other Information
Aukerman	Paul					92			93	053 01	
Aukerman	Barbara					72			73	053 02	
Bear	John	8.27	1836							053 03	aged about 75 years
Bear	Maria	2.06	1845			88			89	053 04	
Bear	Eliza	8.31	1836			7	2.18		8	053 05	
Bear	John	6.06	1866			71	11.02		72	053 06	
Bear	Rebecca	6.01	1860			37	3.08		38	053 07	
Bear	John H.	8.28	1893	11.11	1824				69	053 08	
Bear	Mary Ann	2.08	1897	5.03	1828				69	053 09	Bear, John H., wife of
Bear	Andrew	12.10	1835			18	1.23		19	053 10	
Bear	Maria	1.06	1836			20	0.12		21	053 11	
Bear	Christie S.	3.18	1894	1.18	1894				1	053 12	
Brown	Catharine	8.24	1895			37	5.08		38	053 13	Brown, Jacob, wife of
Desanno	Charlotte G.	5.09	1850	11.16	1811				39	053 14	Desanno, John F., consort of; born in Philadelphia
Diller	David D.	1.14	1845							053 15	Diller, Samuel & C., son of
Eberly	Ann	8.10	1853			23	5.02		24	053 16	Eberly, John, wife of; Bear, John & Elizabeth, daughter of
Gill	Sarah	1.26	1834		1744	89			90	053 17	Gill, W. G., wife of
Givler	Ann	4.28	1848			25	2.29		26	053 18	
Haines	Annie	8.06	1873			64	3.03		65	053 19	Haines, John, wife of
Hays	George	12.15	1835			42	11.15		43	053 20	
Hedden	Mary	11.07	1868	9.30	1792				77	053 21	
Keiser	Rachel	3.27	1863			34	11.21		35	053 22	Keiser, George, wife of
Keiser	Anna	4.12	1857			4	0.09		5	053 23	
Keiser	Mary	4.17	1857				10.06		1	053 24	
Keiser	William	4.23	1857			5	5.06		6	053 25	
Keiser	Mary E.	8.24	1867	2.22	1866				2	053 26	
Kizer	John B.	3.04	1846				1.20		1	053 27	
Kizer	Ann E.	5.19	1851			1	6.07		2	053 28	
Longnecker	Rebecca Jane	11.10	1861			21	10.29		22	053 29	Longnecker, Benjamin F., wife of; Diller, Samuel & Catharine, daughter of
Messimer	Catharine	8.16	1866			71	0.01		72	054 01	Messimer, George, wife of
Musselman	George	9.28	1860	12.24	1775				85	054 02	
Musselman	Mary	12.19	1851	2.26	1802				50	054 03	
Musselman	Caroline	9.16	1848			23	2.02		24	054 04	Musselman, Jacob & Mary, daughter of
Shaw	Susana	5.02	1836			22	0.04		23	054 05	Shaw, Solomon, wife of; Strome, George & Mary, daughter of
Yarlet	Peter	8.25	1902			75			76	054 06	b. in France; d. in U. S. of A.
Zeigler	Isabella	4.25	1848			22	0.03		23	054 07	Zeigler, Charles, wife of
Zeigler	Elizabeth	5.22	1848			62	11.28		63	054 08	

West Pennsboro - Bitner Farm Graveyard
Diller Mennonite Church Graveyard

BITNER FARM GRAVEYARD

Surname	Given Name	Death Mo/Dy	Year	Birth Mo/Dy	Year	Att. Yr	Age Mo/Dy	Cm Ag	Pg	No	Other Information
Myers	Christiana	11.00	1805			72		73	067	01	Myers, John, wife of
Myers	Abraham	10.28	1826			68	5.00	69	067	02	"Preacher of the Gospel"
Myers	Anna Baker								067	03	Myers, Abraham, wife of; Baker, Felty, daughter of; [name is given as M. Anna Baker]

DILLER MENNONITE CHURCH GRAVEYARD

Surname	Given Name	Death Mo/Dy	Year	Birth Mo/Dy	Year	Att. Yr	Age Mo/Dy	Cm Ag	Pg	No	Other Information
Auker	Edward	1.22	1874	1.21	1874			1	171	01	Auker, Isaiah & A., child of
Auker	Adaline	1.22	1874	1.21	1874			1	171	02	Auker, Isaiah & A., child of
Bowman	Jacob	7.04	1820		1751	69	3.14	70	171	08	(b. 1751)
Bowman	Mary	3.24	1814			62	2.14	63	171	09	Bowman, Jacob, wife of
Bowman	Abraham	4.21	1846			57	4.10	58	171	10	
Bowman	Martha	1.09	1855			66	8.11	67	171	11	
Bowman	Samuel	4.08	1868			32	2.15	33	171	12	
Bowman	Catharine	12.15	1893			85	2.07	86	171	13	
Bowman	Jacob	7.25	1863			51	5.21	52	171	14	
Bowman	Christian	9.13	1850			75	9.14	76	171	15	
Bowman	Barbara	8.21	1860			80	7.20	81	171	16	Bowman, Christian, wife of; [text reads "wife of Christian & Henry Warner"]
Brim	Joseph	3.13	1851	6.24	1804			47	171	03	
Brim	Catharine	3.03	1851	10.12	1808			43	171	04	Brim, Joseph, wife of
Brim	John	2.24	1851	5.22	1829			22	171	05	Brim, Joseph & Catharine, child of
Brim	Adam	4.10	1851	4.23	1831			20	171	06	Brim, Joseph & Catharine, child of
Brim	Lydia								171	07	Brim, Joseph & Catharine, child of
Buckwalter	Daniel	2.25	1861		1779	82	7.20	83	171	17	
Buckwalter	Peggy	12.10	1844		1778	66	1.20	67	171	18	Buckwalter, Daniel, wife of; (b. 1778)
Buchwalter	Jonas	11.17	1840			30	10.17	31	171	19	
Buchwalter	Jonas	1.08	1855			13	10.28	14	171	20	Buchwalter, Jonas & Esther, child of
Buchwalter	William	3.10	1841			1	4.17	2	171	21	Buchwalter, Jonas & Esther, child of
Buckwalter	Henry	9.22	1863			45	3.11	46	171	22	
Buckwalter	Margaret		1860			1	1.08	2	171	23	Buckwalter, Henry & M., daughter of
Burkhart	John	7.02	1858			52	4.09	53	171	24	
Burkhart	Leah	9.03	1881	9.23	1814			67	171	25	
Burkhart	Susannah M.	3.11	1846			9	1.09	10	171	26	Burkhart, John & Leah, child of
Burkhart	Elizabeth	1.05	1856			16	7.10	17	171	27	Burkhart, John & Leah, child of
Burkhart	Jacob	3.02	1865			22	4.03	23	171	28	Burkhart, John & Leah, child of

West Pennsboro - Diller Mennonite Church Graveyard

Surname	Given Name	Death Mo/Dy	Year	Birth Mo/Dy	Year	Att. Age Yr	Cm Mo/Dy	Ag	Pg	No	Other Information
Burkhart	Jacob, Sr.	2.27	1863			87	2.15	88	171	29	
Burkhart	Anna	4.21	1848						171	30	Burkhart, Jacob, wife of
Burckhart	Elizabeth	3.07	1818			40	1.07	41	171	31	Burckhart, Jacob, wife of
Burkhart	Jacob	10.08	1846			36		37	171	32	
Burkhart	Martin	12.07	1850			47	0.29	48	171	33	
Burkhart	Hannah	11.09	1874			69	6.15	70	171	34	Burkhart, Martin, wife of
Burkhart	Abraham	12.25	1859	8.31	1820			40	171	35	Rev.
Burkhart	Elizabeth	5.23	1881	6.22	1821			60	171	36	Burkhart, Abraham, Rev., wife of
Burkhart	Bennie	8.04	1872			3	5.09	4	172	01	
Burkhart	J. S.	4.29	1882			39	4.06	40	172	02	
Burkhart	Heber S.	4.27	1882						172	03	Burkhart, J. S. & E. H., son of
Burkhart	Jacob E.	8.11	1877				9.12	1	172	04	Burkhart, J. S. & E. H., son of
Burkhart	Samuel M.	5.22	1864			2	10.08	3	172	05	Burkhart, Joseph & Mary M., son of
Burkhart	Henry W.	12.08	1864			1	5.26	2	172	06	
Burkholder	Abraham	2.24	1855	4.13	1794			61	172	07	
Burkholder	Elizabeth	9.27	1867	7.14	1798			70	172	08	Burkholder, Abraham, wife of
Burkholder	Mary	1.27	1869	9.11	1816			53	172	09	Burkholder, Abraham & Elizabeth, dau. of
Burkholder	Joseph	6.25	1848	2.23	1801			48	172	10	Rev.
Burkholder	Mary	7.31	1843			41	9.02	42	172	11	Burkholder, Joseph, wife of
Burkholder	Abraham	2.28	1835			68	5.08	69	172	12	
Burkholder	Barbara	2.26	1843	12.11	1775			68	172	13	Burkholder, Abraham, wife of
Burkholder	Abraham	8.30	1889			66	0.14	67	172	14	
Burkholder	Mary	1.30	1883			55	8.11	56	172	15	Burkholder, A., wife of
Burkholder	Anna	3.12	1862				0.31	1	172	16	Burkholder, Abraham & Mary, child of
Burkholder	Abraham	12.13	1862			6	7.10	7	172	17	Burkholder, Abraham & Mary, child of
Burkholder	Fanny	8.24	1867				10.24	1	172	18	Burkholder, Abraham & Mary, child of
Burkholder	Mattie	10.07	1868				0.17	1	172	19	Burkholder, Abraham & Mary, child of
Burkholder	Jacob	3.31	1847	5.16	1796			51	172	20	
Burkholder	Elizabeth	5.26	1876	10.30	1801			75	172	21	Burkholder, Jacob, wife of
Burkholder	Nancy	3.08	1875			43	4.28	44	172	22	Burkholder, Jacob & Elizabeth, dau. of
Burkholder	Benjamin	2.14	1866	8.20	1813			53	172	23	
Borkholder	Mary	5.07	1847	2.22	1812			36	172	24	Borkholder, B., wife of; [both last names appear as "Borkholder"]
Burkholder	Mary	4.05	1882			75	10.12	76	172	25	Burkholder, Benjamin, wife of
Burkholder	John	6.27	1886			68	4.18	69	172	26	
Burkholder	Barbara	2.20	1894			74	10.08	75	172	27	
Burkholder	Daniel	5.02	1874			67	6.09	68	172	28	
Burkholder	Nancy	12.30	1889			81	2.21	82	172	29	Burkholder, D., wife of
Burkholder	Samuel	10.20	1869			1	0.11	2	172	30	Burkholder, D. R., Rev. & Susan, ch. of
Burkholder	Martha	8.04	1871				5.06	1	172	31	Burkholder, D. R., Rev. & Susan, ch. of
Burkholder	Ellen	8.18	1875			14	2.00	15	172	32	Burkholder, D. R., Rev. & Susan, ch. of
Burkholder	John	8.08	1863				0.25	1	172	32	Burkholder, Abraham & M., child of
Burkholder	Mary	11.26	1864				0.25	1	172	33	Burkholder, Abraham & M., child of
Burkholder	Samuel R.	4.23	1896	4.09	1840			57	172	35	
Burkholder	Annie	12.30	1882	8.30	1847			36	172	36	Burkholder, Samuel R., wife of
Burkholder	Jacob	7.03	1895	12.27	1828			67	172	37	
Burkholder	Barbara	5.25	1888	11.06	1821			67	173	01	Burkholder, Jacob, wife of
Burkholder	Catharine	11.18	1863			21	6.29	22	173	02	Burkholder, B. & M., child of
Burkholder	Barbara	12.08	1863			28	3.07	29	173	03	Burkholder, B. & M., child of
Burkholder	Elizabeth	6.09	1838				11.07	1	173	04	Burkholder, Jacob & Martha, child of

West Pennsboro - Diller Mennonite Church Graveyard

Surname	Given Name	Death Mo/Dy	Year	Birth Mo/Dy	Year	Att. Age Yr	Mo/Dy	Cm Ag	Pg	No	Other Information
Burkholder	Mary R.	9.15	1842			1	7.06	2	173	05	Burkholder, Jacob & Martha, child of
Burkholder	Elizabeth	10.26	1842			3	0.10	4	173	06	Burkholder, Daniel & Anna, child of
Burkholder	Samuel			8.05	1835				173	07	Burkholder, Daniel & Anna, child of
Burkholder	Daniel E.	4.22	1868				2.01	1	173	08	Burkholder, David & M. A., child of
Burkholder	Joseph Harvey	9.10	1880				10.28	1	173	09	Burkholder, David & M. A., child of
Burkholder	Martha Ellen	12.09	1880			3	7.15	4	173	10	Burkholder, David & M. A., child of
Burkholder	Maggie May	4.03	1883	10.03	1882			1	173	11	
Burkholder	Nancy	1.15	1891			66	5.22	67	173	12	Burkholder, J. R., wife of
Burkholder	Martha	3.09	1897			39	3.16	40	173	13	
Burkholder	Hannah	8.07	1900			50	3.07	51	173	14	Burkholder, Abraham, Rev., wife of
Burkholder	Barbara	5.16	1901			71	1.01	72	173	15	Burkholder, Jacob & Elizabeth, dau. of
Burkholder	Edna Florence						1.01	1	173	16	
Burkholder	Howard W.	11.28	1888				0.13	1	173	17	Burkholder, J. A. & Orrilla, son of
Campbell	Sarah E.	1.09	1847				1.19	1	173	18	Campbell, Andrew & Anna, child of
Campbell	Jacob M.	9.24	1857			2	6.11	3	173	19	Campbell, Andrew & Anna, child of
Campbell	Samuel M.	2.23	1866			18	2.05	19	173	20	
Campbell	John W.	2.28	1881			7	1.01	8	173	21	Campbell, D. M. & S. J., child of
Campbell	Flora E.	8.25	1888			1	10.07	2	173	22	Campbell, D. M. & S. J., child of
Daelhousen	Susanna	2.28	1899	4.27	1817			82	173	23	Daelhousen, John, wife of
Daelhousen	John	4.19	1881	4.17	1817			65	173	24	
Darr	Frederick	10.02	1838			3		4	173	25	
Darr	John (Miller)	12.06	1863			73	3.26	74	173	27	
Derr	Elizabeth	11.19	1885	5.02	1804			82	173	28	Derr, John, wife of [spelling varies]
Derr	David J.	6.10	1874	7.15	1833			41	173	29	
Derr	William M.	8.17	1870				1.14	1	173	30	Derr, David & Sarah, son of
Darron	Samuel	9.29	1838				9.00	1	173	26	
Diller	Frances	2.21	1814			71		72	173	31	[Frances (sic)]
Diller	Elizabeth	10.05	1816			64	2.10	65	173	32	Diller, Frances [sic], wife of; Beam, Jacob, daughter of
Diller	Peter	3.15	1816		1732	84	9.00	85	174	01	
Diller	Magdalene	3.15	1814			82		83	174	02	Diller, Peter, wife of
Diller	Annie	7.00	1803		1707	96	1.00	97	174	03	(b. 1707)
Diller	Mary	3.09	1821			19	6.27	20	174	04	Diller, Miller Francis & Elizabeth, child of
Diller	David	5.28	1842			21	7.00	22	174	05	Diller, Miller Francis & Elizabeth, child of
Diller	M. Francis	5.17	1845			69	9.00	70	174	06	
Diller	Elizabeth	2.02	1846			67	6.08	68	174	07	Diller, M. Francis, wife of
Diller	Susan	8.10	1839			1	0.14	2	174	08	Diller, Francis, Jr., daughter of
Diller	John	3.16	1871	4.29	1788			83	174	09	
Diller	Elizabeth	9.15	1867			71	1.27	72	174	10	Diller, John, wife of
Diller	Anna Amelia	10.26	1857			26	1.17	27	174	11	Diller, Samuel, wife of
Diller	Nancy	6.18	1875	3.20	1803			73	174	12	Diller, Abraham, wife of
Diller	Abraham	4.05	1843	4.18	1840		3		174	13	Diller, Abraham & Nancy, son of
Diller	Martin	1.20	1901			77	7.19	78	174	14	
Diller	Sarah	9.27	1903			79		80	174	15	Diller, Martin, wife of
Dorron	Lidia	5.19	1839			24		25	174	16	Dorron, Jo'n, wife of; [sic]
Emmerich	Mary Ann	8.22	1850	11.03	1830			20	174	17	Emmerich, Peter & Susannah, daughter of
Erford	John W.	12.14	1868				10.07	1	174	18	Erford, J. J. & R., son of
Gring	Daniel	9.14	1860	11.25	1799			61	174	19	

West Pennsboro - Diller Mennonite Church Graveyard

Surname	Given Name	Death Mo/Dy	Year	Birth Mo/Dy	Year	Att. Age Yr	Mo/Dy	Cm Ag	Pg	No	Other Information
Grove	Martha B.	4.11	1862			65	6.06	66	174	20	
Harn	Jeremiah	9.25	1850			4	1.25	5	174	21	Diller, Elizabeth, son of
Hershey	Peter	1.19	1845	1.07	1774			71	174	22	
Kendig	Elizabeth	2.08	1839			8	8.06	9	174	23	Kendig, Emanuel & Anna, daughter of
Koser	Catharine	8.21	1875	7.06	1838			38	174	24	Koser, G. M., wife of
Koser	Edwin G.	5.29	1879	9.03	1863			16	174	25	Koser, George M. & Catharine, eldest son of
Lehman	Benjamin	5.11	1867			73	0.20	74	174	26	
Lehman	Magdalena	5.21	1854	4.03	1791			64	174	27	Lehman, Benjamin, wife of
Lehman	Susan	1.03	1897			59	2.21	60	174	28	Lehman, Benjamin, wife of
Lehman	Samuel	10.04	1877	9.07	1819			59	174	29	
Lehman	Catharine	12.17	1886			88	3.00	89	174	30	Lehman, S., wife of; [d. 188<u>6</u> ?]
Lehman	Magdalena			9.16	1847		0.14	0	174	31	Lehman, Samuel & C., daughter of
Lehman	Esther	8.25	1857			9	11.22	10	174	32	Lehman, Samuel & C., daughter of
Martin	Jacob, Sr.	4.12	1847	12.01	1777			70	174	33	
Martin	Esther	10.15	1863	5.26	1787			77	175	01	Martin, J., Sr., wife of
Martin	Abraham	6.28	1868	4.18	1820			49	175	02	
Martin	Elizabeth	7.31	1855			29	7.02	30	175	03	
Martin	Benjamin	8.04	1850				6.09	1	175	04	Martin, A. & E., child of
Martin	Mary M.	8.25	1857			19		20	175	05	Martin, A. & E., child of
Martin	Jacob H.	8.22	1864				10.03	1	175	06	Martin, A. & E., child of
Martin	Manuel M.	10.30	1871			3	9.26	4	175	07	Martin, Abraham & E., son of
Martin	Elizabeth	9.28	1877	12.08	1824			53	175	08	
Martin	Esther Ann	6.09	1860				0.12	1	175	09	Martin, Emanuel & E., daughter of
Mayberry	Peter	10.03	1883			73	7.22	74	175	10	
Mayberry	Elizabeth	7.30	1880			65	9.13	66	175	11	Mayberry, Peter, wife of
Mayer	Christine	2.23	1770	12.30	1757			13	175	12	Musselman, born; German
Miller	Elizabeth Diller	6.28	1849	4.30	1825			25	175	13	Miller, William, wife of; Diller, Abraham & Nancy, daughter of
Miller	Mary A.	4.04	1855				6.16	1	175	14	Miller, William & Mary J., daughter of
Miller	Edwin	9.01	1871				11.18	1	175	15	Miller, Jacob & Jane, son of
Myers	Samuel	2.19	1829			49	2.04	50	175	16	
Myers	Abraham	3.03	1833			21	3.13	22	175	17	
Myer	John	1.30	1842			59	8.20	60	175	18	[Myer (sic)]
Myers	Judith	4.04	1868			83		84	175	19	Myers, John, wife of [spelling varies]
Myers	John	2.05	1855			42	4.23	43	175	20	Myers, John & Judith, son of
Myers	Samuel	8.15	1888			79	3.13	80	175	21	Dr.
Myers	Barbara	9.18	1860			78	3.17	79	175	22	Myers, Samuel, wife of
Myers	Elizabeth	5.02	1873			65	2.14	66	175	23	Myers, Samuel, wife of
Myers	Joseph	8.11	1868			31	11.22	32	175	24	Myers, S. & Elizabeth, son of
Myers	David	12.21	1868			83	1.22	84	175	25	
Myers	Elizabeth	2.05	1861	1.27	1837			25	175	26	
Myers	Magdalena	6.28	1890			78	3.17	79	175	27	
Myers	Christian	10.29	1870			83	0.14	84	175	28	
Myers	Elizabeth	4.01	1886	8.31	1801			85	175	29	Myers, Christian, wife of
Negley	Joseph	10.24	1895			79	4.23	80	175	30	
Neiswanger	Emanuel	4.15	1840			88	8.00	89	175	31	
Neischwanger	Magdale		1824	11.05	1767			57	175	32	Hershey, born
Null	Arthur B.	1.23	1840			37	6.21	38	175	33	red sand headstone
Nunemaker	Daniel M.	12.29	1875				8.24	1	175	34	Nunemaker, John & Esther, son of

West Pennsboro - Diller Mennonite Church Graveyard

Surname	Given Name	Death Mo/Dy	Year	Birth Mo/Dy	Year	Att. Age Yr	Mo/Dy	Cm Ag	Pg	No	Other Information
Nunemaker	Samuel S.	11.16	1876				0.14	1	175	35	Nunemaker, John & Esther, son of
Nunemaker	Anna	2.03	1890			71	6.09	72	176	01	Nunemaker, Joseph, wife of
Raudabaugh	Samuel	9.24	1885			69	8.05	70	176	02	
Raudabaugh	Bertha F.	8.11	1885				0.08	1	176	03	Radabaugh, William & Mary, daughter of
Roudebaugh	Henry	12.15	1834		1781			54	176	04	red sand headstone
Roudebaugh	Christenia	1.31	1835		1782			54	176	05	Roudebaugh, Henry, wife of
Rhoads	Sarah B.	9.16	1864			1	0.03	2	176	09	Rhoads, Sam... & Sarah A., daughter of
Rice	Benjamin	11.02	1861			75	10.12	76	176	06	
Rice	Nancy	12.08	1861			78		79	176	07	aged 78 years & ----
Rickabaugh	Catharine	10.18	1881			72	4.15	73	176	08	
Shover	Clara Alice	4.11	1871				10.16	1	176	16	Shover, Eli & Mary, daughter of
Stine	Samuel		1895		1824			72	176	10	
Stine	Anna		1860		1826			35	176	11	Stine, Samuel, wife of
Stine	Martha		1895		1840			56	176	12	Stine, Samuel, wife of
Stine	Anna		1860		1860			1	176	13	
Stine	Laura J.		1857		1854			4	176	14	
Stine	Ida		1866		1865			2	176	15	
Stout	Michael	5.19	1876						176	17	aged ? years, 2 months, 12 days
Stout	Rebecca	1.16	1901			72	0.01	73	176	18	Stout, Michael, wife of
Stout	Rebecca Ellen	4.23	1875			22	8.27	23	176	19	Stout, John A., wife of
Stout	Samuel	1.03	1860			4	1.01	5	176	20	Stout, Michael & Rebecca, son of
Stout	Michael	11.17	1862			2	11.22	3	176	21	Stout, Michael & Rebecca, son of
Stout	Adam					66	7.20	67	176	22	
Stout	Catharine	11.11	1857			72	11.07	73	176	23	Stout, Adam, wife of
Stout	Ellie J.	8.25	1875				4.08	1	176	24	Stout, J. A. & R. E., daughter of
Warner	Margaret	6.30	1884			64	8.07	65	176	25	
Whistler	Peter	6.01	1857	5.23	1815			43	176	26	
Whistler	Jacob	10.22	1843				0.21	1	176	27	Whistler, P. & Eas., son of
Whisler	Lizzie L.	3.08	1887				0.18	1	176	28	Whisler, E. & L., daughter of

West Pennsboro - Francis Bear Farm Graveyard
Graveyard on hill

FRANCIS BEAR FARM GRAVEYARD

Surname	Given Name	Death Mo/Dy	Year	Birth Mo/Dy	Year	Att. Yr	Age Mo/Dy	Cm Ag	Pg	No	Other Information
Fishburn	Eliza Showalter								066	01	[no dates given]
Fishburn	John	11.16	1846	3.25	1789			58	066	02	
Fishburn	Peter	2.16	1825			66	10.00	67	066	03	
Fishburn	Catharine	4.17	1840			74	2.15	75	066	04	Fishburn, Peter, consort of
Myers	George	5.05	1828	10.31	1788			40	066	05	

GRAVEYARD ON HILL

Surname	Given Name	Death Mo/Dy	Year	Birth Mo/Dy	Year	Att. Yr	Age Mo/Dy	Cm Ag	Pg	No	Other Information
Greason	Margaret	10.16	1848	8.01	1825			24	055	01	Greason, Thomas, consort of
Greason	Anna	5.19	1854	2.01	1826			29	055	02	Greason, Thomas, consort of
Kistler	Mary C.	6.14	1860			3	11.17	4	055	03	Kistler, William & E., youngest daughter of
McManes	Anna Catharine	3.13	1854	6.24	1774			80	055	04	

West Pennsboro - Heikes Farm Graveyard

HEIKES FARM GRAVEYUARD

Surname	Given Name	Death Mo/Dy	Year	Birth Mo/Dy	Year	Att. Yr	Age Mo/Dy	Cm Ag	Pg	No	Other Information
Baker	Jonathan	10.25	1821			29	4.00	30	056	01	
Bear	Benjamin	12.01	1862			50	8.27	51	056	02	
Bear	Elizabeth	11.12	1832			35		36	056	03	Bear, John, consort of
Diller	John F.	3.12	1875			5	4.12	6	056	04	Diller, S. W. & A. M., child of
Diller	William A.	3.05	1870				4.05	1	056	05	Diller, S. W. & A. M., child of
Doner	infant daughter			3.01	1878				056	06	Doner, W. H. & Anna C., daughter of
Greason	Sarah	2.13	1841			22		23	056	07	Greason, Thomas, wife of
Greider	John	9.28	1887			74	11.27	75	056	08	
Greider	Catharine	1.18	1886			69	2.12	70	056	09	
Greider	Kate	1.22	1861			5	10.11	6	056	10	Greider, John & C., daughter of
Greider	Anna	9.03	1865			84	10.04	85	056	11	Greider, Jacob, wife of
Heigis	Margaret	12.06	1822	7.10	1808			15	056	12	German
Heiges	Elizabeth	7.15	1824		1761	62		63	056	13	German; (b. 1761); red sand head stone
Hikes	Andrew	1.27	1835		1757	78		79	056	14	
Heikes	Mary	1.27	1835			29	4.22	30	056	15	Heikes, Andrew, wife of
Heikes	Susanna	11.01	1838			65		66	056	16	Heikes, Andrew, consort of
Heikes	John	11.03	1856			71	10.11	72	056	17	
Hikes	Catharine	1.13	1828			41		42	056	18	
Heikes	Martha	2.01	1864			73	11.26	74	056	19	Heikes, John, second wife of
Heikes	George	4.02	1882			72	6.08	73	056	20	
Heikes	Catharine	2.26	1898			81	7.03	82	056	21	
Heikes	Mary E.	3.03	1843				0.22	1	056	22	Heikes, George & Catharine, daughter of aged 3 weeks, 1 day
Heikes	William H.	10.13	1857			12	2.22	13	056	23	Heikes, George & Catharine, son of
Heikes	John C.		1904		1840			65	056	24	
Heikes	Anna B.				1845				056	25	Heikes, John C., wife of
Heikes	Lizzie C.	10.23	1877			5	10.07	6	056	26	Heikes, J. C. & A. B., child of
Heikes	Fannie A.	11.03	1877			3	10.18	4	056	27	Heikes, J. C. & A. B., child of
Heikes	Andrew, Jr.	2.26	1835			31	1.10	32	056	28	
Keiser	John W.	12.05	1856			5	5.28	6	056	29	Keiser, David & Mary, son of
Leas	William D.	11.08	1856			3	4.08	4	056	30	
Morrett	Sarah C.	2.17	1859			3	9.04	4	056	31	Monett, S. & A. E., daughter of; [spelling varies]
Porter	Susan B.	8.08	1863		1859	4	8.15	5	056	32	Porter, Commodore & Sarah L., dau. of
Washmood	George	8.06	1872	5.25	1802			71	057	01	
Washmood	Samuel Davis	12.02	1848	10.09	1848			1	057	02	Washmood, George & Ann, son of
Watson	Joseph	10.27	1862			29	4.24	30	057	03	
Watson	Josephine	12.08	1862				8.11	1	057	04	Watson, J. & S., daughter of
Zeigler	William H.	1.17	1848	11.12	1846			2	057	05	Zeigler, Samuel M. & Catharine, son of

West Pennsboro - Jonathan Bear Farm Graveyard
              Ker Farm Graveyard

JONATHAN BEAR FARM GRAVEYARD

Surname	Given Name	Death Mo/Dy	Year	Birth Mo/Dy	Year	Att. Age Yr	Mo/Dy	Cm Ag	Pg	No	Other Information
Bear	Samuel	4.30	1855			67	9.27	68	065	01	
Bear	Sarah	12.26	1871			80	5.03	81	065	02	Bear, Samuel, wife of
Bear	Jonathan	3.21	1895			75	8.17	76	065	03	
Bear	John		1879			66	1.29	67	065	04	d. -- 29, 1879
Bear	Martha (Diller)	1.18	1890			71	0.24	72	065	05	Bear, John, wife of
Bear	William	12.26	1865			18	4.03	19	065	06	Bear, John & Martha, son of
Bear	Maria (Bear)	4.15	1896			72	5.00	73	065	07	
Bear	Rebecca	8.02	1863				8.02	1	065	08	Bear, Jonathan & Maria (Bear), child of
Bear	Catharine	6.29	1864				4.10	1	065	09	Bear, Jonathan & Maria (Bear), child of
Bear	Ellen	9.30	1874			17	3.28	18	065	10	Bear, Jonathan & Maria (Bear), child of
Bear	Emma C.	3.11	1883			16	3.18	17	065	11	Bear, Jonathan & Maria (Bear), child of
Bear	Samuel R.	9.09	1883			19	6.21	20	065	12	Bear, Jonathan & Maria (Bear), child of
Givler	Ellsworth	2.22	1873			11	7.03	12	065	13	Givler, A. A. & S. J., son of
Ricabaugh	John								065	14	Ricabaugh, Jacob & Elizabeth, son of; no dates given

KER FARM GRAVEYARD

Surname	Given Name	Death Mo/Dy	Year	Birth Mo/Dy	Year	Att. Age Yr	Mo/Dy	Cm Ag	Pg	No	Other Information
Bear	Joseph	3.03	1847	8.18	1845			2	061	01	Bear, Ephraim & Elizabeth, son of
Bear	Elizabeth	3.02	1848			24	11.16	25	061	02	Bear, Ephraim, wife of
Bear	Rebecca	12.05	1851			28	4.07	29	061	03	Bear, Samuel, wife of; Myers, Jacob & Lydia, daughter of
Myers	Rebecca	6.12	1851	8.15	1782			69	061	04	

West Pennsboro - Mount Rock Graveyard

MOUNT ROCK GRAVEYARD

Surname	Given Name	Death Mo/Dy	Year	Birth Mo/Dy	Year	Att. Age Yr	Mo/Dy	Cm Ag	Pg	No	Other Information
Adams	Jacob	12.27	1880			58	8.18	59	062	01	
Adams	Mary M.	11.09	1883			65	6.12	66	062	02	
Allen	Josiah M.	12.20	1866				4.23	1	062	03	Allen, J. N & B. W., child of
Allen	S. Edwin	10.31	1870			2	11.19	3	062	04	Allen, J. N & B. W., child of
Black	Jacob	2.02	1870			46		47	062	05	
Black	Martha Jane	4.16	1864			1	3.13	2	062	06	Black, Jacob & E., daughter of
Bleakly	Rachel	2.03	1892			82	8.11	83	062	07	Bleakly, John, wife of
Burkepile	James C.	8.13	1879			1	11.29	2	062	08	Burkepile, Jacob B. & Mary, son of
Carothers	William	7.21	1864	10.03	1790			74	062	09	
Carothers	Fanny	11.30	1871		1787	84	3.15	85	062	10	(b. 1787)
Carothers	Mary	8.29	1850			23	3.20	24	062	11	
Cooper	David Roy		1886				2.12	1	062	13	Cooper, David E. & M. J., son of; d. -- 24, 1886
Crider	Joseph	12.23	1900						062	12	Private, Co. F., 17th Regt., Pa. Cavalry
Crozier	William	7.31	1874			55	10.18	56	062	14	
Crozier	Eliza	8.14	1865			41	1.15	42	062	15	
Danner	Sarah J.	11.29	1884			48	10.09	49	062	16	Danner, Clinton, wife of
Ferguson	Margaret	11.08	1862			71	6.13	72	062	17	Ferguson, William, wife of
Galbraith	Willie G.	2.05	1893				4.22	1	062	18	Galbraith, R. W. & L. J., child of
Galbraith	Laura F.	2.08	1893			2	11.00	3	062	19	Galbraith, R. W. & L. J., child of
Hummelbaugh	Berdella E.	7.11	1875			4	8.23	5	062	20	Hummelbaugh, William & M. E., dau. of
Kuntz	John P.	2.29	1859	1.16	1858			2	062	21	Kuntz, William H. & Nancy, child of
Kuntz	Laura J.	2.05	1863	5.21	1862			1	062	22	Kuntz, William H. & Nancy, child of
Lefever	Jacob	4.26	1875			79	10.25	80	062	23	"Father"
Lefever	Elizabeth	12.10	1871			73	8.10	74	062	24	"Mother"
Lefever	Jacob F.	7.04	1855			25	5.09	26	062	25	Lefever, Jacob & Elizabeth, son of
McCool	Elizabeth	1.03	1864			41	4.04	42	063	14	McCool, Elijah, wife of
McCool	Emma M.	3.09	1864			19	7.00	20	063	15	McCool, Elijah & Elizabeth, daughter of; aged 19 years, 7 months, - days
Mell	Jacob	12.03	1877			44	5.00	45	062	26	
Mell	Jacob	7.05	1883			77	11.10	78	062	27	
Mell	Margaret	2.08	1899			88	6.23	89	062	28	Mell, Jacob, wife of
Mell	David	3.24	1847	2.28	1847			1	063	01	Mell, Jacob & Margaret, child of
Mell	Sarah Martha	5.14	1849	5.08	1849			1	063	02	Mell, Jacob & Margaret, child of
Mell	Elizabeth	1.31	1850	12.01	1835			15	063	03	Mell, Jacob & Margaret, child of
Mell	Jane M.	6.14	1869			37	6.23	38	063	04	Mell, Jacob & Margaret, child of
Mell	Nancy Aurin	12.29	1852			31	10.00	32	063	05	Mell, William, wife of
Mell	G. Keller		1905		1832			74	063	06	
Mell	Caroline				1836				063	07	
Mell	John M.	5.28	1862				11.20	1	063	08	Mell, G. Keller & Caroline, child of
Mell	Anna D.	9.18	1870			13	5.11	14	063	09	Mell, G. Keller & Caroline, child of
Mell	Jacob	3.25	1871			12	2.08	13	063	10	Mell, G. Keller & Caroline, child of
Mell	William	4.08	1872				6.18	1	063	11	Mell, G. Keller & Caroline, child of
Miller	George	8.12	1874	8.12	1807			68	063	12	Captain
Miller	Matilda	8.12	1877						063	13	Miller, George, wife of
Nailor	George	4.20	1851			76	3.12	77	063	16	
Paul	Susie C.	1.29	1884			25		26	063	17	Paul, W. H., wife of
Paul	Harvey R. [?]	1.31	1884			3		4	063	18	Paul, W. H & Susie C., son of

West Pennsboro - Mount Rock Graveyard

Surname	Given Name	Death Mo/Dy	Year	Birth Mo/Dy	Year	Att. Age Yr	Mo/Dy	Cm Ag	Pg	No	Other Information
Ritner	Joseph	10.16	1869	3.25	1780			90	063	19	Governor of Pennsylvania from December 15, 1835 to January 15, 1839; Erected by the State of Pennsylvania; dedicated October 15, 1902
Ritner	Susanna	2.22	1852			72		73	063	20	
Ritner	Emma	3.27	1876			67		68	063	21	Ritner, J. & S., daughter of
Ritner	Mary M.	12.20	1869				10.20	1	063	22	Ritner, W. D. & Frances, daughter of
Shambaugh	Peter	10.17	1845			29	2.16	30	063	23	[two death dates given, both are given as October 17, 1845]
Shannon	Ellen F.	1.08	1845			2	6.08	3	063	24	Shannon, Victor & Hannah, child of
Shannon	Orlando	3.08	1850			3		4	063	25	Shannon, Victor & Hannah, child of
Shearer	Samuel L. L.	2.08	1866				5.15	1	063	27	Shearer, J. P & A. B., child of
Shearer	J. I. Edward	5.05	1880				9.21	1	063	28	Shearer, J. P & A. B., child of
Shetron	Charles E.	1.28	1865			5	0.24	6	063	29	
Shover	David	12.06	1855	11.26	1802			54	063	31	
Shover	Sarah	8.31	1865			66	3.21	67	064	01	Shover, David, wife of
Shover	David	4.01	1853	4.15	1843			10	064	02	Shover, David & Sarah, son of
Shover	Thomas	4.24	1896			65	0.21	66	064	03	
Shover	Mary Ellen	10.21	1871			16	6.08	17	064	04	Shover, Thomas & Rachel, daughter of
Staver	Ida M.	7.21	1887			31	4.24	32	063	26	
Swiler	Mary A. L.	3.05	1872			11	3.00	12	063	30	Swiler, William D. & C. A., daughter of
Throne	Peter	12.04	1899			77	0.21	78	064	07	
Throne	Mary	6.12	1883			56	5.11	57	064	08	Throne, Peter, wife of
Throne	Elizabeth	7.27	1851				7.17	1	064	09	Throne, Peter & Mary, child of
Throne	Margareta	11.25	1862			4	1.25	5	064	10	Throne, Peter & Mary, child of
Throne	Agnes A.	8.20	1865				6.04	1	064	11	Throne, Peter & Mary, child of
Throne	Charles E.						1.04	1	064	12	Throne, Peter & Mary, child of; d. October 30, ---
Throne	Elizabeth	2.06	1864			33	6.21	34	064	13	Throne, William, wife of
Throne	Lydia J.	11.22	1903			51	10.21	52	064	14	
Trego	Levi		1850						064	05	Trego, L. & M., child of
Trego	Virginia	2.28	1854	11.03	1853			1	064	06	Trego, L. & M., child of
VanKirk	John	2.24	1865			82	11.17	83	064	15	
VanKirk	Margaret	2.06	1861			75	1.06	76	064	16	VanKirk, John, wife of
Welsh	William	6.27	1855			62	5.27	63	064	17	
Welsh	Nancy A.	2.02	1872			79	11.02	80	064	18	Welsh, William, wife of
White	Fanny	10.30	1870			34	10.17	35	064	19	White, H. H., wife of
Young	Samuel P.	9.22	1875				5.28	1	064	20	Young, John & Mary, child of
Young	Ida J.	9.05	1873				5.02	1	064	21	Young, John & Mary, child of
Zinn	Mary L.	10.24	1870			7	10.09	8	064	22	Zinn, John & C., daughter of

West Pennsboro - Old Shellenberger Farm Graveyard
Plainfield Bethel Church Graveyard

OLD SHELLENBERGER FARM GRAVEYARD

Surname	Given Name	Death Mo/Dy	Death Year	Birth Mo/Dy	Birth Year	Att. Age Yr	Age Mo/Dy	Cm Ag	Pg	No	Other Information
Sneider	David	2.12	1819	9.14	1761			58	060	01	Rev.
Snyder	Elizabeth	2.12	1826			63	9.00	64	060	02	Snyder, David, wife of; [spelling varies

PLAINFIELD BETHEL CHURCH GRAVEYARD

Surname	Given Name	Death Mo/Dy	Death Year	Birth Mo/Dy	Birth Year	Att. Age Yr	Age Mo/Dy	Cm Ag	Pg	No	Other Information
Albert	Elizabeth W.	5.11	1898	12.27	1856			42	048	01	
Alter	Jacob	6.00	1839	1.00	1773			67	048	02	
Alter	Elizabeth	8.31	1873	3.07	1802			72	048	03	Alter, Jacob, wife of
Atchison	Sarah	3.16	1876						048	04	aged about 80 years
Barrick	Elizabeth	7.18	1886			17	1.19	18	048	05	Barrick, William & A., daughter of
Barrick	Lizzie C.	3.03	1901			30	4.02	31	048	06	
Barrick	Bertha B.	3.10	1904			8	5.03	9	048	07	
Barrick	William J.	12.08	1902			32	9.13	33	048	08	
Barrick	Minnie G.	3.02	1901			7	5.03	8	048	09	Barrick, W. J. & L. C., daughter of
Bear	David	11.12	1875			58	4.08	59	048	11	
Bear	Elizabeth	11.09	1891			62	3.29	63	048	12	
Bear	William S.	12.22	1862			4	6.27	5	048	13	Bear, David & E., child of
Bear	Robert L.	12.03	1862			12	10.02	13	048	14	
Bear	Philip	7.11	1885			63	9.09	64	048	15	
Bear	Rebecca	10.23	1892			66	0.12	67	048	16	
Bear	Catharine	9.12	1894			54	0.04	55	048	17	Bear, Francis P., wife of
Bear	Henry		1895		1824			72	048	18	
Bear	Catharine				1824				048	19	
Bear	Bertha F.	8.16	1893				4.20	1	048	20	Bear, D. G. & L. S., child of
Bear	Emma R.	1.07	1897				5.07	1	048	21	Bear, D. G. & L. S., child of; [R.?-P.?]
Bear	Wilbur		1886		1873			14	048	22	
Bear	Joanna E.	9.13	1878	3.25	1852			27	048	23	
Beidler	John	1.23	1888			85	0.26	86	048	24	
Beidler	Mary	7.26	1873			63	3.28	64	048	25	Beidler, John, wife of
Bixler	Jacob	11.26	1896			72	2.25	73	048	26	
Bixler	Annie H.	7.20	1903			76		77	048	27	
Black	Clara C. Clay	12.30	1898			35	2.20	36	048	10	Black, George W., wife of
Bloser	William	4.03	1887			68		69	048	29	
Bloser	Sarah Ann	11.05	1866			41	9.03	42	048	30	Bloser, William, wife of [11/05?/1886]
Bloser	Mary A.	6.05	1889			55		56	048	31	
Bloser	John						3.12	1	048	32	Bloser, W. & S. A., child of
Bloser	David W.	12.15	1858			1	0.01	2	048	33	Bloser, W. & S. A., child of
Bloser	Sarah Alice	12.18	1866			5	0.08	6	048	34	Bloser, W. & S. A., child of

West Pennsboro - Plainfield Bethel Church Graveyard

Surname	Given Name	Death Mo/Dy	Death Year	Birth Mo/Dy	Birth Year	Att. Age Yr	Att. Age Mo/Dy	Cm Ag	Pg	No	Other Information
Bloser	Nora K.	8.16	1870				6.07	1	048	35	Bloser, William & Mary A., daughter of
Bloser	William E.	10.14	1893	12.12	1871			22	048	36	
Bloser	Ross Vincent	9.28	1893			1	0.28	2	048	37	Bloser, William E. & Jennie M., son of
Bricker	Jacob	11.21	1889			33	11.20	34	048	28	
Burger	-----		1875	2.00	1795			80	048	38	
Burger	infant child			9.29	1884				048	39	Burger, A. C. & H. E., infant child of
Carl	Henry	4.28	1901	4.14	1836			66	049	01	
Carl	C. Edwin	5.06	1901	12.05	1860			41	049	02	
Clay	Catharine	3.28	1882			24	8.20	25	049	03	
Clay	Levi	7.17	1897	12.19	1834			63	049	04	
Clay	Mary A.	9.25	1884	10.10	1835			49	049	05	Clay, Levi, wife of
Clay	Fanny Margaret	1.28	1903				9.12	1	049	06	
Crout	Mary I.	4.07	1875			12	8.22	13	049	07	Crout, John & Catharine, daughter of
Danner	Israel	8.12	1900			74	10.00	75	049	08	
Danner	Elizabeth								049	09	Danner, Israel, wife of [no dates]
Deitch	infant son	9.29	1900						049	10	Deitch, George & Rosie E., son of
Dill	Abraham	1.10	1884	5.16	1821			63	049	11	
Dill	Elizabeth	8.01	1887			74		75	049	12	Dill, Abraham, wife of
Doner	Daniel	2.25	1853	12.15	1781			72	049	13	
Doner	Elizabeth	3.07	1875	1.11	1779			97	049	14	Doner, Daniel, wife of
Doner	David	4.01	1892			71	11.25	72	049	15	
Doner	Susanna	4.05	1885			69	3.17	70	049	16	Doner, David, wife of
Doner	Daniel H.	2.15	1851			3	4.22	4	049	17	
Doner	Joseph C.	9.20	1872			23	8.05	24	049	18	Doner, David & Susan, son of
Doner	Jacob	2.01	1899	2.19	1812			87	049	19	
Doner	Nancy	9.22	1858			39	2.03	40	049	20	Doner, Jacob, wife of; Seitz, Jacob & E., daughter of
Doner	Mattie J.	3.27	1883	2.15	1851			33	049	21	Doner, Daniel, wife of
Doner	Rebecca E.	7.10	1879	9.25	1850			29	049	22	Doner, Jacob C., wife of
Doner	Jacob Edgar	8.27	1875			1	5.01	2	049	23	Doner, Jacob & Rebecca, son of
Doner	Mertle Grace	9.05	1885	8.30	1883			3	049	24	Doner, Jacob C. & Mary E., daughter of
Doner	Francis	12.31	1849			1	9.09	2	049	25	
Doner	Benjamin	12.04	1844						049	26	
Doner	Pearl	8.00	1896	12.04	1894			2	049	27	Doner, Daniel & Carrie, daughter of
Duey	William D.	12.14	1898			72	6.05	73	049	28	
Duey	Elizabeth	9.30	1900			74	5.01	75	049	29	Duey, William D., wife of
Eppley	James Roy	2.11	1880	12.29	1879			1	049	30	Eppley, J. W. & B. B., child of
Eppley	Hoyt								049	31	Eppley, J. W. & B. B., child of; b. Nov. 9, 1879; d. March 27, 1879
Fair	Jacob W.	1.13	1882			66	8.21	67	049	32	
Fair	Margaret	9.22	1882			63	7.19	64	049	33	
Fair	Reuben W.	4.06	1870	7.25	1847			23	049	34	Fair, J. W. & M., child of
Fair	Ezemiah	2.12	1862			16	10.28	17	049	35	Fair, J. W. & M., child of
Fair	Adaline	10.25	1859			7	4.26	8	049	36	Fair, J. W. & M., child of
Fair	Barbara A.	5.05	1859			1	2.27	2	049	37	Fair, J. W. & M., child of
Garman	Mary A.	1.16	1895	10.16	1847			48	049	38	Garman, Daniel E., wife of; Brown, Jesse & Elizabeth, daughter of
Getter	George	2.19	1893	12.27	1818			75	050	01	
Getter	Mary	3.25	1888			68	11.03	69	050	02	Getter, George, wife of; Kendig, Henry, daughter of

West Pennsboro - Plainfield Bethel Church Graveyard

Surname	Given Name	Death Mo/Dy	Death Year	Birth Mo/Dy	Birth Year	Att. Age Yr	Cm Mo/Dy	Ag	Pg	No	Other Information
Givler	Daniel	2.16	1883			49	9.00	50	050	08	
Givler	Mary E.	2.13	1897			61	6.12	62	050	09	
Givler	Annie R.	5.21	1899			40	11.00	41	050	10	
Givler	Rebecca Ellen	8.21	1854				9.15	1	050	11	Givler, Daniel & Mary E., child of
Givler	William K.	12.08	1863				6.10	1	050	12	Givler, Daniel & Mary E., child of
Givler	Harry N.	12.18	1868			1	4.03	2	050	13	Givler, Daniel & Mary E., child of
Givler	Nellie Grant		1873			1	6.13	2	050	14	Givler, Daniel & Mary E., child of; d. February 31, 1873
Green	Daniel	1.18	1895			69	9.04	70	050	04	
Green	Rebecca	12.20	1903			76	9.16	77	050	05	
Green	Laura Ann	8.03	1876			15	10.17	16	050	06	
Green	Myrtle Ireane	12.30	1881				8.03	1	050	07	Green, Daniel W. & M. J., daughter of
Greider	Jacob		1904		1837			68	050	03	
Hall	George	3.16	1894			79	4.24	80	050	15	
Hall	Catharine	3.25	1888			65		66	050	16	Hall, George, wife of
Hassinger	William	11.17	1882	6.08	1838			45	050	17	
Hassinger	Nancy A.	5.29	1904	9.08	1842			62	050	18	
Householder	Eve					83	6.12	84	050	19	
Householder	Jacob C.								050	20	[no dates given]
Householder	Mary					27	5.22	28	050	21	Householder, Jacob C., wife of
Householder	Anna								050	22	Householder, Jacob C., wife of
Jacoby	Sarah Porter		1891		1869			23	050	23	Jacoby, Elmer, wife of
James	Susan	11.08	1864			27	10.02	28	050	24	James, Edwin, wife of; Longnecker, Benjamin & Mary, daughter of
Keck	George H.	8.28	1883			10	5.27	11	050	28	Keck, Daniel & Mary, son of
Keeler	Henry		1900		1821	78		79	050	29	b. Germany; served in and was honorably discharged from the Prussian, Italian, and United States armies; d. at Thomas R. Burgner's, Elliott's Mills
Keiser	John C.		1895		1833			63	050	25	
Keiser	Sarah E.				1837				050	26	
Keiser	David K.		1897		1861			37	050	27	
Knisely	Elmor	1.10	1870	2.06	1863			7	050	30	Knisely, W. & M. A., son of; Elmor (sic)
Kochenderfer	David	6.08	1883			66	10.00	67	050	31	
Kochenderfer	Jacob	1.14	1884			63	1.12	64	050	32	
Lehman	Mary A.	5.22	1873			29	7.16	30	050	33	Lehman, Jeremiah, wife of
Longnecker	Benjamin	3.06	1869	1.15	1796			74	050	34	
Longnecker	Mary	7.11	1883	12.07	1797			86	050	35	
Longnecker	Sarah	3.19	1899	10.11	1829			70	050	36	
Longnecker	William P.	8.13	1872	12.18	1870			2	050	37	
Mayberry	Simon	12.14	1874	6.16	1834			41	051	01	
Mayberry	John A.	6.01	1870			2	9.05	3	051	02	Mayberry, S. & S., son of; [parents may be G. & S.]
Mentzer	B. Franklin		1904		1832			73	051	03	
Mentzer	Maria				1839				051	04	Mentzer, B. F., wife of
Mentzer	Catharine		1904		1826			79	051	05	
Mentzer	Edna Greider		1897		1867			31	051	06	
Musselman	William	9.09	1879	8.17	1800			80	051	07	
Myers	Mary Ellen	11.28	1885	3.16	1876			10	051	08	Myers, Joseph & Amelia, daughter of
Myers	Sarah J.	1.11	1892			46	3.02	47	051	09	

West Pennsboro - Plainfield Bethel Church Graveyard

Surname	Given Name	Death Mo/Dy	Year	Birth Mo/Dy	Year	Att. Age Yr	Mo/Dy	Cm Ag	Pg	No	Other Information
Nickey	Jacob	7.30	1886			30	2.24	31	051	10	
Ocker	Willie S.	10.07	1874			7	4.16	8	051	11	Ocker, J. S. & M. A., son of
Palmer	William	3.13	1902			68	10.13	69	051	12	Rev.
Paul	Henry	3.27	1897	4.05	1827			70	051	13	
Paul	Amand C.	1.09	1899	12.22	1835			64	051	14	[text reads "Paul, Amand c."]
Paul	Edwin Outhauk	8.21	1902				0.25	1	051	15	
Paul	Donald	3.30	1904				0.03	1	051	16	
Paul	Rebecca Workman	7.24	1888						051	17	
Paul	David		1901		1832			70	051	18	
Paul	John		1891		1830			62	051	19	
Paul	Eliza J.		1900		1832			69	051	20	Paul, John, wife of
Paul	Joseph		1903		1836			68	051	21	
Paul	Emma M.				1839				051	22	Paul, Joseph, wife of; d. -
Russel	Thomas	6.05	1903			67		68	051	23	Pvt., Co. C, 158th Regt., Pa. Militia
Seitz	Mary	4.06	1898			73	8.14	74	051	28	Seitz, Tobias, wife of
Shade	Lillie F.	7.29	1882				4.14	1	051	24	Shade, John & Annie C., daughter of
Shambaugh	Philip	2.04	1898			85	1.13	86	051	25	
Shambaugh	Rebecca	9.12	1894			76	0.16	77	051	26	
Sheaffer	Samuel F.	5.26	1902						051	27	Private, Co. F, 208 Regt., Pa. Vols.
Shuff	James M.	9.27	1889			61	7.24	62	051	37	
Shuff	Elizabeth	12.19	1904			74	3.17	75	052	01	Shuff, J. M., wife of
Shuff	Anna A.	8.16	1865			8	9.04	9	052	02	Shuff, James M. & E., child of
Shuff	George Albert	10.29	1881			23	0.04	24	052	03	Shuff, James M. & E., child of
Smith	Levi F.	4.13	1880			35	6.28	36	051	29	
Smith	Minnie V.	10.02	1877			5	1.12	6	051	30	Smith, Levi F. & Kate V., daughter of
Smith	S. M.		1893		1855			39	051	31	(M. D.)
Spotts	Anna A.	9.19	1873			21	11.19	22	051	32	Spotts, John, wife of
Strohm	George	6.23	1897	9.18	1815			82	051	33	
Strohm	Eliza	9.08	1893	7.10	1818			76	051	34	
Strohm	Sadie E. Paul	9.21	1883	3.23	1857			27	051	35	Strohm, D. E., wife of
Sutton	Leroy A. J.	9.13	1886			5	7.13	6	051	36	Sutton, Daniel & L. C., son of
Waggoner	Henry	8.27	1882	9.14	1820			62	052	04	
Waggoner	Sarah	3.23	1864	12.28	1861			3	052	05	Waggoner, Henry & Mary A., child of
Waggoner	James E.	1.25	1875	2.15	1869			6	052	06	Waggoner, Henry & Mary A., child of
Waggoner	John G.	10.12	1872			20	8.01	21	052	07	Waggoner, Henry & Mary A., child of
Wagoner	Lavina		1896		1832			65	052	08	
Wagoner	Phyanna		1901		1858			44	052	09	
Watson	Jehu	11.10	1876	11.17	1804			72	052	10	
Watson	Mary Ann	2.02	1898	1.09	1809			90	052	11	
Worley	Katie	11.23	1904			42	7.25	43	052	12	Worley, W. W., wife of
Yoter	Hezekiah	2.15	1870			54	6.17	55	052	13	
Yoter	Catharine	9.25	1895			81	3.02	82	052	14	
Yoter	John C.	5.23	1868			27	0.00	28	052	15	Yoter, H. & C., son of; aged 27 years, 15 months
Yeoter	Hezekiah	10.10	1873			29	10.29	30	052	16	
Yoter	H. Barston	7.30	1886			12	7.13	13	052	17	Yoter, Hezekiah G. & Sue, son of;

West Pennsboro - Plainfield Lutheran Church Graveyard

PLAINFIELD LUTHERAN CHURCH GRAVEYARD

Surname	Given Name	Death Mo/Dy	Year	Birth Mo/Dy	Year	Att. Yr	Age Mo/Dy	Cm Ag	Pg	No	Other Information
Behrens	Jacob	1.17	1900			80	10.08	81	044	04	
Behrens	Samuel	7.03	1898			25	11.11	26	044	05	
Beidler	H. G.								044	01	Co. F, 17th Pennsylvania Cavalry
Beidler	Maud L.								044	02	b. Apr. 15, 1862, d. Feb. 7, 1833
Bergstresser	Sylvester		1903		1850			54	044	03	
Berry	Wilmina C.	5.10	1880	3.19	1872			9	044	06	
Berry	Mary E.	12.22	1884	12.18	1884			1	044	07	
Bloser	Samuel D.		1894		1824			71	044	09	
Bloser	Annie M.	10.06	1890			29	5.27	30	044	10	Bloser, S. D. & Mary, child of
Bloser	Lizzie G.	1.18	1890			33	4.17	34	044	11	Bloser, S. D. & Mary, child of
Bloser	Mary J.	10.26	1888			42	11.00	43	044	12	Bloser, Benjamin J., wife of
Bloser	James M.	12.04	1879			3	4.07	4	044	13	Bloser, Benjamin & Mary J., son of
Bloser	Samuel Oscar	10.30	1885			6	9.21	7	044	14	Bloser, D. & E. A., son of
Brehm	Margery G.	9.02	1888			1	6.27	2	044	08	Brehm, F. P. & Katie A., daughter of
Brown	Mary E.	11.09	1888			37	11.20	38	044	15	
Burgett	Joseph Martin	1.06	1900			4	11.00	5	044	16	
Burgett	Mobel Odessa	4.15	1893				10.12	1	044	17	Burgett, J. W. & E. E., daughter of; [Mobel (sic)]
Burgett	Maggie R.	3.31	1889			30	11.18	31	044	18	Burgett, James D., wife of
Burget	Jacob T.	12.12	1870	6.29	1859			12	044	19	Burket, Martin & Rosanna, child of; [spelling varies in entries 19-22
Burget	David M.	12.14	1870	4.10	1864			7	044	20	Burket, Martin & Rosanna, child of;
Burget	Isaac H.	12.22	1870	2.28	1854			17	044	21	Burket, Martin & Rosanna, child of;
Burget	Michael	12.31	1870	7.16	1868			3	044	22	Burket, Martin & Rosanna, child of;
Calvert	Isaac H.	12.28	1898	8.04	1851			48	044	28	
Clay	William M.	10.16	1884			8	1.06	9	044	23	
Clay	Jacob M.	10.26	1884			4	7.08	5	044	24	
Clay	Rachel B.	6.07	1892			2	7.11	3	044	25	
Clay	David J.	6.12	1892			6	7.25	7	044	26	
Clay	Mabel C.	4.28	1898			4	9.21	5	044	27	
Cornman	William L.	9.26	1889			36	8.10	37	044	29	
Cornman	Harry L.	9.28	1884			8	0.26	9	044	30	Cornman, William L. & Mary, son of
Davidson	Mary P.		1876		1794			83	044	31	
Doner	Henry	1.21	1890			71	5.17	72	044	32	
Doner	Henry C.	1.29	1880			21	6.20	22	044	33	Doner, Henry & M. A., child of
Doner	Elizabeth	9.27	1857			7	2.22	8	044	34	Doner, Henry & M. A., child of
Doner	Carrie E.	1.02	1883			4	0.15	5	044	35	Doner, W. M. & M. A., child of
Doner	Frances Ann	8.30	1863				9.01	1	044	36	Doner, W. M. & M. A., child of
Finkenbinder	Adam	2.02	1891			65	1.26	66	045	02	
Finkenbinder	Sarah Ann	7.12	1864			36	3.07	37	045	03	Finkenbinder, Adam, wife of
Finkenbinder	Susan E.	3.29	1888			23	11.06	24	045	04	Finkenbinder, Albert M., wife of
Finkenbinder	Adam R.	8.13	1888				5.23	1	045	05	Finkenbinder, A. M. & S. E., son of
Finkenbinder	Adam R.	9.03	1872			3	11.18	4	045	06	Finkenbinder, A. & M., son of
Finkenbinder	Florence	3.11	1897	2.27	1897			1	045	07	Finkenbinder, S. W. & E., daughter of
Frederick	Maud	8.01	1902			16		17	045	01	
Fry	David	8.31	1884			66	5.02	67	045	12	
Fry	James A.	1.12	1885				9.25	1	045	13	Fry, J. M. & A. S., child of
Fry	Annie A.	1.31	1885			5	0.05	6	045	14	Fry, J. M. & A. S., child of

West Pennsboro - Plainfield Lutheran Church Graveyard

Surname	Given Name	Death Mo/Dy	Death Year	Birth Mo/Dy	Birth Year	Att. Age Yr	Age Mo/Dy	Cm Ag	Pg	No	Other Information
Fuget	William	5.04	1872	12.16	1808			64	045	08	
Fuget	Sarah	5.27	1885	4.25	1820			66	045	09	
Fuget	Esther Catharine	4.12	1879	7.29	1851			28	045	10	Fuget, Adam, wife of
Fuget	-----	1.07	1877						045	11	Fuget, Adam & E. C., daughter of
Gebhart	Jacob	10.06	1902	1.20	1823			80	045	15	
Gebhart	Elizabeth	9.04	1894	6.05	1827			68	045	16	Gebhart, Jacob, wife of
Greason	James W.	7.09	1889			35	10.16	36	045	17	
Griffie	Sarah J.	1.25	1875	10.13	1849			26	045	18	Snider, J. D. & B., daughter of
Hart	David J.	2.07	1891			47	9.03	48	045	19	
Heiser	Rebecca	4.13	1894	8.19	1811			83	045	20	Heiser, Peter, wife of
Heiser	Sarah E.	11.06	1892	5.13	1843			50	045	21	Heiser, Peter & Rebecca, daughter of
Hipple	George	3.15	1876			85		86	045	22	
Hornbaker	D. M.								045	23	Co. C, 126th Regt., Pa. Vols.;
Humer	Ella V. Lay	6.08	1896			35	3.00	36	045	24	Humer, W. D., wife of
Keiter	Daisy Ruth	11.20	1897			11	4.10	12	045	25	Keiter, D. F. & E. W., daughter of
Kerns	Mary A.		1896		1828			69	045	26	Kerns, Isaac, wife of
Lepperd	John	4.11	1883	8.27	1819			64	045	27	
Lepperd	Catharine	6.11	1886			58	7.00	59	045	28	Lepperd, John, wife of
Lepperd	Emaline	9.27	1870	9.24	1866			5	045	29	Lepperd, John & Catharine, daughter of
Lesher	John	3.24	1892			53	6.06	54	045	30	
Lindenberger	Susannah	11.29	1892			64	6.12	65	045	31	[text reads "wife of "]
McKeehan	John S.	7.28	1889	2.29	1816			74	046	15	
McKeehan	Rebecca	6.06	1863			37	5.11	38	046	16	McKeehan, Skiles, wife of
McKeehan	David S.	12.13	1868			12	2.06	13	046	17	McKeehan, Skiles & R., son of
McKeehan	Annie R.	7.30	1902	2.16	1849			54	046	18	
Miller	John P.	1.19	1886			68	11.11	69	045	32	
Miller	Mary	7.12	1889			68	2.29	69	045	33	
Miller	Mary E.	2.23	1886	9.23	1858			28	045	34	Miller, George M., wife of
Minnich	Simon	2.02	1876			60	2.22	61	046	01	
Minnich	Elizabeth	9.03	1892	12.24	1816			76	046	02	
Minich	infant son	1.19	1859				0.17	1	046	03	Minich, J. W. & S. E., child of
Minich	Jane Ida	1.12	1862			1	1.14	2	046	04	Minich, J. W. & S. E., child of
Minich	infant son	2.03	1863				3.03	1	046	05	Minich, J. W. & S. E., child of
Minich	Clement G.	2.11	1878			1	5.23	2	046	06	Minich, J. W. & S. E., child of
Minnich	Daniel Amos	12.31	1884	10.07	1882			3	046	07	Minnich, D. F. & Jemima, infant son of
Mourer	John N.	3.05	1884			54	2.04	55	046	08	
Moyer	Benniville	11.17	1889			74	5.01	75	046	09	
Moyer	Susanna R.	5.09	1890			71	1.06	72	046	10	
Moyer	Laura M.	9.09	1884	12.30	1863			21	046	11	Moyer, Riley, wife of
Moyer	Sarah E.	3.14	1888						046	14	Moyer, Cyrus, wife of
Myers	Daniel	9.02	1881	1.04	1817			65	046	12	
Myers	Mary H.	12.28	1897			80	7.01	81	046	13	
Nickey	Samuel C.	7.14	1890				4.14	1	046	19	
Nunemaker	Jared	2.24	1904						046	20	Private, Co. A, 152d Regt., Pa. Vols.
Nunemaker	William		1897		1829			69	046	21	Co. H, 1st Regt., Pa. Res.; Co. G, 130th Regt., Pa. Vols.; Co. B., 188th Regt., Pa. Infantry; enlisted June 5, 1861; final discharge June 15, 1865
Nunemaker	Sarah		1900		1827			74	046	22	Nunemaker, William, wife of
Nunemaker	David	5.03	1891			21	0.14	22	046	23	

West Pennsboro - Plainfield Lutheran Church Graveyard

Surname	Given Name	Death Mo/Dy	Year	Birth Mo/Dy	Year	Att. Age Yr	Mo/Dy	Cm Ag	Pg	No	Other Information
Nunemaker	Elizabeth	1.15	1882			81	8.25	82	046	24	Nunemaker, Samuel, wife of
Paul	Annie Grace	7.06	1888	1.23	1888			1	046	25	Paul, C. P. & M. B., child of
Paul	Frank Wilson	1.26	1895	3.27	1893			2	046	26	Paul, C. P. & M. B., child of
Pechart	Daniel	12.23	1874			70	0.16	71	046	27	
Pechart	Catharine	3.27	1872			65	1.15	66	046	28	
Pie	David	10.25	1893						046	29	Co. G, 130th Pennsylvania Volunteers
Reiber	George W.	6.20	1898			63	1.20	64	046	30	
Reiber	Mary A.	10.13	1904			66		67	046	31	
Rhoads	Jacob	9.27	1894			75	9.13	76	046	34	
Rhoads	Susannah	3.27	1896			78	8.15	79	046	35	
Riggleman	Walter	12.09	1882				0.07	1	046	32	Riggleman, J. B. & A. J., child of
Riggleman	David P.	6.07	1886				0.26	1	046	33	Riggleman, J. B. & A. J., child of
Sauer	Susanna	7.31	1886	6.02	1832			55	046	36	Sauer, John W., wife of
Shughart	Jonas	1.30	1878			20	4.29	21	047	02	
Shughart	Fanny	5.18	1895	3.18	1819			77	047	03	[spelling varies]
Shughart	Fannie	9.13	1889			36	6.00	37	047	04	Shughart, Fannie, Mrs., daughter of
Shughart	Cora Caretta	10.31	1880			5	0.24	6	047	05	Shughart, Susanna, daughter of
Souders	Elizabeth A.	6.30	1898			47	7.11	48	047	01	Souders, Harry, wife of
Sperow	Henry	10.14	1895			86	1.28	87	046	39	
Sperow	Susan	5.09	1875			64	11.20	65	046	40	
Sperow	Lucy	11.21	1874			21	7.01	22	046	41	Sperow, Henry H., wife of
Stahl	Samuel	1.15	1892	4.10	1806			86	046	37	
Stahl	Hannah Short	9.14	1871	2.10	1815			57	046	38	Stahl, Samuel, wife of
Stump	Mary E.	2.09	1883	2.28	1834			49	047	06	
Stump	Thomas	8.24	1877	10.11	1832			45	047	07	
Vanasdal	Martha Ellen	3.16	1886			40	4.06	41	047	08	
Vanasdal	Charles Albert	7.22	1901			24	0.03	25	047	09	
Waggoner	Abraham J.	6.17	1888			55	3.00	56	047	10	
Ward	John	8.20	1902	4.11	1827			76	047	11	
Ward	Catharine			11.00	1832				047	12	
Wert	William J.	8.09	1894				8.00	1	047	13	Wert, W. J. & M. J., son of
Whisler	John S.	5.20	1900	3.27	1842			59	047	14	
Whisler	Lizzie R.	6.07	1902	9.26	1861			41	047	15	
Whisler	Marion Vey	12.09	1887						047	16	Whisler, John S. & Lizzie R., dau. of
Wolf	George A.	2.23	1885			29	1.17	30	047	17	
Wolf	William P.	3.05	1895						047	18	Private, Co. F, 101st Regt., Pa. Vols.
Wolf	Alice C.	11.30	1890			27	5.00	28	047	19	Wolf, W. P. & Eliza, daughter of
Wolf	Julia A.	6.12	1888			28	7.24	29	047	20	
Wolfe	M. T.	4.14	1898			58	11.19	59	047	21	
Wolfe	Beckie A.	8.10	1888			20	5.28	21	047	22	Wolfe, M. T., & Annie, daughter of
Yinger	Anthony	10.31	1881			55	7.05	56	047	23	
Yinger	Lydia	9.19	1898			81	3.01	82	047	24	Yinger, Anthony, wife of
Yinger	Frankie M.	10.23	1882				1.23	1	047	25	Yinger, Anthony & Elizabeth, child of
Yinger	Charles E.	11.14	1882			2	4.00	3	047	26	Yinger, Anthony & Elizabeth, child of
Young	Andrew	12.31	1899			74		75	047	27	
Young	Matilda	2.14	1871			23	8.18	24	047	28	Young, Andrew, wife of
Young	Abraham	7.08	1871			79	7.16	80	047	29	
Young	Elizabeth	6.20	1878			80		81	047	30	Young, Abraham, wife of
Young	Samuel A.	8.03	1896			47	6.07	48	047	31	
Young	Mary E.	4.15	1900			52	8.02	53	047	32	

West Pennsboro - Plainfield Lutheran Church Graveyard
　　　　　　Riggleman Farm Graveyard

PLAINFIELD LUTHERAN CHURCH GRAVEYARD (continued)

Surname	Given Name	Death Mo/Dy	Year	Birth Mo/Dy	Year	Att. Yr	Age Mo/Dy	Ag	Cm	Pg	No	Other Information
Young	Harry M.	10.21	1889				3.09	1		047	33	Young, J. O. & S. J., son of
Young	John J.	8.24	1899			79	2.00	80		047	34	
Young	Sarah	10.01	1890			60	7.07	61		047	35	Young, J. J., wife of
Young	Alfred M.	5.29	1874			18	7.12	19		047	36	Young, John & S., son of
Zug	Mary Ellen	12.23	1885				6.12	1		047	37	Zug, Edgar S. & Ida J., daughter of

RIGGLEMAN FARM GRAVEYARD

Surname	Given Name	Death Mo/Dy	Year	Birth Mo/Dy	Year	Att. Yr	Age Mo/Dy	Ag	Cm	Pg	No	Other Information
Rein	Margaret	11.08	1832	8.11	1764			69		058	03	German
Rine	Henry	5.06	1835	4.23	1754			82		058	04	
Ressler	John	9.13	1820	7.09	1791			30		058	01	[Rossler ?]
Ressler	Samuel	5.29	1834		1787	47	2.00	48		058	02	[Rossler ?]
Washmood	John	9.20	1831		1794	37		38		058	05	(b. 1794);　red sand

SEITZ FARM GRAVEYARD

Surname	Given Name	Death Mo/Dy	Year	Birth Mo/Dy	Year	Att. Age Yr	Mo/Dy	Age	Cm	Pg	No	Other Information
Bear	John Z.	2.22	1848			9	6.04	10		059	01	
Grove	Joseph	8.28	1864			4	10.06	5		059	02	Grove, Jacob & Mary, son of
Grove	Charlie E.	5.16	1876			5	3.06	6		059	03	Grove, Jacob & S. E. Runk, child of
Grove	Mattie May	9.01	1877			1	4.00	2		059	04	Grove, Jacob & S. E. Runk, child of
Lefever	John	9.19	1864	3.11	1799			66		059	05	
Lefever	Lawrence	2.24	1830	12.15	1764			66		059	06	
Lefever	Fanny	11.15	1817	10.29	1769			49		059	07	Lefever, Lawrence, wife of
Lefever	Salome Line	3.05	1866	1.08	1790			77		059	08	Lefever, Lawrence, wife of; Kurtz, Abraham, afterwards wife of
Myers	Mary R.					1	2.16	2		059	09	Myers, David & Elizabeth, daughter of; [R. ?]
Seitz	Jacob	3.30	1856	8.21	1779			77		059	10	
Seitz	Elizabeth	2.24	1872			81		82		059	11	
Seitz	Jacob	10.21	1879			69	3.23	70		059	12	
Seitz	Benjamin	6.28	1882			56	5.21	57		059	13	
Seitz	Rebecca		1901		1837			65		059	14	Seitz, Benjamin, wife of
Seitz	Mary	6.11	1895			60		61		059	15	Seitz, John, wife of
Seitz	Elizabeth	1.03	1861			4	5.00	5		059	16	Seitz, J. & M., daughter of
Seitz	William T.						6.00	1		059	17	Seitz, B. & R. E., child of
Seitz	Charles E.	8.02	1862				4.00	1		059	18	Seitz, B. & R. E., child of

West Pennsboro - Springfield Graveyard

SPRINGFIELD GRAVEYARD

Surname	Given Name	Death Mo/Dy	Year	Birth Mo/Dy	Year	Att. Age Yr	Mo/Dy	Ag	Cm	Pg	No	Other Information
Bowers	Jacob	1.23	1869			74	6.03	75		259	13	
Bowers	Rebecca	11.12	1875			65		66		259	14	Bowers, Jacob, wife of
Bowers	Mary C.	5.28	1858			18	9.08	19		259	15	Bowers, Jacob & Rebecca, daughter of
Bowers	George A.	7.26	1863				3.09	1		259	16	Bowers, D. H. & M. E., son of
Brandt	Elizabeth	3.03	1852		1772	80	1.11	81		259	01	Brandt, Jacob, Sr., consort of (b. 1772)
Brandt	David, Sr.	11.21	1864			82	3.06	83		259	02	
Brandt	Elizabeth	7.19	1865			57	10.10	58		259	03	Brandt, David, wife of
Brandt	William	2.12	1839			3	2.19	4		259	04	
Brandt	Easther	8.13	1867			79	6.13	80		259	05	Brandt, David, wife of [Easther (sic)]
Brandt	Barbara	6.14	1832			23	1.23	24		259	06	Brandt, David, wife of
Brandt	David	2.26	1839			1	0.09	2		259	07	
Brandt	Enos	7.18	1845			3	7.00	4		259	08	Brandt, D. & E., child of
Brandt	Elizabeth	12.02	1859			15	6.08	16		259	09	Brandt, D. & E., child of
Brandt	Annie	5.11	1868			24	3.17	25		259	10	Brandt, David, wife of
Brandt	Martha	2.22	1866			68	2.00	69		259	11	Brandt, Michael, wife of
Brandt	Mary Ann	8.06	1875			28		29		259	12	Brandt, Michael & Martha, daughter of
Burkholder	Nancy J.	5.17	1880	12.25	1866			14		259	17	Burkholder, D. N. & L., daughter of
Bush	Robert A.	1.06	1873							259	18	Bush, W. & M., son of: (a colored child)
Cooper	William P.	5.08	1867			82	2.04	83		259	20	
Cooper	Jane	3.13	1853	3.29	1780			73		259	21	Cooper, William P., consort of
Crider	Catharine	11.10	1858			47	0.23	48		259	19	Crider, Jacob, wife of
Farner	Emma Jane	4.26	1879			22	4.26	23		259	22	Farner, William E., wife of
Farner	David C.	8.10	1879				4.03	1		259	23	Farner, W. E. & E. J., son of
Farner	Mary Edith	1.31	1884				0.01	1		259	24	Farner, D. L. & M. E., daughter of
Finkenbinder	Mary Ellen					4	8.08	5		259	31	Finkenbinder, S. & E., daughter of
Foust	George	1.10	1857			62		63		259	25	
Foust	Catharine A.	9.24	1865			42	1.17	43		259	26	
Foust	Mary	4.11	1865			78		79		259	27	Foust, George, wife of
Foust	Elizabeth	2.17	1866			17	3.06	18		259	28	Foust, John W., wife of
Foust	Sarah E.	9.10	1859			1	10.18	2		259	29	Foust, John W. & Elizabeth, child of
Foust	Jacob M.	2.15	1865			16	7.16	17		259	30	Foust, John W. & Elizabeth, child of
Frownfelter	John	8.15	1868			70	10.15	71		260	01	
Gipe	Joshua	4.14	1891			76		77		260	02	a stone mason; built the fences around the graveyard in which he lies buried
Gipe	Martha	11.10	1892			72		73		260	03	Gipe, Joshua, wife of
Gipe	Alexander		1856			1	3.19	2		260	04	
Gipe	Mary J.	10.06	1866			20	7.00	21		260	05	
Gipe	Martha E.	6.18	1890			32	9.18	33		260	06	
Gipe	William P.	5.08	1879			26		27		260	07	
Gipe	John D.	5.20	1881			33	10.27	34		260	08	
Hamilton	William	12.02	1867			83	4.16	84		260	09	
Hamilton	Ann E.	11.14	1865			23	8.21	24		260	10	Hamilton, William & Elizabeth, dau. of
Hirey	Bion L.	2.05	1870			12	1.05	13		260	11	Hirey, John D. & J. D., son of
Holfarty	John	4.12	1874	3.19	1786			89		260	12	
Holfarty	Anna Sabina	7.07	1866			70	3.06	71		260	13	Holfarty, John, wife of
Keller	Jacob	5.28	1861	10.18	1791			70		260	14	
Keller	Frances	4.22	1864	9.22	1789			75		260	15	Keller, Jacob, wife of
McCaleb	Ella J.	5.23	1863			4	8.01	5		260	19	McCaleb, J. & K., child of

West Pennsboro - Springfield Graveyard

Surname	Given Name	Death Mo/Dy	Year	Birth Mo/Dy	Year	Att. Age Yr	Mo/Dy	Cm Ag	Pg	No	Other Information
McCaleb	Ida C.	5.30	1864			5	8.07	6	260	20	McCaleb, J. & K., child of
McCannen	Caroline M. T.	1.15	1866			37	9.19	38	260	21	McCannen, Peter, wife of
Miller	Susannah G.	1.24	1862			5	0.06	6	260	16	Miller, J. & M., daughter of
Miller	William D.	5.25	1873			22	7.20	23	260	17	
Myers	Nancy	10.10	1868			67		68	260	18	Myers, Jacob, wife of
Palm	David	12.17	1897			70	3.02	71	260	22	
Palm	Caroline	1.08	1900			71	9.20	72	260	23	Palm, David, wife of
Palm	Viola	4.13	1858			4	3.15	5	260	24	Palm, D. & C., daughter of
Palm	Florence M.	2.15	1889			18	1.15	19	260	25	Palm, D. & C., daughter of
Palm	Elizabeth	1.06	1863			75		76	260	26	Palm, Tobias, wife of
Rhinehart	Lizzie M.	8.08	1900	10.13	1873			27	260	27	
Rhoads	Samuel	9.10	1868			77	5.00	78	260	28	
Rhoads	Mary	2.15	1871	4.14	1801			70	260	29	Rhoads, Samuel, wife of
Smith	Howard W.	11.06	1893	9.27	1893			1	260	30	
Snyder	Anna	6.12	1897			19	7.26	20	261	02	Snyder, C. E., daughter of
Stoke	Annie M.	4.16	1872			2	9.25	3	260	31	Stoke, F. M. & L., daughter of
Stumbaugh	John	4.24	1903			69		70	260	32	Co. D, 21st Regt., Pa. Cavalry
Stumbaugh	Lucy A.	3.18	1889			59		60	260	33	Stumbaugh, John, wife of
Stumbaugh	Mervin F.	5.05	1896			2	3.22	3	261	01	Stumbaugh, J. K. & C. E., son of
Troup	John H.	10.26	1891			66		67	261	03	
Troup	Mary Jane	6.06	1859					0	261	04	
Troup	John W.	10.01	1868	8.21	1866			3	261	05	
Troup	Charles A.	3.07	1871	6.30	1870			1	261	06	
Troup	Mary Ellen	6.29	1859	12.01	1858			1	261	07	
Troup	Frank W.	4.03	1874	11.16	1872			2	261	08	
Turns	Matilda	2.01	1871			33	8.26	34	261	09	Turns, John B., wife of
Turns	George G.	9.18	1868			3	7.16	4	261	10	Turns, John B. & Matilda, son of
Waters	F. M.	2.16	1887			39	0.18	40	261	11	Co. D, 187th Pennsylvania Volunteers; Post No. 201, G. A. R.
Woodrow	Susie A.	9.28	1901			50	10.28	51	261	12	
Woodrow	Margaret A.	2.24	1876	3.27	1837			39	261	13	Woodrow, Cornelius, wife of
Woodrow	Mary Agnes	1.04	1886				0.19	1	261	14	Woodrow, E. F. & Susie, child of
Woodrow	Frank L.	2.18	1890				10.29	1	261	15	
Woodrow	L. Esther	2.23	1890				11.05	1	261	16	
Work	James	8.04	1881			78	0.11	79	261	17	
Young	Samuel	12.19	1902			75	6.22	76	261	18	
Young	Elizabeth	6.13	1867			44	3.23	45	261	19	Young, S., wife of
Young	William G.	5.13	1871			5	8.18	6	261	20	Young, S. & E. M., son of
Young	Jane	9.03	1892			64		65	261	21	Young, Samuel, wife of

West Pennsboro - William A. Lindsay Farm Graveyard
unknown location - Oyster's Point Graveyard

WILLIAM A. LINDSAY FARM GRAVEYARD

Surname	Given Name	Death Mo/Dy	Death Year	Birth Mo/Dy	Birth Year	Att. Age Yr	Age Mo/Dy	Cm Ag	Pg	No	Other Information
Abrahams	John Enoch	8.15	1812		1758			55	068	01	
Abrahams	Hannah	9.23	1852	5.25	1766			87	068	02	Abrahams, John Enoch, wife of
Abrahams	John Enoch	7.06	1828		1820			9	068	03	
Abrahams	Sarah	4.01	1832	8.06	1809			23	068	04	
Abrahams	Jacob	2.01	1838			45	2.26	46	068	05	
Abrahams	Maria	8.07	1832			32	11.20	33	068	06	Abrahams, Jacob, wife of

UNKNOWN LOCATION

OYSTER'S POINT GRAVEYARD

Surname	Given Name	Death Mo/Dy	Death Year	Birth Mo/Dy	Birth Year	Att. Age Yr	Age Mo/Dy	Cm Ag	Pg	No	Other Information
Funk	Abraham	6.11	1825	1.27	1751			75	128	01	
Marstzbarger	Jacob	11.30	1785			60		61	128	02	
Markbarger	Anna	3.07	1826	1.13	1743			84	128	03	German
May	Frederick, Sr.	1.08	1837	12.24	1765			72	128	04	
May	Christiana	10.29	1825	11.15	1772			53	128	05	May, Frederick, Sr., wife of
May	Frederick, Jr.	12.05	1842	5.25	1829			14	128	06	
Nichols	Ann	5.30	1845	1.29	1779			67	128	07	
Nichols	Maria	4.30	1885			82	2.13	83	128	08	

NARRATIVE OF JEREMY ZEAMER'S VISITS TO CEMETERIES IN CUMBERLAND COUNTY, PENNSYLVANIA

Narrative and descriptive material in the original text appears before, after, and, rarely, interspersed among the lists of interred persons. Here they are gathered together and arranged in chronological order.

In this section, the date of visit and the name and location of the cemetery have been placed as a heading for each entry, the latest date being used for the ordering if there were two visits. For further information see the introduction.

1901   Ashland Cemetery, Carlisle Borough

     count 1091

May 5, 1902   Zion Reformed Church Graveyard, Hopewell Township

     Graveyard at Zion's Reformed Church, north east of Newburg, Pa. These were taken from the tombstones on May 5, 1902, by J. Zeamer.

May 6, 1902   Newburg Church of God Graveyard, Hopewell Township

     Graveyard at the Church of God in Newburg. Inscriptions taken on May 6, 1902 by J. Zeamer.

May 6, 1902   Hoover Graveyard, Hopewell Township

     Hoover Graveyard, north of Newburg. Inscriptions taken on May 6, 1902 by J. Zeamer.

May 6, 1902   Mount Tabor Church Graveyard, Hopewell Township

     Graveyard at Church of Mt. Tabor in Hopewell Township Taken on May 6, 1902 by J. Zeamer.

     Mt. Tabor Church was built in 1876 by the U. B. in Christ. Rev. Cassel was its pastor in 1902.

May 7, 1902   Stouffer Farm Graveyard, Hopewell Township

     Graveyard on the "Stouffer Farm" in Hopewell Township. Farm in 1902 was occupied by Rolla Baker. Inscriptions taken on May 7, 1902 by J. Zeamer.

May 6, 1904   United Presbyterian Church Graveyard, Newville Borough

     Graveyard of the U. P. Church at Newville. Taken May 6, 1904, by J. Zeamer.

     This graveyard lies to the west, or rear, of the U. P. Church in the town of Newville. I visited it on

Narrative

Friday, May 6, 1904, and took the inscriptions, which were all that were in the burying place at the time, excepting two or three on heavy stones which were lying upon their faces and which I could not turn over. The bodies and tombstones were being removed to neighboring cemeteries with the view of abandoning the graveyard as a place of interment. There were many evidences of recent removals. Some years ago I made a visit to the place and took inscriptions of some tombstones which on my second visit were missing. J. Zeamer

---

June 11, 1904   Letort Spring Church Cemetery, Middlesex Township

   Letort Spring or Kutz Church   Built 1841 Rebuilt 1872   count 317

June, 12, 1904   Wagner's Church Graveyard, North Middleton Township

   b. 1780 - 1887   d. 1851 - 1903 [range of dates]
   count - 127   [cemetery name spelled "Wagoner's" in inscription section, "Wagner's' in Table of Contents]

July 1904   Carlisle Springs Church Graveyard, Middlesex Township

   Graveyard at Carlisle Springs Church in Middlesex Township. Taken in July 1904 by J. Zeamer

   b. 1766 - 1863   d. 1831 - 1903 [range of dates]

   These inscriptions I copied from the tombstones at two different times, the first in May 1902, the last in July 1904. I took great care that I got them correct. J. Zeamer

---

March, 28, 1905 Old Associate Reformed Church Yard, Dickinson Township

   Old Associate Reformed Church Yard at Stone House, Dickinson Township
   b. 1768 - 1850   d. 1834 - 1880 [range of dates]

On the same plot of ground where has long stood the "Shady Grove" school house, in Dickinson township, there was erected in 1803-1804, by an Associate Reformed, or Seceder, congregation a stone church building. In 1803 John Moore deeded to Simon Ross, Robert Criswell, William Hewey, John Woodburn, and John Neal, trustees of the Associate Presbyterian Church of Dickinson twp., one acre of ground for the uses and purposes of a house of worship, a school house, and burying ground. The church building long ago fell into decay and was removed, but some of the interments made in the burying plot on this ground are marked with head stones upon which the inscriptions were legible as late as March 28, 1905, when Capt. Wm. E. Miller and William Dinkle visited the place and obtained the following.

April 7, 1905   Peter Albright Farm Graveyard, Middlesex Township

   Middlesex Graveyard on farm of Peter Albright near Balfour, near banks of the Letort.

   I visited this graveyard on April 7, 1905, and found this the only tombstone remaining in it. There were signs of others having been in it. It is said that bodies were removed from this place to the cemetery at "Kutz's Church". The graveyard is enclosed by a thick wall of heavy limestone, topped with a coping of zinc which on the east side was blown off. The enclosure had an iron gate which stood wide open.   J. Zeamer

Narrative

April 7, 1905   Mennonite Graveyard at Balfour, Middlesex Township

Middlesex Mennonite Graveyard at Balfour

On the right bank of the Conodoguinet Creek, at the south end of the bridge at Balfour, stands a brick Mennonite Church, which was built through the aid and influence of Jacob Stouffer when he owned the Middlesex Mills. In the rear of this church is a graveyard which I visited on April 7, 1905, and in it found tombstones containing the following inscriptions all in good condition.

count - 20

August 10, 1905   Dunker Church Graveyard, Middlesex Township

Dunker Church Graveyard at foot of Sterretts Gap, Middlesex Twp.   count - 32

I visited this place on the afternoon of August 10, 1905, walking from John Rebert's. After finishing copying I walked up to the top of the mountain and then by the east road down to Reberts.

August 30, 1905   Plainfield Lutheran Church Graveyard, West Pennsboro Township

Lutheran Church Graveyard in Plainfield.   West Pennsboro Township.   Taken on August 30, 1905.

The church at this place was built in 1870, and rebuilt in 1895.

August 30, 1905   Plainfield Bethel Church Graveyard, West Pennsboro Township

Bethel Church Graveyard at Plainfield

August 30, 1905   Bear Graveyard, West Pennsboro Township

The Bear Graveyard   North of Plainfield

This burying ground is located on a high bluff near the Conodoguinet Creek, due north from Plainfield, partly on what has long been known as the Bear farm but is now owned by ----- Phillips and tenanted by Parker Morrison; and partly on the farm formerly owned by John K. Longnecker, now by John Hays, Esq. I took the inscriptions on August 30, 1905

August 30, 1905   Graveyard on hill, West Pennsboro Township

Graveyard on hill   West of Plainfield

On a hill on the left hand side of the State Road just west of Plainfield in West Pennsboro Twp., there was once a graveyard. The remains of most of the bodies interred there have been taken up and taken to other burying grounds, but there are yet some headstones there lying among the bushes and briars that now effectually cover the place. On August 30, 1905, I made a visit to the place and found the following.

Narrative

August 31, 1905   Heikes Farm Graveyard, West Pennsboro Township

In West Pennsboro Twp. about one and one half miles west of Plainfield and a short distance north of the State Road.

When I visited this family burying ground--Aug. 31, 1905--it was in bad condition. The board fence around it was erect but old and rotten, and at one side within the enclosure the briars, weeds, and bushes were so high and dense as to effectually hide some of the tombstones. The surface is uneven, containing some deep depressions, and the whole was over run with ivy and weeds. Three cedar trees, two of which are quite large, stand in one corner, and from afar mark the whereabouts of the place.

August 31, 1905   Riggleman Farm Graveyard, West Pennsboro Township

Graveyard on the Riggleman formerly McKeehan Farm, tenanted by Mr. ----- Chronister. This burying ground is a short distance north of Kersville in West Pennsboro Twp.

When I visited this burying place--August 31, 1905--it was simply a clump of briars and brambles in a field, the tombstones completely hidden from view and ground hogs burrowing among them.

August 31, 1905   Seitz Farm Graveyard, West Pennsboro Township

Graveyard on Seitz Farm, about 2 miles east of Newville, in West Pennsboro Twp. I visited it on Aug. 31, 1905.

The Seitz graveyard is situated on the southern slopes of the farm now occupied by Jacob Seitz. It is enclosed by a good post fence and its appearance indicated that it receives attention from some one. The stones are all erect and the inscriptions clear and legible. A large spreading cherry tree stands in the south east corner of the grounds. This graveyard is located directly south and near to Prospect Hill Cemetery, a Newville cemetery.

August 31, 1905   Old Shellenberger Farm Graveyard, West Pennsboro Township

Graveyard on the "Old Shellenberger Farm", near Valley View Mill, now owned by Bloser, in West Pennsboro Twp.

This burying place is located well up in a field. It is enclosed by a post fence that is very old but quite strong. The place is grown up and densely covered with bushes and trees of considerable height forming a clump or wood that can be seen from far away. I visited the place on August 31, 1905 and found it difficult to get into it. The grounds are large enough to have contained many graves but the above two are the only ones I found marked.

August 31, 1905   Diller Mennonite Church Graveyard, West Pennsboro Township

The Diller Mennonite Church on the Conodoguinet Creek, below Newville, in Upper West Pennsboro. Taken on August 31, 1905.

Narrative

September 1905   Big Spring Presbyterian Graveyard, Newville Borough

Taken in September 1905.

September 19, 1905   Newville Cemetery, Newville Borough

Newville Cemetery, lying just west of and close to the town of Newville. Taken September 19, 1905.

The Newville Cemetery contains 20 or 25 acres of land and is located on high ground west of the town of Newville. The cemetery association was chartered on November 28, 1883. It is well kept by Charles Washington, a colored man, who has been superintendent for many years.   September 20, 1905

September 21, 1905   Zion Lutheran Church Graveyard, Newville Borough

Zion's Lutheran Graveyard in Newville. "Old Lutheran Graveyard". The lineal descendent of Zeigler's Graveyard in Mifflin Township. Taken on September 21, 1905.

J. Z.

This graveyard is located immediately to the west and in the rear of where the former Lutheran Church--the first Lutheran Church built in the town of Newville--and a little to the north of where the present Zion's Lutheran Church, built in 1862, stands.

This burying ground is badly neglected and when I copied these inscriptions was in shocking condition. It bore evidence of some graves having been opened and the remains removed.

J. Z.

September 21, 1905   Springfield Graveyard, West Pennsboro Township

Springfield Graveyard in Upper West Pennsboro Twp. U. B. Church. Taken September 21, 1905. Rev. Francis, Pastor of the Church.

The U. B. Church of Springfield is a brick edifice in fairly good condition and makes a pleasing appearance. It faces to a narrow street to the east. The graveyard was grown up with high weeds, grass, and flags, and received little attention. At the time I copied these inscriptions Rev. Francis was Pastor of the congregation. He lived at Springfield and in addition to Springfield also served Oakville, Mt. Pleasant, and Bethany Churches.

William Green, a resident of Springfield, gave me this and other information.   September 21, 1905   J. Z.

September 21, 1905   Stoughstown Lutheran Church Graveyard, Newton Township

Stoughstown Graveyard

The graveyard at Stoughstown belongs to a Lutheran Church built there in 1846. The Church building is of brick and is in good condition judging from outside appearances. The congregation is small and is served by a Lutheran minister who resides at Centerville. The graveyard is in low ground, and grown up with grass, high weeds, and briars. Just back of the church a deep gutter runs across the graveyard, which is an outlet for the

Narrative

water that in wet weather gathers upon and beyond the turnpike.

The interments here are few as most of the people in the vicinity bury at Shippensburg and Newville.

September 22, 1905 Mt. Rock Graveyard, West Pennsboro Township

Graveyard at Mt. Rock in West Pennsboro Twp. Taken Sept. 22, 1908.

The church at Mt. Rock is a brick structure, standing east and west with the entrance at the east end. Stands about 80 yards back from the turnpike and the graveyard lies between it and the turnpike. Church has four windows on the turnpike side. Building is in good condition and makes a nice appearance. I visited this burying ground on the afternoon of September 22, 1905, walking to it from the C.V.R.R. at Alterton, and from there down the turnpike to McAllisters and from there south to Spring Road.

September 22, 1905 Old Line Graveyard, Dickinson Township

The Old Line Graveyard on the North side of the Spring Road, in the north part of Lower Dickinson Twp.

I came to this burying ground at 5 P. M. on the evening of September 22, 1905, from Mt. Rock on foot. Mrs. Line, wife of the owner of the farm, directed me to the place, and informed me that there was another "Line graveyard" in the vicinity, to the south of the Spring Road, on the farm occupied by Oran Long, who was married to a Line, a daughter of George Line.

September 22, 1905 Line Graveyard, Dickinson Township

Line Graveyard, South of the Spring Road, partly on the farm formerly owned by George Line and partly on that owned formerly by the late Henry Line.

This burying ground is small and surrounded by a stone wall. Within the wall is a thick growth of bushes and briars and grass so dense that it hid some of the head stones. The head stones are all in good condition and the inscriptions legible.   September 22, 1905   J. Zeamer

---

September 23, 1905 Francis Bear Farm Graveyard, West Pennsboro Township

Graveyard on Francis Bear's Farm, formerly the John Fishburn Farm, near Hay's Bridge in West Pennsboro Twp.

A re-arrangement of roads and fences left this graveyard in the middle of the field where it was much in the way. The fences surrounding it rotted down and exposed the tombstones to the encroachments of cattle and other stock, and finally a tenant--Robert Galbraith--took them up and set them against the wall of the rear end of his barn, where Francis Bear, the owner of the farm, inspected them on the afternoon of September 23, 1905, and copied from them the above inscriptions. The place where the graveyard was is now farmed over.

September 23, 1905 Jonathan Bear Farm Graveyard, West Pennsboro Township

Graveyard on Jonathan Bear Farm in West Pennsboro Twp. on farm now owned by Samuel Eppley.

I visited this graveyard in company with Francis Bear whose parents are buried here. It is located near the south banks of the Conodoguinet Creek, a short distance below what has long been known as Burgner's Mill. It is surrounded by a well-built low stone wall upon which is a wire fence. It is well kept and presents an agreeable appearance. September 23, 1905

September 23, 1905   William A. Lindsey Farm Graveyard, West Pennsboro Township

Graveyard on William Lindsey Farm, formerly the Charley Weaver Farm, in West Pennsboro Twp.

In company with Francis Bear I visited this graveyard on the afternoon of September 23, 1905. It is grown up with briars and brambles, and infested with groundhogs. The headstones stand erect, are of gray slate, and the inscriptions not deep cut but legible. It is a place seldom seen by outsiders.

September 23, 1905   Bitner Farm Graveyard, West Pennsboro Township

Graveyard on the Bitner Farm in West Pennsboro Twp. now owned by the Gross brothers of Middlesex, and tenanted by Adam Fuget.

I visited this burying place on the afternoon of September 23, 1905, in company with Francis Bear. It is on the northern end of the farm enclosed by a post fence which is old but quite strong. Besides the ones here given, it at one time contained the remains of other persons, but apparently they were taken up and removed to other places of interment. Within the enclosure bushes have grown to the size of small trees, but briars and other undergrowth are not plentiful. The inscriptions on the two red sand headstones that remain are quite distinct.

October 1905   Bethel Church Graveyard, North Middleton Township

Bethel Church at "Beechers"

Bethel Church in North Middleton is on the Waggoner's Gap Road, near Beecher's, three miles north from Carlisle. The land for it and its graveyard was acquired from John S. Lightner, although this is not an absolute certainty. The church edifice is a wooden structure and was built about 1865. The congregation now (October 1905) is small. The graveyard is well kept. Rev. F. Y. Weidenhamer is the Pastor, but has had a call from Harrisburg.

October 4, 1905   Ker Farm Graveyard, West Pennsboro Township

Graveyard on Ker Farm, below Valley View Mills in West Pennsboro Twp.

This burying place is situated at the rear end of a field that extends from the rear of the barn northward to the banks of the Conodoguinet Creek. I visited it on my way to the Upper Frankford Church, early on the morning of Oct. 4, 1905, and found it grown up with bushes, grapevines, and briars so densely that it was almost impossible to get through it. The field through which I had to pass to get to it was grown up with high grass which was heavy and white with dew. My shoes and pantaloons got soaking wet.

October 4, 1905   Lutheran Brick Church Graveyard, Frankford Township

Upper Frankford Graveyard, Brick Church, Lutheran Congregation. Taken October 4, 1905.

Narrative

These inscriptions I copied on October 4, 1905. I went to Newville on the 5:40 A. M. train and walked to the graveyard from there, arriving at 7:50. At 5:10 I left the church and walked via Diller's Bridge, the State Road, West Hill, and Plainfield, arriving in Carlisle at 8:30 P. M.
J. Zeamer

October 6, 1905   Lutheran and Reformed Stone Church Graveyard, Frankford Township

Graveyard of the Stone Church in Lower Frankford Twp., Lutheran and Reformed. Taken on October 6, 1905 by J. Zeamer.

The Lower Frankford Church as shown by an inscription on a larger corner stone, was built of stone in 1820, by the Lutheran and Reformed congregations jointly. It formerly was a high building, containing a gallery. In 1873 it was rebuilt on the original foundations, but the gallery was left out. The Lutherans and Reformeds still (1905) jointly own and use it. It is in good condition and presents a nice appearance. A brick school house stands near it to the south, just across the road from it.

I copied the inscriptions on the grave stones in the burying ground of this church on October 6, 1905. I walked from Carlisle to it, getting there by 8:15 in the morning, and finished copying by 4:50 p. m. Returning home I came with C. P. Snyder, who had been out at his farm in his buggy.   J. Zeamer

---

October 7, 1905   Barnitz M. E. Church Graveyard, Dickinson Township

Graveyard of M. E. Church at Barnitz in Dickinson Township. Taken on October 7, 1905   J. Zeamer

The church at this place is a brick building in good condition and of pleasing appearance. There are a number of interments not marked by tombstones.

October 7, 1905   Martin Farm Graveyard, Dickinson Township

Graveyard on the Martin Farm in Dickinson Twp.

This place I visited on October 7, 1905, a son of the late Simon Martin going with me and pointing out the way. There is now nothing in sight to indicate that it at any time was a burying place, but William H. Gibb says he remembers visiting the place when there was something like a vault there. William Martin, son of the late George Martin, Sen., says it was the family burying ground of the Houks, who owned the farm before his father bought it, and that he remembers having seen tombstones there bearing inscriptions.

October 9, 1905   Huntsdale Dunker Cemetery, Penn Township

Dunker Graveyard at Huntsdale, Penn Twp. Taken on October 9, 1905. J. Zeamer   Finished copying these inscriptions from the tombstones at 3:15 P. M., October 9, 1905.

The Church building at this place is a large one-story brick building with basement of stone. It is in good condition.   J. Zeamer

---

Narrative

October 13, 1905   Cumminstown Campbellite Church Graveyard, Penn Township

Graveyard at Campbellite Church at Cumminstown in Penn Twp. Taken on October 13, 1905 by J. Zeamer

The church at this place is a stone structure, of large proportions, and has long been known as Lefever's Church. The congregation is very small and services are now seldom held.

October 13, 1905   Dickinson Presbyterian Church Graveyard, Penn Township

Dickinson Presbyterian Church Graveyard of Penn Twp. Taken October 9, 1905 and October 13, 1905. J. Zeamer

The names and inscriptions here given are not everywhere in alphabetical order, but they were carefully copied and are all here recorded.

The first day I copied at this burying ground night came before I finished. I returned on October 13, 1905, and then finished by 11 A. M.   J. Zeamer

---

October 13, 1905   Centerville Lutheran Church Graveyard, Penn Township

Lutheran Graveyard at Centerville, in Penn Twp.

Finished copying these inscriptions from the tombstones at 4:35 P. M., October 13, 1908, and then started to walk to the Hisner graveyard in the northern part of Penn Township. This church was formerly known as "Beetem's Church", because of the support given it by Samuel Beetem, Esq., who, with his two wives is buried in its graveyard.   J. Zeamer

---

October 13, 1905   Hisner Graveyard, Penn Township

Hisner Graveyard in the northern part of Penn Twp., near the turnpike. Taken on October 13, 1905, by J. Zeamer.

I reached this burying ground at 5:40 P. M. on October 13, 1905, walking to it from the Lutheran graveyard at Centerville, to which I had walked from the R. R. station at Huntsdale. It was already growing dark when I arrived at the Hisner graveyard and finding it difficult to decipher the inscriptions I called to my aid two boys named Wagoner, who had come to the field in which the graveyard is situated to bring home some sheep. With their assistance I obtained all excepting a few very small stones which probably mark the graves of children. At 6:05 P. M. I bid the boys good-bye and walked to Carlisle via the turnpike, reaching Linder's Park at 9 o'clock P. M.

   J. Zeamer

October 14, 1905   Mt. Zion Graveyard, Dickinson Township

Mt. Zion Graveyard, South Dickinson Township

Along the P. & R. R. R. in South Dickinson township is a Lutheran Church named Mount Zion, which was built in 1868. Its graveyard I visited on the afternoon of October 14, 1905, and copied all the inscriptions it then contained. J. Zeamer   count 181   Began at 2:15 and finished at 4:35 P. M.   J. Zeamer

Narrative

October 31, 1905   Entlerville Graveyard, Frankford Township

Entlerville Graveyard, Frankford Twp. Taken October 31, 1905

The graveyard at Entlerville is not now connected with any church. Formerly there was a Zolleringite Church in the locality, but its membership diminished until finally it gave way to the Church of God or Bethel denomination. The church building of this denomination is of frame and is situated on the north side of the road that leads from Bloserville to McClure's Gap.

On the farm now owned and occupied by Thomas Henry, in Frankford Township, there is an old graveyard. I visited it on the same day I visited the Entlerville burying ground, but found nothing but some sand stone markers that barely protruded above the face of the ground. Several trees had grown to considerable size at the spot and against two of these a huge pile of rails were piled. There was no enclosure around the spot. Mrs. Oiler, a daughter of Thomas Henry, informed me that her father had been living on the farm for 36 years and that a man named Smith was buried there.

J. Zeamer

October 31, 1905   Possum Hill Church Graveyard, Frankford Township

Possum Hill Church Graveyard, Frankford Township

The church at Possum Hill is under the auspices of the denomination known as the Zolleringites. It is a low wooden structure entirely surrounded by a wood, and cannot be seen until ones gets quite near it. Tall chestnut, oak, and pine trees are quite thick around it, giving the place a seclusive air that awakens solemn thoughts. I found the graveyard well kept and surrounded by a strong post fence. A school house bearing the same name is located along the same road three or four hundred yards west of the church.

October 31, 1905   Bethel Church Graveyard, Mifflin Township

Bethel Church Graveyard near Doubling Gap, Mifflin Township. Taken October 31, 1908 by J. Zeamer.

The Bethel Church edifice near Doubling Gap, Mifflin township, is of brick and fronts to the west. It has three windows on the south side, three on the north, two on the east, and two windows and folding doors in the front. Above the doors is a date stone on which is the inscription:

                     "Bethel
              Built   1856
              Rebuilt   1878"

The windows are all stained--the glasses of the upper as well as those of the lower sash, but where glasses have been broken--and there are many-- unstained glass has been put in, which gives the windows a spotted and ridiculous appearance.

I copied the inscriptions in the graveyard of this church on October 31, 1905, beginning at 4:21 P. M. and finishing at 4:56 P. M. At 5:05 I started from there to walk to Newville, where I took the train for Carlisle.

Narrative

October 31, 1905   Bloserville Reformed Church Graveyard, Frankford Township

Bloserville Graveyard, belonging to the Reformed Church of that place. Taken on October 31, 1905.

Completed at 3:04 P. M., October 31, 1905.   J. Zeamer

November 6, 1905   Prospect Hill Cemetery, Newville Township

Prospect Hill Cemetery in West Pennsboro. One mile east of Newville. Taken on September 6, 1906. Joseph Jeffrey, Superintendent.

Dr. David Ahl laid out Prospect Hill cemetery about the year 1875, the landscape engineer laying it out that laid out Prospect Hill Cemetery at York. The engineer charged $600.00 for his work. About 1884 the cemetery went into the hands of the Odd Fellows who now own it. Dr. Ahl, the projector of the cemetery, is buried but his grave is as yet unmarked.

November 7, 1905   Farm Graveyard, Frankford Township

Graveyard on farm occupied by J. H. Gayman, in Frankford Twp., opposite N. Scott Alter.

Taken November 7, 1905, 10:51 a.m., by J. Zeamer.

This is a private graveyard in which no interments have been made in many years. It is on a farm on which J. M. Gayman is only the tenant. It is enclosed by a post fence that is in good condition, but is grown up with briars and brambles which in places are so dense as to obscure the tombstones. Two rabbits ran out of the wilderness while I was at work in it.

J. Zeamer   November 7, 1905

November 8, 1905   Center Church Graveyard, Mifflin Township

Center Church Graveyard, Mifflin Twp.

Services are held at this place three Sundays each month by the Lutherans and one Sunday each month by the Dunkers.

These inscriptions I copied on the morning of November 9, 1905. Began copying at 7:30 A. M. and finished by 10:30 A. M. It was a cold day and snow was in the air so thick that it at times obscured the mountain in places. I went to Newville in the train and from there walked to Center.

November 9, 1905   Snokes Graveyard, Mifflin Township

Snokes Graveyard in Mifflin Twp. Taken on November 9, 1905.   J. Zeamer   [Snoke in Table of Contents]

This is a Dunker graveyard but is not connected with any church, school, or other building.

Narrative

November 9, 1905   Mount Hope Cemetery, Mifflin Township

Graveyard at Mt. Hope in Mifflin Twp.

United Evangelical Church built in 1899. The former church at this place was known as the "Ebenezer" Church. In November 1905 Rev. Snook was the Pastor of this congregation; his home was at Bloserville. Floyd Mowry was teacher of the school nearby. Copied inscriptions on November 9, 1905, 12:32 to 12:45 P. M.   J. Zeamer

---

November 9, 1905   Bethany Church Graveyard, Mifflin Township

Bethany Church Graveyard at "Gisetown", in Mifflin Twp., of the U. B. in Christ.

Inscriptions copied November 9, 1905, 1:37 to 2:25 P. M.

Bethany Church in Mifflin township is a brick structure, low and squat in appearance. It fronts on the north, has two doors in its front and two windows on each side. A fence encloses it and inside the fence in front of the building is a lamp post. The country around it is comparatively level and beautiful. The place is known as "Gisetown" but there is no village anywhere near.

J. Zeamer

November 9, 1905   Irishtown Church Graveyard, Newton Township

[First of two visits. See April 17, 1906 for final visit. (page 230)

November 10, 1905   Mount Victory Graveyard, South Middleton Township

Mt. Victory Graveyard in South Middleton Twp.

Along the Carlisle and Hanover Turnpike, near the Adams County line, is a United Brethren Church named Mt. Victory. I visited it on the afternoon of November 10, 1905, and from the graveyard and adjacent to it, I obtained the following inscriptions.

count - 7

November 10, 1905   Flint Ridge Chapel Graveyard, South Middleton Township

Flint Ridge Chapel in South Middleton Twp.

In South Middleton Township, near Gardner's Store, is an Evangelical Church known as "Flint Ridge Chapel", which I visited on the afternoon of November 10, 1905, and took from the tombstones in its graveyard the following inscriptions.

J. Zeamer   count - 10

Narrative

November 17, 1905   Old Hoffer Farm Graveyard, Middlesex Township

A small graveyard on a farm in Middlesex Township, a short distance north of Hickorytown. The farm is known as the "Old Hoffer Farm", and was formerly owned by Christ Hoffer, who sold it to Abram Weaver who in 1905 sold it to Philip Philebaum. In 1905 it was tenanted by Elmer Beitzel.

I visited the place on the afternoon of November 17, 1905, and found it located just west of the barn and in it two marked graves as follows.

One of these tombstones is a heavy granite slab elevated on carved marble posts. They bear evidences of having been fine and expensive specimens of the stone cutter's art and at the lower end of one is the trade mark "Thos. Mein Facit, Phila.". The Matthew Miller is a slate slab flat upon the ground. The stone fence that once enclosed the ground has fallen down and all round is nearly level with the ground.

J. Zeamer

November 17, 1905   Strickler Graveyard, South Middleton Township

Strickler Graveyard, Lower South Middleton

This burying place is located on farm of John Strickler in the north east corner of Lower South Middleton township, east of Hickorytown. I took these inscriptions in the afternoon of November 17, 1905. Frank Greegor, tenant on the farm.

J. Zeamer   count 14

All the inscriptions in this burying ground are in good condition and the stones were all standing erect when I visited the place. The place was well kept and surrounded by a fence made of wire and wooded rails.

November 23, 1905   Garber Graveyard, South Middleton Township

Garber Graveyard, South Middleton

This burying ground is located on what is known as the "Eichelberger Farm", lying south of the Trindle Road, just west of Hickorytown. The farm is now owned by L. T. Brenneman, who recently bought it.

I visited the place on the afternoon of November 23, 1905. It is enclosed by a well built stone wall, to which there is an entrance on the south side, from which the gate is missing. Locust sprouts have grown up in it, also raspberry bushes, and outside the wall on the north side is a large cherry tree. The ground is in Lower South Middleton township and can be seen from the Trindle Road.

Narrative

April 17, 1906   Irishtown Church Graveyard, Newton Township

Graveyard at the Church at "Irishtown" in North Newton Township.

I reached this place from the Bethany, or Gisetown Church in Mifflin township, at 4:20 P. M. on November 9, 1905, on foot. I copied rapidly until 5:25, by which time it became too dark to read the inscriptions. I then suspended work and walked to Oakville and there took the 9:17 P. M. train for Carlisle.

On April 17, 1906, I visited the place a second time, going to Oakville in the train and walked from there, going the latter part of the journey through the fields. I reached the church at 9:45 A. M. and completed the work by 10:15 and then returned to Oakville by the way I came. J. Zeamer

Finished taking these inscriptions on my second visit to the place at 10:15 A. M., Tuesday, April 17, 1906. There were three unmarked graves apparently made since the previous fall. The unmarked graves in this ground are few, almost all the graves having markers of some kind and most of them very creditable ones.

This Church is located on high ground, at a point that affords a splendid view in all directions. The building is of brick and viewed from the outside is in good condition. It is covered with shingle. The burying ground is well kept and is a nice place for the interment of the dead.

J. Zeamer

April 17, 1906   Oakville U. B. Cemetery, Newton Township

U. B. Graveyard at Oakville, North Newton Township

Inscriptions of the tombstones in the graveyard adjoining the United Brethren Church at Oakville, Newton Township, taken on April 17, 1906. I came to this place on foot from Irishtown, after completing my work at that place. and began work here at 10:10 A. M. Finished taking these inscriptions at 11:50 A. M. on April 17, 1906.

The Church at this place viewed from the outside is in excellent condition. It is of brick with slate roof, and faces the road on the west of it. The date stone over the door in its front bears the information: Built in 185 . [sic] Rebuilt in 1901. The graveyard is well kept.

April 17, 1906   Old Roads Graveyard, Newton Township

Old Roads Graveyard in North Newton Twp.

About a mile east of Oakville, a short distance east of where the road from Shippensburg and the road from Oakville meet, on the south side of the road, is an ancient burying ground known as "The Old Roads Graveyard". Many years ago there was here located a schoolhouse known as "The Roads School House". I visited the place on the afternoon of April 17, 1906, and found the grounds recently cleaned off and surrounded by a new wire fence. Locust and other trees had grown up in it to a large size and these were all cut and sawed down and removed. The place is on, or adjoins, the farm now owned by John T. Kelly. The U. B. congregation which owns the Church at Oakville, has charge of this burying ground and it was they who cleared and fenced it. I ---- the grave stones here the following inscriptions.

Narrative

September 21, 1906   Meeting House Springs Grave Yard, Carlisle Borough

    May 1903 [initial visit]   Again September 21, 1906

    b. 1686 - 1866 [range of birth dates recorded]
    d. 1744 - 1901 [range of death dates recorded]

    Captain William Drennan at one time owned a tract of land that included the Brindle farm, near Carlisle Springs, in the northern part of what is now Middleton township.

    William Drennan was 22 years of age in 1788; 6 feet 1 inch, fair complexion; born in Ireland; occupation "Clark"; under Captain Zeigler. Enlisted April 23, 1788. See 5th Series, Pennsylvania Archives, Volume 14, page 845.

    count 70

June 26, 1908   Eberly's Mills Graveyard, Allen Township

    Eberly's Mills or Milltown in Allen Township

    J. Zeamer

June 28, 1908   Oysters' Point Graveyard, unknown location

    Graveyard at Oysters' Point, where the trolley railway comes upon the turnpike.

    Inscriptions taken on June 28, 1908 by J. Zeamer

September 6, 1909   Monroe Woods Farm Graveyard, Lower Allen Township

    Graveyard on Farm of Monroe Woods, near Lisburn, Cumberland County, Pa.

    Inscriptions taken by J. Zeamer, September 6, 1909.

September 6, 1909   Lisburn Cemetery, Lower Allen Township

    Situated on the banks of the Yellow Breeches above the Bridge.

    Inscriptions taken on September 6, 1909, by J. Zeamer.

September 6, 1909   Lantz's School House Graveyard, Upper Allen Township

    Graveyard at Lantz's School House in Upper Allen Township.

    Inscriptions taken on September 6, 1909, by J. Zeamer.

Narrative

no date given   Zeigler's Church Graveyard, Mifflin Township

Zeigler's Church in Mifflin Township. Tombstone Inscriptions.

About the year 1790, or shortly afterwards, Jacob Zeigler gave a corner of ground near the present Council Bluff school house for church and graveyard purposes. Here the German Reformed and Lutheran congregations built a church and a stable for their minister's horse. The church was of logs, two stories high, with a gallery, well seated and very comfortable. Another congregation was similarly organized about 1796 in Upper Frankford and was long associated with this one in a pastoral charge. About 1823, Rev. G. Heilig, a Lutheran and Rev. D. Hessinger, Reformed, took charge of these two churches and continued until 1827. The Reformed part was always the weaker and was so unfortunate as to get into some trouble with Mr. Hessinger. A division among themselves ensued and they never had another pastor. A few joined with the Reformed church in Hopewell, a larger number were absorbed by the Lutherans, and finally only two or three families remained. The Rev. N. [?] J. Stroh, Lutheran, served the congregation for several years.

In 1832 the Lutherans organized in Newville, built a church, called Rev. D. P. Rosenmiller, and soon absorbed the Mifflin membership, so that the old church was rarely used and finally was wholly closed. About ten years after, the building was sold to the Evangelical Association and removed to Whiskey Run. The Newville church is a lineal descendent of the one in Mifflin.

This is taken from Rev. J. B. Scouller's article on Mifflin township in Wing's History of Cumberland County.

"In 1897 Gilbert E. Swope published in Eagle's "Notes and Queries"-- Annual Vol. for 1897--the inscriptions on the tombstones remaining in the graveyard at this place, and headed them with the following preface:

> Zeigler's Church was a log building erected about 1795, and was the first joint building in
> that vicinity for the uses of German Reformed and Lutheran congregations. The Lutheran
> congregation, being the stronger, absorbed the Reformed and continued to worship in the old
> church until 1832. In that year the congregation abandoned the church and erected a new one
> in Newville, incorporated as Zion's Lutheran Church. The old graveyard, unlike many, is kept
> in excellent condition from the income of the fund realized from the sale of the old church building."

---

no date given   Hanna Graveyard, Hopewell Township

The Hanna Graveyard, a short distance north of Newburg in Hopewell Twp., Cumberland County, Pa.

It is said that this graveyard was located through the circumstances of a flood in the Conodoguinet. A child of the vicinity died and it was intended to bury it at the Middle Spring Church, but the creek being unfordable, the owner of the land offered permission to bury it on his ground. This was done and afterwards other graves were added until it became the burying ground for the neighborhood.

The oldest inscription is that of Elizabeth Beaty, d. October 19, 1815.

INDEX TO SURNAMES OF INTERRED PERSONS

Surname	Twp.	Cemetery	Page	Surname	Twp.	Cemetery	Page
Aberly	CARL	Ashland	1	Auker	FRAN	Bloserville Ref. Church	33
Abrahams	WPEN	William A. Lindsey Farm	216	Auker	WPEN	Diller Mennonite Church	195
Abrahims	CARL	Ashland	1	Aukerman	FRAN	Lutheran & Ref. Stone Church	36
Abrahims	NEWV	Newville	137	Aukerman	WPEN	Bear	194
Abrams	CARL	Ashland	1	Auld	PENN	Centerville Lutheran Church	171
Aby	NEWT	Irishtown Church	108	Auxer	NEWV	Big Spring Presbyterian	114
Achenbaugh	CARL	Ashland	1	Bailey	LALN	Eberly's Mills	74
Adair	PENN	Dickinson Presb. Church	178	Bailey	LALN	Lisburn	77
Adams	CARL	Ashland	1	Bair	MDSX	Letort Spring Church	90
Adams	FRAN	Lutheran & Ref. Stone Church	36	Baird	CARL	Ashland	1
Adams	LALN	Eberly's Mills	74	Baker	CARL	Ashland	1
Adams	MDSX	Dunker Church	88	Baker	FRAN	Lutheran & Ref. Stone Church	36
Adams	NEWV	Big Spring Presbyterian	114	Baker	HOPE	Newburg Church of God	63
Adams	WPEN	Mt. Rock	203	Baker	HOPE	Zion Reformed Church	68
Addams	CARL	Ashland	1	Baker	MIFF	Bethel Church	100
Ahl	CARL	Ashland	1	Baker	NEWV	Newville	137
Ahl	NEWV	Big Spring Presbyterian	114	Baker	NEWV	Prospect Hill	149
Ahl	NEWV	Prospect Hill	149	Baker	PENN	Huntsdale Dunker	184
Albert	CARL	Ashland	1	Baker	WPEN	Heikes Farm	201
Albert	WPEN	Plainfield Bethel Church	205	Baldoser	FRAN	Lutheran Brick Church	46
Albright	MDSX	Carlisle Spring Church	81	Baldwin	PENN	Centerville Lutheran Church	171
Albright	MDSX	Letort Spring Church	90	Balsley	LALN	Eberly's Mills	74
Alexander	CARL	Ashland	1	Baltimore	NEWV	Newville	137
Alexander	FRAN	Lutheran Brick Church	46	Baltozer	FRAN	Lutheran Brick Church	46
Alexander	NEWV	Prospect Hill	149	Barley	FRAN	Lutheran & Ref. Stone Church	36
Allen	CARL	Ashland	1	Barley	NMID	Wagner's Church	166
Allen	FRAN	Lutheran Brick Church	46	Barnhill	MDSX	Carlisle Spring Church	81
Allen	MDSX	Letort Spring Church	90	Barnitz	CARL	Ashland	1
Allen	NEWV	Big Spring Presbyterian	114	Barr	HOPE	Hanna	60
Allen	NEWV	Prospect Hill	149	Barr	NEWV	Big Spring Presbyterian	14
Allen	NMID	Wagner's Church	166	Barrack	MIFF	Bethany Church	98
Allen	WPEN	Mt. Rock	203	Barrick	FRAN	Entlerville	34
Allin	NEWV	Newville	137	Barrick	FRAN	Lutheran Brick Church	46
Allman	MIFF	Zeigler's Church	107	Barrick	FRAN	Possum Hill Church	58
Alter	WPEN	Plainfield Bethel Church	205	Barrick	HOPE	Mt. Tabor Church	62
Anthony	FRAN	Lutheran Brick Church	46	Barrick	MIFF	Bethany Church	98
Arbegast	NEWV	Big Spring Presbyterian	114	Barrick	MIFF	Bethel Church	100
Arbegast	NEWV	Prospect Hill	149	Barrick	MIFF	Mt. Hope	105
Armagast	PENN	Centerville Lutheran Church	171	Barrick	NEWT	Irishtown Church	108
Armold	FRAN	Lutheran Brick Church	46	Barrick	NEWV	Prospect Hill	149
Armold	MIFF	Bethel Church	100	Barrick	NMID	Wagner's Church	166
Armolt	FRAN	Lutheran Brick Church	46	Barrick	WPEN	Plainfield Bethel Church	205
Armstrong	CARL	Ashland	1	Bartley	NEWV	Newville	137
Arnold	FRAN	Lutheran & Ref. Stone Church	36	Barto	NEWV	Prospect Hill	149
Ashenfelter	MDSX	Letort Spring Church	90	Barton	LALN	Lisburn	77
Askin	NEWV	Newville	137	Basehore	FRAN	Lutheran & Ref. Stone Church	36
Asper	MIFF	Zeigler's Church	107	Basehore	MDSX	Letort Spring Church	90
Atchison	WPEN	Plainfield Bethel Church	205	Bashore	MDSX	Letort Spring Church	90
Au	HOPE	Zion Reformed Church	68	Batrum	FRAN	Lutheran Brick Church	46
Auckarman	FRAN	Lutheran & Ref. Stone Church	36	Bauchman	MDSX	Carlisle Spring Church	81

Surname Index

Surname	Twsp.	Cemetery	Page	Surname	Twsp.	Cemetery	Page
Baugher	PENN	Centerville Lutheran Church	171	Berie	CARL	Ashland	2
Baughman	FRAN	Bloserville Ref. Church	33	Berkheimer	MDSX	Letort Spring Church	90
Baughman	FRAN	Lutheran & Ref. Stone Church	36	Berkley	DICK	Mt. Zion	27
Baughman	MDSX	Carlisle Spring Church	81	Berntheisle	MDSX	Carlisle Spring Church	81
Baum	NEWV	Prospect Hill	149	Berrier	NEWV	Prospect Hill	149
Beam	DICK	Mt. Zion	27	Berry	FRAN	Lutheran Brick Church	46
Beam	NEWV	Newville	137	Berry	WPEN	Plainfield Lutheran Church	209
Bear	CARL	Meeting House Springs	24	Bert	HOPE	Hoover Farm	62
Bear	MDSX	Dunker Church	88	Bet	NEWT	Old Roads	112
Bear	MIFF	Center Church	101	Biddle	CARL	Ashland	2
Bear	NEWV	Big Spring Presbyterian	114	Bierbrower	MDSX	Letort Spring Church	90
Bear	NEWV	Newville	137	Bigham	MDSX	Dunker Church	88
Bear	NEWV	Zion Lutheran Church	163	Bigham	NEWV	Newville	137
Bear	WPEN	Bear	194	Billman	FRAN	Lutheran Brick Church	46
Bear	WPEN	Heikes Farm	201	Binnen	NEWV	Big Spring Presbyterian	114
Bear	WPEN	Jonathan Bear Farm	202	Bird	CARL	Ashland	3
Bear	WPEN	Ker Farm	202	Bishop	NEWV	Newville	137
Bear	WPEN	Plainfield Bethel Church	205	Bishop	PENN	Centerville Lutheran Church	171
Bear	WPEN	Seitz Farm	213	Bishop	PENN	Hisner	183
Beaston	NEWT	Irishtown Church	108	Bistline	HOPE	Zion Reformed Church	68
Beatty	CARL	Ashland	1	Bistline	MDSX	Carlisle Spring Church	81
Beaty	HOPE	Hanna	60	Bistline	MIFF	Snokes Graveyard	106
Beaty	NEWV	United Presbyterian	160	Bitner	CARL	Ashland	3
Beecher	FRAN	Lutheran & Ref. Stone Church	36	Bitner	CARL	Ashland	8
Beecher	PENN	Centerville Lutheran Church	171	Bitner	HOPE	Newburg Church of God	63
Beecher	PENN	Huntsdale Dunker	184	Bitner	NEWT	Irishtown Church	108
Beetem	CARL	Ashland	1	Bitzer	PENN	Centerville Lutheran Church	171
Beetem	NEWV	Prospect Hill	149	Bixler	CARL	Ashland	3
Beetem	PENN	Centerville Lutheran Church	171	Bixler	FRAN	Lutheran Brick Church	46
Behrens	WPEN	Plainfield Lutheran Church	209	Bixler	WPEN	Plainfield Bethel Church	205
Beidler	CARL	Ashland	2	Black	CARL	Meeting House Springs	24
Beidler	FRAN	Lutheran & Ref. Stone Church	36	Black	DICK	Old Line	31
Beidler	WPEN	Plainfield Bethel Church	205	Black	LALN	Eberly's Mills	74
Beidler	WPEN	Plainfield Lutheran Church	209	Black	NEWV	Newville	137
Beinhower	FRAN	Gayman Farm	35	Black	PENN	Dickinson Presb. Church	178
Beisel	CARL	Ashland	2	Black	PENN	Huntsdale Dunker	184
Beistlein	FRAN	Lutheran & Ref. Stone Church	36	Black	WPEN	Mt. Rock	203
Bell	NEWV	Newville	137	Black	WPEN	Plainfield Bethel Church	205
Beltshoover	NEWV	Newville	137	Blair	CARL	Ashland	3
Beltzhoover	CARL	Ashland	2	Blair	NEWV	Big Spring Presbyterian	114
Beltzhoover	FRAN	Lutheran Brick Church	46	Blair	PENN	Centerville Lutheran Church	171
Bender	CARL	Ashland	2	Blaney	CARL	Ashland	3
Bender	FRAN	Lutheran & Ref. Stone Church	36	Bleakly	WPEN	Mt. Rock	203
Bender	NEWV	Prospect Hill	149	Blean	NEWV	Newville	137
Bender	PENN	Huntsdale Dunker	184	Blemler	DICK	Mt. Zion	27
Benner	FRAN	Lutheran Brick Church	46	Blessing	FRAN	Lutheran & Ref. Stone Church	36
Bents	NEWV	Newville	137	Bloser	FRAN	Lutheran Brick Church	46
Bentz	CARL	Ashland	2	Bloser	WPEN	Plainfield Bethel Church	205
Bergman	CARL	Ashland	2	Bloser	WPEN	Plainfield Lutheran Church	209
Bergner	CARL	Ashland	2	Blosser	MDSX	Letort Spring Church	90
Bergstresser	WPEN	Plainfield Lutheran Church	209	Blyler	PENN	Centerville Lutheran Church	171

Surname Index

Surname	Twsp.	Cemetery	Page	Surname	Twsp.	Cemetery	Page
Boas	MDSX	Letort Spring Church	90	Braught	MDSX	Carlisle Spring Church	81
Bobb	PENN	Huntsdale Dunker	184	Braught	MDSX	Letort Spring Church	90
Boblitz	HOPE	Newburg Church of God	63	Braught	NMID	Wagner's Church	166
Bohme	CARL	Ashland	3	Brechbill	HOPE	Newburg Church of God	63
Boldosser	FRAN	Lutheran Brick Church	47	Breckenmaker	MDSX	Letort Spring Church	90
Boldosser	NEWV	Prospect Hill	149	Brehm	FRAN	Entlerville	34
Bolen	MDSX	Letort Spring Church	90	Brehm	FRAN	Lutheran & Ref. Stone Church	36
Boll	FRAN	Lutheran Brick Church	47	Brehm	NEWV	Newville	138
Bonner	DICK	Mt. Zion	27	Brehm	WPEN	Plainfield Lutheran Church	209
Book	HOPE	Zion Reformed Church	68	Breneizer	MDSX	Carlisle Spring Church	81
Booth	CARL	Ashland	3	Brenneman	CARL	Ashland	3
Booth	HOPE	Newburg Church of God	63	Brenner	LALN	Eberly's Mills	74
Bosh	CARL	Ashland	3	Bretz	CARL	Ashland	3
Bosler	CARL	Ashland	3	Brewster	NEWT	Oakville United Brethren	111
Botdorf	PENN	Centerville Lutheran Church	171	Brewster	NEWV	Big Spring Presbyterian	115
Boughman	FRAN	Lutheran Brick Church	47	Bricker	FRAN	Lutheran Brick Church	47
Bower	FRAN	Lutheran Brick Church	47	Bricker	FRAN	Possum Hill Church	58
Bower	MIFF	Center Church	101	Bricker	HOPE	Newburg Church of God	63
Bower	NEWV	Newville	137	Bricker	LALN	Lisburn	77
Bower	NEWV	Prospect Hill	149	Bricker	MDSX	Letort Spring Church	90
Bower	NEWV	Zion Lutheran Church	163	Bricker	NEWV	Prospect Hill	150
Bowermaster	NEWV	Zion Lutheran Church	163	Bricker	NEWV	Zion Lutheran Church	163
Bowers	CARL	Ashland	3	Bricker	WPEN	Plainfield Bethel Church	206
Bowers	DICK	Mt. Zion	27	Brightbill	CARL	Ashland	3
Bowers	HOPE	Zion Reformed Church	68	Brill	CARL	Ashland	3
Bowers	MDSX	Letort Spring Church	90	Brim	FRAN	Lutheran Brick Church	47
Bowers	NEWT	Oakville United Brethren	111	Brim	WPEN	Diller Mennonite Church	195
Bowers	WPEN	Springfield	214	Brindle	CARL	Ashland	3
Bowman	CARL	Ashland	3	Brindle	MDSX	Carlisle Spring Church	81
Bowman	FRAN	Lutheran Brick Church	47	Brindle	PENN	Centerville Lutheran Church	171
Bowman	MIFF	Snokes Graveyard	106	Brindle	PENN	Huntsdale Dunker	184
Bowman	NEWV	Prospect Hill	149	Briner	NMID	Wagner's Church	166
Bowman	WPEN	Diller Mennonite Church	195	Brinn	PENN	Centerville Lutheran Church	171
Boyd	HOPE	Zion Reformed Church	68	Broce	NEWV	Newville	138
Boyd	NEWV	Big Spring Presbyterian	114	Brougher	CARL	Ashland	3
Boyd	NEWV	Prospect Hill	149	Brown	FRAN	Lutheran & Ref. Stone Church	36
Boyles	NEWV	Big Spring Presbyterian	115	Brown	MDSX	Carlisle Spring Church	81
Boyles	NEWV	Newville	137	Brown	NEWV	Big Spring Presbyterian	115
Bracken	NEWV	Big Spring Presbyterian	115	Brown	NEWV	Newville	138
Brahm	NEWV	Newville	138	Brown	PENN	Dickinson Presb. Church	178
Brandon	NEWV	Big Spring Presbyterian	115	Brown	WPEN	Bear	194
Brandt	NEWT	Oakville United Brethren	111	Brown	WPEN	Plainfield Lutheran Church	209
Brandt	NEWV	Prospect Hill	150	Brownawell	MDSX	Carlisle Spring Church	81
Brandt	PENN	Dickinson Presb. Church	178	Brownfelter	LALN	Eberly's Mills	74
Brandt	PENN	Huntsdale Dunker	184	Brownsbarger	FRAN	Lutheran Brick Church	47
Brandt	WPEN	Springfield	214	Brubaker	CARL	Ashland	3
Brannan	NEWV	Big Spring Presbyterian	115	Brymesser	FRAN	Lutheran & Ref. Stone Church	36
Brattan	NEWV	Big Spring Presbyterian	115	Bryson	NEWV	Big Spring Presbyterian	115
Brattan	NEWV	Newville	138	Bubb	LALN	Eberly's Mills	74
Bratton	CARL	Ashland	3	Buchanan	NEWV	Big Spring Presbyterian	116
Braught	FRAN	Lutheran & Ref. Stone Church	36	Buchwalter	WPEN	Diller Mennonite Church	195

Surname Index

Surname	Twsp.	Cemetery	Page	Surname	Twsp.	Cemetery	Page
Burkholder	CARL	Ashland	4	Cathcart	CARL	Ashland	4
Burkholder	FRAN	Lutheran Brick Church	48	Chambers	CARL	Meeting House Springs	24
Burkholder	WPEN	Diller Mennonite Church	196	Chambers	NEWV	Prospect Hill	150
Burkholder	WPEN	Springfield	214	Chandler	MDSX	Carlisle Spring Church	82
Burns	NEWV	Prospect Hill	150	Chapman	LALN	Eberly's Mills	74
Burtnett	FRAN	Lutheran Brick Church	48	Charlton	HOPE	Newburg Church of God	63
Bush	WPEN	Springfield	214	Chesnell	PENN	Centerville Lutheran Church	171
Bushman	CARL	Ashland	4	Chestnut	NEWV	Big Spring Presbyterian	116
Bushman	PENN	Centerville Lutheran Church	171	Cheston	CARL	Ashland	4
Butler	CARL	Ashland	4	Chism	NEWV	United Presbyterian Church	160
Butler	NEWV	Big Spring Presbyterian	116	Chisnell	NEWV	Newville	138
Butler	NEWV	Newville	138	Chisnell	PENN	Centerville Lutheran Church	171
Buttort	MDSX	Carlisle Spring Church	82	Chisolm	NEWV	Prospect Hill	150
Buttorf	MDSX	Letort Spring Church	90	Chorpenning	MDSX	Carlisle Spring Church	82
Byers	HOPE	Stouffer Farm	67	Christlieb	MDSX	Carlisle Spring Church	82
Byers	LALN	Lisburn	77	Christlieb	MIFF	Bethany Church	98
Byers	NEWV	Big Spring Presbyterian	116	Christlieb	MIFF	Zeigler's Church	107
Byers	NEWV	Prospect Hill	150	Christlieb	NEWV	Prospect Hill	150
Cain	LALN	Lisburn	77	Chronister	FRAN	Bloserville Ref. Church	33
Caldwell	PENN	Dickinson Presb. Church	178	Chronister	HOPE	Hoover Farm	62
Calvert	WPEN	Plainfield Lutheran Church	209	Chronister	PENN	Huntsdale Dunker	184
Cameron	CARL	Ashland	4	Chronister	SMID	Mt. Victory	170
Camp	DICK	Mt. Zion	27	Clandy	NEWV	Newville	138
Campbell	CARL	Ashland	4	Clandy	PENN	Centerville Lutheran Church	171
Campbell	NEWV	Big Spring Presbyterian	116	Clay	FRAN	Lutheran & Ref. Stone Church	36
Campbell	WPEN	Diller Mennonite Church	197	Clay	FRAN	Possum Hill Church	58
Carbaugh	FRAN	Lutheran Brick Church	48	Clay	WPEN	Plainfield Bethel Church	206
Carbaugh	HOPE	Zion Reformed Church	68	Clay	WPEN	Plainfield Lutheran Church	209
Carbaugh	NMID	Wagner's Church	166	Clendenin	MDSX	Carlisle Spring Church	82
Carl	FRAN	Lutheran Brick Church	48	Clinepeter	MIFF	Bethany Church	98
Carl	NEWV	Prospect Hill	150	Clippinger	HOPE	Newburg Church of God	63
Carl	PENN	Dickinson Presb. Church	178	Clody	NEWT	Irishtown Church	108
Carl	WPEN	Plainfield Bethel Church	206	Clouse	FRAN	Lutheran Brick Church	48
Carmany	PENN	Centerville Lutheran Church	171	Clouse	MIFF	Center Church	101
Carmichael	MDSX	Dunker Church	88	Clouse	NEWV	Zion Lutheran Church	163
Carmony	HOPE	Newburg Church of God	63	Clouser	MDSX	Carlisle Spring Church	82
Carnahan	NEWV	Big Spring Presbyterian	116	Cobean	NEWV	Big Spring Presbyterian	116
Carothers	CARL	Meeting House Springs	24	Coble	CARL	Ashland	4
Carothers	DICK	Old Line	31	Cockley	PENN	Huntsdale Dunker	184
Carothers	MIFF	Bethany Church	98	Coffey	PENN	Dickinson Presb. Church	178
Carothers	NEWV	Prospect Hill	150	Cohic	MIFF	Center Church	101
Carothers	PENN	Dickinson Presb. Church	178	Cohick	MIFF	Center Church	101
Carothers	WPEN	Mt. Rock	203	Cole	NEWV	Newville	138
Carr	CARL	Ashland	4	Coleman	MDSX	Carlisle Spring Church	82
Carson	HOPE	Zion Reformed Church	68	Coleman	MDSX	Letort Spring Church	91
Carson	NEWV	Big Spring Presbyterian	116	Coleman	NEWV	Newville	138
Cart	CARL	Ashland	4	Collins	CARL	Ashland	4
Carter	NEWV	Big Spring Presbyterian	116	Collins	MDSX	Letort Spring Church	91
Casey	MDSX	Carlisle Spring Church	82	Comrey	FRAN	Lutheran Brick Church	48
Cash	PENN	Huntsdale Dunker	184	Condon	CARL	Ashland	4
Cashman	PENN	Centerville Lutheran Church	171	Connelly	CARL	Meeting House Springs	24

Surname Index

Surname	Twsp.	Cemetery	Page	Surname	Twsp.	Cemetery	Page
Conner	FRAN	Lutheran & Ref. Stone Church	36	Criswell	MDSX	Carlisle Spring Church	83
Conner	HOPE	Zion Reformed Church	68	Crocket	CARL	Meeting House Springs	24
Conner	MIFF	Bethany Church	98	Crotzer	MDSX	Letort Spring Church	91
Conner	NEWT	Irishtown Church	108	Crouse	CARL	Ashland	4
Conner	NEWT	Old Roads	112	Crout	WPEN	Plainfield Bethel Church	206
Conrad	DICK	Mt. Zion	27	Crozier	CARL	Ashland	4
Cook	NEWV	Big Spring Presbyterian	116	Crozier	WPEN	Mt. Rock	203
Cooper	HOPE	Hanna	60	Cully	PENN	Centerville Lutheran Church	172
Cooper	NEWV	Prospect Hill	150	Culver	CARL	Ashland	4
Cooper	WPEN	Mt. Rock	203	Cummins	PENN	Dickinson Presb. Church	178
Cooper	WPEN	Springfield	214	Curtis	MDSX	Dunker Church	88
Coover	HOPE	Newburg Church of God	63	Daelhousen	MIFF	Center Church	101
Coover	PENN	Centerville Lutheran Church	171	Daelhousen	WPEN	Diller Mennonite Church	197
Coover	PENN	Huntsdale Dunker	184	Dale	CARL	Ashland	4
Cope	NEWT	Stoughstown Lutheran Church	113	Dales	NEWV	Newville	138
Cope	NEWV	Newville	138	Damuth	PENN	Huntsdale Dunker	184
Corbett	CARL	Ashland	4	Danner	CARL	Ashland	5
Corbett	DICK	Mt. Zion	27	Danner	WPEN	Mt. Rock	203
Cornman	CARL	Ashland	4	Danner	WPEN	Plainfield Bethel Church	206
Cornman	FRAN	Lutheran & Ref. Stone Church	36	Danz	PENN	Huntsdale Dunker	184
Cornman	FRAN	Lutheran Brick Church	48	Dar	FRAN	Lutheran & Ref. Stone Church	37
Cornman	MDSX	Carlisle Spring Church	82	Dare	CARL	Ashland	5
Cornman	MDSX	Letort Spring Church	91	Dare	FRAN	Lutheran Brick Church	48
Cornman	WPEN	Plainfield Lutheran Church	209	Darr	LALN	Eberly's Mills	74
Cornog	NEWV	Big Spring Presbyterian	116	Darr	CARL	Ashland	5
Cornprobst	MDSX	Peter Albright Farm	97	Darr	FRAN	Lutheran Brick Church	48
Cornprobst	NEWV	Newville	138	Darr	MDSX	Carlisle Spring Church	83
Coulson	SMID	Mt. Victory	170	Darr	MDSX	Letort Spring Church	91
Coulter	CARL	Meeting House Springs	24	Darr	WPEN	Diller Mennonite Church	197
Cox	NEWV	Big Spring Presbyterian	116	Darron	WPEN	Diller Mennonite Church	197
Coyle	CARL	Ashland	4	Daugherty	NEWV	Big Spring Presbyterian	116
Coyle	NEWV	Big Spring Presbyterian	116	Davidson	CARL	Ashland	5
Craig	NEWV	Newville	138	Davidson	NEWV	Big Spring Presbyterian	116
Craig	NEWV	United Presbyterian	160	Davidson	NEWV	Newville	138
Craighead	CARL	Ashland	4	Davidson	NEWV	Prospect Hill	150
Cramer	LALN	Monroe Woods Farm	80	Davidson	NEWV	Zion Lutheran Church	163
Cramer	MDSX	Carlisle Spring Church	82	Davidson	WPEN	Plainfield Lutheran Church	209
Cramer	MDSX	Letort Spring Church	91	Davis	DICK	Mt. Zion	27
Crammer	MDSX	Carlisle Spring Church	82	Davis	LALN	Eberly's Mills	74
Crane	CARL	Ashland	4	Davis	SMID	Flint Ridge Chapel	169
Cratzer	NEWV	Big Spring Presbyterian	116	Davor	HOPE	Newburg Church of God	63
Crawford	NEWV	Big Spring Presbyterian	116	Day	DICK	Mt. Zion	27
Creamer	HOPE	Newburg Church of God	63	Deardorf	MIFF	Bethany Church	98
Creamer	PENN	Centerville Lutheran Church	172	Deckard	NEWV	Big Spring Presbyterian	117
Creglow	PENN	Centerville Lutheran Church	172	Deem	PENN	Centerville Lutheran Church	172
Cremer	NEWV	Big Spring Presbyterian	116	DeHaven	NEWV	Prospect Hill	150
Crider	NEWT	Oakville United Brethren	111	Deihl	FRAN	Lutheran Brick Church	48
Crider	WPEN	Mt. Rock	203	Deitch	FRAN	Lutheran & Ref. Stone Church	37
Crider	WPEN	Springfield	214	Deitch	MDSX	Letort Spring Church	91
Crim	PENN	Huntsdale Dunker	184	Deitch	WPEN	Plainfield Bethel Church	206
Crist	LALN	Eberly's Mills	74	Deitzel	PENN	Huntsdale Dunker	185

Surname Index

Surname	Twsp.	Cemetery	Page	Surname	Twsp.	Cemetery	Page
Delancey	CARL	Ashland	5	Diven	CARL	Ashland	5
Delancy	NEWV	Newville	139	Diven	NEWT	Irishtown Church	108
Dell	FRAN	Lutheran Brick Church	48	Dixon	CARL	Ashland	5
Dellinger	PENN	Huntsdale Dunker	185	Dobbs	NEWV	Newville	139
Delp	DICK	Mt. Zion	27	Dobson	CARL	Ashland	5
Demuth	PENN	Huntsdale Dunker	185	Dock	NEWV	Prospect Hill	151
Denning	NEWV	Big Spring Presbyterian	117	Donaldson	PENN	Dickinson Presb. Church	178
Denny	CARL	Meeting House Springs	24	Doner	FRAN	Gayman Farm	35
Derland	CARL	Ashland	5	Doner	FRAN	Lutheran Brick Church	48
Derr	CARL	Ashland	5	Doner	WPEN	Heikes Farm	201
Derr	FRAN	Bloserville Ref. Church	33	Doner	WPEN	Plainfield Bethel Church	206
Derr	FRAN	Lutheran Brick Church	48	Doner	WPEN	Plainfield Lutheran Church	209
Derr	NEWV	Prospect Hill	150	Donnelly	MDSX	Carlisle Spring Church	83
Derr	WPEN	Diller Mennonite Church	197	Donor	PENN	Centerville Lutheran Church	172
Derrick	NEWV	Newville	139	Dorron	WPEN	Diller Mennonite Church	197
Desanno	WPEN	Bear	194	Dovenar	NEWT	Irishtown Church	108
Devor	HOPE	Newburg Church of God	63	Dougherty	NEWV	Big Spring Presbyterian	118
Dewalt	CARL	Ashland	5	Drawbaugh	FRAN	Lutheran & Ref. Stone Church	37
Dewalt	FRAN	Entlerville	34	Drawbaugh	FRAN	Lutheran Brick Church	48
Dewalt	MDSX	Dunker Church	88	Drawbaugh	LALN	Eberly's Mills	74
Dewalt	MDSX	Letort Spring Church	91	Drennan	CARL	Meeting House Springs	24
Dewalt	MIFF	Center Church	101	Drewart	HOPE	Zion Reformed Church	68
Dewalt	NMID	Bethel Church	165	Drewett	HOPE	Zion Reformed Church	68
Dewalt	NMID	Wagner's Church	166	Driver	HOPE	Zion Reformed Church	68
Dey	LALN	Eberly's Mills	74	Drorbaugh	LALN	Lisburn	77
Dice	MDSX	Dunker Church	88	Duck	NEWV	Prospect Hill	151
Dick	NMID	Bethel Church	165	Duey	MDSX	Carlisle Spring Church	83
Dickson	MIFF	Bethany Church	98	Duey	NEWV	Big Spring Presbyterian	118
Diehl	CARL	Ashland	5	Duey	NMID	Wagner's Church	166
Diehl	HOPE	Hanna	60	Duey	WPEN	Plainfield Bethel Church	206
Diehl	HOPE	Newburg Church of God	63	Duffey	NEWV	Prospect Hill	151
Diehl	HOPE	Zion Reformed Church	68	Dull	MDSX	Letort Spring Church	91
Diehl	MIFF	Ziegler's Church	107	Dull	MIFF	Center Church	101
Diehl	NEWV	Newville	139	Dumma	FRAN	Lutheran & Ref. Stone Church	37
Diehner	FRAN	Lutheran & Ref. Stone Church	37	Dunbar	FRAN	Entlerville	34
Diel	FRAN	Lutheran Brick Church	48	Dunbar	MIFF	Bethel Church	100
Diel	MIFF	Ziegler's Church	107	Dunbar	NEWV	Big Spring Presbyterian	118
Diener	FRAN	Lutheran & Ref. Stone Church	37	Duncan	NEWV	Big Spring Presbyterian	118
Diener	NEWV	Big Spring Presbyterian	117	Dunfee	NEWV	Big Spring Presbyterian	118
Dill	FRAN	Lutheran Brick Church	48	Dunkle	CARL	Ashland	5
Dill	WPEN	Plainfield Bethel Church	206	Dunkleberger	NEWV	Prospect Hill	151
Diller	FRAN	Possum Hill Church	58	Dunlap	HOPE	Zion Reformed Church	68
Diller	HOPE	Zion Reformed Church	68	Dunlap	LALN	Lisburn	77
Diller	MDSX	Carlisle Spring Church	83	Dunlap	MIFF	Bethany Church	98
Diller	NEWV	Big Spring Presbyterian	117	Dunlap	MIFF	Ziegler's Church	107
Diller	NMID	Wagner's Church	166	Dunlap	NEWV	Big Spring Presbyterian	118
Diller	WPEN	Bear	194	Dunlap	NEWV	Newville	139
Diller	WPEN	Diller Mennonite Church	197	Dunlap	NEWV	Prospect Hill	151
Diller	WPEN	Heikes Farm	201	Dunlap	NMID	Wagner's Church	166
Dinkle	CARL	Ashland	5	Earley	CARL	Ashland	5
Dinnar	NEWV	Zion Lutheran Church	163	Earnest	FRAN	Gayman Farm	35

Surname Index

Surname	Twsp.	Cemetery	Page	Surname	Twsp.	Cemetery	Page
Earnest	NMID	Wagner's Church	166	Erskine	NEWV	Big Spring Presbyterian	118
Eberly	PENN	Huntsdale Dunker	185	Etter	HOPE	Zion Reformed Church	69
Eberly	WPEN	Bear	194	Etter	PENN	Dickinson Presb. Church	178
Ebersole	MDSX	Letort Spring Church	91	Etter	PENN	Huntsdale Dunker	185
Eberts	FRAN	Lutheran & Ref. Stone Church	37	Evans	CARL	Ashland	6
Eberts	PENN	Centerville Lutheran Church	172	Evans	PENN	Huntsdale Dunker	185
Ebrite	FRAN	Lutheran Brick Church	49	Evarts	CARL	Ashland	6
Eckart	FRAN	Lutheran Brick Church	49	Evelhock	NEWV	Prospect Hill	151
Eckels	CARL	Ashland	5	Evig	MIFF	Bethany Church	98
Eckels	PENN	Dickinson Presb. Church	178	Ewing	CARL	Ashland	6
Ecker	PENN	Huntsdale Dunker	185	Ewing	NEWV	Big Spring Presbyterian	118
Eckert	FRAN	Lutheran Brick Church	49	Ewing	PENN	Dickinson Presb. Church	178
Eckert	PENN	Centerville Lutheran Church	172	Faber	CARL	Ashland	6
Eckert	PENN	Huntsdale Dunker	185	Fagan	PENN	Huntsdale Dunker	185
Eckles	CARL	Ashland	5	Fahler	FRAN	Lutheran Brick Church	49
Eckman	NEWT	Oakville United Brethren	111	Fahnestock	MIFF	Bethel Church	100
Eckman	NEWV	Prospect Hill	151	Fahnestock	NEWV	Prospect Hill	151
Edmonds	CARL	Ashland	5	Failer	FRAN	Lutheran & Ref. Stone Church	37
Edmondson	LALN	Lisburn	77	Failor	CARL	Ashland	6
Egbert	CARL	Ashland	5	Failor	FRAN	Lutheran & Ref. Stone Church	37
Ege	NEWV	Big Spring Presbyterian	118	Failor	FRAN	Lutheran Brick Church	49
Ege	PENN	Dickinson Presb. Church	178	Failor	HOPE	Zion Reformed Church	69
Eichelberger	HOPE	Zion Reformed Church	68	Failor	MIFF	Zeigler's Church	107
Eichelberger	NEWV	Newville	139	Failor	NEWT	Irishtown Church	108
Eichelberger	UALN	Lantz's School House	193	Failor	NEWV	Newville	139
Eisenhower	CARL	Ashland	5	Fair	MDSX	Dunker Church	88
Eisenhower	HOPE	Newburg Church of God	63	Fair	WPEN	Plainfield Bethel Church	206
Eisenhower	NEWV	Prospect Hill	151	Fanus	DICK	Mt. Zion	27
Elicker	FRAN	Lutheran Brick Church	49	Farenbaugh	MDSX	Letort Spring Church	91
Elliott	CARL	Ashland	5	Farner	NEWT	Stoughstown Lutheran Church	113
Elliott	HOPE	Hanna	60	Farner	WPEN	Springfield	214
Elliott	HOPE	Newburg Church of God	63	Faughender	HOPE	Hanna	60
Elliott	NEWV	Big Spring Presbyterian	118	Faust	NEWV	Prospect Hill	151
Elliott	NEWV	Newville	139	Faust	PENN	Centerville Lutheran Church	172
Elliott	NEWV	Prospect Hill	151	Feister	MDSX	Carlisle Spring Church	83
Emerich	NEWV	Prospect Hill	151	Felgner	MDSX	Letort Spring Church	91
Emmerich	WPEN	Diller Mennonite Church	197	Felix	NEWV	Newville	139
Ensminger	FRAN	Bloserville Ref. Church	33	Fellman	CARL	Ashland	6
Ensminger	FRAN	Lutheran Brick Church	49	Fenner	DICK	Mt. Zion	27
Ensminger	MIFF	Center Church	101	Fennicle	CARL	Ashland	6
Eppley	CARL	Ashland	6	Fenton	FRAN	Lutheran Brick Church	49
Eppley	MDSX	Letort Spring Church	91	Fenton	NEWV	Big Spring Presbyterian	118
Eppley	WPEN	Plainfield Bethel Church	206	Fenton	NEWV	Newville	139
Erford	FRAN	Lutheran & Ref. Stone Church	37	Ferguson	NEWV	Big Spring Presbyterian	118
Erford	WPEN	Diller Mennonite Church	197	Ferguson	PENN	Dickinson Presb. Church	179
Ernest	CARL	Ashland	6	Ferguson	WPEN	Mt. Rock	203
Ernest	FRAN	Lutheran & Ref. Stone Church	37	Feris	FRAN	Entlerville	34
Ernst	FRAN	Lutheran & Ref. Stone Church	37	Ferree	DICK	Old Line	31
Ernst	FRAN	Lutheran Brick Church	49	Ferree	NEWV	Newville	140
Ernst	NEWV	Prospect Hill	151	Ferris	FRAN	Entlerville	34
Ernst	PENN	Huntsdale Dunker	185	Fetzer	MDSX	Carlisle Spring Church	83

Surname Index

Surname	Twsp.	Cemetery	Page	Surname	Twsp.	Cemetery	Page
Fickes	CARL	Ashland	6	Fought	MDSX	Letort Spring Church	91
Fickes	FRAN	Lutheran Brick Church	49	Foust	PENN	Huntsdale Dunker	185
Fickes	HOPE	Newburg Church of God	64	Foust	WPEN	Springfield	214
Fickes	NEWV	Big Spring Presbyterian	118	Fralich	FRAN	Lutheran & Ref. Stone Church	37
Fickes	NEWV	Newville	140	Franklin	HOPE	Newburg Church of God	64
Fickes	PENN	Centerville Lutheran Church	172	Franklin	MDSX	Letort Spring Church	91
Fickes	PENN	Dickinson Presb. Church	179	Frants	PENN	Centerville Lutheran Church	172
Fields	HOPE	Newburg Church of God	64	Frantz	PENN	Huntsdale Dunker	185
Fields	NEWV	Big Spring Presbyterian	118	Frederick	CARL	Ashland	7
Fiester	MDSX	Carlisle Spring Church	83	Frederick	WPEN	Plainfield Lutheran Church	209
Finkenbinder	FRAN	Lutheran & Ref. Stone Church	37	Freeland	CARL	Ashland	7
Finkenbinder	FRAN	Lutheran Brick Church	49	Freet	FRAN	Bloserville Ref. Church	33
Finkenbinder	FRAN	Possum Hill Church	58	Freet	FRAN	Lutheran Brick Church	50
Finkenbinder	HOPE	Newburg Church of God	64	French	NEWV	United Presbyterian	160
Finkenbinder	MIFF	Center Church	101	Frost	DICK	Mt. Zion	27
Finkenbinder	NEWT	Irishtown Church	108	Frost	SMID	Flint Ridge Chapel	169
Finkenbinder	NEWV	Newville	140	Frownfelter	LALN	Eberly's Mills	74
Finkenbinder	NEWV	Prospect Hill	151	Frownfelter	NEWV	Big Spring Presbyterian	118
Finkenbinder	NEWV	Zion Lutheran Church	163	Frownfelter	PENN	Dickinson Presb. Church	179
Finkenbinder	WPEN	Plainfield Lutheran Church	209	Frownfelter	WPEN	Springfield	214
Finkenbinder	WPEN	Springfield	214	Fry	FRAN	Lutheran Brick Church	50
Finkey	PENN	Huntsdale Dunker	185	Fry	MIFF	Bethel Church	100
Finney	LALN	Lisburn	77	Fry	MIFF	Center Church	101
Firestine	MDSX	Letort Spring Church	91	Fry	NEWV	Big Spring Presbyterian	119
Fishburn	CARL	Ashland	6	Fry	NEWV	Newville	140
Fishburn	NEWV	Prospect Hill	151	Fry	NMID	Bethel Church	165
Fishburn	WPEN	Francis Bear Farm	200	Fry	WPEN	Plainfield Lutheran Church	209
Fisher	HOPE	Newburg Church of God	64	Frymier	NEWV	Prospect Hill	151
Fisher	PENN	Centerville Lutheran Church	172	Fuget	MDSX	Letort Spring Church	91
Fissel	CARL	Ashland	7	Fuget	WPEN	Plainfield Lutheran Church	210
Fissel	DICK	Mt. Zion	27	Fultin	NEWV	Big Spring Presbyterian	119
Fleager	CARL	Ashland	7	Fulton	NEWV	Big Spring Presbyterian	119
Fleming	CARL	Meeting House Springs	24	Funk	FRAN	Lutheran Brick Church	50
Flickinger	NEWT	Old Roads	112	Funk	NEWV	Prospect Hill	151
Floyd	DICK	Mt. Zion	27	Funk		Oyster's Point	216
Foose	MIFF	Bethel Church	100	Furman	NEWV	Big Spring Presbyterian	119
Forbes	CARL	Meeting House Springs	24	Furst	PENN	Huntsdale Dunker	185
Forbes	PENN	Dickinson Presb. Church	179	Fyler	HOPE	Newburg Church of God	64
Ford	HOPE	Newburg Church of God	64	Fyler	HOPE	Zion Reformed Church	69
Ford	PENN	Centerville Lutheran Church	172	Galbraith	CARL	Ashland	7
Forehope	HOPE	Newburg Church of God	64	Galbraith	PENN	Dickinson Presb. Church	179
Forehope	NEWT	Irishtown Church	108	Galbraith	WPEN	Mt. Rock	203
Foreman	CARL	Ashland	7	Galbreath	NEWV	Big Spring Presbyterian	119
Forney	NEWT	Oakville United Brethren	111	Gamber	HOPE	Newburg Church of God	64
Fortenbaugh	MDSX	Letort Spring Church	91	Gamber	NEWV	Prospect Hill	151
Fosnaught	NEWT	Irishtown Church	108	Garber	CARL	Ashland	7
Fosnaught	NEWV	Prospect Hill	151	Garber	MDSX	Letort Spring Church	91
Fosnot	NEWT	Irishtown Church	108	Garber	NEWV	Newville	140
Fosnot	NEWV	Newville	140	Garber	SMID	Garber	169
Fosnot	NEWV	Prospect Hill	151	Garber	PENN	Huntsdale Dunker	185
Foster	PENN	Dickinson Presb. Church	179	Gardner	LALN	Eberly's Mills	74

Surname Index

Surname	Twsp.	Cemetery	Page	Surname	Twsp.	Cemetery	Page
Gardner	CARL	Ashland	7	Gill	WPEN	Bear	194
Gardner	NEWT	Irishtown Church	108	Gillelen	NEWV	Big Spring Presbyterian	119
Gardner	SMID	Mt. Victory	170	Gillen	LALN	Eberly's Mills	74
Garland	FRAN	Lutheran & Ref. Stone Church	37	Gillespie	NEWV	Big Spring Presbyterian	119
Garland	MDSX	Carlisle Spring Church	83	Gillough	FRAN	Lutheran & Ref. Stone Church	37
Garman	FRAN	Lutheran & Ref. Stone Church	37	Gilmor	NEWV	Zion Lutheran Church	163
Garman	HOPE	Zion Reformed Church	69	Gilmore	MIFF	Bethany Church	98
Garman	MDSX	Carlisle Spring Church	83	Gilmore	MIFF	Zeigler's Church	107
Garman	WPEN	Plainfield Bethel Church	206	Gilmore	NEWV	Newville	140
Garver	MDSX	Carlisle Spring Church	83	Gilmore	NEWV	Prospect Hill	152
Gayman	FRAN	Gayman Farm	35	Gingrich	MDSX	Mennonite Grvyd.--Balfour	97
Gayman	FRAN	Lutheran Brick Church	50	Ginter	CARL	Ashland	8
Gayman	MIFF	Center Church	101	Ginter	NEWV	Prospect Hill	152
Gayman	NEWV	Newville	140	Gipe	WPEN	Springfield	214
Gebhart	CARL	Ashland	8	Giveler	MIFF	Zeigler's Church	107
Gebhart	FRAN	Lutheran Brick Church	50	Given	CARL	Ashland	8
Gebhart	HOPE	Zion Reformed Church	69	Givler	CARL	Ashland	8
Gebhart	NEWV	Big Spring Presbyterian	119	Givler	DICK	Old Line	31
Gebhart	WPEN	Plainfield Lutheran Church	210	Givler	FRAN	Lutheran Brick Church	50
Geddes	NEWV	Big Spring Presbyterian	119	Givler	PENN	Centerville Lutheran Church	172
Gees	MIFF	Center Church	101	Givler	WPEN	Bear	194
Geese	HOPE	Zion Reformed Church	69	Givler	WPEN	Jonathan Bear Farm	202
Geese	NEWV	Big Spring Presbyterian	119	Givler	WPEN	Plainfield Bethel Church	207
Geiling	MDSX	Carlisle Spring Church	83	Gladfelter	MDSX	Letort Spring Church	91
Gelbaugh	PENN	Huntsdale Dunker	186	Glass	SMID	Flint Ridge Chapel	169
Gelvin	NEWT	Oakville United Brethren	111	Glauser	NEWV	Big Spring Presbyterian	119
Gelwicks	HOPE	Zion Reformed Church	69	Glauser	NEWV	Newville	140
Gensler	CARL	Ashland	8	Glenn	CARL	Ashland	8
Gensler	FRAN	Bloserville Ref. Church	33	Glenn	NEWV	Big Spring Presbyterian	119
Gensler	FRAN	Entlerville	34	Gochenauer	HOPE	Zion Reformed Church	69
George	NEWV	Big Spring Presbyterian	119	Gonter	LALN	Eberly's Mills	74
Geremyer	CARL	Ashland	8	Good	CARL	Ashland	8
Getter	NEWT	Irishtown Church	108	Good	LALN	Eberly's Mills	74
Getter	NEWV	Newville	140	Goodhart	NEWT	Stoughstown Lutheran Church	113
Getter	NEWV	Prospect Hill	152	Goodhart	NEWV	Newville	140
Getter	WPEN	Plainfield Bethel Church	206	Goodhart	PENN	Centerville Lutheran Church	172
Gettys	FRAN	Lutheran Brick Church	50	Goodhart	PENN	Dickinson Presb. Church	179
Gettys	NEWV	Big Spring Presbyterian	119	Goodhart	PENN	Hisner	183
Gher	LALN	Lisburn	77	Goodlink	NEWV	Newville	140
Gher	LALN	Monroe Woods Farm	80	Goodrich	CARL	Ashland	8
Gibble	PENN	Huntsdale Dunker	186	Goodyear	CARL	Ashland	8
Gibson	CARL	Ashland	8	Goodyear	PENN	Huntsdale Dunker	186
Gilbert	FRAN	Lutheran & Ref. Stone Church	37	Gootschall	MDSX	Carlisle Spring Church	83
Gilbert	HOPE	Newburg Church of God	64	Gottschall	MIFF	Bethel Church	100
Gilbert	HOPE	Zion Reformed Church	69	Gould	CARL	Ashland	8
Gilbert	NEWT	Irishtown Church	108	Gracey	NEWV	Newville	140
Gilbert	PENN	Centerville Lutheran Church	172	Gracey	NEWT	United Presbyterian	160
Gill	CARL	Ashland	8	Graham	CARL	Ashland	8
Gill	MDSX	Letort Spring Church	91	Graham	CARL	Meeting House Springs	24
Gill	NEWV	Newville	140	Graham	FRAN	Lutheran Brick Church	50
Gill	NEWV	Prospect Hill	152	Graham	NEWV	Big Spring Presbyterian	119

Surname Index

Surname	Twsp.	Cemetery	Page	Surname	Twsp.	Cemetery	Page
Graton	FRAN	Lutheran & Ref. Stone Church	37	Gutshall	MIFF	Center Church	102
Greagor	NEWV	Prospect Hill	152	Gutshall	NEWV	Big Spring Presbyterian	120
Greason	CARL	Ashland	8	Haas	MDSX	Carlisle Spring Church	83
Greason	CARL	Meeting House Springs	24	Hach	MDSX	Letort Spring Church	92
Greason	DICK	Old Line	31	Hackenberger	MDSX	Letort Spring Church	92
Greason	WPEN	Graveyard on Hill	200	Hackenberry	CARL	Ashland	9
Greason	WPEN	Heikes Farm	201	Hackett	NEWV	Big Spring Presbyterian	120
Greason	WPEN	Plainfield Lutheran Church	210	Haddock	CARL	Ashland	9
Greaver	NEWV	Newville	140	Hagey	HOPE	Zion Reformed Church	69
Greeger	MIFF	Center Church	101	Haines	LALN	Eberly's Mills	74
Green	FRAN	Lutheran Brick Church	50	Haines	FRAN	Lutheran Brick Church	50
Green	MDSX	Letort Spring Church	91	Haines	WPEN	Bear	194
Green	NEWV	Big Spring Presbyterian	120	Hains	LALN	Eberly's Mills	74
Green	NEWV	Prospect Hill	152	Haldeman	NEWV	Zion Lutheran Church	163
Green	PENN	Dickinson Presb. Church	179	Hale	FRAN	Lutheran Brick Church	51
Green	WPEN	Plainfield Bethel Church	207	Hale	NEWV	Zion Lutheran Church	163
Greenabaum	DICK	Mt. Zion	28	Hall	FRAN	Lutheran & Ref. Stone Church	37
Greenawalt	LALN	Eberly's Mills	74	Hall	LALN	Lisburn	77
Greenfield	CARL	Ashland	9	Hall	MDSX	Carlisle Spring Church	84
Greider	FRAN	Lutheran Brick Church	50	Hall	PENN	Centerville Lutheran Church	172
Greider	NMID	Wagner's Church	166	Hall	WPEN	Plainfield Bethel Church	207
Greider	WPEN	Heikes Farm	201	Hamaker	NEWV	Prospect Hill	152
Greider	WPEN	Plainfield Bethel Church	207	Hambright	LALN	Eberly's Mills	74
Greybill	MDSX	Letort Spring Church	91	Hamill	NEWV	Big Spring Presbyterian	120
Grier	CARL	Ashland	9	Hamilton	MIFF	Center Church	102
Griffee	DICK	Mt. Zion	28	Hamilton	WPEN	Springfield	214
Griffie	WPEN	Plainfield Lutheran Church	210	Hamman	CARL	Ashland	9
Griffin	NEWV	Prospect Hill	152	Hammer	NEWV	Prospect Hill	152
Gring	WPEN	Diller Mennonite Church	197	Hamsher	HOPE	Newburg Church of God	64
Grissinger	CARL	Ashland	9	Hance	PENN	Dickinson Presb. Church	179
Grissinger	FRAN	Lutheran & Ref. Stone Church	37	Handshew	NEWV	Prospect Hill	152
Gross	HOPE	Newburg Church of God	64	Hanna	HOPE	Hanna	60
Gross	HOPE	Zion Reformed Church	69	Hanna	NEWV	Big Spring Presbyterian	120
Gross	NEWV	Newville	140	Hannon	NEWV	United Presbyterian	160
Gross	NEWV	Prospect Hill	152	Hanshaw	MDSX	Letort Spring Church	92
Grosz	MDSX	Mennonite Grvyd.--Balfour	97	Harbold	PENN	Huntsdale Dunker	186
Grove	CARL	Ashland	9	Hard	NEWV	Big Spring Presbyterian	120
Grove	LALN	Lisburn	77	Harder	NEWV	Big Spring Presbyterian	120
Grove	NEWV	Newville	140	Hardy	HOPE	Newburg Church of God	64
Grove	NEWV	Prospect Hill	152	Hare	MDSX	Carlisle Spring Church	84
Grove	WPEN	Diller Mennonite Church	198	Hargis	CARL	Ashland	9
Grove	WPEN	Seitz Farm	213	Harlacher	PENN	Huntsdale Dunker	186
Grubb	MDSX	Letort Spring Church	91	Harlan	NEWV	Big Spring Presbyterian	120
Grube	CARL	Ashland	9	Harlan	NEWV	Prospect Hill	152
Gruver	NMID	Wagner's Church	166	Harman	HOPE	Zion Reformed Church	69
Guldon	PENN	Centerville Lutheran Church	172	Harmon	FRAN	Lutheran Brick Church	51
Gumpert	NEWV	Big Spring Presbyterian	120	Harmon	HOPE	Zion Reformed Church	69
Gussman	NEWV	Prospect Hill	152	Harmony	NEWT	Oakville United Brethren	111
Gutshall	CARL	Ashland	9	Harn	WPEN	Diller Mennonite Church	198
Gutshall	FRAN	Bloserville Ref. Church	33	Harper	LALN	Eberly's Mills	74
Gutshall	MDSX	Carlisle Spring Church	83	Harper	NEWV	Big Spring Presbyterian	121

Surname Index

Surname	Twsp.	Cemetery	Page
Harper	PENN	Dickinson Presb. Church	179
Harrison	CARL	Ashland	9
Hart	CARL	Ashland	9
Hart	DICK	Mt. Zion	28
Hart	LALN	Eberly's Mills	74
Hart	LALN	Lisburn	77
Hart	WPEN	Plainfield Lutheran Church	210
Hartman	MDSX	Letort Spring Church	92
Hartzell	NEWV	Big Spring Presbyterian	121
Hartzell	NEWV	Newville	141
Hartzler	CARL	Ashland	9
Hartzler	SMID	Strickler	170
Harvey	NEWT	Irishtown Church	108
Harvey	NEWV	Newville	141
Harzok	HOPE	Newburg Church of God	64
Haskell	DICK	Mt. Zion	28
Hassinger	WPEN	Plainfield Bethel Church	207
Hastings	CARL	Ashland	9
Hastings	MDSX	Mennonite Grvyd.--Balfour	97
Hastings	NEWV	Newville	141
Hastings	PENN	Huntsdale Dunker	186
Haun	HOPE	Zion Reformed Church	69
Hayes	PENN	Dickinson Presb. Church	179
Hays	CARL	Ashland	9
Hays	NEWV	Big Spring Presbyterian	121
Hays	PENN	Dickinson Presb. Church	179
Hays	WPEN	Bear	194
Heagy	CARL	Ashland	9
Heagy	MDSX	Letort Spring Church	92
Heagy	NEWV	Big Spring Presbyterian	121
Heagy	PENN	Centerville Lutheran Church	172
Heagy	PENN	Huntsdale Dunker	186
Heannan	NEWV	United Presbyterian	160
Heap	NEWV	Big Spring Presbyterian	121
Heberlig	FRAN	Lutheran Brick Church	51
Heberlig	HOPE	Zion Reformed Church	69
Heberlig	MIFF	Zeigler's Church	107
Heberlig	NEWV	Newville	141
Heberlig	NEWV	Prospect Hill	152
Heck	LALN	Eberly's Mills	74
Heck	LALN	Lisburn	77
Heckendorn	MIFF	Center Church	102
Heckman	MIFF	Bethel Church	100
Heckman	NEWV	Newville	141
Heckman	NEWV	Prospect Hill	152
Hedden	WPEN	Bear	194
Heffelman	NEWV	Big Spring Presbyterian	121
Hefflebower	HOPE	Newburg Church of God	64
Hefflebower	NEWT	Irishtown Church	108
Hefflebower	NEWV	Newville	141
Hefflefinger	FRAN	Entlerville	34
Hefflefinger	FRAN	Lutheran Brick Church	51
Hefflefinger	FRAN	Possum Hill Church	58
Hefflefinger	HOPE	Mt. Tabor Church	62
Hefflefinger	HOPE	Newburg Church of God	64
Hefflefinger	HOPE	Zion Reformed Church	70
Hefflefinger	NEWV	Newville	141
Hefflefinger	NEWV	Prospect Hill	152
Hefflefinger	PENN	Huntsdale Dunker	186
Heffleman	FRAN	Lutheran Brick Church	51
Heffleman	NEWV	Big Spring Presbyterian	121
Heiges	WPEN	Heikes Farm	201
Heigis	WPEN	Heikes Farm	201
Heikes	WPEN	Heikes Farm	201
Heiser	FRAN	Possum Hill Church	58
Heiser	MDSX	Letort Spring Church	92
Heiser	NEWV	Prospect Hill	152
Heiser	WPEN	Plainfield Lutheran Church	210
Heller	NEWV	Prospect Hill	152
Heller	PENN	Huntsdale Dunker	186
Helman	NEWV	Newville	141
Helsel	DICK	Mt. Zion	28
Hemminger	CARL	Ashland	9
Hemminger	DICK	Old Line	31
Hemminger	FRAN	Lutheran Brick Church	51
Hemminger	MIFF	Zeigler's Church	107
Hemminger	NEWV	Newville	141
Hemminger	NEWV	Prospect Hill	152
Hemminger	PENN	Centerville Lutheran Church	172
Hemminger	PENN	Dickinson Presb. Church	179
Hemp	MDSX	Letort Spring Church	92
Hench	CARL	Ashland	9
Hench	NEWV	Prospect Hill	152
Henderson	CARL	Ashland	9
Henderson	CARL	Meeting House Springs	24
Henneberger	NEWV	Prospect Hill	152
Henry	CARL	Ashland	10
Henry	HOPE	Stouffer Farm	67
Henry	MIFF	Center Church	102
Henry	NEWV	Prospect Hill	153
Henry	NEWV	Zion Lutheran Church	163
Henry	PENN	Centerville Lutheran Church	172
Henry	PENN	Dickinson Presb. Church	180
Henwood	CARL	Ashland	10
Hepple	FRAN	Bloserville Reformed Church	33
Herbst	CARL	Ashland	10
Herebwont	CARL	Ashland	10
Herman	CARL	Ashland	10
Herron	NEWV	Big Spring Presbyterian	121
Hershey	MIFF	Center Church	102
Hershey	WPEN	Diller Mennonite Church	198
Hertzler	MDSX	Letort Spring Church	92

Surname Index

Surname	Twsp.	Cemetery	Page	Surname	Twsp.	Cemetery	Page
Hess	NEWV	Prospect Hill	153	Hoover	FRAN	Lutheran & Ref. Stone Church	37
Hettrick	CARL	Ashland	10	Hoover	FRAN	Lutheran Brick Church	51
Hettrick	NEWT	Stoughstown Lutheran Church	113	Hoover	HOPE	Hoover Farm	62
Hickernell	LALN	Lisburn	77	Hoover	HOPE	Newburg Church of God	64
Hicks	LALN	Lisburn	78	Hoover	MIFF	Center Church	102
High	HOPE	Zion Reformed Church	70	Hoover	NEWT	Irishtown Church	109
High	NEWV	Newville	141	Hoover	NEWV	Newville	141
Highlands	PENN	Huntsdale Dunker	186	Hoover	NEWV	Prospect Hill	153
Hikes	WPEN	Heikes Farm	201	Hoover	PENN	Centerville Lutheran Church	173
Hildebrand	NEWV	Newville	141	Hoover	PENN	Huntsdale Dunker	187
Hiltibidle	NEWV	Prospect Hill	153	Horn	NEWV	Big Spring Presbyterian	122
Hilton	CARL	Ashland	10	Hornbaker	WPEN	Plainfield Lutheran Church	210
Himes	PENN	Centerville Lutheran Church	172	Hosfeld	FRAN	Lutheran & Ref. Stone Church	38
Himes	PENN	Huntsdale Dunker	186	Hosfeld	PENN	Huntsdale Dunker	187
Hipple	FRAN	Bloserville Reformed Church	33	Hosfelt	PENN	Huntsdale Dunker	187
Hipple	WPEN	Plainfield Lutheran Church	210	Hosler	CARL	Ashland	10
Hirey	WPEN	Springfield	214	Hosler	MDSX	Letort Spring Church	92
Hiser	FRAN	Lutheran & Ref. Stone Church	37	Hosler	MIFF	Mt. Hope	105
Hiser	FRAN	Possum Hill Church	58	Houk	DICK	Martin Farm	26
Hiskey	NEWT	Old Roads	112	House	NEWV	Big Spring Presbyterian	122
Hisner	PENN	Hisner	183	Householder	NEWT	Irishtown Church	109
Hitner	CARL	Ashland	10	Householder	NEWV	Big Spring Presbyterian	122
Hoch	NEWV	Newville	141	Householder	WPEN	Plainfield Bethel Church	207
Hoch	NEWV	Prospect Hill	153	How	DICK	Mt. Zion	28
Hocker	CARL	Ashland	10	Howard	NEWV	Big Spring Presbyterian	122
Hocker	PENN	Centerville Lutheran Church	173	Howe	DICK	Mt. Zion	28
Hoerner	CARL	Ashland	10	Hower	NEWV	Zion Lutheran Church	163
Hoerner	MDSX	Letort Spring Church	92	Howerter	LALN	Lisburn	78
Hoffer	CARL	Ashland	10	Hoy	MDSX	Carlisle Spring Church	84
Hoffer	SMID	Strickler	170	Hudson	NEWV	Big Spring Presbyterian	122
Hoffman	CARL	Ashland	10	Hughes	FRAN	Lutheran & Ref. Stone Church	38
Hoffman	FRAN	Lutheran Brick Church	51	Hull	CARL	Ashland	10
Hoffman	HOPE	Newburg Church of God	64	Hull	LALN	Lisburn	78
Hoffman	MDSX	Letort Spring Church	92	Humbarger	HOPE	Zion Reformed Church	70
Holby	HOPE	Zion Reformed Church	70	Humberger	MIFF	Bethany Church	98
Holby	NEWV	Zion Lutheran Church	163	Hume	NEWV	Big Spring Presbyterian	122
Holfarty	WPEN	Springfield	214	Humer	CARL	Ashland	10
Hollar	MIFF	Snokes Graveyard	106	Humer	MDSX	Carlisle Spring Church	84
Hollenbaugh	NEWV	Prospect Hill	153	Humer	WPEN	Plainfield Lutheran Church	210
Hollenbaugh	NMID	Wagner's Church	166	Humes	DICK	Mt. Zion	28
Holler	HOPE	Zion Reformed Church	70	Hummelbaugh	WPEN	Mt. Rock	203
Hollinger	PENN	Huntsdale Dunker	186	Hunter	CARL	Ashland	11
Holmes	CARL	Ashland	10	Hunter	NEWV	Big Spring Presbyterian	122
Holmes	HOPE	Hanna	60	Huntsberger	NEWV	Newville	142
Holt	NEWV	Prospect Hill	153	Huntsberger	NEWV	Prospect Hill	153
Honich	MDSX	Carlisle Spring Church	84	Hurley	FRAN	Lutheran & Ref. Stone Church	38
Hood	NEWV	Big Spring Presbyterian	121	Hurley	MIFF	Bethany Church	98
Hood	NEWV	Prospect Hill	153	Hurley	MIFF	Bethel Church	100
Hoon	FRAN	Lutheran Brick Church	51	Hursh	NEWV	Big Spring Presbyterian	122
Hoon	MIFF	Bethany Church	98	Hursh	NEWV	Newville	142
Hoon	NEWV	United Presbyterian	160	Hurting	PENN	Huntsdale Dunker	187

Surname Index

Surname	Twsp.	Cemetery	Page	Surname	Twsp.	Cemetery	Page
Husler	NEWT	Oakville United Brethren	111	Jones	NEWV	Prospect Hill	153
Huston	CARL	Ashland	11	Jones	NEWV	United Presbyterian	160
Huston	DICK	Old Line	31	Jones	NMID	Wagner's Church	166
Huston	NEWV	Big Spring Presbyterian	122	Jones	PENN	Huntsdale Dunker	187
Huston	NEWV	Newville	142	Jumper	FRAN	Bloserville Reformed Church	33
Huston	NEWV	United Presbyterian	160	Jumper	FRAN	Lutheran & Ref. Stone Church	38
Huston	PENN	Dickinson Presb. Church	180	Jumper	FRAN	Possum Hill Church	58
Hutchison	HOPE	Newburg Church of God	64	Jumper	MIFF	Center Church	102
Hutchison	PENN	Huntsdale Dunker	187	Jumper	MIFF	Mt. Hope	105
Huyett	CARL	Ashland	11	Kamarer, Kamerer	FRAN	Lutheran Brick Church	52
Hyer	CARL	Ashland	11	Kammerer	FRAN	Lutheran Brick Church	52
Ickes	FRAN	Lutheran Brick Church	52	Kampher	PENN	Huntsdale Dunker	187
Ickes	MIFF	Bethel Church	100	Kann	LALN	Lisburn	78
Ickes	NEWV	Big Spring Presbyterian	122	Karlskint	NEWV	Big Spring Presbyterian	123
Ilgenfritz	MDSX	Letort Spring Church	92	Karns	PENN	Centerville Lutheran Church	173
Inhoff	CARL	Ashland	11	Kash	FRAN	Lutheran & Ref. Stone Church	38
Irvin	CARL	Ashland	11	Kast	FRAN	Lutheran & Ref. Stone Church	38
Irvine	CARL	Ashland	11	Kauffman	CARL	Ashland	11
Irvine	NEWV	Big Spring Presbyterian	122	Kauffman	HOPE	Newburg Church of God	64
Irvine	PENN	Dickinson Presb. Church	180	Kauffman	MDSX	Letort Spring Church	92
Irwin	NEWV	Big Spring Presbyterian	122	Kechler	PENN	Centerville Lutheran Church	173
Irwin	NEWV	United Presbyterian	160	Kechler	PENN	Huntsdale Dunker	187
Jackson	FRAN	Lutheran & Ref. Stone Church	38	Keck	FRAN	Bloserville Reformed Church	33
Jackson	MDSX	Mennonite Grvyd.--Balfour	97	Keck	FRAN	Entlerville	34
Jackson	NEWV	Newville	142	Keck	FRAN	Lutheran Brick Church	52
Jackson	NEWV	United Presbyterian	160	Keck	WPEN	Plainfield Bethel Church	207
Jackson	NMID	Wagner's Church	166	Keefauver	FRAN	Lutheran Brick Church	52
Jacob	NEWV	Big Spring Presbyterian	122	Keefer	HOPE	Newburg Church of God	64
Jacobs	CARL	Ashland	11	Keefourer	PENN	Centerville Lutheran Church	173
Jacobs	MDSX	Carlisle Spring Church	84	Keefouver	PENN	Centerville Lutheran Church	173
Jacobs	NEWV	Big Spring Presbyterian	122	Keeler	WPEN	Plainfield Bethel Church	207
Jacobs	PENN	Huntsdale Dunker	187	Keene	MDSX	Letort Spring Church	92
Jacoby	MIFF	Center Church	102	Keeny	PENN	Huntsdale Dunker	187
Jacoby	Newton	Irishtown Church	109	Keepers	CARL	Ashland	11
Jacoby	NEWV	Newville	142	Keesaman	HOPE	Zion Reformed Church	71
Jacoby	NEWV	Prospect Hill	153	Keiffer	NEWV	Big Spring Presbyterian	123
Jacoby	WPEN	Plainfield Bethel Church	207	Keiffer	NEWV	Newville	142
James	NEWV	Big Spring Presbyterian	123	Keigley	CARL	Ashland	11
James	NEWV	Newville	142	Keihl	FRAN	Lutheran & Ref. Stone Church	38
James	WPEN	Plainfield Bethel Church	207	Keihl	FRAN	Lutheran Brick Church	52
Jameson	LALN	Lisburn	78	Keihl	MDSX	Carlisle Spring Church	84
Jamison	CARL	Ashland	11	Keihl	PENN	Centerville Lutheran Church	173
Jenkins	NEWV	Big Spring Presbyterian	123	Keiser	MDSX	Letort Spring Church	92
John	PENN	Centerville Lutheran Church	173	Keiser	WPEN	Bear Graveyard	194
Johnson	NEWV	Big Spring Presbyterian	123	Keiser	WPEN	Heikes Farm	201
Johnson	NEWV	United Presbyterian	160	Keiser	WPEN	Plainfield Bethel Church	207
Johnson	PENN	Huntsdale Dunker	187	Keiter	WPEN	Plainfield Lutheran Church	210
Johnston	CARL	Meeting House Springs	24	Kell	FRAN	Lutheran & Ref. Stone Church	38
Jones	CARL	Ashland	11	Kell	MDSX	Carlisle Spring Church	84
Jones	MDSX	Carlisle Spring Church	84	Kell	NMID	Wagner's Church	166
Jones	NEWV	Newville	142	Keller	CARL	Ashland	11

Surname Index

Surname	Twsp.	Cemetery	Page	Surname	Twsp.	Cemetery	Page
Keller	MDSX	Carlisle Spring Church	84	Kirkpatrick	NEWV	Newville	142
Keller	PENN	Huntsdale Dunker	187	Kissinger	CARL	Ashland	12
Keller	WPEN	Springfield	214	Kissinger	NEWV	Newville	142
Kelley	NEWV	Big Spring Presbyterian	123	Kissinger	PENN	Centerville Lutheran Church	173
Kelly	NEWV	Big Spring Presbyterian	123	Kissinger	PENN	Huntsdale Dunker	187
Kelly	NEWV	Prospect Hill	153	Kistler	WPEN	Graveyard on Hill	200
Kelly	PENN	Centerville Lutheran Church	173	Kitch	FRAN	Lutheran & Ref. Stone Church	38
Kelso	PENN	Dickinson Presb. Church	180	Kitch	MDSX	Carlisle Spring Church	84
Kemper	CARL	Ashland	11	Kitner	MDSX	Carlisle Spring Church	84
Kenage	NEWT	Old Roads	112	Kizer	WPEN	Bear	194
Kendig		see additional entries on page 261		Kleber	FRAN	Lutheran Brick Church	52
Kendig	NEWT	Irishtown Church	109	Kleier	LALN	Lisburn	78
Kendig	NEWV	Prospect Hill	153	Kline	MDSX	Letort Spring Church	92
Kendig	WPEN	Diller Mennonite Church	198	Kline	PENN	Huntsdale Dunker	187
Kennedy	FRAN	Entlerville	34	Kling	CARL	Ashland	12
Kennedy	FRAN	Lutheran & Ref. Stone Church	38	Kling	NEWV	Newville	143
Kennedy	FRAN	Possum Hill Church	58	Klink	NEWV	Big Spring Presbyterian	123
Kennedy	MIFF	Bethel Church	100	Knaub	MDSX	Dunker Church	88
Kennedy	NEWV	Big Spring Presbyterian	123	Kneisly	PENN	Huntsdale Dunker	187
Kennedy	NEWV	Prospect Hill	153	Knettle	MIFF	Center Church	102
Kenyon	PENN	Dickinson Presb. Church	180	Knettle	NEWV	Big Spring Presbyterian	123
Ker	NEWV	Big Spring Presbyterian	123	Knight	NEWV	Big Spring Presbyterian	124
Kern	NEWV	Prospect Hill	153	Knisely	FRAN	Lutheran & Ref. Stone Church	39
Kernan	CARL	Ashland	12	Knisely	PENN	Huntsdale Dunker	187
Kerns	WPEN	Plainfield Lutheran Church	210	Knisely	WPEN	Plainfield Bethel Church	207
Kerr	HOPE	Hanna	60	Knouse	FRAN	Lutheran Brick Church	52
Kerr	NEWV	Big Spring Presbyterian	123	Kober	CARL	Ashland	12
Kershaw	NEWV	Prospect Hill	153	Koch	CARL	Ashland	12
Kesler	NEWV	Zion Lutheran Church	163	Koch	FRAN	Lutheran Brick Church	52
Kesnel	MIFF	Bethel Church	100	Kochenderfer	WPEN	Plainfield Bethel Church	207
Ketron	HOPE	Zion Reformed Church	71	Kolb	FRAN	Lutheran & Ref. Stone Church	39
Kiahl	FRAN	Lutheran & Ref. Stone Church	38	Konn	LALN	Lisburn	78
Kieffer	CARL	Ashland	12	Koons	NEWV	Big Spring Presbyterian	124
Kiehl	CARL	Ashland	12	Koons	NEWV	Newville	143
Kiehl	FRAN	Lutheran & Ref. Stone Church	38	Koser	FRAN	Lutheran Brick Church	52
Kiehl	PENN	Huntsdale Dunker	187	Koser	HOPE	Zion Reformed Church	71
Kilgore	NEWV	Big Spring Presbyterian	123	Koser	NEWV	Big Spring Presbyterian	124
Killian	NEWV	Newville	142	Koser	WPEN	Diller Mennonite Church	198
Killian	NEWV	Prospect Hill	153	Kosh	FRAN	Lutheran & Ref. Stone Church	39
Kincaid	PENN	Dickinson Presb. Church	180	Kosht	FRAN	Lutheran & Ref. Stone Church	39
Kinch	FRAN	Lutheran Brick Church	52	Kosht	FRAN	Lutheran Brick Church	52
Kindig	HOPE	Newburg Church of God	65	Kost	FRAN	Lutheran & Ref. Stone Church	39
Kiner	FRAN	Lutheran & Ref. Stone Church	38	Kough	NEWT	Irishtown Church	109
Kinert	FRAN	Lutheran & Ref. Stone Church	38	Kough	PENN	Huntsdale Dunker	187
King	CARL	Ashland	12	Krall	LALN	Lisburn	78
King	FRAN	Lutheran Brick Church	52	Krall	NEWV	Prospect Hill	154
King	NEWV	Zion Lutheran Church	163	Krall	UALN	Lantz's School House	193
King	NMID	Wagner's Church	166	Kramer	CARL	Ashland	12
King	PENN	Centerville Lutheran Church	173	Kramer	FRAN	Lutheran Brick Church	53
Kinkead	CARL	Meeting House Springs	24	Kreider	MDSX	Dunker Church	88
Kinsly	NEWV	Big Spring Presbyterian	123	Kreider	PENN	Huntsdale Dunker	187

Surname Index

Surname	Twsp.	Cemetery	Page	Surname	Twsp.	Cemetery	Page
Kremer	CARL	Ashland	12	Layburn	NEWV	Newville	143
Kriner	FRAN	Lutheran & Ref. Stone Church	39	Leas	FRAN	Lutheran Brick Church	53
Kriner	NMID	Bethel Church	165	Leas	WPEN	Heikes Farm	201
Kronenberg	CARL	Ashland	12	Lechtner	NEWV	Zion Lutheran Church	163
Kuhn	NEWT	Irishtown Church	109	Leckey	NEWV	Big Spring Presbyterian	124
Kuhns	CARL	Ashland	12	Lee	CARL	Ashland	13
Kulp	NEWV	Big Spring Presbyterian	124	Lee	PENN	Dickinson Presb. Church	180
Kunkle	HOPE	Newburg Church of God	65	Leephart	MDSX	Carlisle Spring Church	85
Kunkle	MDSX	Carlisle Spring Church	84	Lefever	PENN	Cumminstown Campbellite	177
Kunkle	NEWV	Prospect Hill	154	Lefever	PENN	Dickinson Presb. Church	180
Kunkle	PENN	Centerville Lutheran Church	173	Lefever	WPEN	Mt. Rock	203
Kuntz	DICK	Mt. Zion	28	Lefever	WPEN	Seitz Farm	213
Kuntz	MDSX	Letort Spring Church	92	Lehman	CARL	Ashland	13
Kuntz	WPEN	Mt. Rock	203	Lehman	FRAN	Lutheran Brick Church	53
Kurtz	PENN	Huntsdale Dunker	187	Lehman	HOPE	Zion Reformed Church	71
Kutz	CARL	Ashland	12	Lehman	MIFF	Center Church	103
Kutz	MDSX	Carlisle Spring Church	84	Lehman	NEWT	Oakville United Brethren	111
Kutz	MDSX	Letort Spring Church	93	Lehman	NEWV	Newville	143
Kutz	NEWV	Prospect Hill	154	Lehman	NEWV	Zion Lutheran Church	163
Kyle	NEWV	Big Spring Presbyterian	124	Lehman	WPEN	Diller Mennonite Church	198
Kyle	NEWV	Newville	143	Lehman	WPEN	Plainfield Bethel Church	207
Kyle	NEWV	United Presbyterian	160	Lehn	FRAN	Lutheran & Ref. Stone Church	39
Kyle	PENN	Dickinson Presb. Church	180	Lehner	HOPE	Zion Reformed Church	71
Lahn	FRAN	Lutheran & Re. Stone Church	39	Leib	FRAN	Lutheran Brick Church	53
Laird	CARL	Meeting House Springs	24	Leib	MDSX	Dunker Church	89
Laird	NEWV	Big Spring Presbyterian	124	Leicey	PENN	Huntsdale Dunker	188
Laird	NEWV	United Presbyterian	160	Leichty	FRAN	Lutheran & Ref. Stone Church	39
Lamb	NEWV	Newville	143	Leidich	CARL	Ashland	13
Lambert	MIFF	Snokes Graveyard	106	Leidich	FRAN	Lutheran & Ref. Stone Church	39
Lambert	UALN	Lantz's School House	193	Leidig	NEWV	Prospect Hill	154
Lamberton	CARL	Ashland	12	Leidigh	NEWV	Newville	143
Landis	CARL	Ashland	12	Lemer	LALN	Lisburn	78
Landis	FRAN	Lutheran & Ref. Stone Church	39	Lemon	NEWV	Big Spring Presbyterian	125
Landis	HOPE	Newburg Church of God	65	Lenhart	NMID	Wagner's Church	166
Landis	MIFF	Center Church	102	Lenney	NEWV	Big Spring Presbyterian	125
Landis	NEWV	Newville	143	Lepperd	NMID	Wagner's Church	166
Lane	CARL	Ashland	12	Lepperd	WPEN	Plainfield Lutheran Church	210
Langry	NEWV	Zion Lutheran Church	163	Lesher	CARL	Ashland	13
Lantz	UALN	Lantz's School House	193	Lesher	MDSX	Carlisle Spring Church	85
Latshaw	NEWV	Zion Lutheran Church	163	Lesher	MDSX	Dunker Church	89
Latshaw	PENN	Huntsdale Dunker	188	Lesher	PENN	Centerville Lutheran Church	173
Laughlin	HOPE	Hanna	60	Lesher	WPEN	Plainfield Lutheran Church	210
Laughlin	NEWV	Big Spring Presbyterian	124	Lewis	NEWV	Prospect Hill	154
Laurich	FRAN	Lutheran & Ref. Stone Church	39	Lewis	NEWV	Big Spring Presbyterian	125
Law	CARL	Ashland	13	Lightner	NMID	Bethel Church	165
Lawrence	NEWV	Big Spring Presbyterian	124	Lindenberger	WPEN	Plainfield Lutheran Church	210
Lawton	CARL	Ashland	13	Lindsay	PENN	Centerville Lutheran Church	173
Lay	HOPE	Zion Reformed Church	71	Lindsay	PENN	Dickinson Presb. Church	180
Lay	MIFF	Center Church	103	Lindsey	CARL	Ashland	13
Lay	MIFF	Mt. Hope	105	Lindsey	CARL	Meeting House Springs	24
Lay	NEWV	Newville	143	Lindsey	HOPE	Newburg Church of God	65

Surname Index

Surname	Twsp.	Cemetery	Page	Surname	Twsp.	Cemetery	Page
Lindsey	NEWV	Big Spring Presbyterian	125	Lutz	NEWT	Irishtown Church	109
Lindsay	NEWV	Prospect Hill	154	Lyter	MDSX	Letort Spring Church	93
Line	CARL	Ashland	13	Lytle	NEWT	Irishtown Church	109
Line	DICK	Line	26	Macafery	LALN	Lisburn	78
Line	DICK	Old Line	31	Macaffrey	LALN	Lisburn	78
Line	MDSX	Carlisle Spring Church	85	Machon	PENN	Centerville Lutheran Church	173
Line	NEWV	Newville	143	Madison	NEWV	Newville	143
Line	PENN	Huntsdale Dunker	188	Maglaughlin	CARL	Ashland	14
Lininger	NEWV	Newville	143	Mahaffey	PENN	Huntsdale Dunker	188
Linn	NEWV	Big Spring Presbyterian	125	Manning	MDSX	Letort Spring Church	93
Linn	PENN	Huntsdale Dunker	188	Manning	NEWV	Big Spring Presbyterian	125
Lipe	MDSX	Carlisle Spring Church	85	Mapes	CARL	Ashland	14
Lipert	FRAN	Lutheran & Ref. Stone Church	39	March	DICK	Barnitz M. E. Church	26
Little	FRAN	Lutheran Brick Church	53	March	PENN	Huntsdale Dunker	188
Livingston	Newton	Oakville United Brethren	111	Marchand	CARL	Ashland	14
Livingston	NEWV	Newville	143	Mark	CARL	Ashland	14
Lloyd	LALN	Lisburn	78	Markbarger		Oyster's Point	216
Lockard	CARL	Ashland	13	Marquart	NEWT	Irishtown Church	109
Lockard	PENN	Centerville Lutheran Church	173	Marsh	DICK	Mt. Zion	28
Logan	FRAN	Lutheran & Ref. Stone Church	39	Marsh	SMID	Mt. Victory	170
Logan	NEWV	Big Spring Presbyterian	125	Marshall	HOPE	Zion Reformed Church	71
Logan	PENN	Centerville Lutheran Church	173	Marstzbarger		Oyster's Point	216
Logan	PENN	Dickinson Presb. Church	180	Martin	CARL	Ashland	14
Long	CARL	Ashland	13	Martin	HOPE	Hanna	60
Long	DICK	Line	26	Martin	HOPE	Hoover Farm	62
Long	HOPE	Newburg Church of God	65	Martin	MDSX	Letort Spring Church	93
Long	HOPE	Zion Reformed Church	71	Martin	MIFF	Bethany Church	98
Long	LALN	Eberly's Mill	75	Martin	NEWV	Big Spring Presbyterian	125
Long	NEWT	Oakville United Brethren	111	Martin	NEWV	Zion Lutheran Church	163
Long	NEWV	Big Spring Presbyterian	125	Martin	PENN	Huntsdale Dunker	188
Long	NEWV	Newville	143	Martin	WPEN	Diller Mennonite Church	198
Long	NEWV	Zion Lutheran Church	163	Martz	NEWV	Prospect Hill	154
Long	PENN	Centerville Lutheran Church	173	Martz	PENN	Dickinson Presb. Church	180
Longnecker	WPEN	Bear	194	Mater	PENN	Huntsdale Dunker	188
Longnecker	WPEN	Plainfield Bethel Church	207	Mathers	NEWV	Big Spring Presbyterian	125
Longsdorf	CARL	Ashland	14	Mathers	NEWV	United Presbyterian	160
Lontz	NEWV	Zion Lutheran Church	163	Mathias	MDSX	Letort Spring Church	94
Loophart	MDSX	Carlisle Spring Church	85	Matthews	CARL	Ashland	14
Lord	CARL	Ashland	14	Maurice	NEWV	Prospect Hill	154
Low	CARL	Ashland	14	May		Oyster's Point	216
Low	MDSX	Carlisle Spring Church	85	Mayberry	FRAN	Lutheran Brick Church	53
Low	MDSX	Letort Spring Church	93	Mayberry	FRAN	Possum Hill Church	58
Low	PENN	Centerville Lutheran Church	173	Mayberry	NEWV	Zion Lutheran Church	163
Loy	NEWV	Big Spring Presbyterian	125	Mayberry	WPEN	Diller Mennonite Church	198
Loy	NEWV	Prospect Hill	154	Mayberry	WPEN	Plainfield Bethel Church	207
Loyd	LALN	Lisburn	78	Mayer	WPEN	Diller Mennonite Church	198
Luck	NEWV	Newville	143	McAllister	CARL	Meeting House Springs	24
Ludt	FRAN	Lutheran & Ref. Stone Church	39	McAlwain	HOPE	Hanna	60
Lusk	HOPE	Zion Reformed Church	71	McBride	DICK	Mt. Zion	28
Lutz	FRAN	Bloserville Reformed Church	33	McBride	MDSX	Letort Spring Church	94
Lutz	FRAN	Lutheran Brick Church	53	McCachran	NEWV	Big Spring Presbyterian	125

Surname Index

Surname	Twsp.	Cemetery	Page	Surname	Twsp.	Cemetery	Page
McCaffrey	LALN	Lisburn	78	McFeely	CARL	Ashland	14
McCafrey	LALN	Lisburn	78	McGaw	HOPE	Newburg Church of God	65
McCaleb	NEWV	Big Spring Presbyterian	125	McGaw	NEWV	Big Spring Presbyterian	128
McCaleb	NEWV	Newville	143	McGlen	NEWV	Big Spring Presbyterian	128
McCaleb	WPEN	Springfield	214	McGlin	MIFF	Center Church	103
McCallister	MIFF	Center Church	103	McGonegal	CARL	Ashland	14
McCandlish	NEWV	Big Spring Presbyterian	125	McGonelgal	CARL	Ashland	14
McCannen	WPEN	Springfield	215	McGowan	CARL	Ashland	14
McCaslin	PENN	Dickinson Presb. Church	180	McIlhenny	CARL	Ashland	14
McCausland	HOPE	Zion Reformed Church	71	McIntire	NEWV	Big Spring Presbyterian	128
McCavitt	HOPE	Zion Reformed Church	71	McIvor	NEWV	Prospect Hill	154
McCleaf	HOPE	Newburg Church of God	65	McKee	HOPE	Zion Reformed Church	71
McClean	PENN	Dickinson Presb. Church	180	McKee	NEWV	Newville	144
McClure	HOPE	Newburg Church of God	65	McKeehan	CARL	Ashland	14
McClure	NEWV	Big Spring Presbyterian	126	McKeehan	NEWV	Big Spring Presbyterian	128
McClure	NEWV	Prospect Hill	154	McKeehan	NEWV	Newville	144
McCommon	CARL	Ashland	14	McKeehan	NEWV	Prospect Hill	154
McCool	WPEN	Mt. Rock	203	McKeehan	WPEN	Plainfield Lutheran Church	210
McCormick	NEWV	Big Spring Presbyterian	126	McKehan	CARL	Meeting House Springs	25
McCoy	CARL	Ashland	14	McKibben	NEWV	Big Spring Presbyterian	129
McCoy	FRAN	Lutheran Brick Church	53	McKinney	HOPE	Hanna	60
McCoy	HOPE	Mt. Tabor Church	62	McKinny	HOPE	Hanna	60
McCoy	HOPE	Newburg Church of God	65	McKinny	NEWV	Big Spring Presbyterian	129
McCoy	HOPE	Zion Reformed Church	71	McKinstry	NEWV	Big Spring Presbyterian	129
McCoy	NEWV	Big Spring Presbyterian	126	McLaughlin	CARL	Ashland	15
McCoy	NEWV	Prospect Hill	154	McLaughlin	HOPE	Zion Reformed Church	71
McCrea	NEWV	Big Spring Presbyterian	126	McLaughlin	NEWV	Big Spring Presbyterian	129
McCulloch	NEWV	Newville	143	McLaughlin	NEWV	Newville	144
McCulloch	NEWV	United Presbyterian	160	McLaughlin	PENN	Dickinson Presb. Church	180
McCullough	NEWV	Big Spring Presbyterian	126	McManes	WPEN	Graveyard on Hill	200
McCullough	NEWV	Newville	144	McMonigal	NEWV	Big Spring Presbyterian	129
McCulogh	CARL	Meeting House Springs	25	McMoor	NEWV	United Presbyterian	161
McCune	NEWV	Big Spring Presbyterian	127	McMullen	NEWV	Big Spring Presbyterian	129
McCune	PENN	Dickinson Presb. Church	180	McMullen	NEWV	Zion Lutheran Church	163
McDannel	NEWV	Big Spring Presbyterian	127	McNeal	NEWV	United Presbyterian	161
McDannell	NEWV	Big Spring Presbyterian	127	McNew	DICK	Mt. Zion	28
McDermond	MIFF	Zeigler's Church	107	McWilliams	NEWV	Big Spring Presbyterian	129
McDermond	NEWV	Big Spring Presbyterian	127	McWilliams	NEWV	Prospect Hill	154
McDermond	NEWV	Prospect Hill	154	Meals	DICK	Mt. Zion	28
McDonald	NEWV	Big Spring Presbyterian	127	Meals	MDSX	Letort Spring Church	94
McDowell	CARL	Ashland	14	Meals	PENN	Centerville Lutheran Church	173
McDowell	NEWV	Big Spring Presbyterian	127	Means	CARL	Ashland	15
McElhenny	NEWV	Big Spring Presbyterian	128	Meckley	LALN	Lisburn	78
McElhinny	HOPE	Hanna	60	Megaw	NEWV	Big Spring Presbyterian	129
McElwain	HOPE	Hanna	60	Mehaffie	PENN	Dickinson Presb. Church	180
McElwain	HOPE	Zion Reformed Church	71	Melester	CARL	Ashland	15
McElwain	NEWV	Big Spring Presbyterian	128	Melester	MDSX	Letort Spring Church	94
McElwain	NEWV	Newville	144	Mell	FRAN	Lutheran & Ref. Church	39
McElwain	NEWV	United Presbyterian	161	Mell	FRAN	Lutheran Brick Church	53
McFarlane	CARL	Meeting House Springs	25	Mell	NEWV	Newville	144
McFarlane	NEWV	Big Spring Presbyterian	128	Mell	WPEN	Mt. Rock	203

Surname Index

Surname	Twsp.	Cemetery	Page	Surname	Twsp.	Cemetery	Page
Mellinger	FRAN	Lutheran & Ref. Stone Church	39	Minnich	NEWV	Prospect Hill	155
Mellinger	NEWT	Stoughstown Lutheran Church	113	Minnich	WPEN	Plainfield Lutheran Church	210
Mellinger	NEWV	Newville	144	Mishler	CARL	Ashland	15
Mellinger	NMID	Bethel Church	165	Mitchell	HOPE	Hanna	60
Mellinger	PENN	Huntsdale Dunker	188	Mitchell	MIFF	Bethel Church	100
Mentzer	FRAN	Gayman Farm	35	Mitchell	NEWV	Prospect Hill	155
Mentzer	FRAN	Lutheran & Ref. Stone Church	39	Mitten	FRAN	Lutheran Brick Church	54
Mentzer	FRAN	Lutheran Brick Church	53	Mitten	NEWV	Prospect Hill	155
Mentzer	MDSX	Carlisle Spring Church	85	Mitten	PENN	Dickinson Presb. Church	180
Mentzer	MIFF	Zeigler's Church	107	Mixel	NEWT	Irishtown Church	109
Mentzer	NEWV	Newville	144	Mixell	MIFF	Bethany Church	98
Mentzer	NEWV	Prospect Hill	154	Mixell	NEWV	Big Spring Presbyterian	130
Mentzer	WPEN	Plainfield Bethel Church	207	Mixell	PENN	Centerville Lutheran Church	173
Merchant	CARL	Ashland	154	Moffitt	MIFF	Bethel Church	100
Messimer	WPEN	Bear	194	Moffitt	MIFF	Center Church	103
Messinger	PENN	Centerville Lutheran Church	173	Moffitt	NEWV	Big Spring Presbyterian	130
Messinger	PENN	Huntsdale Dunker	188	Mohler	FRAN	Lutheran Brick Church	54
Metzler	LALN	Lisburn	78	Mohler	MDSX	Letort Spring Church	94
Mickey	NEWV	Big Spring Presbyterian	129	Mohler	MIFF	Center Church	103
Middleton	NEWV	Prospect Hill	154	Mohler	PENN	Huntsdale Dunker	188
Miles	CARL	Ashland	15	Moist	CARL	Ashland	15
Miller	CARL	Ashland	15	Monosmith	CARL	Ashland	15
Miller	FRAN	Entlerville	34	Montgomery	CARL	Ashland	15
Miller	FRAN	Lutheran & Ref. Stone Church	39	Montgomery	HOPE	Hanna	61
Miller	FRAN	Lutheran Brick Church	54	Montgomery	NEWV	Big Spring Presbyterian	130
Miller	HOPE	Hanna	60	Montgomery	NEWV	Newville	145
Miller	HOPE	Newburg Church of God	65	Montgomery	NEWV	United Presbyterian	161
Miller	HOPE	Zion Reformed Church	71	Monyer	CARL	Ashland	15
Miller	LALN	Eberly's Mills	75	Moore	DICK	Old Associate Ref. Church	31
Miller	MDSX	Dunker Church	89	Moore	LALN	Lisburn	78
Miller	MDSX	Mennonite Grvyd.-Balfour	97	Moore	NEWV	Big Spring Presbyterian	130
Miller	MDSX	Old Hoffer Farm	97	Moore	NEWV	United Presbyterian	161
Miller	MIFF	Bethel Church	100	Moore	NEWV	Zion Lutheran Church	163
Miller	MIFF	Center Church	103	Moore	PENN	Dickinson Presb. Church	180
Miller	NEWT	Irishtown Church	109	Mordorf	FRAN	Lutheran & Ref. Church	40
Miller	NEWT	Oakville United Brethren	111	Mordorf	FRAN	Lutheran Brick Church	54
Miller	NEWT	Stoughstown Lutheran Church	113	Morrett	HOPE	Hanna	61
Miller	NEWV	Big Spring Presbyterian	130	Morrett	HOPE	Zion Reformed Church	71
Miller	NEWV	Prospect Hill	155	Morrett	WPEN	Heikes Farm	201
Miller	PENN	Centerville Lutheran Church	173	Morrison	CARL	Ashland	15
Miller	PENN	Dickinson Presb. Church	180	Morrison	FRAN	Possum Hill Church	59
Miller	PENN	Huntsdale Dunker	188	Morrison	PENN	Centerville Lutheran Church	173
Miller	UALN	Lantz's School House	193	Morrow	CARL	Ashland	15
Miller	WPEN	Diller Mennonite Church	198	Morrow	HOPE	Newburg Church of God	65
Miller	WPEN	Mt. Rock	203	Morrow	NEWV	Big Spring Presbyterian	130
Miller	WPEN	Plainfield Lutheran Church	210	Morrow	PENN	Huntsdale Dunker	188
Miller	WPEN	Springfield	215	Morthland	CARL	Meeting House Springs	25
Minich	FRAN	Lutheran & Ref. Stone Church	39	Mortorff	DICK	Mt. Zion	28
Minich	FRAN	Possum Hill Church	58	Mortorff	SMID	Flint Ridge Chapel	169
Minich	WPEN	Plainfield Lutheran Church	210	Mosser	FRAN	Gayman Farm	35
Minnich	FRAN	Lutheran & Ref. Stone Church	39	Motts	CARL	Ashland	15

Surname Index

Surname	Twsp.	Cemetery	Page	Surname	Twsp.	Cemetery	Page
Mountz	FRAN	Lutheran & Ref. Stone Church	40	Myers	PENN	Huntsdale Dunker	188
Mountz	FRAN	Possum Hill Church	59	Myers	WPEN	Bitner Farm	195
Mourer	WPEN	Plainfield Lutheran Church	210	Myers	WPEN	Diller Mennonite Church	198
Mowery	FRAN	Gayman Farm	35	Myers	WPEN	Francis Bear Farm	200
Mowery	FRAN	Lutheran Brick Church	54	Myers	WPEN	Ker Farm	202
Mowery	HOPE	Hanna	61	Myers	WPEN	Plainfield Bethel Church	207
Mowery	HOPE	Newburg Church of God	65	Myers	WPEN	Plainfield Lutheran Church	210
Mowery	HOPE	Zion Reformed Church	71	Myers	WPEN	Seitz Farm	213
Mowery	NEWV	Prospect Hill	155	Myers	WPEN	Springfield	215
Mowery	PENN	Huntsdale Dunker	188	Nailor	FRAN	Lutheran & Ref. Stone Church	40
Mowreay	FRAN	Gayman Farm	35	Nailor	LALN	Eberly's Mills	75
Mowrer	NEWV	Big Spring Presbyterian	35	Nailor	MDSX	Letort Spring Church	94
Mowry	FRAN	Gayman Farm	35	Nailor	NMID	Wagner's Church	167
Moyer	WPEN	Plainfield Lutheran Church	113	Nailor	WPEN	Mt. Rock	203
Much	NEWT	Stoughstown Lutheran Church	113	Nash	CARL	Ashland	15
Muck	NEWT	Stoughstown Lutheran Church	113	Natcher	CARL	Ashland	15
Mull		see additional entries on p. 261		Naugle	DICK	Mt. Zion	29
Mumau	CARL	Ashland	15	Naugle	PENN	Huntsdale Dunker	188
Mumper	MIFF	Center Church	103	Naylor	LALN	Lisburn	78
Munro	CARL	Ashland	15	Naylor	NMID	Wagner's Church	167
Murphy	NEWV	Prospect Hill	155	Neal	NEWV	Big Spring Presbyterian	130
Murray	CARL	Ashland	15	Nebinger	LALN	Lisburn	78
Murray	DICK	Mt. Zion	28	Neel	LALN	Lisburn	78
Murrey	DICK	Mt. Zion	28	Neff	CARL	Ashland	16
Musselman	CARL	Ashland	15	Neff	FRAN	Lutheran Brick Church	55
Musselman	DICK	Old Line	32	Neff	MDSX	Letort Spring Church	94
Musselman	FRAN	Lutheran & Ref. Stone Church	40	Neff	NEWV	Big Spring Presbyterian	130
Musselman	WPEN	Bear	194	Neff	PENN	Centerville Lutheran Church	173
Musselman	WPEN	Plainfield Bethel Church	207	Negley	NEWV	Prospect Hill	156
Musser	FRAN	Gayman Farm	35	Negley	WPEN	Diller Mennonite Church	198
Musser	FRAN	Lutheran Brick Church	54	Negly	NEWV	Newville	145
Musser	PENN	Huntsdale Dunker	188	Nehf	FRAN	Lutheran Brick Church	55
Myer	WPEN	Diller Mennonite Church	198	Nehf	NEWV	Prospect Hill	156
Myers	CARL	Ashland	15	Neibert	NEWV	Prospect Hill	156
Myers	CARL	Meeting House Springs	25	Neideigh	MIFF	Bethel Church	100
Myers	DICK	Line	26	Neidich	CARL	Ashland	16
Myers	DICK	Mt. Zion	28	Neidich	NEWV	Prospect Hill	156
Myers	FRAN	Bloserville Ref. Church	33	Neidigh	HOPE	Zion Reformed Church	72
Myers	FRAN	Lutheran & Ref. Stone Church	40	Neidigh	NEWV	Prospect Hill	156
Myers	FRAN	Lutheran Brick Church	54	Neischwanger	WPEN	Diller Mennonite Church	198
Myers	HOPE	Hanna	61	Neisley	MDSX	Letort Spring Church	94
Myers	HOPE	Newburg Church of God	65	Neiswanger	MDSX	Dunker Church	89
Myers	HOPE	Zion Reformed Church	72	Neiswanger	WPEN	Diller Mennonite Church	198
Myers	MDSX	Carlisle Spring Church	85	Nelson	LALN	Lisburn	78
Myers	MDSX	Dunker Church	89	Nerons	PENN	Centerville Lutheran Church	173
Myers	MIFF	Zeigler's Church	107	Nevel	MDSX	Letort Spring Church	94
Myers	NEWV	Big Spring Presbyterian	130	Newcomer	HOPE	Hanna	61
Myers	NEWV	Newville	145	Newcomer	PENN	Huntsdale Dunker	188
Myers	NEWV	Prospect Hill	155	Newman	NEWV	Big Spring Presbyterian	130
Myers	PENN	Centerville Lutheran Church	173	Nichols		Oyster's Point	216
Myers	PENN	Dickinson Presb. Church	180	Nicholson	NEWV	Big Spring Presbyterian	130

Surname Index

Surname	Twsp.	Cemetery	Page	Surname	Twsp.	Cemetery	Page
Nickel	DICK	Mt. Zion	29	Owen	PENN	Centerville Lutheran Church	174
Nickey	FRAN	Lutheran & Ref. Stone Church	40	Pague	CARL	Ashland	16
Nickey	HOPE	Zion Reformed Church	72	Palm	NEWV	Big Spring Presbyterian	131
Nickey	MDSX	Dunker Church	89	Palm	PENN	Centerville Lutheran Church	174
Nickey	NEWV	Big Spring Presbyterian	130	Palm	PENN	Dickinson Presb. Church	181
Nickey	NMID	Wagner's Church	167	Palm	WPEN	Springfield	215
Nickey	PENN	Huntsdale Dunker	188	Palmer	WPEN	Plainfield Bethel Church	208
Nickey	WPEN	Plainfield Bethel Church	208	Parker	CARL	Ashland	16
Nickey	WPEN	Plainfield Lutheran Church	210	Parker	CARL	Meeting House Springs	25
Niesley	MDSX	Letort Spring Church	94	Parks	PENN	Dickinson Presb. Church	181
Noaker	CARL	Ashland	16	Patterson	NEWV	Big Spring Presbyterian	131
Noble	CARL	Ashland	16	Patterson	PENN	Dickinson Presb. Church	181
Noel	NEWV	Big Spring Presbyterian	130	Patton	NEWV	Big Spring Presbyterian	131
Noell	LALN	Eberly's Mills	75	Patton	NEWV	Newville	145
Noffsinger	CARL	Ashland	16	Paul	LALN	Lisburn	78
Noggle	CARL	Ashland	16	Paul	MDSX	Letort Spring Church	94
Noggle	PENN	Centerville Lutheran Church	173	Paul	WPEN	Mt. Rock	203
Noggle	PENN	Huntsdale Dunker	189	Paul	WPEN	Plainfield Bethel Church	208
Norcross	CARL	Ashland	16	Paul	WPEN	Plainfield Lutheran Church	211
North	MIFF	Center Church	103	Paxton	CARL	Ashland	16
North	NEWV	Big Spring Presbyterian	130	Paxton	DICK	Mt. Zion	29
Null	NEWT	Stoughstown Lutheran Church	113	Paxton	PENN	Huntsdale Dunker	189
Null	WPEN	Diller Mennonite Church	198	Pearson	CARL	Ashland	16
Nunemaker	WPEN	Diller Mennonite Church	198	Pechart	PENN	Centerville Lutheran Church	174
Nunemaker	WPEN	Plainfield Lutheran Church	210	Pechart	WPEN	Plainfield Lutheran Church	211
O'Donnel	CARL	Meeting House Springs	25	Pecher	PENN	Centerville Lutheran Church	174
O'Donnel	NEWV	Prospect Hill	156	Pechert	PENN	Huntsdale Dunker	189
O'Hara	MDSX	Carlisle Spring Church	85	Peck	FRAN	Entlerville	34
Ober	HOPE	Newburg Church of God	65	Peebles	HOPE	Hanna	61
Ocker	CARL	Ashland	16	Peebles	NEWV	Big Spring Presbyterian	131
Ocker	PENN	Huntsdale Dunker	189	Peffer	CARL	Ashland	16
Ocker	WPEN	Plainfield Bethel Church	208	Peffer	DICK	Old Line	32
Ogden	LALN	Eberly's Mills	75	Peffer	FRAN	Lutheran Brick Church	55
Ogilby	CARL	Ashland	16	Peffer	PENN	Centerville Lutheran Church	174
Oiler	FRAN	Entlerville	34	Peffer	PENN	Dickinson Presb. Church	181
Oiler	FRAN	Lutheran Brick Church	55	Peiffer	NEWV	Newville	145
Oiler	FRAN	Possum Hill Church	59	Peirce	NEWV	Big Spring Presbyterian	131
Oiler	MIFF	Center Church	103	Pennington	CARL	Ashland	16
Oliver	NEWV	Big Spring Presbyterian	130	Penrose	CARL	Ashland	16
Orris	FRAN	Lutheran & Ref. Stone Church	41	Perlet	NEWV	Newville	145
Orris	FRAN	Lutheran Brick Church	55	Perry	NEWV	Big Spring Presbyterian	131
Orris	NEWV	Newville	145	Peterman	LALN	Eberly's Mills	75
Orth	LALN	Lisburn	78	Peters	CARL	Ashland	16
Osburn	CARL	Ashland	16	Peters	DICK	Mt. Zion	29
Ott	PENN	Huntsdale Dunker	189	Phelebaum	HOPE	Newburg Church of God	65
Otto	CARL	Ashland	16	Philips	NEWV	Big Spring Presbyterian	131
Otto	NEWV	Newville	145	Phillips	PENN	Centerville Lutheran Church	174
Otto	PENN	Huntsdale Dunker	189	Phreaner	MIFF	Bethany Church	98
Over	MIFF	Center Church	103	Pie	WPEN	Plainfield Lutheran Church	211
Over	NEWV	Big Spring Presbyterian	130	Pierce	NEWV	Big Spring Presbyterian	131
Owen	NEWT	Oakville United Brethren	111	Pilgrim	HOPE	Zion Reformed Church	72

Surname Index

Surname	Twsp.	Cemetery	Page	Surname	Twsp.	Cemetery	Page
Piper	CARL	Ashland	17	Rebok	NEWV	Prospect Hill	156
Piper	MIFF	Bethany Church	98	Reddig	PENN	Huntsdale Dunker	189
Piper	NEWV	Newville	145	Reed	MDSX	Carlisle Spring Church	85
Piper	PENN	Dickinson Presb. Church	181	Reed	MIFF	Bethany Church	98
Pipher	LALN	Lisburn	79	Reed	NEWV	Big Spring Presbyterian	131
Pislee	HOPE	Hanna	61	Reed	NEWV	United Presbyterian	161
Pislee	HOPE	Newburg Church of God	65	Reed	NMID	Wagner's Church	167
Plank	CARL	Ashland	17	Reed	PENN	Dickinson Presb. Church	181
Platt	CARL	Ashland	17	Reeder	MIFF	Center Church	103
Pleyer	NEWV	Newville	146	Reemer	MDSX	Letort Spring Church	94
Plough	CARL	Ashland	17	Reep	CARL	Ashland	17
Plough	FRAN	Gayman Farm	35	Reep	FRAN	Lutheran Brick Church	55
Plough	PENN	Huntsdale Dunker	189	Reese	FRAN	Lutheran & Ref. Stone Church	41
Ployer	FRAN	Lutheran Brick Church	55	Reiber	NMID	Bethel Church	165
Pollock	NEWV	Big Spring Presbyterian	131	Reiber	WPEN	Plainfield Lutheran Church	211
Porter	CARL	Ashland	17	Reifsnyder	FRAN	Lutheran Brick Church	55
Porter	MDSX	Letort Spring Church	94	Reighter	CARL	Ashland	17
Porter	WPEN	Heikes Farm	201	Reighter	PENN	Huntsdale Dunker	189
Preisler	NEWV	Prospect Hill	156	Reigle	CARL	Ashland	17
Price	LALN	Eberly's Mills	75	Reigle	PENN	Centerville Lutheran Church	174
Prosser	NEWV	Prospect Hill	156	Rein	WPEN	Riggleman Farm	212
Province	CARL	Ashland	17	Reinhardt	HOPE	Hanna	61
Pyke	MDSX	Letort Spring Church	94	Reinhardt	HOPE	Zion Reformed Church	72
Quigley	FRAN	Lutheran & Ref. Stone Church	41	Reside	CARL	Ashland	17
Quigley	NEWT	Oakville United Brethren	111	Ressler	FRAN	Lutheran Brick Church	55
Railing	MDSX	Carlisle Spring Church	85	Ressler	WPEN	Riggleman Farm	212
Railing	MDSX	Letort Spring Church	94	Rex	FRAN	Lutheran Brick Church	55
Railing	MDSX	Mennonite Graveyd.-Balfour	97	Rheem	CARL	Ashland	17
Railing	MIFF	Center Church	103	Rhinehart	WPEN	Springfield	215
Railing	NEWV	Prospect Hill	156	Rhoads	CARL	Ashland	17
Railing	PENN	Huntsdale Dunker	189	Rhoads	FRAN	Lutheran Brick Church	55
Ralson	CARL	Ashland	17	Rhoads	NEWV	Big Spring Presbyterian	131
Ralston	NEWV	Big Spring Presbyterian	131	Rhoads	NEWV	Newville	146
Ramp	HOPE	Newburg Church of God	66	Rhoads	NEWV	Prospect Hill	156
Ramp	HOPE	Zion Reformed Church	72	Rhoads	WPEN	Diller Mennonite Church	199
Ramp	MIFF	Zeigler's Church	107	Rhoads	WPEN	Plainfield Lutheran Church	211
Ramsey	CARL	Ashland	17	Rhoads	WPEN	Springfield	215
Ramsey	CARL	Meeting House Springs	25	Rhodes	DICK	Mt. Zion	29
Randall	NEWV	Big Spring Presbyterian	131	Rhodes	NEWT	Old Roads	112
Randolph	NEWV	Big Spring Presbyterian	131	Ricabaugh	WPEN	Jonathan Bear Farm	202
Rankin	NEWV	Big Spring Presbyterian	131	Rice	FRAN	Lutheran Brick Church	55
Raudabaugh	FRAN	Lutheran Brick Church	55	Rice	WPEN	Diller Mennonite Church	199
Raudabaugh	FRAN	Possum Hill Church	59	Richards	NEWV	Big Spring Presbyterian	132
Raudabaugh	WPEN	Diller Mennonite Church	199	Richardson	NEWV	Big Spring Presbyterian	132
Rea	HOPE	Newburg Church of God	66	Richey	NEWV	Big Spring Presbyterian	132
Rea	NEWV	Newville	146	Richwine	DICK	Mt. Zion	29
Rea	NEWV	Prospect Hill	156	Rickabaugh	WPEN	Diller Mennonite Church	199
Rea	NEWV	United Presbyterian	161	Ricker	CARL	Ashland	17
Reader	HOPE	Zion Reformed Church	72	Rideout	NEWV	Newville	146
Reaghert	MDSX	Letort Spring Church	94	Rider	MIFF	Center Church	103
Rebert	MDSX	Dunker Church	89	Rife	NEWT	Stoughstown Lutheran Church	113

Surname Index

Surname	Twsp.	Cemetery	Page	Surname	Twsp.	Cemetery	Page
Rife	PENN	Centerville Lutheran Church	174	Sanderson	FRAN	Lutheran Brick Church	55
Riggleman	WPEN	Plainfield Lutheran Church	211	Sands	PENN	Dickinson Presb. Church	181
Rine	WPEN	Riggleman Farm	212	Sanlino	HOPE	Newburg Church of God	66
Rinehart		see additional entries on page 261		Sanno	CARL	Ashland	18
Ringwalt	CARL	Ashland	17	Saretell	MDSX	Letort Spring Church	95
Rinker	PENN	Dickinson Presbyterian Ch.	181	Sauer	WPEN	Plainfield Lutheran Church	211
Rippey	NEWV	Big Spring Presbyterian	181	Saxton	CARL	Ashland	18
Ritner	NEWV	Big Spring Presbyterian	132	Saylor	LALN	Eberly's Mills	75
Ritner	NEWV	Prospect Hill	156	Saylor	MDSX	Carlisle Spring Church	85
Ritner	WPEN	Mt. Rock	204	Schneider	FRAN	Lutheran & Ref. Stone Church	43
Ritter	CARL	Ashland	17	Schneider	FRAN	Lutheran Brick Church	56
Ritter	NEWV	Prospect Hill	156	Schwartz	MDSX	Carlisle Spring Church	85
Roads	NEWT	Old Roads	112	Schweitzer	PENN	Huntsdale Dunker	189
Roberts	NEWV	Big Spring Presbyterian	132	Scott	NEWV	United Presbyterian	161
Robinson	NEWV	Big Spring Presbyterian	132	Scouller	NEWV	Big Spring Presbyterian	132
Robinson	PENN	Dickinson Presb. Church	181	Scouller	NEWV	Newville	146
Robinson	PENN	Huntsdale Dunker	189	Scroggs	NEWV	United Presbyterian	161
Rockey	DICK	Mt. Zion	29	Searight	CARL	Ashland	18
Rockey	PENN	Huntsdale Dunker	189	Sease	DICK	Mt. Zion	29
Rodgers	MDSX	Carlisle Spring Church	85	Seavers	PENN	Dickinson Presb. Church	181
Rone	HOPE	Stouffer Farm	67	Seiler	MDSX	Carlisle Spring Church	85
Roney	CARL	Ashland	17	Seilhamer	HOPE	Newburg Church of God	66
Ross	PENN	Dickinson Presb. Church	181	Seitz	FRAN	Lutheran & Ref. Stone Church	41
Roudebaugh	WPEN	Diller Mennonite Church	199	Seitz	MDSX	Letort Spring Church	95
Roush	CARL	Ashland	18	Seitz	NEWV	Newville	146
Roush	MIFF	Zeigler's Church	107	Seitz	WPEN	Plainfield Bethel Church	208
Row	LALN	Eberly's Mills	75	Seitz	WPEN	Seitz Farm	213
Row	NEWT	Irishtown Church	109	Sell	FRAN	Lutheran & Ref. Stone Church	41
Rowe	NEWT	Irishtown Church	109	Sell	FRAN	Lutheran Brick Church	56
Royer	CARL	Ashland	18	Sellers	CARL	Ashland	18
Royer	PENN	Huntsdale Dunker	189	Sellers	LALN	Eberly's Mills	75
Ruch	MDSX	Letort Spring Church	94	Sellers	NEWV	Big Spring Presbyterian	132
Ruff	FRAN	Lutheran & Ref. Stone Church	41	Sellers	PENN	Centerville Lutheran Church	174
Ruhl	MDSX	Letort Spring Church	94	Sells	FRAN	Lutheran & Ref. Stone Church	41
Rupert	PENN	Centerville Lutheran Church	174	Sener	CARL	Ashland	18
Rupp	FRAN	Lutheran Brick Church	55	Sener	NEWV	Prospect Hill	156
Rushmyer	NEWT	Irishtown Church	109	Senk	MDSX	Carlisle Spring Church	86
Russel	WPEN	Plainfield Bethel Church	208	Sennet	PENN	Centerville Lutheran Church	174
Russell	NEWV	Big Spring Presbyterian	132	Sensebaugh	NEWV	Prospect Hill	156
Russell	PENN	Dickinson Presb. Church	181	Sentman	FRAN	Lutheran & Ref. Stone Church	41
Ruth	HOPE	Zion Reformed Church	72	Shade	WPEN	Plainfield Bethel Church	208
Ruth	NEWT	Irishtown Church	109	Shadel	LALN	Eberly's Mills	75
Ruth	NEWV	Zion Lutheran Church	163	Shafer	PENN	Huntsdale Dunker	190
Ryder	MDSX	Letort Spring Church	95	Shaffer	NEWV	Newville	146
Rynard	MIFF	Center Church	103	Shalley	CARL	Ashland	18
Sadler	CARL	Ashland	18	Shambaugh	FRAN	Lutheran & Ref. Stone Church	41
Salisbury	FRAN	Lutheran Brick Church	55	Shambaugh	FRAN	Lutheran Brick Church	56
Salsburg	FRAN	Lutheran Brick Church	55	Shambaugh	MDSX	Carlisle Spring Church	86
Salter	MIFF	Center Church	103	Shambaugh	WPEN	Mt. Rock	204
Saltzgiver	PENN	Centerville Lutheran Church	174	Shambaugh	WPEN	Plainfield Bethel Church	208
Sanderson	CARL	Meeting House Springs	25	Shanabrook	HOPE	Newburg Church of God	66

Surname	Twsp.	Cemetery	Page	Surname	Twsp.	Cemetery	Page
Shanabrough	FRAN	Lutheran & Ref. Stone Church	42	Shoap	DICK	Mt. Zion	29
Shanabrough	FRAN	Lutheran Brick Church	56	Shoap	HOPE	Zion Reformed Church	72
Shank	PENN	Huntsdale Dunker	189	Shoap	NEWV	Prospect Hill	156
Shannon	WPEN	Mt. Rock	204	Shoedler	PENN	Huntsdale Dunker	190
Shapley	CARL	Ashland	18	Shoemaker	HOPE	Newburg Church of God	66
Sharf	NEWV	Prospect Hill	156	Shoemaker	NEWV	Newville	146
Sharp	FRAN	Lutheran Brick Church	56	Shoemaker	PENN	Centerville Lutheran Church	174
Sharp	NEWV	Big Spring Presbyterian	132	Shoemaker	PENN	Huntsdale Dunker	190
Sharp	NEWV	Newville	146	Shopp	FRAN	Lutheran & Ref. Stone Church	42
Sharp	NEWV	Prospect Hill	156	Shopwell	NEWV	Prospect Hill	156
Sharp	NEWV	United Presbyterian	161	Short	PENN	Huntsdale Dunker	190
Sharpe	CARL	Ashland	18	Shover	WPEN	Diller Mennonite Church	199
Sharpe	NEWV	Newville	146	Shover	WPEN	Mt. Rock	204
Shatto	FRAN	Lutheran & Ref. Stone Church	42	Shower	CARL	Ashland	19
Shatto	MDSX	Carlisle Spring Church	86	Shreffler	NEWV	Prospect Hill	157
Shatto	MDSX	Dunker Church	89	Shreiner	MDSX	Letort Spring Church	95
Shaw	LALN	Lisburn	79	Shriner	HOPE	Zion Reformed Church	72
Shaw	NMID	Wagner's Church	167	Shriner	NEWT	Oakville United Brethren	111
Shaw	PENN	Dickinson Presb. Church	181	Shriver	PENN	Centerville Lutheran Church	174
Shaw	WPEN	Bear	194	Shrom	CARL	Ashland	19
Sheaffer	CARL	Ashland	18	Shroyer	PENN	Centerville Lutheran Church	174
Sheaffer	MDSX	Carlisle Spring Church	86	Shuff	MDSX	Letort Spring Church	95
Sheaffer	NEWV	Newville	146	Shuff	SMID	Flint Ridge Chapel	169
Sheaffer	NMID	Wagner's Church	167	Shuff	WPEN	Plainfield Bethel Church	208
Sheaffer	PENN	Centerville Lutheran Church	174	Shufman	MDSX	Carlisle Spring Church	86
Sheaffer	PENN	Huntsdale Dunker	190	Shughart	FRAN	Lutheran & Ref. Stone Church	42
Sheaffer	WPEN	Plainfield Bethel Church	208	Shughart	NMID	Wagner's Church	167
Shearer	FRAN	Lutheran & Ref. Stone Church	42	Shughart	WPEN	Plainfield Lutheran Church	211
Shearer	NMID	Wagner's Church	167	Shulenberger	HOPE	Zion Reformed Church	72
Shearer	WPEN	Mt. Rock	204	Shulenberger	NEWV	Prospect Hill	157
Sheets	NEWT	Oakville United Brethren	111	Shuler	FRAN	Entlerville	34
Sheffer	NMID	Bethel Church	165	Shuler	MDSX	Carlisle Spring Church	86
Sheffler	PENN	Centerville Lutheran Church	174	Shullenberger	NEWV	Big Spring Presbyterian	132
Shellebarger	NEWV	Prospect Hill	156	Shuman	FRAN	Lutheran & Ref. Stone Church	42
Sheller	PENN	Huntsdale Dunker	190	Sidle	LALN	Lisburn	79
Shenk	NEWV	Newville	146	Siler	MDSX	Carlisle Spring Church	86
Shenk	PENN	Dickinson Presb. Church	181	Sipe	CARL	Ashland	19
Shenk	PENN	Huntsdale Dunker	189	Sipe	FRAN	Lutheran & Ref. Stone Church	42
Sherf	NEWV	Prospect Hill	156	Sipe	FRAN	Lutheran Brick Church	56
Sheriff	NEWV	Big Spring Presbyterian	132	Sipe	FRAN	Possum Hill Church	59
Sheriff	NEWV	Prospect Hill	156	Sipe	LALN	Eberly's Mills.	75
Sheriff	NMID	Wagner's Church	167	Sipe	NEWT	Stoughstown Lutheran Church	113
Shetron	MDSX	Letort Spring Church	95	Sites	FRAN	Lutheran & Ref. Stone Church	42
Shetron	NMID	Wagner's Church	167	Sites	MDSX	Letort Spring Church	95
Shetron	WPEN	Mt. Rock	204	Skelly	HOPE	Newburg Church of God	66
Shibley	FRAN	Lutheran & Ref. Stone Church	42	Skiner	NEWV	Newville	147
Shimp	FRAN	Lutheran Brick Church	56	Skinner	NEWV	Newville	147
Shipley	NEWV	Prospect Hill	156	Slaybaugh	NEWV	Zion Lutheran Church	164
Shipp	PENN	Huntsdale Dunker	190	Sleabaugh	FRAN	Lutheran Brick Church	56
Shively	FRAN	Lutheran & Ref. Stone Church	42	Slusser	DICK	Mt. Zion	30
Shively	NEWV	Newville	146	Slusser	PENN	Centerville Lutheran Church	174

Surname Index

Surname	Twsp.	Cemetery	Page	Surname	Twsp.	Cemetery	Page
Smead	CARL	Ashland	19	Sower	CARL	Ashland	19
Smec	MDSX	Letort Spring Church	95	Sowers	DICK	Mt. Zion	30
Smeigh	NMID	Bethel Church	165	Sowers	FRAN	Lutheran & Ref. Stone Church	43
Smiley	CARL	Ashland	19	Sowers	MDSX	Letort Spring Church	95
Smith	CARL	Ashland	19	Sowers	PENN	Centerville Lutheran Church	175
Smith	FRAN	Lutheran Brick Church	56	Spahr	CARL	Ashland	19
Smith	HOPE	Hanna	61	Spahr	MDSX	Carlisle Spring Church	86
Smith	HOPE	Zion Reformed Church	73	Spangler	CARL	Ashland	19
Smith	LALN	Eberly's Mill	75	Spangler	MIFF	Bethel Church	100
Smith	MDSX	Carlisle Spring Church	86	Spangler	NEWT	Irishtown Church	110
Smith	MDSX	Letort Spring Church	95	Spangler	NEWV	Newville	147
Smith	MIFF	Center Church	103	Spangler	NEWV	Prospect Hill	157
Smith	NEWT	Oakville United Brethren	111	Spangler	PENN	Centerville Lutheran Church	175
Smith	NEWV	Big Spring Presbyterian	132	Spangler	PENN	Huntsdale Dunker	190
Smith	NEWV	Newville	147	Speck	CARL	Ashland	20
Smith	NEWV	Prospect Hill	157	Speck	NEWT	Irishtown Church	110
Smith	PENN	Centerville Lutheran Church	174	Spence	PENN	Centerville Lutheran Church	175
Smith	WPEN	Plainfield Bethel Church	208	Spencer	NEWV	Big Spring Presbyterian	132
Smith	WPEN	Springfield	215	Sperow	WPEN	Plainfield Lutheran Church	211
Smyers	DICK	Mt. Zion	30	Spidel	NEWV	Zion Lutheran Church	164
Smyser	LALN	Lisburn	79	Spidle	PENN	Huntsdale Dunker	190
Sneider	WPEN	Old Shellenberger Farm	205	Sponsler	CARL	Ashland	20
Snevely	NEWV	Zion Lutheran Church	164	Sponsler	NEWV	Prospect Hill	157
Snider	FRAN	Lutheran & Ref. Stone Church	43	Spotts	CARL	Ashland	20
Snider	FRAN	Lutheran Brick Church	56	Spotts	WPEN	Plainfield Bethel Church	208
Snodgrass	NEWV	Big Spring Presbyterian	132	Spottswood	NEWV	Big Spring Presbyterian	132
Snoke	MIFF	Bethany Church	98	Sprenkle	LALN	Lisburn	79
Snoke	MIFF	Snokes Graveyard	106	Spriggs	PENN	Dickinson Presb. Church	181
Snoke	NEWT	Irishtown Church	110	Sprout	NEWV	Prospect Hill	157
Snoke	PENN	Centerville Lutheran Church	175	Stahl	CARL	Ashland	20
Snoke	PENN	Huntsdale Dunker	190	Stahl	WPEN	Plainfield Lutheran Church	211
Snowden	NEWV	Big Spring Presbyterian	132	Stake	HOPE	Newburg Church of God	66
Snyder	FRAN	Lutheran & Ref. Stone Church	43	Staller	CARL	Ashland	20
Snyder	FRAN	Lutheran Brick Church	56	Stamy	PENN	Huntsdale Dunker	190
Snyder	LALN	Eberly's Mill	75	Stanton	NEWV	Big Spring Presbyterian	133
Snyder	MDSX	Carlisle Spring Church	86	Starner	DICK	Mt. Zion	30
Snyder	MDSX	Letort Spring Church	95	Starr	LALN	Lisburn	79
Snyder	NEWV	Newville	147	Starrett	NEWV	Big Spring Presbyterian	133
Snyder	NEWV	Prospect Hill	157	Staub	HOPE	Newburg Church of God	66
Snyder	PENN	Centerville Lutheran Church	175	Stauffer	CARL	Ashland	20
Snyder	UALN	Lantz's School House	193	Stauffer	MDSX	Carlisle Spring Church	86
Snyder	WPEN	Old Shellenberger Farm	205	Staver	NEWV	Prospect Hill	157
Snyder	WPEN	Springfield	215	Staver	WPEN	Mt. Rock	204
Sollenberger	MIFF	Center Church	104	Stawart	NEWV	Big Spring Presbyterian	133
Sollenberger	NEWV	Big Spring Presbyterian	132	Stayman	CARL	Ashland	20
Sollenberger	PENN	Huntsdale Dunker	190	Stayman	DICK	Old Line	32
Souder	FRAN	Bloserville Ref. Church	33	Steel	NEWV	Big Spring Presbyterian	133
Souder	FRAN	Lutheran Brick Church	56	Steerick	MIFF	Snokes Graveyard	106
Souders	FRAN	Bloserville Ref. Church	33	Stephen	LALN	Eberly's Mills	75
Souders	PENN	Huntsdale Dunker	190	Stephens	HOPE	Zion Reformed Church	73
Souders	WPEN	Plainfield Lutheran Church	211	Sterner	DICK	Mt. Zion	30

Surname Index

Surname	Twsp.	Cemetery	Page	Surname	Twsp.	Cemetery	Page
Sterrett	CARL	Ashland	20	Strohm	NEWV	Zion Lutheran Church	164
Sterrett	NEWV	Big Spring Presbyterian	133	Strohm	NMID	Wagner's Church	167
Stevens	HOPE	Newburg Church of God	66	Strohm	WPEN	Plainfield Bethel Church	208
Stevenson	NEWV	Big Spring Presbyterian	133	Stroman	HOPE	Newburg Church of God	67
Stevick	HOPE	Newburg Church of God	66	Stuart	NEWV	Big Spring Presbyterian	133
Stewart	NEWV	Big Spring Presbyterian	133	Stuart	PENN	Dickinson Presb. Church	181
Stewig	HOPE	Newburg Church of God	66	Stum	FRAN	Lutheran Brick Church	57
Stichler	FRAN	Lutheran Brick Church	56	Stum	MIFF	Bethel Church	100
Stickle	MDSX	Letort Spring Church	95	Stum	MIFF	Center Church	104
Stickler	FRAN	Lutheran Brick Church	56	Stum	NEWV	Prospect Hill	157
Stine	FRAN	Lutheran & Ref. Stone Church	43	Stumbaugh	WPEN	Springfield	215
Stine	FRAN	Lutheran Brick Church	57	Stump	FRAN	Lutheran & Ref. Stone Church	43
Stine	WPEN	Diller Mennonite Church	199	Stump	HOPE	Zion Reformed Church	73
Stitzel	NEWV	Zion Lutheran Church	164	Stump	MIFF	Mt. Hope	105
Stock	CARL	Ashland	20	Stump	WPEN	Plainfield Lutheran Church	211
Stoke	WPEN	Springfield	215	Stutsman	NMID	Wagner's Church	167
Stone	FRAN	Lutheran & Ref. Stone Church	43	Sumerland	PENN	Huntsdale Dunker	191
Stone	MDSX	Carlisle Spring Church	86	Sutton	WPEN	Plainfield Bethel Church	208
Stone	MDSX	Letort Spring Church	95	Swanger	MDSX	Letort Spring Church	95
Stoneberger	MIFF	Zeigler's Church	107	Swarner	NMID	Bethel Church	165
Stonebraker	CARL	Ashland	20	Swartz	FRAN	Lutheran Brick Church	57
Stoner	FRAN	Lutheran Brick Church	57	Swartz	HOPE	Zion Reformed Church	73
Stoner	MDSX	Carlisle Spring Church	86	Swartz	NEWV	Prospect Hill	157
Stoner	PENN	Centerville Lutheran Church	175	Swartz	NMID	Wagner's Church	167
Stoner	PENN	Huntsdale Dunker	190	Swiger	FRAN	Lutheran & Ref. Stone Church	43
Stouffer	CARL	Ashland	20	Swiger	NMID	Bethel Church	165
Stouffer	HOPE	Newburg Church of God	66	Swigert	CARL	Ashland	20
Stouffer	HOPE	Stouffer Farm	67	Swigert	FRAN	Lutheran & Ref. Stone Church	43
Stouffer	MDSX	Carlisle Spring Church	86	Swigert	MDSX	Carlisle Spring Church	86
Stouffer	MDSX	Mennonite Grvyd.-Balfour	97	Swigert	NEWV	Newville	147
Stough	NEWV	Newville	147	Swigert	PENN	Huntsdale Dunker	191
Stough	NEWV	Prospect Hill	157	Swiler	NEWV	Big Spring Presbyterian	133
Stout	PENN	Cumminstown Campbellite	177	Swiler	WPEN	Mt. Rock	204
Stout	WPEN	Diller Mennonite Church	199	Sword	PENN	Centerville Lutheran Church	175
Stover	FRAN	Bloserville Ref. Church	33	Swords	FRAN	Lutheran Brick Church	57
Stover	FRAN	Lutheran Brick Church	57	Swords	MDSX	Dunker Church	89
Stover	HOPE	Zion Reformed Church	73	Swords	PENN	Centerville Lutheran Church	175
Stover	NEWT	Irishtown Church	110	Swoyer	NEWV	Big Spring Presbyterian	133
Stover	NEWV	Big Spring Presbyterian	133	Swoyer	NEWV	Newville	147
Stover	PENN	Huntsdale Dunker	190	Talhelm	NEWV	Prospect Hill	157
Strausbaugh	MDSX	Letort Spring Church	95	Tanner	NEWV	Prospect Hill	157
Straw	PENN	Huntsdale Dunker	190	Taylor	FRAN	Lutheran Brick Church	57
Strayer	MDSX	Dunker Church	89	Taylor	NEWV	Prospect Hill	157
Strickler	MDSX	Letort Spring Church	95	Tennent	CARL	Ashland	20
Strickler	SMID	Strickler	170	Thoman	MDSX	Carlisle Spring Church	86
Strike	HOPE	Newburg Church of God	66	Thomas	FRAN	Lutheran & Ref. Stone Church	44
Strine	FRAN	Entlerville	34	Thomas	MIFF	Bethany Church	99
Strohm	CARL	Ashland	20	Thomas	MIFF	Center Church	104
Strohm	FRAN	Lutheran & Ref. Stone Church	43	Thomas	MIFF	Mt. Hope	105
Strohm	HOPE	Newburg Church of God	66	Thomas	NEWV	Newville	147
Strohm	NEWV	Prospect Hill	157	Thomas	NEWV	Prospect Hill	157

Surname Index

Surname	Twsp.	Cemetery	Page	Surname	Twsp.	Cemetery	Page
Thomas	NMID	Wagner's Church	167	Underwood	PENN	Centerville Lutheran Church	175
Thomas	PENN	Centerville Lutheran Church	175	Urich	LALN	Eberly's Mill	75
Thompson	CARL	Ashland	20	Utley	FRAN	Lutheran Brick Church	57
Thompson	NEWV	Big Spring Presbyterian	134	Utley	NEWV	Newville	147
Thompson	NEWV	Newville	147	Utley	PENN	Centerville Lutheran Church	176
Thompson	PENN	Dickinson Presb. Church	181	Utly	FRAN	Lutheran Brick Church	57
Thomson	CARL	Meeting House Springs	25	Utz	PENN	Huntsdale Dunker	191
Throne	CARL	Ashland	20	Vanard	NEWV	Big Spring Presbyterian	134
Throne	FRAN	Lutheran & Ref. Stone Church	44	Vanasdal	PENN	Centerville Lutheran Church	176
Throne	FRAN	Lutheran Brick Church	57	Vanasdal	WPEN	Plainfield Lutheran Church	211
Throne	NEWV	Newville	147	Vance	NEWV	United Presbyterian	162
Throne	PENN	Centerville Lutheran Church	175	Vance	PENN	Huntsdale Dunker	191
Throne	PENN	Huntsdale Dunker	191	Vanderbelt	NEWV	Big Spring Presbyterian	134
Throne	WPEN	Mt. Rock	204	Vanderbilt	NEWV	Big Spring Presbyterian	134
Through	NEWV	Prospect Hill	158	VanKirk	WPEN	Mt. Rock	204
Thrush	HOPE	Zion Reformed Church	73	Varner	NEWT	Oakville United Brethren	111
Thrush	NEWV	Newville	147	Von Heilen	CARL	Ashland	20
Thrush	NEWV	Prospect Hill	157	Wade	PENN	Huntsdale Dunker	191
Thrush	PENN	Dickinson Presb. Church	181	Waggoner	CARL	Ashland	21
Thrush	PENN	Huntsdale Dunker	191	Waggoner	FRAN	Bloserville Ref. Church	33
Thudium	CARL	Ashland	20	Waggoner	FRAN	Lutheran & Ref. Stone Church	44
Thumm	FRAN	Entlerville	34	Waggoner	NEWT	Irishtown Church	110
Thumma	FRAN	Lutheran & Ref. Stone Church	44	Waggoner	NEWT	Oakville United Brethren	111
Thumma	FRAN	Lutheran Brick Church	57	Waggoner	NEWV	Big Spring Presbyterian	134
Thumma	FRAN	Possum Hill Church	59	Waggoner	NEWV	Newville	147
Thumma	NMID	Wagner's Church	167	Waggoner	NEWV	Zion Lutheran Church	164
Tobias	MDSX	Letort Spring Church	95	Waggoner	NMID	Wagner's Church	167
Todd	CARL	Ashland	20	Waggoner	WPEN	Plainfield Bethel Church	208
Trego	CARL	Ashland	20	Waggoner	WPEN	Plainfield Lutheran Church	211
Trego	MDSX	Letort Spring Church	95	Wagner	CARL	Ashland	21
Trego	NEWV	Big Spring Presbyterian	134	Wagner	FRAN	Bloserville Ref. Church	33
Trego	NEWV	Newville	147	Wagner	FRAN	Lutheran Brick Church	57
Trego	PENN	Dickinson Presb. Church	181	Wagner	HOPE	Newburg Church of God	67
Trego	WPEN	Mt. Rock	204	Wagner	NEWT	Irishtown Church	110
Trimmer	NEWV	Newville	147	Wagner	NEWV	Big Spring Presbyterian	134
Trine	PENN	Huntsdale Dunker	191	Wagner	NEWV	Prospect Hill	158
Tritt	NEWV	Big Spring Presbyterian	134	Wagner	PENN	Huntsdale Dunker	191
Tritt	NEWV	Newville	147	Wagoner	CARL	Ashland	21
Tritt	NEWV	Prospect Hill	157	Wagoner	HOPE	Hanna	61
Tritt	PENN	Centerville Lutheran Church	175	Wagoner	NMID	Wagner's Church	167
Tritt	PENN	Huntsdale Dunker	191	Wagoner	WPEN	Plainfield Bethel Church	208
Trostle	MDSX	Carlisle Spring Church	86	Waidly	MDSX	Letort Spring Church	96
Trough	NEWV	Prospect Hill	157	Waigal	FRAN	Lutheran Brick Church	57
Troup	MDSX	Letort Spring Church	95	Walker	CARL	Ashland	21
Troup	WPEN	Springfield	215	Walker	FRAN	Lutheran & Ref. Stone Church	44
Turns	WPEN	Springfield	215	Walker	LALN	Monroe Woods Farm	80
Tyson	LALN	Eberly's Mill	75	Walker	NEWT	Irishtown Church	110
Uhler	CARL	Ashland	20	Walker	NEWV	Prospect Hill	158
Ulrich	MDSX	Letort Spring Church	95	Walker	NMID	Wagner's Church	168
Umberger	LALN	Lisburn	79	Walker	PENN	Dickinson Presb. Church	182
Umholtz	PENN	Centerville Lutheran Church	175	Walker	PENN	Huntsdale Dunker	191

Surname Index

Surname	Twsp.	Cemetery	Page	Surname	Twsp.	Cemetery	Page
Wallace	CARL	Ashland	21	Weise	CARL	Ashland	21
Wallace	HOPE	Newburg Church of God	67	Weise	FRAN	Lutheran Brick Church	57
Wallace	NEWV	Big Spring Presbyterian	134	Weiser	NEWV	Prospect Hill	158
Wallace	NEWV	Newville	147	Weiss	NEWV	Big Spring Presbyterian	135
Walmsley	PENN	Dickinson Presb. Church	182	Weist	HOPE	Newburg Church of God	67
Walt	PENN	Centerville Lutheran Church	176	Weitzel	MDSX	Letort Spring Church	96
Walter	DICK	Mt. Zion	30	Weitzel	MDSX	Mennonite Grvyd.-Balfour	97
Walter	FRAN	Possum Hill Church	59	Wells	NEWV	Newville	148
Walters	FRAN	Possum Hill Church	59	Welsh	WPEN	Mt. Rock	204
Walters	MIFF	Bethany Church	99	Wengert	HOPE	Hoover Farm	62
Walters	PENN	Huntsdale Dunker	191	Wentz	PENN	Huntsdale Dunker	191
Wanbaugh	MDSX	Letort Spring Church	96	Wert	CARL	Ashland	21
Ward	CARL	Ashland	21	Wert	FRAN	Lutheran & Ref. Stone Church	44
Ward	MDSX	Carlisle Spring Church	86	Wert	MDSX	Carlisle Spring Church	87
Ward	WPEN	Plainfield Lutheran Church	211	Wert	NMID	Wagner's Church	168
Warden	NEWV	Prospect Hill	158	Wert	WPEN	Plainfield Lutheran Church	211
Wareham	CARL	Ashland	21	Westafer	NEWV	Newville	148
Warner	FRAN	Entlerville	34	Westafer	NEWV	Prospect Hill	158
Warner	FRAN	Lutheran & Ref. Stone Church	44	Westfall	MDSX	Letort Spring Church	96
Warner	WPEN	Diller Mennonite Church	199	Westfall	NEWV	Prospect Hill	158
Washmood	WPEN	Heikes Farm	201	Wetzel	CARL	Ashland	21
Washmood	WPEN	Riggleman Farm	212	Wetzel	FRAN	Lutheran & Ref. Stone Church	44
Wastafer	NEWV	Newville	148	Wetzel	MDSX	Carlisle Spring Church	87
Waters	WPEN	Springfield	215	Wetzel	NMID	Wagner's Church	168
Watson	HOPE	Mt. Tabor Church	62	Whaler	NEWV	Prospect Hill	158
Watson	HOPE	Newburg Church of God	67	Wheeler	NEWV	Prospect Hill	158
Watson	HOPE	Zion Reformed Church	73	Wheler	NEWV	Prospect Hill	158
Watson	WPEN	Heikes Farm	201	Wherry	CARL	Ashland	21
Watson	WPEN	Plainfield Bethel Church	208	Wherry	HOPE	Hanna	61
Weakley	CARL	Ashland	21	Whisler	HOPE	Newburg Church of God	67
Weakley	CARL	Meeting House Springs	25	Whisler	HOPE	Zion Reformed Church	73
Weakley	NEWV	Big Spring Presbyterian	135	Whisler	MIFF	Bethany Church	99
Weakley	PENN	Centerville Lutheran Church	176	Whisler	MIFF	Center Church	104
Weakley	PENN	Dickinson Presb. Church	182	Whisler	MIFF	Snokes Graveyard	106
Weary	FRAN	Lutheran & Ref. Stone Church	44	Whisler	WPEN	Diller Mennonite Church	199
Weary	MDSX	Carlisle Spring Church	86	Whisler	WPEN	Plainfield Lutheran Church	211
Weary	MDSX	Letort Spring Church	96	Whistler	MIFF	Bethany Church	99
Weast	NEWV	Big Spring Presbyterian	135	Whistler	MIFF	Center Church	104
Weast	NEWV	Prospect Hill	158	Whistler	MIFF	Mt. Hope	105
Weaver	HOPE	Zion Reformed Church	73	Whistler	NEWT	Oakville United Brethren	111
Weaver	MDSX	Carlisle Spring Church	87	Whistler	NEWV	Newville	148
Weaver	MIFF	Bethany Church	99	Whistler	NEWV	Prospect Hill	158
Weaver	NEWT	Irishtown Church	110	Whistler	WPEN	Diller Mennonite Church	199
Weaver	NEWV	Prospect Hill	158	White	NEWV	Prospect Hill	158
Weaver	PENN	Huntsdale Dunker	191	White	NEWV	United Presbyterian	162
Weekline	PENN	Centerville Lutheran Church	176	White	PENN	Centerville Lutheran Church	176
Weibley	CARL	Ashland	21	White	WPEN	Mt. Rock	204
Weibley	MDSX	Carlisle Spring Church	87	Whiteside	NEWV	Big Spring Presbyterian	135
Weigle	DICK	Mt. Zion	30	Whitley	NEWV	Big Spring Presbyterian	135
Weigle	FRAN	Possum Hill Church	59	Whitmer	LALN	Eberly's Mills	76
Weirich	HOPE	Newburg Church of God	67	Whitmer	PENN	Centerville Lutheran Church	176

Surname Index

Surname	Twsp.	Cemetery	Page	Surname	Twsp.	Cemetery	Page
Wichlein	NEWV	Prospect Hill	158	Wolf	HOPE	Zion Reformed Church	73
Wickard	FRAN	Lutheran & Ref. Stone Church	45	Wolf	MDSX	Carlisle Spring Church	87
Wickard	MDSX	Carlisle Spring Church	87	Wolf	MIFF	Center Church	104
Wickard	NMID	Wagner's Church	168	Wolf	NEWT	Irishtown Church	110
Wickert	MDSX	Carlisle Spring Church	104	Wolf	NEWV	Big Spring Presbyterian	135
Wickline	NEWT	Irishtown Church	110	Wolf	NEWV	Newville	148
Widder	PENN	Huntsdale Dunker	191	Wolf	NMID	Wagner's Church	168
Widders	MIFF	Center Church	104	Wolf	PENN	Centerville Lutheran Church	176
Wild	NEWV	Newville	148	Wolf	PENN	Huntsdale Dunker	191
Wilder	CARL	Ashland	22	Wolf	WPEN	Plainfield Lutheran Church	211
Wiley	LALN	Lisburn	79	Wolfe	PENN	Huntsdale Dunker	191
Wilkinson	NEWV	Newville	148	Wolfe	WPEN	Plainfield Lutheran Church	211
Willey	CARL	Ashland	22	Wonderlich	CARL	Ashland	22
Williams	CARL	Ashland	22	Wonders	MDSX	Letort Spring Church	96
Williams	DICK	Mt. Zion	30	Woodburn	NEWV	Big Spring Presbyterian	135
Williams	FRAN	Lutheran & Ref. Stone Church	45	Woodburn	NEWV	Newville	148
Williams	NEWV	Big Spring Presbyterian	135	Woodburn	NEWV	United Presbyterian	162
Williams	NEWV	Newville	148	Woodburn	PENN	Dickinson Presb. Church	182
Williams	NEWV	Prospect Hill	159	Woodrow	WPEN	Springfield	215
Williamson	CARL	Ashland	22	Woods	CARL	Ashland	22
Williamson	NEWV	Big Spring Presbyterian	135	Woods	NEWV	Big Spring Presbyterian	136
Williamson	PENN	Centerville Lutheran Church	176	Woods	NEWV	Newville	148
Williamson	PENN	Dickinson Presb. Church	182	Woods	NEWV	United Presbyterian	162
Wills	LALN	Eberly's Mills	76	Woods	PENN	Dickinson Presb. Church	182
Wilson	CARL	Ashland	22	Woods	PENN	Huntsdale Dunker	191
Wilson	MDSX	Dunker Church	89	Woodward	CARL	Ashland	22
Wilson	NEWT	Irishtown Church	110	Work	WPEN	Springfield	215
Wilson	NEWV	Big Spring Presbyterian	135	Worley	WPEN	Plainfield Bethel Church	208
Wilson	NEWV	Prospect Hill	159	Wormley	CARL	Ashland	23
Wilt	NEWV	Big Spring Presbyterian	135	Worst	FRAN	Lutheran Brick Church	57
Wimer	NEWV	Big Spring Presbyterian	135	Worst	NEWV	Prospect Hill	159
Winand	SMID	Flint Ridge Chapel	169	Worst	PENN	Huntsdale Dunker	191
Wing	CARL	Ashland	22	Wright	CARL	Ashland	23
Wink	MDSX	Letort Spring Church	96	Wunderlich	CARL	Ashland	22
Wire	FRAN	Lutheran & Ref. Stone Church	45	Wyke	NEWV	Prospect Hill	159
Wirt	FRAN	Lutheran & Ref. Stone Church	45	Wynkoop	FRAN	Lutheran & Ref. Stone Church	45
Wise	CARL	Ashland	21	Wynekoop	FRAN	Lutheran & Ref. Stone Church	45
Wise	MDSX	Letort Spring Church	96	Yarlet	WPEN	Bear	194
Wise	MIFF	Center Church	104	Yarlets	NEWT	Irishtown Church	110
Wise	MIFF	Zeigler's Church	107	Yarlets	NMID	Wagner's Church	168
Wise	NEWV	Newville	148	Yeager	FRAN	Bloserville Ref. Church	34
Witherspoon	CARL	Meeting House Springs	25	Yeager	NEWV	Zion Lutheran Church	164
Witmer	CARL	Ashland	22	Yeingst	PENN	Huntsdale Dunker	192
Witmer	MDSX	Letort Spring Church	96	Yeoter	WPEN	Plainfield Bethel Church	208
Witmer	PENN	Huntsdale Dunker	191	Yesler	SMID	Flint Ridge Chapel	169
Wolf	CARL	Ashland	22	Yetter	PENN	Huntsdale Dunker	192
Wolf	DICK	Mt. Zion	30	Yhost	PENN	Centerville Lutheran Church	176
Wolf	FRAN	Entlerville	34	Yinger	WPEN	Plainfield Lutheran Church	211
Wolf	FRAN	Lutheran & Ref. Stone Church	45	Yorlets	FRAN	Possum Hill Church	59
Wolf	FRAN	Lutheran Brick Church	57	Yorlets	NMID	Wagner's Church	168
Wolf	FRAN	Possum Hill Church	59	Yost	MIFF	Bethel Church	100

Surname Index

Surname	Twsp.	Cemetery	Page	Surname	Twsp.	Cemetery	Page
Yost	PENN	Huntsdale Dunker	192	Zeigler	MDSX	Letort Spring Church	96
Yoter	FRAN	Lutheran & Ref. Stone Church	45	Zeigler	MIFF	Bethel Church	100
Yoter	WPEN	Plainfield Bethel Church	208	Zeigler	MIFF	Zeigler's Church	107
Young	CARL	Meeting House Springs	25	Zeigler	NEWV	Prospect Hill	159
Young	FRAN	Lutheran & Ref. Stone Church	45	Zeigler	WPEN	Bear	194
Young	LALN	Lisburn	79	Zeigler	WPEN	Heikes Farm	201
Young	NEWV	Prospect Hill	159	Zell	PENN	Huntsdale Dunker	192
Young	NEWV	Zion Lutheran Church	164	Zettler	MDSX	Letort Spring Church	96
Young	PENN	Centerville Lutheran Church	176	Zimmerman	CARL	Ashland	23
Young	PENN	Huntsdale Dunker	192	Zimmerman	FRAN	Bloserville Ref. Church	34
Young	WPEN	Mt. Rock	204	Zimmerman	NMID	Wagner's Church	168
Young	WPEN	Plainfield Lutheran Church	211	Zinn	NEWT	Oakville United Brethren	111
Young	WPEN	Springfield	215	Zinn	PENN	Centerville Lutheran Church	176
Zalar	FRAN	Lutheran Brick Church	57	Zinn	WPEN	Mt. Rock	204
Zearing	CARL	Ashland	23	Zitzer	CARL	Ashland	23
Zeigler	CARL	Ashland	23	Zoller	FRAN	Lutheran Brick Church	58
Zeigler	DICK	Mt. Zion	30	Zug	CARL	Ashland	23
Zeigler	FRAN	Lutheran & Ref. Stone Church	45	Zug	PENN	Huntsdale Dunker	192
Zeigler	FRAN	Lutheran Brick Church	57	Zug	WPEN	Plainfield Lutheran Church	212
Zeigler	MDSX	Carlisle Spring Church	88				

ADDITONS TO THE INDEX

Surname	Twsp.	Cemetery	Page	Surname	Twsp.	Cemetery	Page
Buckwalter	FRAN	Lutheran Brick Church	48	Buttort	MDSX	Carlisle Spring Church	82
Buffington	MDSX	Dunker Church	88	Buttort	MDSX	Letort Spring Church	90
Burger	WPEN	Plainfield Bethel Church	206	Cully	PENN	Centerville Lutheran Church	172
Burget	WPEN	Plainfield Lutheran Church	209	Deihl	FRAN	Lutheran Brick Church	48
Burgett	MDSX	Carlisle Springs Church	82	Deihl	HOPE	Newburg Church of God	63
Burgett	WPEN	Plainfield Lutheran Church	209	Kendig	FRAN	Lutheran Brick Church	52
Burckhart	WPEN	Diller Mennonite Church	195	Kindig	HOPE	Newburg Church of God	64
Burkepile	WPEN	Mount Rock	203	Mowrer	NEWV	Big Spring Presbyterian	130
Burkhart	FRAN	Lutheran Brick Church	48	Mull	NEWV	Big Spring Presbyterian	130
Burkhart	HOPE	Hoover Farm	62	Mull	NEWV	Zion Lutheran Church	163
Burkhart	HOPE	Newburg Church of God	63	Ramp	HOPE	Newburg Church of God	65
Burkhart	MDSX	Carlisle Spring Church	82	Richards	NEWV	Big Spring Presbyterian	132
Burkhart	MIFF	Snoke	106	Rinehart	MDSX	Carlisle Spring Church	85
Burkhart	WPEN	Diller Mennonite Church	195	Rinehart	MDSX	Letort Spring Church	94
Burkholder	CARL	Ashland	4	Rippey	NEWV	Big Spring Presbyterian	132
Burkholder	FRAN	Lutheran Brick Church	48	Stroman	HOPE	Newburg Church of God	66
Burkholder	WPEN	Diller Mennonite Church	196				
Burkholder	WPEN	Springfield	214				
Burns	NEWV	Prospect Hill	150				
Burtnett	FRAN	Lutheran Brick Church	48				
Bush	WPEN	Springfield	214				
Bushman	CARL	Ashland	4				
Bushman	PENN	Centerville Lutheran Church	171				
Butler	CARL	Ashland	4				
Butler	NEWV	Big Spring Presbyterian	116				
Butler	NEWV	Newville	138				

Relative Index

INDEX TO RELATIVES OF INTERRED PERSONS

Relative's Name	Name of Person Interred	Township, Cemetery	
Armstrong, W. K.	Waggoner, Jennie E. Armstrong, wife	North Middleton, Wagner's Church Graveyard	167
Ashenfelter, S. & L.	Strausbaugh, Elminah Ashenfelter, daughter	Middlesex, Letort Spring Chruch Graveyard	95
Baker, Felty	Myers, Anna Baker, daughter	West Pennsboro, Bitner Farm Graveyard	195
Balmer, Christian	Bitzer, Lucia, daughter	Penn, Centerville Lutheran Church Graveyard	171
Beam, Jacob	Diller, Elizabeth, daughter	West Pennsboro, Diller Mennonite Church Grvyd.	197
Bear, John & Elizabeth	Eberly, Ann, daughter	West Pennsboro, Bear Graveyard	194
Biddle, William M. & Lydia	Baird, Lydia M., daughter	Carlisle, Ashland Cemetery	1
Bitner, Adam & Fanny	Zug, Lucetta, daughter	Penn, Huntsdale Dunker Cemetery	192
Breckenmaker, P. & S.	McBride, Annie C., daughter	Middlesex, Letort Spring Church Graveyard	94
Brickley, William & Margaret	Hefflefinger, Mary E., dau.	Hopewell, Zion Reformed Church Graveyard	70
Brindle, George & Elizabeth	Chandler, Catharine, daughter	Middlesex, Carlisle Springs Church Graveyard	82
Brown, Henry & Leah	Bentz, Susan C., daughter	Newville, Newville Cemetery	137
Brown, Jessie & Elizabeth	Garman, Mary A., daughter	West Pennsboro, Plainfield Bethel Church Grvyd.	206
Carothers, W. W. & E. A.	Mitchell, Alice B., daughter	Newville, Prospect Hill Cemetery	155
Clandy, M. & E.	Beecher, Mary Ann, daughter	Penn, Centerville Lutheran Church Graveyard	171
Comp, Stephen & Ann	Sellers, Christiann, daughter	Lower Allen, Eberly's Mills Graveyard	75
Cope, John & Sarah	Clippinger, Elizabeth	Hopewell, Newburg Church of God Graveyard	63
Coyle, David & Martha Linn	McCullough, Betsey, daughter	Newville, Big Spring Presbyterian Graveyard	126
Davidson, William & Mary	Ritner, Mary Jane	Newville, Big Spring Presbyterian Graveyard	132
Deckard, J. B.	Sellers, Susanna, daughter	Newville, Big Spring Presbyterian Graveyard	132
Diller, Abraham & Nancy	Miller, Elizabeth Diller, dau.	West Pennsboro, Diller Mennonite Church Grvyd.	198
Diller, Samuel & Catharine	Longnecker, Rebecca Jane, dau.	West Pennsboro, Bear Graveyard	194
Donor, John & Ann	Keihl, Sarah R., daughter	Penn, Centerville Lutheran Chruch Graveyard	173
Drawbaugh, John & Leah	Heck, Rebecca, daughter	Lower Allen, Eberly's Mills Graveyard	75
Eisenhower, John F.	Shoemaker, Catharine J.	Hopewell, Newburg Church of God	66
Elliot, Thomas & Jane	Williams, Catharine	Newville, Big Spring Presbyterian Cemetery	135
Farenbaugh, George & Elizabeth	Shreiner, Rebecca, daughter	Middlesex, Letort Spring Church Graveyard	95
Forbes, John, Sr.	Black, Ann, niece	Carlisle, Meeting House Springs Graveyard	24
Galbraith, Joseph S. & Sarah	Woods, Mary S., daughter	Penn, Dickinson Presbyterian Church Graveyard	182
Gamber, William	Miller, Fanny Miller, former wife	Hopewell, Newburg Church of God Graveyard	65
Geddes, John, Dr. & Elizabeth	Barr, Sarah, Mrs., daughter	Newville, Big Spring Presbyterian Graveyard	114
Geddes, John, Dr.	Weakley, Eliza, daughter	Penn, Dickinson Presbyterian Church Graveyard	182
Gillespie, George & Sarah	Ewing, Elizabeth, Mrs., dau.	Newville, Big Spring Presbyterian Graveyard	118
Gontner, John & Mary	Heck Christina, daughter	Lower Allen, Eberly's Mills Graveyard	75
Graham, Robert & Elizabeth M.	Cremer, Martha Jane, daughter	Newville, Big Spring Presbyterian Graveyard	116
Harper, John	Harper, Margaret, daughter	Newville, Big Spring Presbyterian Graveyard	121
Harper, William & I.	Russell, Mary Jane, daughter	Penn, Dickinson Presbyterian Church Graveyard	181
Hawk, Abbie O.	Fields, John B., son	Hopewell, Newburg Church of God Graveyard	64
Heap, John	Wilson, John (unknown)	Newville, Big Spring Presbyterian Graveyard	135
Heck, John & Christiana	Price, Catharine, daughter	Lower Allen, Eberly's Mills Graveyard	75
Hefflebower, Henry	Forehope, Nancy, former wife	Hopewell, Newburg Church of God Graveyard	64
Heffleman, Michael & Mary	Dunlap, Elizabeth, daughter	Newville, Big Spring Presbyterian Graveyard	118
Henwood, William & C.	Zeigler, Elizabeth M., dau.	Carlisle, Ashland Cemetery	23

Relative Index

Relative's Name	Name of Person Interred	Township, Cemetery	
Hosler, John & Catharine	Minnich, Mary Ann, daughter	Frankford, Lutheran & Reformed Stone Ch. Grvyd.	40
Huston, William & Mary	Johnson, Jane, daughter	Newville, United Presbyterian Church Graveyard	160
Huston, William & Mary	Mathers, Agnes, daughter	Newville, United Presbyterian Church Graveyard	160
Jackson, Samuel H.	Wise, Anna M., wife	Middlesex, Letort Spring Church Graveyard	96
John, William & Anna	Heagy, Sarah G., daughter	Penn, Centerville Lutheran Church Graveyard	172
Kelso, James & Mary	Green, Mary Jane, daughter	Penn, Dickinson Presbyterian Church Graveyard	179
Kendig, Henry	Getter, Mary, daughter	West Pennsboro, Plainfield Bethel Church Grvyd.	206
Kiehl, Abraham	Minnich, Sarah A., wife of	Frankford, Lutheran & Reformed Stone Ch. Grvyd.	39
Knaub, J. & C.	Fair, Catharine, daughter	Middlesex, Dunker Church Graveyard	88
Knettle, Henry & Hannah	Randolph, Mary, daughter	Newville, Big Spring Presbyterian Graveyard	131
Kremer, James Brainard & Martha Nevin	Goodrich, Mary, daughter	Carlisle, Ashland Cemetery	8
Kurtz, Abraham	Lefever, Salome Line, afterward wife of	West Pennsboro, Seitz Farm Graveyard	213
Law, M. & S.	Saretell, Maria, daughter	Middlesex, Letort Spring Church Graveyard	95
Lehn, John, Esq.	Sentman, Sylvester Lehn, grandson	Frankford, Lutheran & Reformed Stone Ch. Grvyd.	41
Lewis, Diana	Harper, Mary, Mrs., daughter	Newville, Big Spring Presbyterian Graveyard	121
Line, David & Sarah	Huston, Matilda Line, daughter	Dickinson, Old Line Graveyard	31
Line, David	Ralson, Mary, wife	Carlisle, Ashland Cemetery	17
Lloyd, William & Amanda Anderson	Hart, Mary Ellen, daughter	Lower Allen, Lisburn Cemetery	77
Longnecker, Benjamin & Mary	James, Susan, daughter	West Pennsboro, Plainfield Bethel Church Grvyd.	207
Low, M. & S.	Saretell, Maria	Middlesex, Letort Spring Church Graveyard	95
McCachran, Robert, Rev. & Jane	Oliver, Mary, daughter	Newville, Big Spring Presbyterian Graveyard	130
McKeehan, Samuel & Deborah	Sharp, Eliza Ann, daughter	Newville, United Presbyterian Church Graveyard	162
McLaughlin, William & Eliza A.	Kissinger, Flora B., daughter	Carlisle, Ashland Cemetery	12
Mountz, Jacob	Waggoner, Anna M., wife	Frankford, Lutheran & Reformed Stone Ch. Grvyd.	44
Mundorff, Elizabeth	Chronister, Ida Alice, dau.	Frankford, Bloserville Reformed Church Graveyar	33
Myers, Jacob & Lydia	Bear, Rebecca, daughter	West Pennsboro, Ker Farm Graveyard	202
Nevin, William M,, Prof., & McClay, Hannah	Kremer, Martha Ella, daughter	Carlisle, Ashland Cemetery	12
Radabaugh, S. & H.	Morrison, Martha J., adopted daughter	Frankford, Possom Hill Church Graveyard	59
Ramsey, Mary Sterrett	Province, Mary, Mrs., daughter	Carlisle, Ashland Cemetery	17
Row, Peter M. & Anna	Snyder, Elizabeth Row	Lower Allen, Eberly's Mills Graveyard	75
Ruston, James & Sarah	Reed, Agness, daughter	Newville, United Presbyterian Church Graveyard	161
Scherich, Christian & Anna	Lambert, Anna, daughter	Upper Allen, Lantz's School House Graveyard	193
Scroggs, Alexander	Stevenson, Rachel, daughter	Newville, Big Spring Presbyterian Graveyard	133
Seitz, Jacob & E.	Doner, Nancy, daughter	West Pennsboro, Plainfield Bethel Church Grvyd.	206
Shambaugh, Philip, & Anna M.	Orris, Barbara, daughter	Frankford, Lutheran & Reformed Stone Ch. Grvyd.	41
Shambaugh, Philip	Zeigler, Anna M., former wife	Frankford, Lutheran & Reformed Stone Ch. Grvyd.	45
Sharp, John & Jane	McKeehan, Margaret, daughter	Newville, Newville Cemetery	144
Spence, Elihu, Rev., D. D.	Biddle, Lydia, Mrs.	Carlisle, Ashland Cemetery	3
Show-----, Henry & Mary	Salter, Elizabeth, daughter	Mifflin, Center Church Graveyard	103
Snider, J. D. & B.	Griffie, Sarah J., daughter	West Pennsboro, Plainfield Lutheran Ch. Grvyd.	210
Spence, John & C.	Walt, Eleanor Ann, daughter	Penn, Centerville Lutheran Church Graveyard	176
Starr, J. & E.	Hicks, Philemon H., grandson	Lower Allen, Lisburn Cemetery	78

Relative Index

Relative's Name	Name of Person Interred	Township, Cemetery	
Steel, John & Catharine	Heck, Esther, daughter	Lower Allen, Eberly's Mills Graveyard	75
Sterrett, Ralph	Ramsey, Mary, Mrs., daughter	Carlisle, Ashland Cemetery	17
Sterrett, Robert C. & Jane	Sponsler, Agnes, daughter	Carlisle, Ashland Cemetery	20
Stickle, J. & C.	Trego, Rebecca, daughter	Middlesex, Letort Spring Church Graveyard	95
Strohm, H. & Susan	Baker, Catharine E., daughter	Hopewell, Newburg Church of God Graveyard	63
Strome, George & Mary	Shaw, Susan, daughter	West Pennsboro, Bear Graveyard	194
Talhelm, John & Elizabeth	Taylor, Anna E., daughter	Newville, Prospect Hill Cemetery	157
Warner, Burkhart	Sleabaugh, Sarah	Frankford, Lutheran Brick Church	56
Vance, Anna	Pecher, Daniel, son	Penn, Centerville Lutheran Church Graveyard	174
Weekline, Lucretia	Whitmer, Samuel G., son	Penn, Centerville Lutheran Church Graveyard	176
Wherry, Samuel	Beaty, Elizabeth	Hopewell, Hanna Graveyard	60
Wise, Isaac & M. J.	Manning, Sadie C, daughter	Middlesex, Letort Spring Church Graveyard	93
Wise, J. Jacob & Anna Catharine	Line, Rebecca Wise	Carlisle, Ashland Cemetery	13
Wolf, David & M.	Cully, Mary E., daughter	Penn, Centerville Lutheran Church Graveyard	172
Wolf, John & Elizabeth	Jacobs, Jane, daughter	Middlesex, Carlisle Springs Church Graveyard	84
Wolgemuth, J. M.	Neisley, Elizabeth, daughter	Middlesex, Letort Spring Church Graveyard	94
Young, James	Laird, Mary, daughter	Carlisle, Meeting House Springs Graveyard	24
Zinn, George & Mary	Beetem, Hannah, daughter	Carlisle, Ashland Cemetery	2
-----, William & E.	Wickard, Rebecca, daughter	Frankford, Lutheran & Reformed Stone Ch. Grvyd.	45
-----, Thomas W.	Starrett, Martha, daughter	Newville, Big Spring Presbyterian Graveyard	133

INDEX TO CEMETERIES IN NARRATIVE

Cemetery	Page	Cemetery	Page
Ashland Cemetery	217	Martin Farm Graveyard	224
Barnitz M. E. Church Graveyard	224	Meeting House Springs Graveyard	231
Bear Graveyard	219	Mennonite Graveyard at Balfour	219
Bethany Church Graveyard	228	Monroe Woods Farm Graveyard	231
Bethel Church Graveyard (Beechers)	223	Mount Hope Cemetery	228
Bethel Church Graveyard (Doubling Gap)	226	Mount Rock Graveyard	222
Big Spring Presbyterian Graveyard	220	Mount Tabor Church Graveyard	217
Bitner Farm Graveyard	223	Mount Victory Graveyard	228
Bloserville Reformed Church Graveyard	227	Mount Zion Graveyard	225
Carlisle Springs Church Graveyard	218	Newburg Church of God Graveyard	217
Center Church Graveyard	227	Newville Cemetery	221
Centerville Lutheran Church Graveyard	225	Oakville U. B. Cemetery	230
Cumminstown Campbellite Church Graveyard	224	Old Associate Reformed Church Graveyard	218
Dickinson Presbyterian Church Graveyard	225	Old Hoffer Farm Graveyard	229
Diller Mennonite Church Graveyard	220	Old Line Graveyard	222
Dunker Church Graveyard	219	Old Roads Graveyard	230
Eberly's Mills Graveyard	231	Old Shellenberger Farm Graveyard	220
Entlerville Graveyard	226	Oysters' Point Graveyard	231
Flint Ridge Chapel Graveyard	228	Peter Albright Farm Graveyard	218
Francis Bear Farm Graveyard	222	Plainfield Bethel Church Graveyard	219
Farm Graveyard	227	Plainfield Lutheran Church Graveyard	219
Garber Graveyard	229	Possum Hill Graveyard	226
Graveyard on hill	219	Prospect Hill Graveyard	227
Hanna Graveyard	232	Riggleman Farm Graveyard	220
Heikes Farm Graveyard	220	Seitz Farm Graveyard	220
Hisner Graveyard	225	Snokes Graveyard	227
Hoover Graveyard	217	Springfield Graveyard	221
Huntsdale Dunker Cemetery	224	Stouffer Farm Graveyard	217
Irishtown Church Graveyard	230	Stoughstown Lutheran Church Graveyard	221
Jonathan Bear Farm Graveyard	222	Strickler Graveyard	229
Ker Farm Graveyard	223	United Presbyterian Church Graveyard	217
Lantz's School House Graveyard	231	Wagner's Church Graveyard	218
Letort Spring Church Cemetery	218	William A. Lindsey Farm Graveyard	223
Lisburn Cemetery	231	Zeigler's Church Graveyard	232
Line Graveyard	222	Zion Lutheran Church Graveyard	221
Lutheran & Reformed Stone Ch. Graveyard	224	Zion Reformed Church Graveyard	217
Lutheran Brick Church Graveyard	223		

Narrative Index - Miscellaneous

INDEX TO NARRATIVE

Item	Page	Item	Page
Ahl, David, Dr.	227	Line, Mrs.	222
Alter, N. Scott	227	Longnecker, John K.	219
Baker, Rolla	217	Martin, George, Sen.	224
Bear, Francis (Francis Bear Farm Graveyard)	222	Martin, William	224
Bear, Francis (Jonathan Bear Farm Graveyard)	222	McKeehan farm	220
Bear, Francis (Wm. Lindsey Farm Graveyard)	223	Mein, Thos.	229
Bear, Francis (Bitner Farm)	223	Middle Spring Church	232
Beaty, Elizabeth	232	Miller, Matthew	229
Beetem, Samuel, Esq.	223	Miller, William, Captain	218
Beetem's Church	225	Moore, John	218
Beitzel, Elmer	229	Morrison, Parker	219
Bethany Church	221	Mount Pleasant Church	221
Bloser	220	Mowry, Floyd	228
Brenneman, L. T.	229	Neal, John	218
Cassell, Rev.	217	Oakville Church	221
Chronister, Mr.	220	Odd Fellows	227
Council Bluff school house	232	Oiler, Mrs.	226
Criswell, Robert	218	Philebaum, Philip	229
Dinkle, William	218	Phillips, -----	219
Drennan, William	231	Rebert, John	219
Ebenezer Church	228	Roads School House	230
Eichelberger farm	229	Rosenmiller, D. P., Rev.	232
Evangelical Association	232	Ross, Simon	218
Evangelical Church	228	Scouller, J. B., Rev.	232
Fishburn, John	222	Seitz, Jacob	220
Francis, Rev.	221	Shady Grove school house	218
Fuget, Adam	223	Smith	226
Galbraith, Robert	222	Snook, Rev.	228
Gardner's Store	228	Snyder, C. P.	224
Gayman, J. H.	227	Stouffer, Jacob	219
German Reformed & Lutheran Congregations	232	Strickler, John	229
Gibb, William H.	224	Stroh, N. [?] J., Rev.	232
Gisetown	228	Swope, Gilbert E.	232
Greegor, Frank	229	United Brethren Church (Oakville U.B. Cm.)	230
Green, William	221	United Brethren Church (Old Roads Grvyd.)	230
Gross brothers	223	United Evangelical Church	228
Hays, John, Esq.	219	Wagoner boys	223
Heilig, G., Rev.	232	Washington, Charles	221
Henry, Thomas	226	Weaver, Abram	229
Hessinger, D., Rev.	232	Weaver, Charley	223
Heway, William	218	Weidenhamer, R. Y., Rev.	223
Hoffer, Christ	229	Wing's History of Cumberland County	232
Jeffrey, Joseph	227	Woodburn, John	218
Kelly, John T.	230	Woods, Monroe	231
Kutz Church (Letort Spring Church Cemetery)	218	Zeigler, Capt.	231
Kutz Church (Peter Albright Farm Graveyard)	218	Zeigler, Jacob	232
Lefever's Church	224	Zeigler's Graveyard	221
Lightner, John S.	223	Zolleringite Church	226
Line, George	222	Zolleringites	226
Line, Henry	222		

www.ingramcontent.com/pod-product-compliance
Lightning Source LLC
Chambersburg PA
CBHW081418230426
43668CB00016B/2276